Geo*active 1*

STAGE 4 GLOBAL GEOGRAPHY

Third edition

Susan **Bliss** | John **Paine**

Contributing author
Paul **McCartan**

Third edition published 2010 by
John Wiley & Sons Australia, Ltd
42 McDougall Street, Milton, Qld 4064

First edition published 1998
Second edition published 2005

Typeset in 9.5/12.5 pt LinoLetter

© Susan Bliss, John Paine 1998, 2005, 2010

The moral rights of the authors have been asserted.

National Library of Australia
Cataloguing-in-publication entry

Author:	Bliss, Sue, 1944–
Title:	Geoactive 1: stage 4 global geography/ Susan Bliss and John Paine.
Edition:	3rd ed.
ISBN:	978 1 7421 6006 1 (pbk)
	978 1 7421 6141 9 (web)
Notes:	Includes index.
Target audience:	For secondary school age.
Subjects:	Geography — Textbooks.
	Physical geography — Textbooks.
Other authors/ contributors:	Paine, J. (John)
Dewey number:	910.02

Cover image: © Digital Stock/Corbis Corporation; © Photodisc

Internal design images: © Digital Stock/Corbis Corporation;
© Digital Vision

Cartography by MAPgraphics Pty Ltd Brisbane and the Wiley
Art Studio

Illustrated by Phillip Blythe, D'lan Davidson, Stephen Francis,
Mike Gorman, Steve Hunter, Craig Jackson, Terry St Ledger,
Paul Lennon, Janice McCormack, Bronwyn Searle, Graeme
Tavendale and the Wiley Art Studio

Printed in China by
Printplus Limited

10 9 8 7 6 5 4 3

Contents

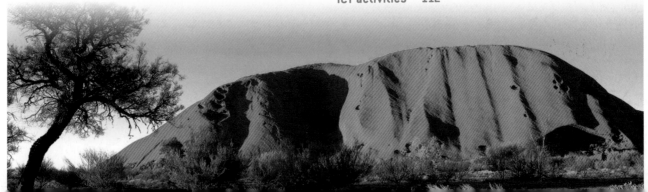

Preface

Geoactive 1, third edition has been written for the NSW Stage 4 Global Geography syllabus. The needs of students and teachers have been carefully researched, with meetings, surveys and reviews used to revise the text, activities, illustrations and layout of this third edition. The core idea of the text is to engage students in different forms of learning as they acquire the skills to work geographically, and to ensure that the activities form the basis of learning how to learn.

The sample spreads on pages viii–ix and the overview of the exciting new eBookPLUS on page vii explain the main features of this print and digital package of student resources and teacher support.

The following are some of the highlights of this new edition of the student text.

- The textbook features a more student-friendly layout, with text, activities and a range of visual information. Particular attention has been paid to literacy and reading level in all chapters, with shorter paragraphs and greater use of bullet points to enhance understanding and highlight concepts.
- Most of the text is in double-page format but, where the topic is large, a four-page format is used.
- *Geoterms* on pages provide definitions of geography-specific terms in context as they are used. As well, a full list of *Key terms* appears in the chapter opener and in a combined glossary at the end of the book.
- *Geofacts* have been included on many pages to interest and engage students in bite-sized geography facts.
- A comprehensive range of *GEOskillbuilder* features is included in relevant sections according to syllabus requirements. These skillbuilders provide a detailed step-by-step guide to important practical geographical skills. *GEOskills toolbox* features provide additional information on key skills.
- The student *Activities* are divided into three sections: *Understanding* revises basic concepts and terms; *Thinking and applying* requires higher levels of understanding and often calls on students to apply different intelligences; and *Using your skills* applies the skills learned in the section or revises those skills learned in previous sections.
- End-of-chapter *Working geographically* pages allow students to practise concepts and skills developed within chapters and to begin preparation for the School Certificate test at the end of Stage 5.
- There are many new, up-to-date and topical sample studies, graphs, statistics, maps and diagrams.
- A new chapter, Climate change, presents this complex global issue at a level that Stage 4 students can understand.
- A new and exciting dimension in the teaching and learning of Geography is provided through a range of online resources for each topic in eBookPLUS (see page vii). These innovative tools for the Geography teacher use the full potential of digital media to integrate ICT and stimulate students in inquiry-based learning.

Next generation teaching and learning

About eBookPLUS

This book features eBookPLUS: an electronic version of the entire textbook and supporting multimedia resources. It is available for you online at the JacarandaPLUS website (www.jacplus.com.au).

Using the JacarandaPLUS website

To access your eBookPLUS resources, simply log on to www.jacplus.com.au. There are three easy steps for using the JacarandaPLUS system.

Step 1. Create a user account

The first time you use the JacarandaPLUS system, you will need to create a user account. Go to the JacarandaPLUS home page (www.jacplus.com.au) and follow the instructions on screen. An activation email will be sent to your nominated email address. Click on the link in this email and your activation will be complete. You can now use your nominated email address and password to log in to the JacarandaPLUS system.

Step 2. Enter your registration code

Once you have activated your account and logged in, enter your unique registration code for this book, which is printed on the inside front cover of your textbook. The title of your textbook will appear in your bookshelf. Click on the link to open your eBookPLUS.

Step 3. View or download eBookPLUS resources

Your eBook and supporting resources are provided in a chapter-by-chapter format. Simply select the desired chapter from the drop-down list. The student eBook tab contains the entire chapter's content in easy-to-use HTML. The student resources tab contains supporting multimedia resources for each chapter.

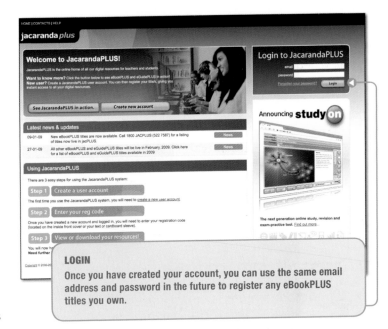

LOGIN
Once you have created your account, you can use the same email address and password in the future to register any eBookPLUS titles you own.

Using eBookPLUS references

eBookPLUS logos are used throughout the printed books to inform you that a multimedia resource is available for the content you are studying.

Searchlight IDs (e.g. int-0001) give you instant access to multimedia resources. Once you are logged in, simply enter the searchlight ID for that resource and it will open immediately.

Minimum requirements
- Internet Explorer 7, Mozilla Firefox 1.5 or Safari 1.3
- Adobe Flash Player 9
- Javascript must be enabled (most browsers are enabled by default).

Troubleshooting
- Go to the JacarandaPLUS help page at www.jacplus.com.au
- Contact John Wiley & Sons Australia, Ltd. Email: support@jacplus.com.au Phone: 1800 JAC PLUS (1800 522 7587)

How to use this book

The following examples highlight the structure and main features of this textbook and eBookPLUS.

Chapters begin with *Inquiry questions* based on the syllabus.

A short section introduces each chapter.

Skills covered are listed at the beginning of each chapter.

The *Key terms* used in the chapter are clearly defined.

Presentation within chapters is in two-page or four-page sections for ease of study and teaching.

To aid literacy, dot points are used to break up blocks of text.

GEOskills toolbox features explain geographical skills and tools. Some chapters have step-by-step *GEOskillbuilder* features to teach skills.

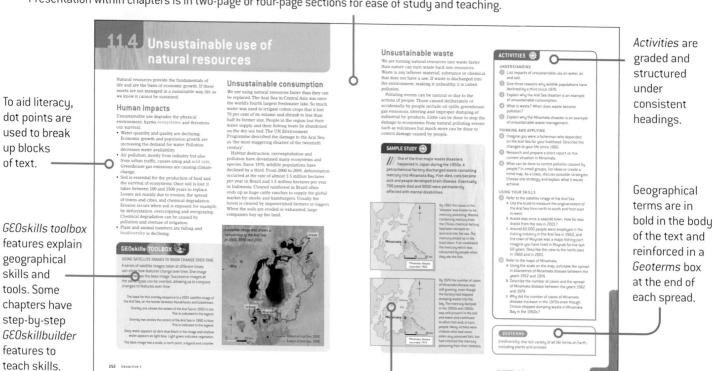

Activities are graded and structured under consistent headings.

Geographical terms are in bold in the body of the text and reinforced in a *Geoterms* box at the end of each spread.

Sample study features provide topical case studies.

End-of-chapter *Working geographically* pages focus on students' understanding and analysis of stimulus material to begin preparation for the School Certificate.

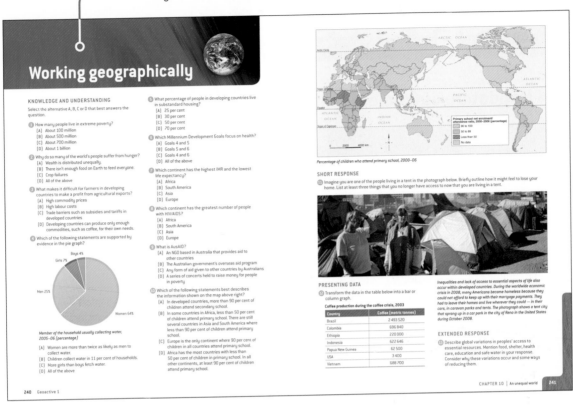

ProjectsPLUS is a new research management system, featuring media, templates and video introductions to a unique ICT project. Each project is specifically designed to inspire and engage students while providing quality assessment support for teachers.

Targeted *ICT activities* are available on eBookPLUS.

Coverage of syllabus

Stage 4 Mandatory outcomes

Outcomes	Focus areas and chapter coverage			
A student:	4G1	4G2	4G3	4G4
4.1 identifies and gathers geographical information	Chapters 1–3	Chapters 4–8	Chapters 9–11	
4.2 organises and interprets geographical information	Chapters 1–3	Chapters 4–8	Chapters 9–11	Chapters 12–16
4.3 uses a range of written, oral and graphic forms to communicate geographical information	Chapters 1–3	Chapters 4–8	Chapters 9–11	Chapters 12–16
4.4 uses a range of geographical tools	Chapters 1–3	Chapters 4–8	Chapters 9–11	Chapters 12–16
4.5 demonstrates a sense of place about global environments	Chapters 1–3		Chapters 9–11	
4.6 describes the geographical processes that form and transform environments	Chapters 1–3	Chapters 4–8		
4.7 identifies and discusses geographical issues from a range of perspectives			Chapters 9–11	Chapters 12–16
4.8 describes the interrelationships between people and environments		Chapters 4–8		Chapters 12–16
4.9 describes differences in life opportunities throughout the world			Chapters 9–11	Chapters 12–16
4.10 explains how geographical knowledge, understanding and skills combine with knowledge of civics to contribute to informed citizenship.	Chapters 1–3	Chapters 4–8	Chapters 9–11	Chapters 12–16

Geographical tools

GEOskillbuilder [a]	Chapter, section, page
Using scale to measure distance on a map	Chapter 2, 2.1, page 21
Constructing a map using symbols	Chapter 2, 2.1, page 23
Reading a picture graph	Chapter 2, 2.8, page 36
Making a line drawing	Chapter 3, 3.5, pages 58–9
Drawing a sketch map	Chapter 3, 3.6, page 60
Understanding contours	Chapter 5, 5.5, pages 96–7
Constructing a column graph	Chapter 5, 5.10, page 109
Interpreting and constructing climatic graphs	Chapter 6, 6.3, pages 120–1
Constructing and interpreting graphs	Chapter 7, 7.11, pages 164–5
Creating a mind map	Chapter 15, 15.7, page 353

(a) *GEOskillbuilder* features take students step by step through key geographical skills.
(b) Working geographically

Acknowledgements

The authors would like to thank Pamela McAlister for assistance with learning theory and student activities. The publisher wishes to thank Paul McCartan for his material on coral reefs in New Caledonia on page 330 in chapter 14. The publishers would like to thank Pamela McAlister for assistance with learning theory and student activities, and John Bliss for his research and support. Thanks also to the staff of John Wiley and Sons Australia for their commitment to quality, particularly Jan Cousens for her dedication and creativity.

The authors and publisher would like to thank the following copyright holders, organisations and individuals for their assistance and for permission to reproduce copyright material in this book.

Images:
• Used under license from Shutterstock.com 2009: /© 3777190317 **72**; /© Aaron Wood **360** (right); /© Anke van Wyk **336**; /© Anne Kitzman **170** (left); /© Anyka **216**; /© Arkady **265** (top); /© clearviewstock **171** (top); /© Dhoxax **242** (bottom); /© Feverpitch **243** (left); /© imageshunter **243** (bottom right); /© JackF **171** (bottom); /© jon le-bon **243** (top); /© JustASC **312**; /© K Thorsen **242** (top); /© Kane513 v, **337**; /© Kevin Tavares **361**; /© Kurhan **217**; /© kwest **313**; /© Len Green **360** (left); /© Liviu Toader **382**; /© Mateo-Pearson **360** (second right); /© Mopic **265** (bottom); /© Qing Ding **73**; /© Regien Paassen **360** (second left); /© Ryan M Bolton **170** (right); /© Sabri Deniz Kizil **84** top, **85** (4 images) /© Sergey Lazarev **264** • Mike Saunders/Aladdin Books **90** (top) • Paul Springett/Alamy **357** • © Alan Moir, *Sydney Morning Herald*, 8–9 November 2008, p. 34 **205** • © Amnesty International **281** (bottom) • Andy Singer, www. andysinger.com **208** (left) • Colin Sale/Atlas Picture Library **77** (centre right); /**79** (bottom) • Auscape/Jean-Paul Ferrero **103** (bottom) • Austral International **282** (top right); /Camera Press/Sarah Errington **271**; /Fox **201** • Map courtesy of the Australian Antarctic Division Data Centre, © Commonwealth Australia 2008 **192** • AusAID: /The Australia Indonesia Basic Education Program, Australia Indonesia Partnership Kemitraan Australia Indonesia, p. 3. Reproduced by permission of AusAID **237**; /Photograph by Jim Holmes **7** • AAP Image: /© AP via AAP/David J Phillip **292** (top); /AFP/Australian Antarctic Division/Gary Dowse **186**; /Anthony Mitchell **368**; /Anupam Nath **238** (top); /AP/Themba Hadebe **234** (top); /AP/Ove Hoegh-Guildberg **44** (bottom right); /Chris Ivin **107**; /Dale Paget **335**; /Jordan Baker **282** (bottom right); /Kevin Frayer **177** (top); /Ross D Franklin **342** (bottom); /Yuri Tutov **379** • Energy Update 2008 © ABARE **301** (2 images) • Adapted with permission from the ACIA. MAPgraphics Pty Ltd, Brisbane **323** (top) • AFP **257** (bottom) • ANTPhoto.com.au: /BG Thomson **320**; /Colin Blobel **174** (bottom); /Dave Watts **45** (bottom); /Fred Parker **98** (top); /Fredy Mercay **169** (bottom); /Jurg Baer **374** (bottom); /Jurgen Otto **62**; /M Cermak **317** (top left); /Martin Harvey **317** (bottom, top right), **318** (photo), **324** (top); /NHPA **144** (bottom right); /Norbert Wu **316**, **329**; /Otto Rogge **332**; /Rob Blakers **144** (bottom left); /Ron & Valerie Taylor **328** (right); /Silvestris **144** (top right) • © ASPO Ireland **257** (top right) • © Brand X Pictures **11** (bottom) • © Tim Freccia/CARE **220** (top) • 'Making water everybody's business. Practice and policy of water harvesting', edited by Anil Agarwal, Sunita Narain and Indira Khurana, p. 69 **370** (bottom) • © Commonwealth of Australia, reproduced by permission: /Australian Bureau of Meteorology **53**; /Budget 2007–2008 **239** (top); /*Garnaut Climate Change Review*, **290**, **300** (left), **304** • Corbis: /© John Noble **180–1**; /Ann Hawthorne **187** (right); /Ashley Cooper **296** (right); /Australian Picture Library /Peter Turnley **257** (top left); /Bernard and Catherine Desjeux **137**; /Bill Ross **4** (glider); /Corbis SABA/Louise Gubb **235** (top left); /Darrell Gulin **76** (bottom left); /David Muench **76** (top left); /Documentary Value/Richard T Nowitz **203** (bottom); /Dominique

Derda/France 2 **381** (top); /Encyclopedia/Jack Fields **244–5**; /epa **223** (top); /epa/Anatoly Maltsev **108**; /epa/Greenpeace **191** (top); /EPA/John Jon Hrusa **326** (top right); /epa/Olivier Maire **44** (left); /epa/Sarah Elliott **222** (top); /epa/Tugela Ridley **212**; /Galen Rowell **181** (top), **187** (left); /Gallo Images/Philip Richardson **211** (bottom right); /Gideon Mendel **228** (top); /JAI/Peter Adams **86–7**; /James L Amos **99** (top); /Jerry Arcieri **235** (top right); /Karen Kasmauski **376**; /Kennan Ward **189**; /Keren Su **14** (panda); /Lattitude/Maria Maria Stenzel **172–3**; /Layne Kennedy **78**; /Lloyd Cluff **91** (top); /Michael S Yamashita **91** (left); /News/Viviane Moos **218–19**; /Owen Franken **150** (bottom); /pa/Soeren Stache **223** (bottom); /Paul A Souders **179**; /Paulo Friedman **279**; /Peter Johnson **251** (right); /Ralph A Clevenger **183**; /Reinhard Eisele **135** (top); /Ric Ergenbright **263** (bottom); /Robert Harding World Imagery/Robert Francis **300** (bottom right); /Robert Harding/Gavin Hellier **45** (top); /Sandro Vannini **43** (bottom); /Star Ledger/Andy Mills **208** (right); /Sygma/ Silva Joao **225**; /Sygma/Christian Simonpietri **135** (bottom); /Terra Standard/Charles O'Rear **211** (bottom left); /W Perry Conway **77** (top); /Wild Country **106**; /Xinhua Press/Du Huaju **370** (top); /Xinhua Press/Gong Lei **344** (top left); /Yann Arthus-Bertrand **79** (top left), **251** (left), **327**; /zefa/Frans Lemmens **129** • Corbis Royalty Free: /© Corbis Images **40** (right); /© Corbis Corporation **41** (bottom, top right), **300** (centre) • Coo-ee Picture Library **58** • CSIRO Marine and Atmospheric Research **331** • © Denise Buchanan **195** • Courtesy of Kakadu National Park. MAPgraphics Pty Ltd, Brisbane **22** • © Diamonds North Resources Ltd **211** (top left) • © Digital Stock/Corbis Corporation **iii**, **35** (4 images), **41** (centre right, top left), **42** (left), **117** (bottom), **178** • © Digital Vision 4 (elephants), **10**, **33**, **102**, **123**, **175**, **261** (bottom), **314–15**, **317** (centre); /Stephen Frink **261** (top left) • © DAJ **188** • © DK Images **91** (centre) • Average global temperature, 1880–2004, with projection to 2100, www.earth-policy. org **289** • Map redrawn by MAPgraphics Pty Ltd, Brisbane. Reproduced with permission of Eric Frost **252** (2 maps with overlays) • ESA, European Space Agency © 2002 **190** (right) • © EyeWire Images **6** • *Ecos*, Dec.–Jan. 2008, p. 140, graph by Peter Seligman **310** • Fairfax Photos **322**; /Matt Wade **299**; /Rick Stevens **349** • *The Age*, 5 Jan. 2006, p. 6, map by MAPgraphics Pty Ltd, Brisbane **296** (left) • Virginia Carter, FogQuest **131** • FSC AC 2009, www.fsc.org **164** (left) • © Geohive, www.geohive.com **278** (top left, top right) • Data supplied and processed by Geoimage, www.geoimage.com.au/ Landsat 2004 **56–7** • © Commonwealth of Australia, Geoscience Australia 2010. This material is copyright Commonwealth of Australia. Map by MAPgraphics Pty Ltd Brisbane **152**, **152–3** • Getty Images **79** (top right), **269**; /AFP **155** (bottom); /AFP/Emmanuel Dunand **211** (top right); /AFP/Jay Directo **268** (top right); /Eric Meola **322–3**; /John Stanton **307**; /Max Whittaker **241** (bottom); /Michael Williams **50**; /National Geographic/Gordon Wiltsie **1**; /Paula Bronstein **151** (right); /Photographer's Choice/ Frans Lemmens **114–15**; /Photographer's Choice/Stuart Dee **76** (bottom right); /Stone/Hugh Sitton **76** (centre left); /Stone/James Balog **177** (bottom); /Stone/David Muench **319** (top); /Stone/Warren Bolster **56** (centre, top); /Tengku Bahar **155** (top); /The Image Bank/Harald Sund **90** (bottom); /The Image Bank/Joseph Van Os **77** (centre left); /The Image Bank/Jerry Driendl **378** (left) • Google Inc. **4** (screenshot) • © Greenpeace: /Daniel Beltra **291** (bottom); /De Agostini/Archivo Museo Salesiano, Patagonia **291** (top) • © Guido Alberto Rossi **134** (inset) • © International Telecommunication Union **202** • www. internetworldstats.com/Miniwatts Marketing Group **203** (top), **209** (top) • Giacomo Rambaldi, © IADAP **283** • Geography Department, IUPUI. MAPgraphics Pty Ltd, Brisbane **96** • John Wiley & Sons Australia: /Carol Grabham **65** (bottom); /Maggy Saldais **65** (top) • Kelly Babcock and Majo Cholich. Reproduced by permission **213** (top) • Kino Studio/Fred Adler **80** (centre), **151** (left) • *National*

Geographic Picture Atlas of the World, 1990, © artist Shusei Nagaoka. Reproduced with permission of Klimt Represents **26** (4 images), **31** • The Kobal Collection/Warner Bros **213** (bottom) • Map courtesy of Land Information New Zealand. Crown copyright reserved **100–1** • © 2009 Alex S MacLean/Landslides **56** (bottom) • Lochman Transparencies/Jiri Lochman **144** (top left) • Lonely Planet Images/ Casey & Astrid Witte Mahaney **328** (left) • AMP Capital Investors Ltd **68** (bottom); AMP/Macquarie Centre **68** (logo) • Dr Max Quanchi, Senior Lecturer, Humanities Program, QUT, Kelvin Grove Campus, Brisbane, Australia, mobile 0402 042 879, private: 1/23 Burns Rd, Toowong 4066, 07 3217 7565 **330** (left) • © 2008 Sydway Publishing Pty Ltd. Reproduced from Sydway Edition 14 with permission **25** • © Mongabay **164** (right), **165** • Map by MAPgraphics Pty Ltd, Brisbane **5** (map), **8**, **9** (Africa, South America), **14** (map), **27** (4 maps), **30**, **32** (2 maps), **34** (2 maps), **37**, **38–9**, **71**, **83**, **88–9**, **97**, **103** (top), **104**, **111** (top), **116–17**, **126**, **130**, **132** (left), **136**, **144** (map), **154**, **156**, **158** (bottom), **161** (2 maps), **174** (top), **176**, **193**, **207** (top, 2 maps), **209** (bottom), **210**, **215**, **220** (bottom), **228** (bottom), **232** (bottom), **234** (bottom), **238** (bottom), **246**, **250**, **256**, **263** (top), **270**, **273** (bottom), **278** (bottom), **305** (bottom), **305** (top), **318** (map), **321**, **326** (top left), **341**, **348**, **351**, **354** (top), **356**, **366**, **367**, **374** (top), **378** (right); /© Tibor Toth/National Geographic Image Collection **325** • © Georg Gerster/Network **77** (bottom) • Reproduced with permission of *New Internationalist magazine*, Sep. 1995, www.newint.org **226** • *New Scientist*, 28 Jun. 2008, p. 36 **275** • *New Zealand Herald* **282** (centre left) • Newspix **159**; /AFP Photo/Philippe Desmazes **91** (right); /AFP **306**; /AFP/Marcus Brandt **207** (bottom); /AFP/Kazuhiro Nogi **350** (left); /Daniel Forster/AFP **5** (yacht); /Kevin Bull **297**; /Rohan Kelly **67** • NASA **294** (2 images), **323** (bottom); /GSFC/Modis Rapid Response Team/Jacques Descloitres. Overlay by MAPgraphics Pty Ltd, Brisbane **252**; /NSIDC **190** (right, labels), **191** (bottom) • NASA Earth Observatory, http://earthobservatory.nasa.gov **190** (left, 3 images) • © NSW Department of Community Services, www. community.nsw.gov.au **66** • Panos Pictures: /Betty Press **282** (centre left); /Hamish Wilson **81**; /Paul Weinberg **344** (top right) • © Paul McCartan **330** (right) • Phil O'Brien **182** (3 images) • © Photodisc **5** (cyclone), **18–19**, **42** (right), **68** (top), **94**, **116** (top), **117** (top), **158** (top), **160**, **167**, **169** (top), **198–9**, **255** (bottom), **260** (top), **261** (top right), **300** (centre right, top right), **308** (5 images), **342** (top) • photolibrary.com: /age fotostock/Andoni Canela **40** (left); /age fotostock/Berndt Fisher **150** (top); /Alain Evrard **105**; /Bildagentur **142–3**; /Bill Bachmann **350** (bottom right); /Claver Carroll **11** (top); /Daniel Thierry **133**; /Geoff Higgins **2–3**; /imagebroker.net/Heiner Heine **362–3**; /imagebroker.net/Norbet Michalke **44** (top right); /Jose Fuste Raga **98–9** (bottom); /Kenneth W Fink **344** (bottom); /Millard H Sharp **166**; /OSF/Mary Plage **346**; /Oxford Scientific/ Ariadne Van Zandbergen **4** (abseiler); /Pacific Stock/Aeder Erik **4** (sailboard); /Paul Thompson **338–9**; /Peter French **350** (top right); /Photo Researchers, Inc./Carl Frank **227**; /Photo Researchers/Bill Bachman **355**; /Photo Researchers/Gregory Ochocki **266–7**; /Photo Researchers/Kenneth W Fink **268** (left); /photononstop/Sebastian Boisse **74–5**; /Professional Sport International **206**; /Richard Shiell **150** (centre); /Rick Strange **371** (top); /Robert Harding Travel **128**; /Robert Harding Travel/Ann & Steve Toon **354** (bottom); /Robert Harding Travel/Ken Gillham **286–7**; /Robin Smith **100**; /SPL **132** (right), **134** (left), **163**; /SPL/David Parker **372**; /SPL/JBI **48–9**; /Thien Do **111** (bottom) • © PhotoEssentials **63**, **116** (bottom) • Picture Media: /Australian Department of Defence/Reuters **239** (bottom); /Reuters/Adnan Abidi **235** (bottom); /Reuters/Adrees Latif **281** (top); /Reuters/Kamal Kishore **43** (top) • Reproduced by permission of Population Reference Bureau **248** (left); /Map by MAPgraphics Pty Ltd, Brisbane **248** (right) • © 2003 Trustees of Princeton University, www.qed.princeton.edu/Image. Map designed by Flaming Toast Productions **215** • Jeff Hornbaker/Quiksilver **5** (diver) • Rob Brittle **292** (bottom) • Robert A Rohde **298** • Robert Estall Photo Agency/© Angela Fisher/Carol Beckwith **247** • Ron Tandberg **268** (bottom right) • © Save the Tiger Fund **324** (bottom) • South American Pictures **157**, **282** (bottom left) • Courtesy Stephen Codrington **80** (bottom), **319** (bottom, centre) • © stevebloom.com **326** (bottom) • Sue Cunningham/SCP **82** • Susan Bliss **80** (top) • SEPA/SOE. MAPgraphics Pty Ltd, Brisbane **9** (China) • © Toyota Industries Corporation **259** • © UNICEF: *Progress for children. A world fit for children statistical review*, no. 6, Dec. 2007, p. 17 **236** (top); *Progress for children. A report card on water and sanitation* no. 5, Sep. 2006, p. 12 **381** (bottom) • © United Nations Development Programme, 2006. All Rights reserved **222** (bottom); *Millennium Development Goals Report 2008*, p 42 © United Nations, 2008. All rights reserved **240** • © UNFPA, *State of world population 2007. Unleashing the potential of urban growth* **229** • Energy Information Administration (EIA), www.eia.doe.gov/iea **301** (top) • University of California, *Atlas of Global Inequality*, www.ucatlas.ucsc.edu. Map redrawn by MAPgraphics Pty Ltd, Brisbane **232** (top) • United Nations Environment Program (UNEP) **249**, **254** (3 graphs), **262** (right); / Redrawn by MAPgraphics Pty Ltd **255** (top), **295**; /© UNEP, http:// maps.grida.no/go/graphic/fifty-million-climate-refugees-by-2010 **311** • UNESCO **369**, **371** (bottom) • © UNICEF: /*Progress for children. A world fit for children statistical review*, no. 6, Dec. 2007, p. 13. This map and all maps in this publication are stylised and not to scale. They do not reflect a position by UNICEF on the legal status of any country or territory or the delimitation of any frontiers. The dotted line in this map and all maps in this publication represents approximately the Line of Control in Jammu and Kashmir agreed upon by India and Pakistan. The final status of Jammu and Kashmir has not yet been upon by the parties. Redrawn by MAPgraphics Pty Ltd, Brisbane **241** (top); /*Progress on drinking water and sanitation*, UNICEF and World Health Organization, 2008, p. 26 © UNICEF and WHO **377** • US Geological Survey. Redrawn by MAPgraphics Pty Ltd, Brisbane **51** • ©Viewfinder Australia Photo Library **64** • Transparency Encyclopedia Geography, © Visual Teach Nijmegen Netherlands **273** (top) • Adapted from World Hunger Map, 2006, World Food Programme. Redrawn by MAPgraphics Pty Ltd, Brisbane **224** • Tourism 2020 Vision, p. 4. Reproduced by permission of the World Tourism Organisation, UNWTO, p. 347 © UNWTO, 9284401609 **341** • World Wildlife Fund: /Reproduced with permission from WWF-World Wide Fund for Nature, Gland Switzerland © text and graphics: 2008 WWF All rights reserved. **258** (2 graphs), **262** (left), **373**; /WWF International. Reproduced by permission **260** (bottom) • © WWF International/www.panda.org **15**

Text:
• *Jacaranda SOSE 2, 2nd edition*, John Wiley & Sons Australia, 2000, © Angelo Calandra **28–9**, **30–1** • Extract from ABC News in Science, 'Climate change affects birds and bees', by Judy Skatssoon, first published by ABC Online, 9 Nov. 2005, reproduced by permission of the Australian Broadcasting Corporation and ABC Online, © 2005 ABC. All rights reserved **311** • 'Green collar army recruits for the solar boom', by Stephanie Peatling and Ben Cubby, *Sydney Morning Herald*, 31 Oct. 2008 **303** • *Garnaut Climate Change Review*, © Commonwealth Copyright, reproduced by permission **290**, **304** • Graham Readfern, *The Courier-Mail*, 23 Aug. 2008 **297** • Ecos, 129, Feb.–Mar. 2006, p. 7, © CSIRO Publishing **331** • Jo Chandler, *The Age*, 19 Jan. 2008 **292** • Paul McCartan **330–1** • Paul Williams, *The Courier-Mail*, 7 Jan. 2009 **335** • © 2005 Reprinted with permission from Reuters. Reuters content is the intellectual property of Reuters or its third party providers. Any copying, republication of redistribution of Reuters content is expressly prohibited without the prior written consent of Reuters. Reuters shall not be liable for any errors or delays in content, or for any actions taken in reliance thereon. Reuters and the Reuters Sphere Logo are registered trademarks of the Reuters group of companies around the world. For additional information about Reuters content and services, please visit Reuters website as www.reuters.com. License # REU-5626-MES **83** • 'Qantas plans to offset its carbon emissions', *The Age*, 2 Nov. 2006 **351** • 'Tree-sitting activist wins high praise from judge', *The Sydney Morning Herald*, 21–23 Dec. 2007, p. 3, News **333** • *Progress for children. A report card on water and sanitation*, no. 5, Sep. 2006, p. 30 © UNICEF **381** • 'Saving the last frontier, by Vincent Ross, *The Sunday Mail*, Escape Supplement, 13 Jul. 2008 **195** • © UNWTO, 9284401609 **342**

Every effort has been made to trace the ownership of copyright material. Information that will enable the publisher to rectify any error or omission in subsequent reprints will be welcome. In such cases, please contact the Permission Section of John Wiley & Sons Australia, Ltd.

Without
geography
you're
nowhere.

Jimmy Buffett

1 The nature of geography

INQUIRY QUESTIONS

+ What is geography?
+ What are the features of the physical and human environments?
+ How do the physical and human environments interact?

Geography is all around us in the air we breathe, the sun that shines on us, the soil and water that nourish us, and the plants and animals who share our Earth. Geography is also concerned with how humans use and interact with environments to meet their needs. Today, when technology gives us instant access to global events, geography can help us make sense of our world and consider important issues from different perspectives. With the help of geographical inquiry, we can participate as informed citizens to help build a sustainable and socially just world.

GEOskills TOOLBOX

+ Gathering geographical information from the internet (page 15)

Physical and human elements of the environment come together at the Gold Coast in Queensland.

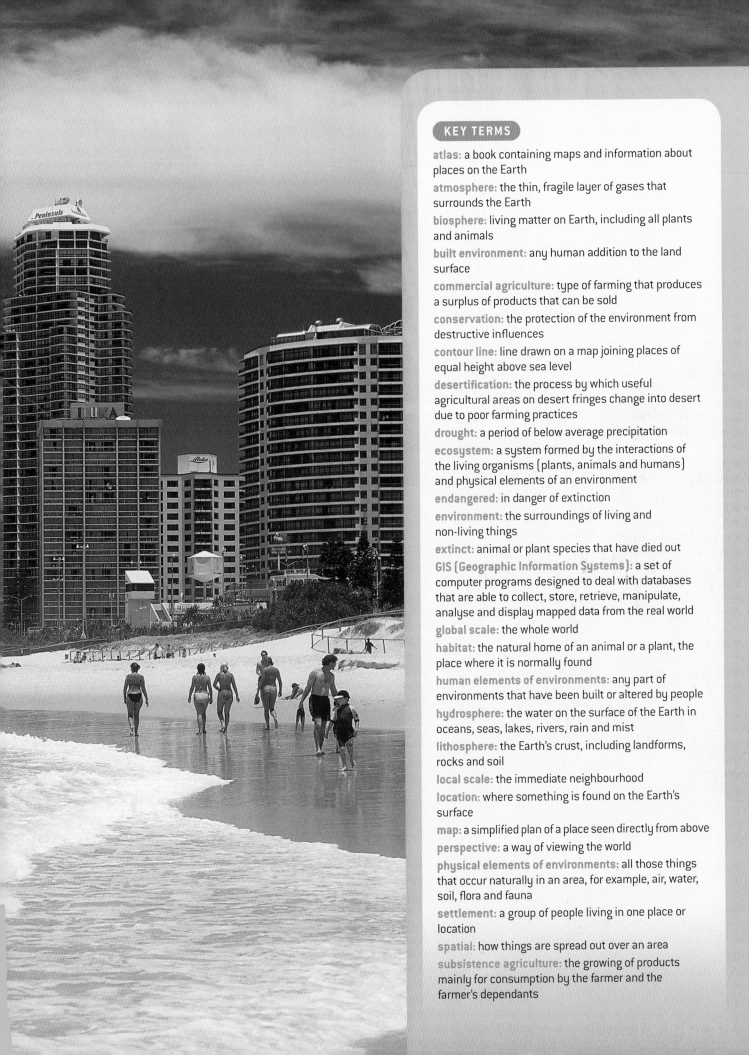

KEY TERMS

atlas: a book containing maps and information about places on the Earth

atmosphere: the thin, fragile layer of gases that surrounds the Earth

biosphere: living matter on Earth, including all plants and animals

built environment: any human addition to the land surface

commercial agriculture: type of farming that produces a surplus of products that can be sold

conservation: the protection of the environment from destructive influences

contour line: line drawn on a map joining places of equal height above sea level

desertification: the process by which useful agricultural areas on desert fringes change into desert due to poor farming practices

drought: a period of below average precipitation

ecosystem: a system formed by the interactions of the living organisms (plants, animals and humans) and physical elements of an environment

endangered: in danger of extinction

environment: the surroundings of living and non-living things

extinct: animal or plant species that have died out

GIS (Geographic Information Systems): a set of computer programs designed to deal with databases that are able to collect, store, retrieve, manipulate, analyse and display mapped data from the real world

global scale: the whole world

habitat: the natural home of an animal or a plant, the place where it is normally found

human elements of environments: any part of environments that have been built or altered by people

hydrosphere: the water on the surface of the Earth in oceans, seas, lakes, rivers, rain and mist

lithosphere: the Earth's crust, including landforms, rocks and soil

local scale: the immediate neighbourhood

location: where something is found on the Earth's surface

map: a simplified plan of a place seen directly from above

perspective: a way of viewing the world

physical elements of environments: all those things that occur naturally in an area, for example, air, water, soil, flora and fauna

settlement: a group of people living in one place or location

spatial: how things are spread out over an area

subsistence agriculture: the growing of products mainly for consumption by the farmer and the farmer's dependants

1.1 Geography at work and play

Geography is a serious study and, yet, knowledge of it can also help you have fun! It may surprise you just how often geography matters in a whole range of fun activities. To participate fully in these activities, it helps to know about the air (atmosphere), water (hydrosphere), soil and landforms (lithosphere), and plants and animals (biosphere).

Geography can teach about natural landforms such as mountains so that you can understand gradients and slopes when abseiling in Swaziland.

Geography can teach about coastal landforms, waves and winds so that you can get the most out of windsurfing at Maui, in Hawaii.

Geography can teach about animals and their so that you can get the most out of travelling on safari in Kruger National Park in Africa.

Geography can teach about weather, wind speed and wind direction so that you know when to go hang gliding in California, in the USA.

Geospatial technologies like Google Earth allow geographers to recognise patterns of interaction between physical and human elements.

A geographer's tools

You have probably noticed that many jobs require tools to help people do their work. Builders use spirit levels and computer drawing software, doctors use stethoscopes and ultrasound machines, journalists use cameras and digital editing tools. Geographers use tools such as **maps**, photographs, graphs and statistics, fieldwork studies and **spatial** technology such as **GIS (Geographic Information Systems)** and Google Earth.

Topographic maps (right) are an essential tool for climbing Mt Everest (below).

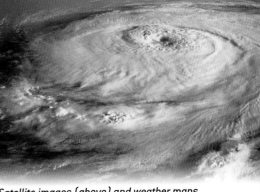

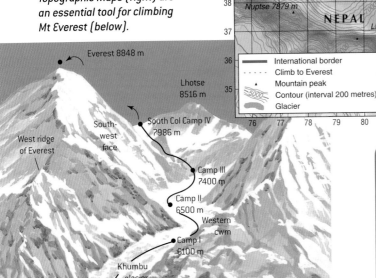

Satellite images (above) and weather maps helped in the rescue of survivors after the capsizing of yachts during the Sydney to Hobart Yacht Race in 1998 (below).

ACTIVITIES

THINKING AND APPLYING

1. What fun outdoor activities do you enjoy? What elements of the air, water, land, plants and animals are involved in these activities?
2. Design a collage of images of world sports that are linked to geography.
3. Think of a recent world event and brainstorm how geography could help to explain it.

Fieldwork (below) is vital for the collection of data (right) to map, measure, observe and record the real world.

Fish species, Great Barrier Reef, 2000–2008

GEOTERMS

atmosphere: the thin, fragile layer of gases that surrounds the Earth

biosphere: living matter on Earth, including all plants and animals

GIS (Geographic Information Systems): a set of computer programs designed to deal with databases that are able to collect, store, retrieve, manipulate, analyse and display mapped data from the real world

habitat: the natural home of an animal or a plant, the place where it is normally found

hydrosphere: the water on the surface of the Earth in oceans, seas, lakes, rivers, rain and mist

lithosphere: the Earth's crust, including landforms, rocks and soil

map: a simplified plan of a place seen directly from above

spatial: how things are spread out over an area

1.2 Geographers investigate the world

Geographers are curious people. Their curiosity leads to them asking endless questions such as: Why are pandas disappearing? What is climate change? Why do volcanoes erupt? Why should we recycle waste? What problems do large cities create? How can we make sure everyone has access to safe water? Geographers use problem-solving skills and tools to answer key geographical questions about issues from a local scale (in the immediate neighbourhood) to a global scale (affecting the whole world).

A geographer will ask, 'Why are pandas disappearing?'.

Geographical skills include:
- locating, gathering and evaluating information from a variety of local sources. Sources include fieldwork, maps, photographs, books, the media and the internet.
- observing and analysing information
- choosing and applying appropriate geographical tools
- presenting and communicating information to others
- participating as informed and active citizens.

Geographical tools include:
- maps
- fieldwork
- graphs and statistics
- photographs.

Perspectives and citizenship

A perspective is a way of viewing the world, the people in it, their relationship to each other, and their relationship to communities and environments. Geography students are asked to imagine what it would be like to see, think, feel or even walk in another person's shoes when they study issues. For example, the photograph opposite shows a child paddling in a river where people bathe, wash clothes, dispose of garbage and urinate and defecate. The local community then drinks this water, which leads to water-borne diseases such as cholera. From one perspective, Australians who have access to a toilet and clean water may be horrified. On the other hand, millions of poor children, living in developing countries without access to a toilet or clean water,

1. What is the geographical issue?

2. Where is it happening?

3. Why is it happening?

4. What are the effects?

5. What action(s) is appropriate? (Citizenship)

6. Who will be involved — individuals, groups, non-government organisations, governments?

7. Why has active citizenship made a difference? If not, why not?

Key geographical questions

1. **What is the issue?** 2.6 billion people, or 40 per cent of the world's population, do not have access to adequate sanitation.

2. **Where is it happening?** In many developing countries such as Indonesia, Nepal and India

3. **Why is it happening?** Poor governments do not have the money to build a sewerage system and provide clean drinking water. Poor people cannot afford to pay for toilets and clean water.

7. **Why has this made a difference?** The contribution of people and money from developed countries in partnership with local organisations in developing countries has led to access to improved sanitation for 1.2 billion people.

4. **What are the effects?** The health of people is affected: low life expectancy, high infant mortality rate, sickness and death from cholera, typhoid and dysentery.

6. **Who will be involved?** United Nations International Year of Sanitation 2008, non-government organisations (e.g. World Vision), AusAID, governments and volunteers.

5. **What actions are appropriate?** Access to basic sanitation is part of the UN Millennium Development Goals (2000–2015).

Key geographical questions about access to clean water

have no choice but to perform all these actions in the source of the local drinking water. Their perspective is different.

After studying this issue, one of the key geographical questions might require students to suggest what action(s) they as citizens could take to make a better life for this child. These actions could range from a local to a global scale. For example, at a global level, a citizen could become a volunteer for AusAID on a project that provides toilets and fresh water to poor people living in developing countries.

At a local level, a citizen could donate money to a non-government organisation such as World Vision.

GEO*facts*

A study of geography is of value in many careers. These include doctors working with patients suffering HIV/AIDS in Asia, engineers building roads in Africa, diplomats working in the Middle East, journalists reporting news from Fiji and defence people working in Afghanistan. People employed as traffic engineers, park rangers, farmers, miners, real estate agents, conservationists, land developers, energy planners, market researchers, builders and marine biologists are also likely to have qualifications in geography.

Many geographers are employed in the tourism industry and in emergency services when there are floods, fires, cyclones or landslides. Others are employed as meteorologists tracking cyclones, vulcanologists researching volcanoes and seismologists monitoring earthquakes. An increasing number are employed by the United Nations and AusAID to help reduce poverty in developing countries, and in businesses and governments for their Geographic Information Systems (GIS) skills.

ACTIVITIES ➡

UNDERSTANDING

1. What are the key geographical questions? Draw your own mind map to display them.
2. List the main factors that might influence the perspectives people have.
3. What is meant by 'local to global citizenship'? Give examples of issues in your local community. What actions could you take on these issues as a citizen of the community?
4. Name two types of geographical tools.

THINKING AND APPLYING

5. Briefly describe how studying geography and asking geographical questions could help people to participate in society as active and informed citizens.
6. Referring to the internet, newspapers or TV, find and list five global geographical issues. Choose one issue and answer the key geographical questions used in the mind map on page 6 as a guide.

GEOTERMS

global scale: the whole world
local scale: the immediate neighbourhood
perspective: a way of viewing the world

An **atlas** is a book containing maps and information about places on Earth. Most atlases also contain photographs, diagrams and graphs. Geographers frequently use an atlas to find detailed information about places. When you use an atlas, there are three different ways you can find places and information:

1. From the list of contents at the front — the contents page is a list of the maps that are found in the atlas. It will help you locate broad areas such as continents or groups of countries.
2. From the index at the back — the index lists in alphabetical order all the countries, towns and cities, and other features found on the maps. The index tells you the page number for the map and the location on the map where you will find the place name you are seeking.
3. From the maps themselves and from other visual material in the atlas.

There are different types of maps in an atlas because they have a variety of purposes. There are four main types of maps:

- physical
- topographic
- political
- thematic maps.

Physical maps

These maps show the physical landforms of a region, including patterns of mountain ranges, rivers and other physical features. Political boundaries are often not shown on physical maps. Variation in colour and shading are used to show height above sea level.

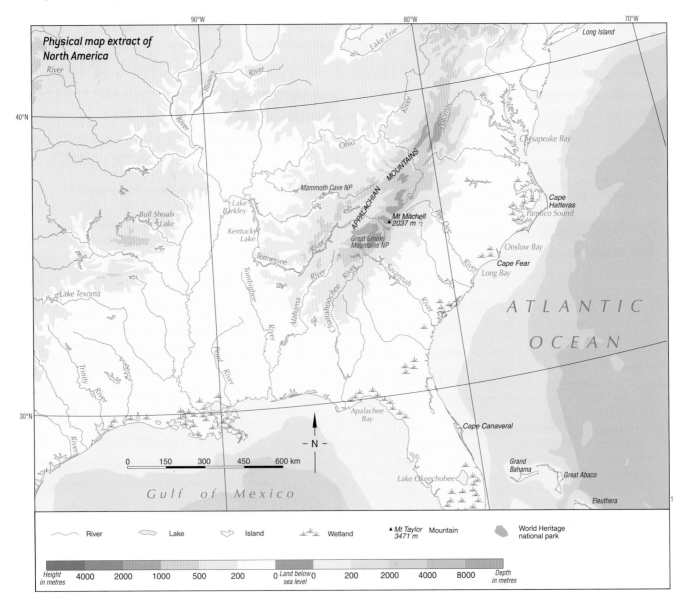

Physical map extract of North America

Political maps

These are maps that show different political regions in a different colour, with their borders marked by lines. The most common political maps are world maps and continent maps showing countries.

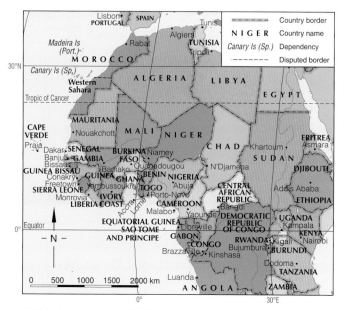

Political map extract of Africa

Topographic maps

These maps show relief or height above sea level using **contour lines**. They also show physical features such as forests, rivers and lakes, and cultural features such as roads, railways and **settlements**. This type of map is useful for bushwalking, planning roads and checking the steepness of slopes. You can see examples of topographic maps on pages 97 and 101.

Thematic maps

A wide range of themes can be shown in map form, such as how temperature, agriculture or incomes vary over an area.

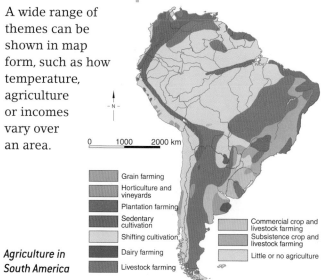

Agriculture in South America

ACTIVITIES

UNDERSTANDING

1. What is an atlas?
2. Describe the ways in which you can find information in an atlas.
3. List the four main types of maps found in an atlas.

THINKING AND APPLYING

4. Refer to the political map of Africa.
   a How can you tell one country from another?
   b Why can't you see the Sahara Desert on this map?
5. Refer to the physical map of North America.
   a Why can't you find Washington DC on this map?
   b List three physical features marked on the map.
6. Refer to the map of agriculture in South America. Identify the four main types of farming. How did you do this?
7. What type of map is the one below? Explain how you reached this conclusion.

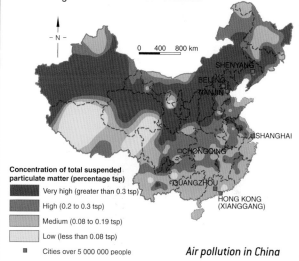

Air pollution in China

USING YOUR SKILLS

8. Use an atlas to answer the following questions.
   a On what page would you find a map of China?
   b On what page would you find the city of Rome?
   c Find an example of each of the four main types of maps.
   d Find an example of non-map material.

GEOTERMS

atlas: a book containing maps and information about places on the Earth

contour line: line drawn on a map joining places of equal height above sea level

settlement: a group of people usually living in one place or location

1.4 Geographers study environments

The **environment** is the surroundings of living and non-living things. Environments consist of three aspects:

- **physical elements of environments**
- **human elements of environments**
- interaction of the physical and human elements of environments.

The physical elements of environments are all those things that occur naturally in an area, for example: air, flora and fauna, soil, solar energy and water.

The human elements of environments are any part of environments that have been built or altered by people such as houses, farms, factories, roads and towns. Human additions to the land surface are referred to as the **built environment**.

Ecosystems and food webs

An **ecosystem** is a system formed by the interaction of living things (plants, animals and humans) and

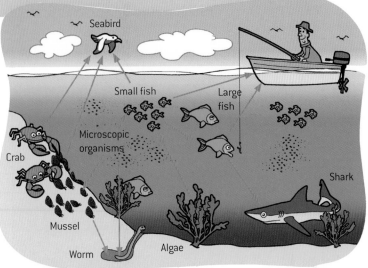

A simplified coastal food web, containing many food chains

physical elements of environments. The energy from the sun enables all living things to grow in the ecosystem. Complex patterns called food chains (who eats who) and food webs (when food chains interlock) are formed within ecosystems.

Air is a mixture of gases, mainly nitrogen, oxygen and water vapour. Most of the air is in the atmosphere.

Solar energy is energy in the form of heat and light from the sun. Solar energy makes all life possible.

Soil consists of fine rock particles and organic material on the Earth's surface. It is the part of the Earth's surface in which plants grow. Soils form a part of the lithosphere.

Flora are plants of a particular area, while *fauna* are the animals of a particular area. Flora and fauna are parts of the biosphere.

Water is a common substance that is essential to all known forms of life. Water exists in three forms: a solid (as ice); a liquid (as water); and a gas (as water vapour). Water is probably humankind's single most important resource. All life depends on water: animals need it for drinking and it is essential for plants to grow. Most water is in the hydrosphere.

Physical elements of environments

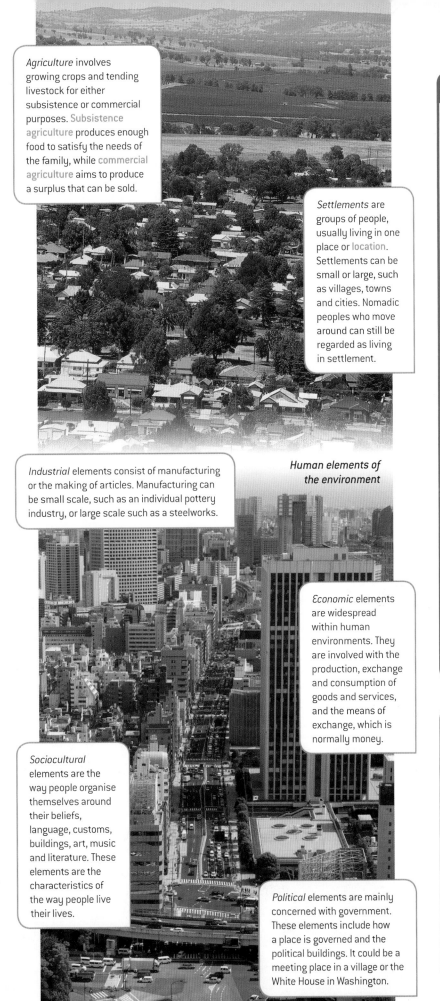

Agriculture involves growing crops and tending livestock for either subsistence or commercial purposes. Subsistence agriculture produces enough food to satisfy the needs of the family, while commercial agriculture aims to produce a surplus that can be sold.

Settlements are groups of people, usually living in one place or location. Settlements can be small or large, such as villages, towns and cities. Nomadic peoples who move around can still be regarded as living in settlement.

Industrial elements consist of manufacturing or the making of articles. Manufacturing can be small scale, such as an individual pottery industry, or large scale such as a steelworks.

Human elements of the environment

Economic elements are widespread within human environments. They are involved with the production, exchange and consumption of goods and services, and the means of exchange, which is normally money.

Sociocultural elements are the way people organise themselves around their beliefs, language, customs, buildings, art, music and literature. These elements are the characteristics of the way people live their lives.

Political elements are mainly concerned with government. These elements include how a place is governed and the political buildings. It could be a meeting place in a village or the White House in Washington.

ACTIVITIES →

UNDERSTANDING

1. Match the element from the list below with the example.
   Elements: air, flora, fauna, soil, solar energy, agriculture, settlement, industrial, water, political, sociocultural
   a a group of people living in one place or location
   b energy emitted from the sun
   c a cottage industry making lavender soaps
   d Parliament House in Canberra
   e a map showing the distribution of the main languages of the world
   f a ploughed paddock
   g a mixture of gases
   h a camel
   i a forest
   j a wheat farm
   k a lake

2. Define an ecosystem.

THINKING AND APPLYING

3. Explain the statement: 'All life depends on water'.

4. Imagine a huge black cloud covering the sun and cutting off all incoming solar energy. Describe what would happen to:
   a the physical environment
   b the human environment.

5. Picture your walk home from school. Briefly describe all of the elements of the human environment that you will see. Have these elements changed over the last five years? If so, how have they changed?

GEOTERMS

built environment: any human addition to the land surface

ecosystem: a system formed by the interactions of the living organisms (plants, animals and humans) and physical elements of an environment

environment: the surroundings of living and non-living things

human elements of environments: any part of environments that have been built or altered by people

physical elements of environments: all those things that occur naturally in an area, for example, air, water, soil, flora and fauna

1.5 Interaction of physical and human environments

Human–physical interactions involve the way people depend on, adapt to, or change their environments. Everything we do as humans interacts with the elements of the physical environment. As well, both the physical environment and the human environment are constantly undergoing changes. Some of these changes are natural and some are caused by the actions of people.

Rising populations

For most of the time that humans have been on Earth their numbers have been small. As recently as 10 000 years ago, the global human population was probably only about one-thousandth of its present size. Humans were primarily hunters and gatherers and, apart from their use of fire, had little impact on the environment.

Today, the world's population is over six billion and many of its environments have been transformed. Vast areas of the natural environment have been cleared to provide food and raw materials. Urban areas are getting bigger.

The physical elements of environments provide people with resources such as coal, oil, timber and minerals. Exploitation of these resources has led to economic development and improved the quality of life for many people. But at the same time overconsumption and misuse of these resources has caused problems such as water pollution, soil degradation and desertification.

Although the power of humans to change their environment has increased dramatically, people must still cope with a wide range of effects from their physical environment. Crops can be destroyed by drought, beaches savagely eroded by storms, towns drowned by floods, lives and forests lost through bushfires and buildings destroyed by earthquakes.

There are two main types of volcanic eruption – those that produce flowing lava such as this one, and those that produce ash. Both types of eruption can destroy huge areas.

An earthquake has created this crack or fissure in the Earth's surface. Earthquakes occur when stress builds up in the Earth's crust and is suddenly released.

Desertification increases when vegetation is lost due to land clearing and overgrazing by animals. When droughts occur and there is not enough vegetation to bind the soil, wind and water can cause large-scale erosion. Dust storms remove topsoil. When rain does fall, rapid run-off causes flooding and erosion.

As waves attack the coastline, coastal erosion can occur. Houses and roads built on cliff tops can collapse into the sea.

UNDERSTANDING

1. Study the scene on these pages and decide where you think the safest place to live would be.
2. Why have vast areas of the Earth's physical environments been cleared?
3. Outline some adverse effects the physical environment can have on the human environment.

THINKING AND APPLYING

4. Study the scene on these pages. Choose any three events and describe their effects on the human and physical environment. Would it have been possible to prevent any of these events from occurring?
5. Discuss as a class how physical elements such as the soil, plants, animals, air and water of your local area have been changed by humans.

Strong winds, torrential rain and high waves caused by tropical cyclones or storms can devastate towns and cities on the coast. Tornadoes present one of the greatest dangers to communities from the atmosphere. Winds of up to 400 kilometres an hour can be generated by a tornado.

Heavy rainfall, earthquakes and volcanic eruptions can all trigger landslides. Clearing forests from steep hillsides increases the risk of landslides. When rain falls on a forested hillside, trees protect the soil. The roots hold the soil and absorb water, reducing erosion, run-off and landslides.

Lightning is a release of electricity from storm clouds to the Earth.

A bushfire has been started by a natural event – a lightning strike. (Some bushfires, though, are started by arsonists.) Bushfires are a common occurrence not only in Australia, but also in parts of the United States and Europe.

Heavy rain in the mountains can cause rivers to flood low-lying areas.

A tsunami is a large wave. Tsunamis are usually created when an earthquake occurs under the ocean.

GEOTERMS

desertification: the process by which useful agricultural areas on desert fringes change into desert due to poor farming practices

drought: a period of below average precipitation

The physical environment is greatly affected by the human environment. The impact of people on the physical environment, for example, its flora and fauna, is enormous. In the following case study, it can be seen how human activities have reduced the habitat of pandas and, as a result, reduced their numbers in the wild.

Distribution of the panda

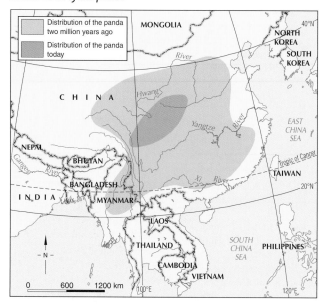

Why are pandas precious?

Pandas have existed in eastern and southern China for about three million years and have been called a 'living fossil'. The World Wide Fund for Nature (WWF) uses the panda as its international symbol to represent endangered animals. Scientists fear that pandas could soon become extinct. This means that your children or grandchildren might never have the opportunity to see one.

There are only about 1500 giant pandas remaining in the panda's wild forest habitat in the mountainous areas of south-western China. On average, a giant panda will eat 3480 stems or 20 kilograms of bamboo shoots each day. It spends between 50 and 75 per cent of each day eating.

How humans have affected panda habitats

Giant pandas live in bamboo thickets. These thickets have been severely reduced by activities of the human environment such as logging and forest

Distribution of the panda two million years ago and today

Female pandas have difficulty becoming pregnant and giving birth. A female may give birth to three cubs, but she will reject two of them.

Some scientists say pandas are in natural decline. Pandas once ate animals and plants. But today they eat mainly bamboo as they have poor eyesight and lack the speed to hunt prey. Pandas have also become less agile. This means their natural predators (leopards, brown bears) can kill them more easily.

Between 60 and 70 per cent of all pandas suffer from roundworm disease. This slows down growth and reproduction. It can also kill pandas.

Other reasons for the decline in giant panda numbers

clearance for agriculture. Cattle, sheep and goats now graze on new bamboo seedlings. This prevents the regrowth of the forest. In the last 30 years, Sichuan Province in China has lost one-third of its forest. Many giant panda populations are now isolated in narrow belts of bamboo. These are sometimes no more than one kilometre wide.

In the late 1970s and early 1980s, many giant pandas died following the flowering and death of arrow bamboo shoots over wide areas. This natural event occurs at intervals of between 30 and 120 years (depending on the type of bamboo). When this happened in the past, giant pandas migrated to other areas with different species of bamboo. Now, human settlement prevents such migration.

Hunting giant pandas is illegal but poaching is still a problem. Their pelts are used to make mattresses and coats, bringing high prices in some Asian markets. Sometimes they are caught in traps set by poachers for musk deer, another endangered species in China.

ACTIVITIES

UNDERSTANDING

1. Where do giant pandas live?
2. Approximately how many giant pandas live in their natural habitat?
3. Why have pandas been described as 'living fossils'?

THINKING AND APPLYING

4. Do you agree that pandas are precious? Justify your answer.
5. Using the map of panda distribution, describe the distribution of pandas in China today compared to two million years ago.
6. Describe how activities from the human environment have reduced the number of giant panda habitats.
7. What natural factors may be contributing to panda decline?

USING YOUR SKILLS

8. Apply the questions from the Geoskills Toolbox to the WWF website on pandas. How well does the website meet the criteria?
9. Think of another question that you have about giant pandas, and then use your favourite search engine to find an answer on a website that meets the criteria. Why do you believe this is a useful website?

GEOskills TOOLBOX

GATHERING GEOGRAPHICAL INFORMATION FROM THE INTERNET

A wide selection of geographical information can be sourced from websites. When gathering information from websites, it is important to be critical about their accuracy and reliability. Many websites have accurate and up-to-date information, while others can be biased, inaccurate and out of date.

Questions to ask when using the internet are:

1. Who is responsible for the website? Is it:
   - the government
   - an educational institution
   - a business or some other organisation
   - a private individual?
2. How reliable is the information?
   - Are there any indications of bias (one-sided opinion) or exaggeration?
   - How current is the information?
   - Can it be verified from another source?
3. How relevant is the information?
   - Does it help answer the questions you are asking?
   - Can you use it in your work or study?

Imagine you would like some information about conservation actions to protect the giant panda. The following is an extract from the internet site of the World Wide Fund for Nature (WWF). It was accessed by using a popular search engine. First, we entered the words 'conservation of pandas'. After trying several sites, we chose WWF, deciding that it satisfied the above three criteria.

GEOTERMS

conservation: the protection of the environment from destructive influences

endangered: in danger of extinction

extinct: animal or plant species that have died out

eBook *plus*

eLesson

GEOGRAPHY CAREERS

Geography is the study of the Earth and how humans interact with their environment. This introductory eLesson immerses you in the world of geography and the people involved in the study of our physical environment. What do geographers do? What kind of tools do they use? What kind of work is there for geographers? Watch a series of case studies and discover all this and more!

SEARCHLIGHT ID: ELES-0160

Interactivity

JIGZONE: 'WORLD'

This interactive Jigzone game will test your knowledge of the locations of the world's landforms. You must drag and drop the landforms to their correct positions in the world outline. Be careful because any wrong move you make will give your enemy more power. You must complete the map of the world and make sure your enemy doesn't end up with more points than you.

SEARCHLIGHT ID: INT-0966

These ICT activities are available in this chapter's Student Resources tab inside your eBookPLUS. Visit www.jacplus.com.au to locate your digital resources.

Interactivity

HOTSPOT COMMANDER: 'WORLD LANDFORMS'

Hotspot Commander challenges your geographical skills and knowledge in a fun question-and-answer format. You will receive the coordinates of a location. When you hit your target accurately, you will be given some secret information and a question to answer. Get it right and part of the mystery image is revealed. Can you conquer all 10 locations and become a Hotspot Commander?

SEARCHLIGHT ID: INT-0967

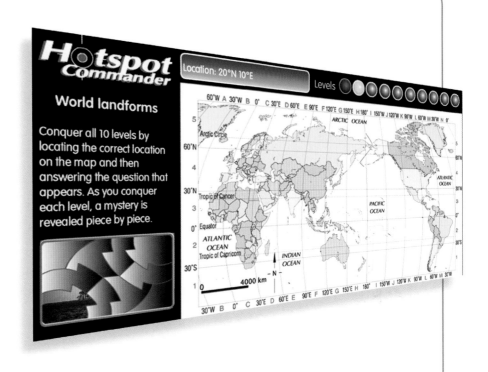

Interactivity

TIME OUT: 'PHYSICAL AND HUMAN ENVIRONMENTS'

This exciting interactivity will test your knowledge of different environments, challenging you to classify a series of scenes as either physical or human environments. You must think hard and fast because the clock is ticking and any wrong answer will lose you time; but get them right and you'll get a bonus chunk. Can you answer all 10 questions before Time Out?

SEARCHLIGHT ID: INT-0927

2 Our world, our heritage

INQUIRY QUESTIONS

+ What are the essential features of a map?
+ What is the influence of latitude on climate?
+ What are the global patterns of physical and human features?
+ What is worth keeping for all time?

The world is an amazing place — as far as we know, the Earth is the only planet in our solar system to support life. Geographers represent the Earth using maps, and locate places using latitude and longitude. The Earth has a wide range of climates that influence the type of vegetation that grows and where people live. It is important that we understand our world so that we can manage the Earth's finite resources sustainably. World Heritage sites, for example, are places of outstanding value that should be preserved for all people and for all time.

GEOskills TOOLBOX

GEOskillbuilder Using scale to measure distance on a map (page 21)

GEOskillbuilder Constructing a map using symbols (page 23)

GEOskillbuilder Reading a picture graph (page 36)

+ Using topographic maps (page 24)
+ Using a time zones map (page 31)
+ Reading line graphs (page 39)

The temple at Angkor Wat in Cambodia is part of a World Heritage site that was inscribed in 1992.

KEY TERMS

alphanumeric grid reference: combination of letters and numbers that locate points on a map

area reference: four numbers used to locate features on a topographic map

cartography: the art of drawing maps. A professional map maker is called a cartographer.

climate: the long-term variation in the atmosphere, mainly relating to temperature and precipitation

climate change: any change in climate over time, whether due to natural processes or human activities

climatic zones: zones where climate is similar; the main zones are the tropics, the polar regions, and the temperate zones, which lie between them

compass: an instrument for determining direction

continents: the seven great landmasses of the Earth

conventional symbols: standard symbols that are commonly used on maps

Greenwich Mean Time (GMT): time at the Royal Observatory in Greenwich, near London, England, which is used as the basis for standard time around the world

grid reference: six numbers used to locate features on a topographic map

insolation: incoming solar radiation or heat from the sun

International Date Line: the line of longitude at 180°

latitude: imaginary lines drawn around the Earth that run east to west

legend: used with a map to explain the meaning of signs and symbols shown on the map, also called a key

longitude: imaginary lines drawn around the Earth from north to south

map projection: a representation of the Earth's surface drawn on a flat grid, using latitude and longitude

ocean: a large body of salt water

plan view: the view from directly above

scale: uses a line, ratio or words to show how distance on a map relates to distance in the real world

precipitation: the condensation in the atmosphere that falls as rain, hail, snow or dew

time zones: the 24 hours of different time into which the Earth is divided

topographic map: a map that shows the height and shape of the land by using contour lines

weather: condition of the atmosphere at a particular time in relation to air pressure, temperature, precipitation, wind and cloud

World Heritage site: a place recognised as being of such great value that it should be preserved for all people and all time

Geographers use maps

The geographer's most important tool is a map. In everyday life too, maps communicate information about places and help us to find locations. From the earliest land and sea explorers' rough maps to the highly accurate digital **cartography** of today, maps have always been an exciting way of exploring the Earth's surface.

from a bird's-eye view, only the tops of objects such as trees and houses can be seen. Maps are drawn from a **plan view**, and this plan or vertical view is different from the view you would get from the ground. You will see this by observing the two views of Holiday Island.

What is a map?

A map is a simplified plan of a place seen directly from above. Features on the Earth's surface can look quite different when viewed from the air. When viewing the Earth's surface

Looking down on Holiday Island from above (aerial perspective)

Looking at Holiday Island from the sea (ground perspective)

Essential features of a map

There are essential features that we must include on maps if they are to be a useful tool for the geographer. These features are:

- border
- title
- scale
- latitude and longitude (see pages 28–9)
- legend or key
- direction or orientation.

Title

The title will tell you the place on Earth the map is representing. It may also give you a clue about what the map is trying to show, for example, 'Australia: landforms', or 'Sydney Harbour and foreshores'. The title for our map on page 23 is Holiday Island.

Scale

Scale shows how distance on a map relates to distance in the real world. Maps show large areas of the Earth's surface on a small piece of paper. Large-scale maps show detailed information about a small area. A map of your bedroom is a large-scale map and it shows a lot of detail. Small-scale maps show broad patterns and large areas such as global weather patterns. On the map of Holiday Island on page 23, the map maker has been able to show the whole island on less than half a page in a book. The shape of the features remains the same, but they are drawn smaller by using a scale.

Scale statement or written scale

The scale of a map can be shown in a statement given in words. For example, 'one centimetre on the map represents one kilometre on the ground'.

Line scale or linear scale

Scale can be shown on a map using a line scale marked at even intervals. On each of the line scales below, each centimetre interval represents one kilometre on the ground.

Representative fraction (RF) or ratio

The scale of a map can also be shown in numbers, using a fraction. This is usually written like a ratio; for example, '1/25 000' or '1:25 000'. This means that one centimetre on the map represents 25 000 centimetres, or 250 metres, on the ground. A 1:100 000 scale means that one centimetre on the map represents 100 000 centimetres, or one kilometre, on the ground.

GEOskillbuilder

USING SCALE TO MEASURE DISTANCE ON A MAP

We can use the scale of a map to work out the distance from one place to another. A line scale is the easiest scale to use. To measure the straight line distance between two points, we should follow four steps.

STEP 1

Place a piece of paper between the two points on the map.

STEP 2

Mark off the distance between the two points along the edge of the paper.

STEP 3

Place the paper along the line scale.

STEP 4

Read off the distance on the scale.

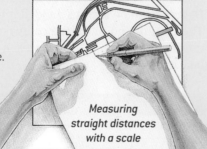

Measuring straight distances with a scale

What happens if we have to measure a winding river or coastline? This is not as difficult as it seems. We could follow the path of a winding river or road with a piece of string or cotton. We could then pull the cotton straight and measure the length as a straight line. Another way to measure the distance between two points on a bend or curve is to use the four steps below.

STEP 1

Place a sheet of paper on the map and mark off the starting point on the edge of the paper.

STEP 2

Then, move the paper so that the edge of the paper follows the curves on the map.

STEP 3

Mark off the end point on your sheet of paper.

STEP 4

Finally, place the paper along the line scale and read off the distance on the scale. The following diagram shows how the winding road between Newtown and Oldtown can be measured.

Newtown

Oldtown

N

How to measure curved distance on a map

Use the tip of your pencil or a pin to keep the paper on the curve. You can then pivot the paper around without losing your place.

Legend or key

A **legend** or key shows the signs that have been used to draw the map and explains their meaning. Map makers use **conventional symbols** to help quickly identify features on a map. These symbols are drawn to look like the object they are representing. The three main types of symbols are:

- *point symbols*. These show a feature of a particular place such as a bridge, shop or toilet block.
- *line symbols*. These form lines such as roads, rivers and railway lines.
- *area symbols*. These represent larger areas such as a lake or forest.

Colours are also used to convey a quick message to the map reader. For example, bushland, forest and other vegetation are usually shown in green. Features associated with water are usually shown in blue.

Tourist facilities at Kakadu National Park

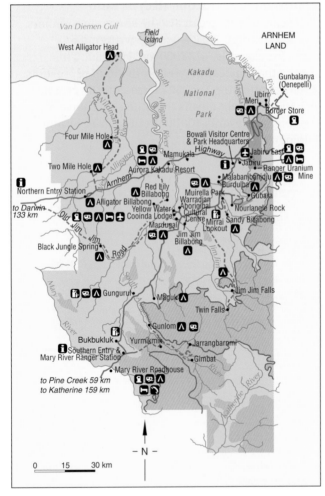

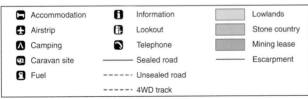

Direction or orientation

Direction on maps is shown using an arrow pointing north. Most maps will have north at the top of the page, but always make sure you look for the north pointer. If north is at the top, then south is at the bottom, east is to the right and west is to the left.

Geographers use the points of a **compass** to give direction from one location to another. Words such as left, right, up, down, top and bottom can be confusing and inaccurate. Using compass points such as north, south, east and west are more accurate because, in whatever direction you are facing, the compass direction always remains the same.

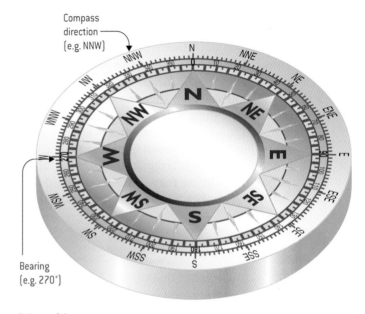

Points of the compass

Compass bearings

Geographers are able to measure the precise direction from one point to another with the use of compass bearings. A bearing is an angle that is measured clockwise from 0° or north. (Note that because a compass is circular, north is also 360°.) Degrees can be further divided into 60 minutes ('). The cardinal points of the compass and the intermediate compass points each relate to a bearing.

Direction	Bearing	Direction	Bearing
North	0°/360°	South	180°
North-east	45°	South-west	225°
East	90°	West	270°
South-east	135°	North-west	315°

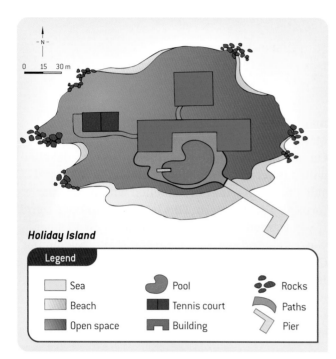

Holiday Island

Legend

▢	Sea	◗	Pool	⬤	Rocks
▢	Beach	▨	Tennis court	◢	Paths
▨	Open space	⊞	Building	▱	Pier

GEOskillbuilder

CONSTRUCTING A MAP USING SYMBOLS

STEP 1

In your workbook, rule two squares four centimetres wide, side by side, on your page. Leave a few centimetres space around each square.

STEP 2

In the first box, construct a map of a town using the features listed below. You must write the locations of each of the features of the map. You may write these wherever you like, but they must be within the border of the first box.

- a major road
- a minor road
- a railway line
- a school
- four houses
- a church
- a post office

STEP 3

Now redraw your map in the second box, but this time use symbols instead of writing. Choose appropriate coloured symbols to show the features, and draw your map neatly and clearly.

STEP 4

Complete your map by drawing a legend or key to show what your symbols represent.

Which map is clearer and better organised? Below your two maps, write a sentence to explain why symbols on maps are useful.

ACTIVITIES →

UNDERSTANDING

1. Define a 'map'.
2. What are the essential features of a map?
3. How does an aerial perspective of the Earth's surface differ from a ground perspective?

THINKING AND APPLYING

4. Draw a map titled 'My dream island'. Include the following essential features: border, title, scale, legend and direction.

USING YOUR SKILLS

5. Show the following written scales as line scales.
   a. One centimetre on the map represents five kilometres on the ground.
   b. One millimetre on the map represents 10 kilometres on the ground.
6. Refer to the Kakadu tourist map on page 22.
   a. What is the representative fraction (ratio scale) and scale statement for the map?
   b. Is the map a large-scale or small-scale map?
7. Refer to the map 'Holiday Island'.
   a. Draw the symbols that have been used for each of the following features: pool, rocks, pier.
   b. Walking in a straight line, what is the distance from the northern end of the pier to the western end of the tennis court?
   c. How long is the pier at its longest point?
8. How many camping sites are marked on the Kakadu tourist map on page 22?
9. Name the most northerly camping spot.
10. Find an example of a (a) point, (b) line and (c) area symbol on the map.
11. What is the distance by:
    a. sealed road from Bukbukluk to Meri
    b. unsealed road from Yurmikmik to Gunlom?
12. What direction is:
    a. Jim Jim Falls from Jim Jim Billabong
    b. Four Mile Hole from Black Jungle Spring?

GEOTERMS

cartography: the art of drawing maps. A professional map maker is called a cartographer.

compass: an instrument for determining direction

conventional symbols: standard symbols that are commonly used on maps

legend: used with a map to explain the meaning of signs and symbols shown on the map, also called a key

plan view: the view from directly above

scale: uses a line, ratio or words to show how distance on a map relates to distance in the real world

'Where is it?' is one of the key questions asked by geographers. Every place on Earth has a specific location. Map makers have developed a way of finding exact locations on the Earth by using a grid. A grid is a system of vertical and horizontal lines. If it weren't for grid references, finding places in detailed books of maps, such as street directories and atlases, would take a long time.

Alphanumeric grid references

Alphanumeric grid references are used to show maps over small areas. A street directory, a tourist map with a guide to a small town or a local area map will use this form of grid. The map extract of Manly, opposite, is divided into a series of squares. On the top of the map page the squares are labelled with a letter of the alphabet, and on the left-hand side of the page they are labelled with numerals, forming a grid pattern. This is an alphanumeric grid. If you wanted your friends from Hornsby to meet you at the Andrew 'Boy' Charlton Manly Swimming Centre, you would give them the grid reference C2. By tracing a line with your finger down from the letter C, and then across the page from the number 2, your friends should be able to find the swimming centre — and you.

GEOskills TOOLBOX

USING TOPOGRAPHIC MAPS

The map below is a topographic map showing contours, grid references and a legend or key. Topographic maps are useful when bushwalking, planning roads and checking the steepness of slopes. They show features of the physical environment, such as lakes, and of the human environment, such as roads, railway lines and settlements.

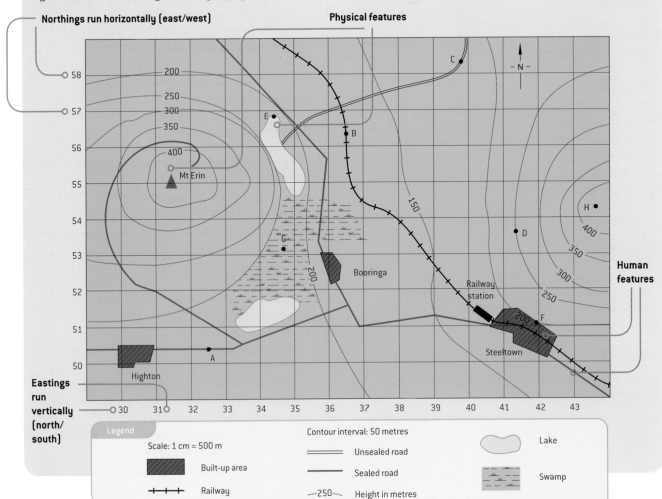

Northings run horizontally (east/west)

Physical features

Eastings run vertically (north/south)

Human features

Legend

Scale: 1 cm = 500 m

Contour interval: 50 metres

Built-up area

Railway

Unsealed road

Sealed road

—250— Height in metres

Lake

Swamp

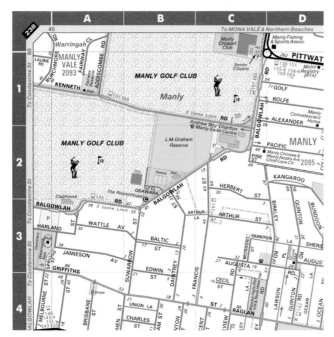

Map extract of Manly from a street directory

Area and grid references

Another detailed type of map where a grid system is used to accurately locate places is a **topographic map**. A topographic map shows relief or height above sea level using contour lines — lines that join places of equal height above sea level.

Topographic maps use lines overprinted to form a grid to help locate places. The grid lines are given as two-digit numbers that appear on the margins of the map. The lines that run up and down the map (north/south) are called *eastings* because the numbers increase the further east they are. The lines that run across the map horizontally (east/west) are called *northings* because the numbers increase the further north they are. When stating location, the eastings are given first, then the northings.

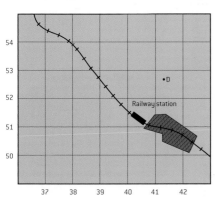

An example of an area reference on a topographic map

An **area reference** is a four-figure reference that tells us the grid square in which to find a feature. On the map above, the railway station is located at area reference 4051. The letters AR are usually placed in front of an area reference, so the area reference for the railway station is AR4051.

A grid reference is a six-figure number that shows an exact point in the grid square. The third and sixth figures represent one-tenth of the distance between the two grid numbers. However, these divisions are not written on the map, so they must be estimated. The letters GR are used in front of a grid reference. The grid reference for point D on the map at left is GR413527. There are no spaces between the digits in references.

ACTIVITIES ➡

UNDERSTANDING

1. What is a grid?
2. Why is a grid a useful tool for reading a map?
3. How does an alphanumeric grid work?
4. In which direction are eastings drawn?

USING YOUR SKILLS

5. Refer to the map extract of Manly at left. What is the alphanumeric map reference for:
   a the tennis court
   b L M Graham Reserve
   c Manly Golf clubhouse?

6. Refer to the simple topographic map opposite.
   a What is the area reference for these points marked on the map? The first one is given.
      • A is in AR3250.   • B   • C
      • D   • E   • F
      • G   • H
   b What are the grid references for the same points?
      A is GR325504.
   c In which direction would you have to travel to reach point D from:
      • B   • G   • F?
   d Using the legend, what is at each of these points?
      • A   • E   • B
      • C   • F   • G
   e Which towns can be found at the following area references?
      i. AR3050   ii. AR4150   iii. AR3652

GEOTERMS

alphanumeric grid reference: combination of letters and numbers that locate points on a map

area reference: four numbers used to locate features on a topographic map

grid reference: six numbers used to locate features on a topographic map

topographic map: a map that shows the height and shape of the land by using contour lines

How can you show a round globe on a flat piece of paper?

A globe is a scale model of the Earth showing the shapes of countries and continents in their true proportions. It is the most accurate way to represent the features of the Earth.

When we try to show a globe on a flat piece of paper, some of the features become stretched and squashed. Area, distance, direction and shape are all accurately represented on a globe. Flat maps are able to show only some of these features accurately while others are distorted.

A **map projection** is a representation of the Earth's surface drawn on a flat grid. The grid is made up of lines of **latitude** and **longitude** (see pages 28–9).

There are four types of map projections:
- Azimuthal or planar
- Conic
- Cylindrical
- Interrupted.

The purpose of the map influences which type of map projection is used. Maps used for navigation must show correct direction. Maps used to compare areas need to show all areas according to their actual size. The extent and location of the area to be mapped also influences which projection is used. Distortion increases as the area being mapped increases.

Different map projections can vary greatly in appearance and can change our view of the world. The four types of projections shown in the diagrams below can be further refined to show particular perspectives. The Mercator, Peters and Mollweide map projections shown opposite are variations of cylindrical projections. The McArthur Projection shows yet another perspective.

Developments in computer and satellite technology are now changing the way that maps are made. Future maps will rely much more on Geographic Information Systems (GIS). These systems are a set of computer programs designed to deal with databases that are able to collect, store, retrieve, manipulate, analyse and display mapped data from the real world.

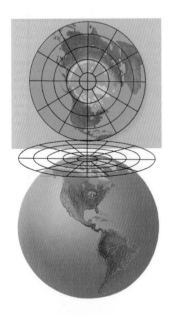

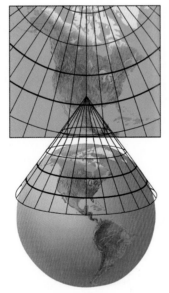

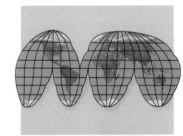

Azimuthal or planar projections
The surface of a globe is projected onto a flat piece of paper that touches the globe at only one point. These projections are often used to show the polar regions.

Conic projections
The globe is projected onto a cone and then unfurled to make a flat map. Conic projections are often used to represent mid-latitude regions because they show these areas with minimum distortion to land and water areas.

Cylindrical projections
Information is projected onto a cylinder wrapped around a globe. The cylinder is then unfurled to create a flat map. Cylindrical projections are often used to show low latitude regions (areas close to the Equator).

Interrupted projections
The globe is peeled like an orange and flattened out. Interrupted projections are very good at showing continents and oceans with little distortion to their shape or size.

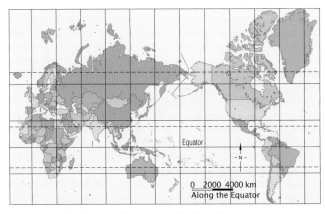

Mercator Projection, a cylindrical projection. *The scale and shape of regions near the Equator are accurate. Regions in high latitudes, such as North America, appear much larger than they actually are.*

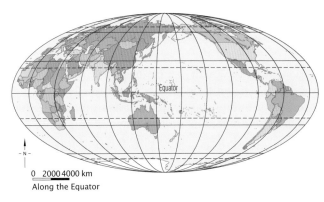

Mollweide Projection, a pseudocylindrical projection, *has curved meridians instead of straight ones. Distortion occurs at higher latitudes and the poles cannot be shown. This type of projection is often used for thematic maps.*

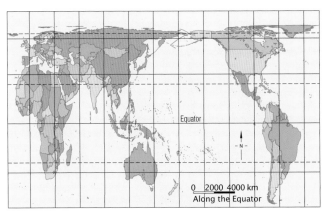

Peters Projection, a cylindrical projection. *The area of the land is more accurate but the shape is exaggerated.*

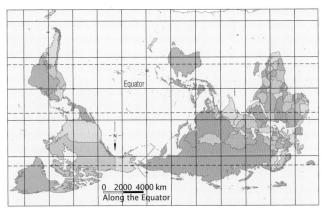

McArthur's Universal Corrective Map of the World *was published by an Australian in 1979. It provides a whole new way of viewing the world.*

GEO*facts*
In the early sixteenth century, Johannes Werner improved on an earlier map projection created by Johannes Stabius. The projection was heart-shaped and was used for world maps throughout the century.

ACTIVITIES ⊙

UNDERSTANDING

1. What is a globe?
2. Define the term 'map projection'.
3. List the four main types of map projections.
4. What are Geographic Information Systems (GIS)?

THINKING AND APPLYING

5. What is the advantage of using globes to show the Earth?
6. Outline why it is difficult to accurately represent the spherical surface of the Earth on a flat piece of paper.
7. Describe the distortions that appear in the size of the continents on the following map projections:
   a Mercator
   b Mollweide
   c Peters.
8. Compare the Mercator and Peters map projections.
   a The Peters Projection shows North America at an accurate size. How does the Mercator projection show North America?
   b Where does the most 'stretching' occur in these two projections?

GEOTERMS

latitude: imaginary lines drawn around the Earth that run east to west

longitude: imaginary lines drawn around the Earth from north to south

map projection: a representation of the Earth's surface drawn on a flat grid, using latitude and longitude

Any location on Earth can be described by two numbers — its latitude and its longitude. These numbers are important when, for example, rescuing people who are lost in a plane crash in the dense jungle or in a sinking boat in the middle of a storm in the Pacific Ocean.

Maps in atlases usually have lines of latitude and longitude printed on them. These lines help us find the exact location of places. If you look in the index of an atlas, you will usually see a series of numbers following the name of a location: these numbers represent latitude and longitude.

Van Diemen, Cape **80 C9** 11.10S 130.22E
Van Diemen Gulf **80 C9**
Vanern, Lake **114 G4** ———————— Latitude
Vanersborg **114 G4** | 58.23N | | 12.19E |
Vangunu, island **89 G3** ———————— Longitude
Vanimo **88 D3** 2.40S 141.17E
Vannes **116 C4** 47.40N 2.44W
Van Rees Range **88 C3**
Vanrhynsdorp **126 B1** 31.36S 18.45E

What is latitude?

Lines of latitude are imaginary lines drawn around the Earth in an east–west direction. These lines are called parallels of latitude because they run parallel to each other. They are measured in degrees (°). The most important line of latitude is the Equator (0°). Latitude lines are written using the letters N (north) or S (south).

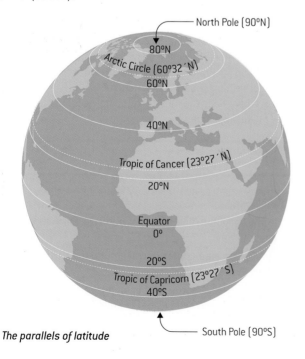

The parallels of latitude

What is longitude?

Lines of longitude are imaginary lines that run in a north–south direction from the North Pole to the South Pole. The lines are called meridians of longitude and they are also measured in degrees (°). The most important line of longitude is the Greenwich or Prime Meridian (0°). This line runs through the Greenwich Observatory in London. All the other lines of longitude are given a number between 0° and 180°. Longitude lines are written using the letters E (east) or W (west).

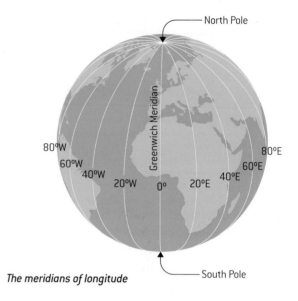

The meridians of longitude

What is a hemisphere?

The Equator divides the globe into the Northern and Southern hemispheres. Australia is located in the Southern Hemisphere, but most of the world's landmass is found in the Northern Hemisphere. The Greenwich Meridian divides the globe into the Western and Eastern hemispheres. The Western Hemisphere contains North America and South America. The Eastern Hemisphere contains most of Africa, Europe, Asia and Australia. Parts of Antarctica are found in both hemispheres.

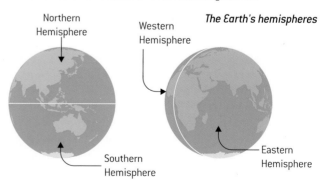

The Earth's hemispheres

Finding a place using latitude and longitude

The intersection of the lines of latitude and the lines of longitude can pinpoint any position on the Earth's surface. The lines of latitude and longitude form a grid pattern on the Earth's surface similar to that shown in the illustration below. The Greenwich Observatory in London can be located at a latitude of approximately 51° north of the Equator and a longitude of 0°.

Today the Global Positioning System (GPS) and Google Earth can calculate latitude and longitude anywhere on Earth.

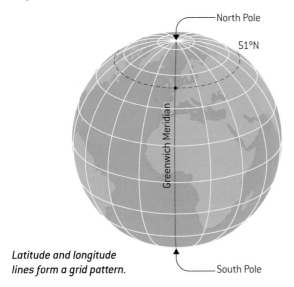

Latitude and longitude lines form a grid pattern.

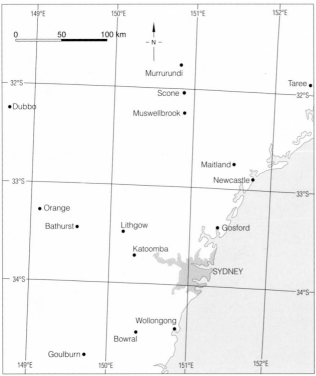

Map of Sydney and environs

To help pinpoint particular locations, each degree of longitude and latitude can be further divided into 60 small sections that are referred to as minutes. For example, the latitude of the town of Bathurst is 33 degrees (°) and 27 minutes (′) south of the Equator. Its longitude is 149 degrees (°) and 35 minutes (′) east of the Prime Meridian. When you look for the location of Bathurst in the index of an atlas, it will look something like this: 33.27S 149.35E.

GEOfacts

The point at which the Equator (0° latitude) and the Prime Meridian (0° longitude) intersect is in the Atlantic Ocean, 611 kilometres south of Ghana.

ACTIVITIES ➔

UNDERSTANDING

1. What is latitude?
2. Name two parallels of latitude.
3. What is longitude?
4. What is the most important meridian of longitude?
5. Refer to the map below left, and give the latitude and longitude to the closest degree for the following places: Lithgow, Taree, Dubbo and Gosford.

THINKING AND APPLYING

6. Use your own atlas to find the capital cities located at the points given below. Estimate the location using the world political map, and then turn to a map of the continent or region to make a more accurate estimate. Check your answer in the index (records of latitude and longitude vary slightly in atlases). The first letters of each correct answer spell the name of a continent.
   a 25°15′S 57°40′W
   b 8°30′N 13°17′W
   c 34°02′N 6°51′W
   d 33°42′N 73°09′E
   e 10°35′N 66°56′W
   f 13°49′S 171°45′W

USING YOUR SKILLS

7. Refer to the map at left. Which towns are located at the following latitude and longitude?
   a 33°17′S 149°06′E
   b 34°45′S 149°43′E
   c 32°55′S 151°46′E
8. Scone and Murrurundi have a similar longitude. Which town is further south? Can you tell this by simply looking at the latitude?

What time is it? If you are reading this at school, it will be sometime during daylight hours. But what time is it on the other side of the Earth?

Why does a day last 24 hours?

The Earth spins on an axis, creating night and day. It takes one day, 24 hours, for the Earth to complete one rotation of 360°. Each hour the Earth turns 15°. The globe opposite shows meridians of longitude spaced at intervals of 15°. Every hour a different meridian is directly opposite the sun. Places on the same longitude see sunrise and sunset at the same time.

What are time zones?

The Earth is divided into 24 time zones based on each 15° of longitude. When the sun is directly over the Prime Meridian (longitude 0°), the time is 12 noon Greenwich Mean Time (GMT). Locations to the east of Greenwich are experiencing afternoon or evening and those to the west of Greenwich have morning. For example, when it is noon in Greenwich, it is 10 pm in Sydney.

We use 15° of longitude to represent a one-hour time difference, but these time zones are often moved slightly so they coincide with international or regional borders. Also, some time zones do not represent an hour — South Australia, for example, is nine and one-half hours ahead of GMT.

International Date Line

The International Date Line is the line of longitude at 180°. It is both 180°E and 180°W of the Prime Meridian, so E or W is not necessary. The line has been 'bent' so it does not pass through land.

The International Date Line represents not only the point at which the time zone changes one hour, but also a change of one day. If you are travelling from the west to the east across the International Date Line, you gain one day. If you are travelling

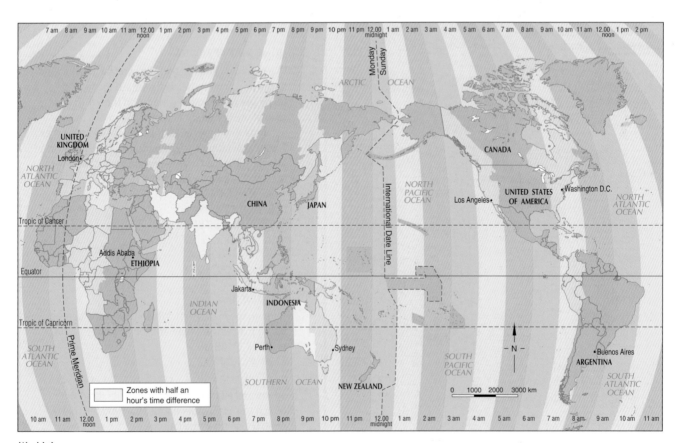

World time zones

from east to west, you move back one day — for example, at 10 am Monday in Sydney, it will be 4 pm Sunday in Los Angeles. To calculate this, count back one hour for each time zone until you reach the left-hand edge of the map. Then count back from the right-hand edge until you reach the Los Angeles time zone.

GEO*facts*

- Because 24 lines of longitude meet at the poles, it means Antarctica is divided into 24 very small time zones. To reduce time problems, scientists working at the poles use Greenwich Mean Time.
- Every spring most of Australia advances its clocks by one hour. This is called Daylight Saving Time. It allows people to take advantage of the longer daylight hours for outdoor leisure activities as well as reduce energy use. They then move the clocks back one hour in autumn.

The globe shows meridians of longitude spaced at intervals of 15°.

GEOskills TOOLBOX

USING A TIME ZONES MAP

If you know the time in one location, you can use the map of world time zones to find times anywhere in the world. For example: if the time in Sydney is 10 pm Monday, what is the time in Addis Ababa, Ethiopia? Locate Sydney on the map of world time zones opposite, then count back one hour for each time zone until you reach the zone in which Addis Ababa is situated. Addis Ababa is seven time zones behind Sydney, so it is seven hours behind Sydney. Therefore it must be 3 pm Monday in Addis Ababa. We have *not* crossed through midnight, so there is no change of day.

ACTIVITIES

UNDERSTANDING

1. What is Greenwich Mean Time? Why is it important?
2. What is the International Date Line? Where is it located?
3. Explain how we lose or gain a day by passing the International Date Line.
4. Find the International Date Line on the time zones map. Rewrite the following statement, filling in the missing words from the box below.

Cook Islands	New Zealand	China
sea	Wednesday	Kiribati
USA	land	west
Prime Meridian	W	line

The International Date Line is a _____ of longitude. Unlike other lines of longitude, it is not necessary to have either E or _____ after it because the line is both 180°E and 180°W of the _____ _____. The International Date Line does not pass through any _____. In fact, the line is deliberately 'moved' so it passes only through _____. If you travel across the International Date Line, you must change not only the time but also the day and date. To the *east* of the line is one day behind areas to the *west* of the line. So if it is Thursday in New Zealand, it will be _____ in Argentina.

USING YOUR SKILLS

5. Refer to the map of world time zones opposite.
   a. If it is 2 am Sunday GMT, what is the time and day in the following locations: Sydney, Perth, Jakarta and Washington DC?
   b. You have a friend living in Los Angeles, United States. You want to telephone her just before she leaves for school at 8 am Tuesday. What time should you telephone?
   c. If the Chinese Government linked its local times to standard time zones, how many time zones would China have?
   d. What advantages and disadvantages would this create for China?
   e. How many time zones are there in the United States? (Don't forget places that are not on the mainland!)

GEOTERMS

International Date Line: the line of longitude at 180°
time zones: the 24 hours of different time into which the Earth is divided

Why are some places in the world hotter than others and is there a general pattern to the world's temperatures? There are several factors that determine the temperature of a particular place. The most important influences on temperature include latitude, altitude and the distance from the sea.

The importance of latitude

Temperature varies with latitude. Most people know that the world's warmest places are in the tropics (near the Equator) and the coldest places are nearer the poles. At higher latitudes on the Earth's curved surface, insolation (incoming solar radiation from the sun) is spread more widely than at places of lower latitudes (see the diagram at right). The sun's rays that reach the Earth near the Equator (that is, at low latitudes) have a smaller area to heat than rays reaching the Earth at higher latitudes. This explains why Darwin experiences higher temperatures than Sydney.

Altitude

Temperatures are usually much lower in mountain areas than they are at sea level for places of the same latitude. The rate of change in temperature that occurs as altitude increases is called the lapse rate. It is generally between 1° and 2° Celsius per 300 metres.

Temperatures and solar radiation

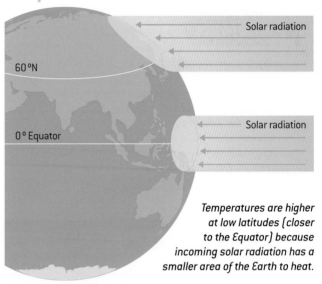

Temperatures are higher at low latitudes (closer to the Equator) because incoming solar radiation has a smaller area of the Earth to heat.

Temperature varies with latitude

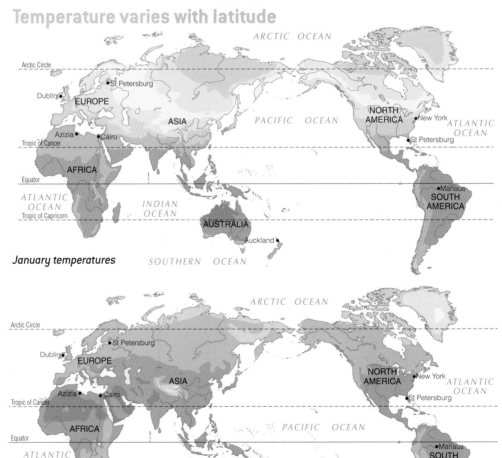

January temperatures

July temperatures

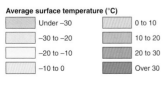

Average surface temperature (°C)

Under –30	0 to 10
–30 to –20	10 to 20
–20 to –10	20 to 30
–10 to 0	Over 30

Insolation and the seasons

At the Equator there are barely any seasons. The length of the day stays almost the same throughout the year, and at midday the sun is always high in the sky. However, a journey away from the tropics will take you to places where the seasons have a gradually greater effect on the climate.

The four seasons that are typical of places such as Sydney occur because of the tilt of the Earth's axis. The Earth rotates on its own axis — which is tilted at an angle of 23.5° to the vertical — and the Earth revolves once around the sun every 365 and one-quarter days. As the Earth completes its orbit around the sun, the tilt of its axis does not change. (It leans either to the right or the left, depending on which way you are 'looking' at the orbit.) This means that at certain times during the Earth's orbit, one hemisphere or the other is leaning more towards the sun.

When a hemisphere tilts towards the sun, it is 'hit' more directly by the sun's rays. So it heats up faster and the days are warmer. This hemisphere experiences summer. When a hemisphere tilts away from the sun, the sun's rays 'hit' it at more of an angle. So insolation from the sun's rays is spread out more, and is not as intense. Days are shorter and colder. This hemisphere experiences winter.

When neither hemisphere tilts towards the sun, which happens in autumn and spring, each hemisphere receives the same amount of insolation.

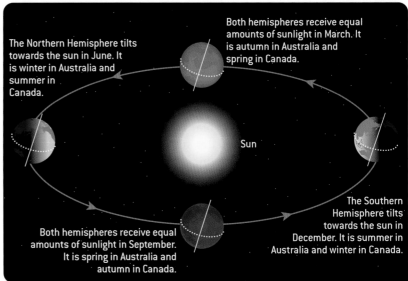

The Northern Hemisphere tilts towards the sun in June. It is winter in Australia and summer in Canada.

Both hemispheres receive equal amounts of sunlight in March. It is autumn in Australia and spring in Canada.

Both hemispheres receive equal amounts of sunlight in September. It is spring in Australia and autumn in Canada.

The Southern Hemisphere tilts towards the sun in December. It is summer in Australia and winter in Canada.

Sun

The tilt of the Earth affects seasonal insolation.

ACTIVITIES →

UNDERSTANDING

1. Identify the most important influences on the temperature of a place.
2. Define 'insolation'.
3. The region that always receives the sun's most direct rays is the:
   a. high latitudes
   b. tropics
   c. temperate zones
   d. middle latitudes.
4. Describe the effect of altitude on climate.

THINKING AND APPLYING

5. What season are we having in Australia when:
   a. it is autumn in England
   b. it is summer in Canada
   c. the sun does not set at the South Pole?
6. If the axis of the Earth were vertical, how would this affect weather patterns at the Equator and at the poles? How would this affect the climate where you live?
7. Refer to the diagram 'Temperatures and solar radiation'. Explain why temperatures are higher at the Equator than at the poles.
8. Refer to the maps 'Temperature varies with latitude'.
   a. Describe the world distribution of temperatures for January.
   b. Explain this distribution.

Altitude also influences temperatures. Mount Kilimanjaro in Africa is located only 3° south of the Equator. Air becomes cooler as it rises, and the peaks of mountains are typically colder than areas close to sea level.

GEOTERMS

insolation: incoming solar radiation or heat from the sun

The world can be divided into three major **climatic zones**: the tropics (near the Equator), which are warm and receive heavy regular rain; the polar regions, which are cold and dry; and the temperate zones, which lie between them.

Climate is the long-term variation in the atmosphere for a given area, as determined over the seasons and the years. Climate is not the same as **weather**. Weather is the condition of the atmosphere at a particular time. It can change very quickly in a short period of time. The two main elements of climate are temperature and **precipitation**.

World average annual precipitation

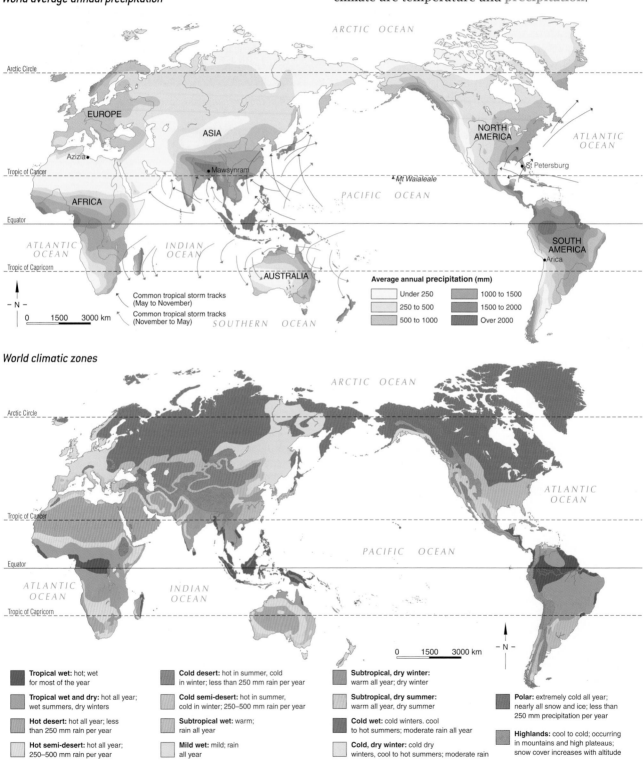

World climatic zones

Average annual precipitation (mm)

Under 250	1000 to 1500
250 to 500	1500 to 2000
500 to 1000	Over 2000

Common tropical storm tracks (May to November)
Common tropical storm tracks (November to May)

Tropical wet: hot; wet for most of the year

Tropical wet and dry: hot all year; wet summers, dry winters

Hot desert: hot all year; less than 250 mm rain per year

Hot semi-desert: hot all year; 250–500 mm rain per year

Cold desert: hot in summer, cold in winter; less than 250 mm rain per year

Cold semi-desert: hot in summer, cold in winter; 250–500 mm rain per year

Subtropical wet: warm; rain all year

Mild wet: mild; rain all year

Subtropical, dry winter: warm all year; dry winter

Subtropical, dry summer: warm all year, dry summer

Cold wet: cold winters. cool to hot summers; moderate rain all year

Cold, dry winter: cold dry winters, cool to hot summers; moderate rain

Polar: extremely cold all year; nearly all snow and ice; less than 250 mm precipitation per year

Highlands: cool to cold; occurring in mountains and high plateaus; snow cover increases with altitude

GEOfacts

Highest average annual rainfall
Mawsynram, Assam, India 11 783 millimetres

Highest recorded temperature
Azizia, Libya
58° Celsius

Most sunny days
St Petersburg, Florida, recorded 768 consecutive sunny days (1967–69).

Lowest average annual rainfall
Arica, Chile
0.8 millimetres

Lowest recorded temperature
Vostok Station, Antarctica
−89.2° Celsius

Most rainy days
Mount Waialeale, Hawaii, has up to 350 rainy days every year.

The Daintree, Queensland — tropical wet

Alberta, Canada — cold wet

South Island, New Zealand — mild wet

Uluru, Northern Territory — hot desert

ACTIVITIES

UNDERSTANDING

1. Identify the world's three major climatic zones.
2. What is the difference between *climate* and *weather*?
3. Which country has the highest recorded average annual rainfall?
4. Which country has the lowest recorded temperature?

USING YOUR SKILLS

5. Refer to the map 'World average annual precipitation'.
   a. Describe the location of three of the wettest regions on Earth.
   b. Describe the location of three of the driest regions on Earth.
6. Refer to the map 'World climatic zones'. Describe the main climatic zones for Africa as you move from the Equator to the southernmost tip of the continent.
7. Make a list in your notebook with all of the climatic zones listed in the map legend. Then, use an atlas to sort the following place names according to the climatic zone in which they lie:
   Helsinki, Cairo, Hobart, Calgary, Edmonton, Oodnadatta, Santiago, Paris, Denver, Manaus, Cooktown and Sydney.

GEOTERMS

climate: the long-term variation in the atmosphere, mainly relating to temperature and precipitation

weather: condition of the atmosphere at a particular time in relation to air pressure, temperature, precipitation, wind and cloud

The Earth is one of eight planets that circle the sun. Seventy-one per cent of the Earth is covered with water in the form of oceans, seas, rivers and lakes. The rest is made up of huge landmasses known as continents. There are six inhabited continents in the world: Africa, Asia, Australia, Europe, North America and South America. The seventh continent is Antarctica. The Earth's oceans are the Arctic, Atlantic, Indian, Pacific and the Southern oceans. The Earth has four main physical environments: lithosphere, atmosphere, hydrosphere and biosphere.

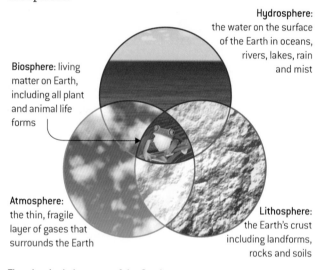

Biosphere: living matter on Earth, including all plant and animal life forms

Hydrosphere: the water on the surface of the Earth in oceans, rivers, lakes, rain and mist

Atmosphere: the thin, fragile layer of gases that surrounds the Earth

Lithosphere: the Earth's crust including landforms, rocks and soils

The physical elements of the Earth

Lithosphere

The lithosphere is the Earth's crust, including landforms, rock and soil. The lithosphere was formed about 4.6 billion years ago. Geographers have noticed that if the continents of the world were rearranged and repositioned, they would fit together like a giant jigsaw puzzle. Scientists believe that about 225 million years ago the continents were all joined together. Since then, they have broken up and moved apart. This process is known as continental drift.

Atmosphere

This is the thin layer of gases that surround the Earth. The mixture of gases in the atmosphere is commonly known as air. The atmosphere protects the Earth from the extremes of the sun's heat and the chill of space, making conditions suitable to support life. Our weather results from constant changes in the air of the lower atmosphere.

Hydrosphere

This is the water on the Earth's surface in oceans, lakes, rivers, rain and mist. Within the hydrosphere, water is stored in locations such as the oceans (liquid), the atmosphere (gas) and the icecaps (solid).

Biosphere

The biosphere is the living matter on Earth, including all plant and animal life forms. The biosphere consists of part of the atmosphere, lithosphere and hydrosphere because various forms of life exist in these spheres.

GEOskillbuilder

READING A PICTURE GRAPH

Picture graphs immediately tell the reader what the graph is about. They are read by carefully taking note of the numbers and/or labels on each axis.

STEP 1

Check the axis label to ensure you are measuring the correct item.

STEP 2

Use a ruler to line up the scale on the axis with the object to be measured.

STEP 3

When the measurement falls between numbers on the axis, estimate it.

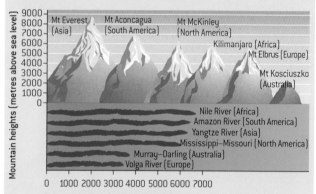

Highest mountain and longest river on each continent

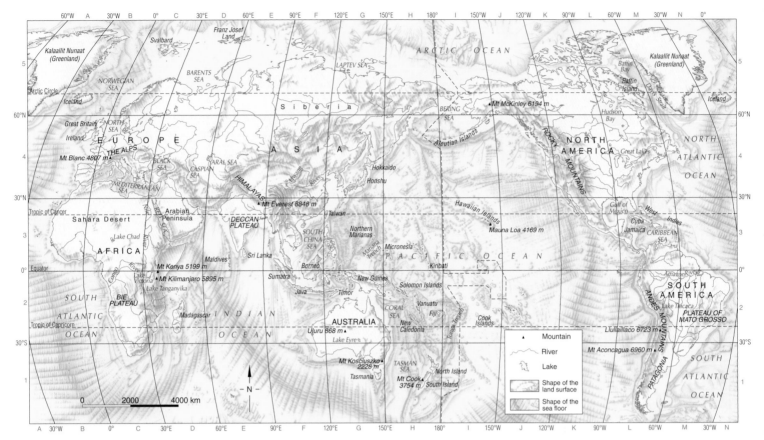

World landforms

GEO*facts*

- Mount Everest, highest mountain: 8848 metres
- Mauna Kea, highest mountain from base to top: 10 203 metres
- Andes, longest mountain range: 7200 kilometres
- Mariana Trench, deepest point on Earth: 11 032 metres in depth
- Dead Sea, lowest point on land: 400 metres below sea level
- Pacific Ocean, largest ocean: 166 241 700 square kilometres
- Nile River, longest river: 6695 kilometres
- Amazon River, greatest river: average flow of 175 000 cubic metres per second
- Caspian Sea, largest lake: surface area of 371 800 square kilometres
- Lake Superior, largest freshwater lake: 84 414 square kilometres
- Greenland, largest island: 2 166 086 square kilometres

GEOTERMS

continents: the seven great landmasses of the Earth

ocean: a large body of salt water

ACTIVITIES

UNDERSTANDING

1. Define the four main physical environments of the Earth.
2. What is continental drift?
3. What percentage of the Earth is covered in water?

USING YOUR SKILLS

4. Refer to the picture graph opposite.
   a. What is the approximate height of Mount Aconcagua?
   b. What is the highest mountain in Africa? Estimate its height.
   c. How many times higher is Mount Everest than Mount Kosciuszko?
   d. Which major river is 6020 kilometres long?
   e. What is the world's longest river? Estimate its length.
5. Refer to the map 'World landforms' above.
   a. Name the largest continent and its highest mountain.
   b. Imagine you are on an expedition travelling along the Equator from west to east in Africa. Outline the significant landforms and water bodies you would observe.
   c. Identify the largest ocean. Briefly describe the sea floor.

The human features of the Earth consist of any parts of an environment that have been built or altered by people (see page 11). Many features of the human environment can be mapped. For example, a political map of the world shows 195 countries. The world's population was approximately 6.7 billion in 2008. Every second, five people are born and two people die. At this rate the world's population is doubling every 40 years.

	Country	Population
1	China	1 324 700 000
2.	India	1 149 300 000
3.	USA	304 500 000
4.	Indonesia	239 900 000
5.	Brazil	195 100 000

100 000 000 people

Top five countries by population, 2008

GEOfacts

- Monaco is the world's most densely populated country with 16 587 people per square kilometre.
- Mongolia has the world's lowest population density with 1.7 people per square kilometre.
- Niger has the world's highest birth rate of 50 births per 1000 population in a year.
- Kuwait has the world's lowest death rate of 2 deaths per 1000 population in a year.
- Angola experiences the world's highest death rate of 25 deaths per 1000 population in a year.
- Swaziland has the world's lowest life expectancy at just 32 years.

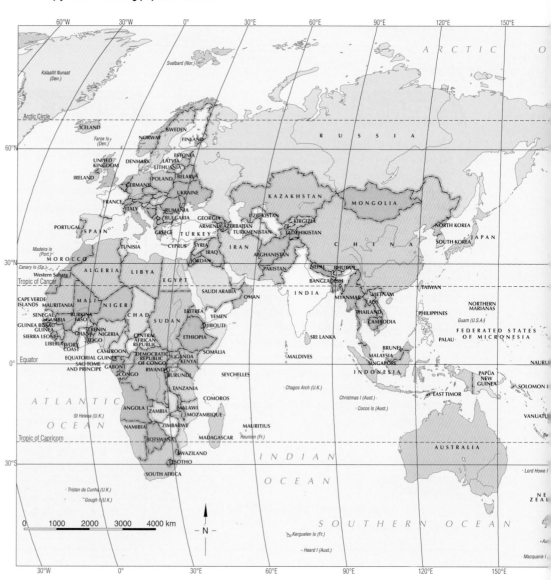

World political map

GEOskills TOOLBOX

READING LINE GRAPHS

Line graphs are best used to show trends or change over time. Usually the horizontal axis will show units of time. The vertical axis will show what changes over time. This example shows how the world's population has grown over time.

2054: 9 billion
2028: 8 billion
2013: 7 billion
1999: 6 billion
1987: 5 billion
1974: 4 billion
1960: 3 billion
1927: 2 billion
1804: 1 billion

World population growth (past and projected)

ACTIVITIES

UNDERSTANDING

1. How many countries are there in the world?
2. How many people are added to the world's population every day?
3. List the top five countries by (a) area and (b) population. Which countries appear in both lists?

THINKING AND APPLYING

4. If the world's current population growth continues, in what year will the population reach 12 billion? When will it reach 24 billion?

USING YOUR SKILLS

5. Refer to the political map of the world.
   a. Name a country located on the Equator, a country located on the Tropic of Capricorn, and a country located on the Arctic Circle.
   b. Australia is located between latitude 10°S and 44°S and longitudes 113°E and 153°E. Work out the locations of Canada, South Africa and Afghanistan.
6. Refer to the line graph 'World population growth'.
   a. Describe the pattern of growth of world population in the period from 1500 to 2000.
   b. How long did the world's population take to grow from one billion to two billion?

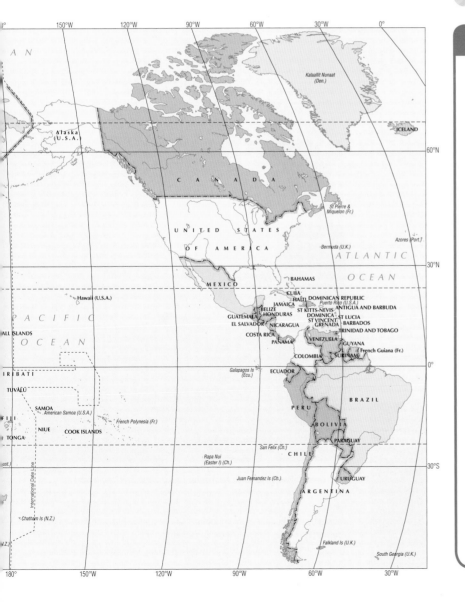

What is worth keeping?

The essence of the concept of World Heritage is that something is of such great value that it should be preserved for all people and for all time. The World Heritage Committee lists sites around the world that should be protected and conserved. There are now more than 878 World Heritage sites in more than 145 countries. Australia has 17 sites on the World Heritage List. The most recent Australian addition, the Sydney Opera House, was listed in 2007 as an example of human creative genius.

Since 2004 UNESCO has used one set of ten criteria for the selection of outstanding and/or unique World Heritage sites. These include:

i.   human creative genius
ii. exchange of human values, over time or within a culture
iii. culture or civilisation that is living or has disappeared
iv. building or landscape that illustrates significant stage(s) in human history
v.   human settlement representing human interaction with the environment, especially if vulnerable to extinction
vi. events, traditions, ideas or beliefs
vii. exceptional natural beauty and importance
viii. major stages of the earth's natural processes such as landforms
ix. ongoing processes in the evolution of living things and developing ecosystems
x.   important natural habitats for conservation of biodiversity.

(C) Mont-Saint-Michel and its bay, France. Mont-Saint-Michel is a Benedictine abbey built on a rocky islet in the midst of sandbanks exposed to powerful tides. It was constructed between the eleventh and sixteenth centuries. Because of its unique location and the problems that its builders had to overcome during its construction, it fulfils three of the criteria for World Heritage listing, most notably, human creative genius. This site was inscribed in 1979 under Criteria (i), (iii) and (vi).

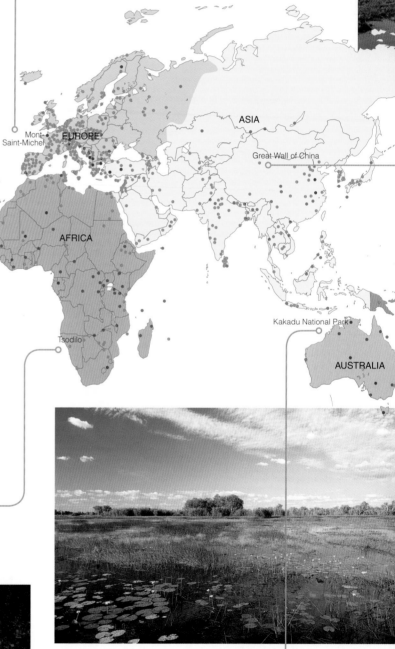

(C) Tsodilo, Botswana. Over 4500 rock art paintings are preserved on rocky outcrops at Tsodilo in the Kalahari Desert in Botswana. Tsodilo has been called the 'Louvre of the Desert' because of the number and richness of the paintings that tell of human activities in the region for over 100 000 years. The site was inscribed in 2001 under Criteria (i), (iii) and (vi). Criterion (vi) recognises that the site continues to have great spiritual and religious significance for the communities who live there today.

(N) Kakadu National Park, Australia. This unique archaeological and ethnological reserve, located in the Northern Territory, has been inhabited for more than 40 000 years by indigenous people. The cave paintings record the way of life of the inhabitants from the hunter-gatherers of prehistoric times. It is also a unique example of a complex of ecosystems. The site was inscribed in 1981 and extended in 1987 and 1992 under Criteria (i), (vi), (vii), (ix) and (x).

(N) Grand Canyon National Park, United States of America.
The Colorado River carved a huge, deep and twisting canyon over centuries as the Earth rose and erosion occurred. There are several important native American sites along the river. It is also one of the world's most popular canoeing, hiking, riding and tourist destinations. The site was inscribed in 1979 under Criteria (vii), (viii), (ix) and (x).

(N) Iguazu National Park, Argentina. This natural site was inscribed in 1984 under Criteria (vii) and (x) and covers an area of 55 000 hectares close to Argentina's border with Paraguay. The Iguazu Falls at the heart of this site are 80 metres in height and 2700 metres in diameter, making them one of the most spectacular waterfalls in the world. The national park is rich in fauna and includes 68 species of mammals, including tapirs, giant anteaters, howler monkeys, ocelots, jaguars and caimans. It is also home to 422 species of birds, 38 of reptiles, and 18 of amphibians, a large number of which are threatened or vulnerable.

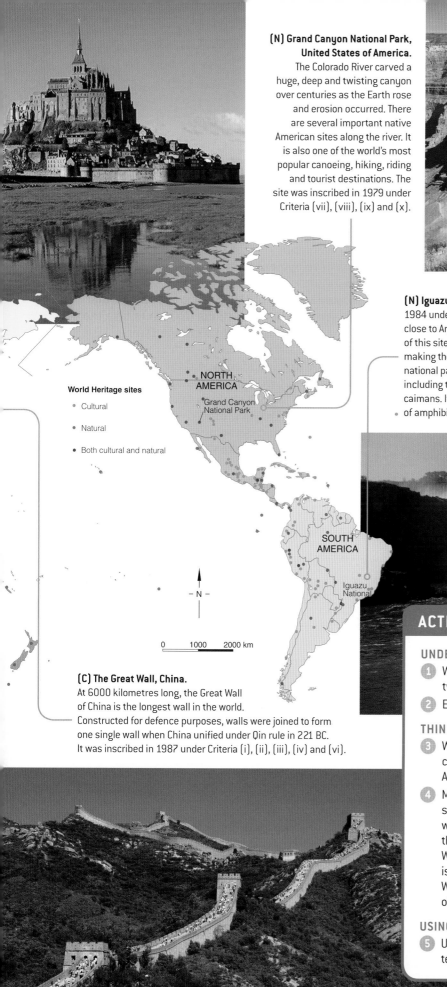

World Heritage sites
- Cultural
- Natural
- Both cultural and natural

NORTH AMERICA

Grand Canyon National Park

SOUTH AMERICA

Iguazu National

– N –

0   1000   2000 km

(C) The Great Wall, China.
At 6000 kilometres long, the Great Wall of China is the longest wall in the world. Constructed for defence purposes, walls were joined to form one single wall when China unified under Qin rule in 221 BC. It was inscribed in 1987 under Criteria (i), (ii), (iii), (iv) and (vi).

ACTIVITIES ➜

UNDERSTANDING

1. What are the requirements for placement in the two categories of World Heritage listings?
2. Explain the importance of World Heritage listing.

THINKING AND APPLYING

3. Why do you think that most of the World Heritage cultural sites are located in Europe rather than Australia or Africa?
4. Make a poster about a World Heritage site. Make sure you answer the key geographical questions: where is the site located (country)? When was the site inscripted (year it was placed on the list)? Why was it included on the list (criteria)? Why is it important to be on the World Heritage List? Who manages the site? What are the legal obligations of governments to preserve the site?

USING YOUR SKILLS

5. Using an atlas and the map on these pages, choose ten sites and give their latitude and longitude.

The World Heritage Convention

A treaty known as the 'Convention Concerning the Protection of the World Cultural and Natural Heritage' was adopted by the United Nations Educational, Scientific and Cultural Organization (UNESCO) in 1972. The aim of the convention is to promote cooperation among nations to protect sites of outstanding value.

Since the 1970s, more than 184 countries have signed this international convention, agreeing to conserve not only the World Heritage sites in their own country but those all over the world. Countries also contribute money, advice and emergency assistance for sites in danger.

Step 4: World Heritage Committee — reads all the reports. The selection is then based on the ten criteria. When the committee meets once a year, it decides which sites will be included on the World Heritage List.

Step 3: Advisory Bodies — the nominated site is independently evaluated by two Advisory Bodies. For a cultural site it is the International Council on Monuments and Sites (ICOMOS), and for a natural site it is the World Conservation Union (IUCN). After the site is evaluated, the Advisory Bodies prepare a report for the World Heritage Committee.

Step 2: Nomination file — the country then presents the nomination list to the World Heritage Centre in Paris for review. The list will include a detailed file of maps and facts about the site. Once the file is complete the World Heritage Centre sends it onto the Advisory Bodies, where it is evaluated.

Step 1: Tentative list — a country makes a list of natural and cultural heritage sites it wants included on the World Heritage List in the next 5–10 years.

Process: steps to becoming a World Heritage site

The World Heritage in Danger List

The World Heritage in Danger List informs the global community of sites threatened by problems such as development, conflict and decay. Increased global awareness has led to the successful coordinated efforts of UNESCO, governments and non-government organisations (NGOs) to take the following sites off the World Heritage Danger List:

- Angkor, in Cambodia, was in danger from illegal excavation and landmines, and the Old City of Dubrovnik, in Croatia, was damaged by artillery fire in 1991. UNESCO helped restore both sites.
- The old city of Fez, in Morocco, with 9000 narrow twisting alleys and decaying historic buildings is being restored under the World Heritage Cities Project, with a loan from the World Bank.
- The Giza pyramids were threatened by a highway project that would damage the site. In 1995, negotiations with the Egyptian Government resulted in an alternative solution.

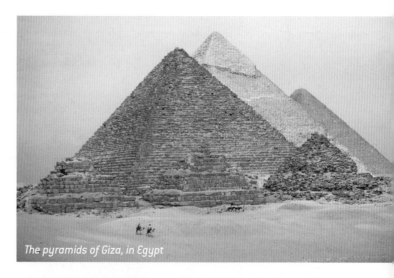

The pyramids of Giza, in Egypt

GEO*facts* Thousands of volunteers and non-government organisations restore World Heritage sites around the globe. The Sea Shepherd Conservation Society protects and conserves marine species and ecosystems. It has agreements with the governments of Ecuador and Costa Rica to survey the seas surrounding the Galapagos and Cocos Islands, both World Heritage sites.

- The Royal Chitwan National Park in Nepal provides refuge for 529 one-horned rhinoceros. In 1990, the World Heritage Committee informed the Asian Development Bank and the Nepalese Government that it was against the proposed Rapti River Diversion Project. The project would have threatened water habitats critical to the rhino inside Royal Chitwan. The project was abandoned.

The one-horned rhinoceros in Nepal

SAMPLE STUDY →

Dracula Park: Sighisoara, Romania

 Sighisoara, a town in Romania located at 46°N, 24°E, is the best-preserved, medieval fortified town in Transylvania. It was inscribed on the World Heritage List as a site of outstanding cultural significance in 1999. Sighisoara is also the birthplace of Dracula or Vlad the Impaler. Most Romanians know Vlad as a fifteenth century hero who fought off the Ottoman invaders and defended the Christians until his death. Vlad was not a vampire, but his cruelty inspired the fictional Dracula character who leaves his castle in Transylvania to feed on blood in the crowded streets of London.

A few years ago, Romanians wanted to create a Dracula Park in Sighisoara. The park offered catacombs and horror rides on vampire roller coasters. It was hoped to create 3000 jobs and attract one million tourists annually. After five years of protests, the Romanian Government drove a stake through the heart of Dracula Park. The theme park did not go ahead and the World Heritage site was preserved.

The clock tower and buildings in Sighisoara

ACTIVITIES →

UNDERSTANDING

1. What is the aim of the World Heritage Convention?
2. Who nominates new sites for the World Heritage List?
3. Which organisation selects sites for the list?
4. Briefly describe the process for World Heritage listing.
5. Discuss the arguments for and against the Dracula Theme Park.

6. Design a photograph collage of ten World Heritage sites. With each photograph include date of inscription, the criteria for selection and who is responsible for its management.
7. Imagine a special place you would like placed on the World Heritage List. Locate the place on a map, provide facts and figures about the place, describe the reason for its inclusion on the list and explain the process you would follow to have the site inscripted.

Protecting World Heritage sites

Population growth, resource exploitation, pollution, war, earthquakes, vandalism, climate change and tourism are all potential threats to World Heritage sites. In 2012, 100 million people are expected to visit World Heritage sites. To protect these sites, the UNESCO World Heritage Tourism Programme encourages sustainable tourism.

Impact of climate change on World Heritage sites

The potential impact of climate change on many World Heritage sites is a subject of growing concern. The following sites affected by climate change require a coordinated management strategy, involving individuals, groups and governments at national and local levels.

Tortin icefield, Switzerland

Melting glaciers: the Jungfrau-Aletsch-Bietschhorn area, in Switzerland, is affected by retreating glaciers due to increasing temperatures. The Aletsch Glacier has retreated 1.4 km over the past 56 years. As a short term solution, the Tortin icefield has been covered with a protective 2000 m² light-blue insulated sheet to reduce glacier melting in summer.

Venice, Italy

Rising sea levels: Venice, in Italy, has been sinking at a rate of 10 centimetres per century as a result of natural subsidence. With rising sea levels and flooding due to climate change, the historic buildings are in danger of disappearing. The building of massive, swinging gates is designed to help keep the marauding sea at bay.

Great Barrier Reef, Queensland

Increasing water temperatures: the Great Barrier Reef, in Queensland, is the largest coral reef ecosystem in the world. Increasing temperatures are already bleaching the coral. The coral turns

SAMPLE STUDY

// In 2000, the UNESCO World Heritage Committee inscribed the Greater Blue Mountains Area under natural criteria (ii) and (iv). This site has unique eucalypt vegetation and relic species such as the *Wollemia*. The NSW National Parks and Wildlife Service is the government agency managing the mountains for future generations.

The Greater Blue Mountains:

- covers over 10 000 square kilometres and is made up of eight conservation reserves
- protects 70 different vegetation communities — 10 per cent of Australia's higher plant species and 13 per cent of the world's eucalypt species
- protects 700 places of Aboriginal significance
- provides clean water to Sydney's water supply catchment of Lake Burragorang.

The Greater Blue Mountains is under stress from urban development, tourism, fires, pests, polluted

The Three Sisters, Blue Mountains, NSW

run-off from agriculture, and climate change. Increased temperature is expected to lead to more wildfires that could destroy the diversity of eucalypts. One of the strategies to protect this environment is controlled burning, aimed to limit the risk of intense and ecologically destructive fires.

white and dies, resulting in the deaths of thousands of fish species that depend on it to survive. Seventy per cent of the world's corals are expected to be affected by rising temperatures by the year 2100. By promoting sustainable tourism and improving the quality of the water that runs off into the ocean, it is hoped corals will be stronger and less vulnerable to climate change.

Protecting Australian sites

In Australia, the federal government is legally responsible for implementing international treaties and conventions. The state governments are the land managers for most World Heritage sites. If these sites are to be protected for future generations, the cooperation of federal, state and local governments is important.

World Heritage listing highlights the conflict between conservation and development.

In 1982, the federal government nominated part of western Tasmania for the World Heritage List. However, the Tasmanian Government wanted to construct a dam in the area. The Wilderness Society and environmentalists protested that this would destroy the area's natural beauty. To stop the dam, the federal government passed the *World Heritage Properties Conservation Act, 1983*.

ACTIVITIES

UNDERSTANDING

1. Name five threats to World Heritage sites.
2. What is climate change? Explain its impact on World Heritage sites.
3. How does Australia protect its World Heritage sites?
4. Explain the conflict over the management of western Tasmania in the 1980s.
5. Create a mind map displaying the reasons the Greater Blue Mountains is under stress.

THINKING AND APPLYING

6. Research and describe the impacts of climate change on five World Heritage sites. How could these sites be protected from the local to the global scale?

Franklin–Gordon Wild Rivers National Park, Tasmania

GEOTERMS

climate change: any change in climate over time, whether due to natural processes or human activities

eLesson

UNDERSTANDING MAP SCALES AND DISTANCE

In this video tutorial, you will gain an understanding of different map scales and how maps have been used throughout history and today. You will learn important geospatial skills, including how to use scale to calculate distance on a map and how you can calculate your driving distance from one place to another with a map, ruler and piece of string.

SEARCHLIGHT ID: ELES-0138

Interactivity

WORLD MAP

This interactivity features a political world map with zoom capability, and the ability to measure distance between two points. Double-click on the map to instantly measure the distance from one location to another or between a series of locations. You can then print the map with annotations included. A worksheet is included to enhance your understanding of key geospatial concepts.

SEARCHLIGHT ID: INT-0772

Interactivity

COMPASS DIRECTIONS

This interactivity will test your ability to complete a virtual journey around Australia. With each attempt you will be provided with three new points of reference. Using the on-screen compass, you must calculate directions for a journey from A to B to C and back to A again. The interactivity will show the path using the directions you have entered. If you are incorrect, you can adjust your answers and try again using the on-screen indicators to help you.

SEARCHLIGHT ID: INT-0774

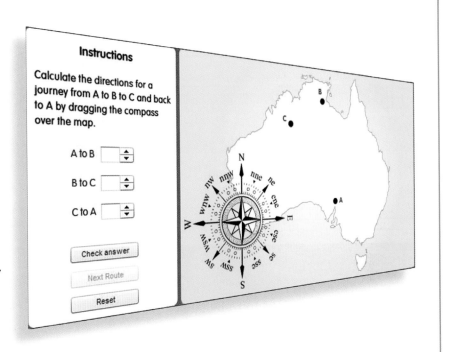

Instructions

Calculate the directions for a journey from A to B to C and back to A by dragging the compass over the map.

A to B

B to C

C to A

Check answer

Next Route

Reset

Interactivity

DAY, NIGHT AND TIME ZONES

This interactivity enables you to calculate the time of the day or night, anywhere in the world, on any given date and time. You can also explore the concept of how nightfall patterns change according to the seasons around the world. A full world map is included, with the international dateline, time zones and lines of latitude and longitude clearly marked. Six key cities are highlighted as points of reference, and a comprehensive worksheet is included to help you make the most of this interactivity.

SEARCHLIGHT ID: INT-0006

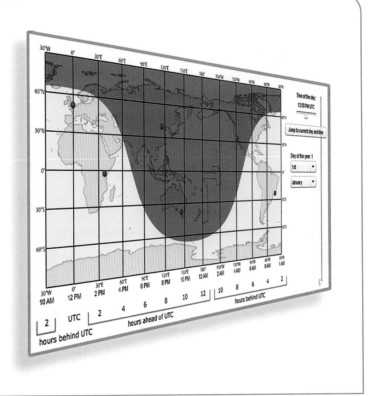

3 Geographical research

INQUIRY QUESTIONS

- How do geographers inquire?
- How do geographers study weather?
- How do geographers use tools in the field to investigate physical and human environments?

Geographers ask, and try to answer, key geographical questions about issues and places from a local scale to a global scale. Geographers use many tools and skills to investigate physical and human environments. For example, geographers can use maps, photographs, graphs and statistics to find out about places. They also carry out fieldwork. Fieldwork is practical geography, where you can find out about the interactions in an environment by observing, recording and analysing information.

GEOskills TOOLBOX

A volcanologist by the lava flow on Mt Etna

Consider the following questions.
- What are the causes and effects of tornadoes?
- Have you ever seen starving children from sub-Saharan Africa on television?
- How can a camel survive in a hot desert without water for 20 days?
- Why must you have injections to prevent cholera before you can travel to some countries?
- Why are expensive and fashionable running shoes manufactured in countries that pay low wages?

These questions and the matters they raise are all part of geography.

An inquiry model

Being curious is the basis of all inquiry. Let's assume you wanted to know about tornadoes. You could give some shape to your curiosity by asking the key geographical questions below about the topic.

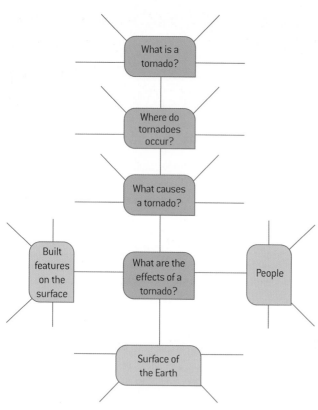

What is a tornado?

Where do tornadoes occur?

What causes a tornado?

Built features on the surface

What are the effects of a tornado?

People

Surface of the Earth

A simple geographical inquiry model

Further questions relevant to some geographical issues might be:
- How has it changed over time?
- Should it be like this?
- What will it be like in the future?

For the topic of tornadoes, this might lead to looking at data to determine whether the incidence of tornadoes is increasing or decreasing, why this might be so and what projections for the future incidence might be; for example, climate change might result in more tornadoes.

Skills and tools

Geographers are not the only ones to use an inquiry approach. However, geographical inquiry focuses on spatial concepts and the use of geographical skills and tools to answer questions. An inquiry into tornadoes, for example, would consider spatial interaction by studying how the location and movement of tornadoes interacts with the location of settlements.

Geographical skills include:
- locating, gathering and evaluating information from a variety of sources. Sources include fieldwork, maps, photographs, books, the media and the internet.
- observing and analysing information
- choosing and applying appropriate geographical tools
- presenting and communicating information to others
- participating as informed and active citizens.

Geographical tools include:
- maps
- fieldwork
- graphs and statistics
- photographs.

A theatre in Ohio, United States, destroyed by a tornado in 2002

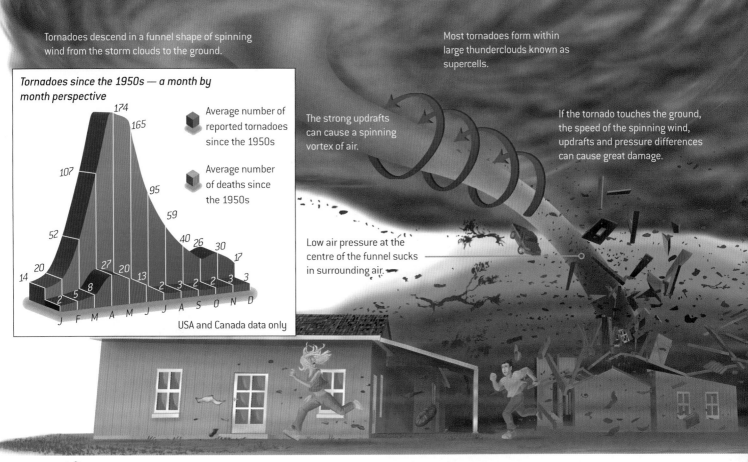

Tornadoes descend in a funnel shape of spinning wind from the storm clouds to the ground.

Most tornadoes form within large thunderclouds known as supercells.

The strong updrafts can cause a spinning vortex of air.

If the tornado touches the ground, the speed of the spinning wind, updrafts and pressure differences can cause great damage.

Low air pressure at the centre of the funnel sucks in surrounding air.

Tornadoes since the 1950s — a month by month perspective

174
165
107
95
59
52
40 26 30
20 17
14 27 20
8 13 2 3 2 3
2 5 2 2 3

J F M A M J J A S O N D

Average number of reported tornadoes since the 1950s

Average number of deaths since the 1950s

USA and Canada data only

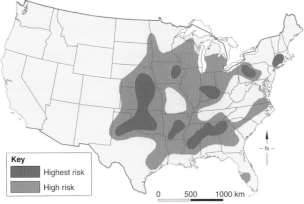

Key
Highest risk
High risk

0   500   1000 km

– N –

Areas in the United States at risk of being hit by a tornado. Every single point in places of highest risk can expect to be hit by a fairly large tornado at least once every 2000 years.

Communities in areas of the United States at high risk for tornadoes respond by:
- building basement shelters in most buildings
- instructing school students in safe evacuation procedures
- training residents, police and fire services in disaster relief.

GEOTERMS

spatial concepts: key ideas in geography including location, distance, direction, scale, region, distribution, movement, spatial interaction, spatial association and spatial change over time

ACTIVITIES

UNDERSTANDING

1 List the different types of geographical tools gathered here on tornadoes.
2 Which piece of information provided here would help answer which geographical question or questions?
3 Which geographical questions would require different information from that provided here?
4 Where might you find more information on tornadoes?

THINKING AND APPLYING

5 Refer to the map on this page and an atlas to work out which American states are most at risk of being hit by a tornado. List ten American cities or towns that lie within the highest risk zone.
6 The cars in the photograph ended up in the front seats of a theatre after a tornado swept through the area in 2002. Use one of the other pieces of information provided to explain how tornadoes can produce this outcome.
7 How could someone survive a tornado?
8 What else would you like to find out about tornadoes? How could you find this out?
9 Think of something you are curious about in your local area. Create a mind map like the one on tornadoes to guide your inquiry. Decide what skills and tools you will use in the inquiry.

Weather affects us every day. The temperature, rainfall, wind speed, cloud cover and humidity are all elements of weather that we might consider when planning our activities for the day. Weather can be studied and measured using a variety of instruments such as a thermometer for temperature and a rain gauge for rainfall. However, we are probably most familiar with the weather maps we see daily on television or in the newspaper.

Pressure systems

One of the most important features of the atmosphere and one that is very frequently measured is *air pressure*, or the weight of the air. All air has weight. While we can't feel it because we are constantly surrounded by it, sensitive instruments called barometers can measure the air pressure. Atmospheric air pressure measurements are given in hectopascals (hPa). Several times a day, air pressure is read at various weather stations around the world. Many observers around Australia measure air pressure and other aspects of the weather and send them to the Bureau of Meteorology. These observations are combined with others made from satellites, aircraft, ships at sea and in other countries to prepare weather maps or synoptic charts.

The main lines that we see on weather maps are called isobars. Isobars are lines joining places of equal pressure.

The average weight of air at sea level is 1013 hPa. If air pressure measures more than 1013 hPa, it is usually an area of sinking air and is generally

GEOskills TOOLBOX

READING SYNOPTIC CHARTS

The table below shows some of the main symbols found on weather maps. The labels and pointers around the weather map opposite show how these symbols might appear on an actual weather map.

Weather system	Name	Description	Associated weather
1020 1018 1016	Isobar	Lines joining places of equal pressure	The closer the isobars are, the stronger the winds.
1014 1016 H	High pressure system	Areas of sinking air	Generally fine weather. Winds rotate around these systems in an anticlockwise direction.
1012 1010 1008 L	Low pressure system	Areas of rising air	Generally cloudy weather and a good chance of rain. Winds rotate around these systems in a clockwise direction.
T.C. Pamela 1002 1000 998	Tropical cyclone	Areas of rapidly rising air	Torrential rain, very strong and destructive winds in a clockwise direction. Given a name (e.g. Tropical Cyclone Pamela).
	Cold front	Separates warm and cold air, with the cold air behind the front	Fall in temperature, may bring rain and storms. Front moves in the direction of the arrowheads.
	Warm front	Separates warm and cold air, with the warm air behind the front	Increase in temperature; may bring light showers. Uncommon in Australia.

an area of high pressure. High pressure systems are often called *anticyclones*. The moving air, known as wind, always moves out of a high and into a low pressure system.

If air pressure measures below 1013 hPa, it is usually an area of rising air, and is generally an area of low pressure. Low pressure systems are often called *cyclones*.

Pressure systems generally move from west to east as they move across Australia and around the world. As they move they change in shape and often change their latitudinal position.

GEOTERMS

atmosphere: the thin, fragile layer of gases that surrounds the Earth

synoptic chart: weather map that uses isobars and other symbols to show the movement of weather systems and patterns of temperature and rainfall

ACTIVITIES ➔

UNDERSTANDING

1. What is another name for a weather map?
2. What instrument measures air pressure?
3. Does an area of high pressure result from sinking or rising air?
4. In which direction across Australia do pressure systems generally move?

USING YOUR SKILLS

5. Refer to the synoptic chart below.
   a. What type of pressure system is dominating southern and eastern Australia?
   b. Name two areas of Australia that have experienced rain in the previous 24 hours.
   c. Why is Sydney experiencing fine weather?
   d. Describe the area on the map where it is likely to be windiest.

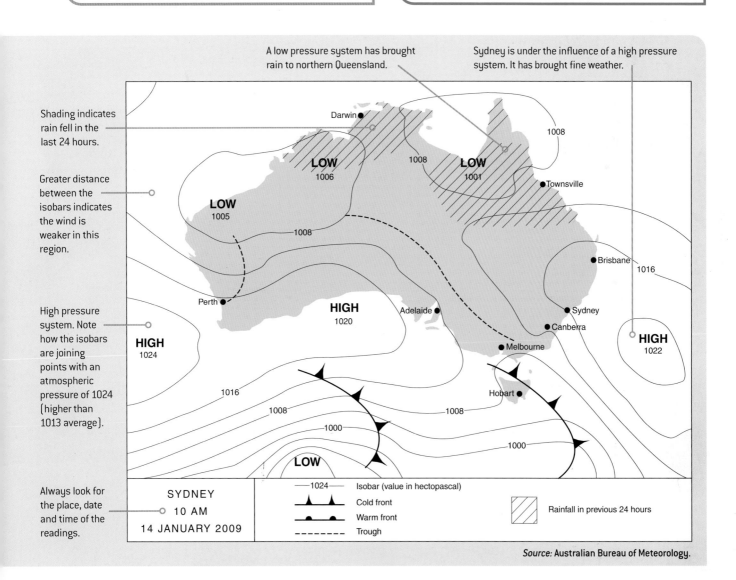

A low pressure system has brought rain to northern Queensland.

Sydney is under the influence of a high pressure system. It has brought fine weather.

Shading indicates rain fell in the last 24 hours.

Greater distance between the isobars indicates the wind is weaker in this region.

High pressure system. Note how the isobars are joining points with an atmospheric pressure of 1024 (higher than 1013 average).

Always look for the place, date and time of the readings.

SYDNEY
10 AM
14 JANUARY 2009

——1024—— Isobar (value in hectopascal)
▲▲▲ Cold front
●●● Warm front
- - - - - Trough

▨ Rainfall in previous 24 hours

Source: Australian Bureau of Meteorology.

There's a rabbit! No, it looks like a mouse! Clouds put on a daily show in our skies. Apart from their interesting shapes and colours, clouds can provide a useful indication of weather conditions. Weather observers around Australia send regular reports to Bureau of Meteorology forecasters on cloud types, height and the amount of sky covered. The official unit of cloud cover is eighths of the sky. When the sky is completely covered by cloud (overcast), the cloud cover is eight-eighths. When the sky is clear the reading is zero-eighths.

Cloud types

Clouds come in a range of textures, shapes and sizes. Some form only at certain altitudes. Others, such as cumulonimbus clouds, may extend right up through the troposphere. Clouds can be roughly described as being one of three main types. The meanings of their Latin names give us some idea of their appearance:

- 'strato' means smooth, flat layer
- 'cumulo' means pile or heap
- 'cirro' means curl.

Altocumulus clouds are found between about 2.5 and 6 kilometres above the ground. These are rippled clouds that may produce light showers.

Stratocumulus clouds are broad and flat at the bottom and puffy on the top. These clouds (whose base lies between about 1 and 2.5 kilometres above the Earth's surface) produce drizzling rain.

Cumulus clouds form fluffy, white piles that often evaporate. They can, however, turn into cumulonimbus clouds. Cumulus clouds lie between about 1 and 2.5 kilometres above the ground.

Tornadoes may form from the meeting of air underneath a developing cumulonimbus cloud. The swirling air is then tilted upwards to form the tornado. Tornadoes range in size from a few metres across to about a kilometre wide.

Stratus are low, greyish clouds whose base can be anywhere between ground level and about 2 kilometres above sea level. Any rain is often drizzle.

Smog (a mixture of fog and air pollution) hangs on the horizons of large cities. It becomes worse when a layer of warm air moves over a layer of cold air, preventing it from rising and spreading the pollutants. This is known as a temperature inversion.

Rainbows appear when sunlight passes through raindrops. As sunlight enters a raindrop, the rays of light are bent at different angles and the colours of light are separated. Rainbows have seven colours. From outside to inside they are: red, orange, yellow, green, blue, indigo and violet.

On clear, still nights the ground temperature can fall to below 0° Celsius. When this happens, water vapour can turn into solid crystals of frost. Frost occurs more often in valleys than higher areas because colder and heavier air sinks.

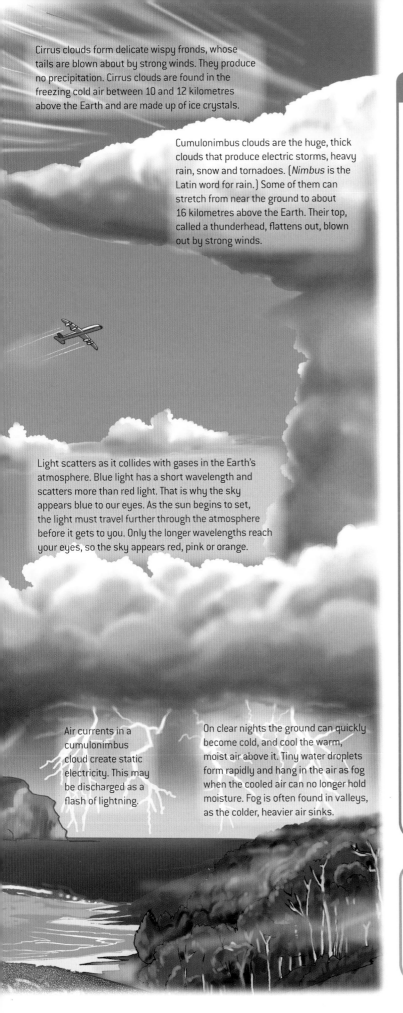

Cirrus clouds form delicate wispy fronds, whose tails are blown about by strong winds. They produce no precipitation. Cirrus clouds are found in the freezing cold air between 10 and 12 kilometres above the Earth and are made up of ice crystals.

Cumulonimbus clouds are the huge, thick clouds that produce electric storms, heavy rain, snow and tornadoes. (*Nimbus* is the Latin word for rain.) Some of them can stretch from near the ground to about 16 kilometres above the Earth. Their top, called a thunderhead, flattens out, blown out by strong winds.

Light scatters as it collides with gases in the Earth's atmosphere. Blue light has a short wavelength and scatters more than red light. That is why the sky appears blue to our eyes. As the sun begins to set, the light must travel further through the atmosphere before it gets to you. Only the longer wavelengths reach your eyes, so the sky appears red, pink or orange.

Air currents in a cumulonimbus cloud create static electricity. This may be discharged as a flash of lightning.

On clear nights the ground can quickly become cold, and cool the warm, moist air above it. Tiny water droplets form rapidly and hang in the air as fog when the cooled air can no longer hold moisture. Fog is often found in valleys, as the colder, heavier air sinks.

ACTIVITIES

UNDERSTANDING

1. Define the term 'troposphere'.
2. What are the three main types of clouds?

USING YOUR SKILLS

3. Refer to the illustration opposite.
   a. Describe what cumulus clouds look like.
   b. Clouds are categorised as low (from the Earth's surface to about 2 kilometres), middle (about 2 to 6 kilometres), or high (above 6 kilometres). Give one example for each category.
   c. Which clouds are made of ice crystals? Why do you think this is so?
   d. What are the similarities and differences between fog and clouds?
   e. What types of clouds can you see today? Will they produce rain? Explain.

4. Work in small groups for this activity. Observe the clouds you can see in the sky above your schoolyard over a two-week period. *Do not look directly at the sun.*
   - On each day, measure the temperature using a thermometer. The thermometer should be placed in a shady location about a metre above the ground and well away from buildings.
   - Estimate the percentage of the sky covered by cloud.
   - Identify the type of cloud using the illustration on these pages.
   - Draw up a table like the one below, and record your results in it.

Date	Time	Temp.	Cloud type	Cloud cover	Rain

   a. Is there a relationship between the percentage of cloud cover and temperature?
   b. Is there a relationship between the type of cloud and temperature?
   c. Did any rain fall during your trial? If so, which clouds produced rain?

GEOTERMS

troposphere: the closest layer of the Earth's atmosphere. It extends about 16 kilometres up from the Earth's surface and is where the Earth's weather occurs.

3.4 Photographs

Photographs are one of the geographer's most valuable tools. They are a record of how a place looks at any one time and often contain information that is not on a map. Photographs from different time periods can also show how a place has changed over time. The most commonly used photographs that geographers work with are those viewed from a:

- ground view
- oblique aerial view
- vertical aerial view
- satellite view.

GEOskills TOOLBOX

INTERPRETING PHOTOGRAPHS
Different views

Ground view

Oblique aerial view

Vertical aerial view

Scene A

This ground view shows how a feature would look if you were standing (or paddling) near it. A ground view gives an excellent impression of the height and shape of objects in the foreground, but those in the background are largely obscured and their scale is greatly distorted.

Scene B

An oblique aerial view gives a better idea of the height and shape of objects, but some of the objects in the background are hidden. Those in the foreground appear larger than those in the background.

Scene C

This view gives a 'bird's eye' view and is taken directly from above. With a vertical aerial view it is easy to see the spatial pattern of the surfers and their location in the water. This is the view from which maps are drawn.

Sandouping

Three Gorges Dam

UNDERSTANDING

1. What is another term for a bird's eye view?

2. In which view do objects in the foreground appear larger than those in the background?

3. Name one advantage and one disadvantage of satellite images as a means of studying the surface of the Earth.

USING YOUR SKILLS

4. Describe what you see in Scene A. Why do you think this type of photograph was used to show this scene?

5. If this was a race to shore, would Scene B or C best show you who was in the lead? Explain.

6. Refer to the satellite image of the Three Gorges Dam.
   a Which colour represents the urban area?
   b Which colour represents the vegetation?
   c What distance on the map is represented by one centimetre?
   d What features might you see in an aerial view or oblique aerial view of the Three Gorges Dam that cannot be seen here? What does the satellite image show that an aerial view or oblique aerial view might not?

Satellite image of the Three Gorges Dam and surrounding region, 2004

Key: vegetation (green); water (dark blue); urban area (purple)

Satellite images

Satellite images help geographers cover a much larger area of the Earth's surface than photographs taken from an aircraft. They are very useful in helping the geographer identify distinct regions but do not allow many smaller features to be identified. To do this, Landsat satellites are positioned 700 kilometres above the ground, orbiting the Earth every 100 minutes. Special cameras detect and record variations in the light reflected in a process known as remote sensing. Digital data is beamed to stations on Earth, where computers are used to enhance the images to enable the study of features such as landforms, farming, urban areas, impacts from disasters, environmental changes and weather.

Google Earth makes use of satellite images to help create its maps. This new map source, now widely used by geographers and other people, also uses high-resolution aerial photographs and GIS. People can find their way around a city, for example, by using Google's street maps overlaid on satellite images and aerial photographs.

Making a line drawing

Setting out a line drawing

Making line drawings from photographs is an important skill for the geographer. Line drawings encourage us to focus on the most valuable information in the photograph and draw attention to it by using labels or making notes.

STEP 1

Carefully observe the main features in the photograph. These features can be grouped under the following headings.

Physical features:
- climate
- landforms
- natural vegetation.

Human features:
- types of land use
- settlement
- transport
- other built features (such as dams).

There is no need to record these observations at first. However, they will help you when you attempt your line drawing.

STEP 2

Draw a frame in the same proportions as the photograph. It could be the same size as the photograph, depending on how large or small the photograph is. The line drawing on page 59 is slightly smaller than the photograph above.

Imagine that the photograph is divided into three areas: foreground, middle ground and background. This is shown on the diagram below.

Background		
Middle ground		
Foreground		
Left	Centre	Right

Each area does not have to be the same size. The proportions will depend on the photograph. Next, divide the area into left, centre and right.

STEP 4

Carefully observe the features in the background and draw and label these. Sketch and label the features in the middle ground and foreground. Remember that it is a line drawing, not a major art work.

STEP 5

You should now attempt to describe the various features shown in the photograph using the following headings.

Physical features:
- climate — are there clues in the photograph?
- landforms
- natural vegetation.

Human features:
- types of land use
- transport
- settlement
- other built features.

Background · Middle ground · Foreground

Coconut trees · Fruit trees · Houses in village · Padi to be harvested · Woman harvesting · Banana trees · Straw · Women bagging rice · Padi recently harvested

Climate
Rice growing indicates a warm climate. Padi fields mean that it is probably a wet climate.

Landforms
Flat and suitable for irrigation and rice farming

Natural vegetation
Mainly cleared except near houses in the background

Land use
Rice padi fields. Houses in the background — could be part of a village

Settlement
Scattered houses in the background

3.6 Local area fieldwork

Fieldwork in the physical environment

Geographers are very observant. In the classroom, as geography students, you observe a wide variety of information sources such as maps, diagrams, photographs and written material. But good geographers extend their skills beyond the classroom, library, office or laboratory to the field. Going outdoors and observing the physical and human environment is fieldwork. Fieldwork is practical geography in which you find out about interactions in an environment by observing, recording and analysing information. Fieldwork may involve anything from a walk around the school to an excursion lasting several days. A good place to start fieldwork is in the area around you: the school, the school grounds, your home and the local neighbourhood.

Location

Where is your school located?

1. Use an atlas to locate your school.
   - Give the latitude and longitude to the closest degree.
   - What type of map projection is the map? What are the advantages and disadvantages of this map projection?
2. Locate your school on a topographic map.
   - Use the legend and linear scale to identify and name the physical and cultural features within 10 kilometres of your school.
3. Locate your school in a street directory.
   - Compare the information shown on the street directory map with the atlas and topographic maps. What are the differences in scale, details and purpose?
4. Draw a sketch map locating your school within the surrounding area.
   - Include your home and features such as transport routes, shopping centres, clubs, churches, parks and sporting facilities.
   - Add a linear scale, legend and north point.
   - Use the scale to measure the straight line distance from school to home. Compare this with the actual distance you travel (use thin string to follow your path on the map, then pull the string straight and measure the length using the linear scale).

GEOskillbuilder

DRAWING A SKETCH MAP

STEP 1

Establish the border of the map. Walk around your school grounds to determine the overall layout of the map.

STEP 2

Distinguish between the physical (for example, plants) and human (for example, buildings) features. Decide on the detail required and show these details on the sketch. Use different symbols and colours to show different features and list them in the map legend.

STEP 3

Walk around the perimeter of the school grounds, counting your steps as you go. Measure the length of your step and calculate the total distance.

STEP 4

Choose a linear scale for your map. For example, 1 centimetre on the map will represent 50 metres on the ground. Walk around the main features and check that their size on the map corresponds to the scale.

STEP 5

Use a compass to add a north point to your map (see page 22).

STEP 6

Complete the map by adding a title.

STEP 7

Check that you have a border, scale, north point and legend. Remember, when using a compass in the field:
- It is important to remember the compass always points to north (or magnetic north).
- To orientate a map, turn the map so that north on the map is in line with the true direction of north on the ground.

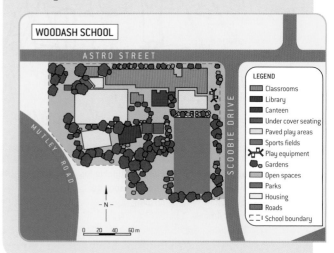

Climate and weather (atmosphere)
How hot, wet, windy and shady is it?

Use the **Bureau of Meteorology** and **Measuring Weather** weblinks in your eBookPLUS. Use information from these weblinks and your own observations to investigate the local climate and weather.

1. Use a thermometer to record the temperature in the coolest and hottest part of the school. Read the temperature at the same time each day.
   – Record your findings on a chart for two weeks.
   – Calculate the average maximum and minimum temperatures, the average temperature and the temperature range.
2. Make two simple rain gauges. Place one under trees and the other one in an exposed area. Each day measure how many millimetres of rain has fallen in each jar.
   – Record your findings on a chart for two weeks then calculate the average **precipitation.**
   – Are the readings different for each jar? Why?

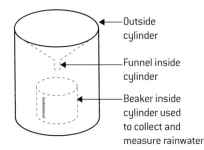

Outside cylinder

Funnel inside cylinder

Beaker inside cylinder used to collect and measure rainwater

Simple rain gauge

3. Compare your results for temperature and precipitation with the daily newspaper or Bureau of Meteorology statistics (use the **Bureau of Meteorology** weblink in your eBookPLUS). Give reasons for the differences.
4. Attach some lightweight material to the end of a broomstick and describe the wind direction, four times a day over two days. Use the Beaufort Scale (explained in the table) to describe the wind speed.
5. Collect synoptic charts over a week and discuss the changes to the weather in your local area. What effects have high and low pressure systems, wind direction, wind speed, fronts and precipitation had on your weather?

What types of clouds cover the sky?

Find out about clouds on pages 54–5 of this chapter and also by using the **Clouds** weblink in your eBookPLUS. Sketch, describe and compare clouds over two days.
– Name the different types of clouds you observe.
– Estimate how much of the sky is covered by clouds over two days. Give reasons for changes.

Water quantity and quality (hydrosphere)
Where does the water flow?

Use the **Landcare** weblink in your eBookPLUS. Which catchment is your school located in?
   Draw a sketch map of your catchment and use your own observations to determine:
– What direction does the water run when it rains?
– What are the names of the creeks near your school? Are the creeks permanent or intermittent? Where do they flow to and in which direction?

The Beaufort Scale

Beaufort number	Description of wind	Effect of wind on objects	Range of wind velocity (km/hr)
0	Calm	Calm, smoke rises vertically	Less than 1
1	Light air	Direction of wind shown by smoke drift; vane doesn't move	2–6
2	Light breeze	Felt on skin; leaves move, vane moves	7–12
3	Gentle breeze	Leaves/small twigs move constantly	13–19
4	Moderate breeze	Raises dust/loose paper; small branches move	20–30
5	Fresh breeze	Small leafy trees sway; crests on small waves on inland waters	31–39
6	Strong breeze	Large branches move; telegraph wires whistle	40–50
7	Moderate gale	Trees sway; uncomfortable to walk against	51–61
8	Fresh gale	Breaks twigs; difficult to move against	62–74
9	Strong gale	Can cause damage to houses e.g. remove tiles	75–87
10	Whole gale	Seldom inland; trees uprooted; considerable damage to buildings etc.	88–102
11	Storm	Very rare; widespread damage	103–120
12	Hurricane	Very rare; widespread damage	Above 120

Do you have good quality water?

1. Use the **Streamwatch** and **Waterwatch** weblinks in your eBookPLUS. Use information from these weblinks and your own observations to investigate whether waterways in your local area are polluted.
   - Take measurements such as pH, velocity, turbidity and temperature. Record and interpret your results.
   - Count plants and water bugs. Small bugs can indicate the level of water pollution. For example, mayfly nymphs indicate the water is not heavily polluted.
   - Research the relationship between water quality and frogs. Did you find any frogs? What does this tell you about your water quality?
2. Use your own observations and information from the **Landcare**, **Community Involvement** and **Oz Green** weblinks in your eBookPLUS to find out about environmental issues in your catchment.
   - List the environmental issues.
   - How are environmental groups managing water quality problems in your catchment?

What is in the gutter?

Stormwater and rubbish eventually flow into rivers, lakes or the sea.
- Carry out a litter survey along a 100-metre length of roadside gutters in different locations (near your school, around shopping centres, near parks and industrial areas).
- Plot this information on graphs and describe the spatial distribution of rubbish.
- Draw a mind map of potential management strategies.

Landforms and soil (lithosphere)

What is on the ground?

1. Use a topographic map to find your school's height above sea level.
2. Use a clinometer and tape to determine the slope of the land in the school grounds (flat, gentle, steep or split-level).
3. How has the slope affected land use, soil erosion and the construction of buildings?
4. How have humans changed the original landforms? For example, have retaining walls been built to stop soil erosion?

What is under the ground?

1. What is the bedrock (for example, sandstone, shale)?
2. Take three soil samples from different places in the school grounds: one exposed to sunlight, one shaded by buildings or trees and one used by most people (for example, a pathway). Place samples in plastic bags and label them.
   - Describe the colour (for example, red, black, brown) and texture (for example, sandy, clay, moist, dry) of each sample.
   - Compare the different samples and give reasons for the differences.
3. Collect a bucket of soil from several places in the school grounds.
   - Count the number of earthworms in each bucket and compare the findings.
   - Record the results: under five earthworms per bucket means poor soil; five to ten good; and over ten excellent.

Severely eroded creek

Plants and animals (biosphere)

What types of plants and animals are found?

1. Collect and press vegetation samples. Place your samples on cardboard and label them.
   – Describe the leaves (for example, thin, broad, waxy, hard) and flowers (colour, number of petals).
   – Determine whether they are native or exotic.
2. Count birds for five minutes, three times a day. Compare the number of native versus introduced species.

Sulphur-crested cockatoo, a native bird

3. Describe problems caused by exotic and introduced species in your local area.

Civics and citizenship

How can I be an active responsible citizen?

1. What do the phrases 'not in my backyard' and 'act locally think globally' mean? Would you protest against a nuclear power station or a garbage dump beside your school? Give reasons for your answer.
2. What level of government (local, state, federal) deals with issues such as disappearing native species and flooding of streets after heavy rain?
3. What are the rules in your local area about clearing native vegetation for housing development, agriculture or other land uses? What are your views on these issues? How can they be managed sustainably?
4. There are many places in Australia that have restrictions on water use. How can you promote the responsible use of water:
   (a) by your own example
   (b) in your household
   (c) in your local area?

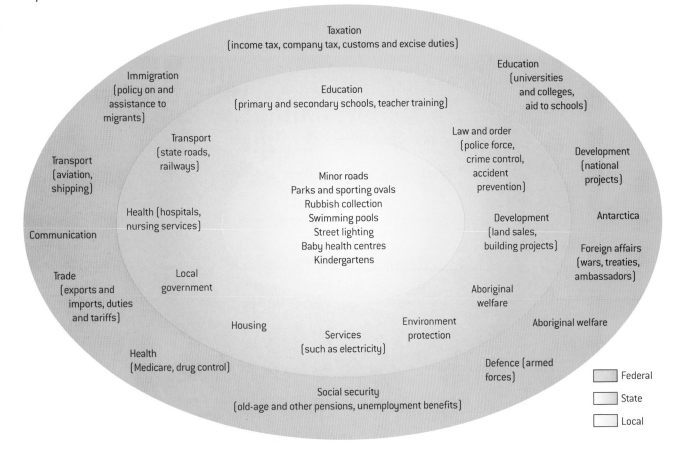

Responsibilities of the three levels of government

Fieldwork in the human environment

Local areas are constantly changing and many possess a colourful history. For example, buildings in the historic Rocks area of Sydney were once warehouses and sailors' homes. Today they are used as art galleries, restaurants and shops. All over Australia there are examples of local areas that were originally Aboriginal sites and consisted of natural vegetation before they were developed into housing, retail and industrial sites.

What makes up the changing built environment?

1. Make a collage of different types of buildings found in your local area. Use a mixture of labelled drawings and photographs from sources such as newspapers, magazines or the internet.
2. Visit the local library or council chambers and research changes to the physical (cleared land) and human (architecture, materials used for buildings, height and size of buildings) environments in the local area over the last 100 years. Divide the class into groups and allocate an area of research to each group. Pool your research and discuss the changes.
3. Research the price range of homes, units, factories, shops and farms in the local area. Compare these prices with another local area. Explain the differences (use the **Real Estate** weblink in your eBookPLUS).

4. Are the homes and schools in your local area environmentally sustainable? Prepare an environmental audit of your home or school (use of water, power, pesticides, native vegetation, insulation and airconditioning). Present this information as an oral report to the class.
5. Describe how your school or home could become more environmentally friendly.
6. Use the **Sustainable House** weblink in your eBookPLUS. Compare and contrast a sustainable home with your own home. Design your own sustainable house and present your plan as a poster for display.

The Rocks area of Sydney

Why are local shopping centres changing?

Shopping centres have changed over the last 50 years. Many small retailers such as the local corner shop have to compete with supermarkets and discount department stores. Shops in towns and in the central business district of cities also compete with large shopping centres or suburban shopping malls. Online shopping is a new source of competition for traditional retailers. All these changes affect local shopping centres and communities.

1. When a local shopping centre goes into decline, it often means vacant and run-down shop fronts and reduced property values. Investigate a declining shopping area in your local district or interview the owner of a corner store. List factors that have led to the decline (for example, the shopping centre has been isolated by a new bypass road) or problems that have made it more difficult to run a successful business. Present your investigation as an oral report to the class.

2. You can now buy a wide range of goods including your food from the internet. Search the internet for two sites that provide online food shopping. Compare and contrast the two sites with each other, and list the advantages and disadvantages of online shopping. Discuss how this technology is changing local communities.

3. Draw a transect of the main shopping centre near your home or school. Label the different types of shops and describe the architecture (for example, modern, 1920s renovated). Discuss whether the shopping centre is growing or declining. Give reasons for the changes.

4. Interview a person who can tell you what the shopping area was like 40 years ago. Present your findings as an oral report to the class.

Conducting an interview

Shops in towns compete with suburban shopping malls.

What is the social and economic profile of your local community?

1. Research the demographics of your local area (population, income, age, religion, education, occupation, birthplace and ancestry). Sources of information include your local council and internet sites (use the **Australian Bureau of Statistics** and **Real Estate** weblinks in your eBookPLUS).

2. Interview a person who belongs to a local group or club, for example, a sporting club, church, volunteer or charity organisation, music or environmental group.
   - Your interview should include the following key geographical questions:
     - What is the name of the group?
     - Where and when do they meet?
     - What does the group do? (function, purpose)
     - What are the members' responsibilities and rights?
     - How does the group help the community?
   - Create a poster about the group using the information you have gathered.

3. Conduct the following class survey on immigration in your local area.
   - How many migrants are in your local community? Where do they come from? Discuss the differences between the generations.
   - Compare these figures with two other local areas (use the **Australian Bureau of Statistics** weblink in your eBookPLUS).
   - What are the advantages of a multicultural local area?

4. How can we help to build stronger local communities? (Use the **COMMUNITY Builders** weblink in your eBookPLUS.) Use this link to design a multimedia presentation for your class about building stronger communities.
   - List 20 different community builders in New South Wales.
   - Research three of the following topics: Drugs and Community Action, Racism No Way Education Resource, Teaching about Human Rights and Responsibilities, and The Choice is Yours board game.

Migrant survey

Country of origin	Students			Parents		Grandparents	
	Self	Brothers	Sisters	Mother	Father	Grandmother	Grandfather
Australia							
United Kingdom							
Italy							
Greece							
New Zealand							
Pacific Islands							
Vietnam							
India							
China							
Indonesia							
Middle East							
Others (list countries)							

COMMUNITY builders website

How do the human and physical elements of environments interact with the local area?

Create a report, multimedia presentation or web page using the following subheadings:

Biophysical
- Describe a disaster in your local area such as a flood, hailstorm, fire, drought, cyclone, landslide or earthquake and how the community responded to the disaster.

History
– Investigate Aboriginal sites or multicultural changes in your local area, and report on how this heritage has affected your community.

Chinese New Year being celebrated with a dragon dance outside Town Hall in Sydney

Social and economic
– Research issues such as poverty, unemployment, crime, inadequate housing, types of businesses (banks, retail, tourism, mines, farms) or the availability of sporting facilities in your local area.

Community associations
– List events that are held in your community such as market days, parades, sporting events and religious activities. How does your community commemorate national events such as Anzac Day or Australia Day? Describe one or more local events that you have participated in.

Political services and local area infrastructure
– Investigate and list government facilities and services in your area such as pools, parks, libraries, postal and communication networks, transport services and garbage disposal. Does your community need more facilities or services such as hospitals, schools, roads, railway lines, buses, ferries, airports or better sewage disposal? How could your community achieve better services or facilities?

Community-based services
– What is available in your local area? List sources of entertainment such as movie theatres, health services such as doctors and dentists, non-government and volunteer organisations such as the Red Cross or Rotary.

Information services
– Does your area have a local newspaper or its own radio and TV station? Are there adequate telephone and internet services available?

Local, state, national and global links
– What links does your community have with other communities? Consider information and communication links such as the internet, cultural links such as music, theatre, food or clothes and links that result from activities such as tourism, sport and education programs.

What are the contemporary geographical issues in your local area?

1. Prepare a media file on ten geographical issues in your local area over the last six months. Include the names of the newspapers or magazines and the dates that the articles were published. Highlight the main points. Determine whether the articles are biased or include a variety of perspectives.
2. Investigate three of the following contemporary issues by using a variety of information sources:
   • feral animals and exotic plants
   • polluted atmosphere, water and soil
   • graffiti and street litter
   • lack of areas for young people — skateboard ramps, theatres, entertainment and sporting facilities
   • poor transport
   • crime (Neighbourhood Watch).

TRAFFIC COUNT			LOCATION: A	
DATE: 20/9/09				
Time Interval	Cars		Bikes	
	To the city	From the city	To the city	From the city
7.30–7.45	₦₦ ₦₦ ₦₦ ₦₦ ₦₦ //	₦₦ ₦₦ ₦₦	///	
7.45–8.00	₦₦ ₦₦ ₦₦ ₦₦ ₦₦ ₦₦ ₦₦ /	₦₦ ₦₦ ₦₦	₦₦	//
8.00–8.15	₦₦ ₦₦ ₦₦ ₦₦ ₦₦ ₦₦ ₦₦	₦₦ ₦₦ ₦₦ /	₦₦ ₦₦ //	////
8.15–8.30	₦₦ ₦₦ ₦₦ ₦₦ ₦₦ ///	₦₦ ₦₦ ₦₦	//	//
8.30–8.45	₦₦ ₦₦ ₦₦ ₦₦ ₦₦ ₦₦ ₦₦ ///	₦₦ ₦₦ ₦₦ ///	///	///
8.45–9.00	₦₦ ₦₦ ₦₦ ₦₦ ₦₦ ₦₦ ₦₦ ₦₦	₦₦ ₦₦ ₦₦	₦₦	/
9.00–9.15	₦₦ ₦₦ ₦₦ ////	₦₦ /	₦₦ /	///
9.15–9.30	₦₦ ₦₦ ₦₦ ₦₦ ₦₦	₦₦ ₦₦ ₦₦	₦₦ ////	

Simple traffic survey

Engineers and architects have built shopping complexes that have become pleasant experiences for communities. They provide not only shops but entertainment, sporting and medical facilities. This is part of the global trend for regional shopping centres to become a focal point for the community.

From small markets to supermarkets

Very few humans produce everything they need, so most people are forced to buy things. In all communities humans buy and sell goods and services in marketplaces. In less developed countries people buy goods, such as food, at local markets. The shops are often at the side of the road and each shop is owned or run by a family. In contrast, people in developed countries tend to buy their food at large supermarkets, owned by large corporations such as Woolworths or Westfield. In the twenty-first century, people are increasingly shopping via the internet, at least for some goods and services.

The increased popularity of shopping online has so far had only a minor impact on major shopping centres.

Today's shopping centres in Australian cities provide a shopping 'experience' rather than simply the basic necessities.

SAMPLE STUDY →

Multifunctional Macquarie Centre

 Macquarie Centre is located opposite Macquarie University in North Ryde, Sydney. It was opened in 1981. The centre is built in a continuously graded mall that spirals upwards. It features over 200 retailers such as Woolworths, Myer, Target, Event Cinema complexes and Borders. Most of the shops are grouped according to their type; for example, most of the fresh food shops are located in the fresh food market. This 'one-stop' shopping experience means visitors can do many things in the centre: buy food and clothes, book a holiday, go to the bank, see a movie, catch up with friends or go to the doctor. The centre also offers a number of services to customers, such as powered scooters and wheelchairs to help people with limited mobility. The centre constantly reviews its retail mix so that it meets the changing needs of the market.

The centre is surrounded by Macquarie Park — a leading high-tech industrial area, attracting electronic, scientific, computing, medical, communication and pharmaceutical companies; examples include Microsoft and Sony. Access to the centre and transport is an attraction for many global companies. The Park employs over 35 000 people and is the fourth largest concentration of jobs in NSW. As most workers shop at the centre, a Macquarie Centre Shuttle transports them to the centre during their daily break between 11 am and 3 pm, Monday to Friday.

Most people travel to the centre by bus, car or rail. There are over 4100 parking spaces, including 3500 undercover spaces. The centre is linked to major roads, and the passing M2 motorway links the Sydney CBD to the outer western suburbs. Macquarie Centre has a bus interchange and a railway station on the Epping to Chatswood railway line.

QUESTIONNAIRE FOR PROPRIETORS

Name of shop or business: _____

Function of this business: _____

Location: _____

1. When did this business first open at this site?

    Before 1980   1986–90   1996–2000

    1981–85   1991–95   2001–present

2. Did the business first open at this site or relocate from another site?

    Always at this site   Relocated

    If relocated, where from? _____

3. Is this one of a chain or group of shops/businesses?

    Yes   No

4. How many people are employed here (including management)?

    1–6   7–10   More than 20

5. Where do most of your supplies come from?

    Local area   Other parts of Australia

    Other suburb or town in New South Wales   Overseas

6. Does your business rely on services from other firms in the local area?

    Cleaners   Milk vendor   Banks

    Insurance   Medical   Carrier/transport

    Couriers   Others

7. What are the advantages of this location for your business? _____

    _____

8. Are there any problems associated with this location?

    _____

    _____

QUESTIONNAIRE FOR SHOPPERS

1. What suburb do you live in? _____

2. How did you get to the centre?

    Taxi   Bus   Bicycle

    Train   Car or motorcycle   Walk

3. Did you use the car park provided by the centre?

    Yes   No

4. How often do you shop at the centre?

    This is the first time   Once a fortnight

    Several times a week   Once a month

    Once a week   Only very occasionally

5. What types of goods and services will you buy today?

    Clothes   Groceries

    Household/electrical goods   Fresh fruit and vegetables

    Financial/banking services   Light meal/refreshments

6. Do you often shop at any other major shopping centre?

    Yes   No   If yes, which one? _____

7. What attracts you to this centre? _____

8. Apart from shopping, are there any other reasons for you coming to the centre?

    Work   Post office   Bank

    Hairdresser   Doctor   Dentist

    Solicitor   Restaurants   Entertainment

    Other _____

ACTIVITIES

UNDERSTANDING

1. Outline the services provided by today's shopping centres.

2. Describe the location of Macquarie Centre. Why is it ideally located for many shoppers?

THINKING AND APPLYING

3. Imagine you are a developer planning a shopping centre.

    a What special features would you like to include? Sketch your shopping centre and how you would arrange the shops. What design do you think would suit both young and old people in your community?

    b Where would you build the centre? Consider the physical environment, where people live and how they would get to the centre.

USING YOUR SKILLS

4. Fieldwork: walk around the main streets surrounding Macquarie Centre (if possible) or your closest regional shopping centre. Draw a sketch map showing streets, businesses, parks, houses and schools.

GEOskills TOOLBOX

USING SURVEYS AND QUESTIONNAIRES

Geographers are interested in where things are, why they are there and how people interact with their environment. Your local shopping centre is an example of these processes.

As a class, decide what you would like to find out about your local shopping centre. You will need to design a questionnaire like the examples on this page to assist you in obtaining the information.

After conducting your surveys, collate your results. Present the class findings using tables, graphs, photographs, sketches and maps.

Working geographically

KNOWLEDGE AND UNDERSTANDING

Select the alternative A, B, C or D that best answers the question.

1 Which is *not* part of the study of geography?
(A) Weather
(B) Physical landforms such as mountains and rainforests
(C) Maps and atlases
(D) Recreational activities

2 The physical elements of the environment are
(A) air, soil, water, flora and fauna.
(B) air, soil, water and solar energy.
(C) air, water, fauna, solar energy and radiation.
(D) air, flora, fauna, soil, water and solar energy.

3 The human elements of the environment are
(A) agriculture, settlements, industry, economy, politics and socioculture.
(B) agriculture, settlements and industry.
(C) settlements, industry, economy and politics.
(D) agriculture, settlements, industry and economy.

4 A map can be most accurately defined as a
(A) record of the Earth's physical features.
(B) drawing of a place.
(C) simplified plan of a place seen directly from above.
(D) scale model of objects.

5 Which of the following lists best describes the essential features a map should have?
(A) Border, title, scale, latitude and longitude, direction
(B) Border, title, scale, direction, legend, perspective
(C) Title, direction, scale, latitude and longitude, physical features
(D) Border, title, scale, latitude and longitude, legend, direction

6 What are the four cardinal points of a compass?
(A) North-east, south-east, east-west and south-west
(B) North, south, west and north-east
(C) North, south, east and west
(D) North, north-east, north-west, and south

7 The Earth's major climatic zones are
(A) the lithosphere, biosphere, atmosphere and hydrosphere.
(B) precipitation, temperature and wind.
(C) the tropics, polar regions and temperate zones.
(D) the Equator, Tropic of Capricorn and Tropic of Cancer.

8 Cumulonimbus clouds are
(A) low, greyish clouds.
(B) delicate, wispy clouds.
(C) storm clouds.
(D) broad and flat at the bottom and puffy on the top.

9 On the Beaufort scale, a strong gale is
(A) 11
(B) 7
(C) 4
(D) 9

10 A photograph that gives a bird's-eye view of a part of the Earth's surface is known as
(A) an oblique aerial view.
(B) a vertical aerial view.
(C) a ground view.
(D) a scale view.

11 Sites around the world that are protected for either their natural or cultural significance are known as
(A) UNESCO sites.
(B) World Conservation sites.
(C) World Heritage sites.
(D) Monument sites.

TESTING YOUR MAPPING SKILLS

Use the map of Tasmania opposite to answer the following questions.

12 What direction is it from Hobart to Launceston?

13 What direction is it from Hobart to Port Arthur?

14 What direction is Hobart from Freycinet Peninsula?

15 What is the southernmost point of mainland Tasmania?

16 What is the distance between
a Hobart and Launceston
b Cape Grim and Cape Portland
c Burnie and Queenstown?

17 What mountain lies 150 kilometres NW of Hobart?

18 What island is located at approximately 40°S and 148°E?

19 What projection has been used to draw this map?

20 What national park can be found at grid reference C2?

21 Use the index in your own atlas to find the following places: Cape Sorell, Hastings, Mole Creek, Hunter Island. Give the latitude and longitude of each place.

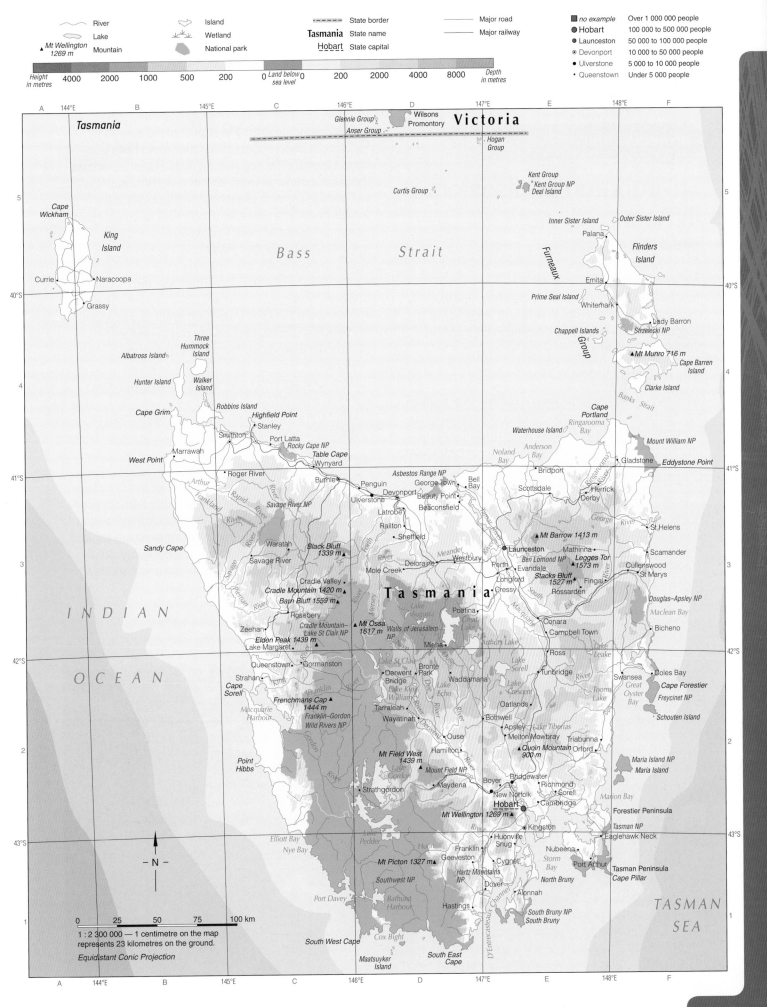

Legend

	River
	Lake
▲ Mt Wellington 1269 m	Mountain
	Island
	Wetland
	National park
– – –	State border
Tasmania	State name
Hobart	State capital
	Major road
	Major railway

■ no example	Over 1 000 000 people
● Hobart	100 000 to 500 000 people
◉ Launceston	50 000 to 100 000 people
◎ Devonport	10 000 to 50 000 people
● Ulverstone	5 000 to 10 000 people
• Queenstown	Under 5 000 people

Height in metres: 4000 2000 1000 500 200 0 Land below sea level 0 200 2000 4000 8000 Depth in metres

Tasmania

Victoria

Glennie Group
Wilsons Promontory
Anser Group
Hogan Group

Bass Strait

Curtis Group

Kent Group
Kent Group NP
Deal Island

Cape Wickham

King Island

Inner Sister Island
Outer Sister Island
Palana

Furneaux

Flinders Island

Currie
Naracoopa

Emita

Grassy

Prime Seal Island
Whitemark

Lady Barron
Strzelecki NP

Three Hummock Island

Chappell Islands

Group

Albatross Island

▲ Mt Munro 716 m
Cape Barren Island

Hunter Island
Walker Island

Clarke Island

Banks Strait

Cape Grim

Robbins Island
Highfield Point
Stanley

Cape Portland
Ringarooma Bay

Smithton
Port Latta
Rocky Cape NP

Waterhouse Island

Noland Bay
Anderson Bay

Mount William NP
Gladstone
Eddystone Point

West Point
Marrawah
Table Cape
Wynyard

Bridport

INDIAN
OCEAN

Roger River
Burnie
Penguin
Asbestos Range NP
George Town
Bell Bay

Scottsdale

Herrick
Derby

Arthur
Rapid
River
Savage River NP
Ulverstone
Devonport
Beauty Point
Beaconsfield
Latrobe

George River
St Helens

Sandy Cape

Waratah
Black Bluff 1339 m ▲
Railton
Sheffield
Mole Creek
Deloraine
Westbury
▲ Mt Barrow 1413 m

Savage River
Cradle Valley
Cradle Mountain 1420 m ▲
Barn Bluff 1559 m ▲
Rosebery

Tasmania

Launceston
Ben Lomond NP
Perth
Evandale
Longford
Cressy
Stacks Bluff 1527 m ▲
Rossarden
Mathinna
Legges Tor 1573 m ▲
Fingal

Cullenswood
St Marys

Zeehan
▲ Mt Ossa 1617 m
Walls of Jerusalem NP
Miena
Poatina
Arthurs Lake
Conara
Campbell Town

Douglas–Apsley NP
Maclean Bay
Bicheno

Eldon Peak 1439 m ▲
Lake Margaret
Cradle Mountain–Lake St Clair NP

Lake Augusta
Great Lake

Ross

Queenstown
Gormanston
Lake St Clair
Bronte Park
Waddamana
Lake Sorell

Tunbridge
Lake Leake

Swansea
Coles Bay
Cape Forestier
Freycinet NP

Strahan
Cape Sorell
Franklin
King
Derwent Bridge
Lake King William
Lake Echo
Lake Crescent
Oatlands
Tooms Lake
Great Oyster Bay
Schouten Island

Macquarie Harbour

Frenchmans Cap ▲ 1444 m
Franklin–Gordon Wild Rivers NP
Tarraleah
Wayatinah
Bothwell
Apsley
Lake Tiberias
Melton Mowbray
Triabunna
Orford

Maria Island NP
Maria Island

Point Hibbs

Mt Field West 1439 m
Mount Field NP
Hamilton
Ouse
▲ Quoin Mountain 900 m

Strathgordon
Lake Gordon
Maydena
Boyer
New Norfolk
Bridgewater
Richmond
Sorell
Cambridge
Marion Bay

Forestier Peninsula

Lake Pedder
Hobart
Mt Wellington 1269 m ▲
Kingston

Tasman NP
Eaglehawk Neck

Elliott Bay
Nye Bay
Huon
Huonville
Snug
Franklin
Geeveston
Cygnet
Nubeena
Storm Bay
Port Arthur
Tasman Peninsula
Cape Pillar

– N –

Mt Picton 1327 m ▲
Hartz Mountains NP
Dover
Alonnah

Southwest NP

Port Davey
Bathurst Harbour
Hastings

North Bruny
South Bruny NP
South Bruny

TASMAN SEA

South West Cape
Cox Bight
South East Cape

Maatsuyker Island

0 25 50 75 100 km

1 : 2 300 000 — 1 centimetre on the map represents 23 kilometres on the ground.

Equidistant Conic Projection

Environmental disasters in Asia

SEARCHLIGHT ID: PRO-0029

YOUR TASK

Your task is to create an interesting slideshow that reviews a natural disaster in Asia and offers some suggestions for what could be done in the future to minimise the impact.

SCENARIO

As a new employee in the Asian Hazards Organisation you are keen to make a good impression on all of your work colleagues. You have just been given the job of presenting on behalf of the organisation at the annual Hazards in Asia conference that will be held in Jakarta, Indonesia, later this year.

Scientists and government representatives from all around the world will attend the conference so your presentation will need to be informative and interesting to a range of knowledgeable people.

Your job will be to talk about a specific hazard, to review the events that led to a disaster caused by that hazard and to describe the impact of the disaster. You should also suggest things that could have been done to reduce the negative impacts of that hazard on the people and environment that were affected. You will need to create a slideshow that includes striking visuals and some notes for you to read as you present.

Your audience will want to know:

- What type of disaster was it?
- Where did the disaster occur?
- How did the disaster occur, and why did it occur where it did?
- What were the social, environmental and economic impacts of the disaster on the people in the immediate area and the country/region as a whole?
- What was done to reduce the negative impacts of the disaster?
- What should have been done and what could be done differently in the future?

PROCESS

- Open the ProjectsPLUS application for this chapter, located in your eBookPLUS. Watch the introductory video lesson and then click the 'Start Project' button to set up your project. You can complete this project individually or invite other members of your class to form a group. Save your settings and the project will be launched.

Your ProjectsPLUS application is available in this chapter's Student Resources tab inside your eBookPLUS. Visit www.jacplus.com.au to locate your digital resources.

SUGGESTED SOFTWARE
- ProjectsPLUS
- Microsoft PowerPoint

MEDIA CENTRE

Your Media Centre contains:
- a selection of maps and images to use in your presentation
- weblinks to sites with information on the disasters you will research
- an assessment rubric.

- Navigate to your Research Forum. A number of recent Asian disasters have been loaded as topics to provide a framework for your research. Choose the disaster you would like to include in your presentation and delete the other topics.
- Research the disaster you have chosen. You should find at least two sources (other than the textbook, and including at least one offline source such as a book or encyclopaedia) to help you discover information about the disaster you are presenting. The weblinks in your Media Centre will help you get started. Enter your findings as articles in the Research Forum. You can also view and comment on other group members' articles and rate the information they have entered.
- When your research is complete, create your slideshow. A selection of images has been provided for you in your Media Centre to download and use in your presentation. If working as a group, assign time for each group member to have access to your slideshow file. Remember to leave time before the final due date so you can review each other's work and make any changes.
- Print out your Research Report from ProjectsPLUS and hand it in to your teacher with your slideshow. You might even like to present your slideshow to your class.

eLesson

UNDERSTANDING A WEATHER FORECAST

You might watch the weather report every day on the evening news, but do you really understand what all the information means? Just what is a high or low pressure system, and what are all those swirly lines and colours all over Australia? This eLesson will help you interpret weather maps for yourself and provide you with an insight into how the experts predict future weather conditions.

SEARCHLIGHT ID: ELES-0161

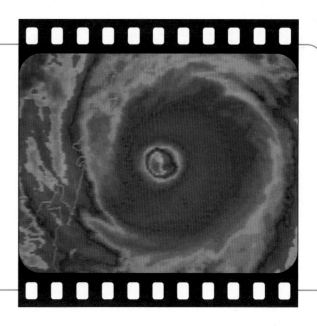

4 Global environments

INQUIRY QUESTIONS

+ What are the locations of the main types of global environments?
+ How do communities adapt to the global environments in which they live?
+ How have global environments been changed by human activities?

Global environments are many and varied. From polar lands situated at extreme latitudes to the coral reefs and rainforests of the tropics, each has unique physical and human features. Geographers study environments and how people adapt to and interact with specific environments. Many global environments have already been significantly changed by humans. Today's challenge is how to manage them sustainably for the future.

GEOskills TOOLBOX

+ Using oblique aerial photographs (page 79)

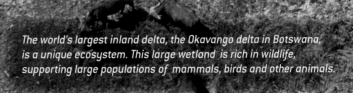

The world's largest inland delta, the Okavango delta in Botswana, is a unique ecosystem. This large wetland is rich in wildlife, supporting large populations of mammals, birds and other animals.

KEY TERMS

biodiversity: the rich variety of all life forms on Earth, including plants and animals

blue-green algae: micro-organisms that grow in water high in nutrients, such as nitrates and phosphates

community: an identifiable group formed by people with something in common; usually based on shared space and social organisation

culture: the body of beliefs, attitudes, skills and tools with which members of a community structure their lives and interact with their environment

deforestation: the process of clearing forest, usually to make way for housing or agriculture

delta: a nearly flat plain between outspreading branches of a river at its mouth

developed country: a country that has high economic productivity, relatively high standards of living and a relatively democratic systems of government

developing country: a country in which most people have a low economic standard of living

estuary: the tidal mouth of a river where the salt water of the tide meets the fresh water of the river current

fossil fuels: fuels that come from the breakdown of organic matter; for example, coal, oil and natural gas. They have formed in the ground over millions of years.

global warming: describes the observable trend of rising world temperatures over the past century

hinterland: the area influenced by any settlement

indigenous: the descendants of the original inhabitants of an area

isotherm: a line joining places of equal temperature

nomadic: a way of life in which people move from one area to another to hunt or find food

permafrost: an area where the subsoil remains frozen throughout the year

pollution: the build-up of impurities likely to be harmful to plants, animals and humans at certain concentrations

river: a large natural stream of water flowing in a definite course

sedentary: staying in one place

slash-and-burn: a method of clearing land for agriculture. Trees and shrubs are cut down, and the remaining vegetation burned.

tundra: barren lands located between isotherms 0° and 10° Celsius. The subsoil is permanently frozen, allowing only small vegetation growth.

wetlands: areas that are covered permanently, occasionally or periodically by fresh or salt water up to a depth of 6 metres

Polar environments are broadly located inside the Arctic and Antarctic circles. They are very cold lands with little or no vegetation. The harsh environment makes polar lands very difficult for settlement and they are sparsely populated. Polar environments are covered in chapter 8.

Icefield in the St Elias National Park, Alaska

Village in the Himalayas

Tundra environments are located between isotherms 0° and 10° Celsius. They are cool to cold throughout the year. Vegetation is small and ground-hugging. Tree growth is impossible because of the **permafrost**. Some settlements in **tundra** environments are discussed in chapter 8.

Mountain environments are the highest areas on Earth and are found in all continents and latitudes. They are generally mild to cold, with steep to rugged land. Precipitation can vary greatly. Some are subject to natural hazards such as volcanoes, earthquakes and avalanches. The environment can be harsh and generally does not support large settlements and population. Mountain environments are covered in chapter 5.

Tundra near Mount McKinley, Alaska

Tropical rainforest on Camiguin Island, Philippines

Rainforest environments need constantly wet conditions. There are three main types of rainforest: tropical, mangrove and temperate. Rainforests are valuable sources of timber. In many areas the forest has been cleared for settlement and large populations. Rainforest environments are covered in chapter 7.

Agricultural land encroaching on the Everglades National Park, Florida

Wetland environments are covered permanently, occasionally or periodically by fresh or salt water up to a depth of 6 metres. They are ecosystems whose formation is dominated by water. They are mostly found in coastal river estuaries but can also be located inland. Wetlands include areas such as swamps and marshes; they occupy around 6 per cent of the world's land surface and are areas of great biodiversity. They are often important agricultural areas and valuable sources of timber. Many wetlands have been drained for agricultural or urban use. In river deltas they are often centres for settlements that support large populations.

Zebras crossing savanna grasslands in Kenya

The Russian steppes are part of the vast temperate grasslands of Eurasia and extend from central Europe eastwards to Siberia. These level plains are generally treeless.

Temperate grasslands are dominated by grasses with few trees and shrubs. They are found in the mid-latitudes in parts of South Africa, Europe, Asia, Australia, North and South America. Temperate grasslands have a greater range of seasonal temperature than savannas and less variation in precipitation. Temperate grasslands are usually fertile and are valuable farming environments.

Grassland environments are dominated by grasses rather than large shrubs or trees. *Savanna* is a type of grassland with scattered trees. Savannas are located in and around the tropics in Africa, Australia, South America and India. The climate is warm to hot, with a wet season followed by a dry season. These can be harsh lands for settlement and savannas, except for India, generally do not have large numbers of people.

Desert environments are areas where there is a shortage of moisture because of low precipitation. There are two main types of deserts: hot and cold. Hot deserts are located in or near the Tropic of Cancer and the Tropic of Capricorn, generally on the western side of continents. Cold deserts are located in the mid-latitudes in the interior of Asia, North America, South America and all of Antarctica. The desert environment is harsh and generally does not support large settlements and population. Desert environments are covered in chapter 6.

Sand dunes engulfing Palm Gardens, an oasis in the Sahara Desert

The force of rushing water on a steep slope cuts a V-shaped valley.

When the river meets resistant rock a waterfall can occur.

The line of mountains that mark the start of rivers is known as a watershed.

Erosion occurs on the outside of a meander.

Sediment is deposited on the inside of a meander.

Billabongs or oxbow lakes occur when a meander is cut off.

On flatter land the river meanders.

Deltas can occur when sediment deposited near the mouth splits the river into smaller distributaries.

Rivers often flow through different environments, such as mountains, rainforests, grasslands and wetlands before they reach the coast.

Rivers

Rivers often flow through different environments on their journey to the sea. Rivers are part of a system that begins with rain falling or ice melting in mountains or hills. The force of the water rushing down the steep slope erodes the mountain vertically into steep-sided V-shaped valleys. As the river reaches flatter land, the eroded stones, sand and soil begin to wear away both the floor and sides of the valley. On the flood plain the river slows and begins to meander. Silt deposited during flooding enriches the soil and provides fertile farmland. Deposits of silt near the mouth of the river can cause the river to split into many smaller branches and form a delta. Settlements occur along rivers because rivers provide fresh water and transport routes, and the surrounding land is often suitable for farming.

The Amazon River in South America flows through the world's largest remaining rainforest.

Coral reefs

Coral reefs are wave-resistant underwater mounds, made up of a variety of species including corals, algae and sponges. Coral sands and limestone also play an important role in the build-up of a coral reef. As one the world's most diverse environments they support a wonderful variety of corals, fish and other organisms. Coral reefs are located in tropical waters along the western coasts of ocean basins (or the eastern side of continents) and around oceanic

Moorea in French Polynesia is a volcanic island with a fringing coral reef.

These colourful coral and fish are part of the extensive coral reef found off the coast of Belize in the Caribbean Sea.

islands. They are located within 30° north and south of the Equator. Many islands and their coral reefs are popular tourist destinations.

Coasts

The coastal environment includes the coastal hinterland, nearby islands, beaches and estuaries. This environment is located around the world, on the edges of continents and islands. Although it is generally flat land, its climate and other physical features vary greatly. This environment has a wide range of communities and includes many of the great cities of the world.

The tropical Pacific coast of southern Mexico is noted for its hilly peninsulas, bays and beaches.

GEOskills TOOLBOX

USING OBLIQUE AERIAL PHOTOGRAPHS

Oblique aerial photographs, like the one of Moorea above, are taken at an angle to the ground. Oblique aerial photographs give us a good idea of the height and shape of the features below. Unlike vertical aerial photographs, which are taken directly above the centre of an area, the scale in an oblique aerial photograph varies from one part of the photograph to another. For more information on photographs, see pages 56–7.

ACTIVITIES

UNDERSTANDING

1. List three natural hazards found in mountain areas.
2. What is the main feature of a wetland?
3. Describe the location of:
   a hot deserts
   b cold deserts
   c polar lands
   d tundra.
4. What are the main differences between savanna and temperate grasslands?
5. List the three main types of rainforests.
6. How is a delta formed?
7. Describe the main features of coral reefs.

USING YOUR SKILLS

8. Refer to the aerial photograph of Moorea and its fringing coral reef.
   a Explain why this is an oblique aerial photograph.
   b Describe the main landform feature in the photograph.
   c Locate the main areas of coral. How can you identify where the coral ends and the ocean begins?
   d Describe the pattern of vegetation. What is the main type of vegetation?
   e In what areas are the main cultural features located?
   f List the features that could make this location an attractive tourist destination.
   g What are the advantages and disadvantages of using oblique aerial photographs?

GEOTERMS

delta: a nearly flat plain between outspreading branches of a river at its mouth

river: a large natural stream of water flowing in a definite course

People with something in common live in groups called communities. Members of a community often share the same space and have similar beliefs or interests.

Geographers study how people adapt to specific environments. Physical environments have had a strong influence on the activities of traditional, indigenous communities.

South America: Lake Titicaca

Lake Titicaca, the world's highest navigable lake, is located in South America on the border of Peru and Bolivia in a mountain environment. On this lake there are floating islands composed of layers of totora reeds, which rot from the bottom and are replaced by new growth at the top. About 600 Uro Indians inhabit these mats of reeds, living a traditional lifestyle. They depend on the reeds for shelter and transport, using them to build cone-shaped huts and boats. A well-constructed boat lasts for six months.

The Uro have a sedentary way of life. They eat potatoes and fish from the lake and rarely leave their islands except for religious or medical purposes.

These traditional communities are undergoing change. Tourists regularly visit the floating islands, and the money they spend there is an important source of income for the Uro Indians. Unfortunately, Lake Titicaca suffers environmental problems, such as blue-green algae. This algae has been caused by sewage and fertilisers washed down from the expanding tourist and agricultural developments in the area surrounding the lake. Blue-green algae is toxic to a wide range of aquatic and terrestrial animals and provides a real threat to the fresh water supply of the Uro Indians.

Above: A Uro Indian girl cooking beside her hut of reeds

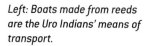

Left: Boats made from reeds are the Uro Indians' means of transport.

Among the many fascinating goods sold at the Witch's market in La Paz, the capital of Bolivia, are llama foetuses. The Indians of Bolivia, Peru, Ecuador, Chile and Argentina keep herds of llamas, which they use as pack animals and for meat, wool, hides and tallow for candles. Dried llama dung is used as fuel. Some of these Indian communities have unique customs, such as the belief that owning a llama foetus will ensure good fortune throughout life.

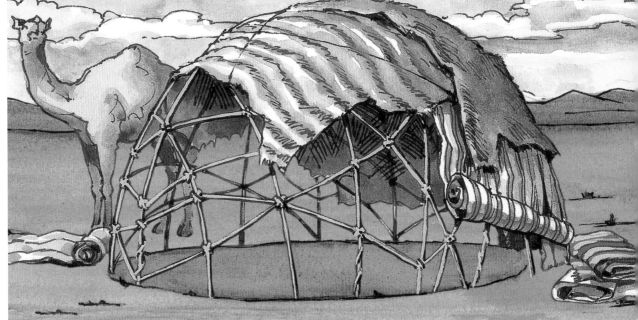

The Somali dwelling called an aqal can be carried from place to place on a camel. Aqals are made from a framework of saplings bound with bark and twine and covered with animal skins.

North-east Africa: Somalia

Traditional social organisations usually have strong family ties or clan links. For example, the four Somali clans that live in north-east Africa can trace their family back to a common ancestor. Husbands may have four wives. Each clan has their own place or homeland, but during dry periods, every three or four years, they move into other homelands in search of water and pasture. Somalis regard pasture and rain as gifts of God to be shared.

These nomadic pastoralists keep camels, galla goats and black head Persian sheep. Men look after the camels and women look after the sheep and goats. The animals provide them with milk, meat and skins, transport, income, marriage gifts and compensation if someone is killed. Women do most of the slaughtering of animals.

The Somali nomads carry all of their household possessions on camels. A Somali dwelling is called an *aqal*. It is perfectly suited to life on the move as it is light to transport and easily assembled.

Unfortunately, these communities suffer from a poorer quality of life than most Australians have. Life expectancy is only 47 years for males and 51 for females. The infant mortality rate (IMR) (deaths in the first year of life) is high at 109 per 1000 (Australia's IMR is fewer than five per 1000).

Traditional indigenous communities are currently undergoing social and economic changes. In many countries, these people have been forced to move from their original source of livelihood. Governments want to make them conform to modern, sedentary ways of living and to use their land for other purposes. Many indigenous communities are trying to seek self-rule and feel that they are the legitimate owners of the land.

Somalis loading an aqal onto a camel before moving south to seek grazing for their livestock

ACTIVITIES →

UNDERSTANDING

1. How has the Uro community adapted to a mountain–lake environment?
2. What are the uses of the totora reed?
3. What are the causes of blue-green algae?
4. How have the Somalis adapted to their physical environment?
5. Describe the different gender roles in a Somali community.
6. Outline the main differences between the nomadic Somali herders and the sedentary Uro Indians.

Many global environments have already been significantly changed by humans. Throughout history, human environments have taken over more and more of the natural environment. Such changes affect environments and communities and can often lead to conflict within or between communities.

Changing rainforest communities

Many of the world's rainforests have been cut down for timber and paper production or have been cleared to make room for farms and mines, towns and cities, dams and transport systems. Today, timbers such as teak, mahogany and ebony are still being exported from rainforests in developing countries to rich developed countries. Indigenous communities living in these environments are under threat. Communities that were once isolated and had developed their own unique culture may not survive if their traditional lands are taken from them or if their environment will no longer support their way of life.

The Kayapo Indians

The Kayapo Indians in the Amazon rainforest adapted to the hot, wet rainforest environment by using slash-and-burn agriculture. They had little contact with the rest of the world until the 1950s. During the last 50 years, the Kayapo's territory has been invaded by loggers and miners in search of valuable rainforest timbers and gold. The activities of the loggers and miners caused deforestation and pollution of the natural environment.

The Brazilian Government set aside land reserves for the Kayapo. However, their traditional way of life remained under threat due to illegal mining and logging, and conflict between community members about these issues. Conflict occurred within the Kayapo community because some members wanted to enter into contracts with mining and logging companies for short-term profits while others saw this as a threat to their culture, their traditional way of life and their rainforest home.

In 1989, the Kayapo Indians faced another threat. The Brazilian Government wanted to build a series of dams that would have flooded thousands of square kilometres of Kayapo rainforest. A huge protest organised by the local Indians gained international support and the dams were stopped.

In 1991, the Kayapo began trading with The Body Shop. The Body Shop uses Brazil nut oil to make hair conditioner. The Brazil nut tree is a tall tree more than 40 metres high. About five nuts grow within an *ourico*, which is like a coconut shell. Brazil nuts are collected between January and March and the trees are not cut down or damaged during harvesting. The oil is extracted by a hand-operated press. The machines are cheap, easy to use and do not harm the environment.

However, the future remains uncertain for the Kayapo. Many indigenous rainforest communities have had to cope with such changes — changes that often threaten their environment, unique cultures and traditional livelihoods.

Climate change

During the twentieth century, the atmosphere warmed by 0.5° Celsius, a trend that is expected to continue. Growing evidence suggests that human activities, such as burning fossil fuels, have contributed to global warming. The resulting climate change (see chapter 13) could cause changes to global environments such as:
- melting of the polar icecaps and the retreat of glaciers in mountain lands

Kayapo Indians participating in an organised protest in the late 1980s against the Brazilian Government's plans to build dams that would have flooded thousands of square kilometres of Amazon rainforest

- rising sea levels and flooding of low-lying areas
- more extreme droughts and storms
- disruption to agriculture and changes to natural habitats such as wetlands.

South America Wetlands May Be 'Next Everglades' — Report

BY ALISTER DOYLE
COUNTRY: NORWAY

Oslo — Giant South American wetlands are under threat from farming and house building, and could shrink like Florida's Everglades last century, a study by UN experts said on Tuesday.

The report also said that global warming of 3–4 degrees Celsius (5.4–7.2 degrees Fahrenheit) could wreck 85 per cent of the world's remaining wetlands from Bangladesh to Botswana, home to thousands of animal and plant species.

Soybean and sugar cane farming, gas pipelines, roads, factories and towns are squeezing the Pantanal, the world's largest freshwater wetlands, that straddles parts of Brazil, Paraguay and Bolivia, the report said.

'The Pantanal is under threat from climate change and human pollution.'

Large parts of the Pantanal, an area bigger than Greece measuring 165 000 sq km (63 710 sq miles), are pristine, Teixeira, leader of the report said.

But there were worries that it could become the 'next Everglades', the wetlands in the US state of Florida, withering under farms and homes since the 1940s and whose national park covers a fifth of their historic territory.

The remote Pantanal, however, does not face comparable pressures from millions of people drawn by Florida's balmy climate and dazzling beaches.

The Pantanal acts as a sponge regulating flows to the Paraguay River and Parana River. Teixeira urged the three nations sharing the wetlands to cooperate closely and avoid damaging a region which is home to 650 species of birds, 190 species of mammals from jaguars to giant anteaters, 270 types of fish and 1100 different butterflies.

'Climate modification may cause some wetlands to dry up, and others to increase in size, fundamentally altering their ecology, biodiversity and species composition,' said the report, published on World Water Day.

The scientific panel to the United Nations projected in 2001 that world temperatures could rise by 1.4–5.8 degrees Celsius by 2100. That could, in turn, trigger catastrophic droughts, floods and storms, and raise sea levels by melting icecaps. Some scientists dismiss those projections as based on unreliable models.

Source: www.planetark.com, 22 March 2005, © Thomas Reuters.

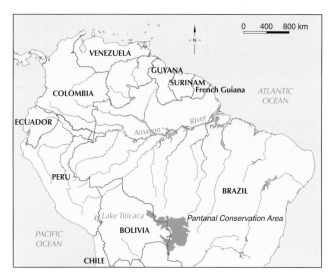

The world's largest wetlands, the Pantanal, stretching across areas of Brazil, Paraguay and Bolivia, is under threat from climate change and human activities.

ACTIVITIES ➔

UNDERSTANDING
Use the media article to answer the following questions.

1. What percentage of the world's wetlands may be destroyed by global warming?
2. What are the two main threats to the Pantanal?
3. What other wetland areas are the Pantanal compared to? Why does the report suggest the Pantanal may be less threatened than this other area?
4. How might climate change affect wetlands generally?

THINKING AND APPLYING

5. The Pantanal is situated across three countries. Why do you think this could make management of the area difficult?
6. What features of the Pantanal make it special? What do you regard as the main arguments for action to ensure its preservation?

USING YOUR SKILLS

7. How balanced a view does the article present? Can you detect any bias in the article?
8. Conduct further internet research on the Pantanal and the Everglades. Write a letter to the United Nations arguing the case for the Pantanal to become a World Heritage site.

GEOTERMS

deforestation: the process of clearing forest, usually to make way for housing or agriculture

global warming: describes the observable trend of rising world temperatures over the past century

projects*plus*

'Planet Valdar'

SEARCHLIGHT ID: PRO-0026

SCENARIO

BlackHoleInc, a production company respected for its realistic film making, is about to make the pilot episode in a new fantasy/ sci-fi series set on an alter-Earth planet named Valdar. You and your production team have been asked to design sample communities that will feature in different episodes of the series. Valdar is similar to Earth and obeys the same basic natural principles as Earth, including the 'rules' related to latitude, altitude, precipitation and wind currents. Planet Valdar's technology predates the invention of electricity, gunpowder and internal combustion engines. The communities have very little knowledge of other continents and cultures, apart from their immediate neighbours.

YOUR TASK

Form small groups and create a profile of each of the communities on the continent of Erehw on the planet Valdar. Each individual is to create a community profile for at least one indigenous community that lives in one of the different environments on the continent.

A map of the continent of Erehw and a sample community profile are provided for you in your ProjectsPLUS Media Centre.

PROCESS

- Open the ProjectsPLUS application for this chapter, located in your eBookPLUS. Watch the introductory video lesson and then click the 'Start Project' button to set up your project. Save your settings and the project will be launched.
- Navigate to your Media Centre and download the map of the continent of Erehw and the sample community profile for the Detrevni people. Note Detrevni's geographic position on the map and its natural features, and think about how its location has influenced the people and their lifestyle.
- Navigate to your Research Forum. Each of the different environments on the continent of Erehw has been loaded as a topic to provide a framework for your research. Using your eBookPLUS and the Hotspot Commander game as your starting point, research and enter information about the daily life of the indigenous communities that exist in each of the global environments now. You should also consider whether these indigenous communities on Earth are using technology that might not be available on the planet Valdar. How would these communities have lived before our society's technological advances?

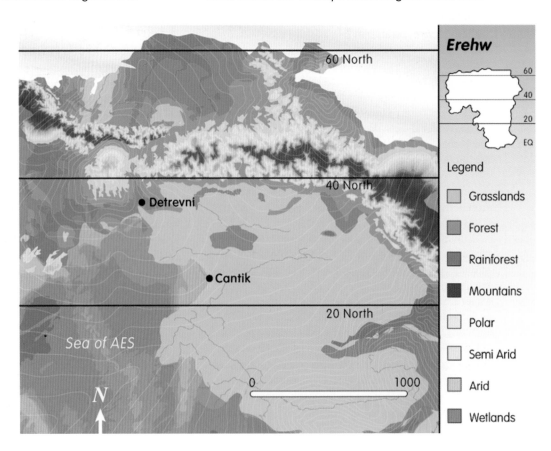

60 North

40 North

● Detrevni

● Cantik

20 North

Sea of AES

N

0   1000

Erehw

60
40
20
EQ

Legend

☐ Grasslands

☐ Forest

☐ Rainforest

☐ Mountains

☐ Polar

☐ Semi Arid

☐ Arid

☐ Wetlands

Your ProjectsPLUS application is available in this chapter's Student Resources tab inside your eBookPLUS. Visit www.jacplus.com.au to locate your digital resources.

- When your research is complete, you should indicate each of the different community profiles that your group will create in their allocated environments on the Erehw map. This will form the cover page for your group's community profiles. Each group member should then begin creating a profile for a different community. Use the headings in the model profile for Detrevni to help you construct your community profile. You will want to consider:
  - Where will your community be located, and how is their lifestyle affected by the natural environment that surrounds them?
  - How will they use the resources available to them in their natural environment?
  - How will they interact with their neighbouring

communities. Are they friendly? Do they trade or share resources?
- When each individual has created their community in Word, you should combine them all into one document, review each other's work and make any necessary adjustments to your full continental communities' profile.
- Print out your research report from ProjectsPLUS and hand it in with your final project.

MEDIA CENTRE

Your Media Centre contains:
- a graphic map of the continent of Erehw
- a sample community profile of the people of Detrevni
- an assessment rubric.

Interactivity

HOTSPOT COMMANDER: 'INDIGENOUS PEOPLE'

HotSpot Commander challenges your geographical skills and knowledge in a fun question-and-answer format. You will receive the coordinates of a location. When you hit your target accurately, you will be given some secret information and a question to answer. Get it right and part of the mystery image is revealed. Can you conquer all 10 locations and become a Hotspot Commander?

SEARCHLIGHT ID: INT-0928

5 Mountain lands

INQUIRY QUESTIONS

+ How have mountains formed?
+ What is a volcanic eruption?
+ What forces shape mountains?
+ How do humans adapt to harsh mountain environments?

Mountains have formed over billions of years due to movements, known as tectonic activity, in the Earth's crust. Where mountains are located, we also find the tectonic forces of earthquakes, fault zones and volcanic activity. Mountain environments are home to many unique plants and animals. Much of the Earth's population relies on mountains as a source of water, timber and mineral resources. This chapter looks at the forces that form and shape mountains, as well as the ways in which communities live in and manage these often difficult environments.

GEOskills TOOLBOX

GEOskillbuilder Understanding contours (pages 96–7)

GEOskillbuilder Constructing a column graph (pages 109)

+ Organising information (page 95)
+ Working with topographic maps (pages 100–1)
+ Understanding cross-sections (page 104)

Mt Veronica above the Sacred Valley, near Cusco in Peru

KEY TERMS

alpine: the area above the tree line in mountains

avalanche: a large mass of ice or snow separated from a mountain slope and sliding or falling suddenly downwards

continental drift: the theory that continents broke away and drifted from an original large landmass

continental plates: the large pieces of the Earth's crust that float on the magma beneath the Earth's surface

contour line: line drawn on a map joining places of equal height above sea level

core: the inner part of the Earth

crater: the opening on top of a volcano through which lava erupts

crust: the outer layer of the Earth's surface

deforestation: the process of clearing forest, usually to make way for housing or agriculture

degraded: reduced in value or quality; for example, land is degraded through erosion and intensive use of the soil

dormant: sleeping, inactive, not erupting

earthquake: series of shock waves that are generated by a disturbance of the Earth's crust

ecotourism: nature-based tourism that involves educating tourists about the natural environment. It is ecologically sustainable tourism.

epicentre: the point on the Earth's surface directly above the focus of an earthquake

erosion: wearing away of soil and rock by natural elements, such as water and soil

faulting: occurs when rocks crack and two sections move vertically, forcing up layers of rock

folding: occurs when a plate in the Earth's crust slides under another, pushing up layers of rock

glacier: moving river of ice

lapse rate: rate of change in temperature that occurs as the altitude increases

lava: molten rock, magma

magma: hot, molten rock under the Earth's surface

mantle: layer of the Earth between the crust and the core

Richter scale: used to measure the energy of earthquakes

rift valley: a valley formed as a result of plate movements, usually long and narrow, with steep-sided mountain walls

seismic waves: a release of energy from the focus of an earthquake that spreads outwards like ripples on a pond

spot height: a point on a map with its exact height above sea level marked

subduction: the process whereby one plate slides under another

supercontinent: the single landmass that existed when all the continents were joined

tectonic activity: the breaking and bending of the Earth's crust

temperature inversion: an increase in temperature with height in the atmosphere, the reverse of the normal decrease in temperature with height

valley: lower land, between hills or mountains

vertical interval: the difference in height between one contour line and the next

volcano: a mountain formed by the eruption of molten rock or lava

weathering: the breakdown of bare rock by water and temperature changes

Mountain ranges are found on all continents and many islands of the Earth's surface. The great mountain ranges, such as the Andes, the Himalayas, the Rockies and the Alps, contain some of the world's most spectacular landscapes. Where mountains are found, we find the tectonic forces of earthquakes, fault zones and volcanic activity. The landforms in mountain areas are also shaped by the forces of weathering and erosion.

The Earth's surface is dynamic and always changing. It is constantly being:
• built up as new mountains form
• worn down through weathering and erosion.

Continental plates

The main reason for the formation of new mountains and some other landforms is the movement of continental plates. The Earth's surface or crust is split into a number of plates. These plates fit together like a huge jigsaw puzzle.

The plates float on the semi-molten rocks of the Earth's mantle. Heating from the Earth's core causes the semi-molten material in the mantle to churn in currents. These currents, called convection currents, carry the crustal plates along up to as much as 15 centimetres per year. Plates beneath the ocean move much more quickly than plates beneath the continents.

The movement of plates is known as the theory of continental drift. Scientists believe that about 225 million years ago all the continents were joined, forming a supercontinent. Since then the continents have moved apart very slowly to form the continents that we know today. The continents are still moving and drifting, with the plates moving up to 11 centimetres in one year. For example, North and South America are drifting apart and the Atlantic Ocean is widening by 3 centimetres each year.

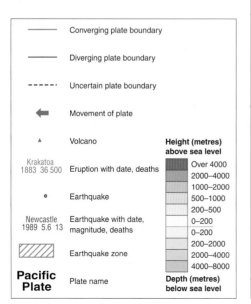

GEOfacts

Fossil seashells have been found high in the Himalayas. The highest mountain range on Earth was under the sea until about 30 million years ago, when India collided with Asia and the rocks were thrust upwards to form the Himalayas.

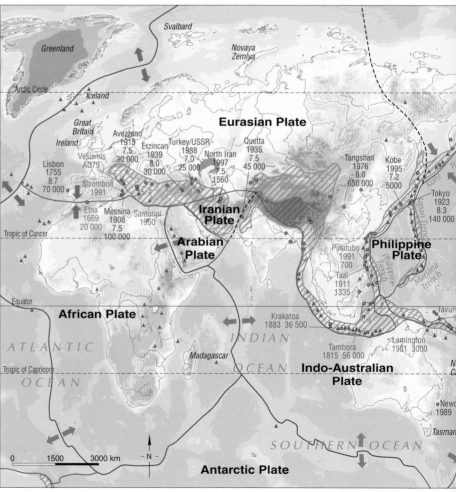

World continental plates

Legend:
- Converging plate boundary
- Diverging plate boundary
- Uncertain plate boundary
- Movement of plate
- Volcano
- Krakatoa 1883 36 500 Eruption with date, deaths
- Earthquake
- Newcastle 1989 5.6 13 Earthquake with date, magnitude, deaths
- Earthquake zone
- **Pacific Plate** Plate name

Height (metres) above sea level
- Over 4000
- 2000–4000
- 1000–2000
- 500–1000
- 200–500
- 0–200

Depth (metres) below sea level
- 0–200
- 200–2000
- 2000–4000
- 4000–8000

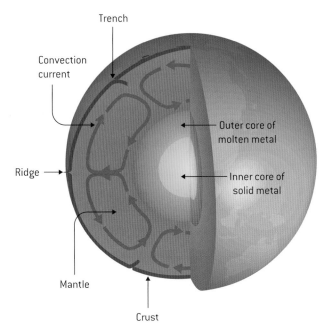

The Earth's layers. The structure of the Earth is a bit like an apple: it has a core at the centre and a thin crust (skin) on the outside.

Labels in diagram: Trench, Convection current, Ridge, Mantle, Crust, Outer core of molten metal, Inner core of solid metal

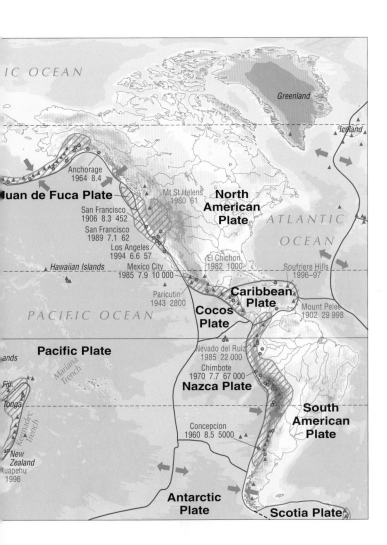

Map labels: IC OCEAN, Greenland, Iceland, Anchorage 1964 8.4, Juan de Fuca Plate, Mt St Helens 1980 61, North American Plate, ATLANTIC OCEAN, San Francisco 1906 8.3 452, San Francisco 1989 7.1 62, Los Angeles 1994 6.6 57, Hawaiian Islands, Mexico City 1985 7.9 10 000, El Chichon 1982 1000, Soufriere Hills 1996–97, Paricutin 1943 2800, Caribbean Plate, Cocos Plate, Mount Pelee 1902 29 998, PACIFIC OCEAN, Nevado del Ruiz 1985 22 000, Pacific Plate, Mariana Trench, Chimbote 1970 7.7 67 000, Nazca Plate, Fiji, South American Plate, Tonga, Kermadec Trench, Concepcion 1960 8.5 5000, New Zealand Ruapehu 1996, Antarctic Plate, Scotia Plate

Sometimes the Earth's plates collide and converge. When this happens it can:

- build up mountain ranges
- cause earthquakes and volcanoes.

This is called **tectonic activity**. Tectonic activity can be sudden and rapid as in the case of an earthquake or volcano. Sometimes it can be very slow, taking many thousands of years, as in mountain building.

ACTIVITIES

UNDERSTANDING

1. Identify the main tectonic forces.
2. What are the Earth's three main layers?
3. What are continental plates?
4. Why do continental plates move?
5. How far can continental plates move in a year?
6. What is continental drift?

USING YOUR SKILLS

7. Refer to the map of continental plates and the legend.
   a. Identify the six largest plates in approximate order of size.
   b. In which two directions is the Indo–Australian plate moving?
   c. How could this affect Australia and New Guinea?
   d. Name two types of tectonic activity that are often located at the boundary of plates.
   e. Explain why there is no large area of tectonic activity marked on Australia.

GEOTERMS

continental plates: the large pieces of the Earth's crust that float on the magma beneath the Earth's surface

core: the inner part of the Earth

crust: the outer layer of the Earth's surface

erosion: wearing away of soil and rock by natural elements, such as water and soil

mantle: layer of the Earth between the crust and core

supercontinent: the single landmass that existed when all the continents were joined

tectonic activity: the breaking and bending of the Earth's crust

weathering: the breakdown of bare rock by water and temperature changes

5.2 Mountain building

The three main forms of mountain building are **folding**, **faulting** and volcanic activity.

Folding

Most of the world's great mountain regions are formed when crustal rocks are buckled as one plate slides under another (**subduction**). Some of the crust is forced down and becomes part of the **magma**; other rocks are forced upwards and bent or folded. These are known as fold mountains.

Large mountain ranges that were formed in this way include the Himalayas in Asia and the Rocky Mountains in North America.

Fault mountains are formed along fault lines, when huge blocks are pushed upwards or sideways (transform faults) by the movement of continental plates. Faults usually occur at the edge of plates where there are weaknesses in rocks.

An anticline valley is an eroded anticline.

Mountain landforms are formed in various ways.

Dome mountains form when volcanic material wells up under the ground, but does not break the surface.

Fold mountains are formed when two continental plates crash together and the rocks in the crust buckle and fold. These mountains normally have pointed peaks.

Erosion mountains result from the erosion of a thick layer of sedimentary rock.

The action of sliding continental plates

Synclines are folds in the Earth's crust that have rocks arching downwards.

Anticlines are folds in the Earth's crust that have rocks arching upwards.

Volcanoes (volcanic mountains) are formed when molten rock, or magma, erupts and is deposited on the Earth's land surface (or as an island within the ocean).

The Rocky Mountains in North America were formed by folding.

Faulting

Faulting occurs when rocks crack and sections move up or down. This process forms both mountains and **rift valleys** (such as those in Africa). Rocks behave differently under pressure, depending on how brittle they are. If the rocks are deep underground and have a lot of weight above them, they will fold when under pressure. Rocks close to the surface tend to be more brittle and will snap under pressure. Faults are formed when these rocks break.

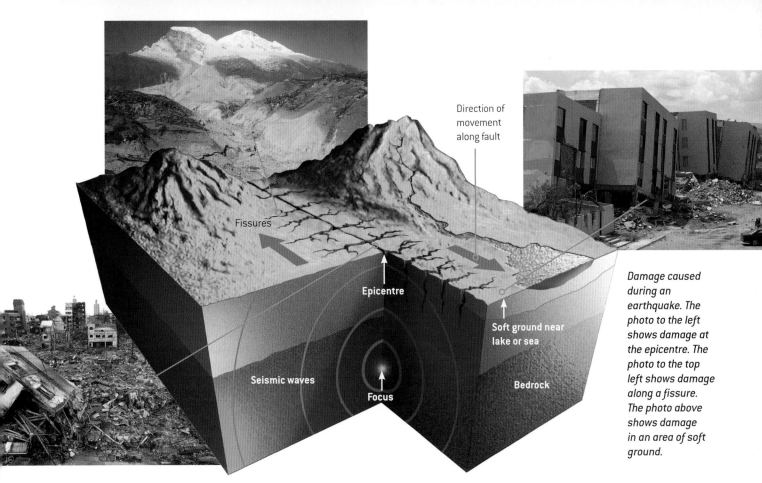

Fissures

Direction of movement along fault

Epicentre

Soft ground near lake or sea

Seismic waves

Focus

Bedrock

Damage caused during an earthquake. The photo to the left shows damage at the epicentre. The photo to the top left shows damage along a fissure. The photo above shows damage in an area of soft ground.

Volcanoes

Volcanoes are formed when molten rock (magma) deep within the Earth erupts and reaches the surface. Mountains that were formed in this way include Mount Fuji in Japan and Mount Etna in Italy.

Earthquakes

Like volcanic eruptions, earthquakes usually occur on or near tectonic plate boundaries. An earthquake is often the result of a sudden movement of the layers of rock at faults near these plate boundaries.

This point of movement is called the focus. The more shallow it is, the more powerful the earthquake will be. Energy travels quickly from this point in powerful seismic waves, radiating outwards like ripples on a pond. The seismic waves decrease in strength as they travel away from the epicentre (the point on the ground directly above the focus). The Richter scale measures an earthquake's strength — the higher the number, the stronger the quake.

GEOTERMS

earthquake: series of shock waves that are generated by a disturbance of the Earth's crust

epicentre: the point on the Earth's surface directly above the focus of an earthquake

magma: hot, molten rock under the Earth's surface

rift valley: a valley formed as a result of plate movements, usually long and narrow, with steep-sided mountain walls

volcano: a mountain formed by the eruption of molten rock or lava

ACTIVITIES →

UNDERSTANDING

1. What are the three main forms of mountain building?
2. What process forms a rift valley?
3. What causes earthquakes?

THINKING AND APPLYING

4. Explain why the effects of an earthquake are less severe away from the epicentre.
5. Would an earthquake measuring 6.5 be stronger or weaker than an earthquake measuring 4.5 on the Richter scale?
6. Refer to the three photos showing damage from an earthquake. Explain why the damage shown in these photos varies in extent.
7. Refer to the diagrams showing the different ways that mountains can be formed. Work in groups of three. Each student uses different coloured plasticine to make a model of a fault, fold or dome mountain. Explain the formation to your group.

5.3 Volcanic mountains

A volcano forms when magma, the hot molten rock from beneath the Earth's crust, emerges on the Earth's surface through a fissure or opening. When it does, this molten rock is called lava. Some volcanoes erupt almost continuously while others go through periods where they are dormant or inactive.

Powerful volcanic explosions occur when the pressure of gases builds up in the main vent and branch pipe, blowing the plug on the crater. Blocks of hot lava and rock explode as lava bombs and are catapulted from the crater. Lava fills the crater and spills down the side of the volcano.

Nearly all active volcanoes occur on or near plate boundaries, where plates are moving towards or away from each other. The Pacific Ring of Fire, located along the edge of the Pacific Ocean, accounts for 75 per cent of the world's active and dormant volcanoes.

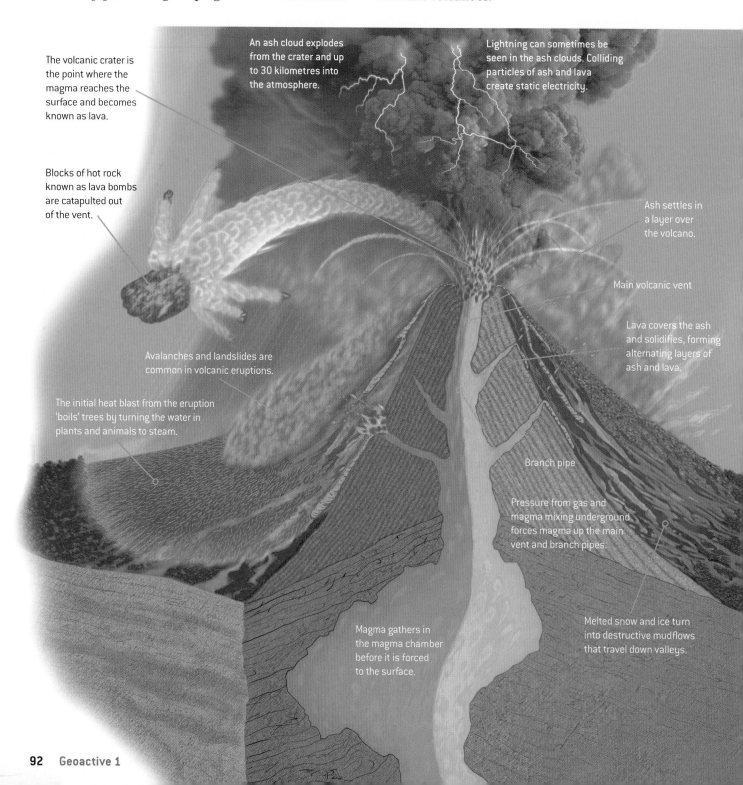

The volcanic crater is the point where the magma reaches the surface and becomes known as lava.

Blocks of hot rock known as lava bombs are catapulted out of the vent.

An ash cloud explodes from the crater and up to 30 kilometres into the atmosphere.

Lightning can sometimes be seen in the ash clouds. Colliding particles of ash and lava create static electricity.

Ash settles in a layer over the volcano.

Main volcanic vent

Lava covers the ash and solidifies, forming alternating layers of ash and lava.

Avalanches and landslides are common in volcanic eruptions.

The initial heat blast from the eruption 'boils' trees by turning the water in plants and animals to steam.

Branch pipe

Pressure from gas and magma mixing underground forces magma up the main vent and branch pipes.

Magma gathers in the magma chamber before it is forced to the surface.

Melted snow and ice turn into destructive mudflows that travel down valleys.

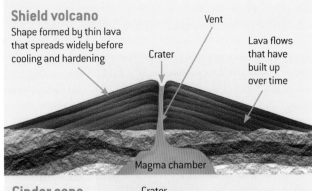

Shield volcano
Shape formed by thin lava that spreads widely before cooling and hardening

Vent

Crater

Lava flows that have built up over time

Magma chamber

Cinder cone
Layers made up of heavier rocks near the vent, and cinders and ash towards the edges

Crater

Vent

Magma chamber

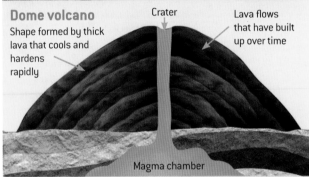

Dome volcano
Shape formed by thick lava that cools and hardens rapidly

Crater

Lava flows that have built up over time

Magma chamber

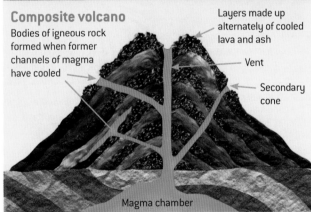

Composite volcano
Bodies of igneous rock formed when former channels of magma have cooled

Layers made up alternately of cooled lava and ash

Vent

Secondary cone

Magma chamber

 **GEO*facts*** The Papua New Guinean town of Rabaul is surrounded by six volcanoes. In 1994, two of the volcanoes, Vulcan and Tavurvur, erupted together. The eruption was triggered by an earthquake that registered 5.1 on the Richter scale.

Types of volcanic cones

Volcanoes have a variety of shapes and sizes, but there are four main types. The shape of the volcano depends on:

- the type of lava that is erupted. If the lava is rich in silica it tends to be very runny and may flow for many kilometres before it cools and hardens to become rock. Volcanoes that erupt runny lava tend to have broad, flat sides (shield volcanoes). Those that erupt thick treacle-like lava tend to have much steeper sides (dome volcanoes).
- the amount and type of ash that is erupted. Heavy material like lava bombs settle close to the crater while lighter ash is carried further away. Volcanoes that are built up through falls of ash are steep-sided *cinder cones*.
- the combination of lava and ash. The most common type of volcano is one built up of both ash and lava, called a *composite volcano*.

ACTIVITIES

UNDERSTANDING
1. How does a volcano form?
2. Where do most of the Earth's volcanic eruptions occur?
3. What is a dormant volcano?

THINKING AND APPLYING
4. The word 'volcano' comes from the Latin word *vulcan*, the name the ancient Romans gave to their god of fire. Write a paragraph to explain why you think volcanoes feature in the belief system of many cultures.

USING YOUR SKILLS
5. Refer to the diagram of an erupting volcano.
   a. Describe four types of material that can be erupted from a volcano.
   b. Which of these materials has the potential to cause the most damage to human activities? Give three reasons for your answer.
6. Refer to the diagram of volcanic cones.
   a. What are the three main factors that determine the shape of a volcano?
   b. Explain in your own words the difference between the shape of a volcanic shield volcano and the shape of a dome volcano.

GEOTERMS
crater: the opening on top of a volcano through which lava erupts

Living with volcanoes

Volcanic eruptions can occur on a massive scale and with little warning. Many times throughout history whole towns have been consumed by ash or lava, and eruptions are responsible for hundreds of deaths every year. While we have little or no hope of preventing eruptions, we may be able to predict their arrival giving nearby residents time to evacuate. In addition, there have been some ambitious attempts made to control the flow of lava from erupting volcanoes.

About half a billion people live in a volcanic zone somewhere near one of the world's 1500 potentially active volcanoes. Most of them will never experience a volcanic eruption during their lifetime and consider the benefits of living near a volcano to be greater than the potential risks. Some of these benefits are described in the table in the Geoskills toolbox opposite.

New Zealand's largest city, Auckland, sits on a volcanic field containing over 20 volcanoes. This is One Tree Hill, a former Maori fort.

A rise in the temperature of a crater lake often precedes an eruption.

Samples of gas can be collected and analysed. An increase in the amount of sulfur dioxide (SO_2) may indicate that magma is moving upwards.

It has been suggested that explosives could be used to breach crater walls, sending lava away from towns. This was first tried in Hawaii in 1935.

In 1973, sea water was sprayed onto lava that was threatening a town in Iceland. The lava cooled quickly and solidified.

As magma rises and collects in the magma chambers, the cone may bulge outwards warning of possible eruptions. Sensitive tiltmetres on the ground and on satellites can detect this bulging.

This bulging can also cause tiny cracks to appear.

Helicopters have been used to drop concrete blocks in front of flowing lava.

Buildings in areas prone to ash eruptions should have steeply sloping roofs so ash does not accumulate.

ORGANISING INFORMATION

It is much easier to understand and remember information that is well organised. One way to do this is to group information that deals with common topic areas in a table. An example is provided below.

Information about volcanoes

Minerals produced	Building materials produced	Other benefits
Magma — rich in minerals needed for healthy plant growth. The rice fields of Java (Indonesia), the grapes of Sicily and the dairy cows of Taranaki (New Zealand) all benefit from these fertile soils.	Basalt — a hard, volcanic rock used in many places for roads and buildings	Electricity can be generated from areas where magma reaches underground water areas. Mexico, Iceland, New Zealand and Italy already generate this geothermal energy.
Sulfur — used in the chemical industry	Softer volcanic rock such as in Bali — used to carve statues	Attract tourists (for example, for skiing)
Spring water — claimed to have particular healing properties for some illnesses such as arthritis		Bring increased rainfall as they increase height of the land

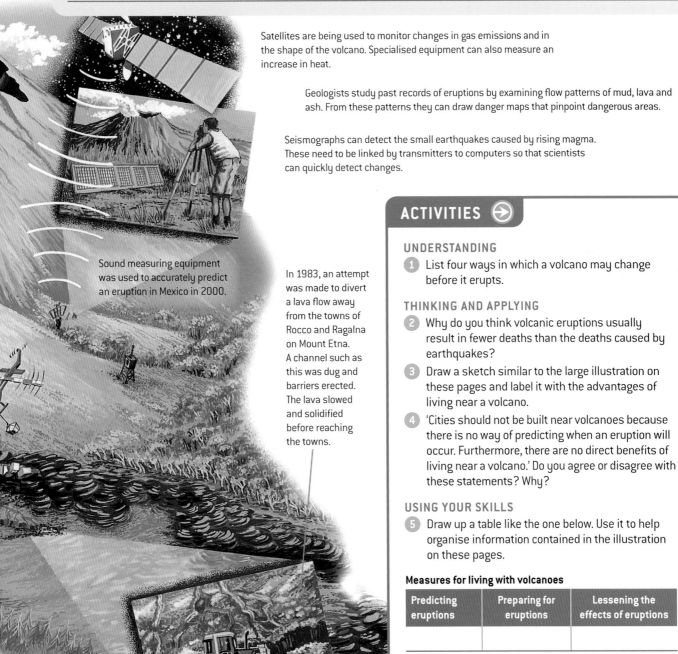

Satellites are being used to monitor changes in gas emissions and in the shape of the volcano. Specialised equipment can also measure an increase in heat.

Geologists study past records of eruptions by examining flow patterns of mud, lava and ash. From these patterns they can draw danger maps that pinpoint dangerous areas.

Seismographs can detect the small earthquakes caused by rising magma. These need to be linked by transmitters to computers so that scientists can quickly detect changes.

Sound measuring equipment was used to accurately predict an eruption in Mexico in 2000.

In 1983, an attempt was made to divert a lava flow away from the towns of Rocco and Ragalna on Mount Etna. A channel such as this was dug and barriers erected. The lava slowed and solidified before reaching the towns.

ACTIVITIES

UNDERSTANDING

1. List four ways in which a volcano may change before it erupts.

THINKING AND APPLYING

2. Why do you think volcanic eruptions usually result in fewer deaths than the deaths caused by earthquakes?

3. Draw a sketch similar to the large illustration on these pages and label it with the advantages of living near a volcano.

4. 'Cities should not be built near volcanoes because there is no way of predicting when an eruption will occur. Furthermore, there are no direct benefits of living near a volcano.' Do you agree or disagree with these statements? Why?

USING YOUR SKILLS

5. Draw up a table like the one below. Use it to help organise information contained in the illustration on these pages.

Measures for living with volcanoes

Predicting eruptions	Preparing for eruptions	Lessening the effects of eruptions

Understanding contours

Contours are very useful for showing the pattern of landforms in an area. Contour lines join points on a map that are at the same elevation or height above sea level. By carefully reading the patterns formed by these lines, you can understand the relief (shape) of the land. When the contour lines on a map are close together, the slope is steep and when they are wide apart the slope is gentle. On a contour map of a mountain area, the contour lines would be close together. The difference in height between one contour line and the next is known as the vertical interval and is always the same on a particular map. Mountain peaks can be shown by using spot heights.

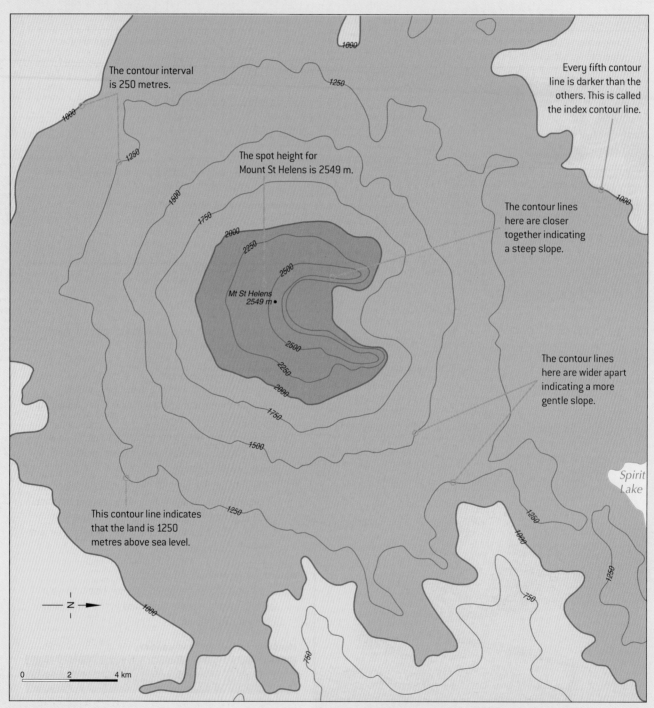

The contour interval is 250 metres.

The spot height for Mount St Helens is 2549 m.

Every fifth contour line is darker than the others. This is called the index contour line.

The contour lines here are closer together indicating a steep slope.

The contour lines here are wider apart indicating a more gentle slope.

This contour line indicates that the land is 1250 metres above sea level.

Spirit Lake

Mt St Helens 2549 m •

Mount St Helens (after the 1980 eruptions)

This map also uses shading to show elevation — from light brown for lower elevation (under 1000 metres) through to medium brown (between 1000 and 2000 metres) and dark brown for the highest elevation (over 2000 metres).

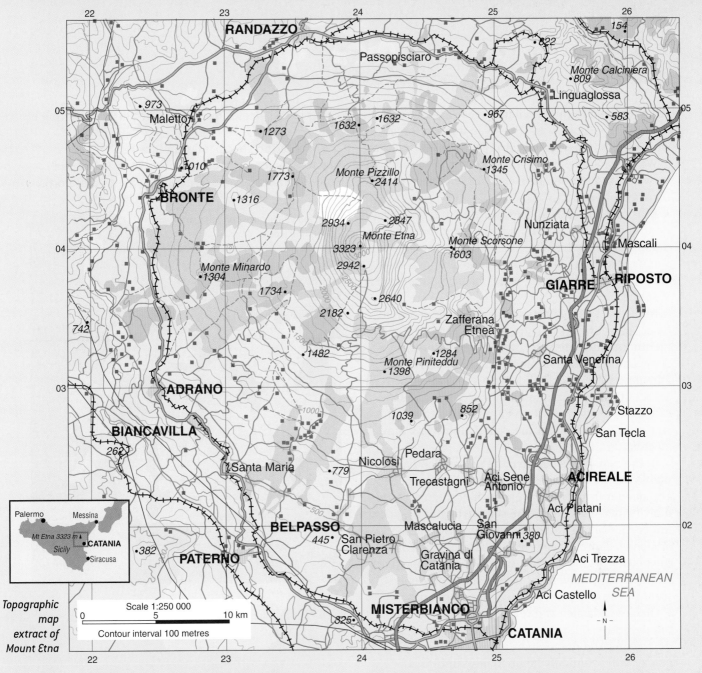

Topographic map extract of Mount Etna

Topographic maps use contours and show physical features such as forests, rivers and lakes, and cultural features such as roads, railways and settlements. This type of map is useful when bushwalking, planning roads and checking the steepness of a slope. Topographic maps use conventional symbols to make it easy for map readers to quickly identify the features shown in the key.

ACTIVITIES →

USING YOUR SKILLS

1 How high above sea level is the summit of Mount Etna?

2 What is the contour interval on the map?

3 What is the steepest part of this landform? Use area references.

4 What is the distance between the summit of Mount Etna and the town of Giarre?

5 Describe how landforms have influenced the location of the main transport routes and settlements.

6 Imagine you work as a tourist guide at Mount Etna. Use the topographic map to design a walk from Belpasso to the summit.
   a How far would you walk?
   b In which direction would you travel?
   c How high would you climb from Belpasso?
   d Does the slope become more gentle or steeper as you climb?
   e What type of land do you walk through on the first half of your journey?
   f At the summit, in which direction would you face to take photographs of the forested slope of the mountains?

We have seen in the previous pages that tectonic forces create mountains. However, it is the forces of weathering and erosion that shape these mountains.

Weathering involves the breakdown of bare rock by water and temperature changes, and prepares the way for erosion.

Erosion is the wearing away of soil and rock by natural elements, such as water, ice and wind. In mountain lands it is water and ice that are the main agents of erosion. Most mountain areas have been eroded by running water, which has cut out deep, V-shaped **valleys**.

In the past, large parts of mountain lands would have been covered by snow and ice. Parts of some mountain lands are still covered permanently by snow and ice, for example, the higher parts of the Himalayas, the Rockies, the Andes and the Alps. Most of the erosion in mountain areas has been caused by glaciers. **Glaciers** are moving rivers of ice. In mountain areas they are called alpine or valley glaciers.

In the mountains where more snow falls than melts over the year, the excess snow becomes deeper and deeper from year to year. As it accumulates, its density increases due to the compacting of the snow under the weight of the upper layers. When the ice and snow depth reaches 60–100 metres in an area, the glacier begins to move, mainly due to the effects of gravity. The movement is very slow and ranges from 1 centimetre per day to 8 metres per day.

Glaciers advance and retreat according to temperature conditions. As a glacier moves downslope and the temperature increases, the glacier will eventually begin to melt until it is feeding water to a normal river or lake.

Like streams, glaciers modify the landscape by erosion. However, they are more powerful than streams. They erode in two ways: by *plucking* and by *abrasion*. Plucking occurs where the glacier freezes onto rock as it passes and slowly pulls rock away as it moves on. Abrasion occurs where the ice and rocks in the glacier move over the surface, eroding it like a giant file.

Some of the spectacular landforms created by glaciers include cirques, horns, arêtes, U-shaped valleys, truncated spurs, hanging valleys and fiords.

V-shaped valleys are cut into mountains by running water.

A glaciated region in the Swiss Alps

GEO*facts* As part of a global trend, glaciers in Alaska, the Andes, the European Alps and the Himalayas are retreating. The Columbia Glacier in Southern Alaska retreated 12 kilometres and reduced its thickness by more than 400 metres between 1982 and 2000. Increasing average temperature and decreasing precipitation are the likely causes.

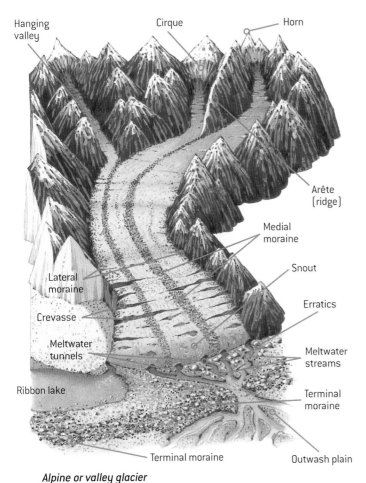

Hanging valley
Cirque
Horn
Arête (ridge)
Medial moraine
Snout
Lateral moraine
Erratics
Crevasse
Meltwater tunnels
Meltwater streams
Ribbon lake
Terminal moraine
Terminal moraine
Outwash plain

Alpine or valley glacier

Milford Sound is located on New Zealand's south-western coast. Glaciers sculptured Milford Sound millions of years ago. The scoured valley was then flooded by the Tasman Sea to produce a fiord. The sheer walls and cascading waterfalls of the 22-kilometre-long fiord draw thousands of visitors each year.

GEOfacts

The world's largest glacier is the Lambert–Fisher Glacier in Antarctica. It is 515 kilometres long and 80 kilometres wide. Antarctica has 244 main glaciers and 87 per cent of them have retreated over the past 50 years.

ACTIVITIES →

UNDERSTANDING

1. Identify the main forces that shape landforms in mountain lands.
2. What are the main agents of erosion in mountain lands?
3. Why do glaciers move?

THINKING AND APPLYING

4. Imagine you are employed as a developer to build a large tourist resort in a mountainous area. Consider such things as transport, accommodation and activities that would attract tourists. What environmental problems would you face?

USING YOUR SKILLS

5. Refer to the photograph of a V-shaped valley.
   a Describe the appearance of this valley.
   b What would be some of the problems and dangers for people living on the slopes of V-shaped valleys?
   c Imagine you are given the task of re-routing the road shown on the photograph to make it shorter and safer. What problems would you face?
6. Refer to the diagram of an alpine or valley glacier.
   a Identify three landform features in the mountainous area above the glacier.
   b Name three features of the glacier.
   c List the main features of the snout and area beyond the glacier under the headings of 'Moraine features' and 'Meltwater features'.

GEOTERMS

glacier: moving river of ice
valley: lower land, between hills or mountains

GEOskills TOOLBOX

WORKING WITH TOPOGRAPHIC MAPS

Using your skills

1. Identify the features of the physical environment located at the following area references (AR):
   (a) 8219   (b) 8418   (c) 8324.

2. Identify the features of the physical environment located at the following grid references (GR):
   (a) 791217   (b) 792206   (c) 798190.

3. Identify the features of the built environment at the following ARs:
   (a) 7614   (b) 7617   (c) 7714.

4. Identify the features of the human environment at the following GRs:
   (a) 814195   (b) 822142   (c) 764185.

5. Estimate the length of the metalled surface of the Tasman Valley Road.

6. What is the shortest distance from the southern shore to the northern shore of the Tasman Lake?

The Tasman Glacier is located in the South Island of New Zealand.

7. Imagine you have joined a group following the walking trail starting to the north-west of the settlement at Mount Cook and finishing at the Hooker Glacier. Describe the main features you would see on your walk.

SCALE 1:50 000

0   1   2   3   4   5   6 kilometres

ROADS

Four lanes or more	
Two lanes	
Narrow road	
Vehicle track	
Foot track	
Road Surface { sealed	
metalled	
unmetalled	
State Highway	①
Tunnel	
Bridge, two lane	
Bridge, one lane	
Footbridge	

WATER FEATURES

Coastal rocks
Sand and mud
Sand
Shingle
Swamp
Dam; waterfall
Cold spring; hot spring
Watercourse; drain
Stream disappearing into ground

RELIEF FEATURES

Index contours 300
Intermediate contours ....
Supplementary contour ....
Depression contours ....
Shallow depressions ....
Trig station beaconed; unbeaconed .... ▲ △
Elevation in metres .... •130 △130m
Cliff, terrace ....
Rock outcrop ....
Stopbank ....
Cutting ....
Embankment ....
Saddle ....
Alpine features
    Moraine ....
    Moraine wall ....
    Scree ....

RAILWAYS

Double or multiple track ....
Single track ....
Station ....
Railway yard ....
Level crossing ....
Road over railway ....
Railway over road ....
Tramway ....

VEGETATION FEATURES

Native forest ....
Exotic forest ....
Scrub ....
Scattered scrub ....
Shelter belt ....
Trees ....
Orchard ....
Mangroves ....
Burnt and fallen bush ....

MISCELLANEOUS

Residential area ....

Large buildings ....

Building .... ▪
Homestead .... Awapuni
Church .... ⌁
Cemetery .... ⊞
Historic sites:
    Monument .... ⚓
    Plaque or signpost .... ★
    Maori Pa .... ⌘
    Redoubt .... ⊠
Wind machine (pump, generator, fan) ... ⚥
Lighthouse; beacon .... ⌂ ⚑
Wreck .... ⋉
Fence (selection only) ....

Power line on pylons (actual positions)	⊶⊷
Power line on poles (away from roads)	
Telephone line (away from roads)	
Masts; radio, T.V., microwave ...	R TV MW
Mine; underground; opencast	◫ ⚒
Cave	▲
Buried gas pipeline	

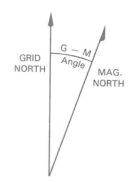

GRID NORTH   G — M Angle   MAG. NORTH

MAGNETIC NORTH on this map is 21° (373 mils) EAST OF GRID NORTH during 1996 increasing at the rate of approx. ½° (9 mils) over 6 years.

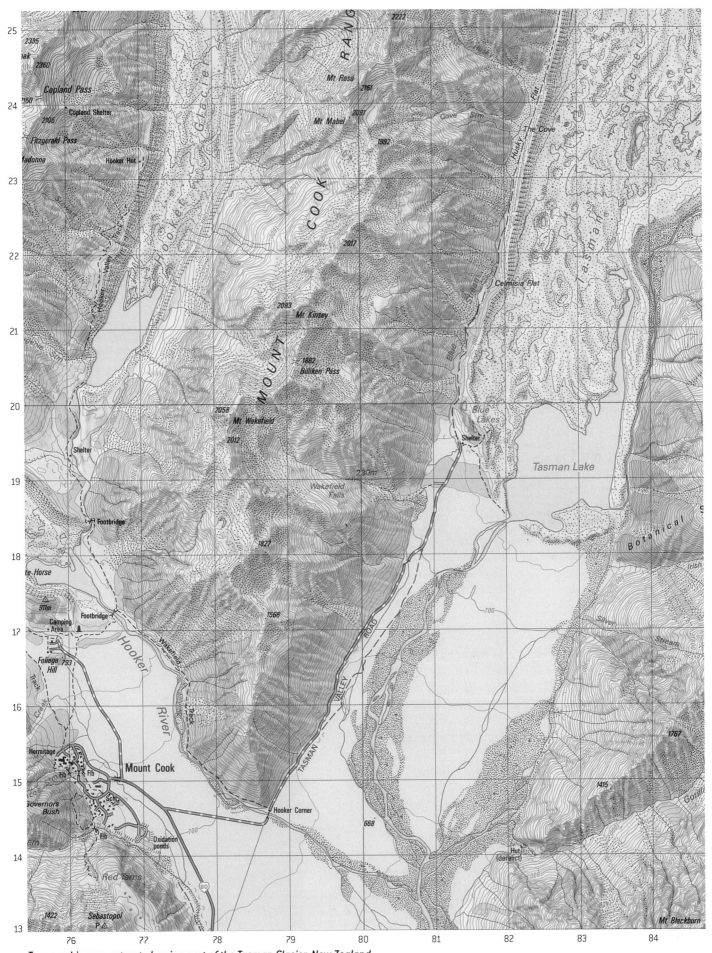

Topographic map extract showing part of the Tasman Glacier, New Zealand

The climate of mountainous regions, wherever they are located, has many elements in common. Generally, temperatures are much lower in mountain areas than they are at sea level for places of the same latitude. Mount Kilimanjaro in Africa, for instance, lies close to the Equator. At its peak, it is so cold that the ground is covered in snow throughout the year. However, in recent years the mountain has been losing its snow cover. Scientists are not yet sure whether climate change is responsible for this trend.

Climate change may mean that Mt Kilimanjaro will not have a snow-covered peak all year round, in spite of its height above sea level.

Temperature

In mountain latitudes, the rate of change that occurs as altitude increases is called the **lapse rate**. It is generally between 1° and 2° Celsius per 100 metres. The reason that temperatures *decrease* as altitude *increases* is the changes that occur in the atmosphere. These changes mainly involve *air temperature* and *air density*.

The highest temperatures usually occur next to the Earth's surface and decrease upwards because very little heating of the atmosphere takes place from the direct rays of the sun.

The sun's rays heat the surface of the Earth and the heat from the Earth in turn heats the atmosphere above it. As well, because mountains have a smaller land area at high latitudes they are less able to heat the surrounding air. The density of air affects the ability of the air to hold heat. Air density *decreases* as altitude *increases* and thus contributes to the lower temperatures.

Precipitation

At higher altitudes on mountains, most of the precipitation falls as snow. Average levels of precipitation also increase with altitude. On very high peaks, snow is a permanent feature all year round. At lower levels, it is seasonal and melts during the warmth of summer. The zone between seasonal and permanent snow is known as the snowline.

Wind speed

Higher wind speeds in mountain areas result from accelerated airflow up and over the mountain range. Winds are generally gusty because of the varied relief. Wind funnelling, where wind is forced through gaps in the mountains, also occurs, producing great variation in wind speed. Valley winds tend to occur under clear and settled conditions and are the result of the variations in heating found in areas of rugged relief.

Climate and vegetation

The changes in temperature and other general climate characteristics also affect the natural vegetation in mountain areas. The higher up mountain plants grow, the smaller they tend to become and, therefore, their growth rates are slower.

Changes in temperature and climate also affect the types of human activities and settlements that occur in mountain lands.

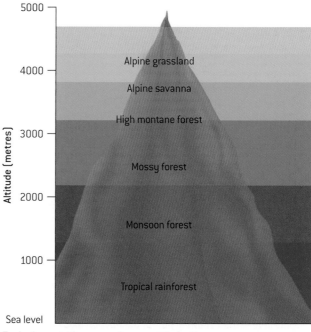

Typical vegetation zones in mountain lands

/// Communities in the Western Highlands of Papua New Guinea

The Western Highlands of Papua New Guinea is an area of mountains and broad highland valleys. Much of the area has an elevation of around 1200 to 2500 metres above sea level.

The main town in the Western Highlands is Mount Hagen, with an elevation of 1600 metres above sea level. Although much of the land is very steep and rugged, there are broader and flatter areas in valleys and plateaus. The annual average temperature in the highlands is around 18° Celsius, which is 8° Celsius cooler than Port Moresby at sea level. In these areas the indigenous people take advantage of the abundant rainfall (around 2500 millimetres), good soils and the cooler highland climate to build settlements, grow crops and raise animals. There are also small areas of commercial plantations in the highlands where the cooler climate is suitable for growing tea and coffee.

Landforms of Papua New Guinea

The soils and climate of the Western Highlands make the area suitable for many crops.

UNDERSTANDING

 1 Explain the term 'lapse rate'.
2 Outline why the temperature decreases as altitude increases.
3 What is the snowline?
4 What are the main physical features that allow settlement in the Western Highlands?

THINKING AND APPLYING

5 How do you think the agricultural activities of the indigenous people in the Western Highlands might be affected if climate change resulted in a warmer annual average temperature?

USING YOUR SKILLS

6 Refer to the map of Papua New Guinea and answer the following.
a Find and state the heights of the two highest mountains.
b Give the approximate latitude and longitude of Mount Hagen.
c Describe the landforms of the Western Highlands of Papua New Guinea.
d Which areas in the highlands would be most suitable for agriculture?

GEOTERMS

lapse rate: rate of change in temperature that occurs as the altitude increases

Nepal is a small, landlocked country in the central Himalayas, situated between India and China. It is about two-thirds the size of the state of Victoria. Although located in the subtropical climate zone between latitudes 27°N and 30°N, Nepal has a wide range of climates. This is because of the great variation in altitude, from as low as 50 metres on the Terai Plain to Mount Everest at 8848 metres, the highest point on Earth.

Nepal is divided into three main landform regions:

- the plains region, with an altitude from 50 metres to 900 metres
- the hills region, across the middle of Nepal, with an altitude of 900 metres to 3000 metres
- the Himalayan region, extending from 3000 metres to 8848 metres.

The hills region

The hills region was formerly forested but, due to Nepal's increasing population and the limited amount of land, the steep slopes have been terraced and are now farmed intensively. The region has been severely degraded due to this pressure on the scarce land.

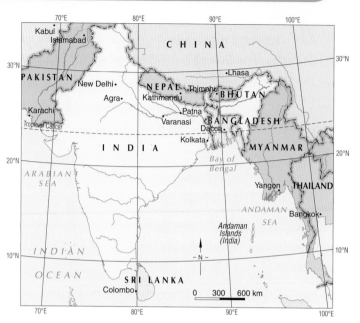

Nepal and its neighbouring countries

Most communities in this region work in agriculture. Rice is grown as the main crop up to 2000 metres. Wheat is planted after the rice is harvested. Mustard is grown for cooking oil, corn is planted up the hills and potatoes are grown up

GEOskills TOOLBOX

UNDERSTANDING CROSS-SECTIONS

A cross-section is a side view or profile that shows the shape of the land. Cross-sections give you the opportunity to imagine what it would be like to walk from one point to another shown on a map. Cross-sections are often drawn from topographic maps using the contours on these maps.

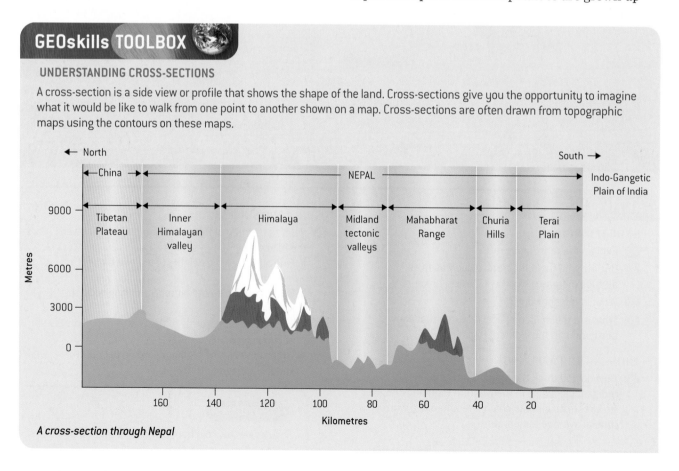

A cross-section through Nepal

to 4000 metres. The growing population has led to a drop in the average size of holdings to only half a hectare. Around half the farmers are tenants and many are in debt to moneylenders and are forced to farm on very poor land. Despite a government recommendation that a 30-degree slope is the limit for cultivation, many farmers have cleared land with a 50-degree gradient. Mud and debris flow down and landslides occur frequently on these steep slopes. Deforestation is also a major problem.

Many former hill dwellers have migrated to the capital, Kathmandu. It is Nepal's major city with a population of 800 000 and is situated at an elevation of 1300 metres. Uneducated rural migrants find it difficult to obtain jobs there. Many sell handicrafts and others might work in hotels as cooks, cleaners, waiters and porters, as day labourers for the wealthy or doing menial work on building construction sites.

A large and growing urban population has placed pressure on both the human and the physical environment of Kathmandu. **Temperature inversions** and the severe smog that accompanies them are a major problem. Kathmandu has an inefficient transport system that pours out pollutants, and the fuel wood used for fires adds to the problem. As Kathmandu is located in a bowl-like valley, surrounded by mountains, this results in little wind and ideal conditions for smog to develop. The smog is a serious health hazard, causing a high percentage of the population to suffer from tuberculosis and lung complaints.

ACTIVITIES ➔

UNDERSTANDING

1. What is meant by the term 'landlocked'? Which countries make Nepal landlocked?
2. What are the three main landform regions in Nepal and what are their altitudes?

USING YOUR SKILLS

3. Refer to the map of Nepal and its neighbours. Describe the location of Nepal, including its latitude and longitude.
4. Refer to the cross-section of Nepal opposite.
   a. What is the direction of the cross-section?
   b. What do you think are the names of the areas that make up the hills region?
   c. What do you think the following colours represent on the diagram: green, brown, and white? Draw a key to explain the use of these colours.
   d. What is the range of the height of the snowline? Why do you think that height varies?

The Himalayan region

The high Himalayan region has become the main centre of mountaineering and trekking in Asia. The local name for this Mount Everest region is Khumbu, and the people who live there are the Sherpas.

Rice terraces near Kathmandu

The environment and the people

Most of Khumbu consists of high-altitude rock, ice and snow. Fewer than 1 per cent can be farmed, but other land is suitable for pasture. Water is plentiful and forest is the natural vegetation in warmer areas. About 3000 Sherpas live here in eight villages and other seasonally occupied settlements at altitudes between 3000 and 5000 metres. The air at these very high altitudes is thinner than at sea level and contains much less oxygen, making it harder to breathe. The Sherpas have adapted to this difficult environment, with a physique that is shorter and lighter than lowland people. They also have larger lungs and a larger heart that pumps more blood. This makes them ideal physically for mountaineering and trekking.

Land use and economy

Traditionally, the Sherpas' land use has been the cultivation of crops and herding of livestock suited to high altitudes. Buckwheat, barley and potatoes are grown on the surrounding terraced hillsides. In summer, the Sherpas take their yaks up to the summer pastures for grazing. These people have also engaged in annual trading expeditions that have extended as far as northern India and Tibet.

Tourism and its impact on Sherpa life

The Mount Everest environment has some of the most spectacular **alpine** scenery in the world. It is the most valuable natural resource of the region. The number of trekking expeditions that visit this region has increased dramatically over recent years.

The Sherpas have adapted their local economy and lifestyle around trekking tourism. It is common for several members of a household to have tourism-based incomes from jobs as guides, cooks or porters. Nearly all of this work is done by men. The work is mainly seasonal, but many men are employed on a full-time basis. Many Sherpa homes

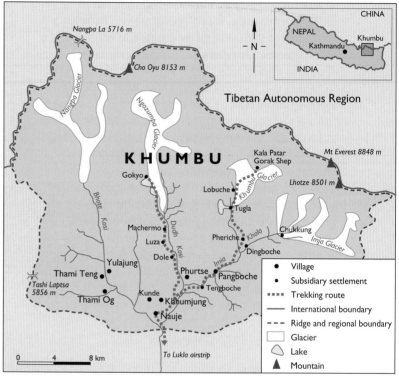

The Khumbu (Mount Everest) region of Nepal

The scenery around the Mount Everest area of Nepal is spectacular.

have been converted to lodges and tea houses to cater for tourists.

The increased incomes from tourism have assisted many of the Sherpas to maintain much of their distinctive lifestyles and customs. Even so, over the last 20 years the Sherpa economy has been transformed from one of subsistence farming and trading to mainly tourism. The cash from tourism has resulted in most of the food and clothing being purchased in shops in villages and towns. Modern houses have been constructed. Many houses have electricity, TV, satellite telephones and the internet. The Nepalese Government has developed schools, better transport systems and a hydro-electric power station.

Conflict over the environment

Sherpas have traditionally used timber from the Himalayan forests for fuel in their cold climate. Tourism has increased this demand. Concern by the Nepalese Government about **deforestation** in the mountains led to the creation of the Sagarmartha National Park (1976), in Khumbu. Originally the Sherpas resisted this attempt to conserve the forest timber. In 1978, the government gave back the management and control to the local Sherpa. The community responded by participating in a reafforestation program.

The Nepalese Government has insisted on:

- trekking and mountaineering parties being self-sufficient in fuel so that they do not rely on local wood supplies
- a ban on cutting of green timber for firewood around villages.

Future ecological sustainability

A form of community-based **ecotourism** is currently being trialled in the Khumbu region

Sherpas can carry extremely heavy loads, even at high altitudes.

where villagers are actively involved in natural and cultural heritage conservation. The government's aim is to reduce trekking tourism's ecological and cultural footprint while maximising its benefit to the community. In 2003, a plan called the 'Sacred Sites Trial to Khumbu' was launched. This community-based tourism initiative tries to integrate conservation needs while spreading the benefits of tourism across the wider community.

ACTIVITIES

UNDERSTANDING

1. Explain the pressure being placed on the human and physical environment in the hills region of Nepal.
2. List some of the crops grown in the hills region of Nepal.
3. Outline the physical environment of Khumbu in the Himalayan region of Nepal.
4. What is the traditional land use of the Sherpas?
5. Outline how the Sherpas have adapted physically to the thin air and lack of oxygen in their environment.
6. Explain why there has been conflict over the physical environment in Khumbu.
7. What is ecotourism? How should Khumbu benefit with ecotourism?

THINKING AND APPLYING

8. With reference to the photograph on page 105, explain terracing. What are the problems of terracing steep hills?
9. Why do you think the Himalayan region has become the main centre for mountaineering and trekking in Asia?

USING YOUR SKILLS

10. Refer to the map of Khumbu on page 106.
    a Imagine you are planning a trekking expedition from Nauje to the Khumbu Glacier. What is the distance? How long might it take?
    b Imagine you want to go further and climb Mount Everest. Would you trek or take a helicopter as far as possible? Give reasons for your answer.

GEOTERMS

alpine: the area above the tree line in mountains

ecotourism: nature-based tourism that involves educating tourists about the natural environment. It is ecologically sustainable tourism.

5.10 Avalanches: a natural hazard in mountain lands

What is an avalanche?

An avalanche is a large mass of loosened snow and ice that moves rapidly down a mountain slope, getting larger as it falls. It is a very sudden event that lasts only a matter of minutes. Avalanches are very powerful and can move at speeds in excess of 300 kilometres per hour, flattening buildings and burying everything in their path.

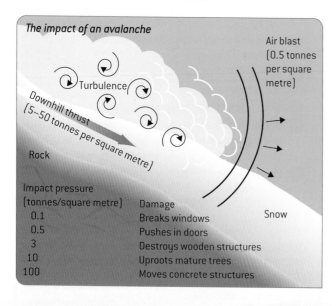

The impact of an avalanche

Air blast (0.5 tonnes per square metre)

Turbulence

Downhill thrust (5–50 tonnes per square metre)

Rock

Snow

Impact pressure (tonnes/square metre)	Damage
0.1	Breaks windows
0.5	Pushes in doors
3	Destroys wooden structures
10	Uproots mature trees
100	Moves concrete structures

In 2002, the Kolka Glacier collapsed, causing a devastating avalanche.

Avalanches are most likely to occur after lengthy snowfalls when large amounts of snow have built up on steep slopes. Earthquakes can cause major avalanches. Other causes include the falling of a tree under pressure from snow, people or animals passing by or the vibrations from trains.

A new cause of avalanches may be developing. In September 2002, over 3 million tonnes of ice broke off from the Kolka Glacier and swept down the Big Caucasus mountain range into the Genaldon valley. The resulting avalanche of water, ice, rocks and other debris buried a Russian village. It left 19 people dead and 106 missing in the biggest avalanche disaster in Russian history. Researchers believe the disaster was a sign of the impact of global climate change in mountainous regions, as glaciers retreat and melt.

Can avalanches be prevented?

On steep, bare slopes, snow can move freely. Trees and obstructions made of wood or metal can be used to slow down or prevent this movement. Further down the slope, structures can be built to divert avalanches away from buildings. In Switzerland, avalanche maps have been produced for tourist areas, showing where avalanches are most likely to occur. Switzerland also has a warning system and emergency evacuation procedures involving specially trained army units and helicopters.

GEOskillbuilder

CONSTRUCTING A COLUMN GRAPH

Geographers use graphs to present and analyse information, especially to make comparisons and determine trends. A column graph is a graph that has vertical columns. The graph below is comparing avalanche fatalities in different countries.

STEP 1

Draw a horizontal axis and select something to compare. In the example below, different countries are compared.

STEP 2

Draw the vertical axis and decide upon the scale. Usually the scale will start at 0 and increase at intervals that suit the data to be graphed. For example, if numbers in the data were in the hundreds or thousands, an interval of 5 would be too small. For this graph, where the highest number in the data is less than 35, intervals of 5 are suitable. Select what you are comparing for the vertical axis. In the example, this is the number of deaths from avalanches in 2000–01.

STEP 3

Decide upon the width and spacing of the columns. Each column should be the same.

STEP 4

Mark the meeting point of the two pieces of information and mark with a dot. Now complete the column. Shade it in with colour or other shading.

STEP 5

Name the vertical and horizontal axes and give the graph a title.

Note: Provide the source of the data at the bottom of the graph. This enables the user to check for more up-to-date statistics when they become available.

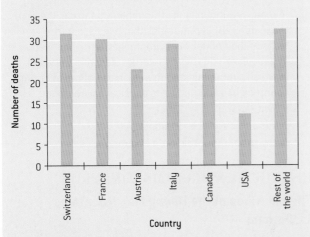

Avalanche deaths, 2000–01

Source: Utah Avalanche Center.

 GEOfacts

- An avalanche can move as fast as 300 kilometres per hour down steep slopes.
- After an avalanche, rescuers probe the snow with long sounding rods for signs of life. Dogs are often used as they can locate people much more quickly.
- An avalanche killed 24 people in Kashmir in 2009. An Australian was also killed by an avalanche in New Zealand.

ACTIVITIES ➜

UNDERSTANDING

1. Define an 'avalanche'.
2. What are some causes that may trigger an avalanche?
3. List three impacts of avalanches. Consider both physical and human environments.

THINKING AND APPLYING

4. Why could the following increase the risk of an avalanche?
   - strong winds
   - strong afternoon sunshine
   - a lack of early snow in winter
   - global warming and climate change
5. Refer to the diagram on the opposite page showing the impact of an avalanche.
   a What are the three forces that together form the impact of an avalanche?
   b Which of these is the most destructive?
   c How important do you think the steepness of the slope is in determining the impact of an avalanche? Explain your answer.

USING YOUR SKILLS

6. Use the information in the column graph of 'Avalanche deaths, 2000–01' to answer the following questions.
   a Which two countries had the highest number of avalanche deaths?
   b Rank the other four countries in decreasing order according to the number of avalanche deaths.
   c Why do you think the first two countries have the highest number of avalanche deaths?
   d Redraw this graph as a pie graph (see page 165).

GEOTERMS

avalanche: a large mass of ice or snow separated from a mountain slope and sliding or falling suddenly downwards

Working geographically

KNOWLEDGE AND UNDERSTANDING

Select the alternative A, B, C or D that best answers the question.

1. The main reason for the formation of new mountains is
   - (A) erosion.
   - (B) the theory of continental drift.
   - (C) heating from the Earth's core.
   - (D) the movement of continental plates.

2. A dome volcano is formed by
   - (A) thick lava that cools and hardens rapidly.
   - (B) thin lava that spreads widely before cooling.
   - (C) layers made up alternately of lava and ash.
   - (D) layers of heavier rock near the vent.

3. The Richter scale measures
   - (A) an earthquake's strength.
   - (B) the epicentre of an earthquake.
   - (C) the strength of seismic waves.
   - (D) the point of the focus of an earthquake.

4. Contour lines that are close together represent
   - (A) a gentle slope.
   - (B) a mountain.
   - (C) a steep slope.
   - (D) a deep valley.

5. Weathering is the breakdown of
   - (A) bare rock by water.
   - (B) bare rock by water and temperature changes.
   - (C) bare rock by water, wind and ice.
   - (D) landforms by water, wind and ice.

6. Glaciers erode by
   - (A) weathering and plucking.
   - (B) abrasion and plucking.
   - (C) grinding and water action.
   - (D) formation of terminal moraine.

7. The lapse rate is
   - (A) the decrease in precipitation as altitude increases.
   - (B) the snowline.
   - (C) the rate of change of temperature as altitude increases.
   - (D) the rate of change of temperature at sea level.

8. The Sherpas live
   - (A) in India.
   - (B) in the region of Khumbu in Nepal.
   - (C) in the hills region of Nepal.
   - (D) in Sagarmartha National Park.

9. The Sherpas are attempting to secure ecological sustainability through
   - (A) conservation of old growth forests.
   - (B) eco-tourism.
   - (C) reduced trekking expeditions.
   - (D) the creation of many national parks.

10. Avalanches can be caused by
    - (A) earthquakes.
    - (B) vibrations from passing trains.
    - (C) people on animals passing by.
    - (D) all of the above.

KEEPING A SCRAPBOOK

11. Volcanoes, avalanches and other natural disasters are often in the news. Begin a scrapbook and collect and record information about such events. Include a map of the event's location, the Richter scale reading (if relevant) and note the effects on people and the environment. Do all reports give as much news time and space to all events? What might make a difference to the coverage given?

RESEARCH

12. In many mountain lands throughout the world, there are many different communities that have adapted in various ways to their physical environments. Using the resources in your library and/or the internet, describe the ways in which a mountain community in one of the following countries has adapted to its physical environment:
    - Switzerland
    - Tibet
    - Iran
    - Ethiopia
    - any other mountain area of your choice.

INVESTIGATE A MOUNTAIN COMMUNITY

The hill tribes of the Hoang Lien Mountains in Vietnam

Minority ethnic groups such as the Tay, H'Mong and Dao live in small communities in Vietnam's highest mountain range at elevations of up to 3000 metres above sea level.

The climate here is monsoonal, with a high level of humidity throughout the year.

This heavily forested mountain environment is rich in biodiversity of species. It contains many plant and animal species that are threatened with extinction such as the rare Taiwania tree and the Western Black Crested Gibbon. The Hoang Lien Nature Reserve was designated in 1986, covering much of the mountain range to the immediate south of the town of Sapa.

The communities are among the poorest in Vietnam. The agricultural land is allocated by the government of Vietnam under a commune system. Traditionally, shifting cultivation and hunting was practised. Today, the people sustain themselves by cultivating rice and maize, fishing, hunting and gathering non-timber forest products such as medicinal plants and orchids. Because of the climate and the steepness of the slopes, only one crop of rice can be grown annually. This sometimes means a shortage of food. Respiratory problems are also common in the misty climate.

Some communities have recently been clearing forested slopes for cardamom cultivation. Cardamom is a plant of the ginger family and when dried is used as a spice. Although its cultivation is bringing income to local communities, it also results in the clearing of the canopy in the forest. Surrounding forest areas are also being used to obtain the wood needed for fires to dry the cardamom fruit.

Consultation with these mountain communities is under way to conserve the forests while developing sustainable incomes for the inhabitants. Tourism is also becoming a factor in the local economies, with many tours offering trekking holidays and accommodation in villages. Villagers can now work as guides, and the resulting income means they can improve the sanitation of their homes. This not only benefits the tourists who stay there but also the long-term health of the villagers.

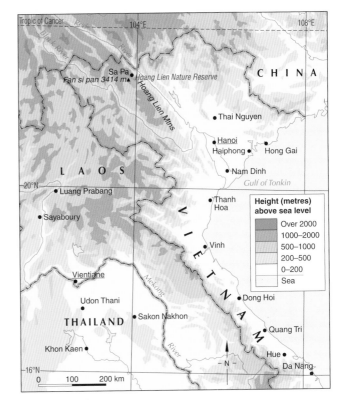

Northern Vietnam

13 How does the environment influence the way the hill tribes of the Hoang Lien Mountains live?

14 Compare the traditional way the communities earned a living with the way they do today.

15 Why is conservation an issue in this mountain community?

16 What are the pros and cons of cardamom cultivation?

17 What benefits is tourism bringing to the hill tribes? What disadvantages might increased tourism bring?

18 Refer to the map above. How high is Fan si pan?

19 Refer to the photograph below. Write a paragraph describing the physical and human elements of the environment shown.

Cat Cat village of the H'Mong ethnic group is located in the Sa Pa region of Vietnam.

eLesson

DRIFTING CONTINENTS

The world hasn't always looked the way it does now. Over millions of years, the giant supercontinent Pangaea broke up to form the continents that we know today. In this eLesson, you will learn about continental drift and watch an animation of how it all happened.

SEARCHLIGHT ID: ELES-0129

PERMIAN
225 million years ago

eLesson

VOLCANOES

Volcanoes have been a source of fascination and fear for people across the world for centuries. There are no active volcanoes on the mainland of Australia, but why is this so? In this eLesson, you will delve into the eruptive world of volcanoes and discover how they are formed, what happens when they blow their tops and how volcanic eruptions have changed the face of the Earth.

SEARCHLIGHT ID: ELES-0130

Interactivity

DRAWING A CONTOUR MAP

Contour lines are used to join places of equal height above sea level. By exploring and interpreting a contour map, you can learn a lot about the shape and slope of a location. In this interactivity, you will create your own contour map of Uluru by following an easy step-by-step process. You can even print your map when you have finished!

SEARCHLIGHT ID: INT-0954

Instructions

How can we show the shape and height of Uluru on a flat piece of paper? By joining spots heights of the same value you can create your own contour map of Uluru. The spot heights start at 500 metres the contour interval is 100 metres. First join the 500 metre spot heights to form a 500-metre contour line. Select a 500 metre spot height as your starting point and click on it to highlight the dot. Click on the next 500-metre dot and the dots will join, eventually completing the 500-metre contour. Follow the same process for all the other heights and then print your map.

Interactivity

MATCH UP: 'CONTOUR PATTERNS'

Match Up is an interactive card game with a twist — the pairs aren't exactly the same. In this exciting interactivity, you will use your geospatial skills to see if you can match the contour patterns with the landscapes they represent. Can you remember where the correct pair is? Can you beat the clock?

SEARCHLIGHT ID: INT-0955

6 Deserts

INQUIRY QUESTIONS

+ Where are deserts located?
+ Why are deserts so hot and dry?
+ How do communities survive in the desert?
+ What changes have humans made to the desert?

Deserts are very dry areas where there is a shortage of moisture because of the low precipitation and high evaporation. Almost one-third of the Earth's land surface is classified as arid or semi-arid desert. Deserts extend to every continent except Europe and may be hot or cold. All deserts have very low rainfall and long dry periods, resulting in only scattered and sparse vegetation. Because of the prevailing harsh conditions, very few people live in desert areas. Flora and fauna have become specially adapted to desert environments.

GEOskills TOOLBOX

GEOskillbuilder Interpreting and constructing climatic graphs (pages 120–1)

+ Interpreting photographs (page 123)
+ Interpreting a satellite image (page 133)

The Sahara Desert near Timimoun, Algeria

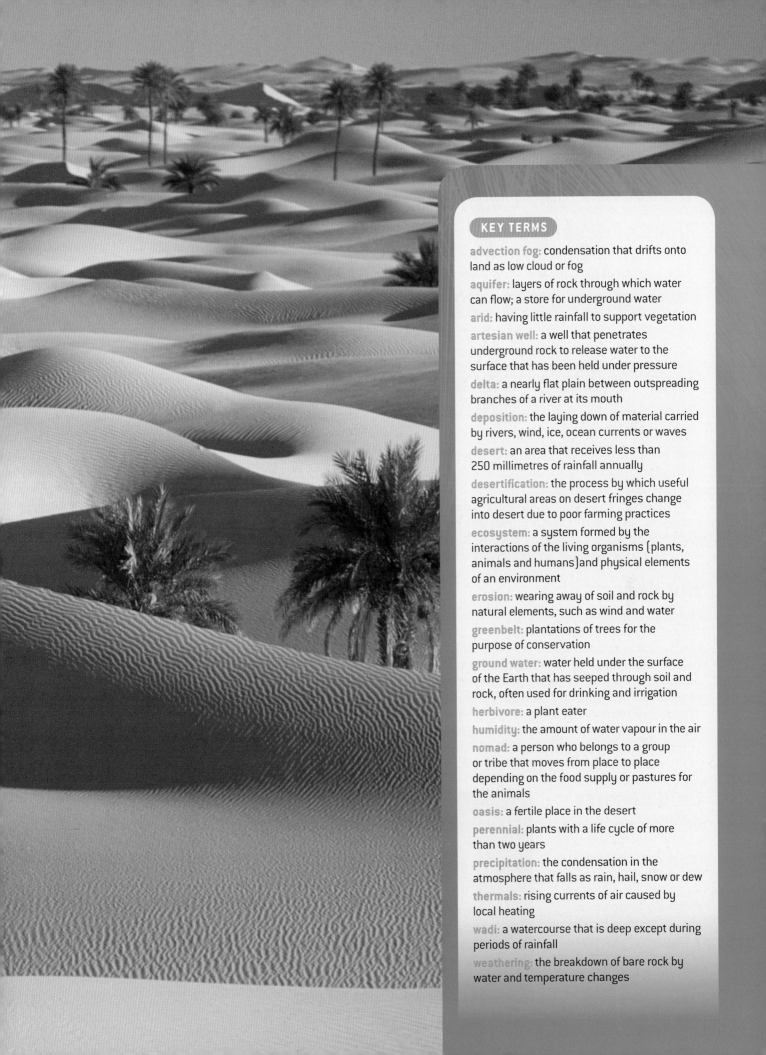

KEY TERMS

advection fog: condensation that drifts onto land as low cloud or fog

aquifer: layers of rock through which water can flow; a store for underground water

arid: having little rainfall to support vegetation

artesian well: a well that penetrates underground rock to release water to the surface that has been held under pressure

delta: a nearly flat plain between outspreading branches of a river at its mouth

deposition: the laying down of material carried by rivers, wind, ice, ocean currents or waves

desert: an area that receives less than 250 millimetres of rainfall annually

desertification: the process by which useful agricultural areas on desert fringes change into desert due to poor farming practices

ecosystem: a system formed by the interactions of the living organisms (plants, animals and humans) and physical elements of an environment

erosion: wearing away of soil and rock by natural elements, such as wind and water

greenbelt: plantations of trees for the purpose of conservation

ground water: water held under the surface of the Earth that has seeped through soil and rock, often used for drinking and irrigation

herbivore: a plant eater

humidity: the amount of water vapour in the air

nomad: a person who belongs to a group or tribe that moves from place to place depending on the food supply or pastures for the animals

oasis: a fertile place in the desert

perennial: plants with a life cycle of more than two years

precipitation: the condensation in the atmosphere that falls as rain, hail, snow or dew

thermals: rising currents of air caused by local heating

wadi: a watercourse that is deep except during periods of rainfall

weathering: the breakdown of bare rock by water and temperature changes

Some of the world's **deserts** are hot and others are cold. All, however, are dry. They make up about one-third of the world's land surface. They are home to some 300 million of its people, as well as to a diverse range of plants and animals.

Types of desert

The world's dry lands are often classified according to the amount of **precipitation** they receive.

Classification	Amount of precipitation
Extremely arid	No precipitation for 12 consecutive months
Arid	Less than 250 millimetres of precipitation per year
Semiarid	Between 250 and 500 millimetres of precipitation per year

Deserts are lands that are either **arid** or extremely arid. They can also form in places where moisture evaporates much faster than it can fall, irrespective of the level of precipitation.

Only about 20 per cent of the world's deserts consist of vast 'seas' of sandy dunes. The rest are either mountainous regions or bare-rock plateaus, stony or gravel plains, or ice-covered landscapes.

Hot deserts

Hot deserts generally lie around the Tropic of Cancer or the Tropic of Capricorn. They have very hot summers and warm winters. What little rain there is often falls in fierce, short bursts that scour out **wadis**. Temperature extremes are common, as cloud cover is rare and **humidity** is very low. This means there is nothing to block the heat of the sun during the day, or prevent its loss at night. Temperatures can range between around 45° and −15° Celsius in a 24-hour period.

Cold deserts

Cold deserts lie on high ground generally north of the Tropic of Cancer and south of the Tropic of Capricorn. They include the polar deserts. Any precipitation falls as snow. Winters are very cold and often windy; summers are dry and mild to warm.

Sahara

The largest hot desert in the world, the Sahara, stretches some 9 million square kilometres across northern Africa over 12 countries. Only a small part of it is sandy. It is the sunniest place in the world.

Arabian

This hot desert is as big as the Australian deserts combined. Towards its south is a place called Rub al-Khali (meaning 'empty quarter'), which has the largest area of unbroken sand dunes, or erg, in the world.

World deserts

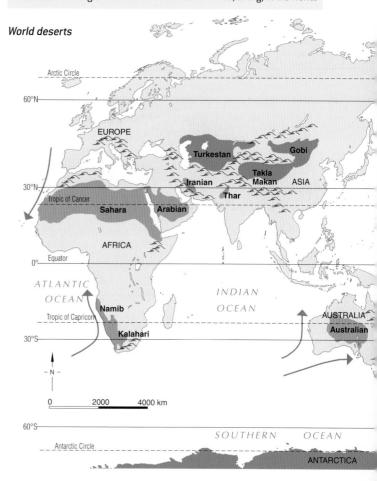

Kalahari and Namib

The Namib Desert stretches for 1200 kilometres down the coast of Angola, Namibia and South Africa. It seldom rains there, but for 80 or so days a year, an early-morning fog streams across the desert from the ocean. The dew it leaves behind provides moisture for plants and animals. It joins the Kalahari Desert, which lies about 1200 metres above sea level.

Australian

After Antarctica, Australia is the driest continent in the world. Its deserts are generally flat lands, often vibrant in colour.

Antarctica

The world's biggest and driest desert, the continent of Antarctica, is another cold desert. Only snow falls there, equal to about 50 millimetres of rain per year.

Takla Makan
The Takla Makan Desert is a cold desert in western China. Its name means 'place of no return'. The explorer Marco Polo crossed it some 800 years ago.

Gobi
Asia's biggest desert, the Gobi, is a cold desert. It sits some 900 metres above sea level and covers an area of some 1.2 million square kilometres. Its winters can be freezing.

Iranian
Two large deserts extend over much of central Iran. The Dasht-i-Lut is covered with sand and rock, and the Dasht-i-Kavir, mainly in salt. Both have virtually no human populations.

Thar
The Thar Desert is a hot desert covering north-western parts of India and Pakistan. Small villages of around 20 houses dot the desert.

North American
The desert region in North America is made up of the Mojave, Sonoran and Chihuahuan deserts (all hot deserts) and the Great Basin (a cold desert). The Great Basin's deepest depression, Death Valley (pictured above), is the lowest point in North America. It is nearly 90 metres below sea level.

Turkestan
The old Silk Road, along which traders travelled between Europe and China, wound through the cold desert regions of Turkestan. The Turkestan deserts cover parts of south-western Russia and the Middle East.

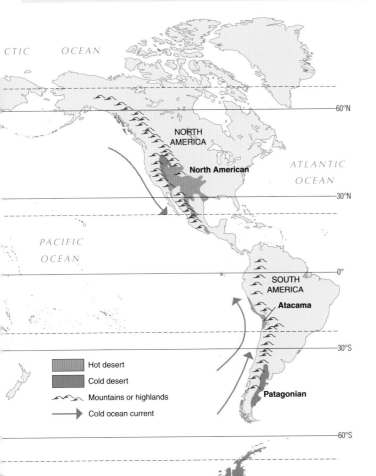

ACTIVITIES ⊙→

UNDERSTANDING

1. Describe the climatic conditions in which deserts form.
2. Explain the main climatic differences between hot and cold deserts.

USING YOUR SKILLS

3. Refer to the map of the world's deserts. Using compass directions, complete the following description of the map.
   Hot deserts are mainly located around the 30° ____ parallel and the ____° south parallel of latitude. The cold deserts are located at latitudes greater than ____° in the northern and ____ hemispheres.
   Deserts cover most of Australia with the exception of the ____ and ____ coasts. Deserts cover most of northern ____. Deserts also cover Antarctica, south-western and central ____, and the west coasts of ____ and ____.
4. The Sahara is the largest hot desert in the world.
   a How large is it?
   b On which continent is it located?
5. Refer to the map and the photographs of deserts.
   a Which continent has the largest area of hot desert?
   b Which continent has the largest area of cold desert?
   c Which is the driest continent in the world?
   d Where is the driest hot desert in the world?
6. Use this map and an atlas to name the 12 African countries covered by the Sahara Desert.

Patagonian
The summer temperature of this cold desert rarely rises above 12° Celsius. In winter, it is likely to be well below zero, with freezing winds and snowfalls.

Atacama
The Atacama Desert is the driest hot desert in the world. Its average annual rainfall is a tiny 0.1 millimetre.

GEOTERMS

arid: having little rainfall to support vegetation
desert: an area that receives less than 250 millimetres of rainfall annually
humidity: the amount of water vapour in the air
wadi: a watercourse that is deep except during periods of rainfall

6.2 Why are deserts so hot and dry?

Why are hot deserts so hot?

Deserts can be found at many different latitudes and altitudes and they can be hot or cold. But why are hot deserts so hot?

Heat and latitude

The sun is so far away from us that its rays may be considered parallel when they reach the Earth. The diagram below shows two of the sun's rays reaching the Earth at the same time but at different latitudes. Both rays have the same amount of solar energy. However, because the Earth's surface is curved, ray 2 (at high latitude near the pole) has to heat a greater surface area than ray 1 (near the Equator).

This different distribution of heat from the sun over the Earth's surface is known as the angle of incidence of the sun's rays.

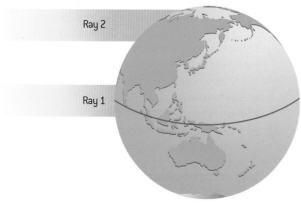

Sun's rays striking the Earth

Cloud cover

The highest temperatures, however, do not occur at the Equator. In general, hot deserts located between 20° and 30° north and south of the Equator have higher temperatures than equatorial lands. The highest temperature ever recorded was 58° Celsius at Azizia in the Sahara Desert.

Equatorial lands often have large areas of cloud that absorb, scatter and reflect incoming solar radiation. Deserts in the tropics have much less cloud cover to block out the sun's rays, so most of the incoming solar radiation is available to heat the Earth's surface. Maximum shade temperatures are often above 40° Celsius.

At night, the warmth quickly escapes because of this same lack of cloud cover. Temperatures drop, even below freezing, resulting in a large daily or *diurnal* range in temperature.

Why are deserts so dry?

Deserts receive very little rainfall. The conditions that lead to low precipitation occur:
- in the tropics and the polar regions
- in the rain shadows of mountain ranges
- in the centres of landmasses
- on the western coasts of continents next to cold ocean currents.

Tropical and polar deserts

Deserts generally lie in regions roughly grouped around the Tropic of Cancer and the Tropic of Capricorn; that is, between latitudes of around 15° and 35° north and south of the Equator. These regions are typically dry due to the general circulation of the Earth's atmosphere.

Hot air from equatorial regions rises high into the atmosphere and flows towards the poles. The higher the air gets, the cooler it becomes. Because cool air cannot hold as much moisture as warm air, it releases it as rain. Areas around the Equator and to the immediate north and south of it (the subtropics) receive frequent heavy downpours. With its moisture gone, the cool, dry air continues moving north and south away from the Equator. At the tropics, the air slowly sinks. As the air descends, it gets warmer. This means it can hold more moisture. Hence, it is likely to absorb what moisture already exists in the environment.

In the polar regions it is generally too cold for precipitation to occur.

Rain shadow deserts

Rain shadow areas form on the leeward side of a mountain range (opposite to the windward side that faces rain-bearing winds). Deserts commonly form in rain shadows. This is how it happens:

- Moist air blowing in from the ocean is forced to rise up when it hits a range of mountains. This cools the air down. As cool air cannot hold as much moisture, it releases it as precipitation.
- By the time the air moves over the top of the range and down the other side, it is likely to have lost most, if not all, of its moisture. It will therefore be fairly dry.
- The more the air descends on the other side of the range, the more it warms up. Hence, it can hold more moisture. So, as well as not bringing any rain to the land, the air absorbs what little moisture the land contains.
- In time, as this pattern continues, the country in the rain shadow of the mountain range is likely to become arid.

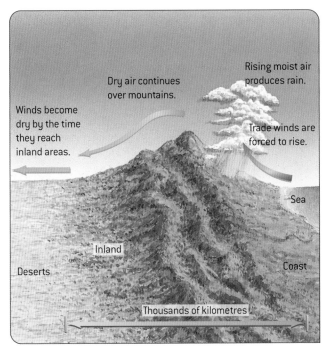

How rain shadow deserts form

Inland deserts

Some deserts form because they are so far inland that they are beyond the range of any rain relief. By the time winds reach these dry centres, they have dumped any rain they were carrying or have become so warm they cannot release any moisture they still hold.

Deserts near cold ocean currents

Currents in the oceans are both warm and cold, and are always moving. Cold currents begin in polar and temperate waters, and drift towards the Equator. They flow in a clockwise pattern in the Northern Hemisphere, and in an anticlockwise pattern in the Southern Hemisphere. As they move, they cool down the air above them.

Sometimes cold currents flow close to the western sides of warm landmasses. If the cool air they create blows in over warm land, it warms up. This means it can hold more moisture. It is therefore not likely to release any moisture it contains unless it is forced up by a mountain range. Hence, warm, flat coastal lands (e.g. the Namib Desert in Africa) often become arid when they are near cold currents.

GEO*facts*

- Australia's largest desert is the Great Victoria Desert in Western Australia and South Australia. It covers an area of 424 400 square kilometres.
- The Sahara Desert is estimated to be 65 million years old.
- Because it is so close to the ocean, the Sonoran Desert in North America receives more rain than any other desert. It has two rainy seasons and plants like the saguaro cactus grow up to 12 metres high.
- The highest sand dune recorded is in the Sahara Desert at over 500 metres high.

ACTIVITIES

UNDERSTANDING

1. How does latitude affect the global distribution of heat?
2. Where are the highest temperatures on Earth recorded?
3. How does the lack of cloud cover in deserts influence temperature?
4. Is the following statement *true* or *false*? 'Temperatures can drop below freezing in deserts at night.'
5. How does the circulation of the Earth's atmosphere influence rainfall in deserts?
6. Explain how cold currents can reduce rainfall.

THINKING AND APPLYING

7. How could a mountain range create a desert? Look in an atlas to find an example of a desert located adjacent to a mountain range.

Interpreting and constructing climatic graphs: understanding desert climates

Interpreting climatic graphs

A climatic graph shows the climate of a place over the twelve months of the year. Climatic graphs include a line graph and a column graph. The line graph shows the average temperature for each month. The column graph shows the average precipitation for each month.

- The **maximum temperature** is the highest average monthly temperature. It is the highest point on the line graph.
- The **minimum temperature** is the lowest average monthly temperature. It is the lowest point on the line graph.
- The **maximum monthly precipitation** is the highest column in the column graph.
- The **minimum monthly precipitation** is the lowest column in the column graph.
- The **temperature range** is the difference between the highest and lowest average monthly temperatures. To calculate the temperature range, subtract the lowest temperature from the highest.

- The **average annual precipitation** is the total precipitation for the year. To calculate it, add up all the monthly precipitation figures.

The heading shows the name of the place.

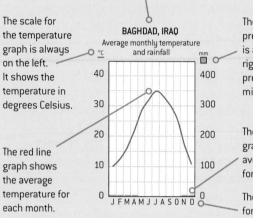

The scale for the temperature graph is always on the left. It shows the temperature in degrees Celsius.

The scale for the precipitation graph is always on the right. It shows precipitation in millimetres.

The red line graph shows the average temperature for each month.

The blue column graph shows the average precipitation for each month.

The letters stand for the months of the year.

Hints for interpreting climatic graphs

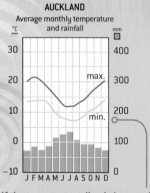

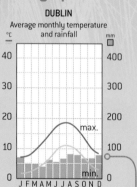

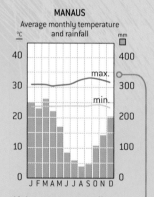

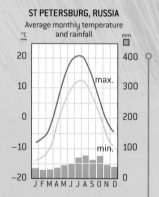

If the temperature line is lowest during June, July and August, the place has winter in the middle of the year so it is in the Southern Hemisphere. If temperatures are lowest in December, January and February, the place is in the Northern Hemisphere.

If the temperature line is almost level (a small temperature range), the place is probably close to the Equator.

If the temperature line has very high and very low points (a large temperature range), the place is either far from the Equator or a long way inland.

If the column graph has a group of higher columns, the place has a wet season.

If the column graph has a group of lower columns, the place has a dry season.

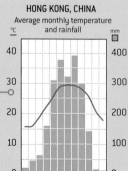

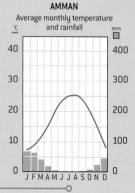

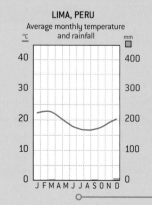

If the column graph shows very little precipitation throughout the year, the place has dry conditions all year round. If the total annual precipitation is less than 250 millimetres, the place is in a desert environment.

Constructing climatic graphs

It is much easier to compare the climates of two places by looking at climatic graphs than by looking at tables of statistics, so drawing and using these simple graphs are important geographic skills.

Follow these steps to draw a climatic graph for Newcastle.

STEP 1

- Look at the data in the table below. Two sets of data are given: average monthly rainfall in millimetres (mm) and average monthly temperature in degrees Celsius (°C) for each of the 12 months of the year.

STEP 2

- Check the range of the data to decide what scales will work for the vertical axes.
- For the right hand axis, find the wettest month. The precipitation scale begins at 0 mm and extends far enough to include the wettest month.
- For the left axis, find the highest and lowest temperatures. A temperature scale of 0°C to 40°C will suit most climatic graphs.
- Use scales that stop the line and column graphs overlapping. (This may not be possible if the place has a very high rainfall.)

STEP 3

- Rule up the horizontal axis and two vertical axes. (Use graph paper and a ruler for an accurate result.)
- Divide the horizontal axis into 12 equal sections to represent the months of the year.

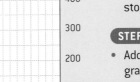

Set of axes for Newcastle climograph

- Label each month.
- Label the temperature on the left vertical axis and rainfall on the right vertical axis.

STEP 4

- Using a pencil, construct a column graph showing the average monthly rainfall for Newcastle. Make sure you use the right hand vertical scale to plot your data. Rule a line across each bar and colour the bars blue.

STEP 5

- Using a pencil, construct a line graph showing Newcastle's average monthly temperature. Plot the temperature by placing a dot in the centre of each month. Make sure you use the left vertical scale.
- Use a red pen or pencil to join the dots with a smooth curve (not with a ruler).
- Complete the temperature line so that it reaches the edges of the graph. Extend the temperature line for January to the left of your graph so that it stops at December's temperature. Extend the temperature line for December to the right so that it stops at January's temperature.

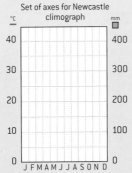

NEWCASTLE
Average monthly temperature and rainfall

STEP 6

- Add a heading that shows the name of the place being graphed. You could also include the latitude, longitude and elevation of the place.
- Add the source of information, such as Bureau of Meteorology, if available.

Climate data for Newcastle, Australia

	J	F	M	A	M	J	J	A	S	O	N	D
Av. monthly temperature (°C)	22	22	21	18	15	13	12	13	15	18	19	21
Av. monthly precipitation (mm)	93	103	121	117	114	116	98	77	76	76	69	83

ACTIVITIES

USING YOUR SKILLS

1. Refer to the climatic graphs on page 120.
   a Which places are clearly in the Northern Hemisphere?
   b Which place is clearly in the Southern Hemisphere?
   c Which place is closest to the Equator?
   d Which place has a desert environment?
   e Which place has a clear wet season?
2. Using the climate data below for Oodnadatta, Australia, construct a climatic graph following the steps shown above.

Climate data for Oodnadatta, Australia

	J	F	M	A	M	J	J	A	S	O	N	D
Av. monthly temperature (°C)	30	29	27	21	17	13	13	15	19	23	26	29
Av. monthly precipitation (mm)	24	32	12	11	13	12	10	8	9	14	11	16

6.4 Desert landforms

We often associate deserts with great expanses of sand dunes. However, sand dunes make up only a small proportion of desert landforms. The grains of sand that make up the dunes were once part of other landforms still to be seen in deserts. These landforms are created by extremes of temperature, water and wind.

Shaping the desert

The landforms and patterns of a desert are created by a number of natural processes:

- Extremes of temperature, together with the impact of rushing torrents that often follow desert rainstorms, cause pieces of rock to split off from larger rocks. This process is called **weathering**.
- **Erosion** removes material such as weathered rock. Most erosion in deserts is caused by running water. During heavy rainfall, water carves out channels in the ground. The torrent carries with it rocks and sand, which help to scour out the sides of the channel. As vegetation is usually sparse or non-existent, there are few roots to hold the soil together. Eventually, deep gullies called wadis form.

Erosion can also result from the action of wind and from chemical reactions. Some rocky formations, such as limestone, contain compounds that react with rainwater and then dissolve in it.

- Materials carried along by rushing water and wind must eventually come to a halt. Over time, this dumped material builds up, forming characteristic shapes and patterns in the desert. This process is called **deposition**. Sand dunes and alluvial fans are formed by deposition.

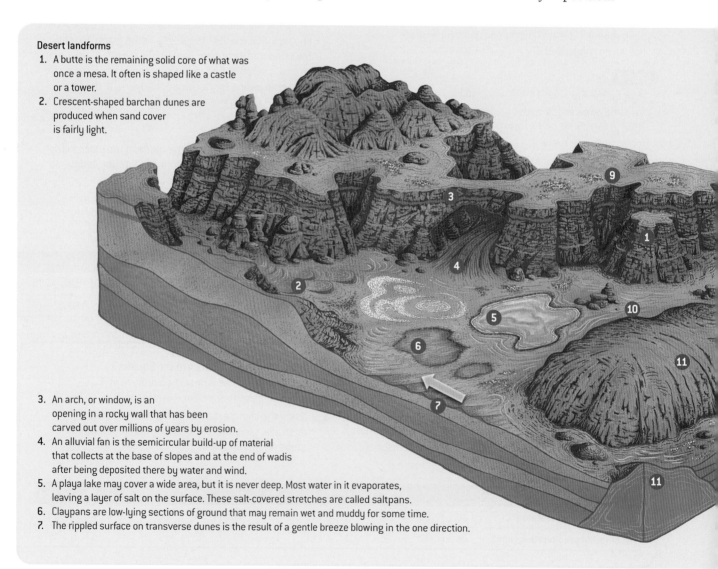

Desert landforms

1. A butte is the remaining solid core of what was once a mesa. It often is shaped like a castle or a tower.
2. Crescent-shaped barchan dunes are produced when sand cover is fairly light.
3. An arch, or window, is an opening in a rocky wall that has been carved out over millions of years by erosion.
4. An alluvial fan is the semicircular build-up of material that collects at the base of slopes and at the end of wadis after being deposited there by water and wind.
5. A playa lake may cover a wide area, but it is never deep. Most water in it evaporates, leaving a layer of salt on the surface. These salt-covered stretches are called saltpans.
6. Claypans are low-lying sections of ground that may remain wet and muddy for some time.
7. The rippled surface on transverse dunes is the result of a gentle breeze blowing in the one direction.

GEOskills TOOLBOX

INTERPRETING PHOTOGRAPHS

Geographers frequently use photographs as a tool when they are studying environments. When looking at photographs geographers:

- *observe*, which means looking carefully to find out *what* it shows and *where* it might have been taken
- *record*, which means *writing* down or *drawing* what we see in the photograph
- *interpret*, which means thinking about what we are observing and recording
- *ask* and *answer* geographical questions about the scene in the photograph.

The photograph here is of part of Monument Valley in Arizona, USA. It is a ground level photograph showing the area as if it were observed at eye level. For more information on interpreting photographs, see pages 56–7.

8. An oasis is a fertile spot in a desert. It receives water from underground supplies.
9. A mesa is a plateau-like section of higher land with a flat top and steep sides. The flat surface was once the ground level, before weathering and erosion took their toll.
10. Sand dunes often start as small mounds of sand that collect around an object like a rock. As they grow larger, they are moved and shaped by wind.
11. An inselberg is a solid monolithic rock formation that was once below the ground level. As the softer land around it erodes, it becomes more and more prominent. Uluru is an inselberg.

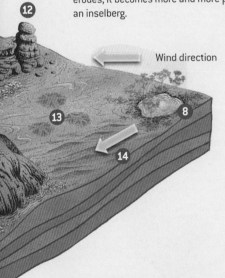

Wind direction

12. A chimney rock is the pillar-like remains of a butte.
13. Star dunes are produced by wind gusts that swirl in from all directions.
14. Strong winds blowing in one direction form longitudinal dunes.

ACTIVITIES

UNDERSTANDING

1. Identify the three natural processes that shape desert landforms.
2. Explain how erosion and deposition are different.

THINKING AND APPLYING

3. Make a list of movies, books and songs that involve deserts. Describe their message.
4. Imagine you are an explorer who has been in a desert for several weeks. One day, there is a huge thunderstorm with torrential rain. Write a report on the appearance of the desert immediately after the storm.

USING YOUR SKILLS

5. Refer to the diagram of desert landforms.
   a Describe the appearance of these landforms: mesa, butte, barchan, and alluvial fan.
   b What wind conditions are needed to create a star dune, a longitudinal dune and a transverse dune?
   c Suggest how playa lakes are formed.
6. Refer to the photograph of desert landforms in Monument Valley.
   a Describe the landforms you can see in the photograph. (Use the diagram to help you identify them.) In your description, use the words: foreground, middle ground and background.
   b How would you describe the vegetation cover? From your knowledge of deserts, explain the reason for the lack of vegetation.
   c Would these landforms be the result of deposition or erosion? Explain.

6.5 A desert ecosystem

Life is rather tough in a desert environment. Desert plants and animals face extremes of temperature, food shortages and a lack of readily available water. To survive, they have to adapt to these harsh conditions.

Animal survivors

The bodies of creatures in desert ecosystems have evolved to help them survive. Many are pale in colour, to reflect the heat. Some desert animals, such as reptiles, can vary their body temperature dramatically to cope with extremes of temperature. Some desert animals have very long legs to increase the distance between their bodies and the hot sand. Others have thick, leathery skins or hard, waxy shells to help them retain water, or thick fur or feathers to insulate their skin from extremes of temperature.

Staying cool

When it gets too hot, most desert birds look for shade. Some take off, to drift on the cool thermals that blow high above the hot sands. Many desert animals dig deep burrows into cooler sand, where they stay during the heat of the day, coming out to hunt at night. Desert storks and vultures urinate on their legs. The evaporating urine cools their skin,

Vultures escape the hot midday temperatures and save energy by soaring high in the cooler thermals of air. They urinate on their legs to allow evaporation to cool themselves down.

The jackrabbit has developed huge ears to draw heat away from its body. The blood vessels in the ears release heat when the animal is resting in a cool, shady location.

North American desert ecosystem

Spadefoot toads construct one-metre-deep burrows and hibernate for up to ten months of the year underground. When the rains come, they leave their burrows for a short period of time to lay their eggs.

The world's only underground owl, the burrowing owl, moves into empty burrows to avoid the daytime sun. To stay cool it opens its beak and rapidly flutters its throat to evaporate water from its mouth.

Kit foxes avoid the heat of the day. They are nocturnal, usually emerging from their dens shortly after sunset to hunt small animals, birds and lizards.

Kangaroo rats have the ability to convert the dry seeds they eat into water. They do not sweat, and they have special kidneys that allow them to dispose of waste materials with very little loss of water.

and the cooler blood then flows back into their body. Some creatures hop to minimise the contact of their feet with hot sand or, like lizards, run extremely fast.

Food and water supplies

Most large desert animals survive because they are herbivores. They obtain moisture from the plants they eat. Others, like scorpions, get their moisture from their prey or from dew. The camel stores food in its hump, and can go for days without drinking. The scarab beetle solves the problem of a scarce food and water supply by eating animal dung!

The coyote is one of the most adaptable animals in the world. It can change its breeding habits, diet and behaviour to survive in a wide variety of habitats. Its skill as a successful hunter for anything ensures this carnivore's success in the deserts of North America.

Saguaro cacti have no leaves. Their spiky thorns reduce the surface area exposed to the sun and the loss of water. When water is absorbed, the stem of the Saguaro cactus can expand to hold the moisture. This ability to store water allows it to flower every year, regardless of rainfall.

Peccaries have sharp teeth and a hardy digestive system that allows them to obtain moisture from prickly desert plants such as cacti. They are nocturnal and spend the heat of the day resting in hollows.

Chuckwallas are large, plump lizards that slide between rocks to avoid the desert sun and predators.

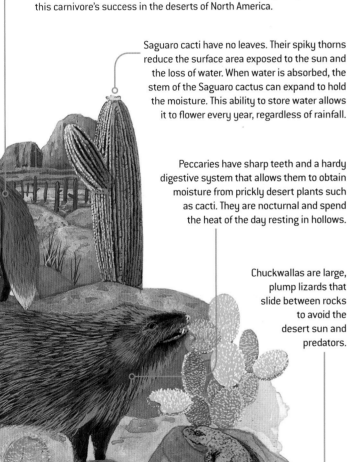

The roadrunner is a fast carnivorous ground bird. It obtains moisture and nutrition from a wide range of foods including insects, scorpions, lizards, snakes, rodents and other birds. The roadrunner reabsorbs water from its faeces before excreting.

Plant survivors

There are two main types of desert plants: perennials and ephemerals. Perennials are plants that have adapted ways to cope with desert conditions and ephemerals are those that have a very short life cycle after rain. Some desert perennials, such as America's mesquite tree or Australia's river redgum, have very long root systems, often stretching down to the watertable. Others, such as succulents, have shallow but widely spread root systems so they can soak up and store lots of water when it rains. Many perennials have small leaves, often waxy, to reduce loss of moisture through transpiration. Some have no leaves at all — just thorns and spikes. During dry periods, plants may drop their leaves, or parts of the plant above the surface may die.

ACTIVITIES

UNDERSTANDING

1. Why is survival a problem for plants and animals in a desert environment?

2. Explain the difference between perennial and ephemeral plants. Provide an example of how each type of plant survives in a desert.

THINKING AND APPLYING

3. Create an imaginary ideal desert animal that can survive in a desert ecosystem. Draw and label a sketch of this creature.

USING YOUR SKILLS

4. Copy and complete the following table in your notebook.

Special plant or animal feature	How it helps to ensure survival
Thorns instead of leaves	
Large ears	
Pale colouring	
Long legs	
Large roots	

GEOTERMS

ecosystem: a system formed by the interactions of the living organisms (plants, animals and humans) and physical elements of an environment

The Bedouin are nomadic Arabs who live by rearing sheep and camels in the deserts of the Middle East and the Sahara. The word Bedouin means 'inhabitants of the desert'. They are communities in that they share space and social organisation. The days of the distinctive Bedouin culture are probably numbered. The discovery of oil under the deserts has brought great and swift change to people's lives in the Middle East. Great wealth has spread through all levels of Arab society, affecting even the most remote Bedouin.

What is life like for the Bedouin?

The desert environment of the Bedouin is barren, stripped bare by the fierceness of the sun and the lack of rain. The traditional Bedouin may live in high mountains or among sand dunes or, most commonly, on the open, stony plains. These stony plains are bleak. They lack shelter and in many areas there is not even a blade of grass. Yet the plains provide the most hospitable terrain in the desert as the surface is firm and easy to travel across. Where there is a little water in wadis, or low-lying areas, there may be a welcome growth of plants. As long as there are a few plants, the Bedouin will camp. They may cross regions where virtually nothing is growing and then camp where there are a few desert shrubs, brought to life by the infrequent rain.

Much of their work involves sitting all day and watching their flocks and herds grazing. The men take out their camels in the morning and the women and children look after the sheep and goats. Traditionally the girls and small children spend part of their time collecting brushwood for fires and bring it home in bundles on their heads. Families with a pick-up truck use this for the task.

Milk and milk products from their flocks and herds form the main part of the Bedouin diet. A Bedouin meal often consists solely of a bowl of milk or yoghurt. The main meal is at night and is usually rice flavoured with butter. Tinned fish or tomato paste can provide welcome variety. Meat is a luxury eaten only a few times a year and then it is usually for a festival or a guest. Locusts are considered a delicacy. Oryx and gazelle were once enjoyed but these are now rare and protected animals.

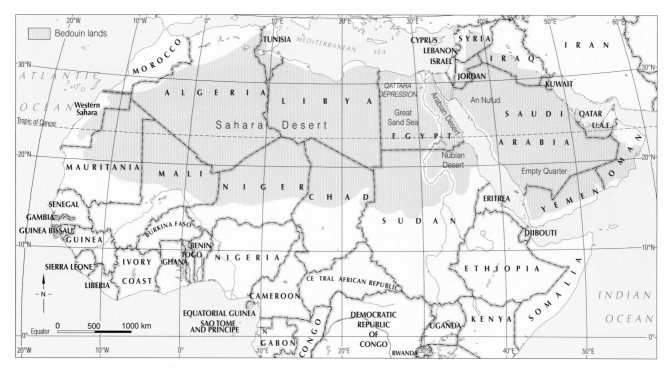

The desert areas inhabited by the Bedouin

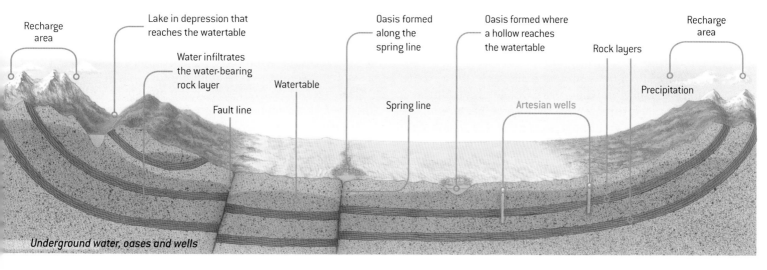

Recharge area

Lake in depression that reaches the watertable

Water infiltrates the water-bearing rock layer

Fault line

Watertable

Oasis formed along the spring line

Oasis formed where a hollow reaches the watertable

Spring line

Artesian wells

Rock layers

Precipitation

Recharge area

Underground water, oases and wells

Water — the key to desert life

For the Bedouin, water is the key to life in the desert and survival depends on finding adequate supplies. Severe drought can mean intense hardship. They try to follow the rain, taking their flocks and herds to places where rain has fallen and some grazing is available. During their seasonal migrations they may travel up to 4000 kilometres.

The Bedouin must have drinking water to sustain both them and their herds. They obtain it from wells that tap into underground water. The Bedouin have always owned wells in the desert. They do not know who made the wells but they are very old. These wells may be as deep as 50 metres. Traditionally, this valuable water is drawn up using hand buckets or by animals hauling a rope and it is transported in camel-skin bags on camels' backs. This method has changed for many Bedouin who now transport water in old oil drums on pick-up trucks.

Community and government

The largest Bedouin community group is the tribe. The tribe is divided into clans. The clan owns wells and grazing lands. The clan is divided into family groupings, which usually camp together for much of the year.

The tribes or clans who own the various wells in their home area usually retreat to them during the severe heat of summer. Because there have been many disputes involving wells, governments in recent years have dug deep wells for the Bedouin, and these are worked by pumps. They are controlled by the government and are free for use by all Bedouin. The establishment of these wells has solved most of the disputes over water and, in some cases, small townships have sprung up around them.

The Bedouin tent — a family home

The Bedouin camp in family groups ranging from two to around 30 tents. Tents are pitched for about a week, or for as long as the grazing for the animals lasts, then they move to a new site. It takes only an hour or two to pack up the tent and its contents.

The black tent is the centre of traditional life. Made from hair and wool, it barely separates the Bedouin from the harsh desert environment but it is superbly adapted to their needs.

When closed, the tent provides shelter from the wind and warmth on cold nights. With the sides rolled up it provides shade from the sun while

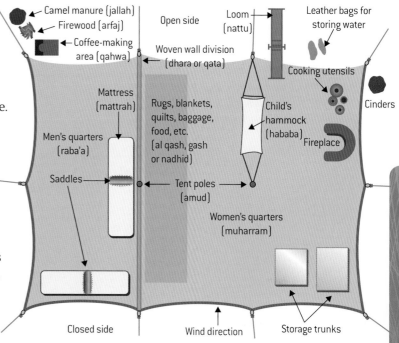

Camel manure (jallah)

Firewood (arfaj)

Coffee-making area (qahwa)

Open side

Loom (nattu)

Leather bags for storing water

Woven wall division (dhara or qata)

Cooking utensils

Mattress (mattrah)

Rugs, blankets, quilts, baggage, food, etc. (al qash, gash or nadhid)

Child's hammock (hababa)

Cinders

Fireplace

Men's quarters (raba'a)

Saddles

Tent poles (amud)

Women's quarters (muharram)

Closed side

Wind direction

Storage trunks

Inside a two-space, two-poled Bedouin tent

permitting any cool breezes to pass through. Within its shelter, the Bedouin have created for themselves a relatively comfortable and happy life.

Going into a Bedouin tent is like entering a cosy home in a barren wilderness. Outside is an almost empty space, threatening because of its extreme aridity and its great heat during the day. Inside is a tidy and well ordered home. Internally the tent is divided by woven wall sections. Piled against these walls are rugs, blankets and quilts. At the back of the tent are leather bags for storing water, dates, coffee beans and yoghurt. Sometimes there are also signs of the modern world — perhaps a radio, a sewing machine or a mobile phone.

The size of tents varies from the one space unit, the *kharbu*, through to the larger eight space or more *msoba*. In the larger tents, two space units are reserved for the kitchen, storage and the daily gathering of women. The remaining spaces are for living, sleeping and receiving family visitors.

A Bedouin family camp today, combining traditional and modern elements.

Bedouin beliefs and cultures

Although seen by others as living in poverty, the traditional Bedouin believe that the desert environment is the best place to live despite its harshness. They reject the city as physically and socially polluted. Their life is organised according to a strict set of rules. To break these rules is considered shameful and this is the worst criticism that can be levelled at a Bedouin. Islam is the basis of their rules, social structure and beliefs. These include: the duty to pray five times a day; give alms to the poor; fast from sunrise to sunset for one month of the year; make a pilgrimage to Mecca once in a lifetime, if possible; the segregation of women; and protection for the rights of orphans and widows. They also include the right of a man to have four wives and to divorce at will, but Bedouin men rarely have more than one wife at a time.

Ecological sustainability

The physical environment of the Sahara Desert is difficult for humans, with its lack of rain and the fierceness of the sun. Traditional Bedouin have adapted well to the environment. Their nomadic way of life has ensured that plants and water are sustainable. The declining population of the nomads ensure the ecology of the area where they roam the desert is sustainable.

What is their future?

Along with the economic development of the countries in the Sahara Desert, life is changing for many Bedouins. Over the

Traditional Bedouin place no pressure on the delicate desert environment.

last 50 years, governments have encouraged the permanent settlement of the Bedouin. Many governments have developed farmland, where there is adequate water for irrigation, for the Bedouin to settle on. Governments and organisations such as the United Nations have provided assistance to construct houses and the famous Bedouin tent is rapidly disappearing — although some enterprising Bedouin have made them tourist attractions.

As well, many Bedouin have settled in towns and cities and adapted to an urban way of life.

GEOTERMS

nomad: a person who belongs to a group or tribe that moves from place to place depending on the food supply or pastures for animals

ACTIVITIES

UNDERSTANDING

1. Who are the Bedouin and where do they live?
2. Describe the environment in which the Bedouin live.
3. Why is the black tent so suitable for the needs of the Bedouin?
4. Explain how the nomadic way of life of the Bedouin is ecologically sustainable.

THINKING AND APPLYING

5. Imagine you are living with a nomadic Bedouin family for a year. Briefly describe your main movements in the year and what factors cause these movements.
6. The Bedouin live according to a strict set of rules. Compare the Bedouin rules with some of the rules we have in our own communities.
7. Think of two ways the life of a Bedouin might change by giving up a nomadic way of life and living in a city.

USING YOUR SKILLS

8. Refer to the diagram on underground water on page 127. Describe how water that falls as precipitation eventually ends up in an oasis or artesian well.
9. Refer to the diagram of the inside of a Bedouin tent on page 127.
   a Why is the open side on the opposite side to the wind direction?
   b What are the main activities that take place outside the open side of the tent?
   c Why are there separate quarters for men and women?

The village of Chungongo is located on the coast of South America, in the northern Atacama Desert of Chile. It is a community based on shared space and social organisation. The main economic activity of the village is fishing.

Community and government

Due to its desert location, there was a serious shortage of fresh water for the village. Some water was obtained from underground sources but the villagers needed to increase their limited supply. A truck would come each week with fresh water and fill up the steel drums outside people's houses. This was so expensive that every drop was rationed.

The community has worked with government scientists to increase the water supply. When the cold Peruvian current cools the air, it sometimes causes a fog. About 6 kilometres from the village, near an abandoned mining settlement, 75 sheets of nylon mesh are mounted like billboards along the steep and dusty side of a hill. They are there to collect moisture from the thick fog that drifts in regularly from the Indian Ocean. The fog condenses on the mesh and the water drips into a trough. The collected water flows from the trough, down through a pipe, to a reservoir near the village of Chungongo, about 6 kilometres away.

What causes the desert fog?

The high Andes Mountains shut off Chungongo from the moist easterlies that bring rain to much of South America. This rain shadow effect and the tropical location result in a hot desert region. However, the area does receive frequent fogs that drift onshore from the west. A cold ocean current from the cold waters of the southern Pacific Ocean moves northwards along the coast of Chile and cools the warm air above it. Condensation occurs and fog (or low cloud) forms. This is called an

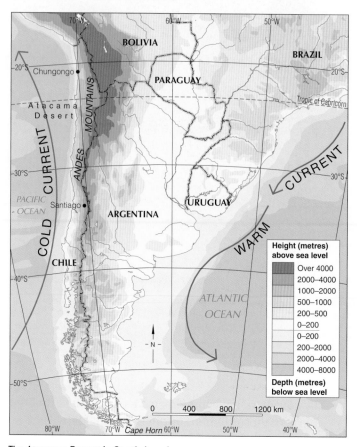

The Atacama Desert in South America

advection fog. On most days, the low cloud drifts onto the coast. It produces a dense morning fog, but very little rain.

Scientists from Chile and Canada looked for ways to capture this fog and built the structures of nylon mesh. As the thick fog drifts in from the sea, drops of water form on the mesh and run down. At the bottom, the water is collected, filtered and piped to the village below. The equipment is simple to maintain and has no motor. On a good day the water collection system can yield as much as 60 000 litres of clean, fresh water.

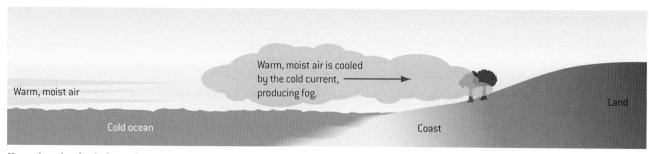

How advection fog is formed

Large nets are used to catch the fog, which drips down into pipes. Then the pipes take the water to a nearby town.

Changes in the community

Now, most houses at Chungongo have taps and running water at a quarter of the price of the supply previously brought in by truck. Washing and small gardens with flowers and vegetables are no longer luxuries. A clean and reliable water supply has brought a better lifestyle for the small community. Since the water began to flow in 1993, the population has grown from 350 to nearly 900 in 2007, but there is more pressure on water supply with a larger population. The scientists who developed the project believe that there are at least 50 sites around the world that have a suitable topography and climate for similar projects.

GEOfacts

- Namibia's Skeleton Coast in south-west Africa also receives dense fog up to 50 kilometres inland. The fog brings much needed water to the Namib Desert, which receives only about 10 millimetres of rain annually.
- For centuries, desert nomads in Africa have put containers under trees to collect water condensed from the air on cold nights.
- The Great Man-Made River Project in Libya is the longest underground pipeline network on Earth. It was built to move water in an underground aquifer from southern Libya to cities on the coast. Over 1300 wells and 3500 kilometres of pipeline were constructed as part of this project.

GEOTERMS

advection fog: condensation that drifts onto land as low cloud or fog

ACTIVITIES →

UNDERSTANDING

1. Why is Chungongo so dry?
2. Why has obtaining fresh water been a problem for the community of Chungongo in the past?
3. How has life in the Chungongo community changed with the increased supply of fresh water?

THINKING AND APPLYING

4. Outline how you think this water scarcity affected life in the village community.
5. The collection of fresh water from fog is a process that takes place in Chungongo whenever conditions are favourable. Draw a flow chart to show this water collection process. The first and second boxes are given below. (Remember to put only one step in each rectangle.)

> Warm, moist air is cooled on lower layers by cold current.

↓

> Condensation occurs and fog is produced.

6. Use the internet or library resources to research how other people use technology to ensure a sustainable water supply.

USING YOUR SKILLS

7. Refer to the map of southern South America.
   a. Describe Chungongo's latitude and longitude.
   b. What is the approximate distance from Santiago to Chungongo?
   c. Which mountain range blocks the flow of moist easterly winds to Chungongo?
   d. What type of ocean current is found on the west coast of South America, and how does it affect weather conditions in Chungongo?
   e. What impact do you think the ocean currents on the west coast have on its climate?

Cairo is a large city of 17 million people located in Egypt on the Nile River. It depends for its existence on the waters of the Nile.

The Nile flows from the Ethiopian Highlands in the south and carries massive amounts of water north through the arid Sahara to its delta in the Mediterranean Sea. For thousands of years the people of Egypt have used the hot climate and the water from this river to grow crops. It is this interaction with physical processes that has made settlement in Egypt possible. Today the river's flow is regulated by the Aswan High Dam, located in southern Egypt. The dam creates a more consistent flow for the river over a period of years.

the turn of the century to nearly 18 million in 2009. It is now a huge settlement in a hot and dry desert.

The recent growth in population has occurred due to the natural increase in the city and also due to the migration of many people from other parts of Egypt seeking employment and a better life.

The rapid growth of the city has created serious housing problems. Much of the old city, or *medina*, can be described as an urban slum, with substandard housing and overcrowding. It has become home to those who cannot afford to live anywhere else, including many new migrants. A neighbourhood in the medina is often a cohesive community, especially if it consists of the buildings and houses around a dead-end alleyway, or *harah*.

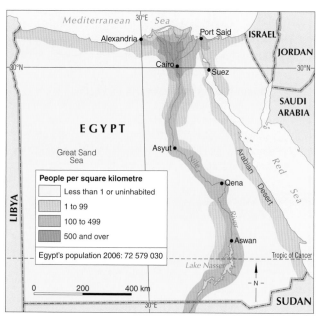

Cairo, Egypt: location and population density

Cairo's growing population

Cairo, throughout its long history, has been one of the most important centres of power and culture in the Arab world. It was established well over a thousand years ago as a walled Muslim city and has since been occupied by many foreign powers, including the Turks, the French and the British. Cairo has always been an important centre of commerce, religion, government and education. More recently it has developed many manufacturing industries. The population grew rapidly during the twentieth century, from approximately 500 000 at

Satellite image of the Nile Desert

GEOskills TOOLBOX

INTERPRETING A SATELLITE IMAGE

Compared with aerial photographs, satellite images show broad features at a much smaller scale. The colours on satellite images are often false colours, which are used to highlight certain features of the landscape. In the satellite image of the Nile delta, healthy vegetation and crops are shown in red, and desert is a pale yellow. Water usually shows as black on a satellite image.

Community in the harah

A *harah* in one of the most densely populated parts of Cairo is Essokkareya. Within this harah is a viable community of over a hundred families with a population of over 600. The housing type varies and includes shanty houses constructed next to the walls of existing houses. Most of the families live in one-room or two-room units. Most do not have taps in their houses and must obtain water from taps in the alleyway. Very few families have electricity and several families might have to share one toilet.

Most of the men work in the harah as craftsmen, peddlers or cart drivers and in domestic services. There are a small number of low-salaried government employees. Most women carry out domestic duties and only a small number have jobs that earn some income.

In the overcrowded conditions of the harah, the alleyway has become an extension of the people's homes. Activities formerly carried out indoors are now conducted in the harah passage, including much of the cooking, washing and socialising. Workshops use the alleyway to store items; poultry, sheep and goats wander around freely; men drink tea and coffee together in the afternoons; boys play soccer in the widest areas; and the women gather in the evening to watch television. House doorways are left open so there is little privacy as people can see from one house into another. Children run freely from house to house and the women speak openly to the male inhabitants of the harah.

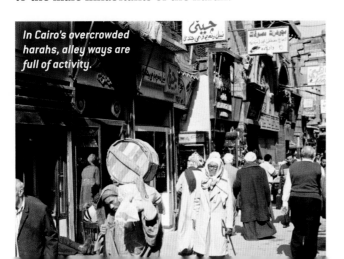

In Cairo's overcrowded harahs, alley ways are full of activity.

ACTIVITIES

UNDERSTANDING

1. Describe the flow of the Nile River.
2. How is the Nile River flow regulated?
3. List the activities that take place in the alleyways in a *harah*.
4. Describe the problems the rapid population growth has brought to Cairo.

THINKING AND APPLYING

5. Decreasing water quality is a contemporary environmental issue in Cairo. Using the internet or your library, research this issue and describe strategies for environmental sustainability.
6. Refer to the photograph of part of old Cairo. What are the main differences between this photograph and where you live?

USING YOUR SKILLS

7. Refer to the map of Egypt on page 132.
   a. Describe the location of Cairo using latitude and longitude.
   b. Where do most of the people live?
8. Refer to the climatic graph for Cairo. Use it to explain the importance of the Nile River for the people of Cairo.

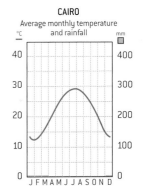

CAIRO
Average monthly temperature and rainfall

9. Refer to the satellite image of the Nile Desert opposite.
   a. The large red triangle on the satellite image is the delta of the Nile River. Deltas form when rivers slow down, and can no longer carry the soil and rock particles. This silt is deposited near the mouth (or end) of the river to form a delta. What evidence can you see on the satellite image that shows that the silt is fertile (productive) land for farming?
   b. Cairo is the light blue area at the narrowest part of the triangular delta. Why do you think that Egypt's largest modern city is located here?
   c. Describe what happens to the Nile River after it passes through Cairo on its way to the Mediterranean Sea.
   d. What is the association between the Nile River and the farmland shown in the satellite image?

GEOTERMS

delta: a nearly flat plain between outspreading branches of a river at its mouth

Modern technology has greatly changed the way people live in deserts. Isolated communities can now easily access water from deep below the desert surface. New heat-resistant breeds of crops are grown in the desert. Even golf courses can be established there! Mining has also caused great change in desert areas rich with fossil fuels and minerals.

Greening the desert

The earliest human settlements in deserts were close to sources of water such as springs or rivers. Technology has allowed desert communities to tap into the large amounts of water deep below the surface. This ground water collects in layers of porous rock known as an aquifer. With modern drilling equipment, people can bore into the deepest aquifers and extract water with mechanical pumps.

The satellite image below shows circular irrigation fields in the Libyan Desert. Water is pumped from the Al Kufrah Oasis, through a rotating irrigation pipe and onto the crops. Without water from beneath the ground or from a dammed river, crops could not be grown.

Mining in the desert

In recent years many riches have been discovered beneath the world's deserts. Desert mining has created wealth for some, but rarely for traditional desert people. Some of these mining resources are:
- bauxite (used to make aluminium) — mined in the deserts of Australia
- phosphates (used to make fertilisers) — mined in the Sahara region
- copper, iron ore and nitrates — in Chile's Atacama Desert
- precious metals such as gold, silver and platinum — found in the deserts of Australia, America and central Asia
- diamonds — found in the Kalahari and Namib deserts of south-western Africa.

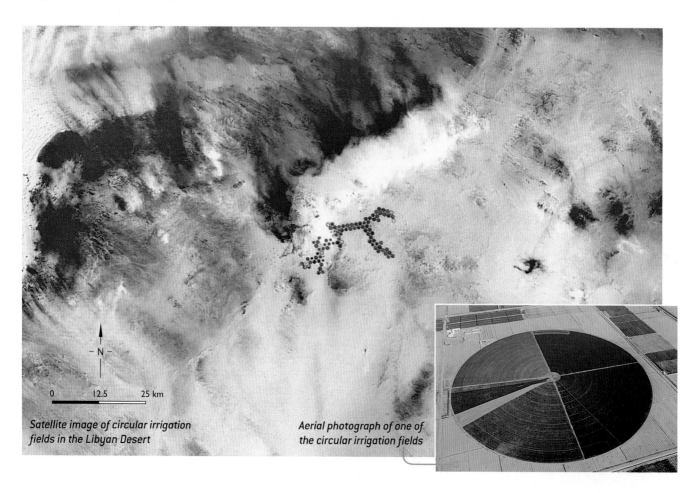

0   12.5   25 km

Satellite image of circular irrigation fields in the Libyan Desert

Aerial photograph of one of the circular irrigation fields

Palm Springs — keeping it green, and providing facilities such as golf courses, requires a lot of precious water.

GEO*facts*

Oil is found in four major areas on Earth:
• desert areas
• arctic areas
• river deltas
• continental areas offshore.

Oil is formed over millions of years by a 'pressure cooker' effect caused by plate tectonics (see chapter 5), which transforms dead microorganisms.

Energy from the desert

More than 65 per cent of the world's oil is found in the desert regions of the Middle East. The main fields are located in Kuwait, Iraq, Iran and Saudi Arabia.

Most of these countries have become dependent on the enormous income generated through oil sales. However, oil and gas resources are non-renewable. Burning fossil fuels also creates enormous amounts of pollution. For this reason, people are looking for cleaner sources of energy. Hot desert areas have large amounts of wind and sunshine, but the technology to harness these has yet to be perfected.

The Middle East has the largest reserves of fossil fuels in the world.

ACTIVITIES

UNDERSTANDING

1. Where does water come from to grow crops in the desert?
2. Where are the world's greatest oil reserves?

THINKING AND APPLYING

3. Oil income is very important for the economies of desert countries in the Middle East. Explain how this could be a future problem for these countries.

USING YOUR SKILLS

4. Satellite images can give a true or false colour image of an area. Refer to the satellite image of the Libyan Desert opposite.
   a. Explain what the little red circles in the satellite image are.
   b. Why are they found in this area of the desert?
5. Refer to the photograph of a golf course at Palm Springs and answer the following questions.
   a. Describe what you can see in the photograph. In your description, use the words: foreground, middle ground and background.
   b. What type of vegetation appears to be planted? Do you think it grows naturally in the area? Why?
   c. What non-renewable resource is needed to maintain this growth? Why?
   d. What features should natural vegetation have to survive in a place like Palm Springs?
   e. Why do you think a facility such as a golf course is constructed at Palm Springs?

GEOTERMS

aquifer: layers of rock through which water can flow; a store for underground water

ground water: water held under the surface of the Earth that has seeped through soil and rock, often used for drinking and irrigation

Nouakchott is the capital city of the western African nation of Mauritania. In 1960, Nouakchott was many days' walk from the desert, but is now entirely surrounded by the Sahara, with sand piling up against walls and fences. The sand is everywhere. Every day, bulldozers push the sand back from Mauritania's Road of Hope, but soon the dunes reclaim the road again.

The advancing dunes have engulfed wells, villages and roads. They sometimes cover whole towns, forcing everyone to move out. Animals and people have been driven southward in search of

Topographic map of Nouakchott

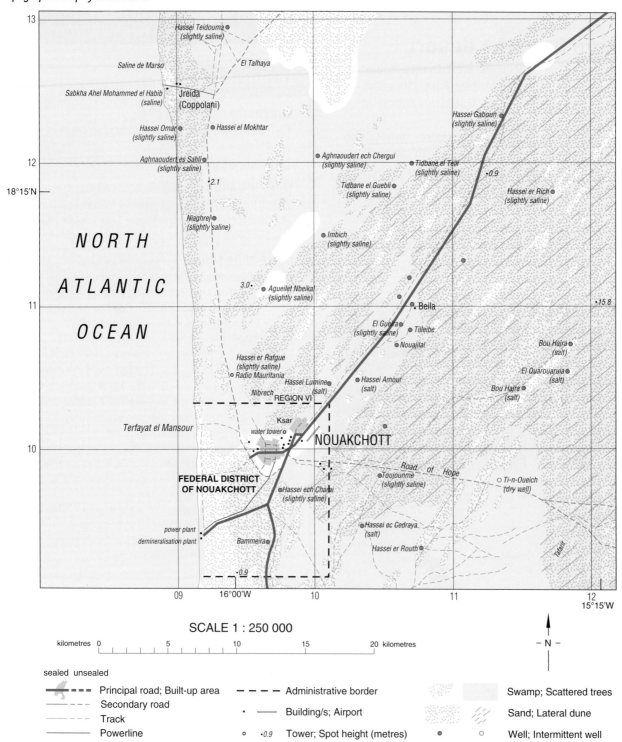

SCALE 1 : 250 000

kilometres 0   5   10   15   20 kilometres

– N –

sealed unsealed

Principal road; Built-up area   — — — Administrative border   Swamp; Scattered trees
Secondary road   • Building/s; Airport   Sand; Lateral dune
Track   o •0.9 Tower; Spot height (metres)   • o Well; Intermittent well
Powerline

Linear dunes of the Sahara (in the foreground) encroach in Nouakchott, the captial of Mauritania (in the background).

food and water. It has led to an exodus of nomads into Nouakchott looking for food and water. Nouakchott's population has increased from 20 000 in 1960 to more than one million today. Currently the city is surrounded by shantytowns.

The Sahara Desert covers 80 per cent of Mauritania. In the 1970s, the country was hit by a drought that caused widespread famine. Land management practices also caused problems. Traditionally, nomadic herders made the most of the erratic rain patterns by constantly moving to find new grazing lands. Today, overgrazing, loss of trees, poor farming methods, and overpopulation have led to **desertification**. During the 1980s, the desert was advancing southward at an estimated rate of 6 kilometres a year. Then, the Mauritanian Government planted 250 000 palm trees to create a barrier against the encroaching desert outside Nouakchott.

Current projects include the planting of small **greenbelts** around villages in order to keep more people from moving into the already overcrowded cities. Local communities are now encouraged to take responsibility for the rehabilitation of their villages. Desert villagers are selling handicrafts to raise money for the expansion of their greenbelts.

ACTIVITIES →

UNDERSTANDING

1. Describe how desertification is affecting Nouakchott.
2. List the steps the Mauritanian Government and local communities have taken to attempt to control desertification.

USING YOUR SKILLS

3. Refer to the topographic map of Nouakchott.
   a What landform features can be seen on the map?
   b Why are there no contour lines marked on the map?
   c Give the grid reference for the highest point on the map. (Use spot heights.)
   d What human features can you list in the Federal District of Nouakchott?
   e What seems to be a problem with the many wells shown on the map? What human feature has been built to deal with this problem?
   f How does the map confirm the problems faced by Nouakchott?

GEOTERMS

desertification: the process by which useful agricultural areas on desert fringes change into desert due to poor farming practices

greenbelt: plantations of trees for the purpose of conservation

Working geographically

KNOWLEDGE AND UNDERSTANDING

Select the alternative A, B, C or D that best answers the question.

1 Hot deserts generally lie
- (A) around the tropics.
- (B) inland.
- (C) where ocean currents are dry.
- (D) close to the Equator.

2 The largest desert in the world is the
- (A) Great Victoria Desert.
- (B) Sahara Desert.
- (C) Gobi Desert.
- (D) Atacama Desert.

3 Heat on the Earth's surface generally varies with
- (A) longitude.
- (B) latitude.
- (C) distance from the sun.
- (D) humidity.

4 Landforms in deserts are created by
- (A) weathering, erosion and wind.
- (B) deposition, erosion and wind.
- (C) wind, erosion and weathering.
- (D) weathering, erosion and deposition.

5 Which of the adaptations listed below is not found in desert animals?
- (A) Thick, leathery skin
- (B) Long legs
- (C) Eyes on stalks
- (D) Hard, waxy shell

6 Ephemerals are plants
- (A) with very short life cycles.
- (B) with long roots.
- (C) with long life cycles.
- (D) characterised by colourful flowers.

7 An oasis is
- (A) located in an aquifer.
- (B) an artesian well.
- (C) a fertile place in the desert.
- (D) a meeting place for Bedouins.

8 Advection fog is condensation
- (A) that forms in a rain shadow.
- (B) that drifts onto land in the night.
- (C) that drifts onto land as low cloud or fog.
- (D) that drifts onto land as cumulus cloud.

9 Hot desert areas have potential for developing renewable energy from
- (A) oil reserves.
- (B) gas reserves.
- (C) wind and sunshine.
- (D) fog.

10 Desertification is caused by
- (A) overgrazing.
- (B) poor farming methods.
- (C) overpopulation.
- (D) all of the above.

INTERPRETING A CLIMATIC GRAPH

Answer these questions using the climatic graph of Alice Springs.

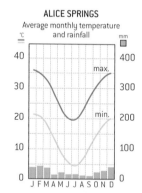

ALICE SPRINGS
Average monthly temperature and rainfall

11 a How can you tell that Alice Springs is in the Southern Hemisphere?
  b Estimate the total annual precipitation.
  c Is Alice Springs in a desert environment?

REPORTS

When you prepare a report it is important to remember there are three main parts:
- a general introductory statement introducing the subject of the report
- a series of paragraphs about the features of the topic. Each new paragraph usually describes just one aspect of the feature and begins with a topic sentence.
- a conclusion that summarises the information presented.

12 Complete a report about desertification. Include the following:
  a how desertification is leading to the expansion of deserts
  b how desertification is affecting one particular desert
  c what you, as an informed citizen, can do about desertification.

SOLAR POWER RESEARCH

In this chapter we have seen that most hot deserts have few natural resources that are useful for the production of agricultural and industrial products or services. This is why most desert areas are sparsely populated. However, deserts are abundant in one natural resource that will be useful for the future — solar power. Solar power produces electricity from the sun.

Select a partner and research this topic in the library or on the internet using your favourite search engine. Present your findings on a large piece of paper suitable for display in the classroom. Provide suitable illustrations in your presentation.

13. Define solar power.

14. Describe the uses of solar power.

15. Describe present solar technologies and problems with their use.

16. Evaluate the potential of deserts to produce solar power.

WHO WILL SURVIVE?

17. Divide the class into small groups. Imagine you are in a plane crash in the desert. You have no shelter and all communication devices have been lost in the crash. You are about 100 kilometres from a settlement and have enough water for about 24 hours. You expect help, but know it could be days before you are found. Fortunately, one of you has three survival aids in their backpack. Discuss how you intend to be found and how you will survive for at least 48 hours. Each group presents their strategy to the class and the class decides which group has the best plan.

Contour map of the area

If lost, find some higher ground and watch/listen for rescuers. The accepted distress signal is three signals together, *regularly* spaced. These may be given by smoke (make a small fire with lots of green leaves), or by shouts, whistles, flashing of mirror or torch, or by waving a cloth. The contour lines show the height, shape and location of hills and other features. Remember that close contours mean a steeper slope and widely spaced contours mean a gentle slope or flat area.

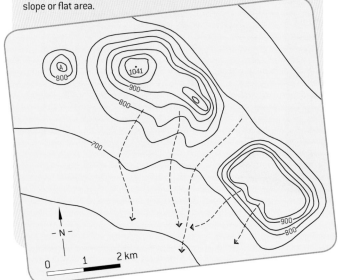

Emergency water supply

In a survival situation, water is more important than food. You can survive many days without food, but less than three days without water. The transpiration method shown below is the most effective way of collecting water.

Emergency water collection using the transpiration method.

- Place a large, clear plastic bag over the leafy end of a tree branch — the more leaves, the better.
- Tie the bag tightly to the branch, sealing the open end of the bag.
- Weigh down one corner of the bag by tying it to a heavy rock. Water will collect in this part of the bag.
- Once enough water has collected, untie the bag and scoop out water with a cup. The bag can then be tied back to collect more water.

Ground-to-air visual code

Valuable information can be signalled to searching aircraft. To avoid misunderstandings, use only the ground-to-air visual code (right). Lay out these symbols by using brightly coloured groundsheets, clothing, sleeping bags, stones, pieces of wood, or any available material. Do not make any signal unless in distress. The aircraft will indicate that signals have been seen and understood by rocking from side to side.

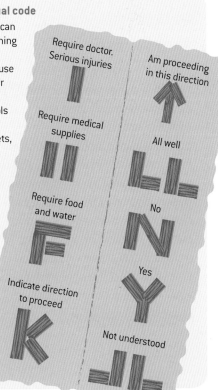

Require doctor. Serious injuries

Require medical supplies

Require food and water

Indicate direction to proceed

Am proceeding in this direction

All well

No

Yes

Not understood

eLesson

DESERTS: WHAT ARE THEY AND WHY DO THEY OCCUR?

A desert is an area that receives, on average, less than 240 mm of rain a year. Before working on this chapter, you probably thought of deserts as the most boring environments out there, but in fact they have an amazing variety of landforms, plants and animals. Deserts cover around 30 per cent of the Earth's land surface and can be hot or cold environments. Almost one-fifth of Australia is classified as desert.

SEARCHLIGHT ID: ELES-0137

Interactivity

FACT FINDER: 'DESERT LANDFORMS'

The sand dunes we associate with deserts take a very long time to form. All those grains of sand were once part of different landforms. In this interactive Fact Finder game, you will race against the clock to identify desert landforms from a series of clues. You must think quickly and carefully. Clicking on the wrong marker in the scene will lose you time, but select the right marker and you'll receive a bonus chunk.

SEARCHLIGHT ID: INT-0778

These ICT activities are available in this chapter's Student Resources tab inside your eBookPLUS. Visit www.jacplus.com.au to locate your digital resources.

Interactivity

FACT FINDER: 'DESERT ANIMALS'

It takes a very special animal to survive in the desert. Searing daytime sun, cold nights and lack of water are just a few of the challenges animals face in this hostile environment. In this interactive Fact Finder game you will race against the clock to identify common desert animals from a series of clues. You must think quickly and carefully. Clicking on the wrong marker in the scene will lose you time, but select the right marker and you'll receive a bonus chunk.

SEARCHLIGHT ID: INT-0779

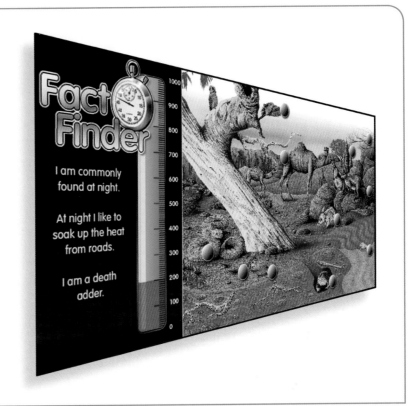

Interactivity

CLIMATE GRAPH: 'TIMBUKTU'

A climate graph, or climograph, is a tool used by geographers to record the minimum and maximum temperatures for an area, and its average rainfall. Timbuktu is a city in the west African nation of Mali. It is located on the southern edge of the Sahara, around 13 km north of the Niger River. Use this interactivity to create your own climograph for the desert city of Timbuktu using the data provided.

SEARCHLIGHT ID: INT-0780

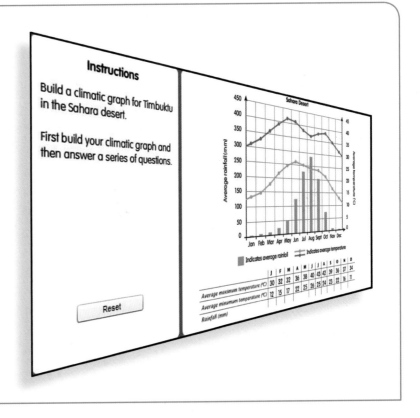

7 Rainforests

INQUIRY QUESTIONS

+ Where are rainforests located?
+ Why are rainforests so hot and wet?
+ Why are rainforests so important?
+ What threats are affecting the Earth's rainforests?
+ How can rainforests be sustainably managed?

Rainforests are very special places: they are the most biologically diverse ecosystems on our planet. They are also important for all people because they produce oxygen, absorb carbon dioxide and provide much of the Earth's fresh water. Rainforests are the source of many foods, medicine and other products. However, during the last 100 years, many areas of rainforests have disappeared due to pressures from logging, farming, mining and transport. These pressures have greatly reduced the numbers of indigenous hunters, gatherers and subsistence farmers living in rainforests.

GEOskills TOOLBOX

GEOskillbuilder Constructing and interpreting graphs (pages 164–5)

+ Interpreting climatic graphs (page 147)
+ Using area and grid references (page 152)
+ Comparing ground-level and aerial photographs (page 155)
+ Comparing maps (page 161)
+ Sketching a satellite image (page 163)
+ Collecting and interpreting electronic information (page 167)
+ Researching and presenting reports (page 169)

Tropical rainforests in the Braulio Carrillo National Park, Costa Rica. These forests are characterised by a diversity of plant species and dense, luxurious tree and plant growth.

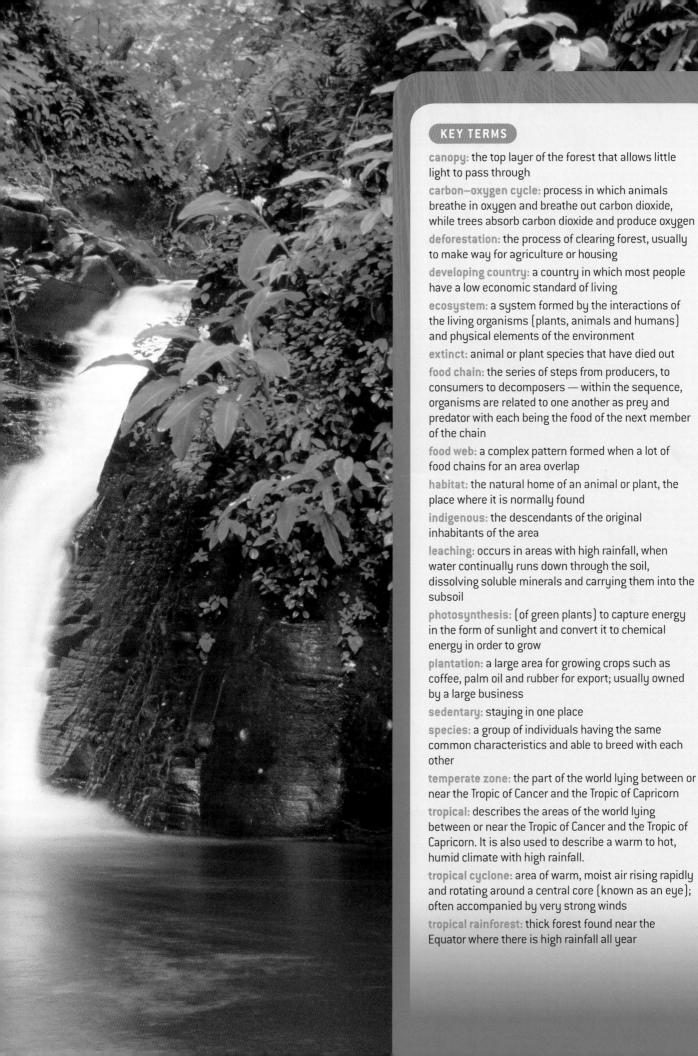

KEY TERMS

canopy: the top layer of the forest that allows little light to pass through

carbon–oxygen cycle: process in which animals breathe in oxygen and breathe out carbon dioxide, while trees absorb carbon dioxide and produce oxygen

deforestation: the process of clearing forest, usually to make way for agriculture or housing

developing country: a country in which most people have a low economic standard of living

ecosystem: a system formed by the interactions of the living organisms (plants, animals and humans) and physical elements of the environment

extinct: animal or plant species that have died out

food chain: the series of steps from producers, to consumers to decomposers — within the sequence, organisms are related to one another as prey and predator with each being the food of the next member of the chain

food web: a complex pattern formed when a lot of food chains for an area overlap

habitat: the natural home of an animal or plant, the place where it is normally found

indigenous: the descendants of the original inhabitants of the area

leaching: occurs in areas with high rainfall, when water continually runs down through the soil, dissolving soluble minerals and carrying them into the subsoil

photosynthesis: (of green plants) to capture energy in the form of sunlight and convert it to chemical energy in order to grow

plantation: a large area for growing crops such as coffee, palm oil and rubber for export; usually owned by a large business

sedentary: staying in one place

species: a group of individuals having the same common characteristics and able to breed with each other

temperate zone: the part of the world lying between or near the Tropic of Cancer and the Tropic of Capricorn

tropical: describes the areas of the world lying between or near the Tropic of Cancer and the Tropic of Capricorn. It is also used to describe a warm to hot, humid climate with high rainfall.

tropical cyclone: area of warm, moist air rising rapidly and rotating around a central core (known as an eye); often accompanied by very strong winds

tropical rainforest: thick forest found near the Equator where there is high rainfall all year

Forests that grow in constantly wet conditions are called rainforests. They can occur wherever the annual rainfall is more than 1300 millimetres and spread throughout the year. While **tropical rainforests** are the most well known, there are also others.

Tropical rainforests

Tropical rainforests are found near the Equator, mostly between the tropics of Cancer and Capricorn. These rainforests grow where conditions are hot and wet. They support a huge number of plants and

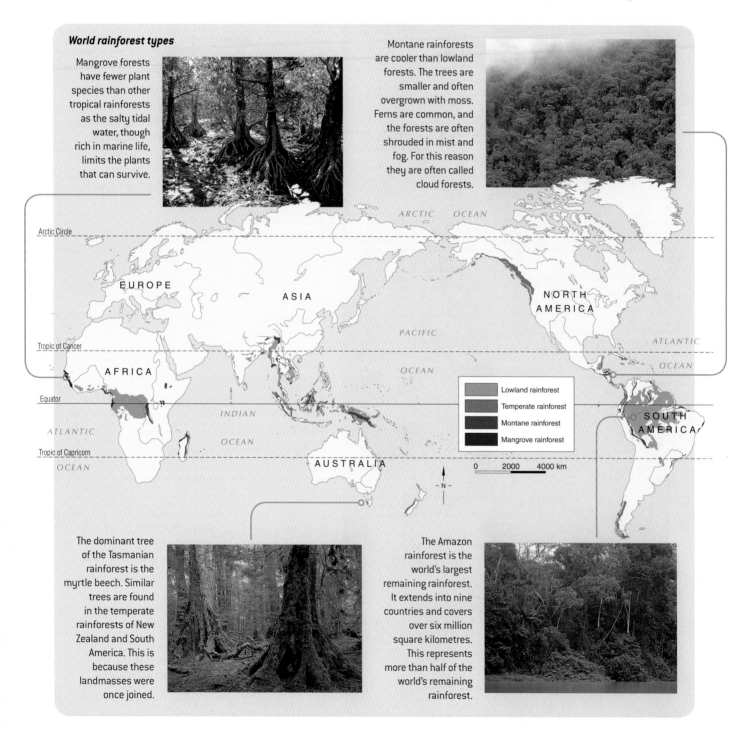

World rainforest types

Mangrove forests have fewer plant species than other tropical rainforests as the salty tidal water, though rich in marine life, limits the plants that can survive.

Montane rainforests are cooler than lowland forests. The trees are smaller and often overgrown with moss. Ferns are common, and the forests are often shrouded in mist and fog. For this reason they are often called cloud forests.

Lowland rainforest
Temperate rainforest
Montane rainforest
Mangrove rainforest

0   2000   4000 km

The dominant tree of the Tasmanian rainforest is the myrtle beech. Similar trees are found in the temperate rainforests of New Zealand and South America. This is because these landmasses were once joined.

The Amazon rainforest is the world's largest remaining rainforest. It extends into nine countries and covers over six million square kilometres. This represents more than half of the world's remaining rainforest.

animals — perhaps as many as 90 per cent of all known species. Poison-dart frogs, birds of paradise, piranha, tarantulas, anacondas, komodo dragons and vampire bats all call tropical rainforests home.

Tropical rainforests are characterised by densely growing trees and plants. The tall trees that make up the canopy grow so close together that they act like an umbrella, allowing very little sunlight to reach the ground. These trees are between 20 and 30 metres high and are often woven together with climbing plants such as lianas. If you fly over a rainforest you cannot see the ground for the canopy. Taller trees, called emergents, occasionally poke up above this layer.

Below the canopy, other vegetation has to compete for light and space. Smaller trees grow here but will reach maturity only if they are under a gap in the canopy. Nearer the forest floor there are very few plants because it is too shady for photosynthesis. Only those plants that have adapted to low light and high humidity, such as ferns, moss, fungi and lichens grow here.

The forest floor consists mainly of dead, decaying plants. Fallen leaves and branches rapidly break down in the constant heat and humidity. On the forest floor are the enormous buttress roots that support the forest giants. These amazing structures grow out from the trunks of the canopy and emergent trees, and can be up to three metres above the ground.

Mangrove forests

Forests that grow along tropical coastlines or salty rivers near the sea have to cope with very difficult conditions. Mangrove forests have developed special roots called pneumatophores that grow up above the surface of the water, allowing the tree to breathe.

Temperate rainforests

The large area of the globe between the tropics and the polar regions is called the temperate zone, and rainforests can flourish there, too. Temperate rainforests occur in North America, Tasmania, on New Zealand's South Island and in China. Giant pandas, Tasmanian devils, brown bears, cougars and wolves all call these temperate rainforests home.

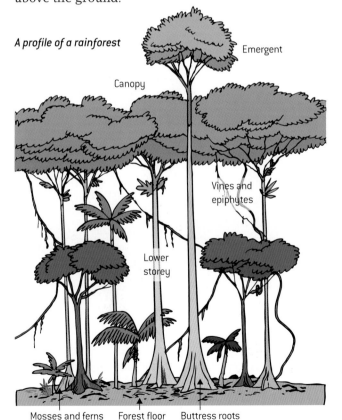

A profile of a rainforest

Emergent

Canopy

Vines and epiphytes

Lower storey

Mosses and ferns   Forest floor   Buttress roots

ACTIVITIES

UNDERSTANDING

1. Where are tropical rainforests located? Why are they found here?

THINKING AND APPLYING

2. Why are there so few plants on the floor of a rainforest?

3. Draw a Venn diagram to show the differences and similarities between the different rainforest types as described in the map.

USING YOUR SKILLS

4. Refer to the diagram 'A profile of a rainforest'.
   a. Describe the appearance of the profile.
   b. Compare the appearance of the canopy with the lower storey.

5. Refer to the map of world rainforest types.
   a. Which continent has the greatest area of rainforest?
   b. Which meridian of longitude runs through the world's largest rainforest?
   c. With reference to latitude, describe the location of tropical lowland rainforests.
   d. What type of rainforest grows closest to the Arctic Circle?

GEOTERMS

temperate zone: the part of the world lying between or near the Tropic of Cancer and the Tropic of Capricorn

tropical rainforest: thick forest found near the Equator where there is high rainfall all year

Tropical rainforests are found where there are both high temperatures and high precipitation. For example, the average temperature in Belem, Brazil, is a high 26° Celsius and annual precipitation is more than 2300 millimetres. Some tropical rainforests receive more than 4000 millimetres per year.

Why are rainforests so hot?

The sun's rays that reach the Earth near the Equator have a smaller area of the Earth and atmosphere to heat than rays reaching the Earth at higher latitudes. It is therefore hotter at the Equator than at higher latitudes. (This is explained in more detail on page 118 'Why are deserts so hot and dry?' You should refer to this now.) Tropical rainforests do not have the very high maximum temperatures that deserts record because they are covered with lots of cloud, which reflects some of the sun's rays during the day. But rainforests are generally warmer at night, because the cloud cover and high humidity help to keep the heat in. Tropical rainforests have a hot climate right throughout the year with no summer or winter.

Why are rainforests so wet?

High precipitation around the Equator is mainly due to convectional rainfall and is often associated with thunderstorms. Convectional rainfall occurs when warm, moist air is heated when it moves over a hot surface on Earth. As the air is heated it expands and becomes lighter than the surrounding air. This causes it to rise. If the air continues to rise, condensation and precipitation occur.

The most widespread form of convectional rainfall is the thunderstorm. The clouds that are associated with thunderstorms are called cumulonimbus clouds. Thunderstorms are most likely to occur in rainforests during the afternoon, but can occur at any time.

There are few sights in nature more awe-inspiring than the lightning and thunder display associated with a thunderstorm. The process that produces lightning is not fully understood, but it is known that an electrical charge builds up at the bottom of large cumulonimbus clouds. This is a negative charge, which causes a positive charge to build up on the ground below. The electricity is then discharged between the positive and the negatively charged areas in the form of a bright flash of light. Each lightning strike that we see is actually made up of several flashes (up to 42) travelling both up and down, but our eyes cannot usually detect these individual strikes. Close to the lightning, the air is heated very quickly to about 30 000° Celsius. This causes the air to expand explosively. This becomes a booming sound wave, which we call thunder. There cannot, therefore, be thunder without lightning.

Thunderstorms occur very frequently in tropical rainforests and are accompanied by lightning, thunder and, often, torrential rain.

Tropical cyclones

Along the Equator and within the tropics there are large areas of low pressure. These are areas of rising air, which are very favourable for the development of convectional rainfall and thunderstorms.

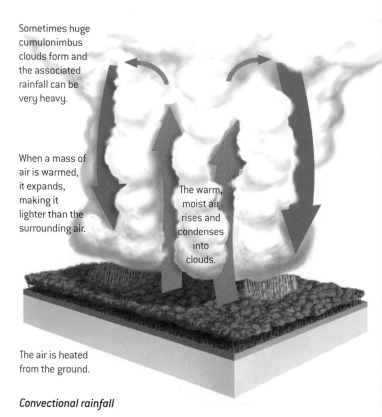

Sometimes huge cumulonimbus clouds form and the associated rainfall can be very heavy.

When a mass of air is warmed, it expands, making it lighter than the surrounding air.

The warm, moist air rises and condenses into clouds.

The air is heated from the ground.

Convectional rainfall

A **tropical cyclone** is a particular type of low pressure system. They often develop in the warmer months in the areas a little north and south of the Equator and close to the tropics. Tropical cyclones are areas of warm, moist air rising rapidly and rotating around a central core (known as the eye). They are often accompanied by very strong winds (gusts of over 300 kilometres per hour have been recorded) and torrential rain (1800 millimetres in 24 hours has been recorded). If these severe storms occur near large population centres, they can cause a lot of damage to property and loss of life.

Tropical cyclones need the energy provided by warm water vapour (sea waters of at least 27° Celsius), so they will usually die out if they move inland away from the water vapour, or out of the tropics, away from the warmth. This is why tropical, coastal areas, such as the Caribbean Sea (central America), the north-west Pacific and north-east Australia are commonly affected by tropical cyclones. Tropical cyclones bring heavy rain to the tropical rainforests that are closer to the tropics than the Equator. They do not form close to the Equator.

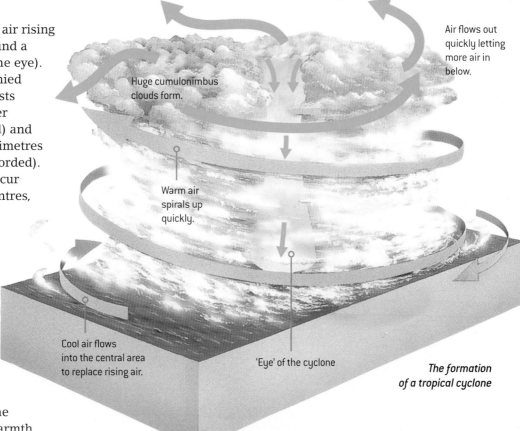

Huge cumulonimbus clouds form.

Air flows out quickly letting more air in below.

Warm air spirals up quickly.

Cool air flows into the central area to replace rising air.

'Eye' of the cyclone

The formation of a tropical cyclone

GEOskills TOOLBOX

INTERPRETING CLIMATIC GRAPHS

Climatic graphs are a combination of a column graph and a line graph. They are used to show the climate of a place over a 12-month period. The line graph section always shows average monthly temperature and the column graph represents average monthly rainfall. Be careful to read from the correct axis when reading climatic graphs. For more on interpreting and constructing climatic graphs, see pages 120–1.

The climatic graph of Belem, in Brazil, shows a climate pattern typical of tropical rainforest areas.

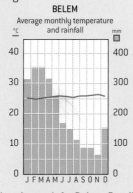

BELEM

Average monthly temperature and rainfall

°C · · mm

Climatic graph for Belem, Brazil

ACTIVITIES ➔

UNDERSTANDING

1 Why are rainforests so hot?

2 Why do tropical cyclones form over water?

3 Describe how convectional rainfall develops.

THINKING AND APPLYING

4 Explain why there cannot be thunder without lightning.

USING YOUR SKILLS

5 Refer to the climatic graph of Belem at left.
   a Describe the temperature pattern throughout the year.
   b Describe the pattern of precipitation throughout the year.
   c In which months do you think the most thunderstorms would be experienced? Why?
   d The latitude of Belem is 1°27'S. What does this tell you about its location? Check your answer in an atlas.

GEOTERMS

tropical cyclone: area of warm, moist air rising rapidly and rotating around a central core (known as an eye); often accompanied by very strong winds

Rainforests provide habitats for more species of plants, animals, insects and birds than any other environment found on our planet. A rainforest **ecosystem** is the interaction of all the living things, such as plants and animals, and the non-living things, such as rainfall and soil. Plants convert energy from the sun, by the process of photosynthesis, into food for animals. Animals cannot live without plants. The removal of a plant species can result in the removal of a food source essential for the survival of an animal.

Some plants and animals are food for others in a **food chain**. Orang-utans eat fruit and jaguars eat small monkeys. Insects join with fungi and bacteria to break down dead matter, which becomes food for plants.

The trees give off oxygen (O_2) as a result of photosynthesis.

Rain

The trees absorb carbon dioxide (CO_2).

The trees store carbon dioxide as carbon.

The forest absorbs the water (H_2O) and releases it gradually.

How a rainforest reduces carbon dioxide gases

Carbon dioxide builds up in the atmosphere, trapping the heat from the sun. This warms the Earth.

The burning vegetation releases carbon dioxide into the air.

With the removal of vegetation, water run-off is increased. This allows the topsoil to be removed by flooding and erosion.

How a cleared rainforest can cause environmental damage

Plants co-exist with animals. Some animals adapt to only one type of fruit and have very simple food webs. Some flowers rely on only one type of pollinator. For example, an orchid in Madagascar has its nectar 15 centimetres down a thin tube. Only the long-tongued hawk moth can reach down the tube of the flower to pollinate it. Such interdependence makes rainforest ecosystems complex.

Rainforests: giant lungs

Rainforests are vital to the Earth because they help to recycle carbon and oxygen. All animals, including humans, breathe in oxygen and breathe out carbon dioxide. Carbon dioxide is poisonous to animals but not to plants, which use it to grow. Plants remove carbon dioxide from the air and return oxygen in its place. This relationship is known as the carbon–oxygen cycle.

Rainforests are major producers of the Earth's oxygen. Rainforests are sometimes called the lungs of the Earth, and scientists believe that half of all the world's oxygen is produced by the Amazon rainforest alone. As rainforests are cut down and burned, carbon dioxide is released into the Earth's atmosphere. This gas traps the sun's heat and warms up the atmosphere, leading to what is called the enhanced greenhouse effect or global warming.

Rainforests and the nutrient cycle

All humans need carbohydrates to grow. But they also need nutrients, such as vitamins, to ensure they are healthy. Plants also need nutrients.

The rainforest depends on the recycling of nutrients for its existence. Leaves, flowers and animals die and fall onto the soil. They decompose and the decomposed material is reused by plants.

Rainforest soils

Rainforest soils give the impression of being fertile because they support an enormous number of trees and plants. But this impression is wrong, as the soil in rainforests is generally poor. Roots of trees must 'snatch' the nutrients from the soil before heavy rain washes them away. Buttress roots absorb nutrients from the leaf litter sitting on top of the ground. This means that the nutrients are caught by the tree roots before it rains. Otherwise nutrients are lost when they are washed down the soil profile. This is called leaching.

GEOfacts

- An astonishing 60 000 species of insects and spiders live in a patch of the Amazon the size of a football field. But there are only 20 000 insect and spider species in the whole of Great Britain and 75 000 in all of Australia.
- Buttress roots are large roots on the sides of tall rainforest trees. Because root systems are shallow due to poor soils, the buttress roots support the trees and prevent them from falling over. Buttress roots can grow up to five metres in height and spread for 30 metres above the soil. Fig trees are one species that rely on a buttress root system.
- Nearly half of the world's species of plants, animals and microorganisms will be destroyed or severely threatened over the next quarter of a century due to rainforest deforestation.

ACTIVITIES ➔

UNDERSTANDING

1. What is a rainforest ecosystem?
2. How does the 'carbon–oxygen cycle' work?
3. What do CO_2 and O_2 stand for?

THINKING AND APPLYING

4. Why are rainforests sometimes called the 'lungs of the Earth'?
5. Explain, in your own words, some of the benefits that rainforests provide to our environment.

USING YOUR SKILLS

6. Explain how a rainforest is able to reduce carbon dioxide and produce oxygen.
7. Refer to the diagram on page 148.
   a Describe what happens to the rainfall absorbed by a rainforest.
   b What happens to carbon dioxide levels in the atmosphere when rainforests are cut down and burned?

GEOTERMS

food chain: the series of steps from producers, to consumers to decomposers — within the sequence, organisms are related to one another as prey and predator with each being the food of the next member of the chain

food web: a complex pattern formed when a lot of food chains for an area overlap

Most of us use rainforest products every day. The next time you eat chocolate, treat your asthma, play a guitar or even breathe, you may have to thank the rainforests.

The rainforest as medicine chest

Your local pharmacy is proof of the healing power of rainforest plants. More than 7000 modern medicines are made from rainforest plants. They can be used to treat problems from nagging headaches to killer diseases like malaria. They are used by people who suffer from multiple sclerosis, Parkinson's disease, leukaemia, asthma, acne, arthritis, diabetes, dysentery and heart disease among many others. The world's first birth control pills were derived from yams in central America, and more than 3000 plants are used to control human fertility.

The green anaconda lives in swamps and marshes in the tropical rainforests of the Amazon. Its venom is used in medicines to treat high blood pressure.

One of the world's most powerful anti-cancer drugs used to fight childhood leukaemia is extracted from the Madagascar periwinkle, a species of the rainforests of Madagascar.

Even rainforest animals can be used to cure human diseases. Tree frogs from Australia give off a chemical that can heal sores, and a similar chemical from a South American rainforest frog can be used as a powerful painkiller. The poisonous venom from an Amazonian snake is used to treat high blood pressure.

Perhaps the greatest benefits to medicine and our own health, however, are yet to come. Only 1 per cent of the known plants and animals of the rainforest have been properly analysed for their potential. The scientists who analyse these plants are known as chemical prospectors.

The rainforest as home

Rainforests are home to the greatest profusion of life on the planet: at least half of all known plants and animals live in these forests, which cover only 7 per cent of the Earth's land surface.

Plants and animals also share their habitat with humans: at least 50 million indigenous people live in rainforests worldwide. From the Kuna people of Panama and the Yanomami of Brazil to the Baka people of Cameroon and the Penan of Borneo, these people have traditionally lived a way of life that has little impact on their forest home.

In the Amazon rainforest, the villagers use its waterways as a means of transport.

The rainforest as supermarket

The people who live in or near the rainforests gain much of their food from the forest. But rainforests also supply the supermarkets of the world with their bounty. Most of these fruits and nuts are now grown by farmers rather than harvested directly from the forest, but it was in the rainforests that they originated.

Chocolate first came from cacao trees native to the Amazon rainforest. Today, the cocoa in the chocolate you eat has most likely come from huge cacao plantations in west Africa. Similarly, brazil and cashew nuts, cinnamon, ginger, pepper, vanilla, bananas, pineapples, coconuts, pawpaws, mangoes and avocados were all originally rainforest plants. Even the gum used in chewing gum comes from a rainforest plant, as does the tree that produces rubber.

An open-air market in South-East Asia

The rainforest as climate controller

Rainforests help keep our climate relatively stable in a few different ways. The rain that falls in a rainforest is quickly drawn up through the plants and then returned to the air as water vapour. This vapour gathers together to create clouds, which in turn provide more rain. Without these plants, the water would not return to the atmosphere as quickly and the area would become drier. This process also cools the surrounding air by up to 5° Celsius.

Rainforests help cool the planet because they absorb much of the sun's heat rather than reflecting it back into the atmosphere. The destruction of rainforests and the burning of trees is now also thought to contribute, along with the burning of fossil fuels, to the enhanced greenhouse effect and global warming (see chapter 13). Rainforests are also major producers of the Earth's oxygen.

The rainforest as timber supplier

The most obvious use for rainforest products is from the timber in the trees. Rainforest trees are generally hardwood trees, making them resistant to decay and attractive for building. Well-known rainforest timbers are mahogany, teak, ebony, balsa and rosewood. Rosewood is particularly interesting, as it is considered the best timber in the world for guitar making. In many tropical countries people also collect timber as fuel for cooking or heating.

Teak logs cut for firewood in Myanmar

ACTIVITIES ➔

UNDERSTANDING
1. Why is the rainforest important to health?
2. Name four indigenous groups from around the world who live in rainforests.
3. Explain how rainforests can partially create their own climate.

THINKING AND APPLYING
4. Which of the uses of rainforests would you consider to be the most important reason for looking after their survival? Explain your answer.
5. Make a list of things in your home that may come from a rainforest. Remember to look in the medicine cupboard and pantry as well as looking at furniture.
6. These pages list only a few of the products we use from rainforests. Conduct some research, using the internet or library resources. Write a short report (about 400 words) on your findings.

USING YOUR SKILLS
7. Refer to the photograph of the open-air market and list the foods that you recognise.

GEOTERMS

habitat: the natural home of an animal or plant, the place where it is normally found

Daintree River National Park features the oldest continuously surviving rainforest on Earth. Along with the other tropical rainforests of the far north-east, the region became the Wet Tropics of Queensland World Heritage site in 1989.

The Daintree includes more than one type of rainforest. Mangrove forest occurs where the forest meets the sea, with inland lowland forest rising behind the mangroves.

The region has warm dry winters. In summer, monsoon rains and cyclones often cause floods.

Indigenous communities

The Kuku Yalanygi Aboriginal tribe have lived in the area for about 50 000 years. They lived as subsistence hunters and gatherers and were conservationists living in harmony with the local ecosystems — the rainforest, the mangroves and the coral reefs. Today, about 1000 members of the tribe survive, living at the Bloomfield River and Mossman Gorge.

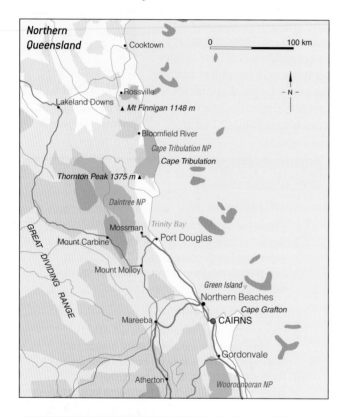

GEOskills TOOLBOX

USING AREA AND GRID REFERENCES

Grid lines running up and down topographic maps (north–south) are called eastings because the numbers increase the further east they are. Lines running across the map (east–west) are called northings because the numbers increase the further north they are. When stating location, the eastings are given first, then the northings.

An area reference is a four-figure number that tells us the grid square in which to find a feature. A grid reference is a six-figure number that shows an exact point in the grid square. The third and sixth figures represent one-tenth of the distance between the two grid numbers. However, these divisions are not written on the map, so they must be estimated. For more on area and grid references, see pages 24–5.

GEOfacts

In an area of the Daintree River National Park called Noah's Creek, 150 species of tree are found per hectare: eight more species than in all of Canada and the United States of America.

ACTIVITIES →

USING YOUR SKILLS

Refer to the topographic map of Daintree River National Park.

1. How would you describe the vegetation and topography of the Daintree River National Park?
2. What features are found at the following locations? GR298835 GR298807 GR268831 GR307760
3. Describe what the scene would look like if you were at: GR195768 GR335765 GR272867.
4. Which of these locations is the highest: GR252763 or GR301759?
5. Give the six-figure grid reference for Dayman Point, Port of Mossman and Miallo.

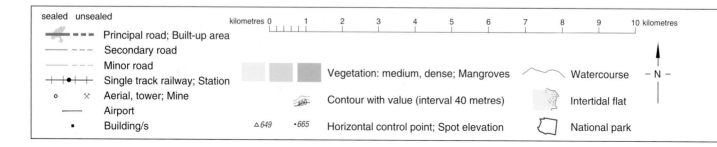

sealed unsealed
— Principal road; Built-up area
— Secondary road
— Minor road
— Single track railway; Station
○ ✕ Aerial, tower; Mine
— Airport
▪ Building/s

kilometres 0 1 2 3 4 5 6 7 8 9 10 kilometres

Vegetation: medium, dense; Mangroves
 Contour with value (interval 40 metres)
△649 •665 Horizontal control point; Spot elevation

Watercourse
– N –
Intertidal flat
National park

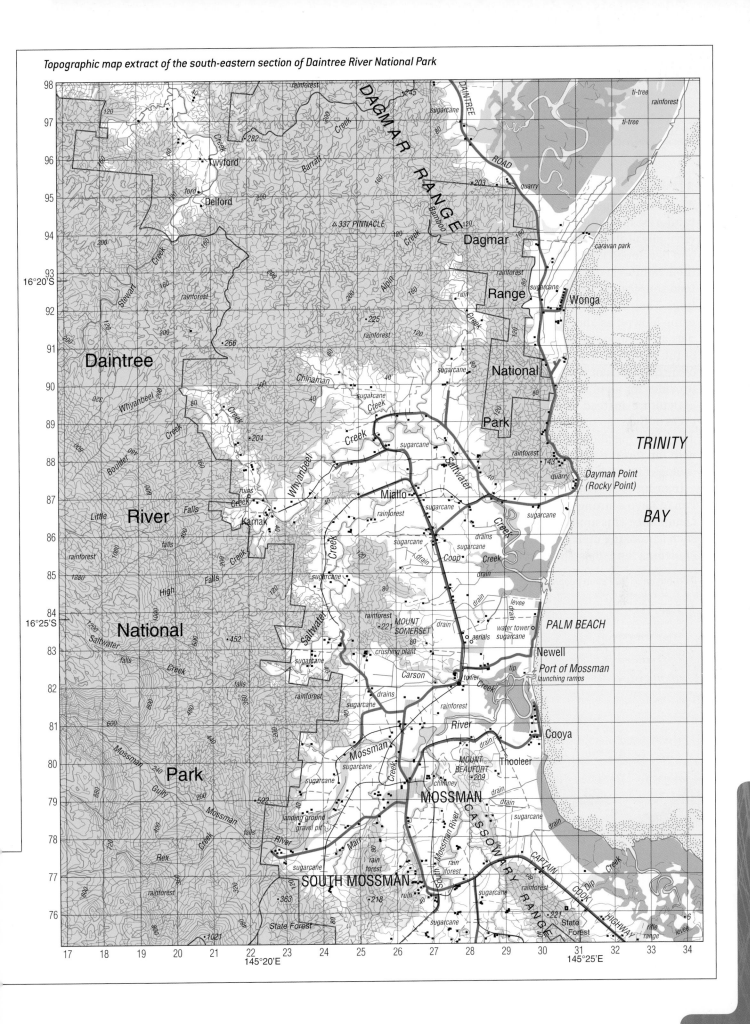

Topographic map extract of the south-eastern section of Daintree River National Park

The rainforest ecosystem

The Penan people have depended on the rainforest for thousands of generations. They have physically adapted to the rainforest ecology and developed knowledge and customs based on their rainforest environment. The Penan's main food sources are the sago palm and other fruiting trees. They are also extremely skilled hunters, using blowpipes and poison darts to kill wild pigs and gibbons (a small ape). Their knowledge of the rainforest ecosystem has been built up over thousands of years. The forest traditionally provides for all of their needs. They do not use agriculture; instead they follow the flowering cycle of the sago palm. Their nomadic hunting and gathering allows them to live in equilibrium with the forest ecosystem and thus ensure ecological sustainability.

In order to survive in this environment, the Penan have a strong culture of sharing in their community. This applies not only to daily objects, such as cooking utensils, but also to land. The idea of owning land does not exist in the Penan culture.

Distribution of the Penan people

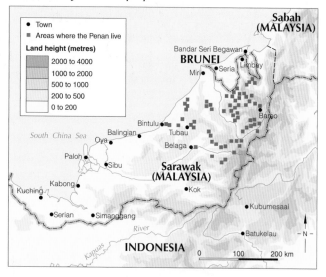

Conflict with government

Many businesses see the rainforest as a valuable resource for logging and, eventually, plantation farming for palm oil. They have had the support of the Malaysian Government, which does not consider the nomadic subsistence lifestyle of the Penan as productive land use. Business interests began logging, damming rivers and establishing palm oil **plantations** in the 1970s. In the early 1980s, many communities, including the Penan, began petitioning the government to halt logging operations on forested land where they and their ancestors had traditionally lived. In the late 1980s, many communities set up blockades in the Malaysian rainforest, temporarily bringing to a halt the logging and clearing operations.

For a short time, there was considerable international attention to the plight of the forest people, and the ecological sustainability of the forests. However, the policy of the Malaysian Government has been to stop the Penan living their traditional nomadic hunting and gathering. They have been forced to abandon their nomadic lifestyle and move to towns, where they suffer poverty and disease. Only a few hundred remain in their dwindling traditional homeland. The Penan have demanded the right to their traditional land. However, the Malaysian Government and large businesses see the forest as a valuable resource to be exploited, so the Penan's demands are ignored. The government has stated that the Penan cannot have any claim to their traditional land unless they settle on it in a **sedentary**, non-nomadic manner.

The government insists that the forest is being logged sustainably, even though it is recognised internationally that the forests are being destroyed at one of the fastest rates on Earth.

Ecological sustainability

The traditional way the Penan lived in the rainforest was ecologically sustainable as they moved from place to place, thereby not imposing any stress on resources. However, the current logging, clearing and plantation farming is clearly unsustainable. Despite international attention by many organisations to the unsustainability of rainforest logging and clearing, Malaysia continues these practices. Most of the Penan people are in urban areas and will never return to the rainforest. If the rainforest is to survive, Malaysia must develop strategies for future environmental sustainability, such as making the area a national park, and promoting ecotourism and research.

GEOskills TOOLBOX

COMPARING GROUND-LEVEL AND AERIAL PHOTOGRAPHS

Geographers use photographs when they are studying environments and communities. They often make line drawings from photographs to record the most important features they observe, adding labels and making notes. Refer to pages 58–9 for a step-by-step guide to making a line drawing from a photograph.

Photograph A: Ground-level photograph showing an oil palm plantation established on former rainforest, Malaysia

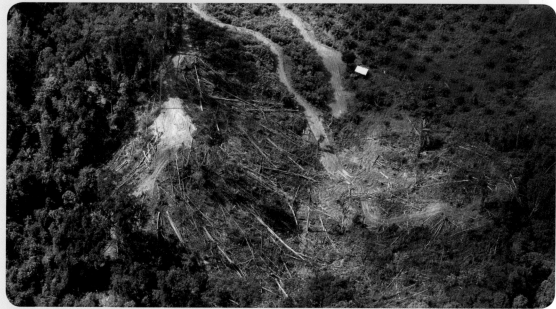

Photograph B: Aerial photograph showing oil palm plantation and heavily logged natural forest, Malaysia

ACTIVITIES ➔

UNDERSTANDING

1. Describe the nomadic lifestyle of the Penan.
2. About how many Penan people still live in the rainforest environment?
3. Describe how the rainforest provides all the needs of the Penan.
4. Why did the Penan conflict with the Malaysian Government?

THINKING AND APPLYING

5. Explain how the Penan traditional life contrasts with their forced life in a town.

6. Describe how development of logging and palm oil plantations are not ecologically sustainable within a rainforest environment.

USING YOUR SKILLS

7. Make a line drawing of the ground-level photograph.
   a Label the features you see on your sketch with reference to foreground, middle ground and background.
   b Describe the scene you see in the photograph.
8. Imagine the scene before the oil palm plantation was established. Outline ways in which the forest was ecologically sustainable.
9. Refer to Photograph B: the aerial view. Outline what you can see in Photograph B that you cannot see in Photograph A: the ground-level view.

Communities in the Amazon rainforest

Where is the Amazon?

The world's largest rainforest is located in the Amazon River basin, which lies mostly in Brazil, in the continent of South America. The Amazon forests cover an area of seven million square kilometres, an area nearly half the size of Australia. This represents about one-third of the world's remaining tropical rainforests. The Amazon rainforest is under increasing threat: a new boom based on timber, agriculture, industry and minerals has caused widespread deforestation. Indigenous communities are also under threat — the environment can no longer support their way of life.

GEO*facts*

- An average of 20 hectares of Amazon rainforest is chopped down every minute.
- Since 1900, more than 90 indigenous tribes have disappeared in Brazil alone.
- The Amazon is the second longest river in the world but it carries more water than the next six largest rivers combined.
- The Amazon rainforest is home to more than 200 000 species of plants.
- The Amazon River and its tributaries contain 4000 species of fish — more than in the Atlantic and Pacific oceans combined.

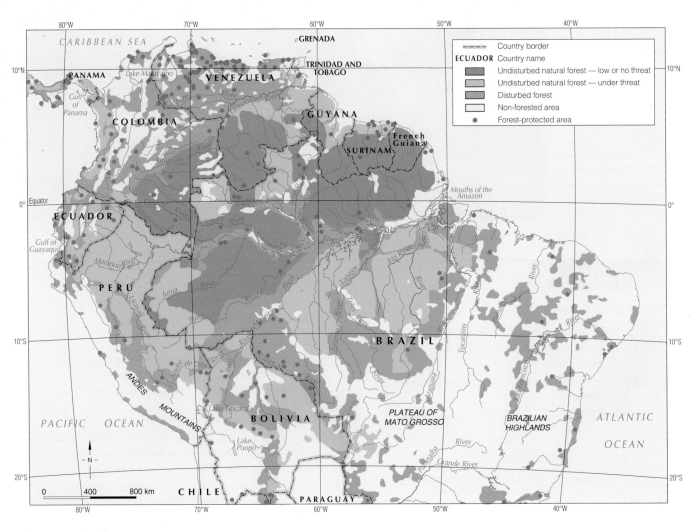

The Amazon basin

The Yanomami Indians

The Yanomami Indians live in the tropical rainforests of northern Brazil and southern Venezuela. The Yanomami Indians adapted to the hot, wet rainforest environment by using shifting cultivation to grow crops such as plantains, cassava, tubers, maize and vegetables. They clear the forest for new gardens for crops every few years when the soil wears out and becomes infertile. The men also hunt and fish over a large area. Because the Yanomami live deep within the rainforests, they remained fairly isolated until recently.

A goldmining boom brought thousands of miners to the Brazilian rainforest in the late 1980s. Large areas of rainforest, and the animals and birds that lived there, were destroyed. Rivers and streams were polluted by mercury, which was used to extract gold from the ore. Stagnant water collected in the holes left in the ground after mining, providing ideal breeding conditions for mosquitos and an increase in malaria. The miners also brought diseases. Many Yanomami died. Armed clashes between miners and Indians occurred when it became clear that the very survival of the Yanomami was threatened. Instead of expelling the miners, the Brazilian Government expelled the missionaries and health workers who were helping the Yanomami.

In 1992, the Brazilian Government set aside land for the Yanomami but this has not stopped miners coming into Yanomami territory. Some politicians and business people are trying to reduce the Yanomami's territory because they want access to its mineral deposits. This would lead to further devastation of the indigenous people and the rainforest.

The Yanomami Indians in Venezuela lost parts of their forest when the government decided to create forest reserves, national parks and protected areas. Slash and burn farming, hunting and building houses were now prohibited in these areas. Today, Indian reserves have been set aside for the Indians. But mining, dam projects, cattle ranches and small farms are still taking their forests and their land.

During the boom in goldmining in the 1980s, the Yanomami Indians could do very little but watch as their rainforest was turned into a hole in the ground.

ACTIVITIES

UNDERSTANDING

1. Describe the location of the Amazon basin.
2. How large is the rainforest area?
3. Explain why the rainforest is being cleared.
4. Describe the effect of goldmining on the rainforest environment.
5. Describe how deforestation has affected the Yanomami Indians in Brazil.
6. What has affected the traditional lifestyle of the Yanomami Indians of Venezuela?

THINKING AND APPLYING

7. Explain why the Yanomami Indians will find it hard to continue their traditional lifestyle in the future.
8. Why do you think there have been few attempts in the past to ensure that the rainforests of the Amazon were managed in a sustainable way? Can individuals do anything to prevent so much of the rainforest being destroyed?

USING YOUR SKILLS

9. Refer to the map on page 156.
   a Which country contains most of the Amazon rainforest?
   b What percentage of the rainforest can be considered (i) low or no threat, (ii) under threat, (iii) disturbed? Construct a pie graph using these percentages.
10. Using a piece of tracing paper, trace the Amazon River and its tributaries. Draw a single line that joins the source of each of the tributaries. Shade this area using a light blue pencil: this area is called the catchment, or basin, of the river. Place your completed diagram over the map of the forest and describe the relationship between the river and the forests.

GEOTERMS

deforestation: the process of clearing forest, usually to make way for agriculture or housing

All around the world, rainforests are being destroyed. The increasing rate at which they are being cut down, and the effects of this deforestation, are perhaps one of the most important issues facing the world today. The main reasons why rainforests are being cleared are described below.

Commercial logging

There are two main types of logging: clear-felling and selective logging. When a forest is clearfelled, all trees are removed either by chainsaw or with heavy machinery such as bulldozers. The most valuable logs are used for furniture and joinery; the rest for woodchips.

In selective logging only the best and most valuable trees are cut down. But in clearing forest to reach these trees, it is estimated that a hectare of forest is destroyed for each log removed.

It is estimated that the world loses about 2 per cent of its rainforest each year, but this differs between countries. At this rate it will all be gone in your lifetime.

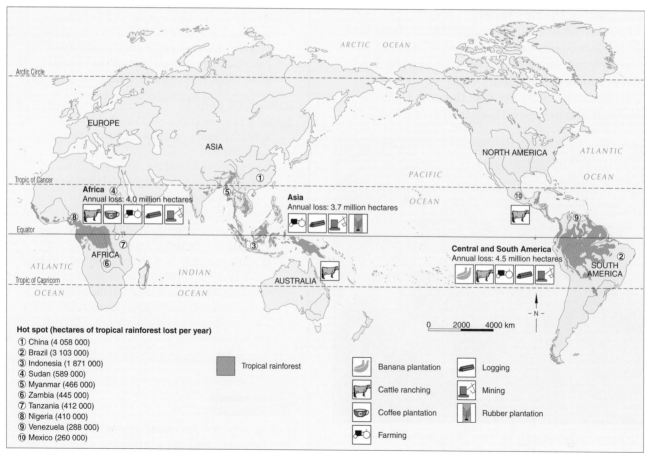

Hot spot (hectares of tropical rainforest lost per year)
1. China (4 058 000)
2. Brazil (3 103 000)
3. Indonesia (1 871 000)
4. Sudan (589 000)
5. Myanmar (466 000)
6. Zambia (445 000)
7. Tanzania (412 000)
8. Nigeria (410 000)
9. Venezuela (288 000)
10. Mexico (260 000)

Tropical rainforest

Banana plantation

Cattle ranching

Coffee plantation

Farming

Logging

Mining

Rubber plantation

Africa ④
Annual loss: 4.0 million hectares

Asia
Annual loss: 3.7 million hectares

Central and South America
Annual loss: 4.5 million hectares

Rainforest destruction hot spots around the world

The Ok Tedi gold and copper mine in the Papua New Guinea rainforest. There have been many concerns raised regarding the impact of this mine on the local streams and rivers.

Mining

Many rainforests are growing on land that also contains large energy and mineral deposits such as oil, gold, silver, bauxite, iron ore, copper and zinc. Mineral companies build roads to the deposits and set up large-scale mining and processing plants. These plants require large amounts of electricity, and this is often supplied by burning trees to create charcoal or by constructing vast hydro-electric dams.

Deep in the Brazilian rainforest, a 2000-square-kilometre dam has been constructed to provide electricity for aluminium smelters. The dam flooded the entire tribal lands of two native tribes, and is so large that it has altered the climate in the area, making it drier.

Another problem created by mining is the pollution of nearby rivers and streams from chemicals used in the processing plants. Rivers downstream from a vast goldmine in Papua New Guinea have been found to contain four times the safe limit of cyanide in the water. Cyanide is used to extract gold from rock.

Farming

Many countries in which rainforest grows are **developing countries**. These countries struggle to provide the basic necessities of life for their people, and their populations are often rapidly growing in size. In these countries, the land on which the forest grows is seen as more valuable than the forest itself. The forests are destroyed and farmers move onto the cleared land, often sowing seed in the still warm ashes of the trees that have been burnt.

In some places, small-scale farmers use the land alongside new roads that have been built through the forest, growing enough to feed their families. In other places, large-scale commercial farms raise beef or crops for export to the richer countries of the world.

 **GEO*facts***

- About one hectare of rainforest is destroyed every second: this is about twice the size of a soccer pitch.
- Scientists estimate that 137 plants and animals are made *extinct* daily: 50 000 each year.
- It is estimated that in the year 1500, up to nine million indigenous people lived in the Amazon rainforest. That number is now fewer than 200 000.
- By 2021, 53 per cent of Papua New Guinea's total forest will be gone.

ACTIVITIES

UNDERSTANDING

1. What are the two main types of logging?
2. Explain why both of these processes are harmful for rainforests.

THINKING AND APPLYING

3. Why is the problem of rainforest destruction so hard to solve in developing countries?
4. Describe what you can do as an informed citizen to reduce the destruction of rainforests.

USING YOUR SKILLS

5. Refer to the map opposite, and then answer these questions.
   a. Which continent is experiencing the greatest destruction of its rainforests on an annual basis?
   b. Name three countries on this continent that are clearing their rainforests.
   c. How many hectares are being destroyed in this continent on an annual basis?
   d. List four reasons why the rainforests are being cleared on this continent.
   e. Give reasons why Australia has not been featured on this map as a rainforest hot spot.

GEOTERMS

developing country: a country in which most people have a low economic standard of living

The major reason that species become endangered is the destruction of their habitat. A habitat is the total environment where an animal lives, including shelter, access to food and water and all of the right conditions for breeding. Clearing native plants for roads, farms and houses creates smaller islands of vegetation. Living in these separate islands makes it difficult for animals to communicate and breed.

Rainforest destruction

The rainforests of the world contain the greatest variety of animal and plant life on Earth. Many rainforest species are now under threat from deforestation carried out for farming, housing and logging. Logging is the major cause of rainforest destruction. The logging companies build roads into the untouched forests to open them up for logging. Farmers clear land on either side of the road to grow crops and graze cattle. As the population of the area grows, more forest is cleared to allow for further housing and agriculture. This continued process of clearing is the major cause of deforestation in countries like Brazil, Indonesia, Malaysia and Bolivia.

Deforestation in Indonesia

Nearly 10 per cent of the world's rainforests and 40 per cent of all Asian rainforests are found in Indonesia. Less than half of Indonesia's original rainforest area remains. Much of this is in Kalimantan, on the island of Borneo. Forests have been cleared for timber, for plantation crops such as palm-oil trees, and to make way for Indonesia's growing population, now more than 200 million. Fires lit to clear land in 1982 and 1997 turned into wildfires that severely damaged large areas of rainforest in Kalimantan. Orang-utans, Sumatran tigers and Javan hawk-eagles may disappear from Indonesia as their natural habitats are reduced.

Endangered orang-utans

Orang-utans are the largest tree-living mammals and the only great ape that lives in Asia. They are perfectly adapted to their rainforest environment. On the ground they eat roots, berries, insects, reptiles and eggs; in the trees they eat leaves, fruits, nuts and even bark.

Orang-utans survive only on the islands of Borneo and Sumatra. Current estimates are that orang-utans have lost 80 per cent of their habitat in the last 20 years. In 1997, wildfires burned through nearly two million hectares of land in Indonesia. Hundreds of orang-utans were burned to death. Orang-utans are also taken from their natural habitat to supply the pet trade. It is thought that some 1000 orang-utans were imported into Taiwan as pets between 1995 and 1999.

The current orang-utan population is estimated at 61 000. There are around 4000 animals protected in national parks. Unless these unique apes are protected in secure parks, and in forest habitats connected by vegetation corridors, they may soon face extinction in the wild. The Indonesian Government has an action plan to preserve their habitat, including conservation education, more controls on logging, laws against mining and patrols against poachers.

Young orang-utans in a Borneo rainforest

GEOfacts

An animal even more threatened than the orang-utan by loss of habitat in Borneo is the sun bear. The rapid disappearance of the forested land and suitable sun bear habitat has seen a decline of wild sun bears to approximately 10 000 individuals. Besides habitat destruction, keeping sun bears as pets, poaching for its body parts for consumption, medicine (gall bladder), and souvenirs, are some of the other threats to the sun bears.

COMPARING MAPS

Comparing two different maps of the same area allows us to identify and explain the patterns of physical and human features shown on the maps.

Legend:
- Lowland rainforest
- Montane rainforest
- Mangrove forest
- Former rainforest
- No data available

Indonesian rainforest

Compare the former rainforest on Borneo with the land use map. Why do you think change has occurred in this area?

Look at the land use map to see what has replaced the rainforest in Malaysia.

Choose one important item from the legend to look at and compare.

Legend:
- Cultivated land
- Irrigated land, rice growing
- Scrub, rough grazing and some cultivation
- Forest and swamp
- Plantation and cash crops

Land use in Indonesia

Check the land use map to see what has replaced the rainforest in Java.

ACTIVITIES

UNDERSTANDING

1. Which activity is the main cause of habitat destruction?
2. Describe the main threat to orang-utans.

THINKING AND APPLYING

3. Indonesia recently granted a licence to a pulp paper producer to clear 50 000 hectares of forest near an orang-utan sanctuary in Sumatra. What impact do you consider this might have on the orang-utan population?

USING YOUR SKILLS

4. Refer to the two maps of Indonesia.
   a Estimate the percentage of Java once covered by rainforests.
   b Identify the main forms of land use now in Java.
   c Rank these forms of land use in importance according to the area they cover. Explain these patterns.
   d Rainforest loss in southern Borneo has mainly occurred along what natural features?
      i. How is the land in these areas now used?
      ii. Why do you think this region of Borneo was chosen?

The Brazilian Government is currently backing a multi-billion dollar scheme designed to 'develop' the Amazon rainforest. A major part of this project is the building of 10 000 kilometres of new highway through the rainforest. Many scientists are concerned that these highways will result in the final destruction of the world's largest rainforest.

1. A typical small farm — mixed crops and a hastily built homestead
2. Small remnant pocket of rainforest, protected as national park
3. Roads give access to poachers.
4. Smoke blankets the forest.
5. Weeds and exotic plants infest rainforest.
6. Newly cleared land — trees cut down and burned. This is called 'slash and burn'.
7. Introduced cattle erode the fragile topsoil with their hard hoofs.
8. A bulldozer clears a new road into the forest, opening up new areas for 50 kilometres on either side of the main road.
9. An endangered macaw

Why do roads destroy the rainforest?

Roads create access to the interior of the rainforest, opening up areas once almost impossible to reach. Soon after the roads are built, settlers (called homesteaders) arrive. There are roughly ten million

10. Large cattle ranch, probably owned by a foreign company
11. Sealed road changes streams and often causes erosion.
12. New settlers arrive from the city to clear land.
13. Logging truck heading towards the pulp mill
14. The river runs brown because it is carrying away topsoil that is no longer protected by the trees.
15. Sweetcorn crop — most farmers can grow only enough to feed their families.
16. Fences stop rainforest animals migrating, and may cut them off from food sources.
17. Tractor spraying pesticide onto crops, which washes into nearby creek
18. Dead golden tamarin, killed by traffic

Effects of roadbuilding on the Amazon rainforest

SKETCHING A SATELLITE IMAGE

Satellite images are used by geographers and cartographers to discover broad patterns on the Earth's surface. Satellite images often use false colours to highlight patterns. Some of the typical colours used are dark blue or black for deep water, blue for shallow water and brown or red to indicate lush vegetation.

The satellite image shows deforestation in Brazil. Areas of dense vegetation appear red. The dark blue areas are marshy savanna. Pale blue rectangles above centre are evidence of deforestation. The pattern of fine blue lines at right is deforestation due to 'slash and burn' farming.

Brazilians who are considered landless and poor, and some of these come seeking a chance to make a living.

Claiming a piece of the forest that borders the road, the homesteaders chop down a few trees as timber for fencing or a house, and then set fire to the rest. In 1998, over 48 000 square kilometres of Brazilian rainforest went up in flames.

Once the initial 'land rush' is over and all the land beside the roads has been claimed, tracks and roads leading off from the highways will push deeper and deeper into the forest, until an area of 50 kilometres either side of the highway has been destroyed and replaced by small farms.

Many of the homesteaders are unable to make much of a living from the poor tropical soils, so they sell their farms to cattle ranchers and return to the cities.

What are the potential problems?

- Thousands of plant and animal species become **extinct**. Some have yet to be discovered!
- The fires will pump millions of tonnes of carbon dioxide into the air, increasing the threat of global warming. At the same time, destroying the trees robs the planet of the natural system that helps regulate the amount of carbon dioxide in the air.
- The area will become much drier, as the cleared land does not return moisture to the atmosphere as quickly as a rainforest does.
- The indigenous people of the area are displaced and their culture may disappear. The homesteaders bring new diseases that indigenous people have no natural immunity to. One tribe, the Nambiquara, lost half of its population when a road was placed through their tribal land.

ACTIVITIES

UNDERSTANDING

1. How many kilometres of new highways are planned for the rainforest by the Brazilian Government?
2. Where do the new settlers come from?
3. How do the settlers clear the land?
4. Explain why most of the land ends up as cattle ranches.

THINKING AND APPLYING

5. In small groups, discuss the following issues.
   a. What are the main environmental problems caused by rainforest destruction?
   b. What alternatives are there to rainforest destruction if the government wants to expand the areas available for agricultural land?

USING YOUR SKILLS

6. Refer to the illustration 'Effects of road building on the Amazon rainforest'. The road was built five years ago.
   a. Describe how this area would have looked ten years ago.
   b. Describe how you think this area will look in ten years' time.
7. Sketch the satellite image. Use a colour legend to show the rivers and tributaries, roads, forested areas, deforested areas.
8. Make a sketch of how you think the area might look in 20 years from now.

Constructing and interpreting graphs

One of the best ways of presenting statistics in geography is by using graphs. A graph is essentially a way of drawing statistics. Graphs help to communicate quickly, showing important information at a glance. Geographers use graphs to visually represent a large range of data.

The important features of graphs

To communicate quickly, graphs should have the following:
- A **title** (name or heading)
- The **source** details (where the information came from)
- A **horizontal axis**. This is the line running across the bottom of the graph with numbers or words on it.
- A **vertical axis**. This is the line running up the side of the graph with numbers or words on it.
- A **scale**, which is commonly on the vertical axis.

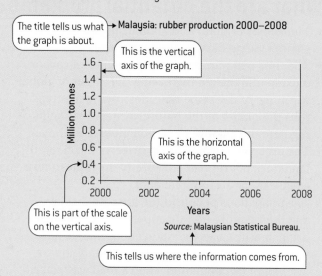

The title tells us what the graph is about. → Malaysia: rubber production 2000–2008

This is the vertical axis of the graph.

This is the horizontal axis of the graph.

This is part of the scale on the vertical axis.

Source: Malaysian Statistical Bureau.

This tells us where the information comes from.

Line graphs

Line graphs show information as a series of points that are joined up to form a line. The line shows a trend or change over time. Line graphs are very useful for showing change over time and for comparing data.

Line graphs can be constructed by hand or by using a spreadsheet program on your computer.

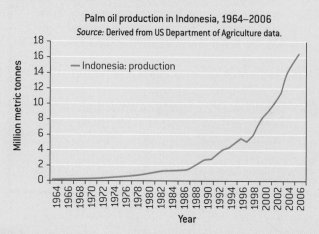

Palm oil production in Indonesia, 1964–2006
Source: Derived from US Department of Agriculture data.

— Indonesia: production

STEP 1
- Draw a horizontal axis and select something to compare. On many of the line graphs you draw, the horizontal axis will show units of time. In the example below left, the unit is in years.

STEP 2
- Draw the vertical axis and decide upon the scale. The vertical axis will show what changes occur over time. In the example, the unit is millions of metric tonnes.

  Usually the scale will start at 0 and increase at intervals that suit the data to be graphed. For example, if numbers in the data were in hundreds or thousands, an interval of 2 would be too small. For this graph, where the highest number in the data is less than 20, intervals of 2 are suitable.

STEP 3
- Plot a series of dots at the points where information meets. For example, in 2000 the production was 8 million tonnes.

STEP 4
- Join the dots with a freehand line. Do not use a ruler.

STEP 5
- Name the vertical and horizontal axes. Give the graph a title. *Note:* Provide the source of the data with the graph. This enables the user to check for more up-to-date statistics when they become available.

Bar graphs

Bar graphs show information in the form of a bar or column. They are useful for comparing quantities. Computer spreadsheets give different ways to present bar graphs.

For a guide to drawing column or bar graphs, see page 109.

The column graph shown below, compares different countries on the horizontal axis. The vertical axis compares the percentage of forest cover lost.

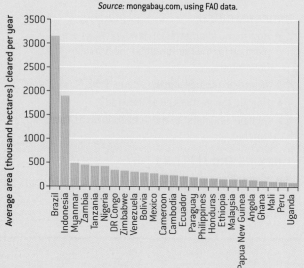

Tropical deforestation rates, 2000–2005
Source: mongabay.com, using FAO data.

Drawing pie graphs

In a pie graph the slices or sectors represent the size of the different parts that make up the whole. The circle of the 360 degrees represents the total or 100 per cent of whatever is being looked at. The size of the slices can be easily seen. The individual parts or components should be presented in order, from largest to smallest, to make it easier to interpret the figures.

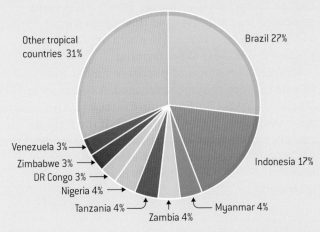

Share of tropical deforestation, 2000–2005

Brazil 27%
Indonesia 17%
Myanmar 4%
Zambia 4%
Tanzania 4%
Nigeria 4%
DR Congo 3%
Zimbabwe 3%
Venezuela 3%
Other tropical countries 31%

Source: mongabay.com, using FAO data.

Create your own pie graph using the following information. You will need a compass, a protractor, paper and colouring pencils.

STEP 1

Order the statistics from largest to smallest. If you have an 'other' catergory, put it last. Make sure you know what the total of all the parts adds up to.

STEP 2

Convert the figures to a percentage of the whole; that is, divide the part's figure by the total figure and multiply by 100.

STEP 3

Convert the percentage to degrees of a circle by multiplying by 3.6. (100% of the circle = 360 degrees, so 1% of the circle = 3.6 degrees.) This gives the angle of each slice of the pie. Study the following example.

Share of tropical deforestation, 2000–2005

Country	Hectares cleared	%	Degrees
Brazil		27	97
Indonesia		17	61
Myanmar		4	14
Zambia		4	14
Tanzania		4	14
Nigeria		4	14
Democratic Republic of the Congo		3	11
Zimbabwe		3	11
Venezuela		3	11
Other tropical countries		31	113
Total		100	360

STEP 4

Use the compass to draw a circle. Don't make it too small or it will be hard to draw and read. Make the radius at least 3 centimetres. Put a pencil dot on the middle of your circle. Steps 5 to 7 are shown below.

STEP 5

Draw a straight line from the centre of the circle up to the 12 o'clock position.

STEP 6

Use the protractor to mark the first and largest slice, working clockwise.

STEP 7

Place the 0 degrees line on your protractor along the line you have just drawn. Now mark in the second largest group. Use the protractor to mark each of the other slices in descending size, marking the 'other' category last.

STEP 8

Label each slice, give the graph a clear title and colour each sector so that it is easy to read. *Note:* A pie graph can also be created using a spreadsheet.

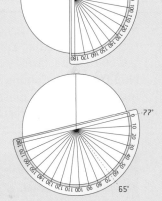

ACTIVITIES →

USING YOUR SKILLS

1. Refer to the line graph 'Palm oil production in Indonesia', 1964–2006 on page 164.
   a What is the production rate for 2002?
   b What is the production rate for 1989?
2. Refer to the bar graph 'Tropical deforestation rates, 2000–2005' on page 164.
   a What is the rate for Brazil?
   b What is the rate for Ecuador?
3. Refer to the pie graph 'Share of tropical deforestation, 2000–2005'. What is the share for Brazil, Indonesia and Myanmar?
4. Use the data below to draw a pie graph.

Causes of deforestation in the Amazon, 2000–2005

Cattle ranches	60%
Subsistence agriculture	33%
Fires, mining, road construction, dams	3%
Logging	3%
Large-scale, commercial agriculture	1%

Source: mongabay.com, based on a variety of sources.

As people begin to realise the importance of rainforests, many of them have started to work towards preserving these 'green dinosaurs'. Some of these methods of conservation are relevant to governments and large companies, but some of them are relevant to you and the choices that you make.

Rescue package 1: protect the remaining rainforests

While only 6 per cent of the world's rainforests are in a national park or reserve, there are many large areas of rainforest under protection. The number and size of these national parks are slowly increasing. The Korup National Park in Cameroon holds 126 000 hectares of Africa's richest untouched rainforest; the Khao Yai National Park in Thailand has 200 000 hectares, where the habitats of tigers, elephants and gibbons are protected; Costa Rica's rainforests are the most protected of all, with national parks and reserves covering almost one-third of that country.

The jaguar lives in the rainforests of Costa Rica. A formidable predator, it is an endangered species. National parks have been established to protect its habitat in an attempt to ensure its survival.

Rescue package 2: using the forest without destroying it

This is called sustainable development. It means that resources are taken from the rainforests but the forest remains largely intact. It has been estimated that a forest used this way is worth $12 000 a hectare, while it is worth only $300 a hectare if it is cleared for farming.

Timber users can now purchase timber from forests that are properly managed. A company in Mexico — Forest Stewardship Council (FSC) — assesses forests around the world. If the forests comply with regulations, the timber is given the FSC stamp. People who purchase that timber know the forest it came from is being responsibly managed.

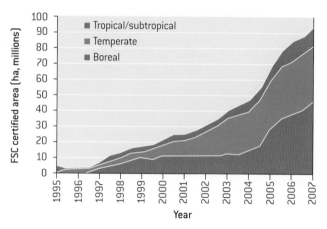

Forest Stewardship Council certified forest area growth

Rescue package 3: using alternative timber

One further step in using timber is not to use rainforest timber at all. Many rainforest trees are now grown in plantations; and using alternative materials such as steel beams in houses and recycled paper in cardboard helps take the strain off the rainforests.

One alternative that has been developed is the processing of old coconut palms to create hardwood. The company that is developing this resource, Tangaloa, claims that there are enough non-productive coconut palms to produce timber equivalent to one million rainforest trees. If this concept proves popular, plantations of coconut palms could be grown specifically for this purpose.

Coconut plantation — could these palms help save the rainforests?

Rescue package 4: you and me

While most of us do not have rainforests growing in our backyards, the choices we make each day can and do make a difference to the way resources are used around the world. There are many organisations that aim to conserve the world's remaining rainforests, and some of their suggestions are:

- use less wood and paper
- write to businesses that destroy the rainforest
- educate yourself about the importance of rainforests
- look for alternatives to rainforest products
- be an ecotourist — visit rainforests where your tourist dollars go towards education and conservation.

GEOskills TOOLBOX

COLLECTING AND INTERPRETING ELECTRONIC INFORMATION

The internet is a good place to collect information on many geographic topics. However, you need to make sure it's reliable because anyone can publish material on the internet without having to prove what they are saying. Much of this information can be wrong. Two useful techniques when using the internet for research are:

- Use at least four different sites to check your information (this is called cross-checking).
- Try to find educational (edu.) or government (gov.) sites. Other reliable sites include those of well-known organisations such as UNESCO and WHO.

ACTIVITIES

UNDERSTANDING

1. List two advantages and disadvantages of each rescue package.
2. What percentage of the world's rainforests is in national parks or reserves?
3. Which country has the most protected rainforests of all?
4. Explain what is meant by sustainable development.
5. Describe the work of the Forest Stewardship Council (FSC).

THINKING AND APPLYING

6. One of the issues the FSC looks at before it certifies a forest is that the right of the indigenous people to own and manage the land is being respected. Explain why this is important.
7. In small groups, discuss which of the four rescue packages offers the most hope for rainforest conservation. Present your choice to the class, giving at least three reasons for your decision.
8. Imagine you are overhearing a conversation between two people about the use of rainforests. One is a wealthy businessman and the other a forest conservationist. Compare and contrast what you think their main arguments would be.

USING YOUR SKILLS

9. Refer to the line graph opposite.
   a Which type of forest had the largest area of FSC in 2007?
   b Which type of forest had the largest growth in the area of FSC classification from 1995 to 2007?
   c Describe the trend for the area of FSC classification for tropical/subtropical forest.
10. Use the internet to find an example of each of the following methods to preserve rainforests:
    a breeding endangered rainforest animals in captivity and then releasing them into the wild
    b providing websites where you can click on a button and a sponsor gives money to buy some rainforest and put it into a reserve
    c employing indigenous rainforest people to pick nuts and berries or even to breed butterflies for collectors.
11. List any other methods of preservation you discover and explain how they are useful.
12. Write a report on your findings. Include information about where you found the information and why this source is reliable.

Working geographically

KNOWLEDGE AND UNDERSTANDING

Select the alternative A, B, C or D that best answers the question.

1. The temperate forests are located between
   - (A) the Equator and the tropics.
   - (B) the two tropics.
   - (C) close to the poles.
   - (D) between the tropics and polar regions.

2. A canopy is
   - (A) the top layer of the forest that allows light to pass through.
   - (B) the middle layer of the forest that allows light to pass through.
   - (C) the top layer of the forest that allows little light to pass through.
   - (D) the middle layer of the forest that allows light to penetrate.

3. The type of rainfall often associated with tropical rainforests is
   - (A) orographic.
   - (B) frontal.
   - (C) cyclonic.
   - (D) convectional.

4. The conditions that tropical cyclones need in order to form are
   - (A) strong winds.
   - (B) warm water vapour.
   - (C) a high pressure system.
   - (D) low temperatures.

5. Rainforest soils are
   - (A) generally low in nutrients.
   - (B) composed of leaf litter.
   - (C) rich and fertile.
   - (D) dependent on leaching.

6. When plants remove carbon dioxide from the air and return oxygen in its place it is known as the
   - (A) carbon–oxygen cycle.
   - (B) leaching.
   - (C) enhanced greenhouse effect.
   - (D) the cycle of regeneration.

7. Hunters and gatherers are usually
   - (A) indigenous people.
   - (B) sedentary people.
   - (C) people who prefer to change their habitat.
   - (D) very healthy.

8. Orang-utans survive
   - (A) in rainforests all over the world.
   - (B) on the islands of Borneo and Java.
   - (C) on the islands of Borneo and Sumatra.
   - (D) only in captivity.

9. The Amazon River basin has around
   - (A) one-third of the world's remaining rainforest.
   - (B) one-half of the world's remaining rainforest.
   - (C) one-quarter of the world's remaining rainforest.
   - (D) three-quarters of the world's remaining rainforest.

10. FSC forests
    - (A) are forests managed in a sustainable way.
    - (B) are to be found only in Mexico.
    - (C) are forests within national parks.
    - (D) are forests with endangered species in them.

DIFFERENT PERSPECTIVES

11. Refer to the photograph at the top of page 169.
    - a Describe this scene from three different viewpoints: a logger, a conservationist and an indigenous person who lived here before logging.
    - b Which of these viewpoints is closest to your own? Give reasons for your answer.

12. What do you think will happen to the world's remaining rainforests in the next 20 years?

13. What do you think should happen to the world's remaining rainforests in the next 20 years?

DISCUSSION

In this chapter we have seen that there is often conflict between communities about the way to use the natural environment in rainforests. Rainforests are a very valuable resource, but different people view them in different ways.

14. With one or more people in your class, brainstorm the ways in which rainforests are valuable to people. Try to come up with at least ten uses.

The desolate landscape of a rainforest after logging

15. Divide each of these rainforest uses into sustainable and unsustainable. List the reasons why it is sustainable or not next to each type of land use.

16. Select two unsustainable uses and then present a short report on how these uses could be managed so that they were sustainable.

17. Which community groups might be affected by your management decisions?

18. How would you attempt to solve any conflict that developed?

CHARACTERISTICS OF SIGNIFICANT REGIONS

19. Test yourself by filling in the spaces in the table.

Type of rainforest	Description of forest	Location of type of forest	Animals and plants found
Lowland tropical forest			
	Smaller trees, often covered in fog and mist		
		Along tropical coastlines, especially in Asia and South America	
			Giant panda, Tasmanian devil, wolves

GEOskills TOOLBOX

RESEARCHING AND PRESENTING REPORTS

When you present a report it is important to remember there are three main parts:
- a general *introduction* that introduces the subject of your report
- a *series of paragraphs* about the subject. Each new paragraph usually describes a different aspect of the subject. Each paragraph should begin with a *topic sentence*. A topic sentence contains the main idea in the paragraph.
- a *conclusion* that sums up the main idea presented in your report.

Reports should also have a heading or title and may include images such as photos as well as text.

Use the following short report as a model to prepare your own report about an endangered rainforest animal. To find out more about endangered species, use the **Red List** weblink in your eBookPLUS.

Tigers at risk

Over the past few centuries, hundreds of animal, bird and plant species have become extinct. Many others are now endangered. Much of this is due to human activities such as land clearing, which destroys the natural habitats of native species.

Three of the eight species of tiger in the world are already extinct. Tiger populations are disappearing due to hunting, poaching for skins, bones for traditional Asian medicine and the destruction of their natural habitat.

The Sumatran tiger is the smallest of the tiger family. It is an endangered animal and there are less than 500 left in the wild. Rainforest clearing in Sumatra is one of the greatest threats to the Sumatran tiger's survival.

In 1995, the Sumatran tiger project was set up to research tiger numbers and try to find ways that tigers can continue to coexist with people. Unless something is done, the Sumatran tiger will join the list of the world's extinct animals.

The Sumatran tiger's shrinking habitat is a serious threat to its survival.

Rainforests: a user's guide

SEARCHLIGHT ID: PRO-0027

SCENARIO

You are an environmental author hired to promote rainforest preservation for a joint promotional campaign between the World Wide Fund for Nature and the Nature Conservancy. The project is to include films, television shows, internet-related resources — and a book.
Your book will be about how useful rainforests are to humans. The publishers would like you to create a user's guide to all the wonderful things that rainforests provide, but they also want you to make clear the importance of conservation of rainforest ecosystems. The intended audience is people aged between 12 and 15.

YOUR TASK

Create a spread from your book for consideration by the publishers. This will include art or photos of three useful rainforest products and some explanatory text

for each. A sample manuscript has been provided for you in Word document format, but you should use a software program like Publisher to give your sample a professional book-finished look. The publishers have also asked you to sprinkle the book with amazing facts about rainforests, such as 'Did you know?' and 'Staggering statistics' boxes. Please incorporate at least one of these in your sample.

PROCESS

- Open the ProjectsPLUS application for this chapter, located in your eBookPLUS. View the introductory video lesson then click the 'Start Project' button to set up your project. You may complete this project individually or invite other members of your class to form a group and create a larger sample. Save your settings and the project will be launched.
- Navigate to your Research Forum. A selection of useful rainforest products have been loaded as topics in the system to provide a framework for your research. You can also add other products of your own as topics.
- Using your eBookPLUS as a starting point, research these useful rainforest products. Wikipedia can be used but is not considered a strongly academic source and should not be relied on as the key information provider. You should find at least three sources (other than the textbook, and including at least one offline source such as a book or encyclopaedia) to help you discover extra information about each of these products. The weblinks in your Media Centre will help you get started. Enter your findings as articles in the Research Forum. You can view and comment on other group members' articles and rate the information they have entered.
- When your research is complete, navigate to your Media Centre and download the sample manuscript for your 'Rainforests: a user's guide' publication. Note that your final pages should be properly designed.
- Work as a group to plan the design of your pages. Think about visual appeal. Consider the font to be used, style and size of headings and whether there will be a visual theme to the text. Don't forget to include at least

Your ProjectsPLUS application is available in this chapter's Student Resources tab inside your eBookPLUS. Visit www.jacplus.com.au to locate your digital resources.

SUGGESTED SOFTWARE
- ProjectsPLUS
- Microsoft Word
- Microsoft Publisher or InDesign

one 'Did you know?' or 'Staggering statistics' box in your design. A selection of images has been provided for you in your Media Centre to help you make a visually appealing spread.

- Draft the sample text for your individual page. Don't forget that the most significant aspect is promoting rainforest conservation — get your facts right and remember your audience. If working in a group, make sure you don't duplicate useful products in your spreads.
- Ask a classmate to edit your manuscript for you and then enter the edited content into your design and finalise your spread. If working as a group, you should end up with a double-page spread for each group member.
- Print out your research report from ProjectsPLUS and hand it in with your 'Rainforest: a user's guide' booklet.

MEDIA CENTRE

Your Media Centre contains:
- a selection of rainforest images
- a sample 'Rainforests: a user's guide' manuscript
- weblinks to informational sites on rainforests
- an assessment rubric.

Interactivity

REVELATION: 'RAINFORESTS'

Forests that grow in constantly wet conditions are called rainforests. They provide habitats for more species of plants, animals, insects and birds than any other environment found on our planet. This interactive Revelation game will challenge you to identify key characteristics of a tropical rainforest. Success rewards you with a video presentation on this unique ecosystem.

SEARCHLIGHT ID: INT-0956

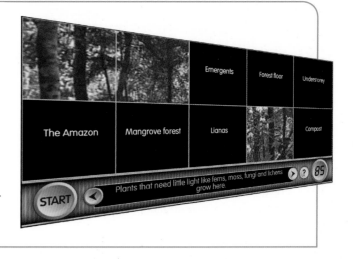

8 Polar lands

INQUIRY QUESTIONS

+ Where are the polar lands?
+ What are the geographical processes that shape the polar lands' environment?
+ How do communities live in this harsh environment?

Polar lands have the most desolate and harsh environment on Earth. It is always cold at the high latitude polar lands.

At the Arctic and Antarctic circles, the daily period of sunlight varies from 24 hours at the time of the summer solstice, to no sunlight at all at the winter solstice.

The plants and animals that live in this environment are well adapted to the extreme conditions. There are very few permanent inhabitants in the north polar lands, and no permanent inhabitants at the south polar lands. While they may seem far away from us, polar lands are an important indicator of the nature and extent of global warming, which will affect us all.

GEOskills TOOLBOX

+ Interpreting climatic graphs (page 175)
+ Annotating (labelling) a photograph or line drawing (page 187)
+ Interpreting and constructing line graphs (page 189)

Antarctica is a land of extremes. It is the coldest, windiest and driest place on Earth.

Location

Polar lands are broadly located between the North Pole and the Arctic Circle and between the South Pole and the Antarctic Circle. In the Northern Hemisphere, polar lands do extend further south. The boundary of these harsh, cold environments is generally agreed to be the isotherm where the mean (or average) temperature of the warmest month is not above 10° Celsius. An isotherm is a line joining places of equal temperature. Trees do not grow further towards the poles than this isotherm. Polar lands have two types of landscape — the icecap and the tundra.

In the icecap lands, the average temperature for all months is below freezing (0° Celsius), so any vegetation growth is very difficult. Icecap lands have a permanent cover of ice and snow.

Tundra is a Lappish word meaning 'barren land'. Tundra areas are located between isotherms 0° and 10° Celsius. In these lands usually only a few months have average temperatures above freezing. Even though the surface snow and ice disappear, the subsoil remains frozen from year to year. This permafrost makes tree growth impossible, but smaller vegetation can grow during the warmer months.

Climate

There are two main reasons the polar lands are so cold:

- The sun's rays hit the Earth's surface at an oblique or sloping angle in the polar lands. At the Equator, the sun's rays are close to vertical. The same amount of sunlight has to heat a greater surface area in the polar lands (see the diagram on page 118).

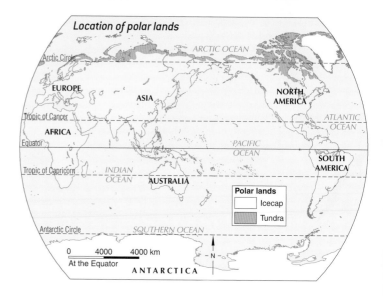

Location of polar lands

- Ice and snow are white so they reflect much of the solar energy that does reach the polar lands. This means warmth from the sun is not absorbed as it is, for example, by the green of forests. Neither the land surface nor the air above it becomes warm.

There is very little information available about precipitation in the icecaps, but it is thought to be very low, probably less than 100 millimetres per year. Precipitation includes rain, hail, snow and dew. In the tundra, precipitation occurs, mainly in summer, but it is also low (approximately 75–450 millimetres per year). Most of the polar lands are actually cold deserts. Precipitation is very low in the polar lands because of the very low temperatures and low humidity. These lands are also dominated by high pressure systems, which provide unfavourable atmospheric conditions for precipitation.

The extreme cold of the high latitude polar lands creates major problems for humans. These problems are greatly increased when the extreme cold is accompanied by strong winds. This causes what is known as wind chill. A wind pulls heated air away from the surface of clothes or skin. Cold air

Tundra means 'barren land' and only the smallest types of vegetation can grow in the frozen subsoil.

replaces the warm air. The faster the air moves, the more heat is taken away from the body. This makes it feel much colder than the temperature shown on the thermometer.

On the icecap there is no vegetation and a permanent ice cover. Emperor penguins are one of the species that have adapted to this environment.

 GEO*facts* While the environments of northern and southern polar lands are similar, they are also different:
- The Arctic Ocean is at the centre of the northern polar lands. At the centre of the southern polar lands, there is a large landmass, the continent of Antarctica.
- Antarctica is more isolated because it is surrounded by ocean. Indigenous people, such as the Sami of Northern Europe and the Inuit of Northern Canada, settled the northern polar lands thousands of years ago. Antarctica has no indigenous people and was first visited by people (whalers and sealers) during the late 1800s.

GEOTERMS

isotherm: a line joining places of equal temperature

permafrost: ground that is permanently frozen

precipitation: the condensation in the atmosphere that falls as rain, hail, snow or dew

tundra: barren lands located between isotherms 0° and 10° Celsius. The subsoil is permanently frozen, allowing only small vegetation growth.

GEOskills TOOLBOX

INTERPRETING CLIMATIC GRAPHS

Climatic graphs or climographs are a combination of a column graph and a line graph, and are used to show the climate of a place over a 12-month period. The line graph section always shows average monthly temperature and the column graph represents average monthly rainfall. Be careful to read from the correct scale when observing climatic graphs. For more information about interpreting and constructing climatic graphs go to pages 120–1.

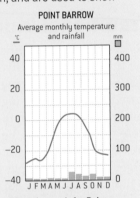

POINT BARROW
Average monthly temperature and rainfall

Climatic graph for Point Barrow, Alaska, 71°N, 156°W

ACTIVITIES →

UNDERSTANDING

1. Where are the polar lands located?
2. Explain why the isotherm 10° Celsius for the **mean temperature** of the warmest month is the boundary used to define polar lands.
3. Explain why the sun's warmth is not absorbed in polar lands.
4. Explain why polar lands are so (a) cold and (b) dry.

THINKING AND APPLYING

5. If you were outdoors in a polar land, explain why it would seem colder on a windy day than on a cold day.
6. Explain why tree growth is impossible in the tundra areas of polar lands.

7. With the aid of your atlas, name five countries that have polar lands within their territory.

USING YOUR SKILLS

8. Refer to the climatic graph for Point Barrow, Alaska.
   a. What is the average monthly temperature in summer?
   b. What is the average monthly temperature in winter?
   c. What type of problems could be experienced in summer when ice and snow melt?
9. Using the data given below, construct a climatic graph for Little America in Antarctica.
   a. Describe the climate of Little America.
   b. How is it different to the climate of Point Barrow?

Little America, Antarctica, 78°S, 161°W

	J	F	M	A	M	J	J	A	S	O	N	D	Mean
Average minimum temperature (°C)	−7	−14	−22	−29	−31	−39	−39	−39	−28	−26	−17	−7	−25
Rainfall (mm)	0	0	0	0	0	0	0	0	0	0	0	0	0

Inuit are communities of people who have lived in and near the Arctic Circle for thousands of years. They were formerly known as Eskimos. The Inuit live in the tundra, one of the coldest and harshest climates in the world where little vegetation can grow. The tundra supports light populations of caribou, reindeer, musk oxen, foxes, wolves and hares. In the sea, on the sea ice and along the Arctic shores are whales, seals, walruses and polar bears.

Land now owned by Canada's Inuit is shown on the map below.

Traditional Inuit communities

Because of the very difficult physical environment, the Inuit have always lived in small communities scattered over a huge region. These communities varied in size from a single family to several hundred people. Often in winter, larger communities were formed to share the food and other necessities provided by the killing of a whale. In spring, these larger communities split into much smaller groups to hunt for fish, seals, caribou, birds and other game. Inuit communities governed themselves by traditional rules, the most important being that everyone helped in the day-to-day activities that ensured the group's survival.

Inuit clothing was made mainly from the skin of seal and caribou. It consisted of a hooded jacket called a parka, trousers, mittens, socks and boots. They often wore a form of goggles made of wood or bone, with small slits or holes to see through. Inuit shelter varied with the season. During summer they lived in wood-framed tents covered with seal or caribou skins. In winter, the Inuit of central and northern Canada built snowhouses made of blocks of hard snow cut with a long knife. We know these houses as igloos. Others built houses of stone and sod (soil held together by the roots of grass). For transport in winter, the Inuit used sleds pulled by dogs. In summer they walked overland and used kayaks and other small boats for water transport.

The Inuit life in Canada changed very little until the 1950s. Then, the hunting of caribou with rifles led to a large drop in the numbers of this animal. At the same time, the fur trade declined. These two changes made a great difference to the livelihood of the Inuit.

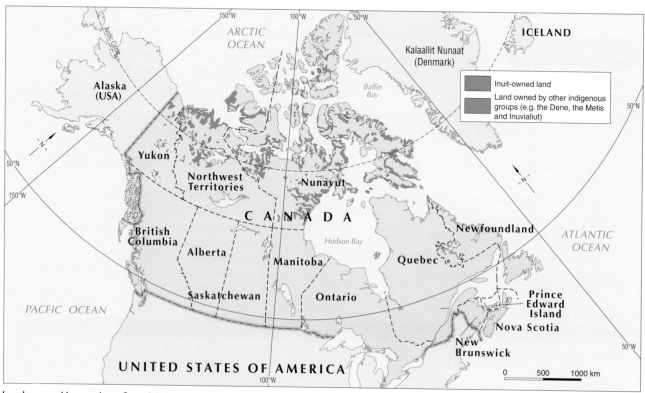

Lands owned by northern Canada's indigenous groups

Response to change

These changes to the Inuit's traditional use of their environment resulted in many of the Inuit people moving to the communities that had grown up around trading posts, government offices and mission churches. Some found work in the construction industry, but many who could not get work began to depend on the Canadian Government for housing and other assistance.

Today the traditional way of life has ended for most Inuit. They wear modern clothing, live in wooden houses and buy most of their food from supermarkets. Most now must adjust to the modern world of work rather than to the physical environment. Unfortunately, about half of the Inuit cannot find permanent employment. The government has assisted Inuit to establish commercial fishing and handicraft cooperatives, such as the one at Cambridge Bay, on Canada's Arctic Victoria Island. Its people live partly off the land, spending varying amounts of time in outcamps where they hunt game such as caribou and musk oxen, and fish for the valuable Arctic char (a fish similar to salmon). They also obtain income from other sources, such as working for the council, their own cooperative and government welfare benefits. Inuit are also expert at making soapstone and ivory carvings and clothing trimmed with exotic furs. They sell these mainly to tourists and they can fetch quite high prices. More recently, Inuit craftwork has found a larger market in Canada and around the world.

Conflict over land rights and the environment

Like many indigenous peoples, land rights have been a problem and a source of conflict for the Inuit community. In 1993, after many years of community action by the Inuit, the Canadian Government passed legislation to create a vast new territory called Nunavut. On 1 April 1999, Nunavut became Canada's third official territory and one of the world's largest native title claims, with the Inuit gaining title to much of this land and the management of its environment.

The traditional Inuit clothing made from animal skins offered most warmth and protection from the harsh environment.

The Inuit believe polar bears are being hunted at sustainable levels. If the polar bear is listed as a threatened species because of climate change, the Inuit will lose income gained by allowing hunters from the US to hunt the animals in Nunavut.

 **GEO*facts***

- Around 55 700 Inuit live in 53 communities across northern Canada.
- Population density is one person per 100 square kilometres.
- Their numbers are growing and may reach about 84 600 by 2016, if present trends continue.

ACTIVITIES

UNDERSTANDING

1. By what name were Inuit people formerly known?
2. Why did the Inuit traditionally live in small communities?
3. Identify the two things that made a difference to the Inuit people's livelihood after the 1950s.
4. Explain how the traditional Inuit lifestyle was adapted to the physical environment.

THINKING AND APPLYING

5. Why do you think that the changes in livelihood resulted in a movement of Inuit from their traditional nomadic hunting activities to living in more permanent settlements. What problems did this bring?

USING YOUR SKILLS

6. Refer to the map 'Lands owned by northern Canada's indigenous groups' opposite.
   a Describe the broad location of Inuit-owned land.
   b Why do you think the Inuit claimed these locations?

GEOTERMS

indigenous people: the descendants of the original inhabitants of an area

Antarctica was the last continent in the world to be discovered. Some parts of it have still not been visited by humans, so we are discovering new things about it all the time. But how much do you know about Antarctica now?

The year is 2014. The front page of your local newspaper is shown below. As you read the main article, some parts of it do not seem true.

You think: 'What great news! Another gold medal for Australia!' But you decide to take a closer look at the 'facts' behind the news report.

- The weather report: could it really be that bad? Well, actually it can. Antarctica is the coldest and windiest place on Earth. The lowest temperature ever recorded was –89.6° Celsius and the maximum about 8° Celsius. Wind speeds during gales can reach 320 kilometres per hour. The Australian explorer Douglas Mawson recorded wind speeds over a period of a month: the average was over 97 kilometres per hour!
- There are no native Antarcticans. The Inuit people are from northern Canada.
- There are no pine forests in Antarctica. The largest plants are a few clumps of grass on the 2 per cent of the continent not covered by ice.
- It snows very little in Antarctica, particularly in the interior, which receives only slightly more snow than the Sahara Desert receives rain. Even so, there have been skiing/snowboarding expeditions in the Vinson Massif.
- It would be extremely surprising to see a polar bear in Antarctica. They live only in the world's northern polar regions.
- Most of Antarctica is too cold for it to rain. Antarctica is the world's driest continent and some of its valleys have received no rain for two million years. Only some of the more northern coastal areas receive occasional rain.
- No roads cross Antarctica. Nor is there a town there called Mawsonia, or any town at all, for that matter. During summer, thousands of scientists live in bases around the continent, but none of them could be called permanent inhabitants.
- Twenty-four hours of sunlight — that can't be right! Well actually it is. For about four months of the year Antarctica receives constant sunlight. The problem with the statement in the 'newspaper' article is that it is said to be occurring in July. July is the middle of Antarctica's winter, when there is no daylight at all.
- Competing in light clothing would be very unwise as the extreme cold can freeze extremities (fingers and toes), causing frostbite. It's not

THE WINTER OLYMPICS

SCOTT BASE   WEATHER –30°C, WINDS TO 120 KM/H

ANTARCTICA — A GREAT SUCCESS

On the second last day of competition at this year's winter Olympics, Australia has picked up its third gold medal in the cross-country skiing. The competition was held in the coastal pine forests of the Ross Ice Shelf and competitors rated the snow conditions as perfect. There is much more snow expected tonight.

In other results, the native Antarcticans, the Inuit, made a clean sweep of the bobsled events. This event was, however, interrupted by the unexpected arrival of a polar bear and her cub.

The outdoor ice-skating events are now set to continue after yesterday's program was washed out in the rain. The 24 hours of sunlight make it easy for organisers to make up time when events are disrupted by the weather.

The ski-jump venue is at Mawsonia, Antarctica's largest city, which has a population of 237 000. Antarctica has proved to be an ideal venue for these games. Daytime temperatures of around –20° Celsius have not been too warm for competitors, who have been able to compete in light clothing. Although much of the continent lies below sea level, there are enough mountains for the alpine events to take place. Antarctica is much smaller than Australia, so spectators can move easily between venues on the excellent roads that criss-cross the continent.

The ski jump venue at Mawsonia, Antarctica's largest city

uncommon for badly frostbitten fingers and toes to later drop off!

- Antarctica is the highest continent on Earth with an average height above sea level of 2300 metres. The highest mountain in Australia, Mount Kosciuszko (2228 metres above sea level) is lower than Antarctica's average height.
- At 14 million square kilometres, Antarctica has roughly twice the area of Australia. In winter it doubles in area as the surrounding oceans freeze. So Antarctica is the coldest, windiest, driest and highest continent. Its features are far too extreme to allow it to host the Winter Olympics! One more thing — the location of the 2014 Winter Olympics is Russia!

Solstices at the poles

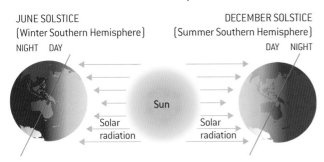

JUNE SOLSTICE
(Winter Southern Hemisphere)
NIGHT   DAY

DECEMBER SOLSTICE
(Summer Southern Hemisphere)
DAY   NIGHT

Sun

Solar radiation

Solar radiation

The Earth's tilt and rotation around the sun causes 24 hours of daylight in summer and 24 hours of darkness in winter at the North and South Poles.

 **GEO*facts*** At the North and South Poles, the sun rises and sets only once each year. During the six months when the sun is above the horizon at the poles, the sun throughout the day constantly moves around the horizon, reaching its highest circuit of the sky in the summer solstice.

ACTIVITIES

UNDERSTANDING

1. Describe the temperature and wind in Antarctica.
2. Why is Antarctica so dry?
3. For how much of the year does Antarctica receive:
   a 24 hours of sunlight
   b 24 hours of darkness?

THINKING AND APPLYING

4. Explain why Antarctica doubles in area every year in winter.
5. Why do you think Antarctica is often described as the world's largest desert?
6. Explain why there are no indigenous Antarcticans.

USING YOUR SKILLS

7. Refer to the diagram 'Solstices at the poles'. Explain why there are 24 hours of daylight in summer, and 24 hours of darkness in winter, at the North and South Poles.
8. Refer to the photograph below.
   a What is the surface the person is walking on?
   b Where do you think he/she is going?
   c Keeping in mind the weather conditions this person is likely to face, describe what you think he/she is wearing.
   d What might this person be carrying in the backpack? What other equipment might he/she be carrying?
   e Explain why this is not a winter scene.

GEOTERMS

solstice: the two times of the year when the sun is furthest from the Equator

Rush hour in Antarctica

8.4 Cold, dry and windy

Antarctica is a land of extremes. It is not only the most isolated continent and the last to be discovered, but also the coldest, windiest and driest place on Earth. The main reason for these climatic extremes is Antarctica's location at the very bottom of the world.

How cold is cold?

On 29 July 1983, Russian scientists at Vostok Base, high on Antarctica's polar plateau, recorded a temperature of −89.6° Celsius, the lowest on record. During the coldest months (July to August), the average temperature at the South Pole is −60° Celsius. During the warmest months (December to January), it rises to a balmy −28° Celsius. At these temperatures your breath freezes and you can see your sneezes fall to the ground as ice!

Why is Antarctica so cold?

There are three main answers to this question:

1. Antarctica's position on the globe means that the sun's rays have to heat much more of the Earth's surface than at other places on the globe.

2. Most of the sun's heat that reaches Antarctica is reflected back into space by the white ice that covers the continent. This also explains why you must always wear sunglasses or goggles in Antarctica.

3. Antarctica is surrounded by the cold waters of the Southern Ocean and this stops warmer water reaching its shores.

Here at the Equator, the sun's rays have to heat only a small piece of the Earth.

Sun's ray

Sun's ray

But down here, each ray has to heat twice as much of the Earth's surface.

How dry is dry?

Most places in Antarctica receive no rain or snow at all. This is because the very cold air contains hardly any of the water vapour needed to create rain or snow. This means that Antarctica is the world's biggest desert. All drinking water in Antarctica comes from melting the ice. Fire fighting becomes very difficult indeed and this is why smoking is banned in most Antarctic bases.

How windy is windy?

Australia's greatest polar explorer, Douglas Mawson, called Antarctica the home of the **blizzard**. He should know. He lived in a wooden hut in the strongest winds ever recorded for two complete Antarctic winters. Mawson's measurements revealed an average wind speed of over 70 kilometres per hour and gusts of over 300 kilometres per hour! His men always carried an ice axe with them to avoid being blown into the sea. One of them, Eric Webb, reported in his diary of having 'lain down flat on the **sastrugi** field, hanging on with fur mitts and fur boots as close as possible to mother Earth and being blown downwind'.

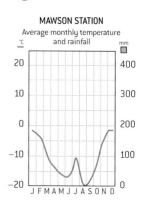

MAWSON STATION
Average monthly temperature and rainfall

Climatic graph for Mawson Station, Antarctica, 67°S, 62°E

Why is Antarctica so windy?

As the air over the polar plateau becomes colder, it becomes denser. Finally, gravity pulls it down off the plateau towards the Antarctic coast. This creates very strong winds, called **katabatic winds**. These can blow continually for weeks on end and carry small pellets of ice. They make life miserable for any human visitor. When these winds are combined with the severe cold, they can be fatal.

At −20° Celsius exposed human flesh begins to freeze when the wind reaches only 14 kilometres per hour.

Blizzard conditions in Antarctica

Sastrugi tend to lie in the direction of the prevailing wind. They certainly remove any idea that Antarctic ice is flat and easy to travel across.

The winds also change the shape of the ice over which they blow, carving it into weird shapes called sastrugi. These shapes range in height from 150 millimetres to two metres. Travelling across sastrugi is extremely difficult because it breaks sledges — and spirits.

Exploring Antarctica

Antarctica's extreme climate has made its exploration extremely arduous and life-threatening.

Early explorers like Shackleton (1907), Mawson (1911), Amundsen and Scott (1910–12) battled blizzards, strong winds, snow and ice, even in the summer months. Scott's fruitless quest to be the first to reach the South Pole was marked by troubles. After failing to reach the South Pole before Amundsen, his party battled gale force winds and blizzards on their journey back to the coast and their ship. Members of the party suffered frostbite, injury and snowblindness. One man, Evans, died after falling into a crevasse and another, Oates, with severe frostbite on his feet, took his own life so that the remaining three in the party might survive. However, a severe blizzard trapped them only 18 kilometres short of a food depot and they all perished.

In 1996, a Norwegian, Borge Ousland, became the first person to cross Antarctica unaided and alone on skis. An attempt the previous year had been abandoned because of severe frostbite.

ACTIVITIES

UNDERSTANDING

1 Describe Antarctica's climate in two sentences.
2 What is the coldest temperature recorded in Antarctica and where did this occur?
3 Describe a blizzard. Use the information in the text and the photograph below to help you.
4 Explain why Antarctica is:
  a so cold
  b so dry
  c so windy.

THINKING AND APPLYING

5 Why is smoking banned at most Antarctic bases?
6 Compare the Antarctic climate with the climate of your local area.
7 Why do you think Antarctic explorers have been prepared to subject themselves to its extremes?

USING YOUR SKILLS

8 a Describe a sastrugi field.
  b Explain how a sastrugi field is formed.
  c How do sastrugi fields make exploring the Antarctic difficult?
9 Refer to the climatic graph for Mawson Station.
  a What is the annual average temperature for the (i) warmest month and (ii) coldest month?
  b What is the annual average rainfall? Why?
10 Refer to the photograph at the top of this page. Explain why the land is not flat and easy to move across.

GEOTERMS

blizzard: a snowstorm accompanied by very strong winds
katabatic winds: strong polar winds that are created as cold air descends from the polar plateau
sastrugi: shapes in the ice that appear due to sculpturing of the wind

It covers 98 per cent of Antarctica. Some of it is millions of years old and five kilometres thick. It crushes mountain ranges, breaks ships, and reflects so much heat that it keeps the planet cooler. It stores 68 per cent of the world's fresh water, but to have a drink you have to spend hours melting it. It is so heavy it holds down Antarctica's mountains. What is it? It is ice — frozen water — and it is the most powerful force in Antarctica. The amount of ice on Antarctica is staggering — 30 million cubic kilometres.

The Antarctic ice sheets

Ice covers the continent of Antarctica to an average depth of about 2500 metres. It has built up over millions of years. Any snow that falls on the surface never melts, but is turned into ice. In Antarctica, the ice has created massive ice sheets. An ice sheet is a large area of ice that completely covers more than 50 000 square kilometres of land. If Antarctica's ice sheets melted, Antarctica would be about half its current size; however sea levels around the world would then be about 60 metres higher, because the melting ice would flow into the oceans.

Scientists are able to measure the thickness of the ice and the shapes of the land below using radar. They have found ice to a maximum depth of 4800 metres near Australia's Casey Station.

Glaciers, shelves, crevasses and bergs

The incredible weight of the Antarctic ice sheets forces them to spread outward. Slow moving rivers of ice called glaciers flow from ice sheets towards the ocean. As they move, glaciers twist and stretch. This causes cracks in the ice called crevasses. Crevasses can be hundreds of metres deep and very dangerous. A thin covering of snow may hide the opening to a crevasse.

The mouth of a glacier spilling into the ocean

Ice shelf in the Antarctic

An iceberg in Antarctica

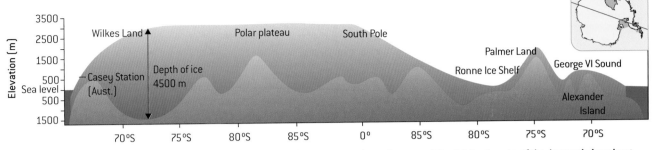

This cross-section, which shows the mountains below the ice sheet, passes through some of the thickest parts of the Antarctic ice sheet.

At the shores of Antarctica, ice sheets and glaciers spill out over the surface of the ocean. Here they form giant stretches of floating freshwater ice that are still anchored to the land. These floating ice sheets are called ice shelves, and they make up 11 per cent of Antarctica's total area.

Icebergs form when chunks break off from glaciers and ice shelves and float out to sea. The biggest icebergs are massive sections of ice shelf. The largest iceberg ever was about 32 000 square kilometres — bigger than Belgium!

Sea ice

As the temperature drops in March each year, the seas around Antarctica freeze solid on the surface. This is called sea ice. It effectively doubles the area of Antarctica each winter.

When summer comes, sea ice breaks up. Older, thicker slabs, or floes, of broken-up sea ice are called pack-ice. Sometimes these slabs float separately; sometimes they are pushed together by winds or currents. If a ship becomes caught in this close pack-ice, and winds blow the floes together, the ship can become stuck and even crushed.

As only one-fifth of an iceberg is visible above the sea, they are a significant shipping hazard. On 14 April 1912, the passenger ship Titanic struck an iceberg in the north Atlantic Ocean and sank, with a loss of 1523 lives.

ACTIVITIES →

UNDERSTANDING

1. How much of the world's fresh water is in Antarctica's ice?
2. Why do Antarctica's ice sheets move?
3. What is an iceberg?

THINKING AND APPLYING

4. Describe what would happen to world sea levels if Antarctica's ice sheets melted.
5. Design a sign warning visitors about the dangers posed by crevasses. Your sign must use pictures and labels.

USING YOUR SKILLS

6. Refer to the cross-section above.
   a Where is the ice thickest?
   b What would happen to this area if the ice were to melt?
   c Suggest a reason for the location of Casey Station.
7. Refer to the three photographs on the page opposite.
   a Are these taken from a ground-level, oblique–aerial or vertical–aerial view?
   b In what season do you think these photographs were taken? Explain your conclusion.
   c What aspects of the information on these pages do you think the photographs best illustrate?
   d Choose one of the photographs and sketch what you would see from an aerial view.

GEOTERMS

iceberg: a huge piece of ice that breaks off a glacier or ice shelf and floats out to sea; most of an iceberg is below sea level

ice sheet: a large area of ice that completely covers more than 50 000 square kilometres of land

ice shelf: the floating edge of an ice sheet that spills out onto the sea; it is composed of freshwater ice

While Antarctica is the world's largest desert, mainly empty of life, the waters that surround it support one of the biggest collections of life on the planet. This is because the very cold waters hold gases such as oxygen much better than warmer waters further north. Also, the windy conditions keep minerals suspended in the water where tiny plants can use them. These plants are eaten by tiny animals. These tiny animals are eaten by bigger animals, which in turn are eaten by bigger animals. The world's biggest animals, the great whales, feed and flourish in these waters. This system, formed by the interactions of the living organisms (plants and animals) and physical elements of environments, is called an **ecosystem**.

To survive in Antarctic waters, animals and birds must be fully protected against the freezing conditions. A human falling into these waters would be dead in minutes. Yet other mammals survive their entire lives here. Antarctic animals survive by:
• having a special layer of fur or feathers to keep them dry
• having a layer of thick fat to keep them warm
• having special chemicals in their blood to stop their blood freezing
• leaving Antarctica (migrating) when it becomes too cold. In fact, only one creature stays on the continent all winter — the amazing emperor penguin (and a few humans, too).

The most numerous of the penguins, the chinstrap penguin nests on the first rocks to become ice-free each spring.

Poorly adapted to Antarctica, with no blubber and very little fur, humans rely on food and shelter brought in from other places in the world. Largely migratory, most flee north for the winter.

Ruthless scavengers, skua prey heavily on the eggs and chicks of penguins and other birds.

Like all penguins, Adelie penguins are designed for life in the sea. Their waterproof feathers, insulating layer of fat, heavy bones and flipper-like wings allow them to hunt for krill.

The crab-eater seal accounts for over half of all of the world's seals. It actually eats very few crabs, preferring krill.

Virtually all Antarctica's wildlife depends on krill directly or indirectly. A single krill is about six centimetres long and looks a bit like a shrimp. It feeds on tiny plants suspended in the water.

The leopard seal eats penguins, other seals, fish and squid. It uses both sonar (sound) and radar (movement) to find food. Its whiskers detect movement, allowing it to find prey in complete darkness.

Sperm whales are toothed whales that feed on squid, fish and octopuses. They are the world's deepest-diving mammal, reaching depths of two kilometres.

Snow petrels breed up to 180 kilometres away from the sea (their feeding ground) on mountain peaks that poke through the ice sheet. Their preferred food is krill.

With a huge wingspan of 3.5 metres, wandering albatrosses have been known to travel 15 000 kilometres in a single flight in search of food.

Like most of Antarctica's flying birds, the southern giant petrel scavenges for food at sea, ripping apart seal and whale carcasses as well as feeding on krill.

Penguins are the only birds that migrate by swimming. Magellanic penguins migrate as far north as Rio de Janeiro in Brazil and Tetas Point near Antofagasta in northern Chile.

Humpback whales have plates of baleen (rather than teeth), which act like a food sieve. They feed on fish and swim circles around schools of krill to produce a 'bubble net'. When the krill are forced into a small area, the whales lunge in with mouths open.

Arctic terns migrate between the polar regions each year, making a journey of 20 000 kilometres each summer — the longest journey made by any bird.

The only Antarctic dolphin, the hourglass dolphin lives in schools of up to 40 animals.

The emperor penguin is the only bird that breeds in Antarctica during the winter. The male incubates the egg by resting it on his feet, huddling together with other males for nine weeks. When the female returns from the sea, the male travels over 100 kilometres to the ocean to feed on squid and fish.

Killer whales are toothed whales that feed on seals, penguins and even much larger whales. They hunt in packs called pods.

ACTIVITIES ⊕

UNDERSTANDING

1. Identify three reasons why Antarctic waters have one of the largest collections of animals on the planet.
2. Define the term 'ecosystem'.
3. Explain how animals survive in the harsh conditions of the Antarctic.

THINKING AND APPLYING

4. All animals in Antarctica are linked by what is called a food web. Each animal eats another and in most cases is food for another. Copy an enlarged version of the following diagram and place these animals into the relevant empty boxes: killer whale, emperor penguin, sperm whale, crab-eater seal and snow petrel. Now add the skua (box and label) to your web.

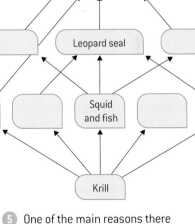

5. One of the main reasons there are so many crab-eater seals now is that humpback whales were hunted almost to extinction. Use your diagram to explain this.
6. Suggest what would happen if krill were to become extinct.
7. Choose one of the animals in the food web diagram above. Use other information on these pages to sketch it in your notebook. Add labels to show how this animal has adapted to life in Antarctica.

It is only recently that people have had an impact on Antarctica. For centuries, the continent lay isolated and protected from the outside world by its remote location and cold climate.

Scientific bases

Antarctica today is the temporary home of over 4000 people in summer and 1000 in winter. Most are scientists and support staff living in one of the Antarctic bases operated by more than 30 countries. Australia has three permanent bases in Antarctica: Casey, Mawson and Davis Stations, and five temporary summer bases. There is even a permanent scientific base at the South Pole: the American Amundsen-Scott Base. You can use a gym, see a doctor, visit a library, hire a DVD and phone home from the South Pole.

Most of Antarctica's scientific stations are located on the coast so that people and supplies can be brought in by boat and helicopter. They are also situated on the 2 per cent of Antarctica not covered in ice, as stations built on ice tend to sink under their own weight. This is because the heat they generate can melt the ice around and under them.

Scientists are prepared to live in the worst conditions in the world because Antarctica is an amazing natural laboratory. They study the world's weather, climate, marine and land biology, glaciers, magnetics, human physiology and geology. Scientists also study the effects of human activities on the environment. Global warming (the warming of the atmosphere, which many scientists believe is caused by burning fossil fuels) is now a very important research area. For example, scientists can find evidence of what the Earth's climate, vegetation and animals were like many thousands of years ago by drilling cores down into the ice (see chapter 13). Another example of research being done is discovering how krill, penguins and other marine life are affected by warmer air and ocean temperatures.

Research also continues into the thinning of the ozone layer over Antarctica, which was mainly caused by global use of chlorofluorocarbon (CFC) gases produced by spray cans, air-conditioners and foam plastics. The ozone layer protects us and other living things from the harmful effects of the sun. Countries have drastically cut back the production of CFCs since the late 1980s, but CFCs already in the atmosphere have a life of over 100 years.

Impact of bases

Most bases are located in ice-free areas on the coast. These sites are the most suitable for people, buildings and the storage of fuels. However, these are the same sites where most of Antarctica's wildlife live, nest or breed. Bases on these sites may have a negative impact on the native flora and fauna.

Bases also produce waste, including sewage, chemicals and rubbish. Fuel to power vehicles, heat buildings, cook food and generate electricity could spill or leak. This could have a major effect on Antarctica's wildlife. In 1989, an Argentine ship, carrying supplies and tourists to an Argentine base, sank three kilometres off the coast of Antarctica. Over one million litres of diesel spilled into the sea, affecting krill and seabird populations.

Mawson Station, Antarctica

All food and equipment must be tightly packed and covered.

Snowmobiles pull the sledges.

GEOskills TOOLBOX

ANNOTATING (LABELLING) A PHOTOGRAPH OR LINE DRAWING

Annotated images enable the reader to absorb a lot of information with just a few words. The information is passed on via both the short label and the visual part of the image (photograph, diagram or map).

- Add labels around the outside of the image. Keep words to a minimum. Labels do not always have to be full sentences.
- Place labels so that they are as close as possible to the relevant item in the image.
- Use arrows to connect each label with the item it refers to in the image.

Members of a geology team pack up their sledges for a practice session in which they will cross the sea ice.

In the days when sledges were pulled by dogs, the driver would have stood here.

This scientist is launching a balloon that carries sensitive instruments high into the atmosphere. These instruments will measure the amount of ozone in the atmosphere and send the data back down to the scientists. The balloon will eventually deflate and fall to Earth. The Earth's ozone layer has developed a hole above Antarctica, leading to an increase in ultraviolet light reaching the oceans. This may kill krill, which would be disastrous for Antarctica's food chain.

GEOTERMS

global warming: the warming of the atmosphere and the Earth, which many scientists believe is caused by the burning of fossil fuels

ozone layer: a layer of gases that surround the Earth and filter out dangerous ultraviolet light from the sun

ACTIVITIES ➔

UNDERSTANDING

1. Why is it only recently that people have had an impact on Antarctica?
2. Name Australia's permanent bases in Antarctica.
3. What do scientists study in Antarctica?

THINKING AND APPLYING

4. Describe the ideal location for a scientific station in Antarctica.
5. Why is the state of the world's ozone layer so important to scientists?

USING YOUR SKILLS

6. Refer to the photograph of Mawson Station opposite. Make a line drawing of the photograph and annotate it to show the important features. (For more information about using photographs and line drawings, see pages 58–9.)

8.8 Antarctica and ecological sustainability

Ecological sustainability means ensuring that we can meet the needs of the present generation of people without compromising the ability of future generations to meet their needs. Using a new resource sustainably means that it can be used forever without ever running out and without damaging the environment.

Antarctica and the seas that surround it contain valuable resources. Many of these have been exploited for profit despite the fact that the continent is protected by extreme isolation, mountainous seas and the world's worst weather.

The Antarctic Treaty

Even though no-one lives permanently in Antarctica, many nations have been involved in the exploration and development of the continent. By the mid 1950s, Australia, New Zealand, the United Kingdom, France and Argentina were actively involved in exploration. These countries declared territorial claims over parts of Antarctica. Other countries continued to carry out fishing, whaling, scientific research and mineral exploration.

Fortunately, people eventually began to realise that this unique wilderness deserved to be protected. In 1958, 12 countries agreed to preserve Antarctica. This led to an international agreement called the **Antarctic Treaty**, which came into force in 1961.

The treaty covers the area south of 60°S latitude. It has been signed by more than 40 countries and they meet regularly to discuss issues affecting Antarctica. The Antarctic Treaty:
- prohibits military activity
- protects the Antarctic environment
- fosters scientific research
- recognises the need to protect Antarctica from uncontrolled destruction and interference by people.

A joint agreement known as the Madrid Protocol was signed by 40 nations in 1991. It outlines a legal framework of environmental standards designed to protect the continent and its ecosystems.

Ocean resources

Whalers and sealers were the first people to recognise that the oceans surrounding Antarctica were a rich and valuable resource. The first whaling station in Antarctica began operation in 1904. That year the whalers used harpoons loaded with high explosives and fired from cannons to kill 195 whales. The protective layer of blubber fat on the whales was melted down to produce oil to burn in lamps. The baleen plates of the toothless whales were used in women's corsets and skirts. Baleen plates are bone-like plates in the mouths of some whales, through which they strain food. Commercial whaling was banned in 1986.

Fur seals and elephant seals were hunted and shot almost to extinction in Antarctica and the surrounding islands in the 1900s. Hundreds of thousands — perhaps millions — of seals were killed for their fur and their blubber. Whaling is now allowed in Antarctica only for scientific purposes. However, Japan and some other countries still kill hundreds of whales each year. They claim the whales are caught for 'scientific purposes', but anti-whaling groups suspect the whales end up in fish markets.

Today, overfishing and krill harvesting have emerged as major problems. Some fish species, such as the Patagonian toothfish, have been hunted almost to extinction. Around 400 000 tonnes of krill are being taken from Antarctica each year to be used mainly for animal feed. This could impact on Antarctic animals such as whales, penguins and seals because krill is their main food source.

Tourism

Antarctica offers one of the last frontiers for tourism. It is seen as a destination that is both different and challenging. It is one of the last real **wilderness** areas in the world. Antarctic tourism started about 35 years ago. The number of tourists visiting Antarctica is increasing each year.

Most tourists reach Antarctica by cruise ship from Chile, and in recent years, from New Zealand and Australia. The most frequent type of air tourism is chartered flights over Antarctica for sight-seeing.

A sperm whale breaching

Minerals and energy

Antarctica has extensive coal, iron ore and oil resources. Of these, oil is by far the most sought-after resource. Extracting Antarctica's resources would be very difficult, due to the depth of the ice cover and the extreme coldness of the region. The risk of environmental damage would also be very high.

The Antarctic Treaty did not control mining activities. In 1982, the treaty nations started developing a Convention on the Regulation of Antarctic Mineral Resource Activities (CRAMRA). Discussions centred around who owned the mineral resources and how environmental damage from mining could be contained. The environmental group Greenpeace supported the view that mining in Antarctica should be banned altogether. In 1991, the Protocol to the Antarctic Treaty on Environmental Protection was signed in Madrid. The Madrid Protocol prohibits all mining activities for 50 years, other than for scientific research.

The number of tourists visiting Antarctica has been rapidly increasing in recent years.

GEOskills TOOLBOX

INTERPRETING AND CONSTRUCTING LINE GRAPHS

Line graphs are very useful for showing change over time, and to compare data.

For more information about interpreting and constructing line graphs go to page 164.

- Include a full title.
- Note any significant rises or falls, and what these depict.
- Lable both axes.
- Plot years on the horizontal axis.
- Mark divisions on axes in even amounts (e.g. 5s, 10s, 100s).
- If there is more than one graph line, use different colours.
- Source line shows where data have come from.

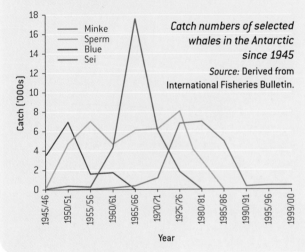

Minke
Sperm
Blue
Sei

Catch numbers of selected whales in the Antarctic since 1945

Source: Derived from International Fisheries Bulletin.

GEOTERMS

wilderness: an unchanged natural area remote from human settlement

ACTIVITIES

UNDERSTANDING

1. What does it mean to use a resource 'sustainably'?
2. Outline the nature and provisions of the Antarctic Treaty.
3. How were whales and seals hunted in the past?
4. Define 'wilderness'. Why do you think an area of wilderness would be a tourist attraction?
5. Identify and name the mineral and energy resources of Antarctica.
6. Describe the significance of the Antarctic Treaty.
7. Outline the present problems with Antarctica's ocean resources. Why is the harvesting of krill a potential problem?

THINKING AND APPLYING

8. If tourism were allowed to develop unchecked in Antarctica, how might it change the region's characteristics?
9. In pairs, design an advertising campaign either to (a) attract tourists to Antarctica or (b) keep tourists away.
10. Discuss as a class: 'Should tourism be allowed in Antarctica?'

USING YOUR SKILLS

11. Refer to the line graph to the left.
    a Which whale was caught in greatest numbers over the period 1945/46 to 1975/76?
    b What is the overall trend for catch numbers of whales?
12. Display the following data on a line graph and continue your line until 2010 (in line with the trend). How many tourists do you think will visit Antarctica in 2010?

Tourists to Antarctica

Year	Tourist numbers
2000–01	12 348
2001–02	11 588
2002–03	13 571
2003–04	19 858
2004–05	22 712
2005–06	26 245
2006–07	28 530

Source: Based on data from International Association of Antarctic Tour Operators.

In the 1770s, Captain James Cook circumnavigated (sailed all the way around) Antarctica without sighting land. He concluded that if land was to be found beyond the sea of ice, 'the world would not be benefited by it'. We now know much more about the value of Antarctica, including the fact that its ice helps keep the world's climate and sea level steady.

The term **climate change** means any change in climate over time whether due to natural processes or human activities. Evidence of the current change in our climate includes an increase in average global temperatures; ice melting in polar and mountain regions; rising sea levels; and an increase in extreme weather events. The observable trend of rising world

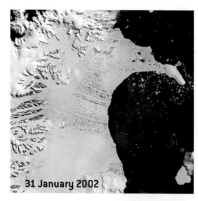

31 January 2002

23 February 2002

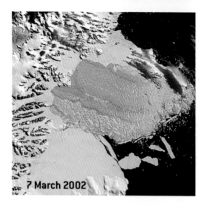

7 March 2002

The sequence of images shows the Larsen B Ice Shelf breaking up in 2002. The main collapse is obvious in the last scene, where the water is shown as light blue amid thousands of icebergs and ice chunks.

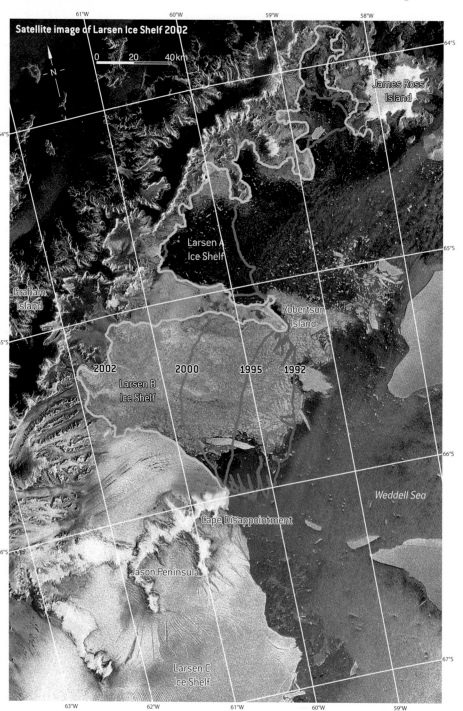

Satellite image of Larsen Ice Shelf 2002

James Ross Island

Larsen A Ice Shelf

Graham Island

Robertson Island

2002   2000   1995   1992

Larsen B Ice Shelf

Weddell Sea

Cape Disappointment

Jason Peninsula

Larsen C Ice Shelf

ESA Envisat, ASAS instrument

temperatures over the last century, particularly during the last couple of decades, is known as global warming. Most scientists agree that this increase in temperature is due to human activities, especially the burning of fossil fuels such as oil, coal and natural gas.

A crack through the Larsen B Ice Shelf

Melting ice

Ice shelves are thick plates of freshwater ice that float on the ocean around the coast of Antarctica. The ice shelves are fed by glaciers moving outward from Antarctica towards the ocean. When the ice reaches the coast, it forms huge ice shelves, many of which are around 200 metres thick. The ice shelves extend northwards to warmer ocean areas where they gradually melt and break up, either forming icebergs or disappearing into the sea.

The ice sheets have been retreating and becoming smaller for over 40 years. Scientists believe that the cause of the retreating ice shelves is strong climate warming in Antarctica. The rate of warming has been approximately 0.5° Celsius every ten years.

In early 2002, a portion of the Larsen B Ice Shelf, a large floating ice mass on the western side of the Antarctic Peninsula, suddenly disintegrated. The floating ice shelf splintered into thousands of icebergs following one of the warmest Antarctic summers on record. More than 3000 square kilometres of floating ice, which had survived for thousands of years, broke up in just 35 days.

 **GEO*facts***

The polar regions at the North and South Poles store 70 per cent of the world's fresh water in the form of ice and snow. If it all melted, the sea level would rise by nearly 65 metres.

ACTIVITIES →

UNDERSTANDING
1. List four indicators of climate change.
2. What do most scientists see as the cause of global warming?
3. How are ice shelves formed?
4. What event in Antarctica, in 2002, supported the theory of global warming and climate change?

USING YOUR SKILLS
5. Refer to the diagrams of glaciers and ice shelves below, and to the satellite images opposite.
   a What do the diagrams show that the satellite images do not?
   b What do the satellite images show that the diagrams do not?
   c Which visual presentation explains it better in your opinion?

GEOTERMS

climate change: any change in climate over time, whether due to natural processes or human activities

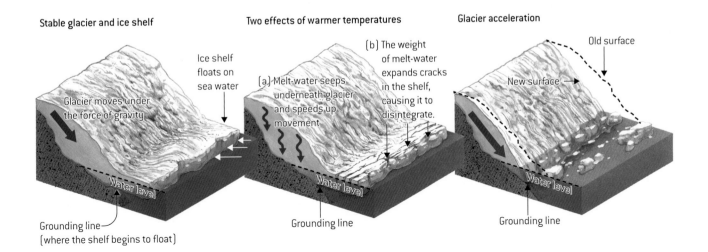

Stable glacier and ice shelf

Glacier moves under the force of gravity

Ice shelf floats on sea water

Water level

Grounding line (where the shelf begins to float)

Two effects of warmer temperatures

(a) Melt-water seeps underneath glacier and speeds up movement

(b) The weight of melt-water expands cracks in the shelf, causing it to disintegrate.

Water level

Grounding line

Glacier acceleration

Old surface

New surface

Water level

Grounding line

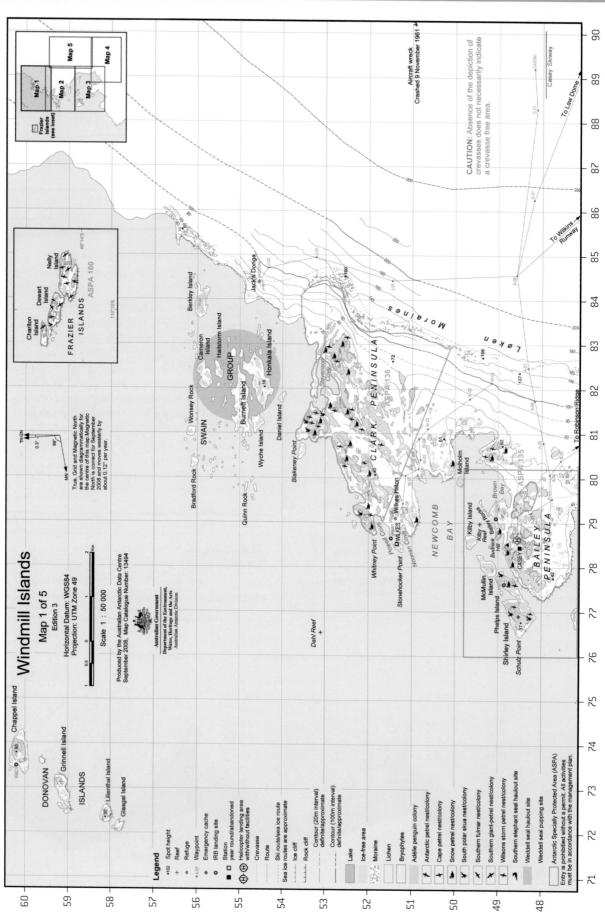

Windmill Islands

Map 1 of 5
Edition 3

Horizontal Datum: WGS84
Projection: UTM Zone 49

Scale 1 : 50 000

Produced by the Australian Antarctic Data Centre
September 2008, Map Catalogue Number: 13494

Australian Government
Department of the Environment,
Water, Heritage and the Arts
Australian Antarctic Division

True, Grid and Magnetic North
are shown diagrammatically for
the centre of this map. Magnetic
North is correct for September
2008 and moves westerly by
about 0.12° per year.

Legend

•102	Spot height
+	Reef
◆	Refuge
◆	Waypoint
◆▲07	Emergency cache
○	IRB landing site
■ □ ⊕ Ⓗ	Station year round/abandoned Helicopter landing area with/without facilities
	Crevasse
	Route
	Ski route/sea ice route
	Sea ice routes are approximate
	Ice cliff
	Rock cliff
	Contour (20m interval) definite/approximate
	Contour (100m interval) definite/approximate
	Lake
	Ice-free area
	Moraine
	Lichen
	Bryophytes
	Adélie penguin colony
	Antarctic petrel nest/colony
	Cape petrel nest/colony
	Snow petrel nest/colony
	South polar skua nest/colony
	Southern fulmar nest/colony
	Southern giant-petrel nest/colony
	Wilsons storm petrel nest/colony
	Weddell elephant seal haulout site
	Weddell seal haulout site
	Weddell seal pupping site
	Antarctic Specially Protected Area (ASPA) Entry is prohibited without a permit. All activities must be in accordance with the management plan.

CAUTION: Absence of the depiction of
crevasses does not necessarily indicate
a crevasse free area.

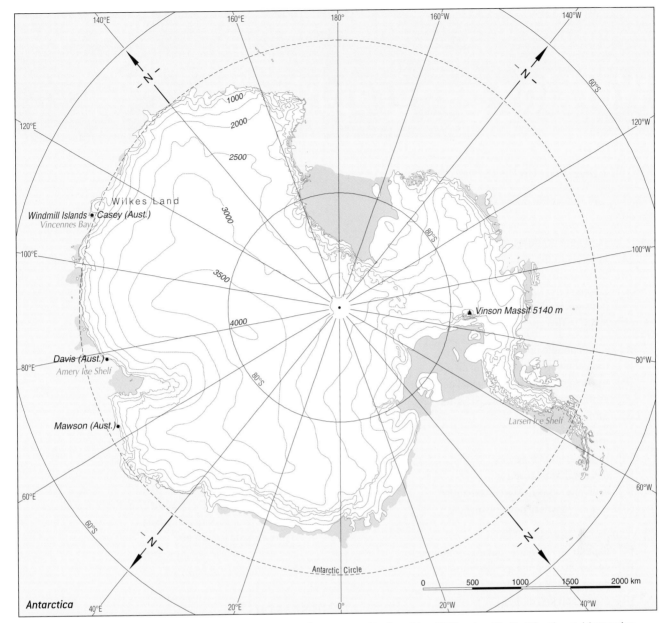

The Windmill Islands (centred 66°15'S, 110°33'E; opposite page) are situated in the midst of Wilkes Land in East Continental Antarctica (above). They lie in the north east of Vincennes Bay, and to the western side of the Law Dome (a small icecap 1300 m high and 200 km in diameter) on a north-south orientated length of coastline.

ACTIVITIES ⊙

USING YOUR SKILLS
Use the topographic map opposite to answer questions 1 to 4.

1. Estimate the distance from Casey Station to the aircraft wreck. In which direction is the aircraft wreck from Casey?

2. Identify the features of the physical environment located at the following area references (AR):
   a. 7653
   b. 7954
   c. 8152.

3. Identify the physical features of the environment at the following grid references (GR):
   a. 821544
   b. 775485
   c. 721578.

4. Identify the features of the human environment located at the following grid references (GR):
   a. 785485
   b. 785514
   c. 844547.

5. Refer to the map above. What direction are the Windmill Islands from Vinson Massif?

Working geographically

KNOWLEDGE AND UNDERSTANDING

Select the alternative A, B, C or D that best answers the question.

1. Polar lands are broadly located
   - (A) at 60° latitude.
   - (B) between the North Pole and the Arctic Circle.
   - (C) between the North Pole and the Arctic Circle and between the South Pole and the Antarctic Circle.
   - (D) in Antarctica and the Arctic.

2. Indigenous people are
   - (A) the people who once lived in an area.
   - (B) the descendants of the original people of an area.
   - (C) ethnic people with territorial rights.
   - (D) former warriors.

3. Antarctica
   - (A) has very little snow.
   - (B) has constant snowfalls.
   - (C) is an area of very high precipitation.
   - (D) is an area where polar bears live.

4. Virtually all Antarctic wildlife
   - (A) depend on krill either directly or indirectly.
   - (B) seasonally migrate to high latitudes.
   - (C) depend on seaweed for a staple food.
   - (D) depend on krill directly.

5. The reason that Antarctica is so cold is that
   - (A) it is surrounded by the cold waters of the Southern Ocean.
   - (B) most of the heat that reaches Antarctica is reflected back into space by the white ice.
   - (C) the sun's rays have to heat much more of the Earth's surface in Antarctica.
   - (D) all of the above.

6. The Madrid Protocol was drawn up mainly to
   - (A) enable scientific whaling.
   - (B) protect the wilderness of the region.
   - (C) monitor exploration of minerals and energy.
   - (D) divide Antarctica equally amongst the global community.

7. A food web is
   - (A) a series of animals dependent on each other in their feeding habits.
   - (B) a series of organisms dependent on each other in their feeding habits.
   - (C) plants being eaten by animals that, in turn, are eaten by herbivorous animals.
   - (D) plants being eaten by a series of predators.

8. Katabatic winds
   - (A) are aerobically based.
   - (B) are gravity-driven winds.
   - (C) increase in intensity with altitude.
   - (D) cause frostbite.

9. Antarctica is at risk from
   - (A) climate change.
   - (B) too many tourists.
   - (C) overfishing.
   - (D) all of the above.

10. An indicator of climate change affecting Antarctica is
    - (A) the disappearance of whales.
    - (B) retreating ice sheets.
    - (C) an increase in windy weather.
    - (D) an increase in snowfall.

RESEARCH

11. Until recently, many people thought that the vast expanses of the Southern Ocean of Antarctica were so rich in marine life that their sustainability would never be in doubt. Research has shown, however, that the population of many species is decreasing rapidly.

    With a partner, select a species (such as whales or seals) and, using your favourite internet search engine, research the sustainability of your chosen species. The topics you should cover are:

    a characteristics of the species

    b threats to the sustainability of the species

    c actions to preserve the species.

ASSESS HOW HUMAN ACTIVITIES CHANGE PLACES

12 Refer to the article 'Saving the last frontier'.

a Explain the title of the news article.

b Who are the 'aliens' in Antarctica and how do they travel there?

c Explain how these aliens have had an impact on World Heritage-listed Macquarie Island.

d What response have governments made to deal with this impact?

e Explain the meaning of the last sentence in the article.

13 Refer to this photo of tourists in Antarctica. What potential impacts might the activity in which they are engaged have on the environment?

Saving the last frontier

BY VINCENT ROSS

There's an alien invasion under way, and the polar regions are in the front line of a fight to protect the world.

ALIENS living in Antarctica and its associated Southern Ocean islands have become the target of intense research by Australian scientists during International Polar Year (IPY).

Covering two polar seasons, from March 2007, to March 2009, IPY includes thousands of scientists from more than 60 nations involved in more than 200 research projects in both the Arctic and Antarctic.

A key project initiated by the Australian Antarctic Division is Aliens in Antarctica, examining the exposure over the past 200 years of the southern polar ecosystems to alien species including microbes, fungi, grasses, sedges, insects and feral mammals such as cats and rats.

Each year, about 40 000 people, including scientists, researchers, technicians and tourists, go to the Antarctic, with the potential of unintentionally carrying alien life in the form of seeds, insects or their eggs, and bacteria in soil particles.

These can be carried on a variety of personal equipment including clothes, shoes, day-packs, camera tripods, as well as on fresh food and other cargo.

Invasive species can have a dramatic impact on habitat, which, coupled with changes in climate, can have a devastating effect on polar mammals and birdlife.

An example is Macquarie Island, 1500 km south of Australia in the Southern Ocean.

It is home to more than four million birds and is one of the world's most-important seabird nesting habitats. It is also a haven for four threatened albatross species, and is the only remaining Australian nesting site of the grey-headed albatross.

Following intense lobbying by World Wildlife Fund–Australia and polar tour-operator Peregrine Adventures, the Tasmanian and Commonwealth Governments jointly committed $24.6 million to a pest eradication program targeting rats and rabbits on the World Heritgage-listed island to help protect its fragile ecology.

Since the eradication of feral cats on the island in the 1980s, rabbit numbers have exploded from 10 000 to 100 000, killing tussock grasses previously used as bird nesting sites and causing major erosion and large landslips. Twenty landslips were recorded in a single month, killing hundreds of nesting king pengiuns.

Rats are also damaging the breeding cycles of petrel by killing both adults and chicks in their nests.

Never in human history have people been made more aware of their impact on the planet and on the animals with which we share it.

Source: The Sunday Mail, 13 July 2008.

Interactivity

FACT FINDER: 'ANTARCTIC ANIMALS'

While Antarctica is the world's largest desert, mainly empty of life, the waters that surround it support one of the biggest collections of life on the planet. In this interactive Fact Finder game, you will race against the clock to identify Antarctic animals from a series of clues. You must think quickly and carefully. Clicking on the wrong marker in the scene will lose you time; but, if you select the right marker, you'll receive bonus time.

SEARCHLIGHT ID: INT-0957

I use both sonar and radar to find my food.

My whiskers detect movement, allowing me to find prey in complete darkness.

I am a leopard seal.

Interactivity

TIME OUT: 'POLAR LANDS'

In this exciting interactivity, you must identify whether a series of images are from the Arctic or Antarctic. While both are polar regions, they have unique characteristics and are home to different plants and animals. You must think quickly before your time runs out.

SEARCHLIGHT ID: INT-0958

Is this scene from the Arctic or Antarctic?

Arctic

Antarctic

These ICT activities are available in this chapter's Student Resources tab inside your eBookPLUS. Visit www.jacplus.com.au to locate your digital resources.

Learning object

VIRTUAL FIELDWORK

The purpose of virtual fieldwork is to investigate the characteristics of a region, and the physical processes and human activities that form and transform the region. Because of its virtual nature, fieldwork can take place on a local, regional or global scale.

Virtual fieldwork is intended to be as real as possible, with the added advantage of interactive design. You are encouraged to participate in virtual activities to enhance your understanding and appreciation of a region and improve your geographical skills. The interactive fieldwork journal in this learning object will help you organise your fieldwork notes and prepare a final report.

Antarctica

Through an inquiry-based approach, you will discover answers to the following questions:

1. What is Antarctica's physical environment like?
2. Who lives in Antarctica?
3. What impact have humans had on Antarctica?
4. How is Antarctica managed?

Download this interactive learning object and install it on your computer to investigate the issues surrounding Antarctica by:

- exploring the plethora of data, photos, maps and drawings
- completing interactive activities
- taking virtual tours.

SEARCHLIGHT ID: LO-0339

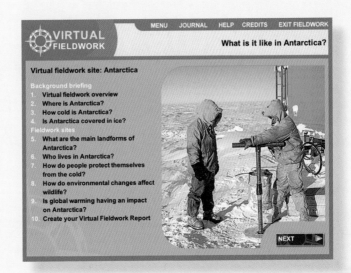

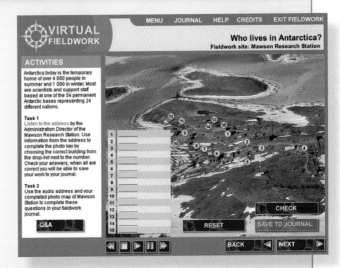

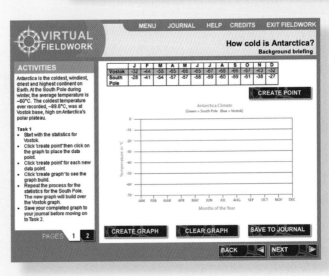

9 The changing nature of the world

INQUIRY QUESTIONS

+ What is globalisation?
+ Why is globalisation occurring?
+ What perspectives do people have about globalisation?
+ What are the impacts of globalisation?

Trade and the movement of people and ideas around the world have occurred for centuries. However, during the last 50 years, vast improvements in transport and in information and communication technologies have encouraged a greater interconnectedness between countries and people everywhere.

Globalisation is the breakdown of traditional barriers between nations. Faster and cheaper flows of goods, money and information around the world have raised standards of living in many countries. But the gains of globalisation are not evenly spread. Many developing countries, for example in Africa, remain in poverty.

GEOskills TOOLBOX

+ Interpreting percentage bar graphs (page 202)
+ Interpreting a cartoon (page 208)

Globalisation brings people around the world closer together through the flow of people, goods, money and information.

As an Australian student living in the twenty-first century, you are part of the global village. Many of your clothes are probably made in China; your tea might come from India or your coffee from Brazil; and your mobile phone and the family car might have been assembled in South Korea. You can move money around the world at the touch of a computer key. In most countries, you can eat McDonald's, drink Coca-Cola, buy jeans and watch your favourite shows on satellite TV.

The globalisation process

Globalisation is the breakdown of traditional barriers between nations. It allows the movement of people, goods, money and information across international borders. Globalisation is not new — people, goods, money and ideas have moved around the world for centuries. But over the last 50 years, the globalisation process has accelerated due to vast improvements in transport, and in information and communication technologies (ICT). This has encouraged a greater interconnectedness between countries and people everywhere.

Factors contributing to globalisation

The following are the main factors contributing to globalisation.
- Advances in transport technology, such as faster air transport and huge container ships, have made it possible to easily and quickly move people and goods between countries.
- Developments in ICT, especially the internet, have slashed the cost and vastly improved the speed at which information and money is moved around the world.
- Growth of world trade, due to advances in transport and ICT, has reduced barriers to trade (such as lower tariffs) and increased trade agreements between countries.

1500–1850

1850–1930

1930–1950s

The shrinking globe — the world grew smaller in the nineteenth century due to improvements in transport and communications. This 'shrinking' has accelerated in the twentieth century.

1960s

2006

Horse-drawn coach and sailing ship: 14 km/h

Steam train: 120 km/h
Steamship: 70 km/h

Propeller aircraft: 600–800 km/h

Jet aircraft: 1000–1500 km/h
Satellite messages: 30 to 60 seconds

Internet message transfers information around the world in one quarter of a second.

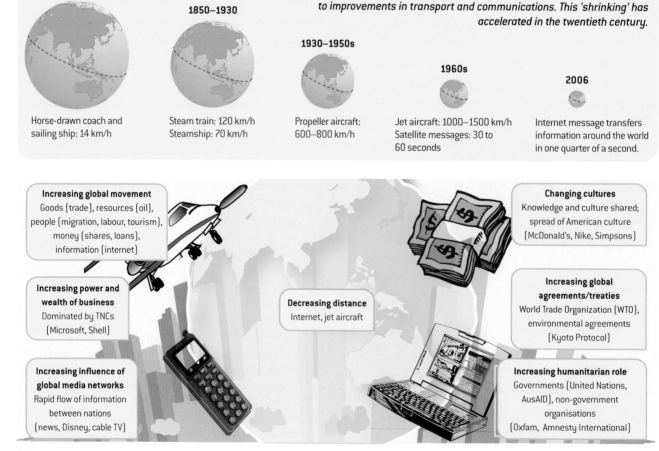

Increasing global movement
Goods (trade), resources (oil), people (migration, labour, tourism), money (shares, loans), information (internet)

Increasing power and wealth of business
Dominated by TNCs (Microsoft, Shell)

Increasing influence of global media networks
Rapid flow of information between nations (news, Disney, cable TV)

Decreasing distance
Internet, jet aircraft

Changing cultures
Knowledge and culture shared; spread of American culture (McDonald's, Nike, Simpsons)

Increasing global agreements/treaties
World Trade Organization (WTO), environmental agreements (Kyoto Protocol)

Increasing humanitarian role
Governments (United Nations, AusAID), non-government organisations (Oxfam, Amnesty International)

The globalisation process

The Simpsons is a hugely successful television show, shown in over 70 countries and dubbed into at least 20 languages.

- Growth of **transnational corporations (TNCs)** — these large companies, who buy their inputs from around the world, tend to manufacture goods in low-cost locations and sell them in many different countries.
- Cultural factors — increasingly mobile populations (tourism, people living and working outside their home country) and the widespread influence of global media networks (global TV news services such as CNN, entertainment channels such as Disney).

Perspectives

As a geographer, it is important to understand different views or **perspectives**. For example, some people think globalisation is a positive process because it leads to economic growth. **Free trade** between countries develops new markets and allows companies to sell more products and hire more workers. Companies and workers become wealthier and standards of living improve.

Others argue that free trade occurs only where there is unrestricted movement of exports and imports. Trade barriers have been reduced for manufactured goods, but many developed countries use tariffs and **subsidies** to protect their farmers from agricultural imports. Eliminating these barriers would greatly benefit the poorest countries because they rely most heavily on agricultural exports.

The rise of global businesses and organisations is sometimes seen as a threat. Some TNCs are wealthier than many countries. International organisations such as the United Nations can set rules and impose penalties on nations. On the other hand, the UN is the driving force behind important international agreements; for example, the Kyoto Protocol aims to limit global greenhouse gas emissions that are causing climate change.

ACTIVITIES

UNDERSTANDING

1. In your own words, define the term 'globalisation'.
2. Why has the globalisation process accelerated during the last 50 years?
3. List five main factors that have contributed to globalisation.
4. What is free trade?
5. Name an important international organisation that attempts to solve global problems.

THINKING AND APPLYING

6. List three different products you use regularly, such as your shoes or your computer.
   a What is the brand name of each product?
   b In which country was each product made?
   c Compare your list with other class members, noting similarities or differences. Did this activity support the idea that we live in a global village? Why or why not?

USING YOUR SKILLS

7. Refer to the diagram of the globalisation process. Explain how globalisation has created a global village that brings people all over the world closer together.
8. Refer to the diagram of the shrinking globe. The distance from Sydney, Australia to London, England is about 17 000 kilometres. Calculate how long the journey would have taken in:
   • 1840   • 1920   • 1950   • 1965.

GEOTERMS

globalisation: the breakdown of traditional barriers between nations and a trend towards faster and cheaper movement around the world of people, goods, money and information

global village: the whole world considered as being like a village, where one individual can communicate with any other and where everyone is part of a web of economic, social, cultural and political relationships

transnational corporation (TNC): a large business organisation that has a home base in one country and operates partially owned or wholly owned businesses in other countries

Technology has played a major role in accelerating globalisation. Breakthroughs in transport technologies and in ICT have increased the speed and reduced the cost of moving people, goods, money and information around the world. Globalisation has raised standards of living in many countries, but the gains of globalisation are not evenly spread.

Changes in transport

Advances in transport have encouraged rapid growth in world travel and trade. Faster air transport and developments in ocean shipping are the most important of these.

Faster air transport

Jet aircraft have brought the world's major cities closer together — to within a day or less in travelling time. This has helped:
- tourism become a boom industry
- workforces become more mobile, as companies can send employees around the world to oversee operations in other countries
- perishable products, such as seafood and flowers, to be sent to distant markets.

Ocean shipping

Two major technologies transformed shipping, making it more efficient and economical. One was the introduction of super tankers for bulk cargoes such as oil and wheat. The other was containerisation, in which goods are packed into huge containers at the factory, taken by train or truck to the port and quickly loaded onto container ships by specialised cranes. The vast majority of goods are transported around the world by sea.

Changes in ICT

In the past, the further apart people were, the longer it took for information to pass between them. Today distance is much less important. We are all linked by an ever-expanding global communications system. An idea that once took years to spread around the world, now takes seconds.

Telecommunications

Fibre-optic cables and satellites are responsible for massive improvements in global communications. Fibre-optic cables were developed in the 1970s. They carry phone calls as well as large amounts of digital information for the internet and cable TV. A network of cables, laid under the sea and on land, connects the world's major cities. Satellites transmit messages, via space, in a fraction of a second and for a fraction of the cost of previous methods. Satellites also make global positioning systems (GPS) possible.

Computerisation

Computers revolutionised the storage, retrieval and movement of information. Personal computers became available in the early 1980s, and the internet was introduced in 1995. The internet allows information to be accessed or shared very quickly. It also enables a wide range of commercial transactions; for example, buying and selling, and advertising.

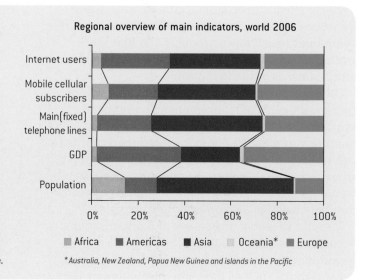

GEOskills TOOLBOX

INTERPRETING PERCENTAGE BAR GRAPHS

A percentage bar graph has a scale of 0 to 100 per cent. Each bar is the same length because each bar represents 100 per cent. Sections within the bar show the percentage of each item that makes up the whole. The bottom bar in this graph shows the percentage of world population in each region. One section of the bar is much larger because the largest percentage of world population lives in Asia. Percentage bar graphs are used to compare data because differences and patterns can be easily seen.

Access to ICT — global overview of the digital divide
Source: ITU World Telecommunication/ICT Indicators (WTI) Database.

Regional overview of main indicators, world 2006

- Internet users
- Mobile cellular subscribers
- Main (fixed) telephone lines
- GDP
- Population

0% 20% 40% 60% 80% 100%

■ Africa ■ Americas ■ Asia □ Oceania* ■ Europe

*Australia, New Zealand, Papua New Guinea and islands in the Pacific

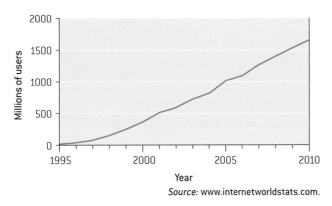

Source: www.internetworldstats.com.

Growth of the internet 1995–2010

The digital divide

The digital divide is the gap between the world's ICT 'haves' and 'have-nots'. Millions of people cannot afford a phone, let alone a computer. In Africa, about 5 per cent of the population is connected to the internet. By contrast, more than 75 per cent of Australians are online.

Fixed phone lines and reliable electricity supplies are often lacking in developing countries. Some communities provide access to telephones and computers at telecentres and internet cafes. However, the technology with the most potential to bridge the digital divide in developing countries is the mobile phone.

Mobiles do not need fixed phone lines, are cheaper than computers and can be connected to the internet. With a mobile phone, people can search for a job, check market prices or build a business by buying and selling online. Access to ICT gives people opportunities to help themselves.

In Kenya's Masai Mara National Reserve, a guide uses a mobile phone in his daily work.

Global citizenship

Advances in ICT mean that people anywhere can be heard and may be able to influence what happens. People can lobby organisations and governments by sending emails or by joining with others in an organised campaign. Non-government organisations (NGOs) often run campaigns to help people in poverty (e.g. World Vision), or to protect **human rights** (e.g. Amnesty International) or the environment (e.g. Greenpeace).

 GEO*facts* By the end of 2008, there were an estimated 4 billion mobile phone users. Africa and the Middle East are the regions where growth of user numbers is fastest.

ACTIVITIES ⊙

UNDERSTANDING

1. Name two advances in transport that have accelerated globalisation.
2. List four advances in ICT that have encouraged rapid globalisation.
3. Explain what is meant by 'the digital divide'.

THINKING AND APPLYING

4. How might low levels of literacy (the ability to read and write) stop people using the internet?
5. How could you use ICT to contribute to global citizenship?
6. Brainstorm things you do that involve ICT. Would your life be different without it? Outline any major differences.

USING YOUR SKILLS

7. Refer to the line graph above left.
   a. How many people used the internet in 1997 and in 2007?
   b. How long did it take for the number of users to reach 1 billion?
   c. Describe the growth of the internet from 1997 to 2007.
8. Refer to the bar graph on the opposite page.
   a. Which region has the greatest percentage of internet users?
   b. Which region has the greatest percentage of mobile subscribers?
   c. Calculate the difference between the percentage of internet users in Africa and in the Americas.
   d. Calculate the difference between the percentage of fixed phone lines in Africa and in Europe.
   e. Does the graph show a link between GDP and access to ICT? Give examples from the graph to support your answer.

Economic globalisation has broken down the walls that separate national economies from each other. Businesses are no longer confined to national borders; they can produce goods in one country and sell them in many others. This has led to the rise of large global businesses called transnational corporations (TNCs) and to the establishment of international organisations.

The rise of TNCs

TNCs are global corporations that buy their inputs from around the world, tend to manufacture goods in low-cost locations, and sell their goods in many different countries. They operate on a worldwide scale, with a head office in one country and branch offices or subsidiaries in other countries. TNCs often own or control the means of production, such as factories, mines or farms in more than one country.

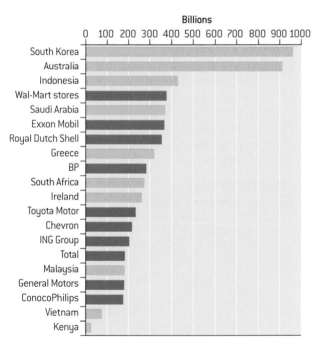

GDP of ten selected countries compared to revenue of the top 10 TNCs, 2007

There are different types of TNC. Retail chains (Wal-Mart stores), oil producers (ExxonMobil), car manufacturers (General Motors), sportswear makers (Nike) and takeaway food outlets (McDonald's) are some of the most successful. The annual sales revenue of some TNCs is more than the gross domestic product (GDP) of many countries.

TNCs and developing countries

TNCs have subsidiaries or manufacturing plants in developing countries for good reasons. These include access to natural resources, lower labour costs and cheaper land. There are also reasons why developing countries welcome TNCs. Employment and investment created by TNCs can raise the standard of living, and development can expand if TNCs share their technologies and expertise.

However, some of the activities of TNCs have attracted criticism, especially the use of sweatshop labour and the damage to the environment through activities such as unsustainable mining, logging and improper waste disposal.

Sweatshops

In sweatshops, adults and children work long hours, often in extreme heat, for very low wages. Working conditions are poor and there are few safety precautions. Sweatshop workers are usually not employed by TNCs. Instead, TNCs purchase goods from companies that do employ the workers. The goods are then marketed through retail outlets, sometimes carrying well known brand names.

NGOs and activists use the internet and public protests to campaign against the use of sweatshop labour. This has brought the problem to the attention of people around the world. As a result of international concerns, the United Nations has identified five key responsibilities for large TNCs:

1. Do not use forced or compulsory labour.
2. Respect the rights of children to be protected from economic exploitation.
3. Provide a safe and healthy working environment.
4. Pay workers enough to ensure an adequate standard of living for them and their families.
5. Recognise the rights of employees to join unions and other collective bargaining organisations.

Many TNCs now publicise their efforts to ensure workers are not exploited and that their operations are environmentally friendly and sustainable.

GEOfacts Wal-Mart stores is the world's largest retailer, with 4100 stores in the USA and more than 3000 in other countries.

International organisations

A number of international organisations oversee the flow of goods, services and money around the world. Two of the most important:

- The **World Trade Organization (WTO)** was established in 1995 to enforce trade agreements. It has nearly 150 member countries, accounting for over 97 per cent of world trade. Its main goal is to reduce or eliminate tariffs and other barriers to international trade. Critics complain that the WTO has not done enough to reduce trade barriers for agricultural products.

- The **International Monetary Fund (IMF)** works to ensure the stability of the international monetary system. It was established after World War II and now has more than 180 member countries. The IMF monitors each country's **exchange rate** and **balance of payments**. Exchange rates tell how much a unit of one currency is worth compared to another; for example, what the Australian dollar is worth against the US dollar. This system is necessary so that nations can pay for the goods and services they buy from each other.

The world economic crisis from 2008 onwards demonstrated the interdependence of national economies. Stock markets crashed and economic growth slowed dramatically in almost every country.

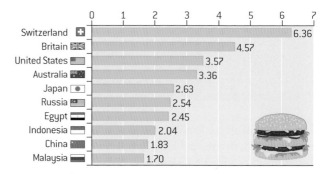

Source: Drawn from data derived from *The Economist* and McDonald's, July 2008.

The 'Big Mac Index' is created by The Economist *financial magazine. It shows the price of a McDonald's Big Mac in different countries and is one way to work out the approximate exchange rate. A Big Mac is generally cheaper in countries with a low GDP, such as Malaysia, and more expensive in countries with a high GDP, such as Britain.*

Cartoon published during the global financial crisis
Source: The Sydney Morning Herald, 8–9 November 2008, p. 34.

ACTIVITIES

UNDERSTANDING

1. What is meant by the term 'transnational corporation'?
2. Give two reasons why TNCs manufacture products in developing countries.
3. What benefits could a TNC bring to a developing country?
4. Describe the working conditions in a sweatshop.
5. What is the role of the WTO?
6. What is the purpose of the IMF?
7. Why are exchange rates necessary?

THINKING AND APPLYING

8. What is the main message being communicated in the cartoon?
9. Jeans manufacturer Levi Strauss & Co. has taken action against suppliers when human rights or environmental codes have not been upheld. Use the internet to research the company's commitment to global citizenship. Give the company a score out of 10. Justify the score.
10. Go to the website of one of the top 10 TNCs. Investigate their commitment to global citizenship, either to fair working conditions or to environmental sustainability. Give the company a score out of 10. Justify the score.
11. Search the internet using the word 'FairWear'. What is the FairWear code for retailers and manufacturers? Investigate a FairWear campaign and prepare a brief report outlining what was achieved.

USING YOUR SKILLS

12. Refer to the graph on page 204.
    a. Are the following statements true or false?
       i. Wal-Mart's sales were more than a third of Australia's GDP.
       ii. General Motors sales were about six times the GDP of Kenya.
       iii. The GDP of the oil-rich country Saudi Arabia was much higher than the sales of the oil giant Exxon Mobil.
    b. Calculate the difference between the sales of Toyota and the GDP of Vietnam.
    c. How many TNCs in the graph had sales greater than the combined GDP of Vietnam and Kenya?
13. Refer to the graph above. What is the price difference of a Big Mac between the cheapest and most expensive countries?

Nike: a case study of a TNC

The global athletic footwear and sportswear market is worth around US$75 billion per year. It is dominated by TNCs such as Nike, Adidas and Reebok. Most companies in the industry manufacture their products in developing countries because of ready access to materials and low-cost labour.

A global company

Nike is a US-based company. It is one of the world's leading suppliers of athletic footwear, apparel, equipment and accessories. Nike employs 30 000 people worldwide. To make its products, it uses more than 800 000 people in almost 700 contract factories in 52 countries. The company sells its products globally through independent distributors, licensees and subsidiaries. In 2008, the company recorded sales revenues of $18.6 billion.

One of the main reasons for Nike's success is its sponsorship of many successful athletes. The Nike logo is worn by top athletes such as golfer Tiger Woods and tennis player Serena Williams. Nike also constantly develops new products. In 2006, they produced a sports shoe that could be linked to an Apple iPod to monitor a runner's performance.

Change over time

The location of Nike manufacturing sites has changed over time. In 1975, most of the company's products were manufactured in the US. Today most of Nike's products are manufactured in developing countries including China, Vietnam, Indonesia and Thailand. Design and development of new products still takes place in the US. The maps above right show the locations of Nike footwear manufacturing plants in 1975 and contract factory sites in 2007. The timeline (left) is a summary of the growth of Nike between 1964 and 2008.

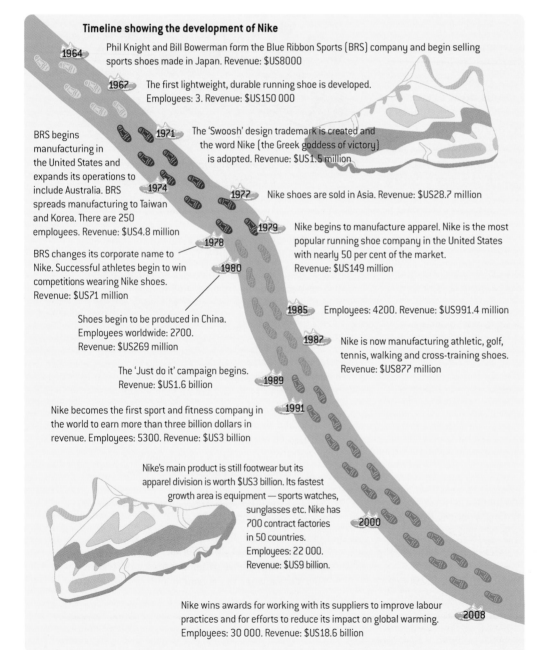

Timeline showing the development of Nike

1964 Phil Knight and Bill Bowerman form the Blue Ribbon Sports (BRS) company and begin selling sports shoes made in Japan. Revenue: $US8000

1967 The first lightweight, durable running shoe is developed. Employees: 3. Revenue: $US150 000

1971 The 'Swoosh' design trademark is created and the word Nike (the Greek goddess of victory) is adopted. Revenue: $US1.5 million

BRS begins manufacturing in the United States and expands its operations to include Australia. BRS spreads manufacturing to Taiwan and Korea. There are 250 employees. Revenue: $US4.8 million **1974**

1977 Nike shoes are sold in Asia. Revenue: $US28.7 million

1979 Nike begins to manufacture apparel. Nike is the most popular running shoe company in the United States with nearly 50 per cent of the market. Revenue: $US149 million

1978 BRS changes its corporate name to Nike. Successful athletes begin to win competitions wearing Nike shoes. Revenue: $US71 million

1980 Shoes begin to be produced in China. Employees worldwide: 2700. Revenue: $US269 million

1985 Employees: 4200. Revenue: $US991.4 million

1987 Nike is now manufacturing athletic, golf, tennis, walking and cross-training shoes. Revenue: $US877 million

1989 The 'Just do it' campaign begins. Revenue: $US1.6 billion

1991 Nike becomes the first sport and fitness company in the world to earn more than three billion dollars in revenue. Employees: 5300. Revenue: $US3 billion

2000 Nike's main product is still footwear but its apparel division is worth $US3 billion. Its fastest growth area is equipment — sports watches, sunglasses etc. Nike has 700 contract factories in 50 countries. Employees: 22 000. Revenue: $US9 billion.

2008 Nike wins awards for working with its suppliers to improve labour practices and for efforts to reduce its impact on global warming. Employees: 30 000. Revenue: $US18.6 billion

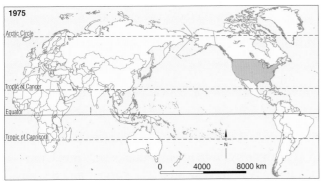

Locations of Nike footwear manufacturing sites in 1975

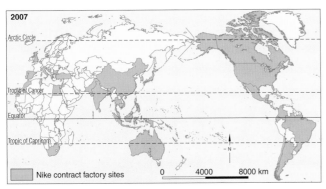

Nike contract factory sites

Locations of Nike contract factory sites in 2007

Perspectives

Manufacturing athletic footwear is labour intensive. For every pair of shoes, workers cut, stitch, shape and pack up to 200 components. Nike does not directly employ most of the people who make their products. Manufacturing is done by hundreds of contract factories, mostly in developing countries.

Like many other TNCs, Nike has been the target of campaigns against exploitation of workers. Sweatshop conditions were discovered in some contract factories. The workers were discouraged from complaining about their conditions or forming trade unions because they were afraid they would lose their jobs. Anti-sweatshop groups ran campaigns to publicise the working conditions, complaining that both the conditions and the pressure on workers not to agitate for better conditions amounted to abuses of human rights.

Tiger Woods is sponsored by Nike.

Nike now works with its suppliers to limit overtime and improve working conditions. In 2008, Nike was named one of the world's most ethical companies for working with its suppliers on ways to treat their workers fairly. From the perspective of anti-sweatshop activists, this is not enough. They want TNCs to stop using factories in countries where the rights of workers are not respected.

ACTIVITIES

UNDERSTANDING

1 What features of Nike make it a transnational company?

2 Name two strategies that have made Nike successful.

3 Who does Nike employ to make most of their products?

4 Why was Nike the target of campaigners for human rights?

5 What was Nike's response to the campaign?

THINKING AND APPLYING

6 In groups, design a survey to find out the answer to this question: Are some sports brands popular because they are associated with top athletes and celebrities?

  a Prepare a short questionnaire to find out:
  • which brands are the most popular
  • if people know which athletes or celebrities are associated with their favourite brands.

  b Conduct the survey among students at your school. Convert the raw data to percentages and present the result as a bar or pie graph.

  c Are students representative of the general population? How might results change if other people were included in the survey?

  d Design a poster to promote one of the brands.

USING YOUR SKILLS

7 Refer to the maps.

  a Describe the location of Nike footwear manufacturing sites in 1975.

  b Where were the manufacturing sites located in 2007? Describe the change in location over time.

  c Give reasons why Nike may have made these changes.

  d What effect would these changes have on the local people in both old and new locations?

8 Refer to the timeline showing the growth of Nike from 1964 to 2008.

  a Draw a line graph of the number of people Nike employed from 1964 to 2008.

  b Draw a line graph of Nike revenues from 1964 to 2008.

  c What do the trends on the line graphs show?

While the world is becoming more interconnected, it is also becoming more standardised. Wherever you travel in the world, there are signs of Western culture. Examples include the familiar golden arches of the McDonald's fast food chain and the colourful advertisements promoting other fast foods such as Kentucky Fried Chicken, Burger King and Starbucks.

Culture includes languages, beliefs, customs and traditions. The cultures of indigenous and national peoples all over the world have been changed by globalisation through trade, migration, tourism, ICT and the media. This can be seen in the spread of Western culture, and in the growing and widespread use of the English language.

GEOskills TOOLBOX

INTERPRETING A CARTOON

Cartoons can be used to make social or political comments. They are intended to stimulate and amuse, but they are not always funny. Cartoonists often use stereotypes to represent a group. In this case, Disney and other TNCs represent groups pushing American culture. Cartoonists also use familiar images and symbols to make a point; i.e. the war scene suggests that American culture is taking over.

'McDonaldisation'

A McDonald's fast food outlet looks very much the same wherever it is located. The service and the way the food is prepared is the same. This standardisation results in efficiency and predictability. Costs can be calculated and operations tightly controlled. Customers know what eating at McDonald's will be like whether they are a block from home or visiting another country.

The American toy Barbie on sale at a Wal-Mart store in Beijing, China, where it is popular and very expensive

The term 'McDonaldisation', invented in the 1990s, means more than the spread of McDonald's restaurants around the world. It includes the idea of standardisation — of making things the same. It refers to the way people in other countries often take on aspects of Western culture, such as food, clothes and music. This happens at the expense of their own culture.

Many different TNCs contribute to the globalised experience of consumers. While people all over the world eat McDonald's, they are also likely to drink Coca-Cola, wear Nike T shirts and Levi jeans, use Microsoft Word, listen to an Apple iPod and watch DVDs made by Time Warner.

Language

There are about 7000 languages spoken worldwide. Each year, about 25 languages die because there are not enough speakers to keep them alive. In a few generations, over half the languages may disappear.

Language preserves cultural heritage. When a language dies, the world loses a source of knowledge.

Where knowledge is passed on through word of mouth, the loss can be total. Information about history, culture and the natural environment, such as the medicinal use of plants, can be lost forever.

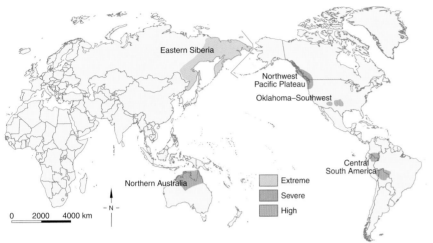

Regions where languages are most at risk of extinction

English has replaced many languages. This process is likely to speed up because it is the main language used on the internet. It is estimated that half the world will be able to speak and write in English by 2050.

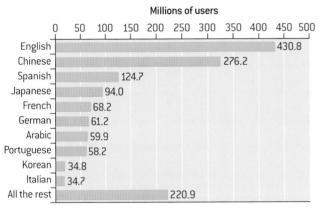

Source: www.internetworldstats.com/stats7.htm, 2008.

Top 10 languages on the internet

Media and entertainment

People around the world can watch the same movies, news channels and television shows. They can listen to the same music and play the same video games. Much of this material originates in developed countries such as the USA and Britain. Control of the media and of entertainment is concentrated in the hands of a few TNCs. The largest are Time Warner, Walt Disney and News Corp. Their influence extends worldwide into television, newspapers, movies, music, magazines, books, amusement parks and retail stores.

Alternatives are growing. The internet allows people to participate instead of just being a spectator. You can set up a website, a **blog** or create content to broadcast on YouTube. Blogs enable people to express views that may not be given space in newspapers or on television. Some blog sites are popular and respected. These services are not available everywhere, for example, China and Iran, where they are blocked or filtered by governments.

There are some signs of a swing back to the local and national. More Australians are listening to community radio. A survey in 2008 found that the number of listeners had grown by more than 20 per cent since 2004. Numbers increased in every age group. The most common reasons given were to: hear specialist music programs, get local news and information, listen to Australian music, and support local artists.

ACTIVITIES →

UNDERSTANDING

1. What is meant by the term 'culture'?
2. How have advances in technology contributed to the spread of Western culture?
3. What is 'McDonaldisation'?
4. Where are the five language hotspots?

THINKING AND APPLYING

5. Explain why the scene shown in the photograph is an example of the cultural impacts of globalisation.
6. How might the internet counteract the 'McDonaldisation' of culture?
7. Why does it matter that languages are disappearing?

USING YOUR SKILLS

8. Construct a sketch map of your local area showing the location of global fast food outlets.
9. Refer to the bar graph.
   a What is the main language used on the internet? Why do you think Chinese is a popular language?
   b List the top Asian languages. How many European languages are in the top 10?
10. Refer to the cartoon of Disney characters.
   a What is the main idea being communicated in the cartoon?
   b List five American TNCs shown in the cartoon.
   c What are the planes dropping on the land? What do you think the cartoonist is trying to say here?
   d What is the reaction of the people to the invasion?

For almost a century, the diamond industry was controlled by De Beers, a company based in South Africa. The situation began to change in the 1990s, partly because other companies challenged De Beers' hold on the market. However, the biggest change to the industry came from another source — growing concern by people worldwide about the role of diamonds in funding conflict and civil wars.

The diamond industry

Diamonds are a natural resource. They are formed in molten rock 120–190 kilometres below the Earth's surface and then transported to the surface in volcanic eruptions. Their distribution varies across the globe. About half of the world's rough diamonds are mined in Africa.

About US$12 billion of rough diamonds are mined each year. They are sold to diamond merchants who cut and polish the stones, turning them into gems before they are sold to the retail market. The retail market is worth about US$70 billion each year.

Diamonds and De Beers

Until the 1990s, De Beers supplied more than 80 per cent of the world's rough diamonds. The company dominated the diamond trade through its Central Selling Organisation (CSO). The CSO was established to sell diamonds from De Beers' African mines, but De Beers persuaded almost every other diamond miner to market through the CSO as well. This made it possible for De Beers to control the worldwide supply of diamonds. By limiting the amount and quality of rough diamonds allowed onto the market, it kept prices high.

The CSO held diamond sales ten times a year in the city of Antwerp in Belgium. Only selected buyers could attend and the price for each parcel of diamonds was not negotiable.

Retail sales

The USA is the largest retail market for diamond jewellery, with half of total world sales. Europe and Japan are also key markets. China, India and the Middle East are emerging as significant markets.

The global diamond industry

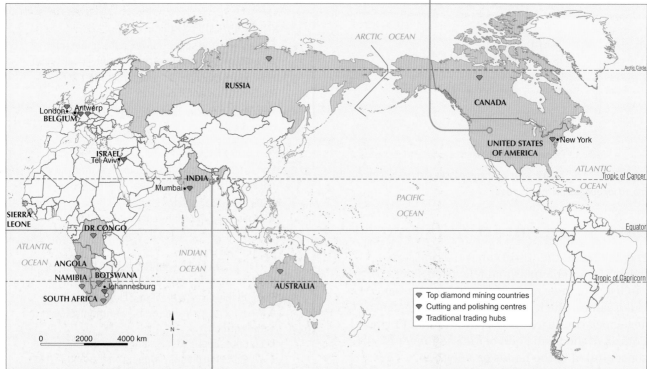

Cutting and polishing centres

India is the most important centre, producing more than half of the world's polished diamonds each year. It employs about a million people. China is emerging as a major centre, with about 25 000 people working in more than 80 factories.

Other diamond-mining countries

Sierra Leone, Liberia, Ivory Coast, Guinea, Ghana, Central African Republic, Tanzania, China, Indonesia, India, Brazil, Guyana, Venezuela, USA

De Beers began to lose its hold on the world market during the 1990s. Other sources of diamonds became available. The Argyle mine, located in the east Kimberley region of north-west Australia, began operating in 1983. Today, the mine produces about one-fifth of the quantity of the world's rough diamonds. New deposits were found in Canada. De Beer's control was further weakened by the break-up of the Soviet Union because it became difficult to enforce contracts with Russian suppliers. Russian diamonds flooded the market, driving prices down.

Argyle originally sold most of its rough diamonds through the CSO. But in 1996, it decided to break with the CSO and sell direct to the international market. It was the first major miner to do so. Others followed. Most of Argyle's diamonds are now sold through their own office in Antwerp to cutters and polishers based in India. It sells its famous pink diamonds worldwide to diamond traders, jewellery manufacturers and luxury retailers.

De Beers now supplies, by value, less than half of the rough diamonds sold on the world market. It remains the largest distributor, but can no longer control the world supply or the industry.

A valuable cut and polished pink diamond from the Argyle mine

De Beers' Big Hole mine in South Africa was once the richest diamond mine in the world until it closed in 1915. In the region, diamonds are found in vertical pipes of kimberlite rock. The 200-metre deep hole was dug out by miners using picks and shovels. Big Hole is the biggest man-made hole on Earth.

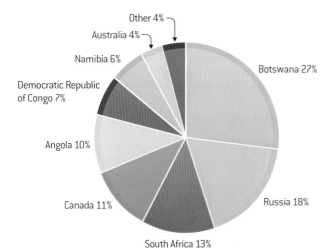

Location of diamond production by value, 2006

- Other 4%
- Australia 4%
- Namibia 6%
- Democratic Republic of Congo 7%
- Angola 10%
- Canada 11%
- South Africa 13%
- Russia 18%
- Botswana 27%

Rough diamonds from the Argyle mine

GEOfacts
- India was the only known source of diamonds before the sixth century. It remained the main source of diamonds until the mid 1700s.
- Diamonds are mined on all continents except Europe and Antarctica (which may be a rich source, but all mining is currently banned in Antarctica).
- The largest rough diamond ever found was discovered in 1905 in South Africa. It was cut into nine major stones and the largest, the Star of Africa, was mounted in the British Royal Sceptre.
- On average, about 250 tonnes of ore is excavated to find one stone big enough to produce a one-carat diamond gem. A carat is a fifth of a gram.
- The famous line 'A diamond is forever' was invented in 1947 by a young copywriter working on the De Beers' advertising account.

Conflict diamonds

Conflict diamonds are used by rebel groups to finance conflict and civil war aimed at undermining legitimate governments. They come from territories controlled by rebels and are sold to pay for guns and other equipment. Armed groups fight for control of diamond-rich areas, terrorising local populations and seizing diamonds. Several long-lasting brutal wars in Africa were funded by conflict diamonds. The worst were in Sierra Leone, Angola, Liberia, Ivory Coast and the Democratic Republic of Congo.

Global Witness, a British non-government organisation (NGO), brought the issue of conflict diamonds to public attention. In 1998, they released a report called 'A Rough Trade'. It exposed how the sale of diamonds was funding terrible suffering and bloodshed. The diamond industry and national governments came under intense international pressure from NGOs and the public to stop the trade in conflict diamonds. During the 1990s, it was estimated that conflict diamonds made up at least 4 per cent of the diamond supply. Some think it could have been as much as 15 to 25 per cent.

The Kimberley Process

The United Nations, diamond-trading countries, the diamond industry and several NGOs worked together to solve the problem of conflict diamonds. In 2000, a conference was held in Kimberley, South Africa, to discuss how to prevent the sale of these diamonds. The discussions included governments of countries that export diamonds such as Botswana, countries that import diamonds such as the USA, industry representatives such as De Beers, NGOs such as Global Witness, and the UN.

The result was the Kimberley Process Certification Scheme (KPCS). It requires governments to certify all rough diamonds traded across their borders. The diamonds must have a certificate that guarantees the diamonds did not come from a conflict area.

The KPCS was implemented in 2003 and proved effective. However, some conflict diamonds continued to get through. Diamonds are small and easy to smuggle. Once out of the country, their origin is hard to trace; once polished they can't be identified. In 2006, another NGO, Partnership Africa Canada, published a report identifying several countries that were still sources of conflict diamonds.

Blood Diamond

In late 2006, the Hollywood movie *Blood Diamond* was released. It is a story about what happens after a man finds a large pink diamond in a rebel-controlled mine in Sierra Leone, Africa. The movie shows the terror and violence suffered by the population during the bloody civil war funded by conflict diamonds.

The movie received a lot of media coverage around the world. People who had never heard of the issue before suddenly realised what was happening. They wrote letters to the media and lobbied politicians. They said they would not buy diamonds if they came from conflict areas.

During 2006, the diamond industry became concerned that negative publicity from groups such as Global Witness and Amnesty International, and by the soon to be released *Blood Diamond* movie, could harm their reputation and their sales. Governments were worried about the consequences of continued sales of conflict diamonds. As a result, they agreed to further strengthen the KPCS. Today, less than 1 per cent of the world's diamond supply is believed to come from conflict areas.

The KPCS is an example of successful international cooperation. Diamonds are now more likely to bring benefits, such as peace and a better standard of living to local people, rather than the horrors of civil war. However, because diamonds are so valuable, groups will always try to find loopholes and ways around the KPCS. Continued public support is necessary to ensure that the KPCS is enforced. If you buy a diamond, ask the retailer if it is certified conflict-free.

Panning for gold, Sierra Leone. When diamond-bearing rock erodes, rough diamonds are washed downhill, eventually ending up on the banks or beds of streams, rivers, lakes and oceans.

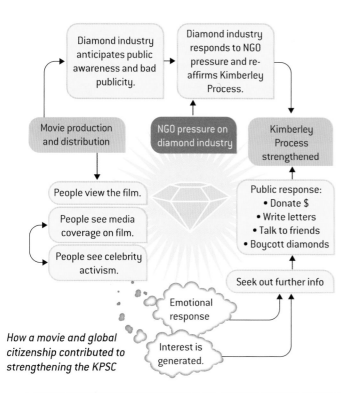

How a movie and global citizenship contributed to strengthening the KPSC

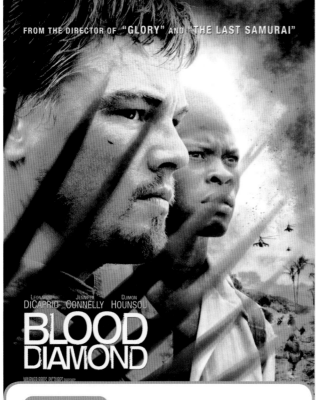

FROM THE DIRECTOR OF "GLORY" AND "THE LAST SAMURAI"

LEONARDO DiCAPRIO   JENNIFER CONNELLY   DJIMON HOUNSOU

BLOOD DIAMOND

WARNER BROS. PICTURES

GEOTERMS

civil war: war between areas or parties within one country

conflict diamond: a diamond used to finance conflict aimed at undermining legitimate governments

rough diamond: a diamond in its original state, before cutting and polishing

ACTIVITIES

UNDERSTANDING

1 Which company controlled the world diamond industry until the 1990s?

2 List three major factors that changed the balance of power in the industry in the 1990s.

3 What is meant by the term 'conflict diamonds'?

4 Describe the KPCS. When was it implemented?

5 Which groups were involved in working on the KPCS?

6 When buying a diamond, what action can you take to help stop the sale of conflict diamonds?

THINKING AND APPLYING

7 Why were most diamonds mined in developing countries but the biggest retail sales were traditionally in developed countries?

8 List examples of the impact of globalisation on the diamond industry at the individual, local, national and global scale.

USING YOUR SKILLS

9 Refer to the map on page 210.
   a Name three major diamond mining countries.
   b Name two cities that are important trading hubs for rough diamonds.
   c Name three cities that are traditional cutting centres.
   d Which country is the most important cutting and polishing centre? Which country is emerging as a cutting and polishing centre?
   e Which country is the largest retail market for diamond jewellery? Where are new retail markets emerging?
   f Is the diamond industry an example of globalisation? Why or why not?

10 Refer to the pie graph on page 211.
   a Which country dominated world diamond production by value in 2006?
   b What percentage of world diamond production by value came from Africa?
   c Which other continents produced diamonds?

11 Refer to the photo of Big Hole mine on page 211.
   a Where is Big Hole mine? Who owned the mine?
   b Create a line drawing of the photo. For more information about line drawings, see page 58. Place information around your drawing that describes natural and cultural features in the background, middle ground and foreground.

12 Refer to the flow chart above left.
   a List the global impacts of the movie *Blood Diamond*.
   b Describe examples of global citizenship that followed the release of the movie.

Working geographically

KNOWLEDGE AND UNDERSTANDING

Select the alternative A, B, C or D that best answers the question.

1. Which technologies rapidly accelerated globalisation?
   - (A) Trade and tourism
   - (B) Transport and trade
   - (C) Trade and computers
   - (D) Transport and ICT

2. Which technologies greatly increased world trade?
   - (A) Super tankers, container ships, jet aircraft, ICT
   - (B) Jet aircraft, fast road transport, fast rail transport
   - (C) Super tankers, container ships, fast rail transport
   - (D) Jet aircraft, super tankers, fast rail transport, ICT

3. Which technologies revolutionised global telecommunications?
   - (A) Satellites and global positioning systems
   - (B) Fibre-optic cables and global positioning systems
   - (C) Fibre-optic cables and satellites
   - (D) Satellites and global media networks

4. What is the digital divide?
   - (A) The population of a country divided by the number of computers
   - (B) The number of computers in a country divided by the population
   - (C) The gap between those who have access to ICT and those who don't
   - (D) The gap between rich countries and poor countries

5. Which of the following is NOT a result of economic globalisation?
   - (A) Economic integration
   - (B) Rise of international organisations to oversee global markets
   - (C) Growth of TNCs
   - (D) Decrease in world trade

6. Where are most of Nike's products manufactured?
   - (A) Contract factories in developed countries
   - (B) Contract factories in developing countries
   - (C) Nike-owned factories in developing countries
   - (D) Nike-owned factories in the USA

7. What are two of the main cultural impacts of globalisation?
   - (A) Spread of American culture and increasing use of the English language
   - (B) Growth of TNCs and increase in world trade

   - (C) Increase in world trade and decrease in the influence of the WTO
   - (D) Increase in world trade and decrease in the influence of American culture

8. Who worked together in 2000 to develop the Kimberley Process Certification Scheme?
   - (A) UN, the diamond industry, the movie industry, NGOs
   - (B) Diamond exporters, diamond importers, the movie industry, NGOs
   - (C) UN, the diamond industry, rebel leaders, NGOs
   - (D) UN, diamond trading countries, the diamond industry, NGOs

9. Which statement sums up how global relationships in the diamond industry changed over time?
   - (A) Control of the industry moved from De Beers to Argyle.
   - (B) De Beers controlled the industry until the movie *Blood Diamond* publicised conflict diamonds.
   - (C) Control moved from one company to many stakeholders including individuals, businesses, governments and international organisations.
   - (D) De Beers controlled the industry until the UN implemented the Kimberley Process.

10. Which of the following do NOT describe the globalisation process?
    - (A) Increasing power of international organisations and decreasing power of national governments
    - (B) Increasing influence of Western culture and decreasing influence of TNCs
    - (C) Increasing global movement of people, goods, information and money
    - (D) Integration of national economies into the global economy

SKILLS REVISION

11. Global cities are large urbanised areas that have gained international importance over the last 40 years. They have a large educated workforce, efficient transport and advanced technological links to the rest of the world. These cities have a variety of functions including finance (stock exchange, banks), entertainment (museums, art galleries), and specialised goods and services. The headquarters for TNCs and intergovernmental organisations (IGO) such as the United Nations and the World Bank are located in global cities, as you will see in the following table.

Global cities with headquarters of the world's largest TNCs, 2009

Rank	City	Country	No. of global 500 companies (TNC)	Rank of GDP (1 highest – 18 lowest)
1	Tokyo	Japan	50	2
2	Paris	France	26	6
3	New York	USA	22	1
3	London	Britain/UK	22	5
4	Beijing	China	18	4
5	Seoul	South Korea	10	12
6	Toronto	Canada	9	9
7	Madrid	Spain	8	8
8	Zurich	Switzerland	7	18
9	Houston	USA	7	1
10	Munich	Germany	6	3
11	Osaka	Japan	6	2
12	Rome	Italy	5	7
13	Atlanta	USA	5	1

a Draw the countries and their number of TNCs as a bar graph. What is the range in the number of TNCs among countries?

b Rank the GDP of countries from highest (1) to lowest.

c Why do you think Switzerland has a global city but a lower GDP?

12 Starbucks is a TNC that specialises in coffee. The raw materials required to make a cup of Starbucks coffee include coffee beans, milk, sugar and paper cups. Study the map and table, and use an atlas to help you answer the following questions.

a Name two countries that supply Starbucks with:
  • coffee beans • sugar • paper for its cups.

b Which country has the largest number of Starbucks stores? Why do you think this is so?

c How many Starbucks are there in Australia?

d Describe the global distribution of Starbucks stores.

e Explain why Starbucks is a global company.

f Visit the Starbucks website and read their annual report to find out where any stores have closed.

Starbucks company-operated retail stores, 2008

Country	Stores open
United States	7238
Canada	731
United Kingdom	664
China	178
Germany	131
Thailand	127
Singapore	57
Australia	23
Other	68
Total	9217

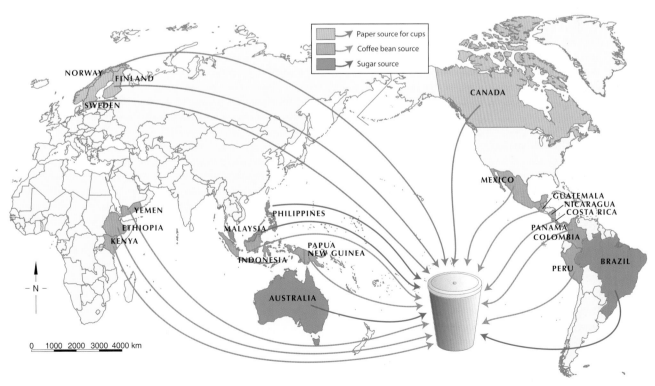

Global supply networks used to make a cup of Starbucks coffee

Source: Mapping Globalization, Princeton University.

The global village

SEARCHLIGHT ID: PRO-0033

SCENARIO

You are the product development manager for a major transnational corporation (TNC). You have been asked to develop a new product to be sold on the global market and present it to the company's board of directors. Your presentation must track the production of the product from the raw material stage to its final point of sale.

You must create a product with a production cycle that spans three different continents. Your raw materials must be sourced from a developing country located on the African continent. You must also select a production location in an Asian country and explain the size and structure of the production plant. Finally, you must identify a location in a developed country (in either Europe or North America) where your product will be sold. You will also need to explain the type of retail enterprise that will sell your product.

YOUR TASK

Your new product is to be presented to the board of directors using Google Maps.

Your interactive global map should pin-point the various locations your production cycle. These should be realistic locations where similar economic activity to what you are proposing actually takes place.

The directors of your company will want to know the following:
- What raw materials will be required to produce this product and where they will be sourced?
- What production process will be used, and what will the primary, secondary and tertiary stages of production involve? Where will this occur, and why was this production location chosen?
- Where will the target market for the product be located? You will need to give reasons why you believe these potential customers will be interested in the product.

Finally, you should write a 500-word report to your shareholders that will encourage them to support your new product by teaching them about global production locations. It should inform them of the advantages and disadvantages of producing in the global village. You should also include in your report a brief explanation of how this process is an example of economic globalisation and the concept of the global village.

PROCESS

- Open your ProjectsPLUS application for this chapter, located in your eBookPLUS. Watch the introductory video lesson and then click the 'Start Project' button to set up your project. You can complete this project individually or invite other members of your class to form a group. Save your settings and the project will be launched.

- Navigate to the Media Centre and preview the sample Google Map provided so you can see the kind of map you will be creating. A document is also available that includes a list of potential developing countries and the raw materials they produce.
- Decide on the product that you would like to create.
- Navigate to your Research Forum. Topics have been loaded in the system to provide a framework for your research. You should research locations in Africa to source your raw materials, locations in Asia to house your production plant, and locations in Europe or North America to sell your product. The weblinks in your Media Centre will help you get started. Enter your findings as articles under each topic. You can view and comment on other group members' articles and rate the information they have entered. Be sure to enter the source of any information you find online. You can include hyperlinks to other websites in your Google Map.
- Make notes of the interesting facts and important ideas you discover about the countries that your product will be produced and sold in. You can insert some of this information as extra 'Amazing facts' or

'Did you know?' boxes in your Google Map or include this information in your report.
- Use the Creating a Google Map guide in your Media Centre to help you create your Google Map. Use pins to add approximately 100 words about each of your chosen sites. Make sure you clearly distinguish between the locations for raw materials, site of production facilities and places where the goods are to be sold. Make sure you use the language of a business executive when accounting for the locations you have chosen: for example, 'India is a rapidly developing country that offers a qualified labour force as well as access to technology including manufactured computer software'. You must ensure that your interactive map is functional and interesting before submitting your assignment. It is important that the pins all work and that the information and images on your map are informative and thought provoking.
- Write your report to the board of directors.
- Email your Google Map to your teacher. Then complete your project by printing the research report from your ProjectsPLUS Research Forum and handing it in with your report to the board of directors.

SUGGESTED SOFTWARE
- ProjectsPLUS
- Google Maps
- Microsoft Word

MEDIA CENTRE

Your Media Centre contains:
- a list of developing countries and the raw materials they produce
- weblinks to sites on global production
- a guide to Creating a Google Map
- a sample Google Map model
- an assessment rubric.

Interactivity

MATCH UP: 'GLOBAL BRANDS'

Match Up is an interactive card game with a twist — the pairs aren't exactly the same. In this exciting interactivity, you will use your knowledge of global brands to see if you can match a series of products with their countries of origin. Can you remember where the correct pair is? Can you beat the clock?

SEARCHLIGHT ID: INT-0965

10 An unequal world

INQUIRY QUESTIONS

+ What is global inequality?
+ Where are the extremes of poverty and wealth?
+ Why do people have different life opportunities and quality of life?
+ How are groups involved in reducing global inequalities?

Living conditions and life opportunities in developed and developing countries are very different. In the developing world, millions of people live in poverty. They do not have enough food to eat and their access to water is inadequate. Their shelter is poor and many have no proper home at all. Due to poverty, rates of disease and death are much higher in developing countries. Access to health care and education is limited.

International organisations, non-government organisations such as World Vision, and national governments and individuals are all working towards a better and fairer world. The Millennium Development Goals are part of a worldwide effort to reduce poverty and inequality.

GEOskills TOOLBOX

+ Using elements of maps (pages 220, 238)

Inequalities between rich and poor are shown starkly in this photograph of slum dwellings against a backdrop of high-rise buildings in Mumbai, India.

KEY TERMS

aid: charitable donations of money, food, goods and services made to countries in need

antiretroviral: a substance that stops or slows the activity of a retrovirus such as HIV

developed country: a country that has high economic productivity, relatively high standards of living and a relatively democratic system of government

developing country: a country in which most people have a low economic standard of living

diarrhoea: a condition leading to loss of fluid through bowel motions, causing dehydration

extreme poverty: surviving on less than US$1 a day

fertility rate: the average number of children a woman is likely to have in her lifetime. A rate of just over two, called the replacement level, keeps population numbers steady.

free trade: occurs where goods and services are traded between countries with no restrictions

gender equity: equal access of females and males to opportunities such as education and employment

gross domestic product (GDP): a measure of a country's wealth; for example, a country with a GDP of $140 billion produces $140 billion worth of goods and services in a year

Human Development Index (HDI): a measure of a country's level of development based on life expectancy, literacy, education and GDP per capita. The highest value is 1 and the lowest value is 0.

infant mortality rate (IMR): the number of deaths per 1000 babies under one year of age

life expectancy: the number of years people can expect to live

literacy: the ability to read and write

malnutrition: the condition suffered when a person does not get enough nutrition to sustain normal bodily functions

obesity: a body weight more than 20 per cent above what is generally considered healthy, increasing the risk of life-threatening diseases such as diabetes

sanitation: the practices in place, such as toilets and sewerage systems, for the disposal of waste products, including human waste

shantytowns: communities that consist of a collection of roughly constructed huts and 'lean-to' structures, and having few conveniences (e.g. running water, toilets, proper roads)

subsidies: grants of money given by governments to producers, which lower the producer's costs and allow the product to be sold at a lower price

tariff: a tax imposed on imports

This young girl lives in rural Malawi, where WHO estimates that 12 per cent of children die under the age of five. With a gross national income per capita of US$690, Malawi is one of Africa's poorest nations. In this young girl's community, CARE is working to improve food security and health services for those affected by HIV and AIDS. By introducing sustainable income opportunities and providing training to community members, CARE is helping communities to overcome poverty.

In rural Malawi, 56 per cent of people live below the poverty line compared to 52 per cent in urban Malawi.

Nearly half of the 13 million people in Malawi live on less than $1 per day. For every 1000 children born in Malawi, 133 die before they reach the age of five. Only 76 per cent of the population has access to clean water, and AIDS is responsible for eight deaths every hour.

Global patterns

We live in an unequal world. About 20 per cent of the world's population uses 80 per cent of the world's resources. The remaining 20 per cent of the world's resources are shared between 80 per cent of the world's population.

The living conditions of people around the world vary enormously. About 1.1 billion of the world's 6.7 billion people live in **extreme poverty**. This means they survive on less than US$1 a day. Nearly half of the world's population lives on less than $US2 a day. Hundreds of millions of people do not have enough food. Even more do not have safe drinking water. In some countries, more than 80 per cent of adults are unable to read and write. The opportunities of many millions of people are extremely limited.

GEOskills TOOLBOX

USING ELEMENTS OF MAPS

Data such as GDP can be mapped to show comparisons between countries. The map at right uses GDP per capita data to illustrate the pattern of global poverty and wealth in 2008. The map uses darker and lighter shades of the same colour group to show a pattern. The darker shades represent 'the most' and the lighter shades represent 'the least'. This map enables the user to easily see global patterns of poverty and wealth.

Gross Domestic Product (GDP) per person, 2008

The darkest shade of *orange* has been used to colour those countries with the highest GDP per capita (over US$10 000). Note these countries.

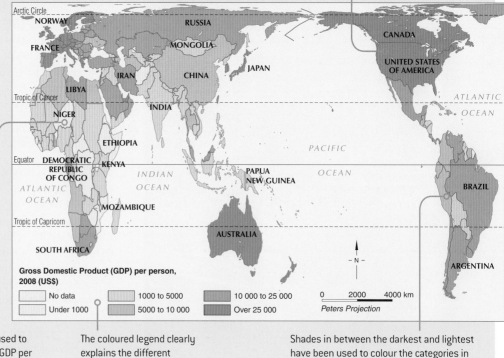

Gross Domestic Product (GDP) per person, 2008 (US$)

No data	1000 to 5000	10 000 to 25 000
Under 1000	5000 to 10 000	Over 25 000

0   2000   4000 km
Peters Projection

The lightest shade of *yellow* has been used to colour those countries with the lowest GDP per capita (under US$200). Note these countries.

The coloured legend clearly explains the different categories being shown.

Shades in between the darkest and lightest have been used to colour the categories in between these two extremes.

Developed and developing

Australia, along with countries such as the United States, France and Japan, is a developed country. This means that the country provides satisfactory living conditions and opportunities for the majority of its people to enjoy high levels of education, health and health care. Developing countries, such as Malawi, Indonesia and India, do not currently provide these benefits for most of their people.

Measuring development

Wealth is one of the most obvious differences between countries. Some, such as the United States, have great wealth; others such as Malawi, are very poor. One measure of a country's wealth is its gross domestic product (GDP) per capita. Australia produced $33 035 of goods and services in 2006 for every person in the country. In contrast, Malawi had a GDP per capita of $703.

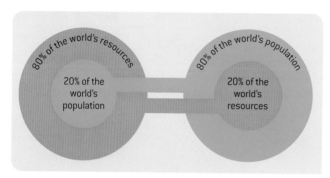

Unequal distribution of global population and resources

Wealth is not the only measure of a country's level of development. The Human Development Index (HDI), devised by the United Nations, attempts to give an indication of living standards beyond simple economic factors. It is calculated by using four measures of development: life expectancy at birth, adult literacy rates, education

standards and GDP per capita. The HDI is used by the UN, governments and non-government organisations (NGOs) such as World Vision and CARE, to target their efforts to help people most in need.

Human Development Index of selected countries, 2007

Country	Human Development Index
Australia	0.962
Brazil	0.800
China	0.777
Indonesia	0.728
India	0.619
Kenya	0.521
Malawi	0.457

Source: Data derived from Human Development Indices: A statistical update 2008.

ACTIVITIES

UNDERSTANDING

1. List three differences between the life of a child in Malawi and your life in Australia.
2. What is meant by extreme poverty?
3. How many people in the world live in extreme poverty?
4. Imagine all of the world's resources as one cake. What proportion of the world's population do you think would get more than three-quarters of the cake?
5. Name four measures of development that are used in order to calculate the Human Development Index.
6. What is Australia's HDI? How does it compare with other countries?

THINKING AND APPLYING

7. Why might rural areas suffer greater poverty than urban areas in a developing country?
8. As a class, discuss what it means to be poor. List comments on the board in point form. Write your own definition of poverty.

USING YOUR SKILLS

9. Refer to the map opposite.
   a Using the country names given on the map, select one example for each category in the key or legend.
   b What is the GDP per capita of the USA?
   c Is China's GDP per capita more or less than Australia's GDP?
   d Give two examples of continents that contain mainly developed countries.
   e Give two examples of continents that contain mainly developing countries.
   f Write a paragraph to describe the pattern of global poverty.

GEOTERMS

extreme poverty: surviving on less than US$1 a day

life expectancy: the number of years people can expect to live

literacy: the ability to read and write

Poverty and unequal access to the essentials of life, such as enough food and safe water, are serious problems in the developing world. This does not mean that the quality of life in developing countries cannot be improved. Some aspects of life *have* improved during the last 25 years:

- infant mortality rates (IMR) fell almost 50 per cent
- life expectancy increased by about nine years
- adult literacy rates increased from less than 50 per cent to more than 75 per cent
- the number of people living in poverty fell by 200 million despite a rapidly growing world population.

However, further improvements are needed if people in all countries are to lead healthy, productive lives. Differences among countries in levels of development and living conditions can be reduced through international cooperation.

The United Nations

The United Nations (UN) was founded in 1945, shortly after the end of World War II. The UN is the most important global organisation. It is made up of 192 member states. Almost every country in the world is a member. The UN is mainly funded by contributions from its member states.

The role of the UN is to:

- maintain peace and security
- encourage friendly relations among nations
- help solve economic, social, cultural, environmental and humanitarian problems
- promote respect for human rights and basic freedoms.

The main bodies of the UN are:

- The General Assembly — a parliament made up of representatives of the world's nations.
- The Security Council — responsible for keeping peace and security in the world.
- The Economic and Social Council — responsible for international economic and social cooperation and development.
- The International Court of Justice — responsible for international law and justice.

International security and peace. *UN peacekeeping troops move into position in the Democratic Republic of the Congo in Africa during civil war in 2008. One of the major roles of the UN is to maintain peace and security. The UN often intervenes to stop disputes between or within countries, or to help restore peace when conflict does break out.*

 1 Eradicate extreme poverty and hunger
Target: Halve the proportion of people who suffer extreme hunger, and the proportion of people living on less than US$1 dollar a day.

 2 Achieve universal primary education
Target: All children everywhere are able to finish primary school.

 3 Promote gender equality and empower women
Target: Girls and women are able to access the same opportunities as boys and men including secondary and tertiary education, and employment.

 4 Reduce child mortality
Target: Reduce by two-thirds the number of children who die before their fifth birthday.

 5 Improve maternal health
Target: Reduce by three-quarters the number of women who die in childbirth.

 6 Combat HIV/AIDS, malaria and other diseases
Target: Stop and begin to reverse the spread of HIV/AIDS and other diseases.

 7 Ensure environmental sustainability
Target: Halve the number of people who do not have access to safe drinking water and basic sanitation. By 2020, improve the lives of 100 million people who live in slums. Reverse the loss of environmental resources and improve sustainability.

 8 Develop a global partnership for development
Target: All countries work together to develop free trade, help developing countries cope with debt and increase aid to poorest countries.

Millennium Development Goals

Humanitarian assistance and emergencies. A survivor of tropical cyclone Nargis carries home a bag of rice from a UN food distribution centre. The cyclone devastated the Asian nation of Myanmar in 2008, killing more than 100 000 people and leaving almost two million people in need of food, water, shelter and medicine. The UN's World Food Programme delivers about one-third of the world's emergency food.

Economic and social development. Children in Bangladesh use a new water pump provided by the UN agency UNICEF. Access to safe water is one of the most effective ways of preventing killer diseases. Most UN resources are devoted to economic and social development in developing countries. UN efforts to improve access to safe water, help expand food production, and fight diseases have had a major influence on the lives and wellbeing of millions of people.

The Millennium Development Goals

In 2000, most nations around the world signed the United Nations Millennium Declaration. Governments agreed to take action to lift millions of people out of desperate poverty by 2015. There are eight Millennium Development Goals (see page 222). To achieve the goals, poor countries improve the way they govern and take responsibility to help their people achieve the first seven goals. They cannot do this, however, unless rich countries fulfil the responsibilities outlined in the eighth goal.

Goal 8 means that rich countries must offer more debt relief to poor countries and increase trade opportunities by reducing trade barriers such as agricultural subsidies.

ACTIVITIES

UNDERSTANDING

1. When and why did the UN form? What was significant about this timing?
2. What are the main aims of the UN?
3. What is the General Assembly?
4. What is the role of the Security Council?
5. Why is the UN the most important of all global organisations?
6. What is the main thing that governments agreed to do when they signed the UN Millennium Declaration?
7. Refer to the information about the Millennium Development Goals. Which three goals do you think are the most important ones to achieve? Give reasons for your choices.
8. Outline what developed countries such as Australia must do to help developing countries reach the goals.

THINKING AND APPLYING

9. Some of the different types of work undertaken by the UN are illustrated by the photographs. Describe how each of these efforts contributes to a better, fairer and more stable world.
10. What type of UN work around the world would you most like to participate in? Explain why.
11. Make a list or draw a mind map of actions taken by the UN that contribute to reducing global inequalities.
12. Use the internet to research what the Australian Government is doing to ensure the Millennium Development Goals will be reached by 2015.

GEOTERMS

aid: charitable donations of money, food, goods and services made to countries in need

free trade: occurs where goods and services are traded between countries with no restrictions

infant mortality rate (IMR): the number of deaths per 1000 babies under one year of age

sanitation: the practices in place such as toilets and sewerage systems for the disposal of waste products, including human waste

subsidies: grants of money given by governments to producers, which lower the producer's costs and allow the product to be sold at a lower price

More than one billion people suffer from extreme poverty and hunger. They cannot buy or produce enough food for their basic needs. Halving the number of hungry people in the world is top of the list of the Millennium Development Goals.

Why are people hungry?

There is enough food to feed everyone on Earth. World hunger is not due to a scarcity of food — it is due to unequal distribution of wealth.

Factors causing hunger include:

- Many people in developing countries are trapped in a cycle of poverty. Families are usually large and few jobs are available, particularly for those without skills. People cannot afford to pay for food, let alone housing, health care and education.
- Natural disasters — for example, droughts, floods and earthquakes can cause famine, which is a severe shortage of food in a region. Famine leads to skyrocketing food prices. Some sections of the population, usually the poorest, are more likely to face starvation than others.
- Wars displace millions of people and cause some of the world's worst hunger emergencies.
- Export of agricultural products to pay debt. Many countries are in debt and reduce their debt by exporting the food they grow.

In developing countries, an estimated 8 million people die each year and about 16 000 children die each day from hunger or hunger-related causes. Many children die from starvation, but most die from treatable diseases, such as measles and malaria, because hunger lowers their resistance to illness.

While many people suffer from hunger in developing countries, **obesity** has become a serious health problem in developed countries. Obesity rates in developing countries are now also increasing. Obesity is largely due to worldwide changes in the types of food that people eat, particularly a substantial increase in the consumption of vegetable oils and animal fats.

Global citizenship

Several UN agencies work to help the hungry. In 2008, the World Food Programme (WFP) provided food assistance to 102.1 million people in 78 countries. WFP's school meals programme helped feed almost 23 million children in 68 countries.

Many NGOs such as World Vision and Freedom from Hunger also provide emergency aid for people in desperate need. World Vision's 40 Hour Famine encourages people to go without food for 40 hours — to experience what it is like to go

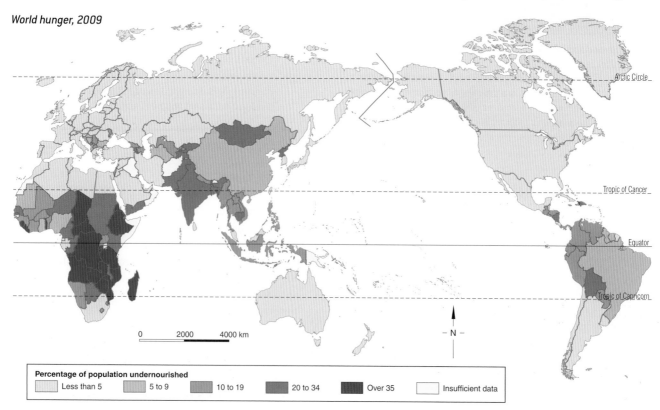

World hunger, 2009

Percentage of population undernourished

Less than 5 | 5 to 9 | 10 to 19 | 20 to 34 | Over 35 | Insufficient data

Source: Data derived from World Food Programme.

without, while at the same time raising money for children in poverty.

Make Poverty History is the largest anti-poverty movement in history. The campaign involves more than 80 countries, thousands of aid agencies, community groups across the world and millions of individuals. The focus of the campaign is to ensure governments honour their commitments to the Millennium Development Goals. It was launched in 2005 and publicised by celebrities such as U2's Bono, Bob Geldof and Brad Pitt. Australians, including TV personality Rove McManus and musicians Missy Higgins and Lior, have also taken a public stand for Make Poverty History.

Are there too many people on Earth to feed?
Birth rates are falling around the world and food production is increasing at a faster rate than population.

How much food does the world produce?
300 kilograms of grain (wheat, rice, millet) per person per year — enough food to feed everyone on Earth. Some countries stockpile surplus food.

Do all countries produce enough food?
Eighty-nine countries do not produce enough food to feed their population and they lack the money to import the shortage. One in five Africans now depends on imported food.

Is there enough farmland to grow food?
The best land is generally used for growing cash crops such as coffee (Ethiopia), cotton (Sudan) and drugs (Afghanistan, Myanmar and Colombia).

Would land reform help?
More land given to poor farmers would help reduce food insecurity. In Bolivia, 85% of the rural population has no land to grow crops; in the Philippines 78%, in Peru 75% and in Mexico 60%.

Is there enough money to buy food?
Despite improvements, there are still 1.1 billion people who live on less than a US$1 a day.

Who grows the food?
Over 2.5 billion people depend on agriculture for an income — 96% live in developing countries. In Africa, women perform most of the agricultural work. They do: 30% of ploughing, 50% of planting, 70% of weeding, 60% of harvesting, 50% of caring for livestock, and 85% of processing and storing crops.

Which countries suffer hunger?
Hungry people are mostly found in the developing regions of the world: 51% of the population in Asia, 33% in Africa, 11% in Latin America and 5% in the Middle East.

Why do countries export food when they have hungry people?
The money earned from food exports is often used to pay debts. India has the largest number of hungry people in the world, but it still sells food on the world market.

How much food is enough?
The average requirement to remain healthy is 2200 to 2400 calories per person per day. Hungry, malnourished people receive less than 2100 calories per day.

ACTIVITIES

UNDERSTANDING
1. If there is sufficient food for everyone on Earth, why does hunger exist?
2. List four factors that cause hunger in developing countries.
3. What is a famine? What can cause famine?
4. Why are hungry people more likely to be sick?
5. Name two global organisations that help the hungry.
6. What does the Make Poverty History campaign want governments to do?

THINKING AND APPLYING
7. Refer to the labelled photograph at left.
   a. How many people can't afford enough food because they live on less than US$1 a day?
   b. Who does most of the farming work in Africa?
   c. Why does India export food when it has such large numbers of hungry people?
   d. Is growing more food for the world's poor the answer? Explain.

USING YOUR SKILLS
8. Refer to the World hunger map.
   a. How does the key or legend on the map help you instantly see the pattern of world hunger?
   b. Which continent has the most undernourished population?
   c. Which three continents have the best access to food?
   d. Refer to the map, and an atlas, to describe the distribution of the world's undernourished people.
9. Compare the World hunger map with the map of GDP per capita on page 220.
   a. List three countries with:
      • high GDP and a low percentage of hungry people
      • low GDP and a high percentage of hungry people.
   b. Can you locate any countries that have a high GDP and a high percentage of hungry people?
   c. Describe the relationships you have found between the two maps.

Food is bought and sold on the global market. Australia exports beef and cheese to Japan, wheat to Iraq and Malaysia, milk and cream to Indonesia and live lambs to Saudi Arabia. At the same time, our local supermarket shelves are filled with mangoes from Kenya, cocoa from the Ivory Coast, tea from India and coffee from Colombia.

The global food market

Several features of the world food market have negative impacts on the poorest countries. The market price of commodities goes up or down depending on supply and demand. High food prices impact most on the poor. Food prices rose sharply in 2008, partly because some food crops, such as corn, are increasingly being used for biofuels (fuels made from organic matter such as plants). Low prices mean that farmers in developing countries receive less for their crops than it costs to produce them.

More than half of the world's poor depend on agriculture for their livelihood. Many of the poorest developing countries depend on just one or two crops for their export earnings. Consequently, developing countries are especially vulnerable to natural disasters such as droughts and the effects of climate change. If harvests fail, food shortages or famine can occur and all export income can be lost.

Many developing countries can grow crops very cheaply — the climate is suitable and labour costs are low. However, tariffs and subsidies in developed countries often make it difficult for developing countries to break into markets or compete. Eliminating trade barriers on farm products would greatly benefit the poorest countries because they rely most heavily on agricultural exports.

The power of TNCs

Much of the world food trade is controlled by transnational corporations (TNCs) such as Nestlé, Unilever and Kraft Foods. Nestlé is the world's largest food manufacturer, recording sales revenues of almost $US90 billion in 2007. TNCs buy and process a lot of agricultural produce and can influence the type of crops that are grown and the price that growers receive. Cash crops such as coffee, cocoa and tea are grown by developing countries because these crops can be sold to the developed world.

TNCs generally buy cheaply from producers and sell dearly to consumers. This increases the corporation's profit and is regarded as good business.

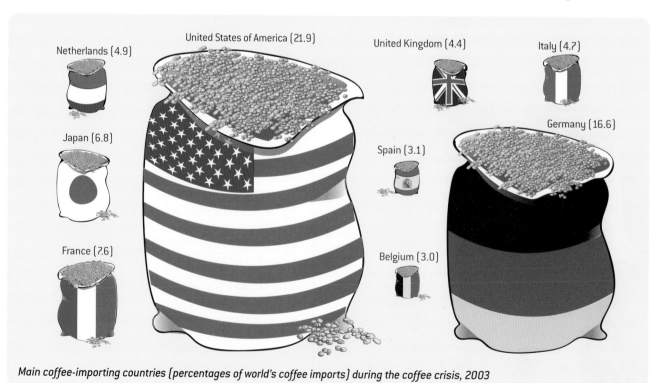

Main coffee-importing countries (percentages of world's coffee imports) during the coffee crisis, 2003

But for growers in the developing world, it means a struggle to earn a living. Increased cash cropping also means that less land is devoted to growing food.

The coffee crisis

Coffee is one of the most valuable agricultural products. In most years, it is second in value only to oil. Coffee is grown in more than 45 countries, located mainly in the tropics. About 25 million small-scale farmers around the world depend on coffee. The retail market is over $US70 billion. However, farmers make as little as 3 cents US for every cup of coffee sold.

When the price of coffee fell dramatically between 2001 and 2004, farmers faced economic ruin. It became a struggle to feed their children, let alone send them to school or pay for health care. At the time, four TNCs — Nestlé, Kraft Foods, Sara Lee and Proctor & Gamble — were the buyers of almost half the world's coffee. While coffee farmers were poverty-stricken, TNCs continued to make large profits.

Many people thought this was unfair. The NGO Oxfam publicised the tragedy and developed the Fairtrade label for coffee. This seeks to ensure that farmers in developing countries are paid a fair price. Concerned coffee drinkers bought Fairtrade coffee. Big companies responded to the pressure and the price received by growers is now generally fairer than it was.

Picking coffee beans, Colombia. Coffee represents a substantial investment for the farmer because plants do not produce beans until they are at least three years old.

Global citizenship

Changes to the global food market could ensure that fewer people suffer hunger. Millennium Development Goal 8 means that rich countries should reduce trade barriers and offer more debt relief to poorer countries so that they do not have to use the food they grow as exports to decrease their debt.

ACTIVITIES

UNDERSTANDING

1. List some foods that Australia exports and imports.
2. Find five items of food in your pantry that were produced in a country other than Australia.
3. Why do droughts usually have a big impact on the economies of developing countries?
4. How do trade barriers contribute to global inequality?
5. Describe the effect of the coffee crisis on farmers. Did the crisis have a similar impact on the incomes of TNCs?
6. What did Oxfam do to try to reduce inequalities in the coffee industry?
7. Explain how the eighth Millennium Development Goal could contribute to a more equal world.

THINKING AND APPLYING

8. Answer these key geographical questions about the global coffee industry.
   a Where is coffee produced and consumed?
   b What role do TNCs play in the coffee industry?
   c What problems and opportunities does the coffee industry give to developing countries?
   d How can inequalities in the coffee industry be reduced?
9. Interview a grandparent about the type of food they ate as a child. Compare their diet with your diet.

USING YOUR SKILLS

10. Refer to the picture graph opposite.
    a Which four countries imported the most coffee?
    b Which four countries produced the most coffee?
    c Refer to the map of GDP on page 220. With the aid of an atlas, compare the GDP of the top four coffee importers and producers. Summarise your findings in a sentence that includes the terms 'developing countries' and 'developed countries'.

GEOTERMS

tariff: a tax imposed on imports

Unsafe water, coupled with a lack of basic sanitation, kills at least 1.6 million children under the age of five each year. Halving the number of people who do not have access to safe water and sanitation is part of Millennium Development Goal 7. According to the World Health Organization, there is a good chance that the world will achieve the safe water target by 2015.

Access to enough water

Like other natural resources, water is unevenly distributed. Many countries, most of them in Africa and the Middle East, do not have enough water. In other countries, especially in Asia, water may be available but unusable because of pollution. Women and children often have to walk for hours to collect water. In developing nations, the daily chore of hauling water is usually carried out by women and girls.

Lack of access to safe water is linked to poverty. Wealthy countries can afford to build dams or use technology to improve water quality. Although Australia is the driest inhabited continent, Australians are among the highest consumers of water in the world — about 350 litres per person per day. People in Asia, Africa and South America use 50–100 litres per day.

Water scarcity is becoming a significant threat to human health, the environment and the global food supply. Climate change is likely to bring more frequent and more severe droughts to many vulnerable regions, further reducing the amount of available water.

Young Zimbabwean girls carry buckets of water to their homes.

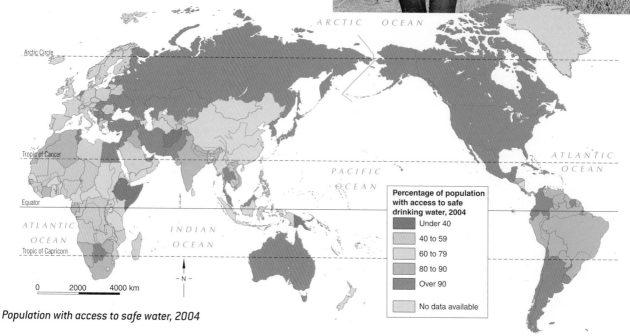

Population with access to safe water, 2004

Percentage of population with access to safe drinking water, 2004

- Under 40
- 40 to 59
- 60 to 79
- 80 to 90
- Over 90
- No data available

Access to safe water

It is not enough for people to have an adequate amount of water. Water also must be of an adequate quality for drinking and washing — it should not be polluted or contain disease-carrying organisms. Toilets and sewerage systems are essential to get rid of waste and prevent disease. Without them, micro-organisms from faeces end up in the water that people drink from rivers, ponds and wells. One in every six people in the world does not have safe drinking water. One in three lacks basic sanitation.

Millions of people die each year from water-borne diseases such as cholera, typhoid and dysentery. Such diseases are caused by drinking contaminated water or by eating food prepared using unsafe water. Many water-borne infections cause diarrhoea, which leads to dehydration. Diarrhoea is a major cause of childhood deaths. These deaths are preventable — diarrhoea does not usually kill people in developed countries.

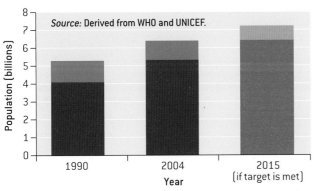

Source: Derived from WHO and UNICEF.

■ Population with access to safe water
■ Population without access to safe water
■ Population with access to safe water if MDG target is met
■ Still without access to safe water if target is met

World population with and without access to safe water in 1990, 2004 and 2015

Global citizenship

AusAID is the agency that manages the Australian Government's official overseas aid program (see pages 238–9). One of its projects is in Vietnam's Cuu Long Delta, bringing safe water to 400 000 rural people and sanitation facilities to another 200 000. Water is plentiful in the region, but it is not suitable for drinking or washing. Waste from industry and households is discharged into the river and each year the river is polluted by floodwaters. AusAID, in partnership with the Vietnamese Government and local communities, is building several water supply and sanitation systems. It is also providing support for local communities to manage and maintain the facilities.

UN agencies involved in improving access to safe water and sanitation include WHO (the World Health Organization) and UNICEF (the United Nations Children's Fund). Many NGOs, such as Global Water and World Vision, are involved in water projects. Such efforts also improve the chances of reaching other Millennium Development Goals, especially Goals 4, 5 and 6, which focus on health. It is estimated that 80 per cent of disease in the developing world is associated with unsafe water and lack of sanitation.

ACTIVITIES

UNDERSTANDING

1. What kills at least 1.6 million children each year?
2. Why is sanitation necessary to prevent disease?
3. Answer these key geographical questions about the Cuu Long Delta project.
   a. Where is the Cuu Long Delta?
   b. Which groups are building the project together?
   c. What is the aim of the project?
   d. Why is the project necessary?
4. Name two global organisations involved in improving access to safe water.

THINKING AND APPLYING

5. What is the difference between access to quantity of water and access to quality of water? Why are they both important?
6. Explain why Australians are water rich, despite living in the driest inhabited continent.
7. Why would reaching Goal 7 increase the chances of reaching Goals 4, 5 and 6?

USING YOUR SKILLS

8. Refer to the map of access to safe drinking water and use an atlas to answer the following questions.
   a. Which continent has the worst access to safe water?
   b. Which three continents have the best access to safe water?
   c. List three countries with the worst access to safe water.
   d. Identify a neighbouring country to Australia with poor access to safe water.
9. Refer to the column graph of world population with and without access to safe water.
   a. Are the following statements true or false?
      • About 4 billion people had access to safe water in 1990.
      • By 2004, the number of people with access to safe water had increased by more than 1 billion.
      • If Goal 7 is reached by 2015, more than 6 billion people will have access to safe water.
   b. The amount of available water has decreased since 1950, yet the number of people with access to safe water is increasing. Why?

Along with food and water, shelter (protection from the elements) is a basic need. Among the 5.5 billion people living in developing countries, about one in four lives in substandard housing. Others have no home at all because they have been displaced by war or must move to search for food, water or employment.

More and more people are moving to cities in search of a better life. One billion people live in over-crowded slums on the edges of cities where there is often no access to safe water and sanitation, resulting in disease and other health problems. Fifty per cent of the world's population now lives in cities. By 2030, the proportion is expected to reach 60 per cent. The largest urban growth is occurring in Africa and Asia.

Millennium Development Goal 7, which aims to improve access to safe water and sanitation, also aims to improve the lives of 100 million slum dwellers. The figure appears huge but it is only 10 per cent of the world slum population.

Case study: Nairobi

Nairobi is the capital city of Kenya. It is one of the largest and fastest growing cities in Africa. Nairobi has a large slum population and a large tourist industry, making it a city of contrasts.

Nairobi's centre lies on a relatively flat plain, while the areas to the west and north are hilly.

Living conditions in Nairobi demonstrate the divide that exists between the rich and the poor in many cities of the world.

Poverty-stricken families may live under bridges, beside rivers, adjacent to landfills and near railways when they first come to Nairobi from surrounding country areas.

Nairobi has one of the world's highest rates of people infected with the AIDS virus.

In general, Nairobi's wealthy residents live to the west and the least wealthy residents live to the east. Shantytowns have grown up next to some residential areas.

Nairobi's slums house 60 per cent of Nairobi's population. The Mathari Valley, built in an old rock quarry, is the oldest, largest and worst slum in the city. Nearly half a million people live in its cluster of tin-roofed shanties.

For the tourist to Nairobi, there are theatres, five-star restaurants, email facilities and first-class accommodation. The entertainment sectors of the city are constantly alive, especially at night.

Kenya's wealth is not evenly distributed and a large percentage of its people live in poverty. Many people from rural areas migrate to the cities each year, hoping to find a better life. Most have low education levels and lack the skills employers want, therefore finding it difficult to gain stable employment. As a result they usually end up living in run-down, disease-infested slums.

Kenya — the statistics (compared with Australia)

	Kenya	Australia
Population (2008)	38 million	21 million
Access to safe drinking water	57%	100%
Infant mortality rate (per 1000 live births)	77	5
Life expectancy	53/53* years	79/84* years
Deaths from AIDS (2003)	150 000	fewer than 200
GDP per capita	$US1700	$US37 300
Unemployment	40%	4.5%

* The first number is for males, the second for females.

Many of the city's streets and highways are regularly in poor condition and subject to floods in times of heavy rainfall.

Places where poor people live are overcrowded. Their shelter is often temporary, and they frequently lack access to water and sanitation, and to health services.

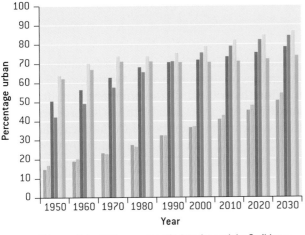

Growth in urban population, 1950 to 2030

Percentage urban (y-axis: 0 to 100)
Year (x-axis: 1950, 1960, 1970, 1980, 1990, 2000, 2010, 2020, 2030)

■ Africa ■ Asia ■ Europe ■ Latin America and the Caribbean
■ Northern America ■ Oceania

Source: UNFPA, State of world population 2007, p. 11.

Some international tourists go on safaris in the surrounding countryside to see lions, elephants and giraffes. People can also visit Giraffe Manor where a giraffe may join them for their meals.

Nairobi has an ultra-modern skyline with many five-star hotels.

International tourists have the services of over 250 cafes, restaurants and snack bars as well as clubs, casinos and discotheques in Nairobi's congested city centre. They can visit the city market, the National Museum and the Kenya National Archives, and horseracing meets.

Nairobi receives significant revenue from tourism.

Houses may be made from cloth cardboard, corrugated iron, scrap wood, boxes, tarpaulins and rope.

Children working on the streets are more susceptible to respiratory infections, pneumonia and other illnesses, and face a high risk of injury of death from motor vehicles. They can be used to assist with drug deals, robberies and extortion. Some are even forced into child prostitution. In the long term, there is little chance of these children gaining meaningful employment.

ACTIVITIES

UNDERSTANDING

1. Outline the reasons why Nairobi is a 'city of contrasts'.
2. Draw a table with two columns headed 'Push factors' and 'Pull factors' (see page 278). Complete it with as many entries as you can for the rural people who migrate to Kenyan cities.
3. Refer to the large illustration. List three examples of how your opportunities in life would be limited if you lived in a place like this.

THINKING AND APPLYING

4. Create a collage of shelters around the world. Include notes or labels that explain the relationship between the type of shelter and wealth.
5. Use the illustration to help you complete one of the following.
   a. Write a short biography about a person who is born in the slums of Nairobi.
   b. Create and perform the lyrics of a song that could have been written by a teenager from a Nairobi slum.
   c. Roleplay, with a partner, what happens when a wealthy tourist takes a wrong turn, walks into a Nairobi slum and comes face to face with a slum dweller.
6. It is not only cities in developing countries that have homeless people. Have a class discussion about:
   a. why a developed country like Australia has homeless people
   b. why young people, in particular, might be homeless
   c. what can be done to help Australia's homeless young people.
7. Form into small groups. Your team has been employed by the Nairobi City Council. Your task is to plan a 15-year strategy to eliminate the slum areas. What will you do? Present your plan to the class.

USING YOUR SKILLS

8. Refer to the column graph above left.
   a. Which regions had the largest percentage of their population living in urban areas in 1950 and 2010?
   b. What is the percentage change of people in urban areas from 1950 to 2010 in Africa, Asia and Europe?
   c. Which region is expected to have less of their population living in urban areas in 2030 than they did in 1980?
   d. Describe the trends shown in the graph.

Most of us expect that we will have enough to eat, that services such as water and sanitation will be provided and that if we are sick, help will be available. But health care and infrastructure such as hospitals cost money. Not all people have access to doctors, hospitals and medicine, or to safe water and sanitation. Access to modern health services is possible for only one in five people in developing countries.

Millennium Development Goals 4, 5 and 6 target inequalities in health. Goals 4 and 5 aim to reduce by two-thirds the number of children who die before their fifth birthday and reduce by three-quarters the number of women who die in childbirth. Goal 6 aims to stop, and begin to reverse, the spread of HIV/AIDS and other diseases.

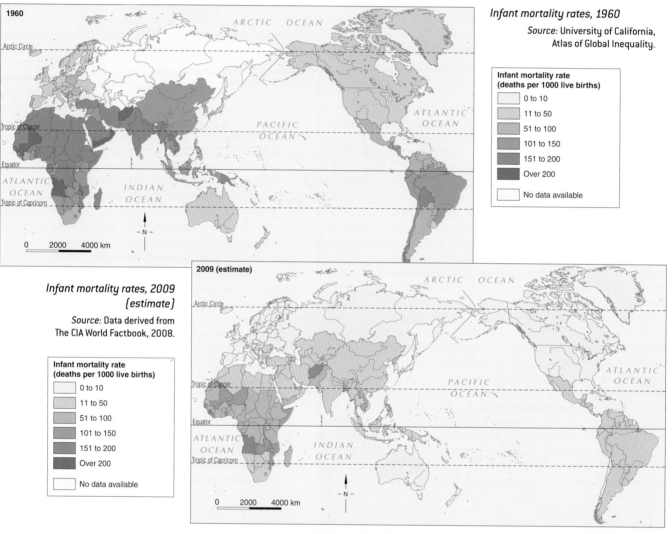

Infant mortality rates, 1960

Source: University of California, Atlas of Global Inequality.

Infant mortality rate (deaths per 1000 live births)
- 0 to 10
- 11 to 50
- 51 to 100
- 101 to 150
- 151 to 200
- Over 200
- No data available

Infant mortality rates, 2009 (estimate)

Source: Data derived from The CIA World Factbook, 2008.

Infant mortality rate (deaths per 1000 live births)
- 0 to 10
- 11 to 50
- 51 to 100
- 101 to 150
- 151 to 200
- Over 200
- No data available

Poverty linked to health services, maternal deaths and undernourishment, 2008

Country	Population living below US$1 a day (%)	Health expenditure per capita ($)	Births attended by skilled people (%)	Persons per doctor	Population with access to affordable essential drugs (%)	Population undernourished (%)	Death of mothers per 100 000 births
Yemen	15.6	82	27	4 100	50–79	38	800
Philippines	14.8	203	60	800	50–79	18	200
Honduras	14.9	197	56	1 100	0–49	23	180
Nicaragua	45.1	231	67	1 055	0–49	27	210
Burkino Faso	27.2	77	38	26 555	50–79	15	1 100
Mali	36.1	54	48	19 232	50–79	29	550
Australia	1.0	3 123	100	410	95–100	0	6

Japan
(82 years)
$34 200

Australia
(82 years)
$38 100

Brazil
(72 years)
$10 100

Papua New Guinea
(66 years)
$2200

Kenya
(58 years)
$1600

Mozambique
(41 years)
$900

Comparing life expectancy and GDP per capita

Source: The CIA World Factbook, 2008.

Health indicators

Health indicators are used to compare the health of populations in different regions or countries. The number of deaths per 1000 babies under one year old is called the infant mortality rate or IMR. The highest IMR is in developing countries, the lowest is in developed countries. There are strong links between poverty and IMR.

How long someone can expect to live is called life expectancy. In developed countries, it is gradually increasing. This is largely due to a drop in infectious diseases such as cholera, measles and influenza. A similar drop is not occurring in the developing world. Africa has the lowest levels of life expectancy and the highest levels of IMR.

Health and development

The health of a nation reflects its level of development. As geographers, it is important to see good health as more than an absence of disease. There is a clear link between where major diseases occur and the region's level of development. There is also a clear link between development and other health indicators such as the number of doctors per person, the number of hospitals and access to safe water. Links between development and health are obvious in the Human Development Index (HDI). All of the countries with the world's lowest HDIs are located in Africa.

A helping hand

Médecins Sans Frontières (Doctors without Borders) gives emergency medical assistance and humanitarian support in 78 developing countries. Often, the doctors work under very difficult conditions. The organisation was one of the first to offer free treatment of diseases to countries trapped in poverty. Eighty per cent of their funding comes from private donors. Médecins Sans Frontières is leading the fight against infectious diseases in Africa, particularly HIV/AIDS.

There is a long way to go before people in developing countries can achieve the essentials necessary for a healthy life. However, due to the efforts of international agencies, such as the World Health Organization, progress has been made. Since 1960, child death rates in developing countries have halved, malnutrition rates have declined by a third, access to safe water has almost doubled and immunisation programs have saved the lives of millions of children.

ACTIVITIES ➔

UNDERSTANDING

1. Why don't more people in developing countries have access to health care?
2. What is the aim of Millennium Development Goal 4?
3. Define infant mortality rate.

USING YOUR SKILLS

4. Refer to the picture graph above comparing GDP with life expectancy.
   a. What is the life expectancy for people in the two wealthiest countries?
   b. What is the GDP for the country with the lowest life expectancy?
   c. What is the relationship between GDP and life expectancy?
5. Rank each of the countries shown in the table from best (1) to worst (7) for each category. Write a report card for the worst performing country, outlining where they are performing well and where they can improve in the future.
6. Refer to the two maps of IMR in 1960 and in 2009. Has there been an improvement in IMR over time? Describe how the pattern of IMR shown on the maps changed from 1960 to 2009.
7. Refer to the maps and an atlas to identify examples of the following:
   a. the country with the worst record of IMR in 2009
   b. a country with little or no improvement to its IMR between 1960 and 2009
   c. a country that reduced its IMR from 51–100 in 1960 to 0–10 in 2009.

Nkosi Johnson, an eleven-year-old orphan, addressed the 2000 World AIDS Conference in Durban, South Africa. He had suffered from HIV/AIDS since the day he was born. Nkosi knew that he had defied the odds to survive so long. He stood on the stage and pleaded for people to show compassion to HIV/AIDS sufferers.

'You cannot catch AIDS from hugging or kissing or holding hands,' he said. 'We are normal, we are human beings.'

Less than 12 months later Nkosi died.

Nkosi Johnson at the 2000 World Aids Conference

A deadly epidemic

HIV/AIDS is the world's fourth largest killer and the leading cause of death in Africa. There are over 30 million people worldwide with HIV. More than two-thirds live in Africa. Three out of four young Africans suffering from HIV are women and girls.

Human immunodeficiency virus (HIV) weakens the body's defences against infection. Acquired immunodeficiency syndrome (AIDS) is the collection of symptoms and infections that occur when HIV defeats the immune system. HIV typically spreads through unsafe drug use (particularly sharing needles) and sexual activity. Babies are exposed to HIV in the womb, during birth and through breastfeeding. At present there is no cure, but antiretroviral drugs can slow down the damage that HIV causes to the immune system, and delay the onset of AIDS.

In Africa, lack of health care and education helps to spread the disease. In some areas, 40 to 70 per cent of young girls do not know how to prevent HIV. Stigma keeps victims from being tested and the social and economic circumstances of girls and women make it difficult for them to avoid unsafe sex (most women are infected during heterosexual sex).

Children and HIV/AIDS

Families coping with HIV/AIDS are burdened by medical bills, lost wages and discrimination. Children often have to drop out of school to take care of the sick and earn additional income. More than 15 million children worldwide, including more than 12 million children in Africa, have lost one or both parents to AIDS. Many orphans have to take on the responsibilities of running the household and caring for younger sisters and brothers.

What can be done?

In recent years, the annual number of AIDS deaths has fallen worldwide, due to education and greater access to treatment. Pregnant women with HIV can now be treated with antiretroviral drugs to prevent mother-to-child infection. From 2005 to 2007, the percentage of pregnant women receiving treatment grew from 14 to 33 per cent. As a result, the number of new infections among children fell from 410 000 to 370 000.

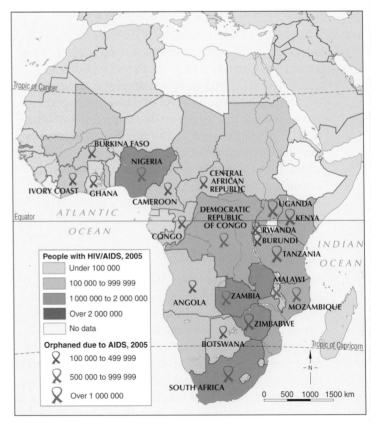

The African AIDS epidemic

AIDS poster in Zambia, Africa

The sixth Millennium Development Goal aims to stop, and begin to reverse, the spread of HIV/AIDS and other diseases. Achieving this goal would also help to achieve other goals, such as reducing poverty, reducing the number of children who die before their fifth birthday and improving the health of mothers. Goals 2 and 3, which emphasise education and gender equality, have a key role to play in the battle against HIV/AIDS.

The red ribbon is an international symbol of AIDS awareness.

Due to the work of UN agencies, governments and NGOs, treatment for HIV has improved remarkably in some African countries. In Rwanda in 2003, only 3 per cent of people with HIV received treatment. By 2007, this had risen to 70 per cent. Educational programs also work. In Cameroon, the percentage of young people having sex before the age of 15 has dropped from 35 to 14 per cent.

Australian captain Ricky Ponting at the ICC Cricket World Cup 2007, promoting the Unite for Children, Unite against AIDS campaign

ACTIVITIES

UNDERSTANDING

1. What is AIDS?
2. Which continent has the greatest number of people with HIV? Which gender is most affected in this continent?
3. Describe some of the impacts that an AIDS epidemic could have on people and on countries.
4. Name two factors that have helped to reduce the number of AIDS deaths worldwide in recent years.

THINKING AND APPLYING

5. Refer to the photograph taken in Zambia above left.
   a Who is the target audience for the sign shown in the photograph?
   b What message do you thing the sign is trying to convey?
   c How effective do you think the sign might be?
6. Conduct a debate on the following: 'HIV/AIDS is largely a disease of poverty'.

USING YOUR SKILLS

7. Refer to the map of Africa opposite.
   a Which African countries have more than 500 000 orphans due to AIDS?
   b For Zimbabwe describe:
     • the number of people with HIV/AIDS
     • the number of AIDS orphans.
   c Imagine you work for a major aid organisation. The map has been presented to you as evidence of the HIV/AIDS crisis in Africa. Which countries would you select for the most urgent action and why?

GEOTERMS

antiretroviral: a substance that stops or slows the activity of a retrovirus such as HIV

Does education matter?

Imagine your life without school, exams and teachers. To many students this sounds great, but the ability to read street signs, your wage slip or a warning label on a poison bottle are important life skills. Without the ability to read, write and calculate, your choice of jobs and access to opportunities in life are limited.

Literacy is the ability to read and write. In the developing world, on average, about 15 per cent of males and 30 per cent of females cannot read or write. Many children leave primary school because they must work so that their family can survive. Global literacy has improved, but some countries and groups are still missing out. Males and people in urban areas have a better chance of going to school.

Education for all?

According to the Universal Declaration of Human Rights, everyone has the right to an education. Improving access to schooling in developing countries helps the poor to increase their earnings and therefore their living standards. Education plays a crucial role in improving health, promoting equality and overcoming gender bias. It helps people make informed choices and share in decision making.

Several factors restrict the life opportunities of girls and women. Many women in developing countries endure a daily struggle to provide food and water for their families. Consequently, there is little time or opportunity for women to access education. Traditional customs may discourage girls from going to school or getting a job, and prevent women from owning land or other items such as cattle.

Millennium Development Goal 2 aims to enable all children everywhere to finish primary school. Goal 3 aims to promote gender equity and empower women. This means that girls and women should have the same opportunities as boys and men, including secondary and tertiary education and employment.

There is a strong relationship between education, fertility rates and poverty. The more education women have, the more likely they are to have small families. As literacy rates increase, poverty declines.

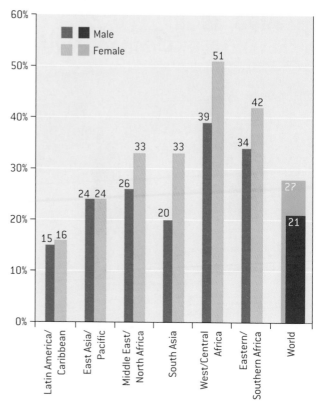

Source: UNICEF, *A fit world for children statistical review*, 2007, p. 17.

Percentage of girls and boys not in secondary school, 2006

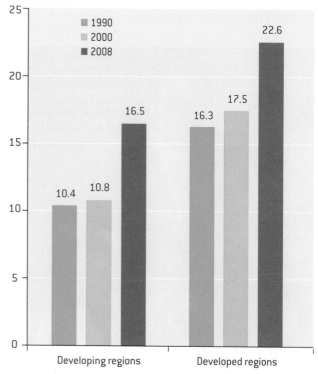

Source: UN, *The Millennium Development Goals Report 2008*, p. 19.

Percentage of seats held by women in national parliaments

Education in Indonesia

/// Indonesia is a developing country with a population of 240 million, the fourth largest in the world. It is also the world's largest Muslim nation and one of our closest neighbours. In 1975, only 72 per cent of Indonesian children attended primary school. By 2005, this had increased to more than 90 per cent. However, only half the children in poor districts are able to attend secondary school.

The Indonesian Government wants every child to have six years of primary and three years of secondary education. To achieve this, more schools are needed, the quality of education has to be improved, and more girls and boys have to attend school and stay at school longer.

AusAID and Indonesia

Through AusAID, Australia is funding the construction of 2000 new junior secondary schools across 19 provinces in Indonesia. Local people are building the schools using locally supplied materials. This building program will create 330 000 new school places for 13–15 year olds. The Australia–Indonesia Basic Education Program began in 2006 and targets districts that are poor, difficult to reach and lacking in educational services. Equal access to education for both girls and boys is central to the program. Gender bias will also be targeted in instructional materials, such as textbooks, and through the professional development of women as education leaders and managers.

In 2009, a supplementary reading materials program was introduced, with the aim of increasing students' interest in reading and writing. Both fiction and non-fiction books have been provided to more than 900 schools. In the more remote provinces, parents would previously have had to travel more than four hours by rented motorbike to get to a town where they could purchase a book.

AusAID is helping to fund the construction of 2000 new junior secondary schools in Indonesia.

ACTIVITIES

UNDERSTANDING

1. What is literacy?
2. How can education break the poverty cycle?
3. Why is there a large drop-out rate from schools in developing countries?
4. What factors contribute to fewer girls having access to education in developing countries?
5. What does gender equity mean?
6. List six facts about Indonesia.
7. List six improvements that the Indonesian Government is making to its education system.
8. What is AusAID doing that will increase access to education in Indonesia? Which groups will benefit the most?

THINKING AND APPLYING

9. Draw a mind map of ways that illiteracy could restrict life opportunities.
10. Explain the links between education, fertility rates and poverty.
11. Why do you think it is a human right to have access to education? How does education empower people?
12. Explain why education is important for the development of a country.

USING YOUR SKILLS

13. Refer to the column graph of children not in secondary school.
    a. Which region has the greatest percentage of boys not in secondary school?
    b. Which region has the greatest percentage of girls not in secondary school? What proportion of girls does not attend secondary school in this region?
    c. Which two regions have achieved gender equity in school attendance?
14. Refer to the column graph of women in national parliaments.
    a. In 1990, what percentage of women were members of governments in developing regions?
    b. Has gender equity been achieved in developed regions?
    c. What do the trends in the graph show?

GEOTERMS

fertility rate: the average number of children a woman is likely to have in her lifetime. A rate of just over two, called the replacement level, keeps population numbers steady.

gender equity: equal access of females and males to opportunities such as education and employment

AusAID: acting to reduce inequalities

The Australian Agency for International Development (AusAID) manages the Australian Government's official overseas aid program. The main objective of this program is to reduce the gap between rich and poor countries by helping developing countries reduce poverty and achieve sustainable development. AusAID works closely with Australian Businesses, non-government organisations (such as World Vision and Care Australia) and international agencies (such as the Red Cross and the United Nations).

Australia's overseas aid

Overseas aid is the transfer of money, food and services from developed countries to developing countries. Australia gives aid to help reduce world poverty and to improve our regional security (aid improves regional security by helping to ensure that neighbouring countries are more stable). Australia's overseas aid program is funded by the federal government and managed through AusAID. From 2007–08, Australia provided $3.7 billion worth of aid — about $2.40 per person per week. This amounts to around 1 per cent of the federal government's total expenditure.

People waiting for aid in the aftermath of a cyclone and storm surge that devastated Bangladesh in 2007

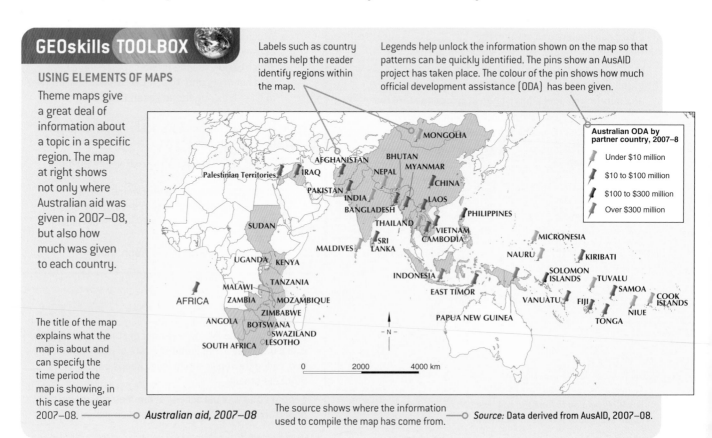

GEOskills TOOLBOX

USING ELEMENTS OF MAPS

Theme maps give a great deal of information about a topic in a specific region. The map at right shows not only where Australian aid was given in 2007–08, but also how much was given to each country.

The title of the map explains what the map is about and can specify the time period the map is showing, in this case the year 2007–08. ——o *Australian aid, 2007–08*

Labels such as country names help the reader identify regions within the map.

Legends help unlock the information shown on the map so that patterns can be quickly identified. The pins show an AusAID project has taken place. The colour of the pin shows how much official development assistance (ODA) has been given.

Australian ODA by partner country, 2007–8

Under $10 million
$10 to $100 million
$100 to $300 million
Over $300 million

MONGOLIA
AFGHANISTAN
BHUTAN
Palestinian Territories
IRAQ
NEPAL
MYANMAR
PAKISTAN
CHINA
INDIA
LAOS
BANGLADESH
PHILIPPINES
SUDAN
THAILAND
VIETNAM
CAMBODIA
SRI LANKA
MICRONESIA
MALDIVES
UGANDA
KENYA
NAURU
KIRIBATI
TANZANIA
SOLOMON ISLANDS
TUVALU
MALAWI
INDONESIA
SAMOA
AFRICA
ZAMBIA
MOZAMBIQUE
EAST TIMOR
VANUATU
FIJI
COOK ISLANDS
ZIMBABWE
NIUE
ANGOLA
BOTSWANA
PAPUA NEW GUINEA
TONGA
SWAZILAND
SOUTH AFRICA
LESOTHO

– N –

0   2000   4000 km

The source shows where the information used to compile the map has come from. ——o *Source:* Data derived from AusAID, 2007–08.

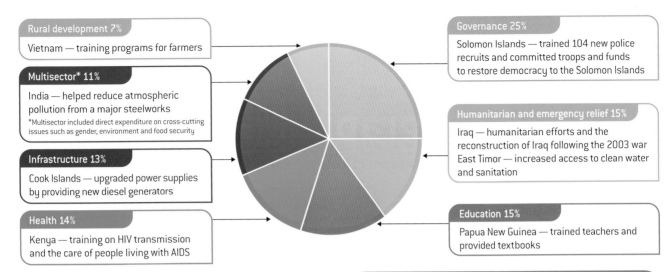

Rural development 7%

Vietnam — training programs for farmers

Multisector* 11%

India — helped reduce atmospheric pollution from a major steelworks
*Multisector included direct expenditure on cross-cutting issues such as gender, environment and food security

Infrastructure 13%

Cook Islands — upgraded power supplies by providing new diesel generators

Health 14%

Kenya — training on HIV transmission and the care of people living with AIDS

Governance 25%

Solomon Islands — trained 104 new police recruits and committed troops and funds to restore democracy to the Solomon Islands

Humanitarian and emergency relief 15%

Iraq — humanitarian efforts and the reconstruction of Iraq following the 2003 war
East Timor — increased access to clean water and sanitation

Education 15%

Papua New Guinea — trained teachers and provided textbooks

AusAID's direct expenditure by sector, 2007–08

Every year the Australian overseas aid program reaches more than 58 million people living in poverty. The program also responds to humanitarian and emergency relief situations such as helping the victims of natural disasters, terrorism, war and famine. A range of growing global issues such as HIV/AIDS, the illegal trade in drugs and small arms, and illegal immigration remain an ongoing priority for AusAID programs. If left unchecked, these issues pose a serious threat to regional development and security. It is, therefore, in Australia's interest and part of its responsibility to global citizenship to continue to have a strong program of overseas aid.

A young Indonesian tsunami survivor receives a container of water from an Australian soldier. The tsunami that hit South-East Asia on Boxing Day 2004 was followed by one of the world's largest peace-time aid efforts.

ACTIVITIES →

UNDERSTANDING

1. What is AusAID?
2. How does AusAID help to reduce global inequalities?
3. Who funds AusAID?
4. How do AusAID activities benefit Australia?
5. Refer to the photographs. Choose one photograph and answer the following questions.
   a What was the cause of the disaster?
   b In which country was the photograph taken?
   c What sort of aid would be desperately needed?
   d Why would this country need help to cope with the disaster?

THINKING AND APPLYING

6. Investigate a non-government aid agency. Include:
   a the name of the organisation
   b the main work done
   c examples of their programs.
   Present your findings as a written report, a multi-media presentation or a poster.

USING YOUR SKILLS

7. Refer to the pie graph.
   a List the top four items in AusAID's budget.
   b Give examples of two countries that have benefited from AusAID activities. What was achieved?
8. Refer to the map of Australian aid opposite.
   a What do the pins on the map represent?
   b Who supplied the aid and when was it distributed to the countries?
   c Which two countries receive the most aid from Australia? Why do you think this is the case?
   d Africa is not a neighbour of Australia. Why do you think Australia offers aid to countries in this region?
   e Why do you think Iraq appears as an exception to the general pattern shown on the map?
   f Rank the countries on the map from those receiving the smallest to the largest amounts of foreign aid.

Working geographically

KNOWLEDGE AND UNDERSTANDING

Select the alternative A, B, C or D that best answers the question.

1. How many people live in extreme poverty?
   - (A) About 100 million
   - (B) About 500 million
   - (C) About 700 million
   - (D) About 1 billion

2. Why do so many of the world's people suffer from hunger?
   - (A) Wealth is distributed unequally.
   - (B) There isn't enough food on Earth to feed everyone.
   - (C) Crop failures
   - (D) All of the above

3. What makes it difficult for farmers in developing countries to make a profit from agricultural exports?
   - (A) High commodity prices
   - (B) High labour costs
   - (C) Trade barriers such as subsidies and tariffs in developed countries
   - (D) Developing countries can produce only enough commodities, such as coffee, for their own needs.

4. Which of the following statements are supported by evidence in the pie graph?

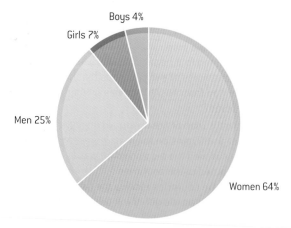

Member of the household usually collecting water, 2005–06 (percentage)

   - (A) Women are more than twice as likely as men to collect water.
   - (B) Children collect water in 11 per cent of households.
   - (C) More girls than boys fetch water.
   - (D) All of the above

5. What percentage of people in developing countries live in substandard housing?
   - (A) 25 per cent
   - (B) 30 per cent
   - (C) 50 per cent
   - (D) 70 per cent

6. Which Millennium Development Goals focus on health?
   - (A) Goals 4 and 5
   - (B) Goals 5 and 6
   - (C) Goals 4 and 6
   - (D) All of the above

7. Which continent has the highest IMR and the lowest life expectancy?
   - (A) Africa
   - (B) South America
   - (C) Asia
   - (D) Europe

8. Which continent has the greatest number of people with HIV/AIDS?
   - (A) Africa
   - (B) South America
   - (C) Asia
   - (D) Europe

9. What is AusAID?
   - (A) An NGO based in Australia that provides aid to other countries
   - (B) The Australian government's overseas aid program
   - (C) Any form of aid given to other countries by Australians
   - (D) A series of concerts held to raise money for people in poverty

10. Which of the following statements best describes the information shown on the map above right?
   - (A) In developed countries, more than 90 per cent of children attend secondary school.
   - (B) In some countries in Africa, less than 50 per cent of children attend primary school. There are still several countries in Asia and South America where less than 90 per cent of children attend primary school.
   - (C) Europe is the only continent where 90 per cent of children in all countries attend primary school.
   - (D) Africa has the most countries with less than 50 per cent of children in primary school. In all other continents, at least 90 per cent of children attend primary school.

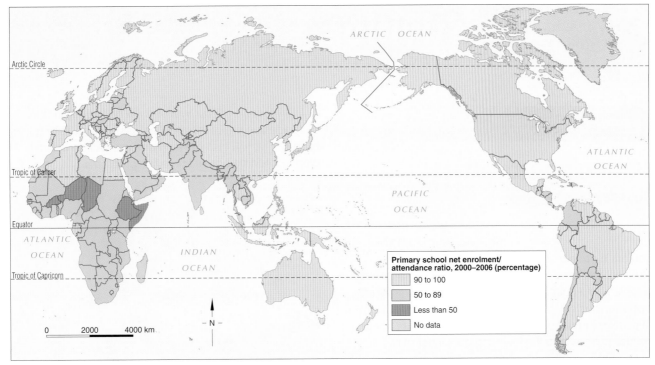

Percentage of children who attend primary school, 2000–06

SHORT RESPONSE

11 Imagine you are one of the people living in a tent in the photograph below. Briefly outline how it might feel to lose your home. List at least three things that you no longer have access to now that you are living in a tent.

PRESENTING DATA

12 Transform the data in the table below into a bar or column graph.

Coffee production during the coffee crisis, 2003

Country	Coffee (metric tonnes)
Brazil	2 493 520
Colombia	696 840
Ethiopia	220 000
Indonesia	622 646
Papua New Guinea	62 500
USA	3 400
Vietnam	688 700

Inequalities and lack of access to essential aspects of life also occur within developed countries. During the worldwide economic crisis in 2008, many Americans became homeless because they could not afford to keep up with their mortgage payments. They had to leave their homes and live wherever they could — in their cars, in caravan parks and tents. The photograph shows a tent city that sprang up in a car park in the city of Reno in the United States during October 2008.

EXTENDED RESPONSE

13 Describe global variations in peoples' access to essential resources. Mention food, shelter, health care, education and safe water in your response. Consider why these variations occur and some ways of reducing them.

projects*plus*

Reducing poverty

SEARCHLIGHT ID: PRO-0034

SCENARIO

You are a project officer working with the United Nations. You have been assigned the task of informing people of the poor living conditions and the limited life opportunities experienced by millions of people living in developing nations. Your project is intended to help reduce poverty and the level of global inequality.

You have identified five key issues that are responsible for millions of people being forced to live in extreme poverty around the world — health, education, food, water and shelter. You are required to create an action plan to address these issues in a country of your choice.

YOUR TASK

Create a website that not only grabs people's attention but also informs them of the plight of a particular developing nation. Visitors to your website will be confronted by images and facts concerning the low standards of living of one of the poorest nations in the world.

A key feature of your website will be the information it provides on five of the most pressing issues facing this country. You will also develop and present an action plan to alleviate one of these five problems.

PROCESS

- Open the ProjectsPLUS application for this chapter, located in your eBookPLUS. Watch the introductory video lesson and then click the 'Start Project' button to set up your project group. You can complete this project individually or invite other members of your class to form a group. Save your settings and the project will be launched.
- Choose a focus nation that is dealing with extreme poverty for your website.
- Navigate to your Research Forum. The five key issues surrounding poverty have been loaded as topics to provide a framework for your research. You should find at least three sources to help you identify the challenges confronted by your country in providing health, education, food, water and shelter for its population. The weblinks in your Media Centre will help get you started. Enter your findings as articles under each topic in your Research Forum. You can view and comment on other group members' articles and rate the information they have entered.
- When you have completed your research, navigate to your Media Centre and download the website-planning template to help you design your site. You should have a home page with at least five linked pages (one for each of the issues). You will also

require another web page to create an action plan that addresses one of the identified issues. Your action plan should include:

– potential solutions that should rectify the problem
– strategies to gain support for this particular cause
– approaches for obtaining the necessary financial, labour and technological resources required to alleviate this problem
– the outcomes you hope to achieve from this plan of action.

Your Media Centre also includes a selection of images that you can download and use to improve the impact of your site.

- Use FrontPage, Dreamweaver, iWeb or other website-building software to build your website. Remember to keep your website simple.

Your ProjectsPLUS application is available in this chapter's Student Resources tab inside your eBookPLUS. Visit www.jacplus.com.au to locate your digital resources.

SUGGESTED SOFTWARE
- ProjectsPLUS
- Microsoft Word
- Website-building software

- Your mission is to make people aware of the problems your country is facing in a thought-provoking and persuasive way. Most importantly, you want people to spend time viewing your website.
- Print your research report from ProjectsPLUS and hand it in to your teacher with your final website.

MEDIA CENTRE

Your Media Centre contains:
- a selection of images to download and use in your website
- a website model
- a website-planning template
- an assessment rubric.

Interactivity

LEGENDS: 'GDP'

This interactivity includes a choropleth map that uses shades of red to show the gross domestic product (GDP) of each country. However, the information for a number of countries is missing. You must use your knowledge of the global market and the GDP of other countries as a guide to predicting the GDP of each of these empty countries. Simply select the correct colour from the legend and drop it into each empty space. Instant feedback is provided.

SEARCHLIGHT ID: INT-0959

11

Global resource use and sustainability

INQUIRY QUESTIONS

+ Where are key natural resources located?
+ Why does access to natural resources vary?
+ What is sustainable resource use?
+ What are the consequences of unsustainable use?
+ How can ecological sustainability be increased?

Natural resources are naturally occurring raw materials that are necessary or useful to people. They include soil, water, mineral deposits, fossil fuels, plants and animals. Access to natural resources influences life opportunities and quality of life throughout the world because they provide the fundamentals of life and are the basis of economic growth.

If natural resources are not managed in a sustainable way, life as we know it cannot be sustained. Unsustainable use degrades the physical environment, harms ecosystems and threatens our own survival. Promoting ecological sustainability is a high priority for geographers.

GEOskills TOOLBOX

+ Using satellite images to show change over time (page 252)
+ Using email for specific purposes (page 260)

Pacific Islanders use traditional methods to fish sustainably in Truk Lagoon where, in 2007, 266 species of reef fish were recorded.

We depend on natural resources to survive — water to drink, soil to produce our food, and forests and mines to supply materials. Natural resources are naturally occurring raw materials that are necessary or useful to people. They include soil, water, mineral deposits, fossil fuels, plants and animals.

There are two types of natural resources: non-renewable and renewable. Fossil fuels are non-renewable. We can't make more of them and eventually they will run out. Renewable natural resources, if carefully managed, can be replenished or regenerated. Forests, soils and fresh water are renewable resources.

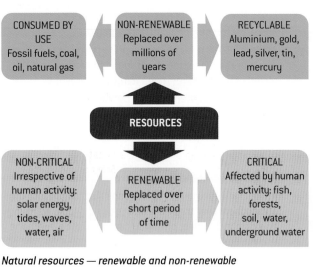

CONSUMED BY USE Fossil fuels, coal, oil, natural gas	NON-RENEWABLE Replaced over millions of years	RECYCLABLE Aluminium, gold, lead, silver, tin, mercury

RESOURCES

NON-CRITICAL Irrespective of human activity: solar energy, tides, waves, water, air	RENEWABLE Replaced over short period of time	CRITICAL Affected by human activity: fish, forests, soil, water, underground water

Natural resources — renewable and non-renewable

Distribution and use

The global distribution of natural resources depends on geology and climate. Several countries in the Middle East, for example, have rich oil resources but are short of water. Many countries in Africa, for example Botswana, have mineral resources but lack the money to process them. Instead, mining is carried out by TNCs so the greatest share of the profits goes to mining companies rather than to local people.

Agriculture, fishing, logging and mining all depend directly on natural resources. In developing countries, traditional forms of agriculture such as shifting cultivation, subsistence farming and nomadic herding are still common. These activities are sustainable if cultivators and herders move on when an area becomes unproductive, allowing the

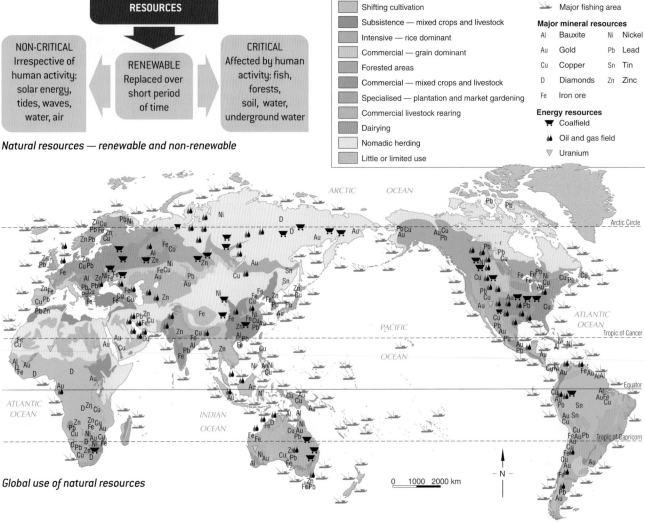

Agriculture
- Shifting cultivation
- Subsistence — mixed crops and livestock
- Intensive — rice dominant
- Commercial — grain dominant
- Forested areas
- Commercial — mixed crops and livestock
- Specialised — plantation and market gardening
- Commercial livestock rearing
- Dairying
- Nomadic herding
- Little or limited use

Fishing
- Major fishing area

Major mineral resources

Al	Bauxite	Ni	Nickel
Au	Gold	Pb	Lead
Cu	Copper	Sn	Tin
D	Diamonds	Zn	Zinc
Fe	Iron ore		

Energy resources
- Coalfield
- Oil and gas field
- Uranium

Global use of natural resources

0   1000 2000 km

— N —

land to recover. However, poverty and population growth mean that many people now clear forests for farms and overgraze or overcrop small plots of land in a desperate effort to survive.

Farms in developed countries are usually much larger. The Anna Creek cattle station in South Australia is 24 000 square kilometres, the size of Belgium. In contrast, an average intensive rice farm in Bali is only about one hectare. Unsustainable agricultural practices in developed countries include overuse of water, fertilisers and pesticides. For example, fertilisers help crops to grow, but when they end up in rivers and oceans, they cause algal blooms and damage coral reefs.

The Dinka people of south-west Sudan are cattle herders. Cattle provide the Dinka with milk, meat, and dung to make fires.

Unequal access

The two main concerns about natural resources are access and ecological sustainability. To survive, everyone must have access to food, water, energy and materials. At the same time, the resources we depend on must be used sustainably, otherwise they will be damaged or lost.

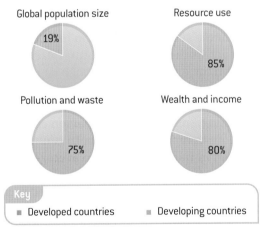

Examples of inequality between developed and developing countries

Poverty is often the result of unequal access to natural resources. Although more than 80 per cent of the world's population lives in developing countries, developed countries consume most of the resources and create most of the environmental pollution. According to the UN, the majority of people who do not have enough to eat are landless, small-scale farmers. Women are the world's poorest people — three-quarters of people living in extreme poverty (living on less than US$1 per day) are women.

ACTIVITIES

UNDERSTANDING
1. What is a natural resource?
2. Outline the difference between *renewable* and *non-renewable* resources.
3. List three examples of non-renewable resources that can be recycled.
4. Which renewable resources are most affected by human activity?
5. What are the two main concerns about natural resources?
6. What does sustainable use of natural resources mean?

THINKING AND APPLYING
7. Collect photographs of unsustainable resource use in developed and developing countries. Select four photos and create captions for them. Include location, type of resource and why the use is unsustainable.

USING YOUR SKILLS
8. Refer to the map of global use of natural resources. With the help of an atlas answer the following:
   a Which type of agriculture is most common around the Equator?
   b Describe the type of farming practised in the Sahara Desert. Suggest why this is the case.
   c Which type of agriculture covers the largest area in Australia?
   d Name three countries that have oil and gas fields.
   e Where is uranium located?
   f Which energy resources are found in Australia?
   g Name two countries that have iron ore resources.
   h Are diamonds more common in Africa or South America?

GEOTERMS

ecological sustainability: the ability to meet the needs of the present generation without compromising the ability of future generations to meet their needs

natural resources: naturally occurring raw materials that are necessary or useful to people. They include soil, water, mineral deposits, fossil fuels, plants and animals.

The population of the world grew steadily until the Industrial Revolution. Since then, it has boomed due to improvements in food production and distribution, sanitation and health care. These advances have increased life expectancy and reduced death rates. In 1950, the total world population was 2.5 billion. By 2008, it had grown to 6.7 billion. It is expected to reach 9 billion by 2050.

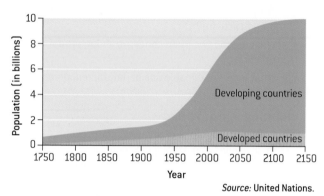

Source: United Nations.

World population growth, developing and developed countries, 1750–2150 (projected)

decades. Africa's population is currently growing faster than any other major region. In 1950, about 9 per cent of the world's population lived in Africa. By 2050, Africa will probably make up more than 20 per cent of world population.

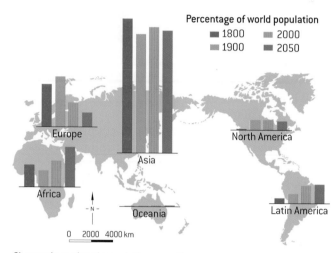

Change in regional population over time

Falling fertility rates

In developed countries, population growth has slowed because the fertility rate has fallen. The fertility rate is the average number of children a woman is likely to have in her lifetime. Women in developed countries are choosing to have fewer children than they did in the past. In the 1950s, the global fertility rate was five children per woman; by 2006, it was 2.7 per woman. Most developed countries now have a low or even a negative birth rate. In contrast, birth rates in developing countries have remained high.

Birth rates are influenced by factors such as education, religious beliefs, cultural practices, urbanisation and employment rates. There is a strong relationship between fertility rates and education. The more education women have, the more likely they are to have smaller families.

Countries with a low fertility rate — below replacement level — will have smaller populations in the future. About 40 countries will decline in population in the next 50 years. Most of these countries are in Europe. The populations of many developing countries, particularly those in Africa and Asia, will increase greatly in the coming

Human impacts

People often think that developing countries have the greatest impact on the world's environment and resources because of their large populations. But it is the people in developed countries who use most of the resources. A person in a developed country, such as the USA or Australia, places more pressure on the environment through consumption and pollution than 20 to 30 people in a developing country. For example, the USA consumes more than 300 kilograms of paper per person each year — more than four trees each. In contrast, each person in India consumes an average of only four kilograms.

Producing the meat-rich diets associated with wealthier countries requires far more water than the cereal-based diets of less wealthy countries. It takes 2000 to 5000 litres of water to produce a kilogram of rice and up to 4000 litres to produce a kilogram of wheat. In contrast, it takes up to 16 000 litres of water to produce a kilogram of beef.

Climate change is expected to increase water shortages and reduce agricultural output in many countries. Developed countries are responsible for more than three-quarters of the greenhouse gas emissions already in the atmosphere. However, as developing countries industrialise and become wealthier, their emissions and their consumption of resources will increase. Overall, industrial development and urbanisation are more responsible for increased resource use than population growth.

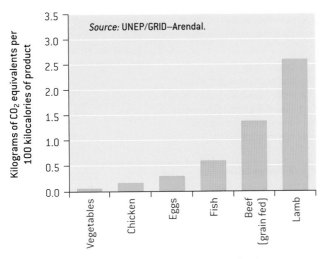

Kilograms of CO_2 equivalent emissions of various foods

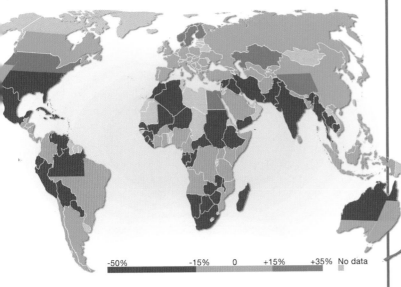

-50%   -15%   0   +15%   +35%   No data

Projected changes in agricultural productivity by 2080 due to impacts on temperatures and precipitation as a result of climate change

GEOTERMS

greenhouse gas emissions: gases discharged into the atmosphere that trap heat and result in global warming and climate change; primarily carbon dioxide, methane and nitrous oxide

---

ACTIVITIES

UNDERSTANDING

1. Outline factors that contributed to the rapid rise in world population during the last two centuries.

2. What was the world's population in 2008? How much has it grown since 1950?

3. Why has population growth slowed in developed countries?

4. The population of the USA in 2008 was just under 304 million. Calculate the approximate number of trees that were used to supply paper for the US population in 2008.

5. Why does eating a lot of meat put more pressure on natural resources than eating cereals and vegetables?

THINKING AND APPLYING

6. Explain why people in developed countries have a greater impact on resources than people in developing countries.

7. Many developing countries are industrialising and becoming wealthier. How will this impact on the use of natural resources?

USING YOUR SKILLS

8. Refer to the line graph of world population growth.
   a. Describe world population growth from 1750 to the present.
   b. Describe population growth in developed countries between 1900 and 2000. Compare this with population growth in developing countries between 1900 and 2000.
   c. What proportion of the total world population lived in developing countries in 2000?

9. Refer to the graphs showing change in regional population over time.
   a. Which region had the largest percentage of global population in 2000?
   b. Describe what happened to the population in Asia and Africa between 1900 and 2000.
   c. Which region's population growth slowed the most between 1900 and 2000? How does this compare with Oceania and North America?
   d. Which two regions will contribute the most to population growth from 2000 to 2050?

10. Refer to the map of projected changes in agricultural productivity by 2080 and an atlas.
    a. Name five developing countries that will experience a decline of 50 per cent in agricultural output by 2080.
    b. Name two developing countries that will experience an increase of 15 to 35 per cent in agricultural output.
    c. Discuss the negative and positive effects of climate change on agriculture in Australia.

The most precious natural resource is fresh water. Without it, life cannot exist. Because the world's population is continuing to grow, the amount of fresh water is diminishing. Therefore, conflicts over the control of water are becoming almost inevitable. This is especially the case in areas where water is scarce or countries share a river. Many countries share a river as an international boundary. Some rivers have their source in one country and then flow through other countries. Conflict over water is occurring in the southern African countries of Namibia, Angola and Botswana.

Namibia, Angola and Botswana are aware that a conflict among them over water could be very damaging, and they are trying to improve life opportunities for all of their people. These countries are developing a management plan to look at a range of options and their environmental impacts. This annotated map of southern Africa highlights this complex issue.

① Angola

The Okavango River begins in the southern highlands of Angola, a water-rich country with good rainfall and many rivers. It is, however , a relatively poor country that has been devastated by the 1975–2002 civil war. Up to 1.5 million people were killed and the economy is in disarray. About one-fifth of the Okavango River basin lies within Angola. As peace returns, industry and agriculture are developing, placing greater demands on the river. Angola wants to build ten new dams.

② Namibia

Namibia is a rapidly growing country that is desperately short of water. The only reliable source of running water in the country is the Okavango River. About 100 000 Namibians gain their livelihoods from the river and associated wetlands.

③ Proposed Namibian pipeline

To provide water to the rapidly growing capital city Windhoek, Namibia intends to build a pipeline from the Okavango River to the city. This will essentially starve the Okavango delta of its lifeblood: water. Botswana has hotly contested the proposal, which Namibia sees as essential.

④ Okavango River

The river is the only source of running water for Namibia and Botswana. As it lies in an arid region, approximately 97 per cent of its water is lost due to evaporation.

⑤ Caprivi Strip

This area is a heavily settled part of Namibia. Namibia and Botswana both maintain a military presence here due to tension and conflict over control of an island.

⑥ Okavango Delta

The Okavango River flows into the world's largest inland delta (some 5000 square kilometres). The delta supports abundant wildlife and attracts thousands of international tourists (and their income) into Botswana. The area is home to over 100 000 people.

⑦ Botswana

Botswana is a rapidly growing developing country. The only reliable source of running water is the Okavango River. This water supports cattle farms and several industries, including tourism and profitable diamond mines.

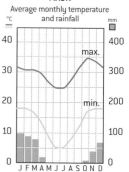

Climatic graph for Maun, Botswana

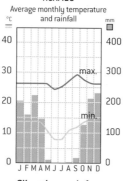

Climatic graph for Huambo, Angola

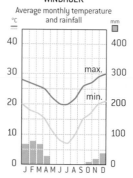

Climatic graph for Windhoek, Namibia

Okavango River basin

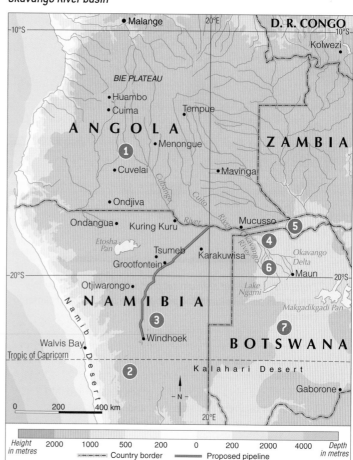

Okavango Delta

In Botswana, water usually has to be carted for many kilometres, often by children.

ACTIVITIES

UNDERSTANDING

1. Name the country where the Okavango River has its source.

2. Name the country where the Okavango Delta is located.

3. What does Angola want to do that would reduce the amount of water available downstream in Namibia?

4. What does Namibia want to do that would reduce the amount of water available downstream in Botswana?

5. List potential effects on the Okavango Delta and on Botswana's economy if Angola and Namibia diverted large amounts of water from the river upstream.

THINKING AND APPLYING

6. Form groups of three people. Each person should represent one of the countries: Angola, Botswana or Namibia. Your task is to discuss the situation and resolve it before it leads to an outbreak of fighting. Each individual should outline their point of view while the others listen. Record common points and brainstorm solutions to points of difference. Decide on the best course of action. As a class, discuss the alternatives presented by the different groups.

7. One of the reasons for this potential conflict is that these three countries share a river as an international border. Use a map of Africa to investigate if this is a common or a rare situation. Complete the following table showing all African countries that use a river as an international border.

Country 1	Country 2	Country 3
Namibia	Angola	Okavango
Botswana	Namibia	Chobe

Explain how using a river as an international border may lead to conflict.

USING YOUR SKILLS

8. Refer to the three climatic graphs.
   a Use the graphs to complete the table below.
   b Describe Windhoek's climate. How does this help to explain the need for sources of water other than rainfall?

9. Refer to the aerial photograph of the Okavango Delta.
   a Describe the geographical features you can see in the photograph.
   b Describe how the delta might change if the Okavango River is dammed.

	Highest temperature	Lowest temperature	Temperature range	Maximum temperature January	Minimum temperature June	Driest months	Wettest months	Precipitation March	Annual precipitation
Huambo									
Windhoek									
Maun									

Natural resources provide the fundamentals of life and are the basis of economic growth. If these assets are not managed in a sustainable way, life as we know it cannot be sustained.

Human impacts

Unsustainable use degrades the physical environment, harms ecosystems and threatens our survival.

- Water quantity and quality are declining. Economic growth and population growth are increasing the demand for water. Pollution decreases water availability.
- Air pollution, mostly from industry but also from urban traffic, causes smog and acid rain. Greenhouse gas emissions are causing climate change.
- Soil is essential for the production of food and the survival of ecosystems. Once soil is lost, it takes between 100 and 2500 years to replace. Losses are mainly due to erosion, the spread of towns and cities, and chemical degradation. Erosion occurs when soil is exposed; for example, by deforestation, overcropping and overgrazing. Chemical degradation can be caused by pollution and overuse of irrigation.
- Plant and animal numbers are falling and biodiversity is declining.

Unsustainable consumption

We are using natural resources faster than they can be replaced. The Aral Sea in Central Asia was once the world's fourth largest freshwater lake. So much water was used to irrigate cotton crops that it lost 70 per cent of its volume and shrunk to less than half its former size. People in the region lost their water supply and their fishing boats lie abandoned on the dry sea bed. The UN Environment Programme described the damage to the Aral Sea as 'the most staggering disaster of the twentieth century'.

Habitat destruction, overexploitation and pollution have devastated many ecosystems and species. Since 1970, wildlife populations have declined by a third. From 2000 to 2005, deforestation occurred at the rate of almost 3.5 million hectares per year in Brazil and 1.5 million hectares per year in Indonesia. Cleared rainforest in Brazil often ends up as huge cattle ranches to supply the global market for steaks and hamburgers. Usually the forest is cleared by impoverished farmers or loggers. When the soils are eroded or exhausted, large companies buy up the land.

GEOskills TOOLBOX

USING SATELLITE IMAGES TO SHOW CHANGE OVER TIME

A series of satellite images taken at different times can show how features change over time. One image is selected as the base image. Successive images at the same scale can be overlaid, allowing us to compare changes to features over time.

The base for this overlay sequence is a 2001 satellite image of the Aral Sea, on the border between Kazakhstan and Uzbekistan.

Overlay one shows the extent of the Aral Sea in 1990 in red. This is indicated in the legend.

Overlay two shows the extent of the Aral Sea in 1960 in blue. This is indicated in the legend.

Deep water appears as dark blue-black in the image and shallow water appears as light blue. Light green indicates vegetation.

The base image has a scale, a north point, a legend and a border.

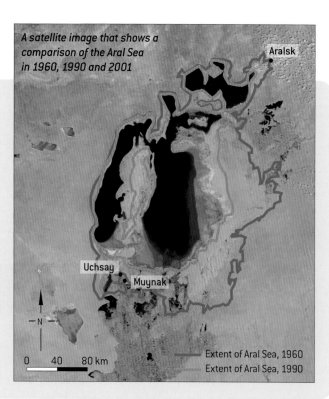

A satellite image that shows a comparison of the Aral Sea in 1960, 1990 and 2001

Aralsk

Uchsay

Muynak

— N —

0   40   80 km

Extent of Aral Sea, 1960
Extent of Aral Sea, 1990

Unsustainable waste

We are turning natural resources into waste faster than nature can turn waste back into resources. Waste is any leftover material, substance or chemical that does not have a use. If waste is discharged into the environment, making it unhealthy, it is called pollution.

Polluting events can be natural or due to the actions of people. Those caused deliberately or accidentally by people include oil spills, greenhouse gas emissions, littering and improper dumping of industrial by-products. Little can be done to stop the damage to ecosystems from natural polluting events such as volcanoes but much more can be done to control damage caused by people.

SAMPLE STUDY

One of the first major waste disasters happened in Japan during the 1950s. A petrochemical factory discharged waste containing mercury into Minamata Bay. Fish died, cats became sick and people developed brain disease. Eventually 700 people died and 9000 were permanently affected with mental disabilities.

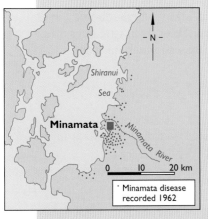

Minamata disease recorded 1962

By 1962 the cause of the 'disease' was known to be mercury poisoning. Wastes containing mercury from the Chisso chemical factory had been dumped on land and into the sea. The mercury ended up in the food chain. Mercury was swallowed by fish and was then consumed by people when they ate the fish.

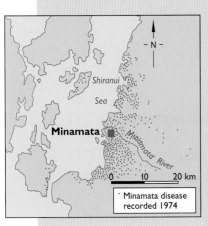

Minamata disease recorded 1974

By 1974 the number of cases of Minamata disease was still growing, even though the factory had stopped dumping waste into the bay. The mercury dumped in the 1950s and 1960s was still present in the soil and water and continued to affect fish and, in turn, people. Many victims were children who had never eaten any poisoned fish, but had inherited the mercury poisoning from their mothers.

ACTIVITIES

UNDERSTANDING

1. List impacts of unsustainable use on water, air and soil.
2. Give three reasons why wildlife populations have declined by a third since 1970.
3. Explain why the Aral Sea disaster is an example of unsustainable consumption.
4. What is waste? When does waste become pollution?
5. Explain why the Minamata disaster is an example of unsustainable waste management.

THINKING AND APPLYING

6. Imagine you were a fisherman who depended on the Aral Sea for your livelihood. Describe the changes to your life since 1960.
7. Research and prepare a short report on the current situation in Minamata.
8. What can be done to control pollution caused by people? In small groups, list ideas or create a mind map. As a class, discuss possible strategies. Choose one strategy and explain what it would achieve.

USING YOUR SKILLS

9. Refer to the satellite image of the Aral Sea.
   a Use the scale to measure the original extent of the Aral Sea from north to south and from east to west.
   b Aralsk was once a seaside town. How far was Aralsk from the sea in 2001?
   c Around 60 000 people were employed in the fishing industry in the Aral Sea in 1960, and the town of Muynak was a major fishing port. Imagine you have lived in Muynak for the last 60 years. Describe the view to the north-east in 1960 and in 2001.
10. Refer to the maps of Minamata.
    a Using the scale on the map, estimate the spread in kilometres of Minamata disease between the years 1962 and 1974.
    b Describe the number of cases and the spread of Minamata disease between the years 1962 and 1974.
    c Why did the number of cases of Minamata disease increase in the 1970s even though Chisso stopped dumping waste in Minamata Bay in the 1960s?

GEOTERMS

biodiversity: the rich variety of all life forms on Earth, including plants and animals

The world's oceans provide many valuable resources and services. Food, income, energy, transport, climate regulation and enjoyment are some of the most important.

- Fisheries — over 200 million people rely on fishing for their livelihoods. The most important fishing grounds are usually within 300 kilometres of the coast and around islands. More than 80 per cent of fish (by value) are consumed in developed countries.
- Coastal tourism — tourism is one of the world's fastest growing industries and millions of people rely on it for their livelihoods.
- Offshore oil and gas — about 20 per cent of the world's oil and natural gas comes from offshore drilling installations.
- Trade and shipping — about 90 per cent of the goods traded around the world are carried by sea.

Human impacts

Even though the world's oceans are so important to us, we are overexploiting and degrading them. The main threats to ocean resources include overexploitation, climate change, pollution and poor management. Many people depend on the sea for their livelihood, especially in coastal communities in the developing world. They will suffer most from the loss of ocean resources.

Overexploitation

Overharvesting and destructive and illegal fishing are removing massive quantities of marine life from the ocean. Up to 80 per cent of commercial fish species are already close to full exploitation. Other fish and marine creatures caught by netting and trawling are often wasted — the 'by-catch' is thrown dead or dying back into the sea.

Climate change

Warmer ocean temperatures are a threat to corals. The ocean is also becoming more acidic as it absorbs more carbon dioxide. Acidification is likely to harm marine life that uses calcium carbonate to build skeletons and shells, such as corals, seashells and crabs. Losing coral reefs, the breeding and feeding grounds for many fish species, is a threat to the world's food supply.

Pollution

Oceans are used as convenient dumping grounds. Pollution from industry, sewage and storm water, and sediments and nutrients from deforestation and agriculture pour into the ocean. Millions of creatures such as birds, dolphins, seals and turtles die each year entangled in discarded packaging, fishing nets and plastic bags. Others die after swallowing bits of plastic. Many people do not realise that leaving fishing lines or plastic bags and bottles on a beach can cause so much damage.

GEOfacts

- An estimated 7 billion tonnes of rubbish ends up in the world's oceans each year.
- Ships dump 5.5 million items of waste into the ocean each day.
- Between 700 000 and 1 million seabirds are killed from entanglement or ingestion of rubbish each year.

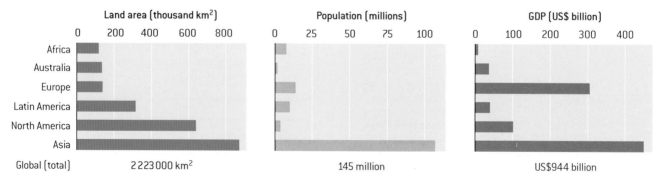

Changes in the ocean will also affect the availability of another resource — land. The three graphs show the effects of a 1-metre sea level rise on land area, population and GDP.

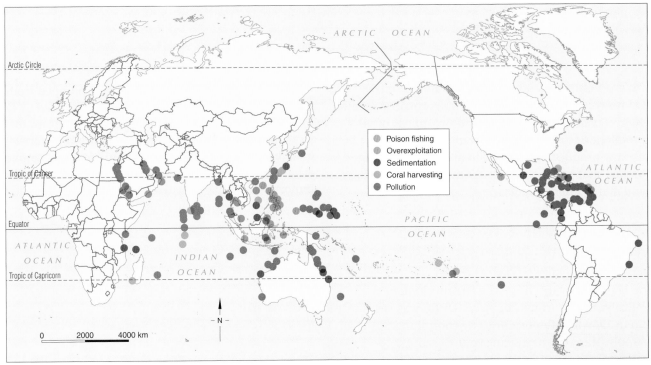

Location of major threats to coral reefs. Coral reefs in all locations are likely to be affected by climate change. If greenhouse gas emissions are not reduced, more than 80 per cent of coral reefs may die within decades.

Management

Better management is needed at global, national and local scales to conserve fish species, reduce pollution and establish more protected areas. Doing nothing is likely to result in a widespread collapse of marine systems and fisheries within the next few decades.

International protection and whaling bans since the 1960s are allowing Humpback whale numbers to slowly recover.

ACTIVITIES →

UNDERSTANDING

1. List three examples of how oceans can benefit people.
2. Explain what by-catch is.
3. List three threats to ocean resources that result from human activities.
4. Why are fish stocks declining rapidly? Give at least two reasons.
5. Describe the possible consequences of leaving litter on a beach.

THINKING AND APPLYING

6. In groups, design a persuasive slogan to influence shoppers to stop using plastic bags.
7. Research and present a report about a coral reef in a tropical location. Include the condition of the reef, threats, who is responsible for looking after it, existing management or conservation strategies, a map and photos.

8. Research the current situation on whale numbers. Which species are still at risk and why?
9. Write a letter or send an email to the Federal Minister for the Environment arguing for greater conservation of marine species.

USING YOUR SKILLS

10. Refer to the map of coral reefs.
    a List threats to Australian coral reefs.
    b What is the main threat to coral reefs in North and Central America?
    c What is threatening coral reefs in southern Africa? How could this damage local economies?

11. Refer to the graphs.
    a How many people are threatened by sea level rise?
    b Which continent will be most affected?
    c How much land is likely to be lost in North America?
    d Describe the economic impact on Europe.
    e Use the graphs to describe impacts on Australia.

Oil is a fossil fuel and a non-renewable resource. Oil reserves will eventually run out, probably within 40 to 80 years. Between half and two-thirds of oil production is used to power transport. It is also used to produce energy and to manufacture plastic bottles, nail polish, lipstick, synthetic clothing fibres and many other products.

Distribution and use

Oil is unevenly distributed. Most reserves are located in the Middle East. About 40 per cent of oil is produced by OPEC, the Organization of Petroleum Exporting Countries. OPEC was set up in 1960 to influence price by controlling supply. Many oil-producing countries are vulnerable to world oil prices because oil is their main, or only, export. In 2008, OPEC had 11 member countries, including Saudi Arabia, Iran, Iraq and Venezuela.

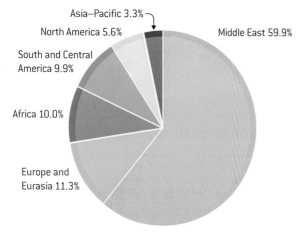

Source: BP Statistical Review of World Energy, June 2008, p. 7.
Distribution of oil reserves (percentage), 2008

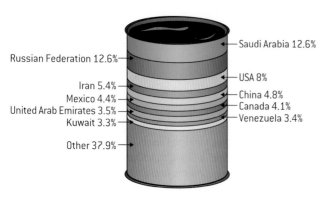

World's top ten oil producers, 2007

Every day, billions of litres of oil are pumped from the ground; 1258 billion barrels were produced in 2007. Oil is exported to countries that can afford to pay for it. For example, even though the USA has only 5 per cent of the world's population, it consumes around 25 per cent of global supplies. Countries import oil because they use more than they produce.

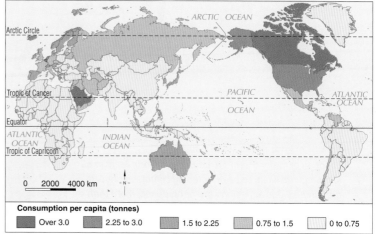

Oil consumption per capita, 2008

Winners and losers

Governments, oil companies and individuals make billions from oil. Saudi Arabia's crown prince and the Sultan of Brunei are oil billionaires. Brunei is a tiny country with a population of only 300 000 but the Sultan's palace has almost two thousand rooms. The Sultan bought an Airbus as a gift for one of his daughters. Large oil companies are some of the most profitable companies in the world. In 2008, six of the top ten global companies were involved in oil, mainly refining petroleum.

Oil generates economic growth and can improve the living standards of people in producer countries. However, while oil may bring wealth to governments and corporations, wealth does not always trickle down to local populations. Venezuela is one of the top ten oil producers but 23 per cent of its population live in extreme poverty. Oil-rich countries are often plagued by conflicts over ownership and control of oil. As a result, money from oil is spent on the armed forces rather than on safe water supplies, health care or education.

Oil consumption is a major contributor to global warming. To avoid dangerous climate change, the use of renewables, such as solar and wind, must begin to replace oil. Other environmental problems associated with oil include oil spills and air pollution.

Oil wells burning in Kuwait during the 1991 Gulf War

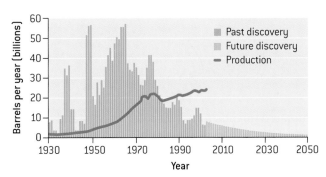

Discovery and production of oil, 1930–2050

SAMPLE STUDY

Exxon Valdez disaster

/// One of the worst oil spills in history occurred in 1989. Forced by the presence of dangerous icebergs to leave the shipping lanes of Canada's western coastline, the tanker *Exxon Valdez* ran aground on Bligh Reef. The collision tore eight of the ship's 11 tanks, spilling 11 million barrels of oil into the nearby Prince William Sound. This volume of oil would fill 125 Olympic-sized swimming pools!

The north-west coast of Canada is a wild and rugged region that has abundant wildlife. The oil spill killed over a quarter of a million birds and more than 3000 other marine creatures, including whales, otters and seals. Over $2 billion was spent over four years on cleaning up the 2000 kilometres of coastline affected by the spill. This huge effort employed 10 000 people, 100 aircraft and around 1000 boats. Even today, remnants of the spill remain on some beaches.

ACTIVITIES

UNDERSTANDING

1. Why is oil a non-renewable resource?
2. What is OPEC?
3. Just because your country has oil does not mean you are rich. Explain why wealth from oil does not always benefit poor people.
4. Explain why oil is not a sustainable energy source. In your answer, refer to the trends shown by the column graph of oil discovery and production, 1930–2050.

THINKING AND APPLYING

5. Read the sample study about the *Exxon Valdez*.
   a Where did the disaster occur?
   b Describe the distribution of the oil spill.
   c How much oil ended up in the ocean?
   d Describe the impacts of the oil spill.
6. Explain what could be done to reduce the world's dependence on oil. What could you do as an individual?

USING YOUR SKILLS

7. Refer to the pie graph opposite.
   a Which region has the largest reserves? What percentage of reserves is held by this region?
   b What percentage of reserves is located in the Asia–Pacific region?
8. Refer to the diagram of the top ten oil producers.
   a Which two countries produce the most oil?
   b How many of the top ten producers are located in the Middle East?
   c What percentage of oil is produced by the USA? Why is Saudi Arabia important to the USA?
9. Refer to the map of oil consumption. Use an atlas to answer the following.
   a List the countries that use more than 3 tonnes of oil per person each year.
   b How much oil do people in Australia and China consume per capita?
   c Name three countries that consume less than 1.5 tonnes per capita. Are these developed or developing countries?

Human demands for food, water, energy and materials are already exceeding the capacity of the Earth. By 2035, if we keep using resources at the current rate, we will need two planet Earths to provide enough resources for everyone.

What is an ecological footprint?

Everyone has an ecological footprint that reflects their dependence on natural resources. An ecological footprint measures the area of productive land and sea required to provide the resources we use, and to absorb our waste. In 2005, the average global footprint per person was 2.7 hectares. However, the total productive area available was only 2.1 hectares per person.

Who has the biggest footprint?

The footprint of a person living in India is 0.9 hectares compared to 9.2 hectares for a person in North America and 7.8 for an Australian. Although the population of Africa has tripled since 1960, the average footprint per person in Africa fell by almost 20 per cent. Meanwhile, average footprints in the wealthiest countries grew by 75 per cent. Much of this increase was due to increased use of fossil fuels. The countries with the five largest national footprints per person are the United Arab Emirates, the USA, Kuwait, Denmark and Australia. The smallest are Bangladesh, Congo, Haiti, Afghanistan and Malawi.

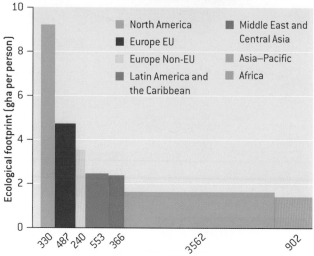

Ecological footprint and population by region, 2005

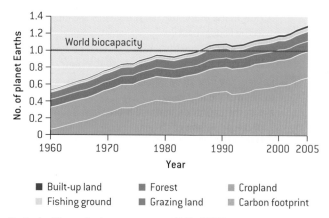

Ecological footprint by component, 1961–2005

What can be done?

Being aware of your personal footprint helps you save energy and water, and reduce waste. Limiting the amount of time spent travelling by car substantially cuts emissions. You can reduce your food footprint by choosing food that needs the least amount of transportation such as locally grown fruit and vegetables. You can reduce your waste footprint by reducing consumption, reusing and recycling.

On average, more than 40 per cent of paper is recycled worldwide. Recycling aluminium cans is helpful because smelting aluminium is one of the worst emitters of greenhouse gases and other pollutants. Reducing the use of plastic bags and bottles is essential. Plastic bags take from 20 to 1000 years to biodegrade in the environment. Most plastic bottles don't biodegrade; they just eventually break up into smaller pieces.

Governments and companies are working on strategies to reduce their footprints. Products require inputs of raw materials and energy. Transporting raw materials and finished items uses energy and emits greenhouse gases. Making products and packaging produces waste. At the end of their life, products must be disposed of if they cannot be reused or recycled. Some companies are actively promoting sustainability. Toyota Motor Corporation, for example, is working on several strategies to reduce the environmental impacts of producing and using motor vehicles.

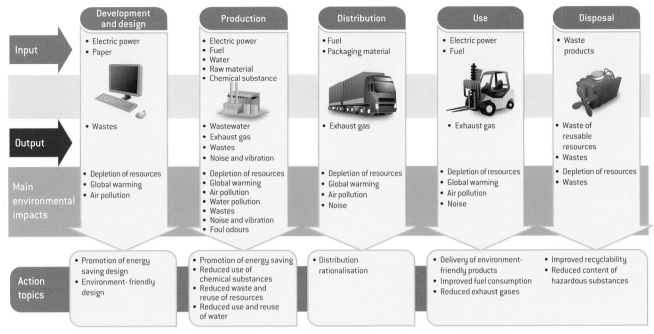

Toyota Motor Corporation's action plan for a cleaner, greener world

At the global scale, Millennium Development Goal 7 aims to reverse the loss of environmental resources and improve sustainability. Global organisations that promote sustainability include:
- United Nations — oversees global agreements such as the Kyoto Protocol to reduce greenhouse gas emissions
- United Nations Environment Programme — uses satellite imagery to observe and manage environmental changes such as water quality
- Australian Government (AusAID) — helps developing countries to conserve forests, restore soils and use sustainable energy sources

- World Wide Fund for Nature (WWF) — publishes the *Living Planet Report*, which regularly updates the state of the global ecological footprint
- Planet Ark — organises campaigns to recycle greeting cards, paper, cartridges and phones.

GEOTERMS

ecological footprint: measures the dependence of an individual or region on natural resources; for example, how much land and water is needed to supply energy, build roads and buildings, grow food, dispose of waste and grow forests for wood and paper

ACTIVITIES

UNDERSTANDING

1. Use your own words to define the term 'ecological footprint'.
2. What is the average global ecological footprint per person? How many global hectares are available per person?
3. What will happen to the Earth's resources if the present rate of consumption continues?

THINKING AND APPLYING

4. Refer to Toyota's action plan above.
   a List the natural resources that are used to produce a motor vehicle.
   b List the environmental impacts of producing a motor vehicle.
   c How does Toyota aim to reduce the environmental impacts of (i) producing motor vehicles, and (ii) using motor vehicles?

5. Should everyone in the world be able to live the way Australians do? Why or why not? Write a summary statement about the impact of the rich and poor on ecological footprints.
6. Many developing countries are industrialising and experiencing economic growth. How will this development affect the global ecological footprint?

USING YOUR SKILLS

7. Refer to the graph of the ecological footprint by component.
   a What makes up the largest component of the ecological footprint?
   b Describe the trends shown by the graph.
8. Refer to the graph of ecological footprint by region.
   a Which region has the largest ecological footprint? Which has the smallest?
   b Calculate the difference (in global hectares) between the largest and smallest regional footprints.

The World Wide Fund for Nature (WWF) is a global non-government organisation (NGO) that promotes ecological sustainability. Its mission is the conservation of nature. It protects natural areas and wild populations, and promotes the sustainable use of renewable resources and the maximum reduction of pollution.

The founder of the WWF, Sir Peter Scott, said *'We shan't save all we should like to, but we shall save a great deal more than if we had never tried'*. The WWF, like Greenpeace, exists *'because the fragile Earth deserves a voice. It needs solutions. It needs change. It needs action.'*

Known by its cute panda logo, the WWF has five million members worldwide. The WWF's approach combines science with local, national and global action. It achieves innovative solutions that meet the needs of both people and nature by working with local communities, scientists, industries, the World Bank and other NGOs. The WWF uses a diversity of methods to influence the global community to donate to its projects and encourages people to follow a sustainable lifestyle. These methods include environmental education, advising governments on environmental policy and organising international campaigns.

The WWF focuses on six major areas for long-term conservation — forests, fresh water, oceans and coasts, climate change, toxic chemicals and species.

Climate change

The WWF is lobbying for a new UN climate change agreement in 2013 that reduces greenhouse gas emissions by 80 per cent by 2050, halts deforestation, promotes investment in clean energy and makes clean technologies available to developing countries.

WWF is promoting investment in renewable energy sources such as wind.

GEOskills TOOLBOX

USING EMAIL FOR SPECIFIC PURPOSES

The WWF and many other NGOs use email campaigns and their websites to promote ecological sustainability. In 2002, the WWF's 'Stop Overfishing' campaign became one of the world's first demonstrations of the power of the internet. People around the world, via email, submitted their names in support of the WWF campaign. In Brussels, a six-metre-high lighthouse was erected outside a meeting of European Union ministers. The lighthouse displayed names, photographs and videos of the 22 000 people who had signed the WWF's digital petition. The campaign was a success. The ministers agreed to a new fishing policy that met most of the WWF's demands.

The WWF involves the users of their website in their campaigns and scientific research. The Polar Bear Tracker website is part of a study on the impact of climate change.

WWF is lobbying for changes to protect fish stocks.

WWF helps to protect endangered species, such as the Siberian tiger.

Oceans and coasts

The WWF wants fundamental change in the fishing industry so that fish stocks can recover and fishing does not harm non-target species. The Coral Triangle project aims to ensure protection and sustainable management of at least half the reefs in the seas around Indonesia, Malaysia, PNG, the Philippines, the Solomon Islands and Timor-Leste.

Fresh water

The WWF is working to conserve wetlands, manage river basins and influence strategies to save water. In 2007, the WWF worked with the Chinese Government to establish the first network of wetland conservation areas along the Yangtze River.

Toxic chemicals

The WWF is concerned about the production, trade and disposal of toxic chemicals. Environments from the tropics to the poles are contaminated with chemicals. Wildlife suffering the effects include polar bears, frogs, birds, panthers and whales.

Forests

The WWF aims to preserve 200 million hectares of tropical forests in Africa, Asia and the Americas. Increasing the number and size of protected areas in South America is saving 50 million hectares of Amazon rainforest. In Africa's Congo basin, the WWF is protecting forests by promoting more sustainable logging and by helping local people manage their own resources.

WWF aims to preserve tropical forests.

Endangered species

The WWF targets human impacts on species including illegal trade and hunting. In cooperation with governments, other NGOs and local communities, the WWF has saved several species from extinction. The WWF helped establish reserves for giant pandas in China. In 2007, two new Russian national parks were established to help protect Siberian tigers.

ACTIVITIES ⊖

UNDERSTANDING

1 What is the WWF?

2 Describe the main aims of the WWF.

3 The WWF uses various methods to influence the global community. List three of their methods.

4 Using information given on these pages, outline successes achieved by the WWF in the Amazon rainforest, China and Russia.

5 What does the WWF want the world to do about climate change?

THINKING AND APPLYING

6 Why is the WWF a successful global organisation?

7 Research a WWF project.
   a Where is the project?
   b What is the aim of the project?
   c What problems do they face?
   d What progress have they made?
   e Design a campaign poster that could be used to promote the project.

USING YOUR SKILLS

8 How did people use email for an ethical purpose in the 'Stop Overfishing' campaign?

9 What is the advantage of using email to circulate a petition?

10 What do you think is unethical use of email and the internet?

11 Find the Polar Bear Tracker on the internet.
   a Read the latest information on the site and prepare an email update on the project.
   b Who would you mail the update to, and why?

Working geographically

KNOWLEDGE AND UNDERSTANDING

Select the alternative A, B, C or D that best answers the question. Use the source materials where appropriate.

1. Unequal access to natural resources often result in
   - (A) climate change.
   - (B) shifting cultivation.
   - (C) poverty.
   - (D) algal blooms.

2. Which of the following best describes Australia's ecological footprint per capita?
   - (A) Less than the average per capita footprints of either the USA or the UK
   - (B) Twice the size of China's per capita footprint
   - (C) More than twice the size of the average world per capita footprint
   - (D) Less than 7 hectares per person

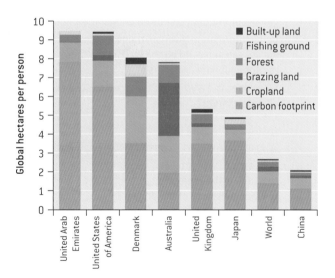

Ecological footprint per capita for selected countries, 2005

3. The graph top right shows the population and resource use of five developed countries. Which of the following statements describes the information shown by the graph?
   - (A) The five countries make up more than a quarter of the world's population and they use more than a quarter of all the resources shown on the graph.
   - (B) The five countries make up 10 per cent of the world's population and they use more than 40 per cent of most of the resources shown on the graph.
   - (C) The five countries make up 10 per cent of the world's population and they use about 10 per cent of all the resources shown on the graph.
   - (D) The five countries make up only 10 per cent of the world's population so the amount of resources they use is relatively small.

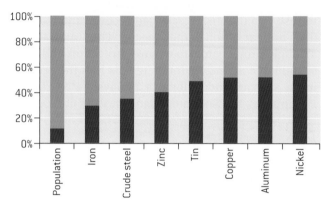

- France, Germany, Japan, United Kingdom and United States (5 countries)
- Rest of the world (188) countries

Consumption of natural resources for selected developed countries compared with global population

ECOLOGICAL SUSTAINABILITY AND EASTER ISLAND

Easter Island, or Rapa Nui, is a UNESCO World Heritage site because of its cultural importance. The site was established to protect the distinctive stone monuments known as *moai*, which stand around the coastline of the island. More than a thousand *moai* were carved from rock quarries at Rano Raraku by the ancestors of the present inhabitants. Many statues remain unfinished.

Easter Island is in the Pacific Ocean about 3600 kilometres from the coast of Chile. It is one of the most isolated inhabited islands in the world and covers an area of just 160 square kilometres. When first settled, the island was a forested land covered with palms and small trees.

Easter Island shows the result of unsustainable use of natural resources. The society that flourished on Easter Island from the year AD 400 onwards gradually used all the island's natural resources. By about 1600, the island was completely deforested. Trees had been cut down to provide fuel, housing materials, canoes, space for agriculture and to use as a means of moving the *moai* from the quarry.

Removal of the trees also affected the soil, eroding it and removing nutrients so that crops failed. By the 1870s, only 111 Easter Islanders remained.

Today the island has around 4000 inhabitants. Tourism is an important source of income for the island as people from all over the world come to see the *moai*. The island also has volcanic craters and beautiful beaches.

4 What was the main reason for the ecological disaster on Easter Island?
- **(A)** Population growth
- **(B)** Isolation
- **(C)** Unsustainable use of non-renewable resources
- **(D)** Unsustainable use of renewable natural resources

5 What is the approximate maximum width of the island from north to south and from east to west?
- **(A)** 25 km and 12 km
- **(B)** 20 km and 15 km
- **(C)** 20 km and 12 km
- **(D)** 12 km and 20 km

6 If you walked from the airport to Vaitea, which direction would you travel?
- **(A)** North
- **(B)** North-east
- **(C)** East
- **(D)** South-east

7 What is the temperature range on Easter Island?
- **(A)** 12° Celsius
- **(B)** 2° Celsius
- **(C)** 15° Celsius
- **(D)** 7° Celsius

8 What is the average annual precipitation on Easter Island?
- **(A)** Less than 1000 mm
- **(B)** More than 1500 mm
- **(C)** 1168 mm
- **(D)** 1267 mm

9 Which months are the wettest on Easter Island and during which seasons do they occur?
- **(A)** April, May, June and July during autumn and winter
- **(B)** April, May, June and July during spring and summer
- **(C)** January, February, March and April during summer and autumn
- **(D)** January, February, March and April during winter and autumn

10 What is now the main source of income for the islanders?
- **(A)** Agriculture
- **(B)** Constructing *moai*
- **(C)** Tourism
- **(D)** Fishing

Easter Island
Average monthly temperature and rainfall

Climatic graph for Easter Island, 27°07' south, 109°22' west

Moai statues on Easter Island

ICT activities

Different sized feet!

SEARCHLIGHT ID: PRO-0035

SCENARIO

It is Global Environmental Week and the NGO 'Think Big, Act Small' is releasing an educational blog site. The purpose of the blog is to enable individuals to post different perspectives, experiences and lifestyles that result from variations in living standards around the world. Through the blog, students are to illustrate a cause-and-effect relationship on the impact that individual lifestyles have on both the environment and the living standards of others.

YOUR TASK

Working in a team of three, develop blog entries for three different characters. Each character must have three blog entries as well as two responses from fictional readers.

Write the blog entries in the first person and from the perspective of an assumed character. Your posts must make reference to the ecological footprints of the different characters your group has created.

Your characters could be a range of people from different continents. You could also write from the perspective of a plant or animal. A plant could explain their experience of how their life has changed; a tribal person could talk of the impact of environmental changes on their lifestyle; and a polar bear might explain the impact of global warming.

Each entry should effectively illustrate both the direct and indirect impacts that the other character's actions have had on their own lifestyles.

Each blog should present at least two complex questions or viewpoints by two different fictional readers. These readers are different from the three assumed characters that you have selected. Responses to the blogs by your fictional readers should include probing questions or statements that add depth to the discussion.

The information you post in your blog can include images, charts, facts, interviews or other means of engaging your audience. Be sure to include a reference to where you obtained such information.

When your group's blog is complete, work individually and assume the role of a news reporter who will use the facts that your group has researched, and the perspectives of the different stakeholders, to write a feature article about the issues described in your blog.

Your feature article should incorporate the main facts of the issues and the different perspectives of the characters to show clearly the relationship between the actions of the different stakeholders and their impacts on each other.

PROCESS

- Open the ProjectPLUS application for this chapter in your eBookPLUS. Watch the introductory video lesson and then click the 'Start Project' button to set up your project. You will write your blog entries individually, but you should work in groups of three to share your research in the ProjectsPLUS Research Forum and create your blog. Save your settings and the project will be launched.

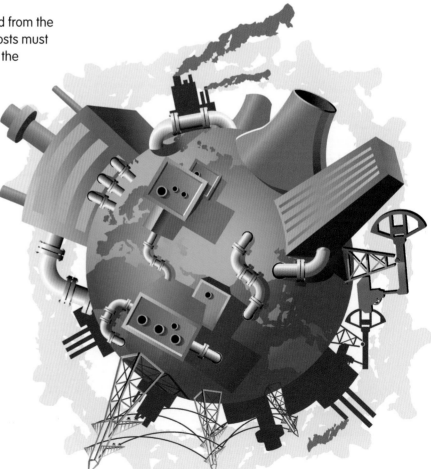

- Navigate to your Research Forum. Here you will find several issues that you might like to focus on. Note that, if you would like to focus on a particular issue that is not on the list, obtain permission from your teacher before starting the task.
- Research. For each character you decide to assume, research their geographical location (continent, country, geographical position), their exports and imports, GNP per capita, living standards of the people, infant mortality, education rates, computers per hundred people, environmental issues and problems that the country might be prone to, political stability of the country, the country's currency and the size of the standard home.
- Visit your Media Centre and download the blog planning template to help you to develop your blog. You will also see a sample blog on which you can model your own task.
- Use an online blogging site to set up your group's blog and then enter all of the required blog entries.
- When your blog is complete, download the Feature Article Scaffold from your Media Centre. You can use this scaffold to complete the last component

SUGGESTED SOFTWARE
- ProjectsPLUS
- Microsoft Word
- An online blogging site

of the task. Be sure to create a headline for your article and add relevant pictures. Your article should emphasise important facts.
- Print out your Research Report from ProjectsPLUS and hand it in with a copy of your group's blog and your three individual newspaper articles.

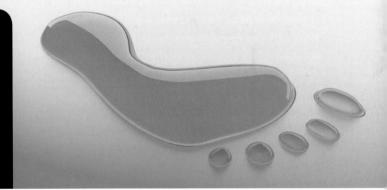

MEDIA CENTRE

Your Media Centre contains:
- a blog model
- a feature article scaffold
- a selection of images of potential characters for your blog
- weblinks to research sites and blogging websites
- an assessment rubric.

Interactivity

TIME OUT: 'RESOURCES'

In this exciting interactivity, you must identify whether a series of resources are renewable, recyclable or non-renewable. You are presented with images depicting each of these resources and you must think quickly before your time runs out.

SEARCHLIGHT ID: INT-0960

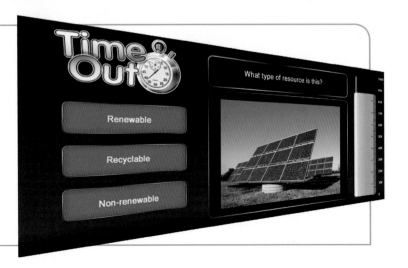

12 Global geographical issues and citizenship

INQUIRY QUESTIONS

+ What are global geographical issues?
+ What is active citizenship?
+ Why is ecological sustainability important?

Global geographical issues are matters that concern us all. They include issues about changes in environments, and how people interact with environments and with each other. Some issues, such as climate change, are relatively new and some, such as human rights and access to fresh water, are as old as time. All are pressing issues, now, and must be dealt with to achieve the best possible outcomes for the Earth and its citizens. As global citizens, we need to understand more about how the planet can be managed in a sustainable way for the sake of our own and future generations.

GEOskills TOOLBOX

+ Using a geographical issues scaffold (page 269)
+ Interpreting a thematic map (page 270)

A wind farm in southern California

KEY TERMS

active citizenship: involves individuals and groups influencing decision making at local, state, federal and global scales, and actively participating in community activities and public affairs

bias: a perspective that has a particular slant reflecting a preference or prejudice

biodiversity: the rich variety of all life forms on Earth, including plants and animals

deforestation: the process of clearing forest, usually to make way for housing or agriculture

degraded: reduced in value or quality; for example, land is degraded through erosion and intensive use of the soil

desertification: the process by which useful agricultural areas on desert fringes change into desert due to poor farming practices

drylands: any area of dry climate or semi-desert

ecological dimension: how humans interact with environments

ecological sustainability: the ability to meet the needs of the present generation without compromising the ability of future generations to meet their needs

fossil fuels: fuels that come from the breakdown of organic matter; for example, coal, oil and natural gas. They have formed in the ground over millions of years.

human rights: based on the idea that all human beings are equal, and deserve fair and equal treatment

indigenous people: the descendants of the original inhabitants of an area

land degradation: the decline in quality of the land

megacity: very large city with a population of over 10 million people

perspective: a way of viewing the world

pull factors: positive characteristics of an area that attract people to move to it

push factors: negative characteristics of an area that cause people to leave it

self-determination: the right of a nation or group of people to form their own government

social justice: situation where individuals or groups in a society are treated justly and fairly

spatial dimension: where things are and why they are there

urbanisation: the process by which the proportion of a country's population in the urban areas increases

Although we live in different countries, we all share the same planet. Global geographical issues are matters that concern us all. They include issues about changes in environments, and how people interact with environments and with each other. Global geographical issues include:
- climate change (see chapter 13)
- energy use
- land degradation
- use of ocean resources
- urbanisation
- human rights
- indigenous people and self-determination
- threatened habitats (see chapter 14)
- tourism (see chapter 15)
- access to fresh water (see chapter 16).

Geographical issues make headlines in newspapers and on the television news. They are part of everyday conversations. For example: Do you think the climate is getting warmer? How can governments solve the refugee crisis?

Global geographical issues can be investigated from a spatial and an ecological dimension. The spatial dimension explains where things are and why they are there. The ecological dimension describes the relationship between people and the environment, and the effects they have on each other. The need to promote ecological sustainability is a major geographical issue at both local and global scales.

Active citizenship

We are all responsible for the management of global issues. As active citizens we aim to move from being part of the problem to being part of the solution by promoting ecological sustainability and social justice. Ecological sustainability means ensuring that we can meet the needs of the present population without endangering the ability of future generations to meet their needs. Social justice means that the individuals and groups in a society are treated justly and fairly.

Active citizenship is participating in community activities and being involved in decisions about what happens in communities and environments. Participation can be at a local, national or global scale.

Activists in the Philippines hold an Earth Day protest in Manila.

Local issues can result in an individual, group or government response. Global issues often require cooperation between national governments and responses by organisations such as the United Nations, or non-government global organisations such as Greenpeace. Even on global issues, individuals can play their part and take

The Californian Condor is endangered as a result of urbanisation and land degradation.

Participating in local clean-up days is one way in which citizens can improve their local environment.

action. Global citizenship represents an individual's commitment to the whole world and to being aware that our responsibilities really do go beyond our local area and our country.

Global laws and agreements are gradually being developed on a range of issues, such as **human rights** and the protection of the environment. All nations do not always support them but these are important first steps towards ensuring the survival of our global community.

Collecting information

Newspapers, television and the internet are all useful sources of information about global issues. However, care must be taken when using information sources because they are sometimes inaccurate and can contain **bias**. Think about where the information was published and who prepared the report. Is the information distorted, or even false? Has something been left out? Consider different people's **perspectives** about particular issues. For example, the people in a community who support the development of local tourism are usually those who think they will benefit from it. Those who don't support it probably are the people who think they will be worse off.

GEOskills TOOLBOX

USING A GEOGRAPHICAL ISSUES SCAFFOLD

A geographical issues scaffold provides a useful way of analysing and summarising information sources. It helps geographers to focus on the main points and compare different perspectives about an issue. The scaffold below can be used for any geographical issue and for different types of information sources such as newspapers, magazines and the internet.

Geographical issues scaffold
Name and date of source
Author
Geographical issue
Spatial dimension (Where? Why?)
Ecological dimension (How do humans interact?)
Impacts
Key interest groups and contrasting perspectives
Responses (individuals, groups and governments)
How successful are their strategies?
What are the implications of these processes for ecological sustainability and social justice?

ACTIVITIES

UNDERSTANDING

1. Define the term 'global geographical issues'.
2. What is ecological sustainability?
3. What does social justice mean?

THINKING AND APPLYING

4. Describe what you can do as a global citizen to make a difference at local, national and global scales.
5. Distinguish between bias and perspective in sources of information.

USING YOUR SKILLS

6. Use newspapers or the internet to find information about six global geographical issues. Collect one article for each global issue. Copy the scaffold into your workbook, and then complete it for each of your articles.

GEOTERMS

ecological dimension: how humans interact with environments

spatial dimension: where things are and why they are there

Environmental crisis

There is growing concern about the way in which humans are using the world's resources. Many conservationists believe that we will not be able to continue using our physical environment in the ways that we have in the past. This environmental crisis is a result of the limited amount of resources that the Earth contains and the rate at which they are being used or destroyed. For example:

- fish in all of the world's major fisheries are being caught faster than they can be replaced
- more than 70 per cent of the world's drylands are degraded
- one in ten of Earth's 300 000 plant species are threatened with extinction.

  Biodiversity and ecological sustainability are closely linked. Much biodiversity is being lost through the destruction of ecosystems and the natural habitats of plants and animals. At the same time as this destruction is taking place, scientists are finding new uses for biological diversity. Biological diversity provides opportunities to produce better food, fibres, medicine and a range of industrial products. As we wipe out species, we could be destroying a plant or an organism that might have helped provide a cure for cancer or migraine headaches — or even the common cold!

The great divide

The crisis is even more complex when we consider the following facts: 20 per cent of the world's population lives in developed or rich countries and they consume about 80 per cent of the world's resources; the 80 per cent who live in the developing or poor countries consume only about 20 per cent of the world's resources. Many of the resources that are consumed in developed countries come from developing countries. For example, nearly all of the timber produced in developing countries is consumed in developed countries.

Living standards

As well as the concerns about the environment, many people are also concerned about living standards throughout the world. Living standards are judged according to the amount of goods and services, such as food, shelter and education, available in the community per head of population. There are concerns that we should at least be able to maintain existing living standards in the world and make real progress towards improving the living standards of the world's poor people.

The world's population is now almost seven billion and is growing at a rate of 75 million per year. The UN estimates a global population of more than 9 billion by 2050. Currently around one-fifth of the world's people live in very poor conditions,

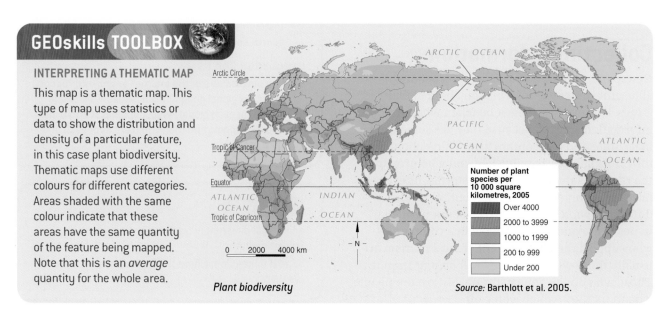

GEOskills TOOLBOX

INTERPRETING A THEMATIC MAP

This map is a thematic map. This type of map uses statistics or data to show the distribution and density of a particular feature, in this case plant biodiversity. Thematic maps use different colours for different categories. Areas shaded with the same colour indicate that these areas have the same quantity of the feature being mapped. Note that this is an *average* quantity for the whole area.

Number of plant species per 10 000 square kilometres, 2005

- Over 4000
- 2000 to 3999
- 1000 to 1999
- 200 to 999
- Under 200

0   2000   4000 km

Plant biodiversity

Source: Barthlott et al. 2005.

Australia — 100% of people

Indonesia — 78% of people

Ethiopia — 24% of people

These percentages of people in three countries show that the availabilitiy of fresh water is very different throughout the world.

without enough food, safe drinking water, clothing and shelter. They are always facing the threat of an outbreak of disease or famine, or both. These people are the global underclass or the global poor. Within this underclass some groups are worse off than others, in particular women, children and indigenous people.

Across the globe many people are denied their human rights. Human rights are based on the idea that all human beings are equal and deserve fair treatment.

What is sustainable development?

Ecologically sustainable development is development that meets the needs of the present population without endangering the ability of future generations to meet their own needs. This means using the world's resources in ways that ensure the resources will still be around to meet the needs of people in the future. It also means trying to ensure that the living standards of present generations, particularly the world's poor, are improved.

Most countries now recognise that almost all environmental problems, at a local, national and global scale, arise from unsustainable use of resources. In 1992, 178 countries at the United Nations Conference on Environment and Development agreed on a comprehensive action plan for sustainable development. This has

become known as Agenda 21. In the twenty-first century, environmental management will become an even more important issue.

GEOfacts

In most years, around 15 million children under five years of age will die in developing countries. In very bad years, when there are wars, famine or severe outbreaks of disease (plagues), many more will die.

ACTIVITIES

UNDERSTANDING

1. What is the environmental crisis faced by the Earth and its people?
2. Give two examples of the environmental crisis.

THINKING AND APPLYING

3. Explain what is meant by the term 'living standards'. Draw a picture showing what you think sustainable development is.
4. Explain why biodiversity and sustainable development are closely linked.

USING YOUR SKILLS

5. Refer to the diagram showing availability of fresh water. Why do you think these three countries have different availability of fresh water?
6. Refer to the map showing plant biodiversity. With reference to latitude describe:
   a the areas of highest plant biodiversity in the world
   b the areas of the lowest plant biodiversity in the world.
   Account for this pattern of distribution.

A shantytown in São Paulo, Brazil

GEOTERMS

biodiversity: the rich variety of all life forms on Earth, including plants and animals

drylands: any area of dry climate or semi-desert

Land degradation is the decline in the quality of the land. Land degradation means that the land is less able to produce crops, feed animals or renew its natural vegetation.

Land degradation can result from land clearing, agricultural activities, urban and tourist developments, industrial and mining activities, logging, disposal of wastes and the introduction of feral animals and exotic plants. Erosion, salinity, decreased water quality and decreased biodiversity are some of the issues that result from poor land management.

Land degradation has a spatial dimension — we can map the extent of land degradation and locate areas with particular problems. It also has an ecological dimension — how people interact with the environment has a major impact on the quality of the land.

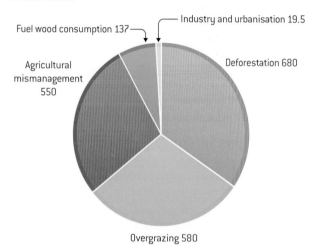

Causes and extent (million hectares) of land degradation worldwide

- Fuel wood consumption 137
- Industry and urbanisation 19.5
- Agricultural mismanagement 550
- Deforestation 680
- Overgrazing 580

Deforestation

When rain falls on a forested hillside it is absorbed by the roots or held in the soil. On a deforested hillside the soil is not held together by the roots of trees. Gullies form, and the unprotected soil is washed into rivers. Deforestation causes the hillside to become unstable and prone to landslides.

Desertification

Many of the world's deserts are spreading. It is estimated that 50 million people could be displaced due to desertification within the next ten years. The main areas affected are sub-Saharan Africa and Central Asia. Desertification occurs when agricultural areas on the fringes of deserts change into desert due to unsustainable farming practices. When farmers cultivate land in semidesert areas, or when fragile drylands are overgrazed, natural vegetation is lost. When droughts occur, winds blow away the topsoil resulting in dust storms and erosion. When rain does fall, it can cause large-scale erosion.

The obvious way to stop desertification is to reduce unsustainable farming and overgrazing. This would allow the land to return to its natural state, which might be grassland or woodland. However, people who occupy the land are usually reluctant to move unless they have an acceptable alternative. In rich countries, governments can pay farmers not to grow crops and carry out campaigns to encourage soil conservation and tree planting. Poor countries, however are unable to do this without aid from other countries.

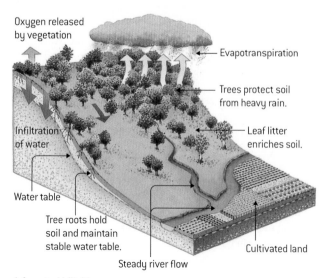

- Oxygen released by vegetation
- Evapotranspiration
- Trees protect soil from heavy rain.
- Leaf litter enriches soil.
- Infiltration of water
- Water table
- Tree roots hold soil and maintain stable water table.
- Steady river flow
- Cultivated land

A forested hillside

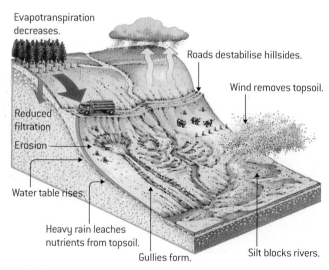

- Evapotranspiration decreases.
- Roads destabilise hillsides.
- Wind removes topsoil.
- Reduced filtration
- Erosion
- Water table rises.
- Heavy rain leaches nutrients from topsoil.
- Gullies form.
- Silt blocks rivers.

A hillside after deforestation

The Sahel

The region called the Sahel is located in Africa, between the Sahara Desert to the north and savanna grasslands to the south. Desertification and famines are major problems in the Sahel.

The Sahel suffered severe droughts in the 1970s and 1980s. Recently rainfall has increased, along with vegetation. However, with global warming and the resulting climate change, scientists predict that rainfall will become even less reliable. Land available for crops and grazing is decreasing, so many of the region's young men have left to seek work in wealthier countries such as Libya.

Reclamation of damaged land has been successful in some areas. Using government and foreign aid money, dunes have been stabilised, trees cultivated and rock walls built to stop erosion. Natural fencing made from the branches of shrubs and grasses stops sand blowing onto cultivated land. To catch rain, pits are dug and seeds are sown in the pits.

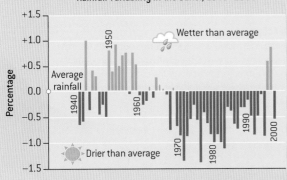

Rainfall variability in the Sahel, 1940–2000

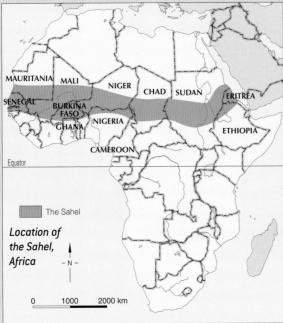

The Sahel

Location of the Sahel, Africa

– N –

0   1000   2000 km

GEO*facts*   Every year on June 17, the United Nations'
World Day to Combat Desertification is celebrated to promote public awareness of the issue. The common aims of the 193 participating countries and organisations are:
• preventing, controlling and reversing desertification and land degradation
• contributing to the reduction of poverty while promoting sustainable development.

ACTIVITIES ➡

UNDERSTANDING

1. Define land degradation.
2. Why is it so important to reduce the loss of topsoil?
3. Outline the main causes of desertification.
4. Briefly explain how humans have helped to increase the rate of land degradation.
5. What methods are used in the Sahel to stop the erosion of crop and grazing land?

THINKING AND APPLYING

6. Work in small groups to develop an action plan to address the problems faced by the Sahel or another area of the world experiencing land degradation. Think about what needs to be done and the resources required. Think about the priorities — what needs to be done first? Share your completed plans with the class.

USING YOUR SKILLS

7. Refer to the diagrams on deforestation. Explain the impact the loss of vegetation has on an environment.
8. Refer to the map of the Sahel region. List the countries that make up the Sahel region.
9. Refer to the rainfall graph of the Sahel from 1940–2000.
   a In what decades has it been (i) drier than average and (ii) wetter than average?
   b How would you expect the graph to look in the decades after 2000 if global warming continues as predicted?

GEOTERMS

deforestation: the process of clearing forest, usually to make way for housing or agriculture

desertification: the process by which useful agricultural areas on desert fringes change into desert due to poor farming practices

Fossil fuels

Will our energy sources ever run out? Every year, the world consumes energy equivalent to about 10 million tonnes of crude oil. The bulk of the energy we use comes from fossil fuels such as coal, oil and natural gas. We burn these fuels in power stations to make electricity, and to power cars and other forms of transport. This reliance on fossil fuels creates two major problems:

- these energy sources are non-renewable. Much of the easily accessible oil will be gone in less than 50 years and coal will be scarce in 200 years.
- perhaps more critically, burning these fossil fuels releases gases into the atmosphere that are responsible for global warming (see chapter 13).

To deal with these problems, we need to develop alternative ways to harness the energy that is all around us. Many of these alternative sources of energy are non-polluting and are readily available, although at present more expensive than traditional fossil fuels.

World energy production, 2005

Pie chart: Oil 37%, Coal 25%, Gas 23%, Nuclear 6%, Biomass 4%, Hydro-electricity 3%, Other 2%

Alternative energy sources

Solar panels in the desert
A series of 1900 curved mirrors, computer controlled to follow the sun, concentrate the rays of the sun onto the top of a 100-metre-high tower. Molten salt heated to 560° Celsius is stored in the tower. The salt slowly releases the heat that is then used to run a generator.

Windmills
Modern windmills, hollow towers with turbines on the top, can be used to generate energy from the wind. A generator converts the spinning motion into electricity. Wind turbines need to be located in areas where the wind blows at a constant speed.

Wave power
This is a floating platform that converts wave energy to electricity. The platform contains three air chambers in which the water level rises and falls as waves pass through the platform. This forces the air to pass over a turbine, thereby creating electricity.

Hot rocks
Australian scientists believe they can drill down to hot rocks that lie deep below the Earth's surface. A pipe will carry water down to these rocks where steam will be produced. Another pipe will transport the steam to the surface where it will be used to turn turbines and produce electricity. Australia contains some of the best sites in the world for this type of geothermal energy.

Hydro-electric power station
A dam blocks the flow of a river, creating a lake. Water rushes through giant pipes across turbines inside the dam. As the turbines spin, the energy of the falling water is converted into electricity. In the Snowy Mountains area of New South Wales, Australia's largest engineering project involved constructing a system of dams, tunnels and power stations to produce hydro-electricity.

Tower of power
Greenhouses radiate seven kilometres outwards from the one-kilometre-tall tower. They will heat and trap air that then rises through the tower to the cooler air above. The rushing air will turn turbines in the giant tower, creating electricity.

Tidal power station
These operate in a similar way to the hydro-electric power station. They convert the energy from both the incoming and outgoing tides to turn turbines and generate electricity. They are best located at the mouth of a bay that has a large difference in water level between high and low tides.

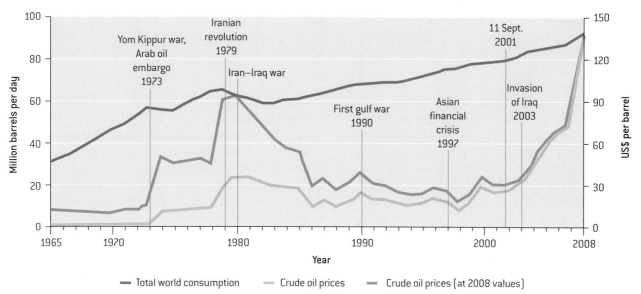

Oil price, 1965–2008

Source: *New Scientist*, 28 June 2008, p. 36.

Legend:
— Total world consumption
— Crude oil prices
— Crude oil prices (at 2008 values)

Biomass farming
This involves growing plants that can be used to produce electricity. Trees of course can be burnt as fuel but other plants such as canola and sunflowers that produce burnable oils may prove to be more useful in the future.

Landfill waste and sewage treatments
These produce gases that can be used to generate electricity. In Queensland, plant fibre that is a waste product in sugar production is burnt to produce steam, which is then used to produce electricity to power the sugar refineries.

Solar panels on buildings
Solar panels on the north-facing roofs of all buildings could produce electricity through sets of photovoltaic cells within the panels. This electricity can be fed into the national power grid, which serves as a battery (storing excess energy during sunlight hours and feeding it back at night and on cloudy days).

GEO*facts* China will become the world's top energy user by 2010, leading the USA. Global energy demand will increase by 50 per cent between 2008 and 2030, with high-growth countries China and India accounting for 45 per cent of this increase.

ACTIVITIES ⊙

UNDERSTANDING
1. Why are fossil fuels important?
2. Describe two problems with our continued use of fossil fuels.
3. Why don't we use alternatives to fossil fuels?

THINKING AND APPLYING
4. Rank the ten methods of electricity generation shown in the illustration from the most promising for the future to the least promising. Justify your rankings.
5. Imagine one week in your life without fossil fuels. How would your life change?
6. Developed countries have built their wealth on 200 years of cheap fossil fuels. They now fear the growth in demand for cars and appliances in developing countries. What are the fears? Can we do something about it?
7. Management of natural resources is at the head of the struggle for more sustainable and equitable development. Discuss the actions of individuals, groups and governments in this issue.

USING YOUR SKILLS
8. Refer to the graph of oil prices from 1965–2008.
   a Describe the trend for total world consumption of oil.
   b Describe the trend for the world price of oil.
   c Suggest reasons for the differences in the trends as shown on the graph.
9. Refer to the pie chart to estimate the percentage of energy resources produced from fossil fuels.

Nearly three-quarters of the Earth's surface is covered by oceans. Fisheries supply almost 20 per cent of the world's protein, and fishing provides a living for millions of people around the world. About one-quarter of the world's oil comes from offshore wells drilled into reserves beneath the sea.

Humans have also used oceans as a convenient way to dispose of wastes. Many countries have dumped all kinds of pollutants into the oceans, including sewage and nuclear and toxic wastes.

Fishing

Today, overfishing, wetlands destruction and pollution threaten world fish stocks.

Modern fishing fleets can locate and catch very large numbers of fish. They can also catch fish from areas deeper in the ocean than ever before. Modern methods of fishing include:

- purse-seine nets, which close around and trap surface-swimming fish
- trawl nets, which catch bottom-swimming fish
- long-line nets, which have hooks attached over a large area
- driftnets, which are often operated by many vessels working together. Many sea creatures (such as turtles and dolphins) are drowned by driftnetting. Several environmental groups are protesting about this method of fishing.

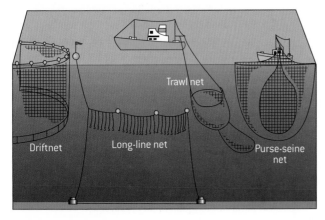

Modern fishing methods

Global action

Over the last 20 years or so, there have been attempts at a global level to prevent and control the overexploitation of fisheries. The decision to set a 320-kilometre fishing zone around countries was one of the most important outcomes of the United Nations Law of the Sea Conference in 1982. This meant that other countries now had to get permission from a country to fish inside that country's zone.

Some countries have introduced management schemes within their territorial waters based on quotas. The European Union (EU), for example, sets quotas for amounts of various fish species that its member countries are allowed to catch. The quota system has been moderately successful in reducing overfishing within these areas.

International agreements to protect marine life have also resulted in whale sanctuaries in the Indian and Pacific oceans. Many countries have now also agreed to end the dumping of industrial and nuclear wastes into the oceans.

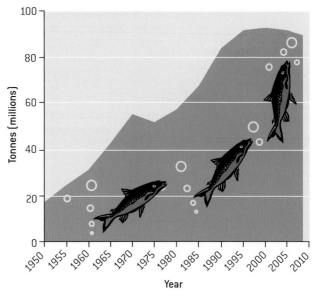

Source: Data derived from www.fao.org.

World-capture fisheries production

GEOfacts

- Fish are Uganda's second biggest export earner after coffee. However, fish stocks are declining in Uganda's lakes, and export earnings for 2007 have dropped by almost 50 per cent since 2005.
- In Asia in the 1950s, it took a fisherman one hour to catch 1 kilogram of fish; today, it takes four hours to catch the same amount. Estimates are that fish stocks have declined by 30 per cent since the 1970s due to overfishing.
- Commercial fishing consumes 1.2 per cent of the oil used globally every year.
- About one-fifth of all fish caught and killed in US waters are thrown back because they are the wrong type.

/// The cod wars

North Atlantic cod

The use of ocean resources can lead to conflict, especially when a resource becomes scarce. During the 1970s, there were bitter disputes between Iceland and Great Britain over who had the right to fish for cod. For Great Britain, the conflict was about fishing industry jobs; for Iceland, it was about economic survival.

Fish and fish products make up around 70 per cent of Iceland's exports. In the mid 1970s, Iceland became worried about falling cod populations. It recognised fishing quotas were essential. But it argued that other countries should bear the cut-backs in cod numbers, as fishing was so crucial for its economy. One solution was to prevent foreign vessels fishing in waters over which it had exclusive rights, so Iceland extended its exclusion zone to 200 miles (321.86 kilometres).

Great Britain did not agree that Iceland had the right to impose this new limit. British trawlers continued to fish in the newly declared exclusion zone. Iceland sent Coast Guard vessels to patrol the zone. Great Britain sent frigates and supply ships to protect the British trawlers that continued to fish these waters. The two NATO allies were on the brink of armed conflict. The UN Security Council was consulted but no progress was made.

When Iceland threatened to close the NATO base on its soil, the Secretary-General of NATO finally interceded to resolve the dispute. Iceland agreed to allow British trawlers to fish inside the exclusion zone for the next six months. When this period ended, Great Britain was no longer allowed under international law to fish in Iceland's waters.

Iceland retained its vital fishing industry. It has also gone on to set a good example of how a finite natural resource, such as cod, can be managed. A quota applies to each Icelandic fishing boat, and catches must be carefully recorded. Areas set aside as cod nurseries are now permanently off limits to fishermen.

UNDERSTANDING

1. How important are oceans for resources?
2. What are the main threats to world fish stocks?
3. Explain the different ways that fish are taken from the ocean. What might be the advantages and disadvantages of each type of fishing?

THINKING AND APPLYING

4. Explain the reasons why some people protest against driftnetting. What do you think about this method of fishing? You could find out more about driftnetting in your library, in newspapers and on the internet.
5. 'Iceland was prepared to go to war over its fishing rights, even to the extent of risking international security.' Discuss this statement in a paragraph, clearly pointing out Iceland's motives.
6. Predict the consequences if this conflict had not been resolved for:
   a cod populations
   b Iceland's economy
   c Iceland's population
   d international attitudes and behaviours.
7. Suggest why each of the rules now in place for cod fishing in Icelandic waters will help to ensure the future availability of this important resource.

USING YOUR SKILLS

8. Refer to the graph of world-capture fisheries production.
   a Describe the trend in production from 1950 to 2000.
   b Explain what this means for world fish stocks.

Along with the growth in world population, there has been an even more rapid growth in **urbanisation**. Urbanisation is the process by which the proportion of a country's population in urban areas increases.

A major reason for the growth of large cities is rural–urban migration. People move to cities for many reasons. These reasons are generally a combination of **push factors** and **pull factors**.

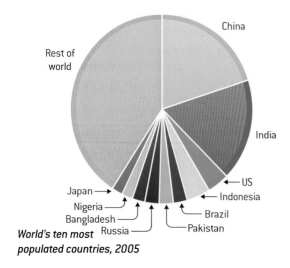

World's ten most populated countries, 2005

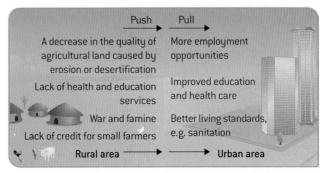

Both push and pull factors result in a drift in population from rural to urban areas.

Growth of cities

About half of the people in the world now live in cities. There has been an extraordinary growth of large cities in the last 50 years, particularly in the developing world. A **megacity** is a city with a population of over 10 million. The world's largest city, Tokyo has more people than the entire population of Australia. By 2015, the world will have 482 cities with one million or more residents.

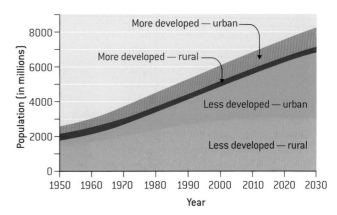

Source: Geohive, www.geohive.com/earth/pop_rururb.aspx.

The increase in urban and non-urban population since the 1950s

Location of the world's 20 largest cities

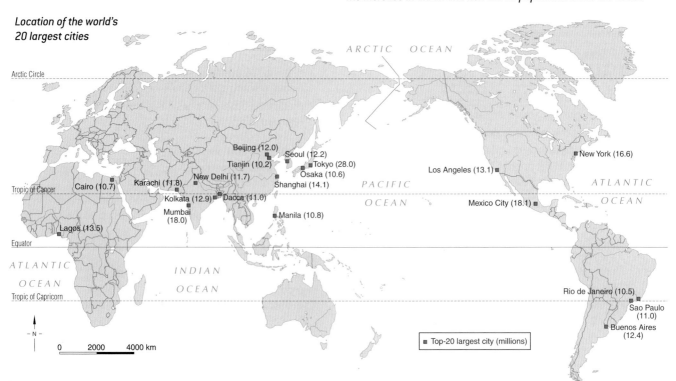

Issues and problems

Some problems caused by urbanisation are:
- Cities use up resources and create huge amounts of waste including heat and domestic and industrial wastes, which must be recycled or removed. One of the greatest problems is air pollution, such as occurs in Beijing.
- Overcrowding, poverty and shantytowns occur in cities such as Mumbai, Lagos and São Paulo.
- Traffic congestion makes movement difficult and adds to pollution.
- Valuable agricultural land is often lost to urban development.

SAMPLE STUDY

/// São Paulo

São Paulo is the largest and fastest growing city in South America, with a population of approximately 11 million. People have moved to the city attracted by the prospect of better jobs, education and health services. This influx has led to the creation of *favelas* or illegal shantytowns on the edges of the city. It is estimated that between 1.5 and 2 million people live in the *favelas*, without adequate sewerage, water or electricity. The promise of employment and a better life has not materialised for many of these people.

Alongside the many poor in São Paulo are the very rich. A wealthy elite lives in luxury, using helicopters to avoid the traffic congestion that plagues the city. A shortage of clean water, very few green spaces, a lack of infrastructure and pollution are other problems caused by the sheer numbers of people in the overcrowded city.

Growth of São Paulo state's population, predicted to 2015

Year	Population, 1950–2015	Year	Population, 1950–2015
1950	2 528 000	1985	13 844 000
1955	3 521 000	1990	15 100 000
1960	4 876 000	1995	16 469 000
1965	6 380 000	2000	17 962 000
1970	8 308 000	2005	19 591 000
1975	10 333 000	2010	20 514 000
1980	12 693 000	2015	21 229 000

Favelas in São Paulo

ACTIVITIES

UNDERSTANDING

1. What percentage of the world's population now lives in cities?
2. Describe the push/pull factors that have resulted in urbanisation.
3. Outline some of the problems caused by the rapid growth of cities.
4. What are favelas and in what city are they located?

THINKING AND APPLYING

5. How do you feel about the fact that some residents of São Paulo live in luxury while others live in poverty? Can you think of any solution?

USING YOUR SKILLS

6. Refer to the pie graph of the world's 10 most populated countries. Estimate the percentage for each country shown.
7. Refer to the map of the world's 20 largest cities.
   a. Rank the cities from 1 to 20 from the largest population to the lowest population.
   b. Which continent has the most cities in this category?
8. Make a line drawing of the photograph of the favelas and label it.
9. Refer to the graph showing the increase in urban and non-urban population since the 1950s.
   a. In which of the four sectors shown on the graph is population increasing most rapidly?
   b. Estimate when the world might reach a population of seven billion.
10. Make a line graph using the data in the table of population growth in São Paulo state.

GEOTERMS

megacity: very large city with a population of over 10 million people

urbanisation: the process by which the proportion of a country's population in the urban areas increases

Importance of human rights

What are human rights?

Human rights are based on the idea that all human beings are equal and deserve fair and equal treatment. It is an idea that has taken many centuries to be accepted and there are still some people who do not agree with it.

Individual countries over time have developed a range of laws to protect human rights. These laws vary across the globe, not only in their protection of human rights but also in the extent to which they are observed and enforced.

A major global breakthrough on human rights took place on 10 December 1948, when the General Assembly of the United Nations (UN) adopted the Universal Declaration of Human Rights. This Declaration sets out in a series of articles the basic human rights of all people. Some of the rights set out in the Declaration are as follows.

Extract from the Universal Declaration of Human Rights

Article 1 All human beings are born free and equal in dignity and rights. They are endowed with reason and conscience and should act towards one another in a spirit of brotherhood.

Article 7 The law is the same for everyone. It should be applied in the same way for all.

Article 13 You have the right to come and go as you wish in your country. You have the right to leave your country for another one and you can return to your country if you wish.

Article 18 You have the right to choose your religion freely, to change it, to practise it as you wish, on your own or with other people.

Article 25 Everyone has the right to a standard of living adequate for their own health and wellbeing and that of their family, including food, clothing, housing and medical care and necessary social services.

Countries can choose to either ratify or sign international human rights agreements. Those countries that ratify international agreements are bound to observe the provisions of such agreements. Countries that only sign, rather than ratify, such agreements undertake not to act in any way that is contrary to the aims of the agreement.

Types of human rights

Human rights can be divided into two main types:
- social, economic and cultural rights, which are concerned with quality of life and having a decent standard of living
- civil and political rights, which cover the right to choose how one's country is run and to conduct one's life free from interference.

Social, economic and cultural rights
- the right to have enough food, clothing, medical care, welfare or social security, education and housing
- the right to enjoy the culture of one's people

Civil and political rights
- the right to choose how a country is run
- no wrongful arrest
- the right to a fair trial
- the right to own property
- the right to work
- the right to freedom of thought and religion
- the right to leave and return to any country
- the right to freedom of opinion and expression
- the right to hold meetings
- the right to join groups
- the right to life
- freedom from slavery

Abuse of human rights

Abuses of human rights occur around the world. This abuse can take many forms: people may be arrested and held without being charged for any crime, political opponents may 'disappear' or be tortured, civilians may be killed or executed, and police may treat prisoners with brutality. Each year the worldwide voluntary human rights organisation, Amnesty International, publishes a report on human rights abuses around the world. The 2008 report documented the human rights situation in 155 countries and territories.

Myanmar (Burma) 2007

Human rights and democracy in Myanmar (Burma) is a dream. This small South-East Asian country is ruled by a dictatorship. The people of Myanmar do not enjoy freedom of expression or assembly. Death, jail, torture and forced labour are common. Freedom of the press is restricted. Anyone who protests against the regime is arrested or imprisoned. The opposition leader Aung San Suu Kyi lives under extended house arrest.

In 2007, Burmese democracy activists and monks took to the streets of the capital, Rangoon, to peacefully challenge two decades of dictatorship by the government. Many were killed. Since the crackdown, the military has hunted down protest leaders in night raids. Monks have been stripped of their religious robes.

There are other human rights abuses in Myanmar:
- children are bought and sold to fight in the army
- ethnic minority villagers have been forced to flee their homes in the country's border areas
- landmines are used by the Burmese army to terrorise civilians and hamper their annual harvest
- child labour is common in the gem industry.

As an informed global citizen you could help to reduce human rights abuses in Myanmar. For example, you could write letters to newspapers and politicians, and support human rights organisations, like Amnesty International.

Amnesty International

Amnesty International is a worldwide human rights movement with members in more than 150 countries. Campaigns run by Amnesty International are guided by the Universal Declaration of Human Rights and include:
- the release of prisoners of conscience
- fair and prompt trials for political prisoners
- the abolition of torture and executions.

Amnesty International send special missions to observe trials, meet prisoners and interview government officials. Once evaluated and checked, the information is distributed to members with recommendations for action. The organisation seeks to be an impartial supporter of human rights and therefore does not take a stand for or against any political system, religion, ideology or economic system.

One way that individuals can help in gaining the release of prisoners of conscience is by joining Amnesty International's letter-writing campaigns. In such campaigns, Amnesty International supporters from all over the world send letters to government leaders appealing for the release of specific prisoners of conscience.

 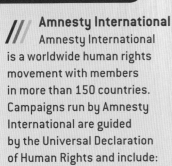
UNDERSTANDING

1. Define the term 'human rights'.
2. What is the Universal Declaration of Human Rights?
3. Why do you think that Article 1 is considered to be so important?
4. What form of government does Myanmar have?
5. How are human rights restricted in Myanmar?
6. Why do you think the Burmese government responded so brutally to monks taking to the streets and protesting in Rangoon in 2007?

THINKING AND APPLYING

7. Refer to the list of social, economic and cultural rights.
   a Can you think of any individuals or communities who do not enjoy these rights?
   b What actions could be taken by governments to ensure that people have these rights?
8. Refer to the list of civil and political rights.
   a Can you think of any circumstances under which you might be deprived of these rights?
   b What would you do as an individual?
9. How could you help to reduce human rights abuses in Myanmar?
10. Suggest reasons why human rights are less likely to be abused in the wealthy countries of the world.
11. Children have rights too. Research child soldiers or child labour, and describe the situation in one country. Explain why these practices are an abuse of human rights.

12.8 Indigenous people and self-determination

The Tuareg live in Africa's great Sahara Desert. About 900 000 Tuareg live a nomadic way of life, moving with their camels, goats and household goods in search of water and pasture. This traditional nomadic existence has limited the pressure on the environment where fertile water and land are scarce. Today, government programs in countries like Niger, Mali and Burkina Faso are taking over much of the Tuareg land, threatening their livelihood.

The Cheyenne is one of 266 American Indian tribes negotiating for a better future for indigenous people in the United States.

Maoris protesting on Waitangi Day. Less than 200 years ago New Zealand's population and culture was Polynesian. Today the population is dominated by people of European origin. New Zealand's Maoris face problems with high unemployment, illiteracy, poor housing and ill health. They are challenging successive New Zealand governments' failure to honour the terms of the Treaty of Waitangi, signed in 1840, which recognised indigenous Maori rights.

The Kayapo Indians live in the Amazon rainforest in Brazil and rely on farming, hunting and gathering for their livelihood. The forest is both their spiritual and physical home. The area is under increasing threat from deforestation, dam construction and pollution. With other Amazon Indians, the Kayapo recently asked for world support to halt the construction of a dam on the Xingu River.

The 6000 inhabitants of the Torres Strait islands live in a narrow strait between Cape York Peninsula and Papua New Guinea. They rely on the ocean for their livelihood. These young boys from Mer Island are dressed in traditional warrior costume. Since the 1970s, the islanders have been linked to Aboriginal people in Australia, while still recognised as a separate community. In 1992, the Mabo case upheld the islanders' claim as original landholders. Currently the Torres Strait islanders are seeking a form of self-government within Australia.

/// The Philippines

Indigenous people in the Philippines can now create a 3D model (relief map) to use as evidence when applying for a Certificate of Ancestral Domain Title. The model shows the relief and boundaries of the area claimed as traditional lands. The certificate gives the indigenous people more control over the land and its resources.

Making a model involves several stages. First, the community members carry out ground surveys and draw sketch maps of the area. The data are checked for accuracy using a global positioning system (GPS). Next, geographic information systems (GISs) are used to prepare a base map that includes contour lines and grid lines. Community members then use all of this information to build the 3D model. The model includes boundaries and contour lines, locations of interest, the current resource base, a legend, scale and north point.

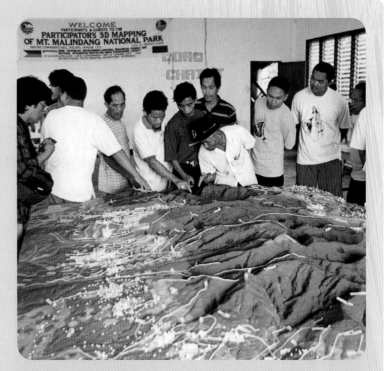

A 1:10 000 scale model of Mount Malindang, Mindanao, Philippines. One-quarter of the Philippines' indigenous people live on the island of Mindanao. The island's resources include gold deposits and stands of old growth forest.

The indigenous experience

Indigenous people are the descendants of the original people of a country or place. Some examples are Aboriginal Australians, the Sami of northern Europe, the Inuit of northern Canada and the Maoris of New Zealand. Indigenous people have their own culture, which usually includes language, religion, social and political organisation and technology.

During the expansion of European power across the world from the sixteenth to the early twentieth century, and the great migrations associated with it, many indigenous people lost their land and culture through conquest and settlement. This was mainly achieved through the newcomers' superior military technology. For example, the indigenous Indian tribes of North America and the Maoris of New Zealand were no match for Europeans with their guns.

In addition, the Europeans introduced new diseases, to which the indigenous peoples had no resistance. This resulted in many deaths.

Many indigenous people became minority groups. Minority groups are often singled out from other people for different and unequal treatment. They therefore regard themselves as objects of collective discrimination.

Self-determination

Often, if indigenous groups are concentrated in a particular part of the country, they will seek self-determination as a way of protecting their human rights. Self-determination is the right of a nation or group of people to form their own government. In Canada, Sweden and the United States there have been movements towards self-determination for indigenous groups.

ACTIVITIES

UNDERSTANDING

1. Define the term 'indigenous people'.
2. What is self-determination?

THINKING AND APPLYING

3. Read the article on the Philippines in the sample study. Explain how the 3D model empowers the local indigenous community.
4. Create a poster, multimedia presentation or a web page about the efforts of an indigenous group of people to achieve self-determination. Search the internet or use other resources such as your library to collect information, photographs and maps.

Interactivity

HOTSPOT COMMANDER: 'ENVIRONMENTAL ISSUES'

HotSpot Commander challenges your geographical skills and knowledge in a fun question-and-answer format. You will receive the coordinates of a location. When you hit your target accurately, you will be given some secret information and a question to answer. Get it right and part of the mystery image is revealed. Can you conquer all 10 locations and become a Hotspot Commander?

SEARCHLIGHT ID: INT-0961

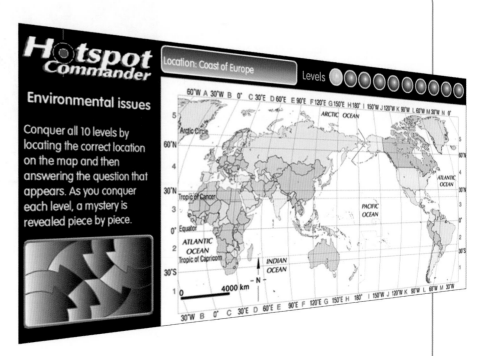

Interactivity

TOP RANK: 'WORLD POPULATIONS'

In this Top Rank interactivity, we test your knowledge of population density around the world by challenging you to correctly list the 10 largest populations in the correct order. Drag each number to underneath the correct flag to rank the countries, and see if you can work out which country holds the Top Rank.

SEARCHLIGHT ID: INT-0963

Interactivity

TOP RANK: 'OIL CONSUMPTION'

In this Top Rank interactivity, we test your knowledge of oil consumption around the world by challenging you to list the top 10 consumers of oil by country in the correct order. Drag each number to underneath the correct flag to rank the countries, and see if you can work out which country holds the Top Rank.

SEARCHLIGHT ID: INT-0964

eLesson

AMNESTY INTERNATIONAL

Amnesty International is a global movement of over 2.7 million people committed to defending those who are denied justice or freedom. It works with people in Australia and all over the world to protect those facing abuse and promote a culture where human rights are embraced, valued and respected. It mobilises people, campaigns, conducts research and raises money to do this important work. In this eLesson, you will meet a representative of Amnesty International and learn how you can get involved in its campaigns and help inspire hope for a better world.

SEARCHLIGHT ID: ELES-0164

13 Climate change

INQUIRY QUESTIONS

+ What is causing climate change?
+ Where is climate change occurring?
+ How is climate change affecting physical and human environments?
+ What can we do about climate change?

Climate change is the environmental challenge of the century. Its impact is already being felt on communities around the globe. Evidence shows that temperatures are increasing, ice is melting in polar and mountain regions and sea levels are rising. Extreme weather events are occurring in more places, more often.

Most scientists believe that many human activities are contributing to climate change. We know it is crucial that we act urgently to slow global warming. Locally and globally, we must meet this challenge to ensure the long-term survival of Earth's ecosystems and humankind.

GEOskills TOOLBOX

+ Using and comparing thematic maps (page 305)

An aerial view of Christmas Island, Kiribati, in the Pacific Ocean. This low-lying island is threatened by sea level rise caused by global warming.

alluvial plain: an area where rich sediments are deposited by flooding

carbon footprint: the total amount of carbon dioxide (CO_2) produced to directly and indirectly support human activities. It can be measured for a country or an individual.

climate: the predicted weather at a particular place, based on the average of weather events over many years

climate change: any change in climate over time, whether due to natural processes or human activities

deltaic plain: flat area where a river(s) empties into a basin

ecotourism: nature-based tourism that involves educating tourists about the natural environment. It is ecologically sustainable tourism and injects money into local economies.

emissions: substances such as gases or particles discharged into the atmosphere

emissions trading scheme: buying and selling of permits to emit greenhouse gases. A permit allows emissions up to a prescribed cap or limit.

enhanced greenhouse effect: increased ability of the Earth's atmosphere to trap heat

fossil fuels: fuels that come from the breakdown of organic matter; for example, coal, oil and natural gas. They have formed in the ground over millions of years.

global warming: describes the observable trend of rising world temperatures over the past century, particularly during the last couple of decades

greenhouse effect: the result of the sun's heat being trapped in the atmosphere rather than reflected out into space. This causes a significant increase in temperature.

greenhouse gases: gases in the atmosphere that trap energy emitted from the Earth's surface; primarily carbon dioxide, methane and nitrous oxide

ice sheet: area of freshwater ice that completely covers more than 50 000 square kilometres of land. There are only three ice sheets in the modern world, the Greenland ice sheet and the East and West Antarctic ice sheets.

mitigation: implementing policies to reduce greenhouse gas emissions and enhance sinks

monsoon: a wind system that brings heavy rainfall over large climatic regions and reverses direction seasonally

photosynthesis: process in plants using the energy from sunlight to convert water and carbon dioxide into carbohydrates and oxygen

renewable energy sources: energy sources that can be easily replaced in a short amount of time, such as solar and wind; non-renewable sources include fossil fuels

sea ice: frozen sea water

sink: any process, activity or mechanism that removes a greenhouse gas from the atmosphere

storm surge: temporary increase in sea level from storm activity

sustainable: describes actions that meet the needs of the present population without endangering the ability of future generations to meet their needs — for example, sustainable energy, resources and development

Climate change

We are all familiar with the climate of where we live. Climate is the predicted weather at a particular place, based on the average of weather events over many years. For example, Sydney has a temperate climate with warm summers, mild winters and rainfall spread throughout the year.

Scientists know that climates do change. Climate change is any change in climate over time. For example, the climate of the area around Sydney has changed throughout the centuries. The Earth experiences colder periods called glacials and warmer periods called interglacials. Eight times in the past 500 000 years the Earth entered a glacial period that reduced global temperatures by at least 5° Celsius and covered areas that are temperate today with ice.

The greenhouse effect

The Earth is heated by the sun, but without the atmosphere the Earth's surface would be about 14° Celsius cooler. Gases in the atmosphere, like the glass shell of a greenhouse, trap the sun's warmth. This is called the greenhouse effect. Water vapour and greenhouse gases, such as carbon dioxide, methane and nitrous oxide, are responsible for trapping the heat and the resulting greenhouse effect.

Natural sources of greenhouse gases include respiration from living organisms, volcanic eruptions, forest fires and the decomposition of dead animals and plants.

The enhanced greenhouse effect

During the last 200 years, the composition of the atmosphere has changed. Greenhouse gases have accumulated in the atmosphere. More greenhouse gases mean that more heat is trapped. The increased ability of the Earth's atmosphere to trap heat is called the enhanced greenhouse effect.

Carbon dioxide is the main gas responsible for the enhanced greenhouse effect. It is mainly produced by burning fossil fuels (coal, oil and natural gas). In addition, the capacity of the atmosphere to eliminate carbon dioxide is reduced when forests are cleared because trees convert carbon dioxide to oxygen during photosynthesis.

The Earth absorbs energy radiated from the sun. Some of this energy is radiated back into the atmosphere, then absorbed and re-emitted in all directions by greenhouse gases. The greenhouse gases trap heat in the near surface layers of the atmosphere, causing the Earth's surface to be considerably warmer than if there were no greenhouse effect.

Sun

Light energy penetrates atmosphere and heats Earth.

Earth's atmosphere

Earth

How the greenhouse effect works

The enhanced greenhouse effect

1. Heat from the sun
2. Heat trapped by greenhouse gases
3. Heat radiating back into space
4. Greenhouse gases produced by power stations burning fossil fuels
5. Greenhouse gases produced by industry burning fossil fuels
6. Greenhouse gases produced by transport burning fossil fuels
7. Greenhouse gases released by logging forests and land clearing
8. Methane escaping from waste dumps
9. Methane from ruminant (cud-chewing) livestock, e.g. cattle, sheep
10. Nitrous oxide released from fertilisers and by burning fossil fuels

Global warming

Since 1860, average temperatures around the world have climbed by about 0.8° Celsius. Some minor drops occurred during that time but the general trend was upward. Much of the increase has occurred in recent decades. Most scientists expect this upward trend to continue. The rising temperature of the Earth is called global warming.

Global warming is causing human-induced climate change. Average global land and ocean temperatures are rising. Higher temperatures are affecting other aspects of climate such as precipitation and storms.

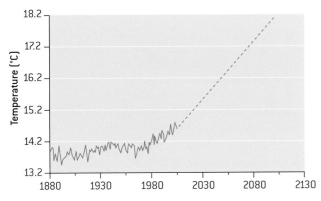

Average global temperature, 1880–2004, with projection to 2100
Source: Earth Policy Institute.

Human activities

The majority of scientists agree that the climate change we are experiencing now is the result of human activities. In 1750, before the Industrial Revolution, the concentration of carbon dioxide in the atmosphere was about 280 parts per million (ppm). In 2007, it was 383 ppm. Natural processes cannot account for such a large increase in such a short period of time.

The extra greenhouse gases are mainly the result of industrialisation and land use changes. Concentrations have increased rapidly, mainly due to the burning of fossil fuels for energy, industry and transport. The clearing of forests and some types of agriculture, such as raising livestock, have also released extra greenhouse gases into the atmosphere.

If greenhouse gas concentrations keep rising at this rapid rate, there is a high risk of hazardous climate change. To meet the challenge, we need alternative methods of powering our homes and industries, new approaches to transport and building design, and more sustainable ways to use resources.

For many years, scientists and geographers have been piecing together evidence of the climate changing. Weather records since the mid 1800s show changes in temperature, the amount of snow and ice cover, precipitation and the intensity of storms.

Long-term trends

Numerous long-term trends are now clear:

- From 1906 to 2005, the average global temperature rose by 0.74° Celsius. Cold days became less common while hot days became more common. Heatwaves became more frequent.
- In 2007, 11 of the previous 12 years were the warmest since reliable records began in 1850.
- Melting of snow and ice during the last 150 years was widespread. The vast area of sea ice that radiates out from the North Pole became smaller. Snow cover in mountain areas decreased and glaciers retreated.
- More powerful storms became more frequent over most land areas. A greater proportion of total rainfall occurred in heavy falls, with longer dry periods in between.
- Droughts became more common in some regions, while precipitation increased in others.
- Average sea levels rose by almost 1.8 millimetres per year from 1961 to 2003. The rate from 1993 to 2003 increased to just over 3 millimetres per year.

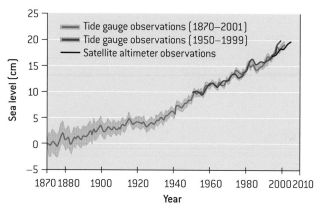

Global average sea level rise, 1870–2005

Source: The Garnaut Climate Change Review 2008, p. 80.

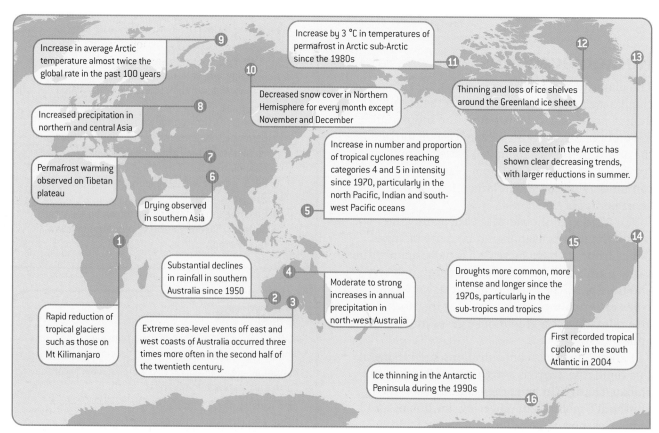

Observed evidence of climate change

Source: The Garnaut Climate Change Review, 2008, pp. 76–7.

Evidence from the past

Today, weather variables such as temperature, rainfall and wind speed are collected from measuring stations all over the world, as well as from weather balloons and satellites. However, most instrumental records date back only to the nineteenth century. For analysing climate change before that time, scientists must rely on other methods.

Ice cores extracted from the ice sheets covering Antarctica and Greenland contain a record of climate change going back hundreds of thousands of years. Bands in ice cores reflect climatic conditions — dark bands indicate warmer temperatures, while light bands indicate colder conditions. Air bubbles in the ice hold information about the state of the atmosphere when the ice formed.

Ice core analysis shows a remarkable connection between carbon dioxide levels and temperature over the past half-million years. The present amount of carbon dioxide in the atmosphere is the highest it has been for 650 000 years.

Tree rings indicate growing conditions, providing a record of the climatic conditions during the tree's life. Trees grow a new layer of wood each year. In good growth years, the new layer or ring in the tree's trunk and branches is wide; in poor growth years the rings are narrower. Using these growth rings, scientists can construct an approximate record of past climates. Some trees live for thousands of years. The study of tree rings to reconstruct past climates is called dendrochronology.

Historical records such as ship logs are useful, as are diaries and letters if they contain detailed information about the weather at the time.

Other data such as fossil records and the landscape can reflect past climates. Many plants and animals exist only in specific climatic conditions. Evidence of past ice ages can be seen in glaciated landscapes. Glaciers carve out landforms such as U-shaped valleys that remain after the ice has gone.

How much hotter?

The projected increase in global temperature by 2100 is in the range of 1.5° to 5° Celsius. Scientists cannot say exactly how much hotter the Earth's temperature may get. It depends on many variables — human and physical. If greenhouse gas emissions are radically cut, it is thought the increase can be kept to about 1.5° Celsius. The concern is that a 'tipping point' might occur — where even a slight rise in global temperature may cause changes that trigger far greater rises.

Future environmental changes

Increases in temperature will trigger environmental changes — the larger the increase, the greater the changes are likely to be. Changes are likely to include:
- more heatwaves and droughts, causing more bushfires
- more violent storms and wider variation in rainfall and snowfall
- the further retreat of glaciers in mountain lands, Greenland and Antarctica
- flooding of some river deltas, low-lying islands and coastal areas through sea level rise
- faster growth rates for some plants due to higher temperatures. This may improve crop growth, but in areas of less rainfall there would be no improvement.
- the possible extinction of many plants and animals as their habitats change. For example, animals in mountain lands that rely on cold temperatures may find conditions too warm for survival. Up to a quarter of plant and animal species are at risk of extinction if temperatures rise by 2° Celsius.

Impacts on people

As environments change, people face serious threats. The people at greatest risk are the poor in developing countries. Developed countries, due to their wealth, have a much greater ability to adapt to impacts. The major impacts will be on food, water, settlements and health. Climate change will result in millions of climate change refugees.

The impacts of climate change on agriculture, such as changes to temperature, precipitation and sea levels, will substantially increase the risk

These photographs of the Upsala Glacier in South America were taken in (a) 1928 and (b) 2004. Although scientists put forward different theories as to why glaciers advance and retreat, many today believe that dramatic change such as this is due to the Earth's rising temperature.

of food shortages. Water scarcity will increase due to reduced snow and ice cover, changes in precipitation and contamination by floods or sea level rise. Many settlements in mountain regions rely on water stored in glaciers or snow for all or part of their water supply. Glaciers and snow feed river systems so less water will be available for settlements and agriculture downstream.

Rising sea levels pose a severe threat to coastal settlements. There may be massive population shifts because people have to move away from affected areas. Millions of people who live in large river deltas, particularly in Asia and Africa, are threatened by sea level rises, storm surges and river flooding.

Damaging effects to human health include malnutrition, spread of diseases and death or injury due to extreme weather events such as storms.

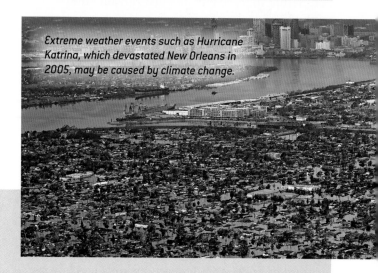

Extreme weather events such as Hurricane Katrina, which devastated New Orleans in 2005, may be caused by climate change.

Icy work may hold key to a brighter future

BY JO CHANDLER

FLAT on their bellies, and frequently scrambling on their knees on Antarctic ice 1000 metres deep and 100 000 years old, the two glaciologists drilling into the summit of Law Dome represent the front-line of climate change science. They are taking the planet's temperature, extracting the data that underpins global debate on what is happening and what might be done.

Labouring in minus 31 degrees over six hours, Tas van Ommen and Mark Curran are gouging a column 10 metres deep into the ice, extracting cores in one-metre lengths which they then painstakingly bag, label and pack into boxes for rapid shipment back to their laboratory. The data they take home may be invaluable — Law Dome is renowned for the penetrating clarity of its climate record — but the hole they leave behind is beautiful, exposing ice time as white through the spectrum of blue to deep indigo.

. . .

They work late into the night taking advantage of the unsetting sun, which hovers long and low on the distant horizon. Despite the plummeting temperatures these are good conditions, they say, shaking their hands to life between tasks. On previous trips wind and snow have made the work unbearable, frozen fingers immovable, forcing them to shelter in tents or the cabin of the Hagglund.

It will be almost 24 sleepless hours before Rob Brittle, a field guide, negotiates the bump and slush of the frozen track back into Casey with the cores. They thaw out, shed glacier boots and goose down coats and find their bunks as the rest of the station rouses.

Their prize today seems relatively modest — two boxes of ice holding about a decade of data. But used in conjunction with other recent climate measurements — taken by satellites and weather stations — and deeper Law Dome cores holding remnants of climate dating back 80 000 years, it becomes immensely powerful.

Salt residue from sea spray reveals the strength of long-exhausted winds, sulfur traces track the vigour of the biological world, and chemical signatures provide a record of past temperature changes. What it means, Dr Curran says, is that we can travel back in time to reconstruct climate history, and throw forward to anticipate its future. Every core, for instance, is exposing closer links between Antarctic conditions and the weather patterns affecting the Australian continent.

. . .

Source: The Sydney Morning Herald, 19–20 January 2008.

Deep history — Tas van Ommen, drilling, and Mark Curran, at right

ACTIVITIES

UNDERSTANDING

1. Complete the following sentences using the words in the box below.

   Scientists use _____ dating back to the nineteenth century to gather evidence of _____. The records show changes in _____, precipitation, the amount of snow and ice cover and the intensity of _____.

   > temperature
   > weather records
   > storms
   > climate change

2. Under each of the following headings, list one long-term trend that shows the climate is changing.

Temperature	Snow and ice	Sea levels

3. What methods do scientists use to identify climate change before the nineteenth century?

4. Who are the people at greatest risk from future environmental changes?

5. List four major impacts that climate change is likely to have on people in the future.

THINKING AND APPLYING

6. Refer to the map 'Observed evidence of climate change' on page 290.

   a Give one example of evidence for each of the following:
   - rising temperatures
   - changes in precipitation
   - more intense tropical cyclones.

   b Use an atlas to name a country likely to be affected by:
   - rising temperatures
   - changes in precipitation
   - more intense tropical cyclones.

   c Several observations detailed on the map are about ice and snow. Why would snow and ice be affected by current climate change?

7. Compare the photographs of the Upsala Glacier on page 291. Describe the impact of climate change on this glacier.

8. How much hotter do scientists think the Earth's temperature may become? What can be done to ensure the temperature increase is as small as possible?

9. What good news and bad news might global warming bring to future farmers?

10. Imagine the environment of your local area in 2050. In the following table, describe the changes that might have taken place.

Temperature	Precipitation	Plants	Animals

USING YOUR SKILLS

11. Refer to the graph 'Global average sea level rise, 1870–2005' on page 290.

   a Describe the changes over the period of the graph.

   b What type of data has been added to the observations in recent decades?

12. Read the newspaper article 'Icy work may hold key to a brighter future' opposite.

   a Outline what the scientists are doing at Law Dome.

   b Describe the harsh weather conditions they face in their work.

   c Outline the information that can be gathered from ice cores. Why are they such a valuable contribution to climate change research?

   d Imagine you are a research scientist in Antarctica. Describe:
   - the qualifications you would need
   - the preparations you would make for the investigations
   - the difficulties you would encounter in your research.

   e In small groups investigate the value of Antarctic research in understanding past climates. Use ICT tools and techniques to assist your investigation.

GEOTERMS

ice sheet: area of freshwater ice that completely covers more than 50 000 square kilometres of land. There are only three ice sheets in the modern world, the Greenland ice sheet and the East and West Antarctic ice sheets.

sea ice: frozen sea water

The regions that are likely to be most affected by climate change are the Arctic, Africa, large river deltas in Asia and low-lying islands. Climate change is happening faster in the Arctic than anywhere else.

Melting ice

During the past 100 years, the Arctic warmed at almost twice the average global rate. Satellite images, available since 1978, reveal a dramatic retreat of Arctic sea ice during the last 40 years. Scientists agree that the loss of so much sea ice so quickly is the result of global warming. The sea ice could disappear altogether during summer within the next couple of decades.

These rising temperatures are threatening ecosystems. In 2008, the polar bear was listed as an endangered species. Polar bears are carnivores (meat eaters) and most of their food comes from the ocean. Sea ice provides a platform for hunting seals,

Satellite image of Arctic sea ice, 1979

Satellite image of Arctic sea ice, 2005

their main diet. Polar bears travel over large areas to find food and, although they are good swimmers, they drown if sea ice isn't available as resting places. Sea ice is vital to the survival of polar bears.

Permafrost (permanently frozen ground) is also beginning to thaw. This makes the ground unstable and can cause infrastructure such as roads and pipelines to collapse.

Methane levels on the rise

The real concern with permafrost is that it contains organic carbon in the form of long-dead plants and animals. If permafrost thaws, the carbon that is released can enter the atmosphere, either as carbon dioxide or methane. Methane is a far more potent greenhouse gas than carbon dioxide.

Shallow Arctic Ocean sediments are also rich in methane. This methane would also be released if the Arctic waters became warmer. Many scientists believe that the increased methane in the atmosphere is contributing to Arctic warming. If the Arctic becomes warmer, even more methane will be released, and this will have an accelerating effect on the warming process.

Possible consequences

Some of the potential consequences of accelerated climate change in the Arctic are described below.

- A predicted global temperature rise of 3 °C this century could be as much as 10 °C in the far north.
- There could be a more rapid change in world sea levels.
- A rapid change in world ocean currents could cause a change in world rainfall patterns. This would threaten the rain-bearing monsoon in southern Asia and the livelihoods of millions of people who depend on these rains.
- If melting continues at the current rate, by 2030 it may be possible to sail straight across the North Pole. New shipping routes create opportunities to exploit Arctic resources. Countries such as Canada, Russia and the United States are hoping to expand their oil and gas fields. It is estimated that the area north of the Arctic Circle contains 22 per cent of the Earth's undiscovered fossil fuel resources, including 13 per cent of oil and 30 per cent of natural gas.
- Increased development and competition for resources may lead to political conflict and negative impacts on indigenous people and wildlife.

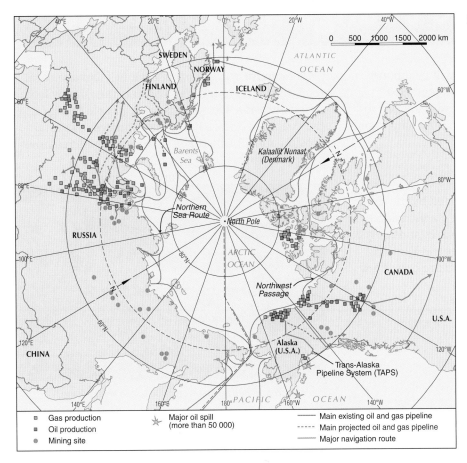

0 500 1000 1500 2000 km

SWEDEN
NORWAY
FINLAND
ICELAND
ATLANTIC OCEAN
Barents Sea
Kalaallit Nunaat (Denmark)
Northern Sea Route
North Pole
RUSSIA
ARCTIC OCEAN
CANADA
Northwest Passage
U.S.A.
Alaska (U.S.A.)
Trans-Alaska Pipeline System (TAPS)
CHINA
PACIFIC OCEAN

■ Gas production
■ Oil production
● Mining site

✶ Major oil spill (more than 50 000)

— Main existing oil and gas pipeline
--- Main projected oil and gas pipeline
— Major navigation route

 GEO*facts*

The UN Convention on the Law of the Sea allows a country's sovereign territory to extend 12 nautical miles beyond its shore. A country also controls resources in a zone that extends for 200 nautical miles from its coast or to the outer edge of its continental shelf, whichever is greater. This zone is called an exclusive economic zone, or EEZ.

ACTIVITIES

UNDERSTANDING

1 Describe the change in average Arctic temperatures during the last 100 years.

2 Explain why ice is melting in the Arctic.

3 What is permafrost? List the negative effects on the human and physical environments if permafrost continues to thaw.

4 Outline how climate change could accelerate development in the Arctic.

THINKING AND APPLYING

5 In small groups, copy the blank flow chart below and use it to sort out the causes, effects and consequences of climate change in the Arctic. Include effects and consequences for the physical environment (including wildlife) and for people (including indigenous people).

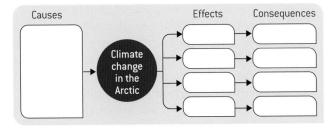

Causes | Effects | Consequences

Climate change in the Arctic

USING YOUR SKILLS

6 Refer to the satellite images of Arctic sea ice.
  a Use an atlas and the map above to name the countries surrounding the sea ice.
  b Use tracing paper to sketch the outline of the sea ice in 1979. Place this over the image for 2005. Estimate the percentage of change in the area covered by sea ice between 1979 and 2005.
  c List some of the consequences of the change in sea ice from 1979 to 2005.
  d What are the advantages of satellite images in learning more about our world?

7 Refer to the map of Arctic development above.
  a Name three examples of resource exploitation shown on the map.
  b Locate the Northern Sea Route and the Northwest Passage. Why are these routes crucial for further Arctic development?
  c Can you find examples on the map of an environmental problem associated with development?
  d How might differing perspectives on developing the Arctic be resolved?

People living on low-lying islands will be among the first wave of climate change refugees. Due to rising sea levels, some people have already had to move — many more could be without a home in our lifetimes.

Rising sea levels

Many low-lying islands will be flooded by the sea as a result of climate change. Some Pacific Island countries are particularly vulnerable. Islands at risk include Kiribati, Kabara in Fiji, Tegua in Vanuatu, the Marshall Islands and Tuvalu. All are only a few metres above sea level.

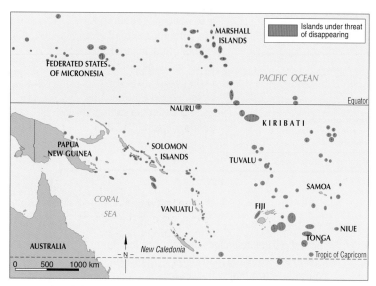

Low-lying islands in the Pacific are under threat.

The majority of Pacific Islanders depend on limited natural resources, especially agriculture, fishing and tourism. Climate change is threatening water supplies, affecting food sources and also destroying buildings.

Many Pacific islands are small and have very few streams; some have none at all. The inhabitants rely on ground water for their drinking supply and to irrigate crops. Ground water is water that is stored naturally within a layer of rock in the ground. It is being contaminated with salt water as a result of higher sea levels and more frequent storm surges.

Crops are ruined when they are flooded by sea water. Soil contaminated with salt is much less able to produce food or cash crops. Fish stocks are at risk because warmer ocean temperatures combined with increased concentrations of carbon dioxide in sea water bleach and kill coral reefs — the most important habitat for fish to breed and feed.

Destructive waves during cyclones damage coral reefs that act as barriers to protect the islands from coastal erosion. On some islands, people living on the coast have already lost their homes to coastal erosion and storm surges generated by increasingly powerful storms.

Poulaka crops killed by salt water due to sea levels rising

What can the islanders do?

The islanders have little choice about what to do or where to go. The islands are a long way from anywhere else, so the costs of importing items such as rainwater tanks are high because of high transport costs. The people cannot simply move inland, away from the waves. Many islands have very little spare land available.

Like other developing countries, the Pacific Island countries are particularly vulnerable to climate change. They do not have the technology, knowledge and money more readily available to developed countries to adapt to or cope with the results of global warming. In recent years, the islanders and their governments have used international forums such as the United Nations to try to raise global awareness of the issues they face.

Can global actions save the islands?

Pacific Island countries are responsible for less than 1 per cent of global greenhouse gas emissions. Unless the international community agrees to large cuts in emissions, the problems facing the islanders will get worse. Numerous people will have to seek refuge in other countries. Without global action, eventually the islanders will lose their countries. Australia has a special responsibility to assist these Pacific neighbours.

Climate of menace

BY GRAHAM READFEARN

Wendy Tekee speaks through lips which until now had formed infectious smiles: 'We face a problem with global warming. They say there will be no more Kiribati.'

The young generation of Kiribati — the Equator-straddling nation of 33 coral atolls halfway between Australia and Hawaii — is the human face of climate change.

Along with more than 50 other young Kiribati women, Tekee has swapped the uncertain shores of her home for the concrete drives and landscaped grounds of Griffith University's Logan campus, south of Brisbane.

Sometime in the next 50 to 100 years, the island nation these young people and their ancestors have called home for more than 1500 years is predicted to disappear under rising sea levels.

Ten years ago, one islet of the Tarawa atoll, which includes the nation's capital, slipped beneath the ocean.

But before other islands are submerged, scientists believe climate change will reduce rainfall on the atolls, where people already struggle to access fresh water.

The island's inshore fisheries become less productive in drought, and there are fears that climate change will force tuna — a staple diet on the island — to move north.

In an effort to build lives away from Kiribati, its government has been working with other nations to find opportunities for its young people.

Tekee, 22, is part of one such attempt — an Australian-funded aid program to teach young Kiribati women nursing skills and English.

...

The Australian government, through AusAID, has put more than $12 million into projects to help Kiribati, including $6 million for the nursing initiative at Griffith University and $2.9 million to help the country adapt to climate change.

...

Source: The Courier-Mail, 22 August 2008.

ACTIVITIES

UNDERSTANDING

1. Refer to the map opposite and then describe the location of the Pacific Islands. Use geographical terms such as latitude, distance, directions, and proximity to coastlines, seas and cities.

2. Why are many islands in the Pacific under threat from rising sea levels?

3. Describe the impacts of climate change shown in the photograph of poulaka crops.

4. What actions can the governments and peoples of the islands take to adapt to or solve the problems they face as a result of climate change?

5. Why does Australia have a responsibility to help Pacific Island nations?

6. Read the newspaper article 'Climate of menace'.
   a Why did Wendy Tekee leave her home?
   b Use the article to list the problems facing Kiribati as a result of climate change.
   c What is the Australian government doing to help the people of Kiribati?

THINKING AND APPLYING

7. Think of a place on the coast you know of, live near or have visited recently. Draw a sketch of how its coastal landforms and other features might change if sea levels were 1 metre higher.

USING YOUR SKILLS

8. In small groups, discuss the following five questions, which relate to climate change in the Pacific. Present your answer using a flow chart.
   a Situation: what has actually happened so far?
   b Background: why has it happened?
   c Solutions: what are all the possible solutions you can think of? What are the consequences, good or bad, of each solution?
   d Choices: what are the best possible solutions?
   e Actions: what can we do about the issue? How can we influence decisions in the future?

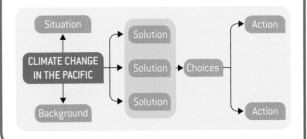

GEOTERMS

storm surge: temporary increase in sea level from storm activity

The country of Bangladesh is a large **alluvial plain** crossed by three rivers: the Ganges, Brahmaputra and Meghna. Each river carries massive volumes of water from its source in the Himalayas, spreads out along the **deltaic plain**, and empties into the world's biggest delta, the Bay of Bengal. This makes Bangladesh one of the most flood-prone countries in the world. The Sundarbans region, a World Heritage site, is just one area of Bangladesh at risk from the increased flooding expected as a result of global climate change.

Why the Sundarbans are important

The Sundarbans are the largest intact mangrove forests in the world. Mangroves protect against coastal erosion and land loss. They play an important role in flood minimisation because they trap sediment in their extensive root systems. Mangroves also defend against storm surges caused by tropical cyclones or king tides, both common in the Sundarbans.

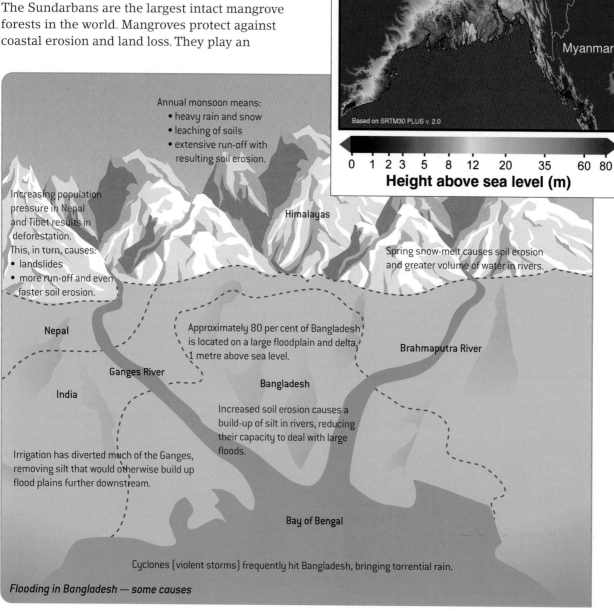

Sea level risks — Bangladesh

India

Bangladesh

India

Myanmar

Based on SRTM30 PLUS v. 2.0

0 1 2 3 5 8 12 20 35 60 80

Height above sea level (m)

Annual monsoon means:
- heavy rain and snow
- leaching of soils
- extensive run-off with resulting soil erosion.

Increasing population pressure in Nepal and Tibet results in deforestation.
This, in turn, causes:
- landslides
- more run-off and even faster soil erosion.

Himalayas

Spring snow-melt causes soil erosion and greater volume of water in rivers.

Nepal

Ganges River

India

Approximately 80 per cent of Bangladesh is located on a large floodplain and delta, 1 metre above sea level.

Brahmaputra River

Bangladesh

Increased soil erosion causes a build-up of silt in rivers, reducing their capacity to deal with large floods.

Irrigation has diverted much of the Ganges, removing silt that would otherwise build up flood plains further downstream.

Bay of Bengal

Cyclones (violent storms) frequently hit Bangladesh, bringing torrential rain.

Flooding in Bangladesh — some causes

The Sundarbans also provide a breeding ground for birds and fish, as well as being home to the endangered Royal Bengal tiger. By sheltering juvenile fish, the mangrove forest provides a source of protein for millions of people in South Asia. Recently, the Sundarbans have also attracted a growing human population as Bangladeshis flee overcrowding in the capital city, Dhaka, or flooding and poverty in rural areas.

Increasing human occupation poses a severe threat to the Sundarbans. Most Bangladeshis rely on wood as a source of energy, and mangroves are being cleared to make charcoal for cooking. Aquaculture industries also have a negative impact. Mangroves are cleared to accommodate huge ponds, which quickly become poisoned by antibiotics, waste products and toxic algae. This damage to the Sundarbans destroys Bangladesh's natural defence against flooding.

The impact of climate change

As icecaps melt due to global warming, sea levels rise, land is lost and people are displaced. Many islands fringing the Bay of Bengal are already under water, producing 'climate refugees', people who have literally nowhere to go. Increasing temperatures are melting glaciers and snow in the Himalayas at a faster rate, which will cause further extreme flooding in Bangladesh. Climate change also causes shifts in weather patterns. If the monsoon season (from June to October) coincided with an unseasonal snow-melt, flooding would occur on a scale never before seen.

Because of these risks, Bangladesh needs to plan for climate change. The government encourages farming methods that avoid deforestation, and a ban is proposed on heavy-polluting vehicles. A proposed economic solution is ecotourism, as it attracts foreign currency while preserving the natural ecosystems and promoting sustainable development.

Boats now sail where this man's 100-year-old ancestral home once stood on the island of Bhola in southern Bangladesh.

GEO*facts* The United Nations Inter-governmental Panel on Climate Change (IPCC) predicts rising sea levels will overtake 17 per cent of Bangladesh by 2050, displacing at least 20 million people.

ACTIVITIES ➡

UNDERSTANDING

1. How do mangroves minimise the impact of floods?
2. List the factors that are displacing Bangladeshis and forcing them to move to the Sundarbans.
3. Name two reasons mangroves are being cleared in the Sundarbans.
4. What are 'climate refugees'?

THINKING AND APPLYING

5. Refer to the diagrams opposite. Explain how the geography of Bangladesh makes it so vulnerable to the threat posed by climate change.
6. How can ecotourism play a role in preserving Bangladesh's ecosystems and help lessen the impact of climate change?

USING YOUR SKILLS

7. Identify the physical and human features shown in the photograph of flooding in Bangladesh.
8. Refer to the diagram 'Flooding in Bangladesh — some causes'.
   a Describe how cyclones can contribute towards flooding in Bangladesh.
   b List some short-term and long-term actions that neighbouring nations Tibet, India and Nepal could implement to lessen the impact of flooding in Bangladesh.
   c Divide a table into three columns headed 'Food production', 'Transport' and 'Settlement', and list the consequences of flooding for each category.

GEOTERMS

alluvial plain: an area where rich sediments are deposited by flooding

deltaic plain: flat area where a river(s) empties into a basin

ecotourism: nature-based tourism that involves educating tourists about the natural environment. It is ecologically sustainable tourism and injects money into local economies.

monsoon: a wind system that brings heavy rainfall over large climatic regions and reverses direction seasonally

Burning fossil fuels emits greenhouse gases, which contribute greatly to global warming. Fossil fuels account for about 60 per cent of global greenhouse gas emissions each year. From 1970 to 2004, global emissions grew by 70 per cent. The largest increases were from energy supply, industry and transport. Replacing fossil fuels with energy sources that do not emit greenhouse gases is an effective way to slow down global warming.

Fossil fuels

Fossil fuels are used to generate electricity and to power transportation. Coal is burned in power stations to boil water, producing steam that drives turbines to generate electricity. Most forms of transport run on oil. In developed countries, our standard of living is based on easily available and relatively affordable energy. Fossil fuels have been widely used since the Industrial Revolution because they are relatively cheap, easy to transport and store, and because our existing technologies are designed to use them.

Sustainable energy

There are two types of energy sources: non-renewable and renewable. Fossil fuels are non-renewable because they were formed in the ground over millions of years under very particular conditions. We cannot make more of them and eventually they will run out. Fossil fuels are unsustainable because their use produces greenhouse gases that harm the environment.

Renewable energy sources include the sun, wind and water. Renewables are replenished naturally and over shorter periods of time. Generating electricity from renewables such as wind, solar and geothermal power emits no greenhouse gases.

Some sources of renewable energy — solar, hydro-electric, wind and geotherm...

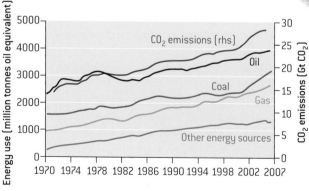

Global energy use and carbon dioxide emissions, 1970–2007

Source: *The Garnaut Climate Change Review 2008*, p. 68.

Some countries, such as Germany, already have a strong sustainable energy industry. Germany has invested in developing solar and wind power. Solar panels and wind generation turbines are now one of their major export industries. Although Australia has abundant sunlight, Germany is well ahead of Australia in the development and utilisation of solar-powered technology.

Alternative energy sources can power transport too. Manufacturers are producing hybrid cars that run partly on petrol and partly on electricity. Others can be recharged overnight like a mobile phone. Ethanol, a renewable fuel produced by fermenting crops such as grains and sugar cane, is being used as a petrol substitute. Brazil is currently the world's largest ethanol producer from its vast sugarcane crops. This may not be a sustainable solution because ethanol's raw materials are normally used as food or are grown on land usually devoted to food crops — raising concerns about food shortages.

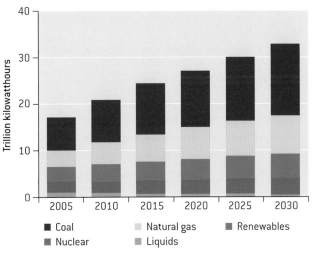

World electricity generation by fuel, 2005–2030

Source: Energy Information Administration (EIA).

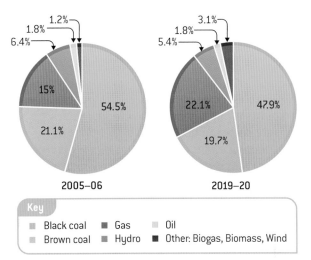

Shares in Australian electricity generation by fuel, 2005–06 and 2019–20 (not including solar, wave or geothermal)

Energy choices for Australia

In Australia, most of our electricity is generated from the burning of coal. Reasons for this include:
- Coal is abundant in Australia and a relatively low cost resource. Using coal results in low electricity prices — an advantage to industries, businesses and individuals.
- Coal exports are an important contributor to our gross domestic product (GDP). They help to support the economy and our standard of living. The coal industry is also a large employer. Consequently, the industry is a strong lobby group in favour of fossil fuels.
- In 2009, the Australian government passed legislation outlining a target of 20 per cent of Australia's electricity to be provided from renewable energy sources by 2020.

Reducing emissions

Countries need ways to generate electricity that are affordable, produce large amounts of power and do not produce high emissions. The need is urgent — before the impacts of climate change become too dangerous. To reduce emissions we could:
- use renewable energy sources — renewables such as solar and wind need more development to match the affordable and massive amounts of power generated by coal.
- develop 'clean coal' technology — a process that captures emissions and stores them underground. This technology is in the early stages of development and is not likely to be used on a large scale for decades.
- use nuclear power — a nuclear reaction releases energy. The energy is used to boil water to produce steam that drives a turbine to generate electricity. Uranium is used in a nuclear reactor. There are no nuclear power plants in Australia, but nuclear energy is used in about 30 other countries. France, for instance, uses nuclear power to produce more than three-quarters of its electricity. The nuclear power option is the subject of wide debate in many countries because of its potential for misuse in the manufacture of nuclear weapons, and the problem of safe waste disposal.
- use less energy and use it more efficiently — this is the fastest and easiest way to reduce emissions. It cannot solve the problem alone, but it does buy extra time to develop other energy sources. Strategies include energy-efficient light bulbs and appliances, switching to solar hot water systems, better building designs that take advantage of natural light and temperature control, and improving public transport so that it is widely available, economical and more attractive to users.

Comparing energy sources

Energy source	Advantages	Disadvantages
Wind power	• Generation doesn't release greenhouse gases. • Will never run out • Technology is well developed. • Safe for people and the environment	• Less affordable than coal at present • Amount of energy varies with wind speed • The largest wind farm in Australia, in 2008, produced one-thirtieth of the output of an average coal-fired power plant. • Some people object to turbines in the landscape.
Solar power	• Generation doesn't release greenhouse gases. • Will never run out • Safe for people and the environment	• Less affordable than coal at present • Not available at night, energy varies with weather conditions
Geothermal power	• Generation doesn't release greenhouse gases. • Available at all times	• Less affordable than coal at present • Can release air pollutants and destabilise the ground if not well designed and operated • Supplies may be limited.
Water power	• Generation doesn't release greenhouse gases. • Tidal or wave power will never run out.	• Constructing dams for hydro-electricity can harm the environment and restrict water availability downstream. • Constructing tidal or wave generators can harm the environment. • Amount of available water and energy varies
Nuclear power	• The reaction itself releases no greenhouse gases. • Australia has large reserves of uranium. • Can generate a reliable and constant supply of electricity • The mining, refining and transporting of uranium, transporting and storing of nuclear wastes and the construction of power plants produce emissions, but only a fraction of those produced by burning coal.	• Less affordable than coal at present (research and development of renewables needed to establish if nuclear power is more or less expensive than renewables) • Takes years to build new installations • Large amounts of water are required. • Nuclear waste is highly radioactive; there is no known safe way to dispose of it; it must be stored for thousands of years. • Generally not popular with the public because of fears about potential dangers such as contamination of mining sites, accidents and leaks from nuclear power plants and storage sites, and proliferation of nuclear weapons

Making it work

Changing the basis of our energy system is beyond the power of individuals. Governments, backed by public support, must take a leading role in achieving the large-scale changes needed to substantially reduce emissions. Key strategies include:

• *Government policies that support reductions in emissions.* A government policy is a course of action designed to achieve a specific result; for example, a policy to limit emissions from power stations and transport to achieve reductions in national emissions.

• *Counting environmental damage as part of the cost of goods and services.* This cost is low for most renewables and much higher for fossil fuels.

• *Research and development to reduce the cost and dramatically increase the output of energy from renewables.* Governments need to invest large amounts of money and provide incentives for the private sector to do the same.

• *Information about why and how quickly emissions must be reduced, which is necessary to achieve sufficient public support.* Companies with vested interests in fossil fuels will not welcome the changes. People will worry about electricity costs, job losses and export earnings.

Climate-friendly energy technologies are not important only in Australia. Developing countries are becoming industrialised and their emissions are rapidly increasing. At present, coal is their lowest cost energy option. To avoid dangerous climate change, the world needs to fuel economic growth in developing and developed countries with energy that is available, affordable and sustainable.

Green-collar army recruits for the solar boom

BY BEN CUBBY AND STEPHANIE PEATLING

Leah Callon-Butler gave up a career in fashion last year to become a solar panel saleswoman, joining a surge towards green jobs predicted by the Federal Government.

Modelling done by Treasury on the cost of climate change found there would be an explosion in 'green-collar' work with the introduction of an emissions trading scheme, with renewable power industries like solar and wind expected to be 30 times their current size by the middle of the century.

Ms Callon-Butler, a sales executive with the Sydney solar hot-water company Endless Solar, intends to stick around for the expected boom. The company has installed 5000 rooftop solar hot water systems in five years, using technology developed at the University of NSW, and it is looking for more staff.

By 2050, Treasury predicts, renewable energy could make up as much as half the energy mix in Australia, replacing the current reliance on coal. 'Renewable technologies will become increasingly competitive, and production methods will switch to less emission-intensive technologies and processes,' the Treasury report said. More jobs will be created by demand for cleaner cars, and Treasury estimates one in four people will be driving a hybrid or plug-in electric car by 2050.

The Clean Energy Council said the Treasury modelling showed immediate public and private investment in renewable power would pay off.

'The smarter and more dynamic we are right now, the more options we will have in terms of deploying technologies commercially five years down the track in 2012 and 2013,' said a spokesman, Matthew Warren. Unions and environment groups called on the Federal Government to pave the way for a green jobs boom.

Half a million new jobs could be created in renewable sectors of the economy by 2030, said a report yesterday by the ACTU and the Australian Conservation Foundation. The ACTU president, Sharan Burrow, said: 'The report shows Australia must act swiftly to make the most of its natural advantages or our economy will be left behind. We can't afford to miss the boat.'

Source: The Sydney Morning Herald, 31 October 2008.

GEOfacts

- If it could be collected, enough sunlight falls on the Earth in just one hour to meet world energy needs for a whole year.
- One wind turbine can produce enough electricity to power up to 300 homes.
- The world still has very large reserves of coal, but oil reserves may run out this century. As reserves run low, the price of oil will rise.

ACTIVITIES

UNDERSTANDING

1 What percentage of annual greenhouse gas emissions is produced by using fossil fuels?

2 Why isn't the use of fossil fuels sustainable?

3 List some major differences between *non-renewable* and *renewable* energy sources.

4 Why might renewable fuels such as ethanol be unsustainable?

5 List reasons why fossil fuels have been the preferred energy source for Australia.

6 Apart from switching to renewable energy sources, what else can Australia do to reduce greenhouse gas emissions?

7 Why are the actions of governments important in developing alternatives to fossil fuels?

THINKING AND APPLYING

8 What would the negative impacts be if all fossil fuels were banned tomorrow?

9 Read the newspaper article 'Green-collar army recruits for the solar boom'.
   a According to the Australian Treasury, what will be the effect of an emissions trading scheme?
   b How many jobs are expected to be created in the renewable sector by 2030?
   c How much of the energy mix is renewable energy expected to make up by 2050?
   d List the non-government organisations mentioned in the article. Are they optimistic or pessimistic about the future?

USING YOUR SKILLS

10 Use the information in the column graph of world electricity generation to estimate the percentage growth in renewable fuels from 2005 to 2030.

11 Refer to the pie graphs of Australia's electricity generation on page 301. What percentage of Australia's energy currently comes from renewable sources? By how much is this projected to increase by 2019–20?

How to avoid dangerous climate change is the challenge of the century. If no action is taken to reduce greenhouse gas emissions, global warming will increase and climate change will accelerate. All countries will be affected, some very badly. To reduce emissions on a global scale, we need strong, coordinated and urgent global action.

Different futures

The impacts of climate change on environments, species and people depends on:

- how much the climate changes
- how quickly it changes
- how vulnerable the environment, species or community is, and how adaptable it is to change
- how quickly and effectively global action can reduce emissions.

The Garnaut Climate Change Review 2008, commissioned by the Australian government, examined three future cases based on different levels of mitigation:

1. No mitigation — no action to reduce emissions or enhance sinks.
2. 450 mitigation — reduce emissions enough to stabilise emissions at 450 parts per million (ppm) in the atmosphere.
3. 550 mitigation — stabilise emissions at 550 ppm.

If the amount of emissions in the atmosphere can be stabilised at 450 ppm, the rise in temperature by 2100 can probably be kept to about 1.5° Celsius. At 550 ppm, it can probably be kept below 3° Celsius.

With no mitigation, the rise in temperature by 2100 will be more than 3° Celsius. The consequences of an increase of 3° Celsius or more are likely to include:

- melting of the Greenland ice sheet, eventually raising the sea level by 7 metres
- extinction of at least one-third of the world's species
- destruction of coral reefs, including the Great Barrier Reef
- environmental changes that pose serious threats to people, including major impacts on food and water supplies, settlements and human health
- huge movements of people away from affected areas resulting in tens of millions of climate change refugees.

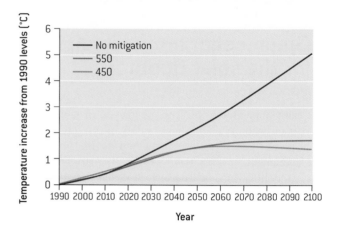

Global average temperature outcomes for three emissions cases, 1990–2100. Temperatures remain high until about 2030 in all cases as a result of emissions already in the atmosphere.
Source: The Garnaut Climate Change Review 2008, p. 88.

Potential impacts for each of the three emissions cases by 2100

Emissions case	450	550	No mitigation
Likely range of temperature increase from 1990 level	0.8–2.1°C	1.1–2.7°C	3–6.6°C
Percentage of species at risk of extinction	3–13%	4–25%	33–98%
Area of reefs above critical limits for coral bleaching	34%	65%	99%
Likelihood of starting large-scale melt of the Greenland ice sheet	10%	26%	100%
Threshold for starting accelerated disintegration of the West Antarctic ice sheet	No	No	Yes

Source: The Garnaut Climate Change Review 2008, p. 102.

Meeting the challenge

There are three strategies that can substantially cut greenhouse gases in the atmosphere:

1. Development of technologies that reduce emissions, such as renewable energy sources.
2. Helping the world's natural sinks to continue absorbing carbon dioxide from the atmosphere, by preserving forests and increasing forest areas.
3. Setting global emissions targets to reduce emissions and cooperate to achieve them. Targets will reduce the risk of disastrous consequences.

USING AND COMPARING THEMATIC MAPS

Thematic maps often use shading or colours to show patterns of information. The first map below shows the nations of the world and carbon dioxide emissions per person, per year. The second map shows the amount of energy used per person, per year.

By comparing the thematic maps below, we can establish if there is a relationship between energy use and carbon dioxide emissions.

A strong positive relationship means that there is an obvious pattern; for example, high carbon dioxide emissions and high energy use, or low carbon dioxide emissions and low energy use. A strong negative relationship would be a general pattern that shows high carbon dioxide emissions and low energy use, or vice versa. A medium relationship would show a pattern, but with some variation. A weak relationship would show little or no pattern.

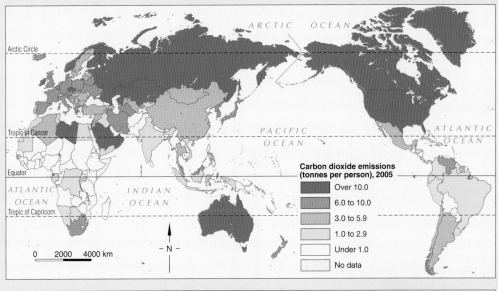

The darker the colour, the higher the average CO_2 emissions per person

Carbon dioxide emissions (tonnes per person), 2005

Over 10.0
6.0 to 10.0
3.0 to 5.9
1.0 to 2.9
Under 1.0
No data

0   2000   4000 km

Carbon dioxide emissions, per person

Source: Data derived from UN Millennium Development Goals Indicators.

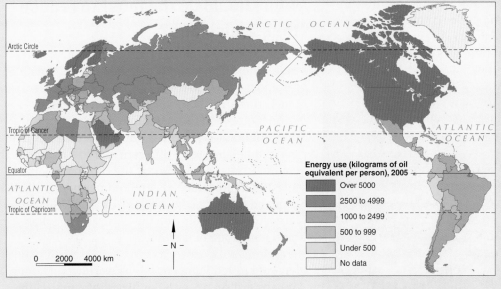

The darker the colour, the higher the average energy use per person

Energy use (kilograms of oil equivalent per person), 2005

Over 5000
2500 to 4999
1000 to 2499
500 to 999
Under 500
No data

0   2000   4000 km

Energy use per person

Source: Data derived from International Energy Agency (IEA).

GEOfacts Coral reefs are sensitive to changes in water temperature and ocean acidity, both of which are now higher than at any time in the last 420 000 years. The ocean becomes more acidic as it absorbs more carbon dioxide, slowing the growth of coral skeletons.

GEOfacts Australia is working with developing countries to encourage them to maintain their forests rather than cut them down for short-term profits. Global deforestation causes 20 per cent of global emissions annually, second only to the burning of fossil fuels.

International action

The international community already has some systems in place that can help the world avoid dangerous climate change.

- **The Intergovernmental Panel on Climate Change (IPCC)** was established in 1988 by the UN and the World Meteorological Organization. Its reports are based on scientific evidence. The IPCC regularly reports on causes of climate change, its impacts and ways we can adapt to and reduce these.
- **The Kyoto Protocol** is an international agreement that aims to limit emissions. Targets were set for developed countries for the first period of the agreement, from 2008 to 2012. Developed countries agreed to reduce their emissions by an average of 5 per cent based on 1990 emissions. This is only the first step. Much larger cuts are necessary.

    The protocol came into effect in 2005 when it was ratified by most developed countries, not including Australia and the United States of America.
- **International forums** are essential so that countries can communicate and cooperate. In 2007, over 180 countries attended the UN Climate Change Conference in Bali, Indonesia. It was proposed that developed countries should cut their emissions by 25 to 40 per cent by 2020. The United States called for developing countries to reduce their emissions. Other countries disagreed because the largest share of greenhouse gases already in the atmosphere was emitted by developed countries. By the end of the conference, there was still no agreement on the new emissions targets to start in 2013.

There was thunderous applause at the Bali Conference when Australia announced it would accept limits on its emissions. The Rudd Labor Government ratified the Kyoto protocol after it was elected in 2007.

A global agreement to substantially reduce emissions requires cooperative and coordinated international action on a scale never seen before. It is difficult to achieve agreement between so many countries. Each country naturally wants to put its own interests first — questions about what is fair and just also have to be taken into account. In December 2009, the United Nations Convention on Climate Change took place in Copenhagen without developing a new global climate change agreement.

Who will be most affected by climate change?

Developing countries are more vulnerable to many impacts. For example, millions of people in Asia and Africa live in vulnerable areas such as large river deltas. Due to a lack of money and technology, developing countries have less capacity to adapt to climate change.

Who should do the most to reduce their emissions?

Some countries emit far more greenhouse gases than others. Developed countries are responsible for about three-quarters of the human-caused emissions already in the atmosphere. China's annual emissions, for example, are ten times higher than Australia's. However, emissions measured on a per capita basis tell a different story — it divides the country's total emissions by the country's population to estimate how much is emitted per person. This is referred to as a carbon footprint. The US has the largest carbon footprint, but Australia also has very high per capita emissions.

A global emissions trading scheme can play a key role in reducing emissions worldwide. Limits or caps are set on each country's total emissions and permits are issued. The number of permits is fixed, limiting the total emissions that can be made in any one period. Once a permit is issued to an emitter, it can be traded. A permit allows emissions up to a prescribed limit. Countries that exceed their limit can decide to either invest in technologies that control emissions or buy permits from other countries.

Delegates participate in the UN Climate Change Conference 2007 in Bali.

Action in Australia

The Garnaut Report recommended the following policies to the Australian government:

- Support for an effective global agreement
- Development of mitigation policies, particularly a national emissions trading scheme
- Large increases in research and development
- Equitable distribution of the burden of mitigation; for example, assisting low-income households if electricity costs rise substantially.

Making the future

People make a difference to what will happen. The Australian Conservation Foundation and the World Wide Fund for Nature are well known examples of environmental organisations. The Pacific Calling Partnership works with schools and community groups to raise awareness of climate change threats facing people in the Pacific Islands.

People across the world, including more than 150 rock and pop groups, joined together to stage Live Earth concerts across seven continents in 2007. The concerts launched a global campaign to spread the word about climate change. Before the Sydney concert, Missy Higgins told *The Sydney Morning Herald* that she had 'greened' her current tour as much as possible.

'We have made our tour carbon neutral by purchasing green energy to power the venues and hiring hybrid cars wherever possible,' she said. 'Everything that's left over, we buy carbon offsets.' … 'Maybe the younger you are, the more willing you are to change your ways,' Higgins says.

Missy Higgins onstage at the Live Earth concert in Sydney, 2007

People have many different perspectives about climate change. The important debate now revolves around the future impacts of climate change and how to reduce the emissions that are causing it. Climate change has created many special interest groups, each arguing their case or solution. Discussion and decision-making are examples of active citizenship. Some possible views are presented below.

Leader of developed country

My government accepts the science of global warming and we think global emissions should be reduced. But we are concerned this could weaken our economy; for instance, if we have to use different or more expensive energy sources.

Instead, we should concentrate on other solutions to reduce emissions such as clean coal technologies. We are also looking at building nuclear power stations.

Climate change needs an international plan that will work. The Kyoto Protocol is an important step, but it requires only developed countries to reduce emissions.

Developing countries should also reduce their emissions, especially China and India who have fast-growing economies. A global emissions trading scheme is central to the effort to reduce emissions.

Leader of developing country

Developed countries should take responsibility for climate change and make big cuts to their emissions. Developing countries have produced significant emissions for only a few decades. The developed world has done so for well over a century.

Even China, for example, whose total emissions are now among the highest of any country, still has very low emissions per capita. Each person in China is responsible for less than 20 per cent of the emissions of a resident in the USA.

The developing world needs economic growth to raise people out of poverty and to meet their basic needs. We should not have to restrict economic growth to solve an environmental problem caused by the developed world.

Perhaps developed countries could think about changing their lifestyles and reducing their consumption to make a contribution to the global climate.

Renewable energy representative

It is essential that we develop large-scale use of renewable energy and energy-efficient technologies. Governments and businesses should invest in sustainable energy such as solar and wind power. Some countries already have rapidly growing solar and wind power industries because of strong investment by governments and businesses.

Green businesses help to reduce global emissions; for instance, we produce renewable energy, capture greenhouse gases from landfills and organise tree planting schemes. A global emissions market could be worth billions of dollars and is the best way to make polluters pay for their emissions.

Environmental groups' representative

It is time for all governments to admit the scale of the problem and develop policies to tackle it. We need long-term wisdom, not short-term political and economic gains.

Consider what the cost will be if we do nothing. Without big cuts to global emissions, we will lose unique environments and many species. Life will be very difficult for us as well. There is still time to avoid the worst impacts of climate change.

Unfortunately, governments and businesses do not always look at the big picture, but often have short-term goals. If they introduce higher taxes or prices to combat global warming, governments may lose votes and, potentially, elections. If businesses cut emissions or divert money to new technologies, they may not make as much profit and may lose shareholders.

We cannot wait for the issue to be solved for us. We can all make changes to reduce global warming, with little effect on our lifestyle.

Fossil fuel company representative

The world still has reserves of fossil fuels, especially large amounts of coal. For some countries, such as Australia, coal is a very important export. Coal is relatively cheap and provides the power for many essential industries. Reducing emissions by too much too quickly will be a great shock to the economy of many countries.

We are looking at ways to reduce emissions. Governments should help us by investing in technology that can use fossil fuels more cleanly. We support research into technologies such as clean coal that will take carbon dioxide from coal emissions and safely dispose of it. It is not a matter of limiting the use of fossil fuels, but of investing in technology to make fossil fuels cleaner.

Bias and misconceptions

These are some of the most common misconceptions:

1. *It's natural — the world switches between ice ages and warm periods.*
Ice ages and warmer interglacials are thought to result from changes in the Earth's orbit, which affects the amount of solar radiation reaching the Earth. The increased warming during recent decades cannot be due to this because the Earth's orbit has been stable since the 1970s.

2. *A few degrees warmer won't matter; it could be a good thing.*
Crop yields could increase and fewer people might die from cold-related causes. But within 20 years, crop yields in some African countries are likely to be halved. When temperatures in the past were 3° Celsius higher, sea levels were tens of metres higher. Extreme rising of sea levels could take hundreds of years, but will be more rapid if ice sheets melt.

3. *What about the Medieval Warm Period?*
There was a period of unusual warmth in the Northern Hemisphere from about AD 900 to 1200. In the Southern Hemisphere, there were both cold and warm periods during this time. The Earth is now warmer than that period and is still warming.

4. *People aren't responsible for global warming.*
The vast majority of scientists agree human activity is the main driver of climate change and that reducing emissions is the only way to slow it. Only a very small minority do not agree. Alternative theories should be considered if they can be supported by evidence.

ACTIVITIES

UNDERSTANDING

1 Refer to the different perspectives about climate change presented on these two pages.
Copy the table below and complete it by using the different perspectives about climate change. The first one has been started for you.

Perspective	Opinion about problem	Suggested solution	Possible future impact
Leader of developed country	• Emissions should be reduced without weakening the economy	• Clean coal technologies • Developing countries must reduce emissions too • Global emissions trading scheme	• Might increase cost of fossil fuels • Difficult for developing countries to reduce emissions without also reducing the quality of life
Leader of developing country			
Renewable energy representative			
Environmental groups' representative			
Fossil fuel company representative			

2 Complete a futures chart like the one below by thinking about the following points:
  • what do you think the future will be like
  • what would you prefer the future to be like
  • what could you do to influence the future so that it is what you would prefer?
  Display the future charts in the classroom.

Level of influence	Situation What is the perceived future problem?	Likely future Why does this event seem likely to happen?	Preferred future What would I like to happen?	Involvement and action What can I/we do about it?
Local				
National				
Global				

Working geographically

KNOWLEDGE AND UNDERSTANDING

Select the alternative A, B, C or D that best answers the question.

1. The enhanced greenhouse effect is
   - (A) the trapping of the sun's warmth in the atmosphere.
   - (B) the increased ability of the Earth's atmosphere to trap heat.
   - (C) the change in climate over time.
   - (D) the unpredictable weather at a particular place.

2. Fossil fuels are
   - (A) the remnants of prehistoric creatures.
   - (B) oil, gold, natural gas.
   - (C) oil, coal, methane.
   - (D) oil, coal, natural gas.

3. Ice cores provide a record of climate change over
   - (A) the last 1000 years.
   - (B) hundreds of thousands of years.
   - (C) millions of years.
   - (D) the interglacial periods.

4. Greenhouse gases include
   - (A) oxygen, methane and hydrogen.
   - (B) methane, carbon dioxide and neon.
   - (C) carbon dioxide, methane and nitrous oxide.
   - (D) nitrous oxide, oxygen and carbon monoxide.

5. Ice shelves are
   - (A) glaciers.
   - (B) thick plates of sea ice that cover the Arctic.
   - (C) thick plates of freshwater ice that float on the ocean.
   - (D) icebergs that have joined together.

6. An example of sustainable energy is
   - (A) tidal power.
   - (B) natural gas.
   - (C) liquefied coal.
   - (D) electricity.

7. A country like Bangladesh is at risk of climate change because
   - (A) it relies heavily on tourism.
   - (B) it has large rivers that flow into a delta.
   - (C) it is close to the Arctic.
   - (D) its economy is underdeveloped.

8. Which of the following is not a likely result of increased global warming?
   - (A) The destruction of coral reefs
   - (B) The extinction of some species
   - (C) The creation of climate refugees
   - (D) An increase in the Arctic and Antarctic ice cover

9. A global emissions trading scheme is designed to
   - (A) limit a country's total emissions.
   - (B) help a country invest in new technologies.
   - (C) increase a country's total emissions.
   - (D) make fossil fuels sustainable energy sources.

10. The key report on climate change for Australia is the
    - (A) Kyoto Protocol.
    - (B) Garnaut Report.
    - (C) Intergovernmental Panel on Climate Change.
    - (D) Bali Agreement.

INTERPRETING COLUMN GRAPHS

11. Refer to the graph 'Domestic CO_2 emissions'.

    a What do you understand by the phrase 'Business as usual'?

    b What is the largest emitter under 'Business as usual'? How can this emission be reduced?

    c What do you understand by the term 'green electricity'?

    d List high energy devices or equipment:
    • in your home • at school • in your community.
    Suggest how these could be replaced to reduce emissions.

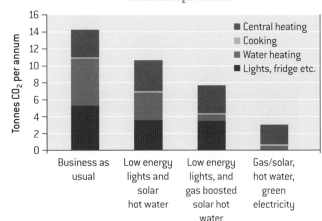

Domestic carbon dioxide emissions

Climate change affects birds and bees

BY JUDY SKATSSOON

Changes in temperature and rainfall are changing the breeding behaviour of magpies ...

... Heather Gibbs from Melbourne's Deakin University is one of a group of scientists investigating climate-driven changes in the migratory and reproductive patterns of Australia's flora and fauna.

Gibbs says evidence over the past 30 years shows that fluctuations in climate can vary the breeding season of the Australian magpie (*Gymnorhina tibicen*) by up to three weeks. ...

But while warmer weather in the northern hemisphere is causing birds to start breeding earlier, Gibbs found that in the southern hemisphere magpies are twice as likely to be seen breeding, and start breeding earlier, in colder, wetter years ...

Climate change has been affecting flowering plants too, says Dr Marie Keatley of the University of Melbourne, who has examined records for more than 20 years.

That timeframe, from 1983–2004, includes 13 of the warmest years ever recorded in Australia.

In her presentation to the Greenhouse2005 climate change conference in Melbourne next week, she will describe how records of 56 plant species in Victoria show a shift in all their flowering dates, which could affect cross-pollination.

Some 24 of the species began flowering at an average of almost 2 weeks earlier over the past 22 years, while the remaining flowered about 3 weeks later.

Source: www.abc.net.au/science/, Wednesday, 9 November 2005.

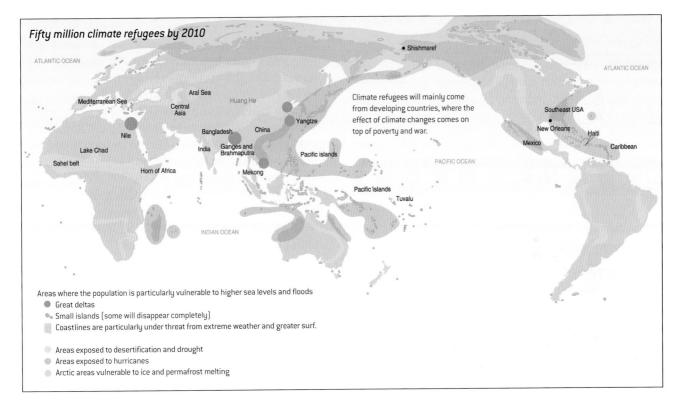

Fifty million climate refugees by 2010

Climate refugees will mainly come from developing countries, where the effect of climate changes comes on top of poverty and war.

Areas where the population is particularly vulnerable to higher sea levels and floods
- Great deltas
- Small islands (some will disappear completely)
- Coastlines are particularly under threat from extreme weather and greater surf.

- Areas exposed to desertification and drought
- Areas exposed to hurricanes
- Arctic areas vulnerable to ice and permafrost melting

CLIMATE CHANGE AND ITS IMPACTS

12 Read the article 'Climate change affects birds and bees'.
   a What evidence of climate change is there in the article?
   b Using the internet and library resources, research evidence that climate change is affecting plants and animals or the spread of disease. Present your research as a short report or poster.

13 Human-induced climate change is likely to make some parts of the world uninhabitable, creating climate change refugees. Use the world map above to answer the following questions.
   a Name the continent that is likely to suffer the most from flooding in river deltas.
   b List the climate change impacts that may affect Africa.
   c Which continents are vulnerable to sea level rise?
   d Which continents are vulnerable to desertification and drought?
   e List climate change impacts that may affect Australia.
   f What are the main threats to North and South America?

ACTIONS AND PERSPECTIVES

14 Create a mind map to present the actions that individuals, groups and governments can take to address the impacts of global warming and climate change.

15 Use the different perspectives on climate change on pages 308–9 as a basis for a class forum on this topic. Choose five students to take on each role and form a panel. The rest of the class should prepare three questions for each panel member. Each panel member should respond to the questions, depending upon their role, and maintain their character's perspective on this topic.

Small acts, big changes

SEARCHLIGHT ID: PRO-0036

SCENARIO

As a member of generation Y, climate change is an issue that is very important to you. Nearly every day you hear frightening statistics about what the world will be like by 2050 unless we all make dramatic changes to our lifestyles. You are also getting frustrated by how slowly change is being initiated. Therefore, you have decided to take action yourself and create a persuasive video that will inform households and local communities of actions they can take personally to help stop the consequences of climate change.

Your project brief includes a sample viral video on climate change.

OMAR'S TOP 10 TIPS FOR REDUCING YOUR CARBON FOOTPRINT

YOUR TASK

Your task is to create a three-minute internet video to be distributed online. Your aim is for this video to become 'viral' — for it to be good enough that people want to pass it on to their friends. Your video should provide the viewer with practical advice on reducing their carbon footprint, but it should also be entertaining enough to appeal to a wide range of people who use the internet. Remember, the consequences of climate change have already begun, so your video should not only create a

sense of urgency about the seriousness of the problem but also be persuasive enough to encourage its viewers to take immediate action. Therefore, you need to provide convincing and accurate facts while appealing to the emotional and intellectual capacities of your audiences.

PROCESS

- Open the ProjectsPLUS application for this chapter in your eBookPLUS. Watch the introductory video lesson and then click the 'Start Project' button to set up your project. You can complete this project individually or invite other members of your class to form a group. Save your settings and the project will be launched.
- Navigate to your Research Forum. A number of issues surrounding climate change have been loaded as topics to provide a framework for your research. Choose the issues you would like to include in your video and delete the other topics. You will need to research facts about what climate change is and the environmental problem it causes.
- Research. You should find at least two sources (other than the textbook, and including at least one offline source such as a book or encyclopedia) to help you discover extra information about the issues your video will present. The weblinks in your Media Centre will help you get started. Enter your findings as articles in the Research Forum. You can also view and comment on other group members' articles and rate the information they have entered.
- When your research is complete, navigate to your Media Centre, download the 'Shooting Script' template, and use it to create a script and shot list for your video. When planning your video, consider how different organisations are promoting action on climate change to a wide audience and which techniques are most effective.

Your ProjectsPLUS application is available in this chapter's Student Resources tab inside your eBookPLUS. Visit www.jacplus.com.au to locate your digital resources.

- A selection of media has been provided in your Media Centre for you to download and use in your video. You can also create animations, or you might like to incorporate other media. Don't forget to record the source of any information or image that you use in your movie as you always need to acknowledge other people's work.
- When your shooting script is signed off, record your voiceover and then use video-editing software to create your final production.
- Print out your Research Report from ProjectsPLUS and hand it in to your teacher with your shooting script and your final video. You might even like to post your video on YouTube or hold a school screening.

SUGGESTED SOFTWARE
- ProjectsPLUS
- Microsoft Word
- Audacity, GarageBand or other voice-recording software
- Windows Movie Maker, iMovie or other editing software

MEDIA CENTRE

Your Media Centre contains:
- a bank of media to use in your video
- a 'Shooting Script' template
- weblinks to sites on climate change and free recording and editing software
- an assessment rubric.

eLesson

GLOBAL WARMING IN AUSTRALIA

This video lesson looks at the phenomenon of global warming. Learn about greenhouse gases and why many scientists believe the Earth is getting hotter. Discover some of the potentially catastrophic effects this could have on the Earth and learn how governments and individuals can address this global problem. A worksheet is included to further your understanding.

SEARCHLIGHT ID: ELES-0057

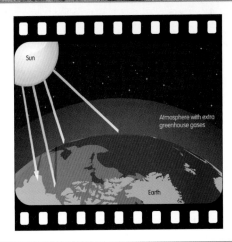

14 Threatened habitats

INQUIRY QUESTIONS

+ Where in the world are habitats under threat?
+ Why are habitats under threat?
+ What can be done to protect threatened habitats?

Threatened habitats make news; deforestation in Indonesia, disastrous fires in Australia, oil spills, tigers facing extinction. They are important everyday news items because both physical and human environments are changing. The human population of our planet has grown rapidly over the last few centuries. No other species on Earth has our capacity to change our world and its habitats. Changes to habitats, for example those brought about by climate change, are dangerous for animals (including humans) and plants that live in these environments. Threatened habitats are a global geographical issue.

GEOskills TOOLBOX

+ Interpreting a group bar graph (page 321)
+ Interpreting a thematic map (page 321)
+ Interpreting change over time maps (page 325)
+ Using grid references (page 327)
+ Analysing a newspaper article (page 333)

The Siberian tiger is one of many animals whose habitats have been threatened by human activities.

KEY TERMS

aerial survey: the tracking and counting of large species of animals from an aeroplane or helicopter

deforestation: the process of clearing forest, usually to make way for housing or agriculture

ecological sustainability: the ability to meet the needs of the present generation without compromising the ability of future generations to meet their needs

endangered: in danger of extinction

extinction: the dying out of an entire species of animal or plant

food chain: a group of plants and animals that feed off living things while, in turn, being eaten by others

GIS (geographic information system): a set of computer programs designed to deal with databases: able to collect, store, retrieve, manipulate, analyse and display mapped data from the real world

global warming: the warming of the atmosphere and the Earth, which many scientists believe is caused by the burning of fossil fuels

green movement: the name often given to people and groups who strongly support the protection of the environment

habitat: the natural home of an animal or plant; the place where it is normally found

ivory: a hard white substance taken from the tusks of elephants and walruses

poaching: hunting or removing animals or fish illegally

predator: living thing that catches and kills another living thing for food

range: to move about an area in all directions

threatened habitat: a habitat that faces the possibility of real harm being done to it

tropical cyclone: area of warm, moist air rising rapidly and rotating around a central core (known as an eye); often accompanied by very strong winds

wetlands: areas that are covered permanently, occasionally or periodically by fresh or salt water up to a depth of 6 metres

14.1 How would it feel to lose your home?

We all have a place that we call home. It could be a house in the suburbs or a country town, or perhaps it is a caravan. Whatever it is, home is the place where we go to eat, sleep, watch television, do homework, wash, and keep our clothes and special things. Our home is the place where we are normally found — our special part of the environment. It is our habitat.

Within our home there are special places where we go to do certain things necessary for our survival. We sleep in our bedroom, we wash in the bathroom, cook meals in the kitchen and so on. Our habitat also extends beyond our house. We go out of the house to school, to the shops, to play sport and for the other things we do regularly in our lives. Within our habitat we depend on other people — parents and others who care for us. They are part of our habitat. The clean air we breathe is part of our habitat, as is the fresh water we drink.

A habitat is the natural home of an animal or plant. It is the place where it is normally found. The habitat of the giraffe is the savanna areas of central Africa, which are grasslands with scattered, short trees. The giraffe thrives in this habitat where its long neck enables it to reach the leaves, twigs and fruit of the bushes and small trees.

The habitats of coral reefs are found where the ocean water temperature is between 21° and 30° Celsius, the water is shallow enough for sunlight to penetrate to the ocean floor and there is a suitable, relatively shallow, firm base less than 100 metres below the surface on which to grow. They also require high oxygen input and low levels of silt, sediment and other impurities that could make the sea water dark. Without these conditions the coral cannot grow and thrive. This habitat would become endangered if any of these conditions changed. For example, large-scale logging in the catchment area of a stream could result in widespread erosion and the deposition of large amounts of sediment in the habitat of the coral. This would make the water dark and the coral would be seriously affected. It would be threatened.

A threatened habitat is one that faces the possibility of real harm being done to it. If the threat to the habitat was so serious that it was facing extinction, it would be an endangered habitat. So how would you feel if you went home this afternoon and your parents told you that the house in which you live — the place you call home — was to be demolished to make way for a freeway? Your home would be made extinct.

This is the situation for many plants, animals and parts of the built environment in different corners of the world. Many habitats are endangered. Sometimes the endangered habitat is small in scale, such as the habitat of frogs that is endangered by the use of insecticides around their pond. Sometimes the habitat is on a global scale — for example, it appears that the whole world could be affected by global warming and climate change during the twenty-first century.

Many examples of threatened habitats exist in both the physical and human features of the environment and we will be studying some of them in this chapter.

Coral reefs are unique marine environments found around tropical and sub-tropical shores. They are a habitat for many marine plants and animals.

Frill-necked lizards live in the dry woodlands and deserts of Australia. In deserts much of the ground is bare. Drought-resistant plants grow in some areas.

The Arctic fox lives in the tundra of Europe, Asia and North America. Small shrubs, grasses, lichens and mosses grow there. Mountainous areas have some trees and shrubs.

Giraffes live in the savanna areas of Africa. The area is mostly grassland with scattered, short trees, which are mainly deciduous.

The mountain gorilla is the largest primate on Earth. The 300 mountain gorillas living in the high forests of the Virunga Mountains in Rwanda represent half of all remaining mountain gorillas. The preferred habitat is forests on quiet, cool mountain slopes with an open canopy and dense ground and shrub layers.

ACTIVITIES →

UNDERSTANDING

1 Define the term 'habitat'.

2 Describe your home habitat.

3 Draw a picture of a part of your habitat that you particularly like being in.

THINKING AND APPLYING

4 Is any part of your habitat threatened or could it be threatened in the future? Describe this part of your habitat and explain why it could be threatened.

5 Name and describe an animal or plant with which you share part of your habitat. Why does this plant or animal live in its habitat? Are there any threats to this animal or plant in its habitat? Describe these.

6 Describe how you would feel if you arrived home from school and the place where you live had been burned down.

USING YOUR SKILLS

7 Refer to the photographs on this page and answer the following.

a Suggest reasons why each animal is suited to its habitat. (*Hint:* look at the type of vegetation, the colour of the animal and so on.)

b Think of another animal that might be suited to this habitat.

c Select one habitat from the photographs and suggest what might happen if the area was to be cleared for a new tourist resort.

GEOTERMS

endangered: in danger of extinction

habitat: the natural home of an animal or plant; the place where it is normally found

threatened habitat: a habitat that faces the possibility of real harm being done to it

Wetlands: ecological balance under threat

They used to be called 'swamps'

Wetlands are areas that are covered permanently, occasionally or periodically by fresh or salt water up to a depth of 6 metres. Wetlands were often called swamps and were thought to be of little use. Many areas of wetlands have been drained and converted to rural and urban use. However, we now know that wetlands are vital to the health of the coastal ecosystem; that is, the system of interactions between the living plants and animals and the environment. They purify polluted water, provide recreational areas, act as buffers against floods and help to protect coastal regions from damage by storms. Wetlands are not only centres of great biodiversity; they are also rich fishing grounds, important grazing areas and valuable sources of timber.

Planners can be interested in draining wetlands to develop valuable new sites. If they are near cities they offer opportunities for urban expansion, while those in rural areas can provide agricultural land. In tourist areas, wetlands have potential for recreational development.

Many wetlands around the world are under constant threat from developers who want to drain them or fill them in. In the past, some wetlands around parts of the Parramatta River in Sydney have been used as tips and filled in during 'land reclamation' programs. Inland wetlands are under threat from dam builders who want to channel water into irrigation areas that would normally flow into wetlands. The Macquarie Marshes and Murrumbidgee Wetlands in New South Wales are good examples of this.

Degradation of the Everglades

The Everglades in South Florida is the largest freshwater wetland in North America. It is so flat and low that no part of the Everglades is more than 2.5 metres above sea level. It once was a 400 kilometre-long area of lakes, marshes and rivers that reached the sea in Florida Bay.

The Everglades developed over a period of between 6000 and 8000 years and was an area of great biodiversity. The animals and plants of the Everglades were species that had adapted to the wet conditions. The region was infested with alligators, supporting around two million in 1950. The alligators were at the top of the food chain and fed on other creatures, such as turtles and fish, which, in turn, fed on shrimps and small marine organisms. It was a delicately balanced ecosystem in which plants and animals were in harmony with each other and their physical environment. However, humans have changed parts of the physical environment, upset this balance and turned large areas into threatened habitats for many species of plants and animals.

In 1947, after a hurricane (a severe tropical storm) had drowned more than 2000 people in the Everglades area, the government decided to change the natural environment to make it more 'hurricane

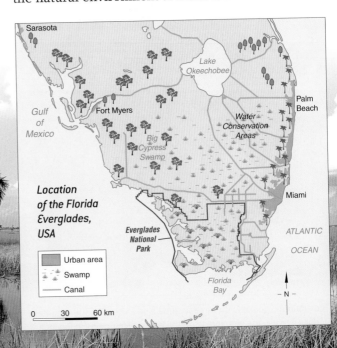

Location of the Florida Everglades, USA

Urban area
Swamp
Canal

0   30   60 km

The Everglades in South Florida, USA

proof'. Over 2000 kilometres of canals and levee banks were built, the northern part of the area was drained for cattle and dairy farming and an area was set aside for growing sugarcane. Only one-third of the Everglades was allowed to remain in its natural state.

The work was completed by the mid 1960s and turned out to be an environmental disaster. Much of the area's water had been polluted by fertilisers used by farmers in the northern part. This affected the growth of the natural vegetation and led to the largest lake being infested by algae. The natural saw grass was replaced by cattails, a plant that thrives on fertiliser-rich water. More significantly, the natural cycles of flood and drought had all but disappeared and with them had gone the flow of water that was essential for the natural cleansing of the wetlands.

Farming was one of the human activities that endangered the natural habitats of the Everglades.

Management

The US Government was so concerned about the damage to the sustainability of the Everglades and its unique physical environment that it filed a lawsuit against local officials. There are now 14 000 hectares of farmland being converted back to wetlands. This is designed to trap some of the fertiliser-polluted water before it enters the southern parts of the area. However, much of the problem of water flow and natural cleansing still remains and large areas of the habitat continue to be threatened.

The water level in many parts of the Everglades is now so low that the soil is dry and hardened.

The habitat of the alligator was threatened by changes and numbers decreased.

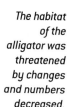

ACTIVITIES

UNDERSTANDING

1 Define the term 'wetlands'.

2 Describe how the Everglades area was 'hurricane proofed' by the government. Why was this an environmental disaster?

3 What has the US Government done to protect the ecological sustainability of this threatened habitat?

THINKING AND APPLYING

4 Why are planners so interested in draining wetlands?

5 Imagine you are a television reporter sent to the Everglades to prepare a report on the success of the present management practices. Make a list of the type of things you would be investigating. Describe how you would go about obtaining your information.

6 There are many other wetlands that are threatened. Using the resources in your library and/or the internet, write a report on another threatened wetland area using the following headings: location, natural environment, biodiversity, management for ecological sustainability.

USING YOUR SKILLS

7 Refer to the map of the Everglades opposite and use an atlas to locate it in its wider setting of North America.

a Why do you think the urban areas are situated where they are on the map?

b What is the latitude and longitude of the Everglades?

c What direction is Sarasota from Miami?

d List the human features visible on the map.

GEOTERMS

wetlands: areas that are covered permanently, occasionally or periodically by fresh or salt water up to a depth of 6 metres

Orang-utans live in the rainforests of Borneo.

Tropical rainforests are the habitats for half the world's known plant species and a large number of animals. Within the rainforest there is a great variety of habitats. For example, some plants and animals live on the forest floor, others live higher up in the canopy. One of the species that lives in the forest is the orang-utan. This large and intelligent animal lives in communities in the canopy of the rainforest. It is a habitat that orang-utans share with many other plants and animals.

Clearing of the forests

It has been estimated that around half of the world's rainforests have been cleared in the last 50 years. If the present rate of deforestation continues, there will be little or no tropical rainforests left in just 30 years. While much rainforest clearing has been for agriculture, an increasing proportion is now being cleared for timber. This deforestation has done much to make the orang-utan an endangered species.

Malaysia and Indonesia together are the world's largest suppliers of tropical timber and most of it comes from the island of Borneo, on which both countries have territory. Many of the rivers of Borneo are lined with logging camps and are a constant muddy brown as topsoil is eroded from slopes that have been cleared of timber. Many environmentalists believe that the present rate of logging will result in the Malaysian territory of Sarawak being largely cleared of rainforest in 20 years. The state government maintains that it is logging only on a sustainable basis. In the Indonesian territory of Kalimantan the situation is not much better, as logging and the clearing of land for plantations and subsistence agriculture continues at an unsustainable pace.

Islands in the forest

In many areas when forests are cleared it has become a practice to leave behind 'islands' of rainforest. This is meant to assist in the natural regeneration of the forest and also to leave sufficient areas of the natural habitats of plants and animals that live in the rainforest. It's not that simple!

First, the islands that are left are unlikely to be big enough to ensure the survival of the large numbers of species that live there. But there is also a second problem. When the forest is cleared, the exposed earth can quickly erode, making the regrowth of vegetation slow. During drought, the bare ground can become hot and barren. With the removal of the forest there is little moisture stored in the ground and a much lower rate of evapotranspiration (see page 364). This in turn reduces the rain that falls on the remaining 'islands' of rainforest. They quickly dry out with the destruction of the habitat.

(a) Rainforest trees are cleared, with 'islands' left for regeneration.

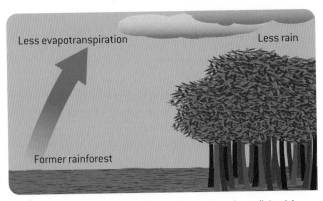

(b) There is less evapotranspiration and less rain on forest 'islands'.

The islands are endangered by the reduced rainfall and cannot survive drought conditions.

What can be done?

Much larger areas that are clearly sustainable need to be protected. Logging must be reduced and carried out in a sustainable way. The World Bank now reviews development funding to ensure that it is environmentally sound. Hopefully, more of the rainforests will now survive and species such as the orang-utan will have a secure habitat.

Legend:
- Lowland rainforest (below 910 m)
- Montane rainforest (above 910 m)
- Mangrove forest
- Former rainforest

Clearing of Borneo's rainforests

ACTIVITIES

UNDERSTANDING

1 What percentage of the world's rainforest has been cleared since the 1950s?

2 Outline how the Malaysian and Indonesian governments are contributing to the destruction of rainforests.

THINKING AND APPLYING

3 Refer to the diagram showing 'islands' of rainforest. Explain why these 'islands' are not preserving forest habitats.

USING YOUR SKILLS

4 Refer to the map of Borneo.
   a What is the main vegetation type found in Borneo?
   b Imagine you are in a small plane flying across Borneo. Your journey follows the Equator from west to east. Describe the main types of vegetation that you see.
   c There are large areas of former rainforest in Borneo. Observe these areas on the map. Can you see a clear pattern in the location of former rainforests? Describe this pattern.
   d Why do you think the rainforest has been cleared in these areas and not in other areas?

5 Refer to the graph of the world's disappearing rainforests.
   a Which three countries had the largest percentage of their original rainforest remaining in the late 1980s? Can you think of reasons for this?
   b Which countries had the lowest percentage of their original rainforest remaining in the late 1980s? Can you think of reasons for this?
   c Which three countries are expected to lose the largest percentage of their original rainforests by 2010? Can you think of reasons for this?

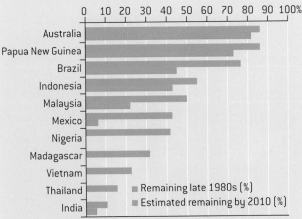

Percentage of original rainforest — selected countries

Countries (top to bottom): Australia, Papua New Guinea, Brazil, Indonesia, Malaysia, Mexico, Nigeria, Madagascar, Vietnam, Thailand, India

- Remaining late 1980s (%)
- Estimated remaining by 2010 (%)

World rainforests, the habitats that contain the majority of animal and plant species, are rapidly declining. Innocent victims of the loss of rainforest have been the animals, birds and plants that depend on the rainforest for survival. Mammals that rely on the rainforest habitat such as orang-utans, Javan leopards and Sumatran tigers are now threatened with extinction.

GEOTERMS

deforestation: the process of clearing forest, usually to make way for housing or agriculture

14.4 Polar bears and global warming

Polar bears are among the largest predators in the world. Mature males are around 3 metres in height and weigh over 400 kilograms. They are perfectly suited to their Arctic habitat with adaptations such as:

- thicker fur than any other bear species. Fur even covers their feet for warmth and traction on ice.
- a thick layer of blubber to provide insulation from the cold and buoyancy in the water
- a long neck and narrow skull to aid in streamlining the animal in water
- flat oar-like front feet to make them strong swimmers.

Threatened Arctic habitat

There are an estimated 25 000 polar bears in the world. They are distributed throughout the Arctic region, with about 40 per cent in Canada and the remainder in Alaska, Russia, Greenland and Norway. Polar bears rely on sea-ice platforms to hunt seals and to move from hunting grounds in winter to summer resting

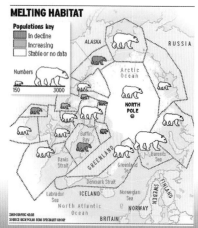

Polar bear populations

areas. When the edge of the ice moves north in summer, the bears will travel many kilometres to stay on the ice and near seals. Any bears stranded on land must wait until the next freeze-up in the autumn to get back onto the ice.

In the last few decades, there has been a gradual loss of the polar ice pack (see chapter 13, page 294). As well, permanent sea ice in the Arctic has been reduced by over 14 per cent since the 1970s. This thinning and moving offshore of the sea ice has reduced the essential polar bear habitats. Loss of the sea ice leads to higher energy requirements for locating prey and a shortage of food. This in turn causes a higher mortality rate among cubs and the reduction in size among first year cubs and adult males.

Global warming has resulted in longer ice-free periods; the sea ice melts earlier and forms later. The bears are left with less and less time to hunt for food. As their habitat shrinks away, polar bears face a grave threat to their survival. Scientists estimate that for every week that freeze-up is delayed, the bears lose at least 10 kilograms of their fat reserves. Weight loss in pregnant females means that they fail to produce enough milk for their cubs. Polar bears have lost approximately 15 per cent of their body weight over the last 20 years.

Polar bears are threatened not only by the global warming that is shrinking their habitat,

Polar bear populations are threatened by global warming, water pollution, hunting and gas and oil developments.

but also by water pollution, hunting, and gas and oil developments. The current and future exploitation of oil and gas leases by the five Arctic powers of Canada, Russia, the US, Norway and Denmark, in what has been termed the 'Cold Rush', places the fragile habitat at risk. It is estimated that the area north of the Arctic Circle contains 13 per cent of the world's undiscovered oil and 30 per cent of undiscovered natural gas.

These factors have led scientists to predict that polar bears may be extinct in areas like Southern Hudson Bay in Canada by the year 2050.

Temperature change

Source: Based on map by ACIA.

Extent of Arctic sea ice, 1900–2003

Source: NASA.

ACTIVITIES

UNDERSTANDING

1. Describe the ways in which the polar bear is adapted to its physical environment.
2. Where do polar bears live?
3. What happens if a polar bear is stranded on land when the ice melts?
4. List the main threats to polar bear habitats.
5. What are the effects on polar bears of longer ice-free periods?

THINKING AND APPLYING

6. How do you feel about the Arctic being opened up to gas and oil exploration and drilling? Draft an email to the United Nations stating your views.
7. Would it matter if polar bears became extinct? Justify your answer.
8. What can you do to save polar bears from extinction?

USING YOUR SKILLS

9. Refer to the map of polar bear populations.
   a Describe the location of the areas where polar bear populations are (i) in decline and (ii) increasing. Use an atlas to help if needed.
   b Estimate the number of polar bears where populations are stable or there is no data. Why is this hard to do?
10. Refer to the graph showing the extent of Arctic sea ice, 1900–2003.
   a Describe the average change in the extent of summer sea ice between 1900 and 2003.
   b In what season has decline been most dramatic in the last 50 years?
   c How will this affect the habitat of the polar bear?
11. Refer to the map of temperature change.
   a Use latitude, longitude and scale to describe the areas of greatest temperature change by 2070.
   b How will this affect the habitat of the polar bear?

GEOTERMS

global warming: the warming of the atmosphere and the Earth, which many scientists think is caused by the burning of fossil fuels

14.5 | Disappearing tigers

The Chinese tiger is on the brink of extinction.

A century ago tigers were found through much of Asia. Killed by hunters and driven from their habitat by farmers and timber cutters, their numbers have rapidly declined. At the start of the twentieth century, there were an estimated 100 000 tigers in the world. Today, as few as 5000 to 7000 are thought to survive in the wild, 4500 of them in India.

Tigers are now protected as an endangered species. However, they are still shot for sport by hunters, and by poachers for their skins, bones and body parts to be used in traditional Chinese medicines.

How did this happen?

Tigers need a lot of meat to survive. They generally prefer large prey such as deer, antelope, buffalo and even elephants, but will also 'snack' on monkeys, birds and frogs.

A serious threat to tigers is competition with people for food. Deer are their staple diet in many areas but deer have disappeared from the forests. With the human population expanding into tiger territory, livestock sometimes becomes a tiger meal. Though most tigers avoid people, ill or injured tigers will sometimes attack humans. At least 50 people are killed by tigers each year.

Estimated tiger populations

Country	Estimated range of tiger numbers	Year of estimate
Bangladesh	200–419	2007
Bhutan	67–81	2008
Cambodia	11–50	2006
China	37–50	2007
India	1165–1657	2008
Indonesia	441–679	2007
Malaysia	300–493	2007
Thailand	250–270	2006

Source: IUCN Red List of threatened species.

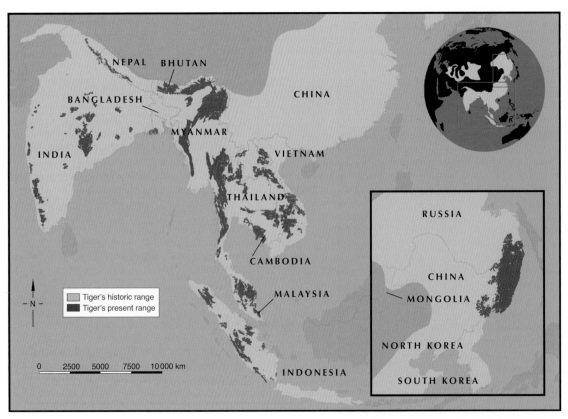

Past and present distribution of tigers

Source: Save the Tiger Fund.

All tigers belong to the *Panthera tigris* species. The Caspian, Balinese and Javan subspecies are now extinct and the Chinese tiger, hunted as vermin, is on the brink of extinction. The four other surviving subspecies — Bengal, Indochinese, Sumatran and Siberian — are all endangered.

Found only in Asia, about 60 per cent of the world's wild tigers are thought to live in India, Nepal and Bangladesh. India's Bengal tiger population fell from 40 000 in 1930 to less than 2000 in 1972. Shooting of tigers was banned in India in 1970, and Project Tiger, set up by Prime Minister Indira Gandhi in 1973, set aside nine national parks for special protection. By 1984 the number of tigers had more than doubled.

After Mrs Gandhi's death many of her efforts to protect the tiger were lost. Human populations rose and some protected areas were turned over to farmers, flooded by dams or disturbed by coalmines. Tiger habitats began to shrink and there were more and more conflicts between tigers and people. Tiger numbers also began to fall because they were being killed so that their bones and other parts could be smuggled out of India to supply manufacturers of Chinese medicines.

What is being done?

Using satellite imagery, the World Wide Fund for Nature and the Wildlife Conservation Society have defined 159 tiger conservation units, which are areas of forest best able to support tigers. 'A tiger in Siberia behaves differently from one in the subtropical grasslands of Nepal,' said scientist Ginette Hemley of the World Wide Fund for Nature. 'Effective tiger conservation involves protecting them in distinct bioregions, ecosystems and habitat types.'

GEO*facts*

- A tiger census in 2001 found 271 Bengal tigers in the Sundarbans Tiger Reserve in India. Officials there have begun projects to improve the economic conditions of the villagers close to the reserve. Instead of killing tigers that stray from the forest, villagers now help officials capture them.
- According to a 1999 report, a Taiwanese factory was importing 2 tonnes of tiger bones annually, representing the death of 100–200 tigers.

GEOskills TOOLBOX

INTERPRETING CHANGE OVER TIME MAPS

Maps can be used to show the change in distribution of a feature over time. The map on the opposite page shows the past and present distribution of the tiger.

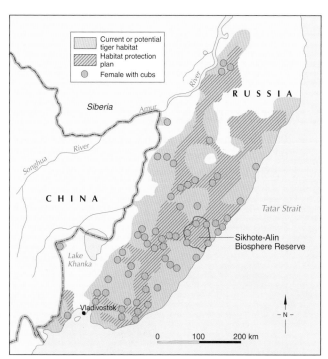

The Siberian Tiger Project has been developed to form a habitat protection plan for tigers in Russia's far east. It identifies the areas best able to sustain tigers in the wild.

Source: Adapted from National Geographic.

ACTIVITIES ➔

UNDERSTANDING

1. Describe the habitat of the tiger. Why is it under threat?
2. Describe the tiger's food supply. Why is it decreasing?
3. How many species of tiger are there and how many are in danger of extinction?

THINKING AND APPLYING

4. Why is the tiger worth saving? Outline a management strategy to save the tiger.
5. Investigate the use of tiger body parts in traditional Chinese medicine. What is your opinion of this practice? Justify your response.

USING YOUR SKILLS

6. Refer to the map and table on page 324 and then answer the questions below.
   a In which country are tigers most widely distributed?
   b Name five countries that no longer have wild tigers.
   c Why do estimates of tiger populations vary?

Endangered African elephants are the largest of all land animals. They are found throughout much of Africa, living in both grasslands and the forests of central and west Africa.

Seventy years ago, the African elephant was common in nearly all African countries south of the Equator. Since then, the number and range of animals have dramatically declined due to the threats of:

- **poaching**
- disappearing habitat.

Poaching

In the early 1970s demand for **ivory** soared to record levels. Most of the ivory leaving Africa was taken illegally. Between 1979 and 1987, Africa's elephant population was halved from 1.2 million to 600 000. It was estimated that at this rate the African elephant would become extinct by 2010. Worldwide concern over this decline led to a ban on all ivory trade in 1989. This action saw a steep decline in illegal killing, especially where elephants were protected by national parks.

Ivory poachers remain a potent threat.

Disappearing habitat

Elephants are such large animals that they need a lot of food and freedom to **range** if they are to survive. Adult elephants require a daily food intake of over 200 kilograms of plant matter. Since the 1940s, farms have steadily replaced elephant habitats. Elephants have been confined to smaller areas of their natural habitat such as national parks. Elephants confined in parks have often destroyed the land. They damage trees by stripping bark and destroy crops on neighbouring farmland. Elephants that damage crops are often shot by farmers or national parks officers.

Counting elephants

The 2002 elephant population estimate for Africa was 500 000. Since then the estimates have gone up to around 600 000. The main reason for the

Tropic of Cancer

Equator

Elephant range

Protected area

~ N ~

Tropic of Capricorn

Elephant range and protected areas

0   1000   2000 km

Oblique aerial photograph of elephant herds

USING GRID REFERENCES

It is easy to find and describe the location of a place on a map or aerial photograph if you use a grid. Straight or curved lines divide maps into smaller parts. Letters and numbers placed along the sides of the grid help you give the grid reference for a place or feature. On the aerial photograph at right, the leader of the herd of elephants is found at A3. Place your right pointer finger on the letter 'A' and your left pointer finger on the number '3'. Move your right finger up and your left finger across until they meet. This is grid reference A3.

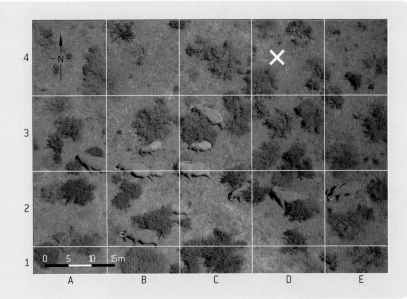

increase has been because elephants are thriving in national parks. Accurate knowledge of African elephant numbers and their habitat is the key to planning for their protection. Aerial surveys can be accurate, but are only suitable for counting elephants in open habitats. It is much more difficult to count elephants in forests, where ground surveys involving the counting of the number of dung piles are used. Researchers store data from ground and aerial surveys in a GIS (geographic information system) that is capable of displaying this research in map form.

Field diary — Re-collaring of Goya, June 2001

... Goya is ... a tall, distinguished elephant with five known calves ... Goya's herd usually consists of her calves ... and two other adult females, Rodan and Matisse, together with their calves.

Iain Douglas-Hamilton flew (over) and located Goya and her herd ... From the air Iain directed the two vehicles onto the herd ... As the darting vehicle approached, Goya kept herself hidden in a thick patch of bush and was reluctant to venture out ... After half an hour we still had no opportunity for a clear shot and, with the plane and vehicles circling, Goya began to get agitated and moved her family away from the disturbance. This gave us an opportunity to move in and fire the dart, which startled her and she ran off with her herd ... Luckily Iain was able to follow her from the air, and after four minutes reported that she was down and directed the two vehicles to the sleeping elephant. The team moved fast to remove the faulty collar and replace it with a new collar, as her family watched us from about 30 metres away. Within ten minutes we had fitted the new collar, collected tail hair samples, ear biopsy and blood samples, measured her tusks and injected the antidote. As Goya raised herself slowly onto her legs, she rumbled to her family ...

The incredibly detailed data we are collecting from these **GPS (global positioning system)** collars is providing us with valuable information ... that will ultimately be used to ensure the long-term conservation of these elephants and their habitat.

ACTIVITIES

UNDERSTANDING

1. Outline the two main threats to the elephant.
2. Why is the elephant's range decreasing?
3. How effective is confining elephants in national parks?
4. What methods are used to count elephants?
5. What can be learnt from using GPS collars on elephants?

THINKING AND APPLYING

6. Explain how elephant herds might change the environment.
7. Over which parts of their range would elephants be easier to count from a helicopter?
8. Research the uses of ivory. Do you agree with the ivory trade? Why or why not?

USING YOUR SKILLS

9. Refer to the map of elephant range and protected areas. Where are most elephants found? Suggest why.
10. Refer to the oblique aerial photo of elephant herds. Write a paragraph describing what you see.
11. Refer to the vertical aerial photograph of elephants in Botswana. Imagine there is a veterinarian at point 'X' (D4) on the ground who needs to treat the large elephant located at B2.
    a Why can't she see it from her location?
    b In which direction and how far is the elephant from the veterinarian?

Coral reefs are some of the most beautiful places on Earth. They are also some of the world's most diverse ecosystems with a wonderful variety of species, including many types of corals, fish and other organisms. Coral reefs cover about only 0.17 per cent of the ocean floor, but they provide a habitat for more than 25 per cent of all marine species.

A coral reef is a diverse ecosystem with a wonderful variety of species. A single coral reef may contain 3000 species of coral, fish and shellfish.

Habitat — a place to grow

Coral reefs need very specific environmental conditions to grow and thrive. They require specific temperature and sea conditions and an area free of sediment. Because of these habitat requirements, they grow only around suitable tropical and subtropical shores.

Coral reefs are built by tiny animals called coral polyps that live together in groups. These polyps have soft, hollow bodies shaped like a sac with tentacles around the opening. They cover themselves in a skeleton of limestone and divide to form new polyps. Therefore, a reef is basically a layer of living corals growing on the remains of millions of dead coral.

Threats to coral reef ecosystems

Coral reefs are fragile ecosystems. They thrive only in very specific temperature and sea conditions. There are two major threats to coral reef ecosystems: natural and human-induced.

Natural threats

Some of the natural threats to coral reefs include cyclones, diseases and predators.

- **Tropical cyclones** (or hurricanes) are naturally occurring weather events in coral reef habitats. Cyclones can bring large seas and torrential rain. The destruction caused by cyclones has increased recently due to the type of settlement in these tropical areas. Where there is farming and urban development, there is accelerated run–off and greatly increased sediment. The sediment is a particular threat to coral reefs.
- **Diseases** appear to have increased significantly over the last ten years, causing widespread mortality among reef-building corals. Many scientists believe that the increase in disease is associated with deteriorating water quality because of pollutants and rising sea temperatures.
- **Predators** are living things that catch another living thing for food. The most well-known predator of coral is the Crown of Thorns starfish. This organism preys on coral polyps. Scientists cannot agree whether this starfish is

This Crown of Thorns is eating coral polyps. When it finds a suitable coral, it pulls its stomach out through its mouth and releases its digestive juices over the coral. This breaks down the coral and also allows other reef creatures such as algae and worms to invade the coral. A plague of this starfish can devastate a coral reef.

an introduced species or a natural member of coral reef communities. These spiny and toxic starfish can wipe out large areas of coral reef. An individual starfish can consume up to 6 square metres of living reef per year. Outbreaks of the species often occur when ocean temperatures and levels of sea pollution increase. Overfishing, which has resulted in a decline of the starfish's major predators, may be a contributing factor.

Human-induced threats

Some of the human-induced threats include: global warming, urban development, agriculture, fishing and tourism.

- **Global warming** is warming of the atmosphere, which many scientists believe is caused by the burning of fossil fuels. Global warming has caused a gradual but noticeable increase in sea temperatures, sometimes making them too warm for the delicate ecology of the reefs. A small, but prolonged, rise in sea temperatures forces coral colonies to expel their food-producing algae, a process known as *bleaching*. The coral becomes a bleached white, cannot grow and eventually dies. Reefs can recover but only if cooler water temperatures return. In 2005, reefs in the Caribbean suffered massive bleaching, killing up to one-third of the coral in some places.
- **Urban development** involves the clearing of natural forest. Urban development greatly increases run-off with increasing pollution of the ocean. Many urban developments involve the draining of coastal wetlands. This, in turn, results in more coastal erosion, more run-off and polluted water.
- **Agriculture** also results in land clearing. The removal of natural vegetation increases run-off, erosion and pollution of the ocean. The run-off of fertiliser pollutes the ocean and causes a severe problem for the coral reef ecosystem.
- **Fishing** — the coral reefs are highly desirable locations for professional and amateur fishing. They contain a wide range of species, many of which are popular for eating. Commercial fishing has depleted many species and caused a problem with the food chain. This has allowed the increase in destructive predators such as the Crown of Thorns starfish. There have been recent global movements to seriously limit and sometimes ban fishing on coral reefs.
- **Tourism** to coral reefs has been rapidly increasing. Coral reefs are a natural wonderland with many attractions. Tourism leads to land clearing and urban development, with their associated problems. Damage is caused to natural ecosystems by simply removing coral souvenirs or by carelessly walking in these fragile areas. Boat anchors can cause significant damage.

This anchor is damaging the coral reef.

ACTIVITIES

UNDERSTANDING

1. Describe the habitat of coral reefs.
2. Briefly outline how coral reefs grow.
3. What are the two main types of threats to coral reef ecosystems?
4. How is global warming a threat to coral reefs?

THINKING AND APPLYING

5. Draw two graphic organisers to show the physical and human threats to coral reefs.
6. Draw a diagram to show how land clearing can affect coral reefs.
7. Create a slogan or message that could be used in an education program for tourists, to help ensure they do not damage coral reef ecosystems.

GEOTERMS

tropical cyclone: area of warm, moist air rising rapidly and rotating around a central core (known as an eye); often accompanied by very strong winds

14.8 Protecting coral reefs

Coral reefs face problems with naturally occurring events such as storms and hurricanes. There is little that can be done to protect reefs from these natural events. However, threats posed by human activities such as tourism and mining can be monitored and reduced.

Reefs threatened in New Caledonia/Kanaky

New Caledonia lies to the north-east of Australia. It is an overseas territory of France and the site of the world's largest unbroken barrier reef and lagoon. The coral reefs surpass the Great Barrier Reef in coral and fish diversity, and they have the world's most diverse concentrations of reef structures. Also found there is the third largest population of dugongs, an endangered sea mammal. In July 2008, UNESCO declared the vast majority of New Caledonia's coral reefs a World Heritage Site.

Threats to the reef

New Caledonia has some of the world's largest deposits of nickel, which is used to make coins and armaments and to strengthen steel. The method of extracting nickel can be extremely hazardous to the marine environment, as torrential rains wash tonnes of unprotected soils straight onto the reefs, smothering the coral and preventing photosynthesis. Nickel mining also uses toxic chemicals to extract the nickel from the ore.

Environmentalists and the indigenous Kanak peoples are concerned that the nickel mining might further damage the pristine terrestrial and aquatic ecosystems of New Caledonia. New Caledonia is a 'biodiversity hotspot', with plants and animals found nowhere else on Earth. Human activities, such as land clearance for nickel mining and farming, have led to severe bushfires. These fires damage the reefs because ash and smoke settle on them, causing acidification. Scientists believe that pollution from the giant nickel smelter in Noumea, New Caledonia's capital, is also contributing to coral reef destruction.

Fighting to save the reef

Because of their physical location just inside the Tropic of Capricorn, New Caledonia's coral reefs are less susceptible to widespread coral bleaching that occurs in more tropical waters. Tourism has also had a relatively minor impact on the reefs because of the role played by responsible dive operators and environmental organisations. For example, Ile de Canard (Duck Island) lies just 500 metres off Anse Vata beach in Noumea and is visited by tens of thousands of tourists yearly, most of whom come to snorkel the clear waters. And yet the coral reef surrounding the island is in remarkably good shape because visitors are encouraged to protect the reef. This is done through signs erected on the island and an underwater trail that identifies different corals and fish.

To Kanak people, their land and sea is sacred and held in common for all to share. However, Kanak people are a minority in their own land; real power lies in France. Kanak tribes have repeatedly petitioned the French government to seek World Heritage status for the whole reef. To date, these requests have been ignored and preference given to the nickel mining industry, which earns export dollars for the local economy.

Recently, Kanaks have also clashed with the Canadian multinational mining company INCO. Fearing destruction of their sacred lands, Kanak tribes occupied the land intended for the nickel mine at Goro and took out an injunction in a French court. The Goro mine was scheduled to begin operating by 2008 but is not yet open because of Kanak protests against a pipeline that would pump sediments and chemicals straight onto the reef.

Nickel mine in New Caledonia

The pristine beauty of New Caledonia's coral reefs

Vast snapshot of the Barrier Reef's deep life rewards collaboration

After more than 300 days sampling at sea, scientists for four major research agencies have begun compiling a rich picture of seabed life across the length and breadth of Australia's Great Barrier Reef Marine Park to form the basis of maps, databases and management tools that will help marine resource managers conserve important habitats and biodiversity, and ensure that fisheries are ecologically sustainable.

Principal investigator, Dr Roland Pitcher of CSIRO, said, 'This has been the most intensive scientific exploration of the lesser known, deeper seabed of the world's largest marine protected area.'

The next stage of the Great Barrier Reef Seabed Biodiversity Project is now the processing of thousands of plant and animal samples, hundreds of gigabytes of electronic data, and thousands of hours of video data taken from 1400 sites on the continental shelf.

Some 50 scientists and technicians from the four research agencies have contributed skills in biology, ecology, geology, physics and mathematics to the joint effort.

Source: Ecos, 129, February–March 2006, p. 7.

A large deepwater sponge and gorgonian corals off the Great Barrier Reef

Protecting coral reefs

Individuals, groups and governments can take action to protect coral reefs.

Individuals

Individuals should be caring and responsible. They should be cautious about touching coral, avoiding anchor damage, polluting or leaving rubbish, and should read and obey signs.

Groups

Many research organisations such as universities and governments contribute to caring for and ensuring the sustainability of our reefs (see article from *Ecos* above).

Governments

Most coral reefs, such as the Great Barrier Reef in Australia, have been declared marine parks. Most management of marine parks is based on the following principles:
- Management to achieve protection of the ecosystem
- Conservation and reasonable use so that the ecosystem provides opportunities for sustainable use and enjoyment of its resources while being protected

- Public participation and community involvement in the development and implementation of management
- Monitoring and performance evaluation of management.

ACTIVITIES ⊛

UNDERSTANDING

1. What is special about New Caledonia's reefs and surrounding environment?
2. List the main factors threatening coral reefs in New Caledonia.
3. What have been the impacts of tourism on the reefs?
4. Briefly describe the activities of the Great Barrier Reef Seabed Diversity Project.

THINKING AND APPLYING

5. Imagine you are representing the Kanak people in a submission to the French government about the need to protect the coral reefs. What arguments would you present?

USING YOUR SKILLS

6. Describe how individuals, groups and governments can contribute to sustainable management of coral reefs.

What can you do to protect threatened habitats?

Environmental groups are usually way ahead of governments in identifying areas of environmental concern. The 'green movement' is the name often given to people and groups who strongly support the protection of the environment. There are now many green organisations that are very active around the world. They include Friends of the Earth, the World Wide Fund for Nature (WWF) and Greenpeace. These organisations and many others are experiencing rapid growth as people become more aware of environmental issues. They have been very active in presenting environmental concerns to a wide and increasingly active public. In some nations, including Australia, green political parties or groups have representation in parliament.

Active citizenship

We don't have to join an organisation to show our concern. We can do it in small and meaningful ways in our own habitat. Disposing of rubbish in an environmentally friendly way is a good contribution. People should try to recycle whenever and as much as they can. It means we use less resources and helps to reduce the strain on precious resources, such as forests.

When we visit any habitat, we must always leave everything as we found it. This way habitats are not disturbed and sensitive species within them will not be threatened.

Some people make a living from trading in wildlife products or products from threatened habitats. We can make an effort not to buy items that we think may have been obtained through the unnecessary death of a plant or animal.

One of the best things you can do as an active global citizen is to make sure you are aware of what is going on. This means reading newspapers, watching the news and current affairs programs on television, and taking an interest in what is happening in your community. If you are not happy, you can make your concerns known. You can:

- write letters to newspapers
- send emails or write letters to politicians or members of your local council
- 'lobby' particular politicians or members of your local council — that is, meet with them and try to influence them
- become involved in public protest meetings
- add your name and address to a petition indicating support (or otherwise) for some government action
- join or support an organisation such as the World Wide Fund for Nature or Landcare.

Obey the law

There are many laws around the world to protect habitats. They are designed to protect human habitats as well as the habitats of plants and animals. National parks in New South Wales have the following simple code for people to follow when in a national park.

- All native flora, fauna, Aboriginal sites and rock formations are protected.
- Wildfires can destroy lives and property, so be careful — especially during the bushfire danger period. Use only the fireplace provided and observe Total Fire Bans.
- Leave pets and firearms at home — they are not permitted in national parks.
- Drive carefully. Vehicles, including motorbikes, must keep to formed public roads.
- Please use rubbish bins if provided, or take rubbish with you when you leave the park.

The Three Sisters in the Blue Mountains, west of Sydney, is a popular tourist spot and World Heritage area.

Tree-sitting activist wins high praise from judge

BY STEVE BUTCHER

To some, the young woman atop the tree-sit tripod in the Victorian old-growth forest — defiant of authority yet dedicated to a cause — was just another unemployed greenie disrupting legitimate workers.

If so glibly dismissed, then 23-year-old Holly Creenhaune is arguably Australia's best-credentialled forest protester.

Her appearance last week in a Melbourne court, after her arrest on January 17 last year in the Goongerah forest logging coupe in East Gippsland, moved one of Victoria's most senior magistrates to exercise a rare discretionary act of judicial power.

Not only did Jelena Popovic, the Deputy Chief Magistrate, dismiss charges of obstructing a road and obstructing an officer — after Creenhaune's pleas of guilty — and refuse an order for Creenhaune to pay $1900 compensation, she described her as a 'remarkable young woman'.

'I have to say I've never had the opportunity to meet someone like Miss Creenhaune,' Ms Popovic said, 'who has worked consistently and effectively in relation to improving our environment and maintaining the environment in a sustainable way so that it isn't further degraded.'

She continued: 'I don't know that I'll ever meet anyone again with the same passion, drive and ability, and I suspect that it won't be the last time I hear the name.

'Next time I'll know how to pronounce it.'

The curriculum vitae of the Victorian-born Sydney resident, tendered by her lawyer, Vanessa Bleyer, first alerted Ms Popovic she had a unique offender before her.

At 12 she started a school conservation club, as a teenager she worked for Rotary in a Brazilian orphanage, and later she co-ordinated 2000 young people for an environmental sustainability conference.

Creenhaune won a human rights award from the University of Technology, Sydney, this year for her commitment to a range of social justice and human rights organisations and activities, including indigenous rights, climate change and environmental justice.

Soon to complete a law and journalism degree, Creenhaune said her parents, both teachers, were not 'greenies or lefties' or even activists. 'What they fostered in me as teachers was to use critical thinking skills, to read a newspaper and look beyond and take a critical eye to issues.'

Politics does not excite her — 'my feet are firmly planted in organising' — but she believes the Rudd Government offers 'wriggle room' for a stronger voice for communities, unions and ecosystems.

'I am looking towards the new area of climate law,' she says.

Ms Popovic said Creenhaune's 'exemplary' character was a factor in dismissing the charges against her, but warned 'similar reasoning may not be applied' if Creenhaune reoffends.

And as a final piece of advice, she said such behaviour in the forest was 'best an activity that's relegated to the past'.

Source: The Sydney Morning Herald, 21–23 December 2007.

GEOskills TOOLBOX

ANALYSING A NEWSPAPER ARTICLE

Newspapers often provide valuable information about geographical issues. Daily newspapers are usually up-to-date and accurate. Be aware that news reports can have some bias, either because of the editorial policy of the newspaper or the individual journalist's point of view.

Newspaper articles are generally written with the most important information early in the article, with less important information or more background information following. Headlines are chosen to summarise the main content of the news being reported and to attract the attention of the reader. The article at left is about one individual's campaign to save a forest from logging.

ACTIVITIES

UNDERSTANDING

1. What is the 'green movement'?
2. Make a list of things you do to help protect threatened habitats and conserve the environment (for example, Clean Up Australia Day, recycling).

THINKING AND APPLYING

3. How can you make sure that you are an aware global citizen?
4. As a class, discuss the ways in which people of your age contribute — either deliberately or accidentally — to the destruction of habitats.
   a Why do you think each one happens?
   b What messages encourage teenagers to be more concerned about protecting the Earth? Why?
5. Work in small groups for this field excursion. Investigate your school grounds and report on the following.
   a Can you find any natural habitats?
   b What proportion of the grounds is still natural habitat?
   c Is there anything your school could do to preserve or restore habitats?

USING YOUR SKILLS

6. Read the news article and answer the following questions.
   a List three facts in the news article.
   b Find the quotes from the judge. Are these fact or opinion?
   c Consider the headline. Does it attract your attention and make you want to read the article? Why or why not?
   d Make a list of all the words or phrases in the article that you associate with 'geography'.
   e What is the tone of the article? Do you think the journalist approves or disapproves of the protester?

Working geographically

KNOWLEDGE AND UNDERSTANDING

Select the alternative A, B, C or D that best answers the question.

1. A habitat is
   - (A) the natural home of an animal or plant.
   - (B) the place where an animal or plant is normally found.
   - (C) the natural home of an animal or plant, the place where it is normally found.
   - (D) the home of a plant or animal.

2. Extinction is
   - (A) the dying out of a species.
   - (B) the disappearance of an entire species or plant.
   - (C) the disappearance of a species from their habitat.
   - (D) the dying out of an entire species of animal or plant.

3. The coastal ecosystem is the system of interactions between
   - (A) living plants and animals of the environment.
   - (B) living plants and humans of the environment.
   - (C) plants and animals of the environment.
   - (D) the tide and water of the environment.

4. The habitat of the orang-utan is threatened by
   - (A) anacondas.
   - (B) deforestation.
   - (C) afforestation.
   - (D) giraffes.

5. Global warming is
   - (A) an excess of carbon in the air, which many scientists believe is caused by the burning of fossil fuels.
   - (B) an excess of carbon dioxide in the air, which many scientists believe is caused by the burning of fossil fuels.
   - (C) gradual heating of the atmosphere.
   - (D) the warming of the atmosphere, which many scientists believe is caused by the burning of fossil fuels.

6. Tigers need a lot of
   - (A) meat to survive.
   - (B) space to survive.
   - (C) grassland to survive.
   - (D) range to survive.

7. Aerial surveys can count elephants
   - (A) accurately.
   - (B) innacurately.
   - (C) accurately, but only in open habitats.
   - (D) accurately, but only in their natural habitat.

8. Ocean water with a temperature between 21° and 30° Celsius is the natural habitat of
   - (A) sharks.
   - (B) coral reefs.
   - (C) sea lions.
   - (D) dolphins.

9. The world's largest unbroken coral reef is in
   - (A) the Great Barrier Reef.
   - (B) Fiji.
   - (C) the Caribbean.
   - (D) New Caledonia.

10. When we visit a habitat we must always
    - (A) leave everything as we found it.
    - (B) clean and dispose of litter.
    - (C) ensure the animals are fed.
    - (D) cover our tracks.

GEOGRAPHICAL INQUIRY

11. The California condor (see photograph on page 268) is the largest flying land bird in North America. Condor numbers were greatly reduced during the last century and it is now an endangered species. In 2001, there were 126 condors living in captivity and an estimated 54 in the wild. Scaffolds provide useful ways of analysing and summarising the issue of the endangered condor. Use the following scaffold and your favourite search engine to research the endangered condor.

California condor
Description of the condor:
Present and past distribution of the condor:
Habitat of the condor:
Food of the condor:
Breeding habits of the condor:
Threats to the condor:
Responses of groups, individuals and governments to help save the condor:
How successful are these strategies?

ANALYSING A NEWSPAPER ARTICLE

12 Read the following newspaper article and answer the questions below.

a Explain the geographical issue that is covered in this article.

b Does the headline correctly reflect the content of the article?

c Why is the mahogany glider's habitat threatened? Is the source of the threat human or physical?

d Why is captive-breeding of gliders not likely to be successful?

e What groups are mentioned in the article and what perspective does each have on the issue?

f The journalist who wrote the article is the environment reporter. Do you think this would mean he may have some bias in his reporting of the issue? Can you detect any bias?

g Create a two column table with headings FACT and OPINION. List all the facts and opinions you can find in the article in the relevant column. Rate this article in terms of the usefulness and reliability of its information.

INTERPRETING GRAPHS

13 Study the graphs below.

a Which two countries have high numbers of both endangered mammals and birds?

b What is Australia's record in relation to endangered mammals and birds?

c Which continent has the greatest number of countries represented in the mammal graph?

d Which continent has the greatest number of countries represented in the bird graph?

Green groups fight to save glider

BY BRIAN WILLIAMS, ENVIRONMENT REPORTER

Habitat cleared for cane ... a recovery plan for the mahogany glider has stalled and species extinction is feared.

Conservationists believe the nation's rarest glider, the mahogany glider, is headed for extinction unless the State Government does more to preserve its habitat.

With fewer than 1500 believed left, the wildlife Preservation Society has sought help from the International Union for the Conservation of Nature.

With 80 per cent of its north Queensland habitat cleared for cane farming, the IUCN has the glider on its red list.

Society president Simon Baltais said yesterday the Environmental Protection Agency glider-recovery plan had not been put into action.

Daryl Dickson, a wildlife carer who looks after gliders at Tully in north Queensland, also wants the Environmental Protection Agency to abandon any plans to release gliders bred at Fleahy's Wildlife Park on the Gold Coast because of their limited chance of survival.

Ms Dickson has managed the only successful release of a captive-bred mahogany glider.

In a letter to Sustainability Minister Andrew McNamara, Ms Dickson said the EPA release was doomed to failure.

'We have an ethical obligation to ensure the projects we undertake are beneficial for the species,' she said. 'This project does not meet those criteria.'

Ms Dickson said it has been found that captive-bred animals would fly but they had problems landing, needed time to develop strength for aerial work, had to battle for territory and were at risk of starvation and disease.

An EPA spokesman rejected suggestions the glider was headed for extinction, saying the Government had taken substantial steps to address habitat loss.

Source: Paul Williams, The Courier-Mail, 7 January 2009.

Number of threatened mammal species

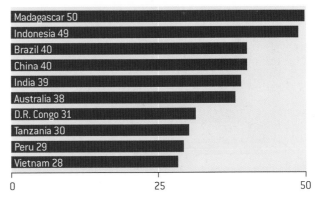

Madagascar 50	
Indonesia 49	
Brazil 40	
China 40	
India 39	
Australia 38	
D.R. Congo 31	
Tanzania 30	
Peru 29	
Vietnam 28	

Scale: 0 — 25 — 50

Number of threatened bird species

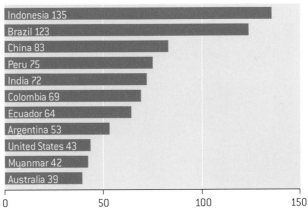

Indonesia 135	
Brazil 123	
China 83	
Peru 75	
India 72	
Colombia 69	
Ecuador 64	
Argentina 53	
United States 43	
Myanmar 42	
Australia 39	

Scale: 0 — 50 — 100 — 150

projects*plus*

Endangered animals viral video

SEARCHLIGHT ID: PRO-0017

YOUR TASK

Your task is to create a three-minute internet video to be distributed online. Your aim is for this video to become 'viral' — for it to be good enough for people to want to pass it on to their friends. Your video will focus on one or more endangered animals and encourage viewers to take up the cause to help protect the animal's habitat.

Your project brief includes a sample viral video on endangered species.

PROTECT ENVIRONMENT FOR FUTURE

SCENARIO

You are a freelance digital filmmaker and have been engaged by the Australian Wildlife Assistance Organisation (AWAO) to shoot a video for them. They are creating a series of videos that will be released online to help raise awareness about species whose survival is threatened.

You will choose one or more animals from a list provided by the AWAO to focus on in your video. Your audience will want to know:

- What does this animal eat?
- Where is it found?
- What are its natural threats?
- How is it threatened?
- Why has it become threatened?
- What would be the impacts on Australia if this animal became extinct?
- What is being done to protect this animal?
- What should be done to help remove it from the threatened species list?

Your movie must be between 2½ and 3½ minutes long and include a voiceover or text on screen. It should interest and appeal to the wide range of people who use the internet. You should discuss current methods of helping to manage this threatened species and suggest at least two future strategies that could be implemented.

ENDANGER
SPECIES
HABITAT

Haleakalā National Pa

PROCESS

- Open the ProjectsPLUS application for this chapter located in your eBookPLUS. Watch the introductory video lesson and then click the 'Start Project' button to set up your project. You can complete this project individually or invite other members of your class to form a group. Save your settings and the project will be launched.
- Navigate to your Research Forum. A number of suggested animals have been loaded as topics to provide a framework for your research. Choose the endangered animals you would like to include in your video and delete the other topics.
- Research the animals you have chosen. You should find at least two sources other than the textbook

and at least one offline source, such as a book or encyclopaedia, to help you discover extra information about your chosen endangered animals. The weblinks in your Media Centre will help you get started. Enter your findings as articles in the Research Forum. You can also view and comment on other group members' articles.

- When your research is complete, navigate to your Media Centre and download the 'Shooting Script' template to use to create your script and shotlist. When planning your video, consider how different organisations promote wildlife and conservation issues to a wide audience, and what techniques are the most effective. A selection of media has been provided for you in your Media Centre to download and use in your video. You may also choose to create animations or source other media to incorporate. Don't forget to record the source of any information or image you use in your video, as you always need to attribute other people's work.
- When your shooting script is signed off, record your voiceover and then use video editing software to create your final production.
- Print out your Research Report from ProjectsPLUS and hand it in to your teacher with your shooting script and your final video. You might like to post your video on YouTube or hold a school screening.

SUGGESTED SOFTWARE
- ProjectsPLUS
- Microsoft Word
- Audacity, Garage Band or other voice-recording software
- Windows Movie Maker, iMovie or other editing software

MEDIA CENTRE
Your Media Centre contains:
- a bank of media to use in your video
- a 'Shooting Script' template
- weblinks to sites on endangered animals and free recording and editing software
- an assessment rubric.

Interactivity

HOTSPOT COMMANDER: 'ENDANGERED SPECIES'

Hotspot Commander challenges your geographical skills and knowledge in a fun question-and-answer format. You will receive the coordinates of a location. When you hit your target accurately, you will be given some secret information and a question to answer. Get it right and a part of the mystery image is revealed. Can you conquer all 10 locations and become a Hotspot Commander?

SEARCHLIGHT ID: INT-0781

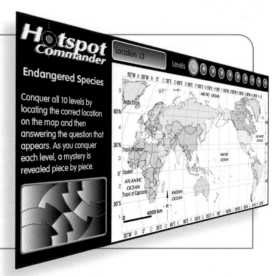

15 Tourism: a geographical issue

INQUIRY QUESTIONS

+ Why is tourism such a huge global industry?
+ What are the patterns of tourism?
+ What are the impacts of tourism?
+ How can tourism be a sustainable industry?

Tourism is travel for pleasure and is one of the world's fastest growing industries. Many people work in the tourism industry to provide transport, accommodation and access to attractions for people to enjoy. Tourism is an enjoyable activity and can increase understanding between different communities around the world. However, it can also be resented by locals, reinforce prejudices and damage environments. In this chapter we will look at the growth and impacts of tourism, including the increasing interest in ecotourism. Sustainable tourism does not damage physical or human environments.

GEOskills TOOLBOX

GEOskillbuilder Creating a mind map (page 353)
+ Interpreting statistics (page 342)
+ Using fieldwork (page 359)

Palma Nova Beach in Majorca, Spain, is a popular tourist destination.

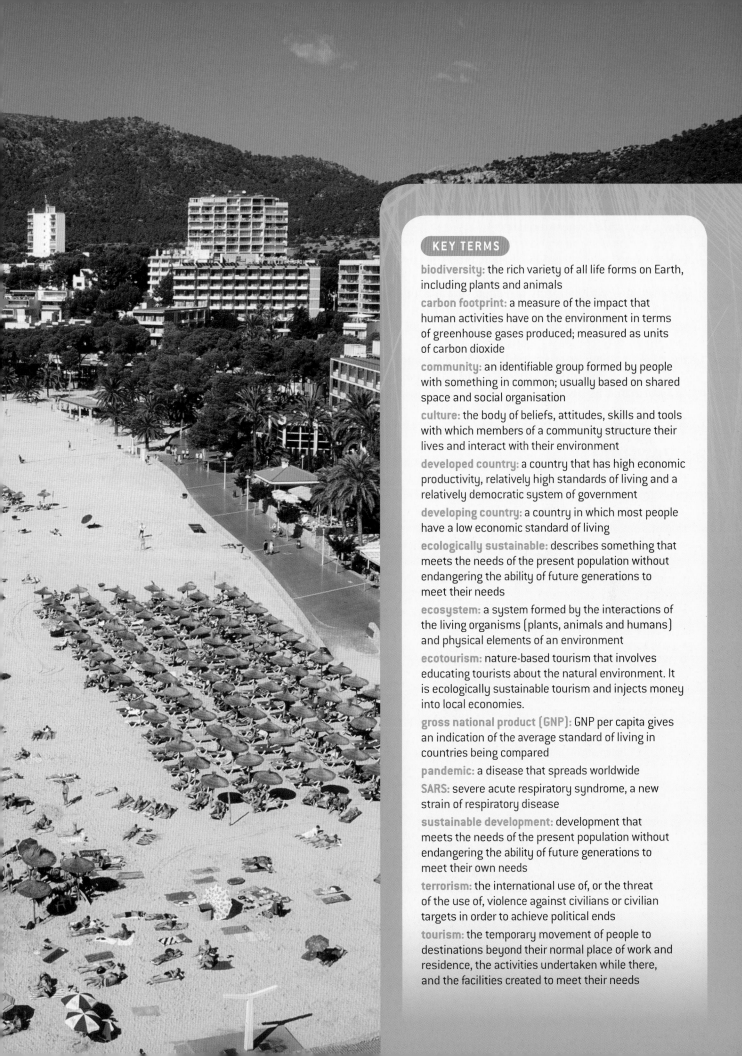

Over 600 million people travel overseas each year, generating more than $1000 billion in revenue and providing work for 200 million people. Tourism is now the world's largest industry.

Tourism is not a new industry. People have always been curious about what lies just around the corner, over the next hill or across the ocean. However, in earlier times, people rarely travelled very far for relaxation, enjoyment or curiosity. Instead they travelled for work, to make religious pilgrimages, to fight wars or to flee dangers. Even so, early travellers and explorers were driven by the same desire that many tourists have — a curiosity about the world and its people.

The growth of tourism over time

During the second half of the twentieth century, mass tourism gradually became established in developed countries. There were a number of reasons for this:

- widespread ownership of motor cars and the development of roads
- increase in leisure time plus paid holiday leave and long-service leave
- development of jet aeroplanes and wide-body jets, resulting in faster, cheaper travel
- development of worldwide direct telephoning
- development of worldwide credit cards, which allowed easy payment for purchases
- development of the internet, resulting in quicker and cheaper booking of travel arrangements and accommodation.

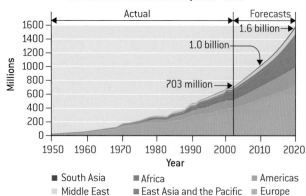

International tourist arrivals, 1950–2020

The growth in global tourism

Source: World Tourism Organization.

Why do people become tourists?

People become tourists for many reasons:

- *To enjoy a break from everyday life*. People often want to get away from their usual environment or routine. Being a tourist allows us to have different experiences such as living in a different climate. It can also be an opportunity to relax.
- *Cultural pursuits*. Many tourists want to find out about the way other people live and learn about their culture. Tourists might have an interest in architecture, art, dance, food or history.
- *To have new experiences*. People like to travel to places they are curious about, or to places where they can do things they like to do. For example, a trip to the snowfields will take people to a new place and give them the opportunity to ski.
- *Sport and physical activity*. Some tourists travel to participate in sport. Many people travel to see sporting events such as tennis or cricket.
- *To learn about the physical environment*. This includes natural wonders such as mountains and forests, and ecotourism, which is concerned with preserving the natural environment.

There are other possible categories. Not everyone fits into a particular tourist type and many people travel for more than one reason.

Planning a holiday

When planning a holiday you would probably consider:

- *Personal interests*. Choice of destination depends on your age and interests. For example, you could go surfing, to a live concert or a resort.
- *Transport and accommodation costs*. If you are a domestic tourist, cost will vary. If you are an international tourist, you will probably go by plane. Your accommodation could vary in cost — from camping, to youth hostels and right through to five-star hotels.
- *Distance*. This will affect your cost, the time you can spend at your destination and whether you will travel through time zones.
- *Available time*. How much time will you have to spend at your destination, and how much time will you spend travelling?
- *Climate and season*. This will affect what you can do and the clothes you need.

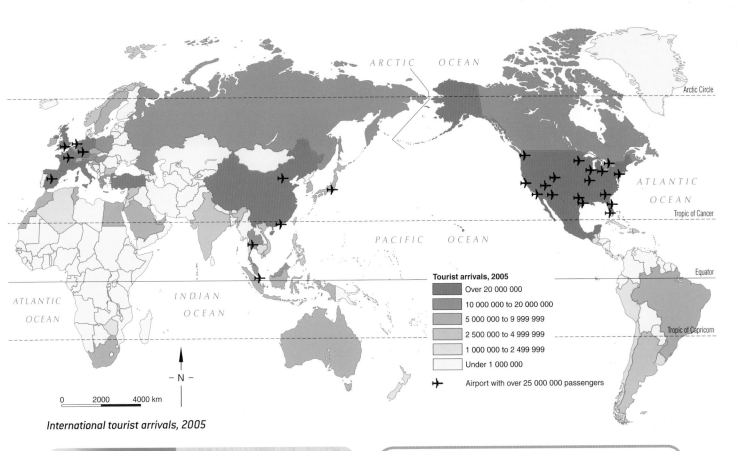

International tourist arrivals, 2005

Tourist arrivals, 2005
- Over 20 000 000
- 10 000 000 to 20 000 000
- 5 000 000 to 9 999 999
- 2 500 000 to 4 999 999
- 1 000 000 to 2 499 999
- Under 1 000 000
- ✈ Airport with over 25 000 000 passengers

 GEOfacts The average backpacker travels further, stays longer and spends more than any other type of tourist. The typical backpacker is aged between 18 and 35 and enjoys adventure holidays. Backpackers often choose budget accommodation provided by hostels. In Australia, around 10 per cent of all international visitors are classified as backpackers. Almost 70 per cent of these come from the United Kingdom, Europe and the USA.

GEOTERMS

culture: the body of beliefs, attitudes, skills and tools with which members of a community structure their lives and interact with their environment

ecotourism: nature-based tourism that involves educating tourists about the natural environment. It is ecologically sustainable tourism and injects money into local economies.

ACTIVITIES ➡

UNDERSTANDING

1. Outline the main reasons people become tourists.
2. Describe the factors people often consider when they plan a holiday.

THINKING AND APPLYING

3. Many developments and inventions have led to the huge increase in tourist numbers around the world. What do you consider to be the most important? Give three reasons for your answer.
4. Imagine there is a competition called 'My dream holiday' run by a large tourist organisation. To enter, you must write 200 words on 'how I'd plan my trip to cater for all members of my family'. Complete your entry.

USING YOUR SKILLS

5. Refer to the graph of international tourist arrivals, 1950–2020.
   a Which area was the most popular for tourist arrivals in 1970?
   b Which area is forecast to be the most popular for tourist arrivals in 2015?
   c Estimate the number of tourist arrivals in 2008 and 2015.
6. Describe the pattern of global tourism shown on the map. Suggest three possible reasons for this pattern. Use the map key and an atlas to help you in your description.
7. Go to Google Earth and select a place you are keen to visit. Describe the place as it appears on Google Earth. What experiences and activities could you participate in there?

There are many different reasons why people travel and why they choose to visit particular places. The three main types of tourist attractions are:

- natural attractions (for example, mountains or coral reefs)
- cultural attractions (for example, the way of life of the local people, art galleries, historic buildings)
- event attractions (for example, shows, festivals, the Olympic Games).

The Arc de Triomphe, a cultural attraction

Viewing platform over the Grand Canyon, a natural attraction

As each tourist enters a new country, he or she is counted by the customs and immigration officials in that country. The World Tourism Organization collects all these data. The tables above right show which countries were the world's most popular tourist destinations in 2006, and how much money tourists spent in each country. Although tourism is the world's largest industry, it is not spread evenly around the globe. Some countries receive and produce more tourists than others.

Top international tourist destinations, 2006

Country	International tourist arrivals, 2006 (millions)
France	78.9
Spain	58.2
United States	51.0
China	49.9
Italy	41.1
United Kingdom	30.7
Germany	23.5
Mexico	21.4
Ukraine	18.9
Turkey	18.9

Source: World Tourism Organization (UNWTO), 2008.

Top international tourism receipts, 2006

Country	Receipts (US$ billions)
United States	85.7
Spain	51.1
France	46.3
Italy	38.1
China	33.9
United Kingdom	33.7
Germany	32.8
Australia	17.8
Turkey	16.9
Austria	16.6

Source: World Tourism Organization (UNWTO), 2008.

GEOskills TOOLBOX

INTERPRETING STATISTICS

Statistics deal with the collection, classification and use of numerical data. Statistics are usually gathered by counting or measuring things. A lot of the information geographers use is in the form of numbers.

When similar pieces of information are grouped together in a table, it is easier to compare numbers and see patterns and trends. You can also get information from tables of statistics by adding numbers, or by finding the average or range of a set of numbers. The range is the gap between the highest and lowest number. To calculate the range, subtract the lowest from the highest.

The information in tables can often be displayed as a graph, like those on the following page.

Top ten tourism spenders

So now we know which countries tourists go to, but which countries do they come from? The column graph below shows the top ten countries in terms of the money they spend as tourists. The line graph below shows the relationship between income and air travel.

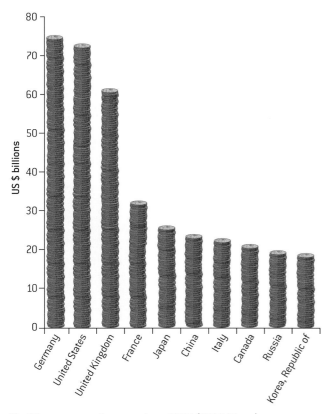

World's top ten tourism spenders, 2006 (US$ billions)

Source: Derived from World Tourism Organization data.

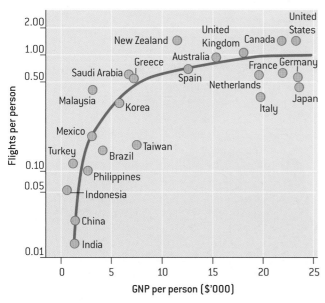

Correlation between income and air travel

ACTIVITIES →

UNDERSTANDING

1. List the three main types of tourist attraction and give an example of each.
2. What is the function of the World Tourism Organization?

THINKING AND APPLYING

3. On a blank outline map of the world, locate and label the capital cities of the top ten tourist destinations (use the table on page 342). Imagine you have a round-the-world air ticket that allows you to stop in each city. The ticket states you must travel in an easterly direction and leave from, and return to, Sydney. On the map, plot your trip to complete this journey in the shortest possible distance. Use the scale on the map to estimate the total distance travelled.

USING YOUR SKILLS

4. Refer to the line graph showing the correlation between income and air travel.
   a What was the **gross national product (GNP)** per person in the United Kingdom? What was the number of flights per person in the United Kingdom?
   b What was the GNP per person in Indonesia? What was the number of flights per person in Indonesia?
   c Explain why the United States and Canada have the most number of flights per person.

5. Refer to the column graph of the world's top ten tourism spenders in 2006.
   a List the top three tourism spenders.
   b What was the total amount of money spent by the top three?

6. Refer to the table of tourist destinations and tourism earners in 2006.
   a Which country had the most tourist arrivals?
   b Name the countries that attracted more than 40 million tourists each during 2006.
   c Which country had the most receipts from tourism? Explain how a country could have the highest receipts but not the highest arrivals.
   d Which two continents are the most important for both arrivals and receipts? Suggest reasons for this.
   e Calculate the range between the tourist receipts for the highest and lowest ranked countries.
   f Use the table to create a column graph that shows the world's top ten tourist destinations.

Tourism sometimes seems to be the perfect industry. Tourists have a holiday and the hosts have a boost to their finances. Greater mobility, larger incomes and more leisure time have led to the rapid growth of tourism. It now employs about 200 million people worldwide and has the potential to benefit us all.

Economic benefits

Tourism is big business. Along with the big crowds comes big money. Income generated from tourism in 2007 ($130 billion) made it the world's number one export earner. In order to attract tourists, local and national governments often improve facilities such as roads, electricity, public transport, water and sewerage. These benefits are also enjoyed by the local people. An example of this type of spending is the money that goes into the Olympic Games. The British Government, for example, expects to spend around $20 billion (Australian dollars) on new facilities for the 2012 Olympic Games in London.

A new subway system was developed in Beijing for the Olympics in 2008. High-speed trains now run at an interval of 3–5 minutes.

Social benefits

Travelling to different places can increase our understanding of each other's values and way of life. It can strengthen some cultural traditions — especially if tourists become interested in these traditions. The revenue that tourism generates can be used to raise living standards within a community.

The survival of animals like the white rhinoceros is threatened by many human activities such as deforestation and farming. However, another human activity — tourism — may be what saves them.

Environmental benefits

The money that tourism brings to a community can also be used to help conserve or repair the environment. This can then lead to more tourists wanting to visit the area. In some areas of the world, phyical environments such as rainforests and reefs have been preserved because they are popular with tourists. The mountain gorillas of Africa, the orang-utans of Indonesia and Kenya's elephants all rely on tourism for their long-term survival. Kenyan authorities estimate that a single lion can generate $7000 a year in tourist income, while a herd of elephants is worth over $600 000. Quite simply, they are worth more alive than dead.

Tourism has allowed the San people (also known as Bushmen) of Namibia to maintain control of a small area of their traditional lands.

The human environment can also benefit from tourism. This is most obvious when historic buildings are restored in order to attract more tourists. Tourist dollars have helped to restore sites such as the famous ruins of Pompeii in Italy and the convict settlement at Port Arthur in Tasmania.

Sustainable tourism

We are all tourists at one time or another and many of our most enjoyable times are when we are on holidays. We want tourism to continue but in a way that does not damage the environment or local culture. Sustainable tourism involves a relationship between three key elements:
• the place
• the host community
• the visitor.

The aims of sustainability tourism are to protect the environment and respect the needs of the local people.

Large cities in Europe such as London, Paris, and Rome can cope fairly well with large numbers of people. Problems created by unsustainable tourism occur more often in the tourist areas in **developing countries** and in places where the physical environment is the tourist attraction.

Sustainable development is development that meets the needs of the present population without endangering the ability of future generations to meet their own needs.

Principles of sustainable tourism

• Tourism is a positive activity that can bring benefits to the local community as well as the tourist.
• The environment has a value for both present and future generations. Tourism should not be allowed to damage the environment or threaten its future enjoyment. The relationship between the environment and tourism is a very delicate one and must be managed for the long term.
• Tourist developments and activities should respect the scale, nature and character of any area in which they are found.
• In any place, the needs of the environment, the local community and the visitor need to be reconciled.
• It is inevitable that there will be change. Adapting to change should not be at the expense of any of these principles.
• It is essential to have cooperation between interested parties to achieve sustainable tourism.

ACTIVITIES

UNDERSTANDING

1. Why does tourism seem to be the perfect industry? Consider people employed and income generated.
2. How large is the tourism industry?
3. What factors have led to the rapid growth of the tourism industry?
4. Outline the main benefits of tourism.
5. Using your own words, describe sustainable tourism.

THINKING AND APPLYING

6. The diagram shows how the tourist dollar can flow from one job to the next. Jobs in the centre of the diagram deal directly with the tourist, those on the outside only indirectly. Complete the diagram by putting appropriate jobs in the blank boxes.

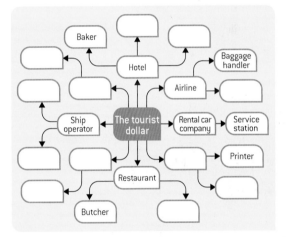

7. List three tourist attractions in a city that attracts large numbers of tourists. Explain how one of these attractions does meet or does not meet the six principles of sustainable tourism.
8. In groups, select a tourist destination that all members of your group would like to visit. Brainstorm ideas about how this place would be sustainably managed and then exchange them with other groups. Would any of these ideas contribute to sustainable management of a tourist attraction in your local area? List useful ideas and note if they require individual, group or government action.

GEOTERMS

developing country: a country in which most people have a low economic standard of living

Tourism can encourage greater understanding between people, and bring prosperity to some **communities**. It can also destroy people's culture and the places in which they live. For many communities, tourists have become not only their best guests but also their worst customers.

Much of the money spent by tourists in foreign countries, especially developing countries, goes back into the pockets of the overseas companies that own the hotels and airlines. A recent study showed that 70 per cent of the money spent by tourists in Thailand ended up leaving the country.

Tourism's potential for destruction — a snapshot

Tourists on safari in Kenya disturb the animals so much that the animals sometimes neglect their young. In Africa predators are often disturbed in their hunt for food.

Land traditionally used for grazing cattle and local festivals in Java has been sold to make way for a five-star tourist hotel. The local people are therefore deprived of this resource.

The smog in Yosemite Valley in California can be so thick that the valley cannot be seen from passing aircraft. This is owing to the large number of visitors who arrive by car — up to 8000 vehicles a day.

Rubbish left by expeditions at Everest base camp

In Hawaii, sacred burial grounds are being excavated to make way for new tourist resorts.

Air travel significantly increases the release of harmful gases into the atmosphere, adding to global warming.

On the Inca Trail in Peru, tourists are damaging the ancient Inca ruins by lighting camp fires in them.

In Nepal, one of the most heavily deforested countries in the world, tourists use 4 to 5 kilograms of wood a day for heating and cooking.

A global explosion in golf tourism has severely reduced the freshwater resources of local residents in many tropical countries. In Thailand, for example, an average golf course uses as much water as 60 000 local villagers.

Child prostitution is an increasing problem in many countries, such as Cambodia and Thailand. Some tourists, including Australians, travel to these countries to take advantage of local children.

Growth in tourism often leads to growth in crime as rich tourists come into contact with poor locals. This is the case in Rio de Janeiro, Brazil, where hotel owners often need to hire machine-gun-carrying guards to warn off potential pickpockets.

In the Maldives, coral reefs have been dynamited and mined for building materials for new tourist resorts.

Cruise ships in the Caribbean Sea produce over 70 000 tonnes of rubbish a year. While many shipping companies that cruise this area are working to improve their environmental record, some of the waste still washes ashore.

THE RESPONSIBLE TOURIST AND TRAVELLER

Travel and tourism should be planned and practiced as a means of individual and collective fulfilment. When practiced with an open mind, it is an irreplaceable factor of self education, mutual tolerance and for learning about the legitimate differences between peoples and cultures and their diversity.

Everyone has a role to play creating responsible travel and tourism. Governments, business and communities must do all they can, but as a guest you can support this in many ways to make a difference:

 Open your mind to other cultures and traditions — it will transform your experience, you will earn respect and be more readily welcomed by local people. Be tolerant and respect diversity — observe social and cultural traditions and practices.

Respect human rights. Exploitation in any form conflicts with the fundamental aims of tourism. The sexual exploitation of children is a crime punishable in the destination or at the offender's home country.

 Help preserve natural environments. Protect wildlife and habitats and do not purchase products made from endangered plants or animals.

Respect cultural resources. Activities should be conducted with respect for the artistic, archaeological and cultural heritage.

 Your trip can contribute to economic and social development. Purchase local handicrafts and products to support the local economy using the principles of fair trade. Bargaining for goods should reflect an understanding of a fair wage.

Inform yourself about the destination's current health situation and access to emergency and consular services prior to departure and be assured that your health and personal security will not be compromised. Make sure that your specific requirements (diet, accessibility, medical care) can be fulfilled before you decide to travel to this destination.

 Learn as much as possible about your destination and take time to understand the customs, norms and traditions. Avoid behaviour that could offend the local population.

Familiarize yourself with the laws so that you do not commit any act considered criminal by the law of the country visited. Refrain from all trafficking in illicit drugs, arms, antiques, protected species and products or substances that are dangerous or prohibited by national regulations.

Practical guide for responsible tourism

GEOTERMS

community: an identifiable group formed by people with something in common; usually based on shared space and social organisation

ACTIVITIES

UNDERSTANDING

1. What are two positive impacts of tourism?
2. What are two negative impacts of tourism?

THINKING AND APPLYING

3. The impact of tourism can be classified into three broad categories:
   i. environmental impact — by which tourists can change the quality of the land, air, plants, animals or man-made structures
   ii. cultural impact — by which tourists change the normal way of life of the people with whom they come in contact
   iii. economic impact — by which tourists change the income, employment or standard of living of the people with whom they come into contact.

   a Study the information on these pages. List two examples of each type of impact.
   b Which type of impact do you think is the most serious? Why?
   c Refer to the photograph of Everest Base Camp opposite. What type of impact does this photograph show?

USING YOUR SKILLS

4. On a blank outline map of the world, locate each of the places mentioned on these pages. Decide on an appropriate symbol for each of the three types of impact listed in activity 3 and show these in your legend. Use these symbols to show where each type of impact occurs in the world. Stick your completed map in the centre of an A3-sized poster. Illustrate it with images cut from tourist brochures.

Many countries rely heavily on tourism and any reduction in the numbers of tourist arrivals has a large impact on these countries' economies. This means that for some countries any interruption to tourism, as a result of world events, can be economically devastating. In developing countries like Tanzania, for example, tourism accounts for nearly 50 per cent of export earnings.

Terrorism and tourism

In recent years, one of the biggest issues affecting global tourism has been that of terrorism. The terrorist attack on the World Trade Center in New York on September 11 2001 heralded a new era in world history. Since then, terrorist attacks have targeted tourists at popular tourist destinations all over the world. Many international travellers are from developed countries, such as the United States, the United Kingdom, Germany and Australia, and the terrorist attacks have caused many of these travellers to cancel or adjust their travel plans.

In Bali, for example, tourist arrivals fell by over 65 per cent after the 2002 terrorist attack, which killed 202 people, including 88 Australians. About 630 000 Balinese, one-third of the workforce, were

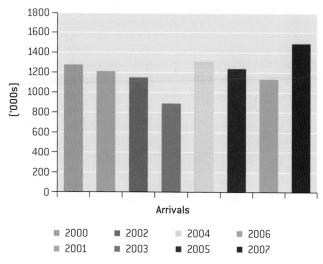

Source: Data derived from Bali Tourism Board.

Foreign tourist arrivals to Bali, 2000–2007

Major terrorist attacks since 2002

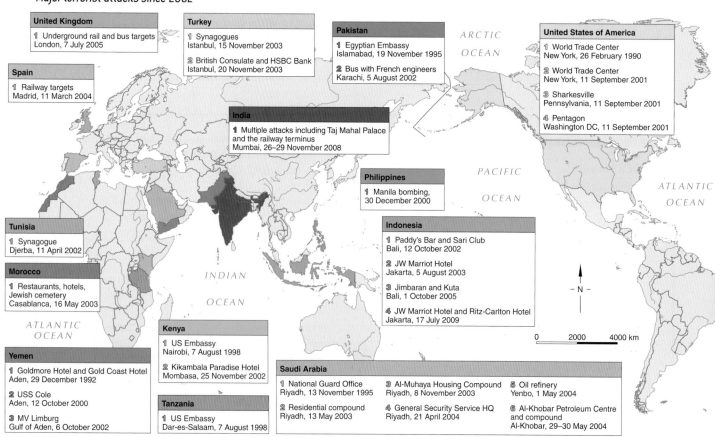

Source: Based on data from www.dfat.gov.au.

employed in the tourism industry at the time and many lost their livelihoods. The industry was recovering when a second attack in 2005 meant that many tourists again decided against holidaying there. The graph opposite shows how Bali's tourism fortunes have fluctuated after terrorist attacks. Owing to Bali's reliance on tourism, the Indonesian island has provided terrorists with two essentials: large numbers of easy tourist targets and the potential to cause lasting economic disruption.

Aerial photograph of Legion Street, Kuta, after the 2002 terrorist bombing

New infectious diseases

Terrorism is not the only issue that impacts upon tourism and people's willingness to travel internationally. In 2003, a new and easily transmitted disease called severe acute respiratory syndrome (SARS) created a tourism crisis in parts of Asia. Similarly, avian influenza (H5N1), a viral infection found mainly in birds, caused a number of deaths in Asia in 2008–2009 with adverse consequences for the tourism industry there. Then, in 2009, a new disease commonly known as swine flu (H1N1) began infecting humans. The disease began in Mexico and soon spread. In June 2009, the World Health Organization (WHO) declared a pandemic as the strain of influenza spread worldwide, with over 60 000 people contracting the disease in 74 countries, including Australia. While the disease seemed mild with deaths only in the hundreds, governments reacted strongly, introducing isolation measures in an attempt to halt the spread. As with avian influenza, if the swine influenza virus mutates into a new strain that is more deadly, there is concern among health authorities worldwide that it could be spread rapidly by international travel, killing millions and severely damaging the global economy, including the tourism

industry. In Mexico, for example, the country most affected by swine flu, tourist revenue experienced its largest fall since records began.

ACTIVITIES

UNDERSTANDING

1. Name two issues that can affect the number of tourists willing to travel internationally.
2. Why did the terrorist attacks in Bali have such a large impact on the local economy?
3. How did governments respond to the SARS epidemic of 2003?
4. In what ways would an outbreak of swine or avian flu be potentially devastating?

THINKING AND APPLYING

5. Bali's largest source of tourists is currently from Japan, Russia and South Korea. Why might tourists from these countries be arriving in larger numbers than, for example, Australian tourists?

USING YOUR SKILLS

6. Refer to the bar graph showing Foreign Tourist Arrivals to Bali from 2000–2007.
   a. What year on the graph shows the lowest number of tourist arrivals? What event the previous year explains this number?
   b. From what you know about the date and effect of the second terrorist attack, what year would you expect the graph to show another drop in tourist arrivals? Does it?
   c. The Banda Aceh tsunami occurred in Indonesia in 2004. Does the graph show any impact from this natural disaster?
   d. How many tourists arrived in Bali in 2007? What percentage increase does this number represent over 2006 numbers? What can you conclude from this increase?
7. Refer to the map of major terrorist attacks since 2002.
   a. Which country has had the most attacks?
   b. Can you see any pattern in the location of the countries that have suffered terrorist attacks?
   c. Which of the terrorist attacks does not appear to have tourists as a target?
8. Use an atlas to locate three countries that have not had terrorist attacks. Suggest why these countries may have escaped an attack.

GEOTERMS

pandemic: a disease that spreads worldwide
terrorism: the international use of, or the threat of the use of, violence against civilians or civilian targets in order to achieve political ends

The physical environment

Tourism has the potential to cause many effects on the physical environment, both globally and locally. To deal with the threat of climate change, the United Nations has established a framework for a worldwide sustainable tourism industry. Its main aims are to:
- reduce greenhouse gas emissions
- help tourism businesses and destinations adapt to changing climate conditions
- use technology to improve energy efficiency.

The role of governments

The role for governments and international organisations will include actions to provide financial, technical and training support to tourist destinations and operators in developing countries. In addition, actions to reduce greenhouse gases in transport, particularly in air travel, will be required. Education and awareness programs for all tourism stakeholders, including tourists themselves, will play a crucial role.

The attraction that coral reefs and beaches have for tourists has meant the construction of beachside hotels, resorts, marinas, golf courses, roads, shopping malls and airports. Tourist developers and tourists are being challenged to consider how best to protect fragile coastal habitats.

The human environment

Unlike the physical environment, large cities are often able to handle large numbers of tourists. They already have hotels, shops, restaurants and transport networks. Even so, the influx of large numbers can still create problems, especially with the local residents. In Venice, for example, the local citizens have protested against a new regional tourism law that would create even more hotels. Venetians say they cannot afford to live in their own city with the minimum price of a two-bedroom apartment now well over US$1 million. Over the last 20 years, the permanent population has halved to around 62 000. Every day, approximately 60 000 visitors arrive and are known as 'hit-and-run' tourists: they spend little and then leave by evening so that Venice resembles a ghost town.

The new Airbus is more fuel efficient than its predecessor, reducing greenhouse gas emission into the atmosphere.

The role of the tourism industry and tourists

Tourism operators will be asked to strive to conserve biodiversity, natural ecosystems and landscapes in ways that ensure a long-term sustainable use of tourist attractions such as rainforests and coral reefs. Tourists will be encouraged to make travel choices that, where possible, reduce their carbon footprint. Preservation of the physical environment and cultural heritage should be their goal.

Venice is crowded with tourists every day.

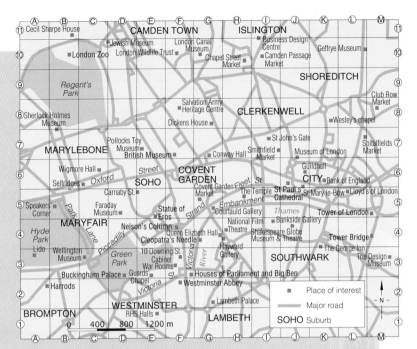

Map of central London

SAMPLE STUDY

Central London

London is considered by many to be the premier tourist destination in the world. Its cultural heritage and instantly recognisable architecture attract millions of tourists every year. Over 16 000 hectares of the inner city are devoted to parks such as Hyde Park and Regent's Park. However, it is London's historic buildings that capture the interest and imagination of the tourist. A tour of Buckingham Palace, Westminster Abbey and the Houses of Parliament, with its distinctive Big Ben clock tower, is on every tourist's 'must see' list.

Qantas plan to offset its carbon emissions

BY ROD MYER

QANTAS is designing a program to allow passengers to offset the carbon emissions from their flights.

Industry sources say it is examining a range of environmental programs, which are becoming increasingly important due to climate change.

Qantas's code-share partner, British Airways, already has a carbon-emissions program in place that allows passengers to pay a fee to cover the cost of the emissions created by their journey. For example, the fee for a return flight to Madrid is £5 (A$12.30) and for a return flight to Johannesburg £13.30. Passengers can choose to pay the fee via a link on BA's website.

BA has chosen to channel the money raised from the carbon offset fee into sustainable energy projects via a company called Climate Care.

Climate Care's projects include a South African scheme to distribute energy-efficient lamps, and an Indian project to provide biomass fuels for stoves.

Neither Singapore Airlines, Emirates nor Virgin Blue offer carbon offsets. However, all three say they are focused on fuel savings.

Qantas says the introduction of the Airbus A380 and Boeing 787 aircraft will cut emissions per passenger by up to 20 per cent.

BA has pledged to cut 30 per cent from its emissions levels between 1990 and 2010.

According to the International Air Transport Association, the airline industry accounts for 2 per cent of global carbon dioxide emissions and 13 per cent of transport emissions. Road vehicles account for 75 per cent of transport emissions.

The industry is aiming to cut its emissions by 10 per cent by 2010, which in turn would shave 350 million tonnes from global carbon dioxide pollution.

A return flight from Melbourne to Singapore on a 747 produces about 1.36 tonnes of carbon dioxide. BA's charge to offset this amount is £10.23.

Source: www.theage.com.au, 2 November 2006.

ACTIVITIES

UNDERSTANDING

1. In your own words, list the aims of the United Nations framework for sustainable tourism.
2. What actions will governments, tourist operators and tourists be asked to take?
3. How does air travel contribute to climate change?

THINKING AND APPLYING

4. How do you think education and awareness programs can help tourism deal with climate change challenges?

USING YOUR SKILLS

5. Read the newspaper article about Qantas's plan to reduce carbon emissions.
   a. What are carbon offset programs?
   b. Name two projects British Airways is funding through money raised from carbon offset fees.
   c. By what percentage does the airline industry aim to cut its emissions before 2010?
6. Read the sample study and refer to the map. The map of London has a grid system to find the location of places, a north point and a scale bar.
   a. What is located at G8, F2 and M4?
   b. Give the grid references for St Paul's Cathedral, the British Museum and Cleopatra's Needle.
   c. What direction would you travel in a direct line from:
      • Buckingham Palace to Westminster Abbey?
      • Tower Bridge to St Paul's Cathedral?
   d. How far would you travel if you walked in a straight line from:
      • Buckingham Palace to Westminster Abbey?
      • Tower Bridge to St Paul's Cathedral?

Tourism can offer many benefits for environments and cultures. It can also destroy them. Ecotourism has developed in response to this dilemma. It is nature-based tourism that involves educating tourists about the natural environment they are visiting and enjoying. All genuine ecotourism attractions are managed so that they are ecologically sustainable.

Ecotourism differs in two main ways from traditional tourism. Firstly, it recognises that many tourists wish to learn about the environment that they are visiting. This refers to both the natural environment (such as reefs, rainforests and deserts) and the human or cultural environment (such as local indigenous people). Secondly, it attempts to limit the impact of tourist facilities and visitors on the environment. This type of tourism is sometimes called 'soft tourism' (meaning it is 'soft' on the environment).

The travelling public have responded very well to this type of tourism. Ecotourism is now the fastest growing sector in the tourism industry, increasing at 10–30 per cent every year compared with 4 per cent for tourism overall.

Features of ecotourist resorts

The natural bush is retained as much as possible, and native plants are used in landscaping.

Composting toilets treat human waste, and worm farms consume food waste. Water is treated with ultraviolet light rather than chlorine. Recycling is encouraged.

Visitors are encouraged to improve the environment — perhaps by planting trees.

Buildings blend in with the natural landscape. Colour, location, height, shape and materials are all carefully selected with this in mind.

Vegetables are grown organically.

Low-impact, non-polluting means of transport, such as bicycles, are provided for guests.

Walking trails are lined with information and education boards.

Many eco-resorts do not have a golf course because of their high use of water and pesticides.

An interpretive centre helps visitors understand the environment. Some eco-resorts include research laboratories that examine plants and animals of the area. Local indigenous people are employed to educate visitors about their culture.

GEOskillbuilder

CREATING A MIND MAP

Mind maps are good for jotting down your ideas on a particular issue. Drawing links between these ideas helps you to organise your thoughts and develop your point of view.

For example, a mind map could be used to explore further changes to the resort shown in the illustration, making it even more environmentally friendly.

STEP 1

Put ideas down even if you're not sure that they're correct.

STEP 2

Put your key idea in the centre.

STEP 3

Add arrows and labels as you think of them.

STEP 4

Don't worry about the layout — it's your ideas and the links between them that are important.

STEP 5

Keep adding ideas until you reach a logical conclusion.

Electricity is generated through solar panels on the roofs of the cabins. Each visitor group may be given an 'energy target' — a set amount of electricity that they may use. Those who use more have to pay for it.

Boardwalks are built over sensitive areas such as sand dunes to protect them from being damaged.

Marine biologists accompany tourist cruises to nearby coral reefs to educate visitors about the reef and show them how to minimise their impact on it.

ACTIVITIES ⊙

UNDERSTANDING

1 Outline how an eco-resort differs from other tourist resorts.

2 At what rate is ecotourism growing each year?

THINKING AND APPLYING

3 Visitors to resorts such as the one in the illustration on the left are often attracted by brochures that emphasise the resort's environmental policies. These brochures also give visitors a set of guidelines to follow to minimise their own impact. Design a brochure for the eco-resort illustrated.

USING YOUR SKILLS

4 Create a mind map to explore your ideas on ways to develop ecotourism in a rainforest or a wetland environment.

GEOTERMS

ecologically sustainable: describes something that meets the needs of the present population without endangering the ability of future generations to meet their needs

15.8 Ecotourism as sustainable tourism

Ecotourism is widely seen as a very acceptable form of tourism and sustainable development. Unfortunately, a lot of what is called ecotourism is no more than an expensive packaged holiday cleverly marketed with the 'eco' label.

Ecotourism developed when many people began to realise that mass tourism was having adverse impacts on many physical environments and the culture of local communities, and many wealthy and experienced tourists became dissatisfied with normal packaged holidays.

Originally, people who took ecotourism holidays were happy to accept very simple accommodation and facilities, and become involved in activities that did not harm the environment. This form of tourism was sustainable, as it did no damage to the environment. However, with the growing popularity of some locations, larger and more luxurious accommodation was built and the numbers coming to an attraction increased until the carrying capacity was exceeded. This is the maximum number of people a tourist destination can contain without damaging the environment or decreasing visitor's satisfaction.

Ecotourism in South Africa

The north-east of South Africa has much to attract the ecotourist. The climate is subtropical, with hot, wet summers and mild, dry winters. The vegetation is savanna, with a mixture of trees and high grasses. There is an extraordinary diversity of wildlife in this area, as the savanna is the natural habitat of some of the most magnificent animal species in the world, including elephants, lions, leopards, cheetahs, giraffes, zebras, buffalos, baboons and birds. Rhinoceroses and crocodiles are found in the rivers and waterholes.

The South African Government has established many national parks and game reserves to protect native animals and their habitats. The largest and most famous of these is the Kruger National Park (KNP), which was established in 1926. These public reserves and other private reserves are favourite destinations for many ecotourists.

In KNP and most other reserves, the main way of limiting potential damage to the environment is to limit the number of tourists who can stay there. The facilities for tourists in KNP are comfortable but not excessive. For example, there is only one swimming pool and no plans to build more.

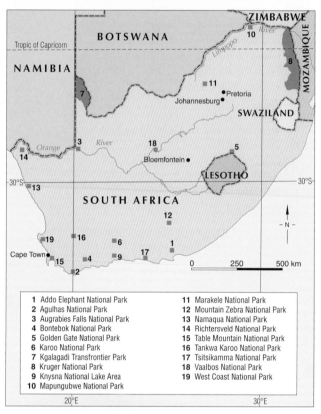

National Parks of South Africa

1 Addo Elephant National Park
2 Agulhas National Park
3 Augrabies Falls National Park
4 Bontebok National Park
5 Golden Gate National Park
6 Karoo National Park
7 Kgalagadi Transfrontier Park
8 Kruger National Park
9 Knysna National Lake Area
10 Mapungubwe National Park
11 Marakele National Park
12 Mountain Zebra National Park
13 Namaqua National Park
14 Richtersveld National Park
15 Table Mountain National Park
16 Tankwa Karoo National Park
17 Tsitsikamma National Park
18 Vaalbos National Park
19 West Coast National Park

Lion in Kruger National Park.
There is a code of conduct for tourists in the national park.

Ecotourism: some pros and cons

Ecotourism mostly takes place in pristine areas, where the untouched nature of the physical environment and the native wildlife are the very reasons ecotourists want to visit.

However, biologists are concerned that contact with humans, even considerate ones, could endanger the survival of the animals that they come to see. For instance, in Manitoba, Canada, vehicles have been taking tourists to watch polar bears at a time of the year when the bears should be resting and waiting for the water to freeze so they can hunt seals. Instead, the bears now remain alert when the vehicles arrive. Experts believe that this change to their behaviour could affect their heart rate and ultimately, their fitness for breeding. Given the threat of climate change to polar regions, any further stress could mean the extinction of the species.

On the other hand, in Africa, ecotourism has helped to save the gorilla from extinction. As a result of a conservation and ecotourism project in Rwanda, gorilla poachers have become ecotourism guides. Poaching of gorillas has been reduced by 60 per cent as the local people now gain a sustainable income from the community-based program. A recent census of the Virunga Volcano mountain gorillas has found gorilla numbers have increased by 17 per cent.

Strategies to manage human–animal interaction in ecotourism include:
- avoiding direct contact
- restricting the use of flashbulbs from cameras
- no-flight buffer zones over animal habitats
- use of webcams for observation.

ACTIVITIES

UNDERSTANDING

1. Why is ecotourism seen as a form of sustainable development?
2. How is Kruger National Park managing potential damage to the physical environment?
3. How might ecotourists unintentionally influence the survival of the wildlife species they come to see?

THINKING AND APPLYING

4. What other strategies can you think of that could be implemented to protect wildlife from the adverse effects of ecotourism?

USING YOUR SKILLS

5. Refer to the map showing national parks of South Africa. Describe the location of Kruger National Park.
6. Which is the most southerly of the parks? What direction is it from Kruger National Park? What approximate distance is it from Kruger National Park?

GEOfacts

- South Africa receives approximately over 1 million foreign tourists a year.
- Kruger National Park covers an area close to 20 000 square kilometres. It is home to more than 145 mammal species, 450 bird species, 114 reptile species and 33 amphibian species.
- In Kruger National Park, research has shown that lions have a diet consisting of 29 per cent impala, 16 per cent Burchell's zebra, 14 per cent blue wildebeest, 13 per cent warthog and 13 per cent porcupine.

Two polar bears play next to a Tundra Buggy full of tourists in Manitoba, Canada.

www. **tundrabuggy** .com

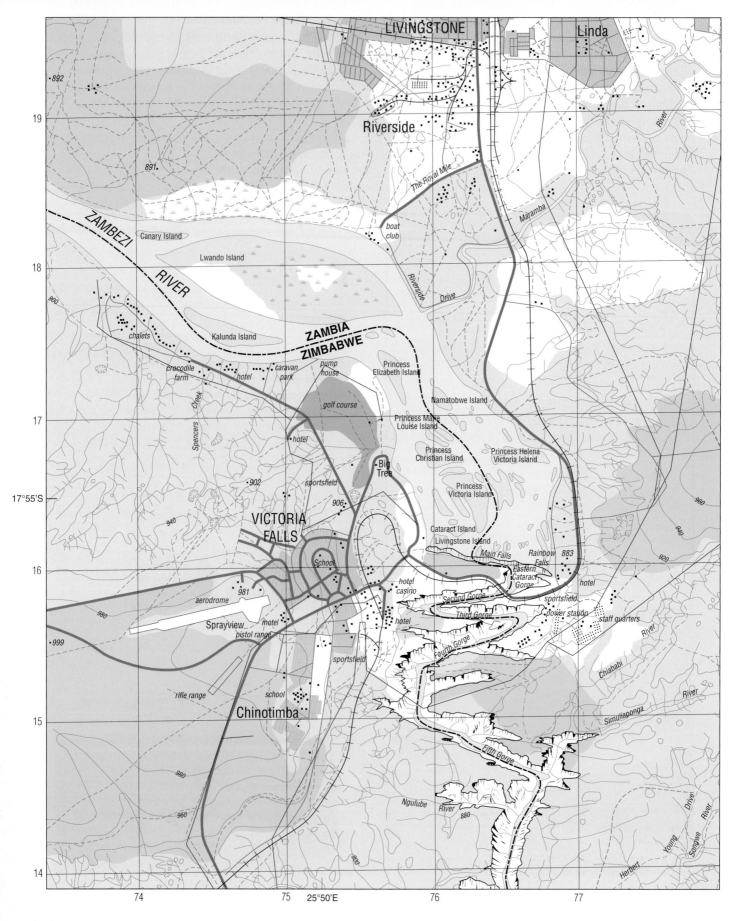

Oblique aerial photograph of Victoria Falls

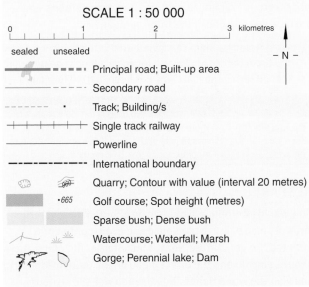

SCALE 1 : 50 000

0   1   2   3 kilometres

sealed   unsealed

– N –

Principal road; Built-up area
Secondary road
Track; Building/s
Single track railway
Powerline
International boundary
Quarry; Contour with value (interval 20 metres)
Golf course; Spot height (metres)
Sparse bush; Dense bush
Watercourse; Waterfall; Marsh
Gorge; Perennial lake; Dam

Topographic map of Victoria Falls, Zambia and Zimbabwe. Victoria Falls is one of the world's most spectacular landforms. The tourism industries in the towns of Livingstone (Zambia) and Victoria Falls (Zimbabwe) have grown in response to large numbers of international visitors.

ACTIVITIES

USING YOUR SKILLS

Refer to the topographic map and photograph to answer the following questions.

a Describe the main landforms on the map.

b What physical feature can be found at area reference AR7715?

c Give the area reference for the spot height of 891 m.

d What is the contour interval of the map?

e What direction is Lwando Island from the Main Falls?

f Calculate the distance by road from Livingstone to Big Tree.

g What physical feature forms a natural boundary between Zambia and Zimbabwe?

h What human features on the map may have been built because Victoria Falls is a tourist destination?

i What features visible in the photograph show why tourists would visit Victoria Falls?

Working geographically

KNOWLEDGE AND UNDERSTANDING

Select the alternative A, B, C or D that best answers the question.

1 During the second half of the twentieth century, mass tourism gradually became established in
- (A) developing countries.
- (B) underdeveloped countries.
- (C) developed countries.
- (D) areas of sustainable development.

2 The world's top tourist destination is
- (A) France.
- (B) Spain.
- (C) the United States.
- (D) Bali.

3 An economic benefit of tourism is
- (A) increased employment.
- (B) increased cultural understanding.
- (C) the restoration of historic buildings.
- (D) increased leisure time.

4 Sustainable tourism involves a relationship between
- (A) the place, the host community and the infrastructure.
- (B) the place, the host community and the visitor.
- (C) the infrastructure, the law and the visitor.
- (D) the law, the government and the host community.

5 Tourist arrivals fell in Bali in 2003 and 2006 because of
- (A) a global financial crisis.
- (B) the avian flu epidemic.
- (C) terrorist attacks in previous years.
- (D) severe acute respiratory syndrome (SARS).

6 Sustainable tourism can help deal with the problem of climate change by
- (A) using aeroplanes that reduce greenhouse gas emission.
- (B) making tourists plant trees.
- (C) asking tourists not to travel to developing countries.
- (D) educating stakeholders.

7 Another term for ecotourism is
- (A) soft tourism.
- (B) environmental tourism.
- (C) a safari.
- (D) caring tourism.

8 Using webcams for observation of animals is a strategy to
- (A) save polar bears from extinction.
- (B) minimise human–animal contact.
- (C) allow biologists to study endangered species.
- (D) make wildlife documentaries.

9 An example of a positive impact of tourism on the physical environment is
- (A) cruise ships that tip their waste into the sea.
- (B) the mining of coral reefs for building materials for tourist resorts.
- (C) the burning of forest wood for tourist camp fires.
- (D) the rise in the number of gorillas because poachers can earn money as tourist guides.

10 The local name for Victoria Falls means
- (A) the white water that falls.
- (B) the smoke that thunders.
- (C) the mist that flies.
- (D) the spray that thunders.

WORKING WITH A PMI CHART

PMI stands for Plus, Minus and Interesting. PMI is a good tool to use when attempting to solve a problem. It works well when a group brainstorms an idea and each person's ideas are then put into one of the three categories.

11 What would happen if a major tourist attraction such as the Great Barrier Reef was banned as a tourist destination for one year? The PMI chart has been started for you.

Plus	Minus	Interesting
The reef would have a period to recover.	There would be a loss of jobs and income.	The reef could still have environmental problem.

RESEARCH

How would international tourism be affected if a mystery virus developed into a pandemic and every continent was affected? To get started, search the internet for information about swine flu and the effect it had on the tourism industry, and visit the World Health Organization website. In your answer you should include the following:

- the nature of the virus
- how the virus is spread
- the industries that would be affected
- how this global disaster could be managed.

USING FIELDWORK

Geographers are interested in where things are, why they are there and how humans interact with the environment. Fieldwork allows you to investigate tourism issues by observing, measuring, asking geographical questions and collecting and analysing data.

Tourist questionnaire

Select a particular tourist attraction in your local area (for example, a national park, an art gallery, a local market or festival, a farm).

- Carry out a tourist survey based on the one shown to the right.
- Ask the organisation in charge of your selected tourist attraction how many people visit the attraction and what are the busiest months of the year. Work out a way to graph this information.
- Draw a map of the area showing the location of the attraction and transport routes used to get to it.
- Analyse the information you have collected and prepare a report summarising your findings.

Tourism survey

- Survey 20 people of different ages in your local area. Use the rating scale and statements in the box below right.
- Collate the answers and graph the results.
- Summarise your findings; compare the results with those of other class members.

Using your own experience

1. List three places you have visited as a tourist in Australia (they could be local sites). Explain why each is a tourist attraction and list the main natural and/or cultural features.
2. Go on a bushwalk. Locate and map your walk. Describe what you saw, heard and smelt. What are the advantages and disadvantages of bushwalking compared with spending the same amount of time at a resort?
3. Collect articles about travel and tourism. List the words and phrases that are used to make a place seem attractive. Then describe your local area using similar language to attract tourists.
4. You have a friend coming from interstate to visit you for a long weekend. Plan a tourist itinerary for your friend in your local area.

Tourist questionnaire

Name of site ....
Location of site (include latitude and longitude) ....
Hours open .... Entrance fee ....

Please answer the following questions by ticking the correct response, and provide information where indicated.

1. What is your usual place of residence?

   NSW ☐   Another state of Australia ☐
                   Which state? ....
   Not Australia ☐   Which country? ....

2. What type of area do you live in?
   City ☐   Town ☐   Rural ☐

3. What is your age?
   6–10 ☐ 11–17 ☐ 18–30 ☐ 31–50 ☐ 50+ ☐

4. What transport did you use to come here?
   Car ☐   Aeroplane ☐   Bus ☐   Bicycle ☐
   Train ☐   Other ....

5. What is the main reason for your visit to this region?
   Natural attractions ☐   Shopping ☐
   Cultural attractions ☐   Weather ☐
   Visiting friends or relatives ☐   Other ....

6. How would you rate this tourist attraction?
   High ☐   Average ☐   Poor ☐

Tourism survey

Rating scale:

   Strongly agree 1
   Agree 2
   Neutral... 3
   Disagree 4
   Strongly disagree 5

Statements:

1. Tourism is good for Australia.
2. Tourism creates employment.
3. Tourism leads to environmental degradation.
4. Tourism disrupts small communities.
5. Governments should spend more money promoting Australian tourism to people overseas.
6. The tourism industry should encourage more ecotourism.
7. The benefits of tourism outweigh the costs.
8. Tourism leads to more costs for the local community because of the need to provide facilities and services.

projects*plus*

The holiday of a lifetime

SEARCHLIGHT ID: PRO-0025

SCENARIO

Congratulations! You have won the holiday of a lifetime. You and three of your closest friends will jet off on an around-the-world adventure visiting some of the world's most amazing tourist destinations.

Your holiday voucher allows you to travel up to 60 000 km in one direction around the world and make up to 10 stops. As this is your first overseas holiday, you and your friends plan to make the most of it and expose yourself to as many different tourism experiences as possible. Your trip should take you to at least four different continents and should include:

- a stop in a country that welcomes lots of tourists
- a stop in a country that welcomes very few tourists
- a visit to one of the world's natural wonders
- a visit to a terrorism memorial
- a visit to a cold environment
- a visit to an eco-tourism resort
- a volunteer experience helping the needy in another country
- a sporting activity.

YOUR TASK

Create a photo slideshow to present your holiday to your class. It should include images of all the destinations you intend to visit and a world map that displays your journey. You can use PowerPoint to create your slideshow or any other software that you may have. You should record a voiceover to play with your slideshow, or you could present your slideshow live to the class. Ask your teacher how they would like it presented.

PROCESS

- Open the ProjectsPLUS application for this chapter, located in your eBookPLUS. Watch the introductory video lesson and then click the 'Start Project' button to set up your project. You can complete this project individually or invite other members of your class to form a group. Save your settings and the project will be launched.
- Navigate to your Research Forum. Topics have been loaded to provide a framework for your research and to help you ensure that you complete each of the activities on your wish list.
- You should use the internet and at least one offline source, such as a brochure from a travel agent, to help you plan your dream holiday. The weblinks in your Media Centre will help you get started. Enter your ideas for destinations as articles in the Research Forum. If you are working as a group, you can view and comment on other group members' ideas.

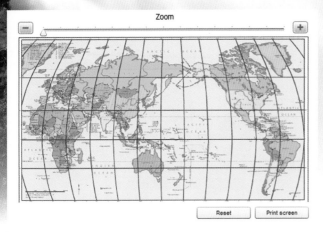

- Create your slideshow. Begin with your journey map, and then show images and key information about each of your destinations in the order you plan to visit them. If you are going to present your journey to the class, be sure to write notes for your presentation. Alternatively, use voice-recording software to record a voiceover that provides information about all of the exciting destinations you have chosen to visit.
- Print out your Research Report from ProjectsPLUS and hand it in to your teacher with your slideshow.

- Once you have all your destinations decided, use the World Map interactivity from chapter 2 to plot the course of your journey. Make sure you are travelling less than 60 000 km and going in only one direction around the world. Print your journey map as a file and include it in your slideshow.
- Navigate to your Media Centre. A selection of images from popular tourist destinations have been provided for you. You should also source images of any other places that you have decided to visit.

MEDIA CENTRE

Your Media Centre contains:
- a selection of images from popular tourist destinations
- weblinks to tourist information sites
- an assessment rubric.

Interactivity

HOTSPOT COMMANDER: 'MODERN WONDERS'

Hotspot Commander challenges your geographical skills and knowledge in a fun question-and-answer format. You will receive the coordinates of a location. When you hit your target accurately, you will be given some secret information and a question to answer. Get it right and a part of the mystery image is revealed. Can you conquer all ten locations and become a Hotspot Commander?

SEARCHLIGHT ID: INT-0962

16 Access to fresh water

INQUIRY QUESTIONS

+ What is the water cycle?
+ How much fresh water is there?
+ Why is fresh water so scarce?
+ How can we reduce water scarcity?
+ What is water pollution?

The human population has grown rapidly over the last two centuries. The world today has no more fresh water than it had 2000 years ago, when the world's population was less than 3 per cent of its current size. As the world's population grows, most countries will struggle to meet their population's need for fresh water.

Water is a vital resource — without it, there is no life. All life depends on it: people and animals need it for drinking, and water is essential for plants to grow. Threats to supplies of fresh water include pollution arising from human activities. Climate change is also affecting rainfall predictability. Water is a unique and limited natural resource. Access to fresh water is a major geographical issue.

GEOskills TOOLBOX

+ Interpreting choropleth maps (page 367)
+ Making a line drawing from a photograph (page 375)
+ Interpreting patterns in graphs (page 377)

Women getting water from a well in Cameroon, Africa

aquifer: layers of rock through which water can flow; a store for underground water

desalination: making salt or brackish water pure by removing the dissolved salts

effluent: the waste from a range of human activities that is discharged into water bodies

fresh water: water that is not salt water

grey water: water that can be used for a second time (e.g. bath water used to water the garden)

ground water: water under the surface of the ground that has seeped through soil and rock, often used for drinking and irrigation

monsoon: the seasonal change in wind direction that is experienced in much of Asia

monsoon Asia: part of Asia that comes under the influence of monsoons

NGOs: non-government organisations, such as Red Cross and Oxfam International, usually involved in humanitarian aid

pollution: the build-up of impurities likely to be harmful to plants, animals and humans at certain concentrations

precipitation: the condensation in the atmosphere that falls as rain, hail, snow or dew

run-off: the water from precipitation that runs off the surface of the land and into streams and lakes

water cycle: the circulation system that carries water from the oceans, through the atmosphere, to the land and back to the sea

water harvesting: collecting, storage and management of water run-off

water table: the upper point at which water can be found in the ground. At times of flooding the water table is at the surface.

The **water cycle** is the circulation system that carries water from the oceans, through the atmosphere, to the land and back to the sea. Water is transferred between various storages, such as oceans and the atmosphere; however, no water actually leaves the circulation system. The water cycle is powered by energy from the sun. This energy passes into, through and out of the system, and, in doing so, transfers water from the various stores. The water cycle consists of a complex system of relationships involving changes in the position of water in the environment. The basic processes in the system are evaporation, condensation, **precipitation**, infiltration and run-off.

Evaporation

Evaporation is the process by which water changes from a liquid into a gas and becomes water vapour. The oceans are by far the most important source of water vapour. From them comes almost all of the water vapour contained in the air. The main evaporating areas are the oceans with clear skies and high temperatures. Evaporation occurs in much smaller amounts from rivers, lakes and streams.

Plants also discharge water vapour into the atmosphere. This is called transpiration. The combined water loss into the atmosphere from evaporation and transpiration is called evapotranspiration.

Condensation

Condensation is the reverse of evaporation. It occurs when water vapour changes from a gas to a liquid. This results in water appearing as visible droplets in the atmosphere. These droplets can be so small that they are supported by the air, and we recognise them as clouds or fog.

Precipitation

Precipitation is the descent of some form of water (rain, hail, snow or dew) through the air to the

Condensation occurs when water vapour in air cools and turns into droplets of water that we see as clouds or fog. It is the reverse of evaporation.

Evapotranspiration is the combined water loss into the atmosphere from evaporation and transpiration. Transpiration is the loss of water from plants into the atmosphere.

Precipitation is the rain, hail, sleet or snow falling from clouds. It occurs when water droplets increase in size and the air can no longer support them.

Surface run-off occurs when precipitation falls on areas higher than sea level and does not soak into the ground. It runs off the surface into streams, lakes or the sea.

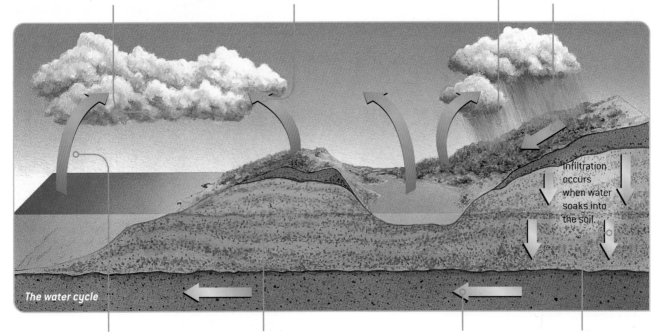

Infiltration occurs when water soaks into the soil.

The water cycle

Evaporation occurs when liquid water turns into water vapour (gas) when heated. Oceans are the most important source of water vapour.

The water table describes the upper point at which water can be found in the ground.

Ground water is water under the surface that has seeped through soil and rock. Most ground water makes its way into streams, lakes or the sea. Some remains in the ground and can be tapped from springs or wells.

Percolation occurs when moisture filters down through soil and rock due to gravity.

ground. For precipitation to occur, the very small water droplets have to increase in size to the point where the air can no longer support them. This normally occurs when the droplets are taken higher into the atmosphere.

There are four main causes of air moving upwards to result in precipitation:
- Convectional, caused by convection currents (see page 146)
- Cyclonic (see page 147)
- Orographic (see below)
- Frontal (see below).

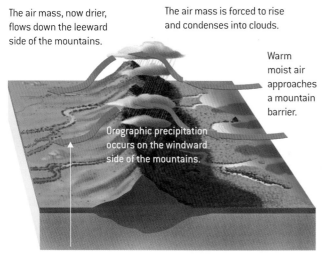

The air mass, now drier, flows down the leeward side of the mountains.

The air mass is forced to rise and condenses into clouds.

Warm moist air approaches a mountain barrier.

Orographic precipitation occurs on the windward side of the mountains.

The dry air mass becomes warmer, with little chance of rain. Deserts are often found on the leeward side of large mountain ranges.

Orographic precipitation is caused by the shape of the land.

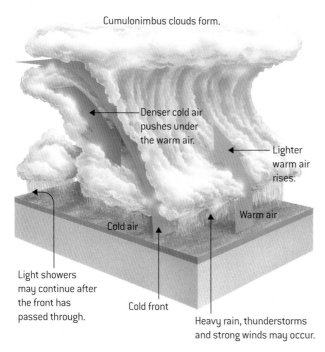

Cumulonimbus clouds form.

Denser cold air pushes under the warm air.

Lighter warm air rises.

Warm air

Cold air

Light showers may continue after the front has passed through.

Cold front

Heavy rain, thunderstorms and strong winds may occur.

Frontal precipitation

Infiltration and run-off

Some of the water that falls on the Earth will be stored as snow and ice and in lakes and storages made by humans, but much of it will continue through the cycle in the processes of infiltration and run-off. If precipitation occurs on areas higher than sea level, and if the water does not infiltrate the ground, it will move overland towards the sea as surface run-off. Most of this run-off will find its way into streams and rivers. This is a most important part of the cycle for communities, as a lot of fresh water is obtained from rivers. However, excessive run-off in times of heavy rains also brings with it the hazards of floods.

Infiltration occurs when water seeps into the soil. When water passes through soil and rock it becomes ground water. Most of this water will eventually make its way into rivers and streams and into the oceans. Some will remain in the ground for long periods as underground water, which can be tapped at the surface at springs and wells.

ACTIVITIES

UNDERSTANDING
1. Define the water cycle.
2. What are the main processes of the water cycle?
3. Identify the four main causes of precipitation.

THINKING AND APPLYING
4. Imagine you are a droplet of water making your way through the water cycle. Use the diagram of the water cycle to describe your journey from the ocean and your return.

USING YOUR SKILLS
5. Refer to the diagram of orographic precipitation. Explain how orographic precipitation occurs.
6. Refer to the diagram of frontal precipitation. Explain how frontal precipitation occurs.

GEOTERMS

ground water: water under the surface of the ground that has seeped through soil and rock, often used for drinking and irrigation

precipitation: the condensation in the atmosphere that falls as rain, hail, snow or dew

water cycle: the circulation system that carries water from the oceans, through the atmosphere, to the land and back to the sea

How much fresh water is there?

Water covers about 71 per cent of the Earth's surface. About 97.5 per cent of all water in circulation is found in the oceans in the form of salt water. The remaining 2.5 per cent represents the supply of **fresh water**. Some two-thirds of this fresh water is locked up in glaciers and permanent snow cover and just 1 per cent is easily accessible fresh water. In addition to this accessible fresh water in rivers, lakes and aquifers, there are small man-made storages in reservoirs and dams. Water resources are largely renewable (except some ground water), with huge differences in availability throughout the world.

The availability of fresh water

Even though fresh water represents only a small proportion of the world's water supply, there is a lot of it — much more than is likely to be needed in the foreseeable future. The supply of fresh water is only a problem on parts of the Earth's surface because water and people are unevenly distributed. The areas where there is an abundant supply of fresh water are not always the same as the areas of greatest population density and greatest demand. Because of this uneven distribution, some areas and people have available and consume far more water than others.

It is estimated that about 80 litres of water per person per day are needed to sustain a reasonable lifestyle. Average consumption per person ranges from 5.4 litres per day in Madagascar to more than 500 litres per day in the United States and Australia. Despite the abundance of water, modern technology and engineering, a secure supply of fresh water for much of the world remains a problem.

There are two main factors that determine the availability of fresh water to humans on a global scale — precipitation and evapotranspiration.

Precipitation

Precipitation is the main source of water for all human uses and for ecosystems.

On a global scale, precipitation is very unevenly distributed. The areas of very high precipitation (more than 2000 millimetres per year) tend to be in the low latitudes, while the areas of low precipitation (less than 250 millimetres per year) are mainly in the tropical deserts and in the high latitudes.

Evapotranspiration

Generally, warm areas in the low latitudes have higher levels of evapotranspiration than cooler areas in the mid to high latitudes. This means that low latitude areas need more precipitation than mid and high latitude areas in order to have the same availability of fresh water.

Uneven distribution: water and population

Fresh water is distributed very unevenly over the Earth with huge differences in availability in different parts of the world. The areas of greatest fresh water availability are often very different to the areas of greatest population density, with many areas facing critical shortages. More than 60 per cent of the world's population must get by on an average of 50 litres per day per person — one-tenth the amount used by the average Australian.

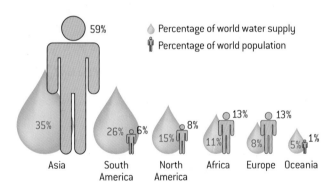

Water availability compared with population distribution

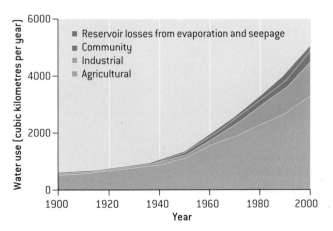

Increased water use during the twentieth century

The lightest shade has been used to colour the countries with lowest availability (under 1000 cubic metres per person per year).

Shades in between the darkest and lightest have been used to colour the categories in between these two extremes.

The darkest shade has been used to colour countries with the highest water availability (over 100 000 cubic metres per person per year). Note these countries.

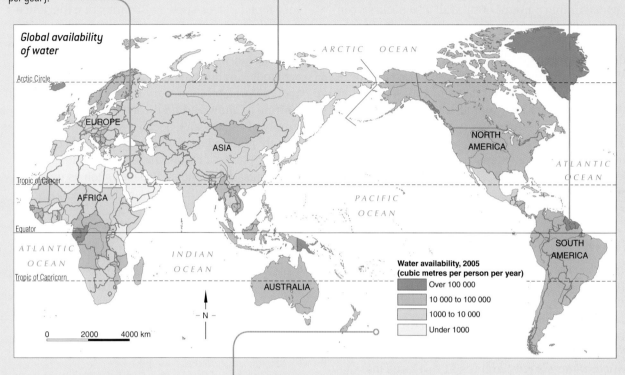

Global availability of water

Water availability, 2005
(cubic metres per person per year)

- Over 100 000
- 10 000 to 100 000
- 1000 to 10 000
- Under 1000

The coloured legend clearly explains the different categories being shown.

Can you see any patterns? For example, which continent has the lowest water availability per person per year?

INTERPRETING CHOROPLETH MAPS

Choropleth maps provide an instant visual depiction of distribution patterns.

Choropleth maps use darker and lighter shades of the same colour group to show a pattern. The darker shades represent 'the most' and the lighter shades represent 'the least'. Choropleth maps enable users to see overall patterns very quickly.

GEOfacts
By 2025, the world will need to make available 20 per cent more water to supply the extra 3 billion people expected on the planet.

GEOTERMS
fresh water: water that is not salt water

ACTIVITIES

UNDERSTANDING
1 What percentage of the world's supply of water is fresh water?
2 Where is the world's supply of accessible fresh water found?

THINKING AND APPLYING
3 Even though the world's supply of fresh water is abundant, a problem still exists. Why?

USING YOUR SKILLS
4 Refer to the map of global availability of water.
   a Outline the main areas with the lowest water availability.
   b Outline the areas with the highest water availability.
   c Suggest two factors that might contribute to each of these distribution patterns.
5 Refer to the graph of water use.
   a What are the main uses of water now?
   b Describe how the uses have changed over the last century.

Why is fresh water scarce?

Much of the rainfall that occurs over the Earth falls during heavy storms and monsoons. Much of this water is quickly lost in run-off and floods. A considerable amount of rainfall also occurs over uninhabited areas where it cannot be used. Even so, the global supply of fresh water should be adequate for the global population.

There are many reasons for water scarcity. There is the obvious reason that many places, such as hot deserts, have very low rainfall, and many people live in these areas. Arid areas, which are defined as having an average annual rainfall of less than 300 millimetres, are extensive. More than 600 million people live in arid areas. The other main reasons for water scarcity are: variations in climate, land degradation, population growth and water pollution.

Variations in climate

There are two main variations in climate that affect the supply of fresh water. They are drought and floods.

A drought is a period of below average precipitation. It can vary in length.

Droughts can cause great hardship in areas of critical water scarcity, and result in a large loss of human life. Drought frequently occurs in African countries such as Ethiopia and causes widespread devastation. One of the worst droughts of modern times occurred in Ethiopia during the 1980s and lasted for years. It was followed by a severe drought in 2006–07. The drought spread beyond Ethiopia to nearby countries and affected over 10 million people. There was a coordinated effort at emergency relief by the United Nations organisation UNICEF, the Ethiopian Government and many NGOs (non-government organisations such as the Red Cross). The aid took many forms including bringing in water and mobile health teams.

Drought in Ethiopia has caused great hardship.

Much of monsoon Asia has droughts. The drought normally is caused by the late arrival of the wet season, decreased precipitation or both. Even very moist places such as Britain can experience drought conditions. During the 'great drought' in Britain during May 1975 to August 1976, there was widespread water rationing.

Floods can be caused by a period of well-above-average precipitation, very heavy storms, the rapid melting of snow and tidal waves. This affects the supply of fresh water because water often becomes heavily polluted during a flood and little clean water is available. As a result, there can be widespread outbreaks of infectious diseases such as cholera.

> **GEOfacts** Australia had its worst drought for 100 years early in the twenty-first century. Most parts of Australia were drought declared at some time during 2001 to 2007. The drought caused widespread loss of livestock and crops and severe financial hardship. The cause was El Niño, a phenomenon that causes a reversal of normal air pressure across the Pacific so that moist tropical air masses that bring rain are prevented from reaching Australia.

Climate change is the variation in climate patterns over a period of time. This may be caused by global warming as a result of human activities that release increased amounts of carbon dioxide and other greenhouse gases into the atmosphere. One effect of this climate change in some locations is the increase in frequency and severity of both droughts and floods. Lower rainfall will mean that less water will be available for human and agricultural use.

Land degradation

Land degradation can be caused by the excessive destruction of natural vegetation through deforestation, overgrazing and farming. If this occurs, especially on slopes, it greatly reduces the ability of the soil to store water. In a well-vegetated area, the soil acts like a giant sponge, absorbing rainfall and releasing it slowly. If this sponge-like action is destroyed, heavy rains run off the land in flash floods, to be lost into rivers and eventually the sea.

Some agricultural practices require more water than others. Raising livestock, for example, uses much greater amounts of water than growing crops such as maize or wheat.

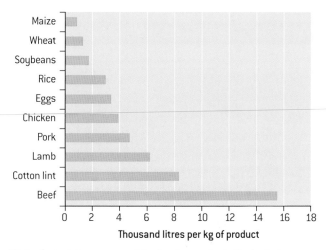

Water footprints: average virtual water content of selected crops
Source: UNESCO.

Population growth

The population of the world has grown rapidly during the twentieth century and has put a great strain on fresh water supplies in many parts of the world. Population growth results in a rapid increase in the amount of water needed for agricultural, industrial and domestic uses. As water is a limited resource, more cannot be created. Every time the population doubles, the amount of water available per person is halved. Countries with rapid population growth such as India, Niger, Syria and Ethiopia are finding it increasingly difficult to meet basic water requirements.

Water-scarce countries in 1955, 1990 and 2025 (projected), based on the availability of less than 1000 cubic metres per person per year

Water-scarce countries in 1955	Bahrain Barbado Djibouti Jordon	Kuwait Malta Singapore
Additional water-scarce countries in 1990	Algeria Burundi Cape Verde Israel Kenya Malawi Qatar	Rwanda Saudi Arabia Somalia Tunisia United Arab Emirates Yemen
Additional countries projected to become water scarce by 2025 under medium or high United Nations population growth projections	*Cyprus Peru	Tanzania Zimbabwe
Additional countries projected to become water scarce by 2025 under all United Nations population growth projections	Comoros Egypt Ethiopia Haiti Iran	Libya Morocco Oman South Africa Syria

*Only on high population growth projection

Water pollution

Water pollution reduces the amount of available fresh water. Polluted river systems also now take longer to recover because river flows have been reduced. Many of today's rivers have been dammed or diverted. Huge amounts of water are removed from river systems for purposes such as irrigation and water supplies for towns and cities. Less water in a river means that it will flow more slowly and pollutants in the river will take more time to disperse. Pollutants are more likely to settle on the river bed as sediment. Much of the water in China's rivers, for example, is too polluted to drink. The Ganges River in India is also heavily polluted, in spite of constant flooding.

ACTIVITIES

UNDERSTANDING

1. List the main reasons for water scarcity.
2. Define the term 'drought'.

THINKING AND APPLYING

3. What types of hardships do you think that a drought would cause if you were living in a poor country such as Ethiopia?
4. How does land degradation reduce the availability of water?
5. How does water pollution reduce the supply of fresh water?

USING YOUR SKILLS

6. Refer to the table of water scarce countries. Using a photocopy of a blank world map and an atlas, complete these activities.
   a Provide a colour legend for water-scarce countries in (i) 1955, (ii) 1990 and (iii) 2025.
   b Use an atlas to locate the countries in each category, then colour them on your blank world map.
   c Describe the pattern shown on your completed map (i.e. which continents are the most and least affected).
7. Refer to the bar graph of 'water footprints: average virtual water content'.
   a Outline what is meant by 'water footprint'.
   b List the three food products with the (i) largest water footprint and (ii) smallest water footprint.

GEOTERMS

monsoon: the seasonal change in wind direction that is experienced in much of Asia

There are two main ways that the scarcity of fresh water can be reduced. The first is to increase supplies, and the second is to manage water more efficiently.

Increasing supplies

Supplies of fresh water can be increased by:
- using water **run-off**
- using more of the world's underground water
- using new technology.

Using water run-off

The main source of water run-off is river catchments. River catchments are land areas from which water drains to a river or lake. Some of the great river catchments of the world are those of the Nile, Ganges, Amazon, Huang Ho and Chang Jiang rivers. Water is available over the catchment in the form of precipitation. Natural vegetation and crops mainly depend on precipitation in order to grow. However, fresh water for human use mainly depends on the amount in ground water storages, the amount of run-off into streams and the way in which this water is collected and distributed.

Building a reservoir (dam) to store water is a way of turning a destructive hazard — a flood created by heavy rainfall — into a productive resource. Dams not only provide a stable water supply, but are also a good way of controlling floods.

Since 1960, more than 36 000 large dams have been built around the world. In Europe, Africa and North America, more than 40 per cent of reliable run-off is now controlled by dams. Most of the world's large cities and many major irrigation areas source their fresh water supplies from dams. Recently, dam construction has slowed considerably. There have been two main reasons for this:
- most suitable dam sites now have dams and it would be very difficult and expensive to build dams at remaining sites — the opportunities are limited for new dams. However, some dams are still being built, including massive projects such as the Three Gorges Project in China.
- more people are questioning the environmental and equity issues of dam construction. The health of rivers and catchments suffers if too much water is taken out of them. Dams and irrigation water reduce flows and can reduce water quality. Equity issues arise because when dams cover an area, the people there have to move, while people downstream often lose access to water they had before the dam was built.

The Three Gorges Dam spans the Yangtze River near Yichang in China. On completion, the 663 kilometre-long dam will be the world's largest. It will provide hydro-electricity and fresh water. The dam will drown river valleys and 1.2 million people will be relocated.

Apart from reservoirs, there are many possible **water harvesting** techniques. Some of these are:
- ploughing along contours or placing lines of stones along contours to hold back run-off
- using a series of embankments to direct water from flash floods to small fields to provide water for irrigation
- constructing underground storage, for example, *kundis* in India to collect water in wells
- collecting rainwater off roofs in rainwater tanks.

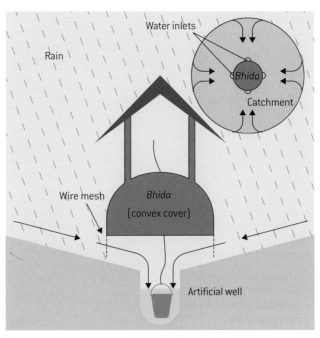

The sides of kundis *are plastered with lime and ash. They are approximately 6 metres deep and 2 metres wide.*

Using more of the world's underground water

Apart from the huge quantities of fresh water stored in icecaps and glaciers, most of the world's fresh water is stored underground. Vast aquifers lie under parts of the Sahara and Arabian deserts. Many countries including India and China rely on underground water to satisfy their fresh water needs.

Underground water is a good way to satisfy water needs as long as it is not extracted faster than nature replenishes (replaces) it. Unfortunately, most underground aquifers are replenished very slowly, the process often taking thousands of years. This is very slow when compared to rivers that are normally replenished within a few weeks.

In many parts of the world, underground supplies of fresh water are being used at an unsustainable rate. This means that the water is being used faster than it can be replenished. This results in a falling water table and wells and bores that have reliably served for centuries begin to dry up. Wells and bores are often sunk deeper and pumping costs increase. This causes a further fall in the depth of the water table. As the water table falls, the land above it can slowly subside. In Mexico City, the overpumping of ground water is causing parts of the city, including its famous cathedral, to sink. Around the Mediterranean, sea water has been seeping into aquifers making the ground water unusable.

In Mexico City, the overpumping of ground water is causing this famous cathedral to sink.

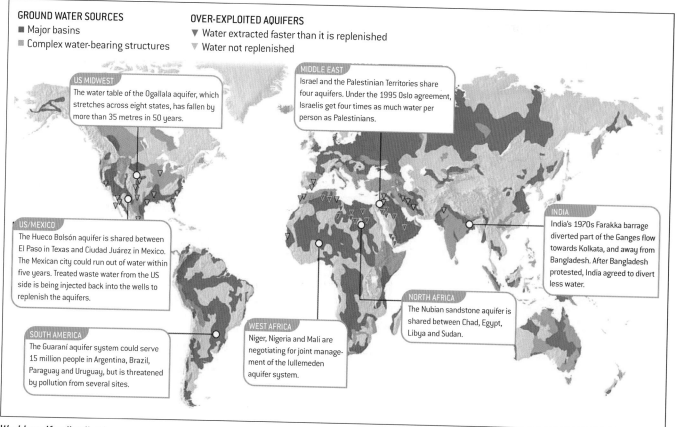

World aquifer distribution

Source: New Scientist.

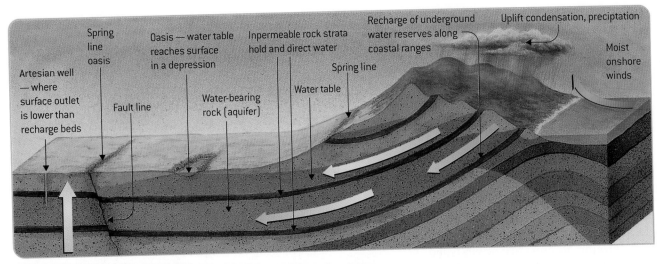

Aquifers and the formation of an oasis

Labels in diagram:
- Spring line oasis
- Oasis — water table reaches surface in a depression
- Inpermeable rock strata hold and direct water
- Recharge of underground water reserves along coastal ranges
- Uplift condensation, precipitation
- Artesian well — where surface outlet is lower than recharge beds
- Fault line
- Water-bearing rock (aquifer)
- Water table
- Spring line
- Moist onshore winds

In areas where underground water has been used for long periods of time, even many centuries, there can be sudden and unexpected falls in the water table. So much water was being pumped in the Beijing area in one year that the water table fell by 4 metres. This led to a fall in rice production. It appears that, in most areas, ground water supplies are already being fully used and even overused, and there are few opportunities to obtain more water from this source.

GEOfacts

- Aquifers supply about half the world's drinking water, 40 per cent of the water used by industry and up to 30 per cent of water used for irrigation.
- The United Nations has proposed new global water laws to provide for equitable use by countries who share aquifers that cross national borders.

A desalination plant in the Nevada Desert USA

Using new technology

Two new technologies that have the potential to increase fresh water supply are low-cost desalination and using recycled water.

- *Sea water desalination.* This is rapidly emerging as one of the major new sources of fresh water. The world is now realising that larger populations and climate change mean that fresh water will be in short supply. This is increasing the interest in desalination as a technique for tapping the vast water supplies of the sea. Improvements in technology, reducing the cost of desalination and using renewable energy such as wind power, have made desalination a more attractive means of restoring fresh water supplies. There has been a large increase in desalination plants in the Middle East and some European countries. However, there are considerable problems with the high cost of the technology and disposal of the salt.
- *Using recycled water.* Recycled water is storm water, grey water, rainwater or effluent that has been purified and made suitable for human consumption and agricultural purposes. Many countries use recycled water for a variety of

purposes. Since 2003, people living in Singapore have had new water coming through their taps. It is reservoir water mixed with recycled waste water from air conditioners, sinks and toilets. The government insists that it is cleaner than the water that previously came out of the tap.

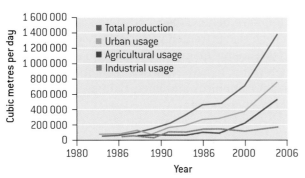

Note: The production of desalinated water in Spain doubled from 2000 to 2004. The Spanish Government predicts that production will double again in another five years.

Use of desalinated water in Spain

Managing water more efficiently

Water is a scarce resource in many countries. There are many ways in which water can be managed more efficiently including these strategies:

- The pricing of water could help prevent waste and encourage conservation. This has been used in many developed countries, but there are problems in developing countries with very poor rural people.
- Rationing is a fair method of water management as it does not depend on ability to pay. Rationing is a method used by many countries.
- Regulating domestic supply, such as using water-saving toilets and shower heads, flow regulators in plumbing and drip irrigation, can help save water.
- Regulating water for agriculture can be achieved by drip irrigation. Industry should be required by law to provide equipment that uses less water.
- Education to change wasteful practices and to encourage conservation has proved successful in many countries.

GEOTERMS

aquifer: layers of rock through which water can flow; a store for underground water

desalination: making salt or brackish water pure by removing the dissolved salts

run-off: the water from precipitation that runs off the surface of the land and into streams and lakes

water table: the upper point at which water can be found in the ground. At times of flooding the water table is at the surface.

ACTIVITIES

UNDERSTANDING

1 What are the two ways that the scarcity of fresh water can be reduced?

2 List the three main ways to increase fresh water supply.

3 What are water catchments?

4 Define the following terms: water harvesting, aquifer and water table.

5 Outline the problems of increasing water supply by using water run-off.

6 Describe ways in which the supply of water could be increased by using run-off.

7 Outline the problems of increasing water supply by using more of the world's underground water.

8 How can using new technologies increase the world's supply of fresh water?

THINKING AND APPLYING

9 Imagine you are in charge of water supplies for a country with a water scarcity problem. How would you attempt to solve this problem?

10 With regard to controlling the use of aquifers that lie under a number of countries, how should a country's share be decided? Should it depend on the country's population or other factors?

USING YOUR SKILLS

11 Refer to the map showing the location of aquifers in the world.
   a Which continents appear to have the most aquifers?
   b What areas of the world have aquifers that are the most over-exploited?
   c Which countries share the Nubian sandstone aquifer?

12 Refer to the diagram of aquifers and the formation of an oasis. Describe the two ways in which an oasis forms.

13 Refer to the graph of the use of desalinated water in Spain.
   a By how much has total production increased since about 1990?
   b Which sector uses the most desalinated water now?
   c Which sector uses the least desalinated water now?
   d Judging by the trend in the graph, what would you expect it to show in 2010?

Bali is a small, fertile island that is part of Indonesia. It has a population of approximately four million people, 95 per cent of whom live in village communities. Bali has a monsoonal climate with a wet summer and drier winter. Temperatures range from warm to hot throughout the year. Bali is covered in deep, fertile, volcanic soils and tropical rainforest.

The most striking feature of the Balinese landscape is the ever-present rice field or *sawah*. The *sawah* is a small patch of land flooded with water that is held back by banks of earth cut out of the red soil. Many rice fields are cut into the sides of hills and mountains, forming terraces. Starting from the coastal plains, these terraces spread up the slopes like flights of gigantic stairs. The recently flooded fields are mirror-like, while those with growing crops are lush and green. Fields with ripening crops are yellow-green. Rice fields that have been recently harvested consist of stalks and cracked mud; the newly ploughed terraces are a mass of brown ooze. The *sawah* reflect the care and attention Balinese farmers give them.

Rice is a very important part of the Balinese diet. The Balinese believe their body and soul are built from it, so rice is treated with reverence and respect. There are many 'magic' ceremonies to ensure enough water, to make the rice grow strong and to protect it from birds and mice. Balinese farmers work closely together.

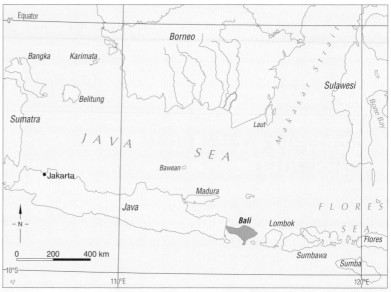

The location of Bali in Indonesia

Rice terraces in Bali

The subak management system

Rice is grown in places where rainforest has been cleared. An elaborate system of terraces to grow rice replaces the forest. Under the natural rainforest vegetation, water run-off would have been slowed by the vegetation cover and thick litter layer. Eventually, however, the run-off would have been channelled into swiftly flowing rivers on the slopes of hills. Normally, removing the natural vegetation would have greatly accelerated the rate of run-off, leading to massive soil erosion. However, the Balinese have adapted the natural ecosystem to create a new ecosystem based on the cultivation of rice. Water is channelled from the mountains to the various levels of terraces by a system of canals, dams, bamboo pipes and even long tunnels cut through solid rock to the dikes that allow the terraces to be flooded or drained at will.

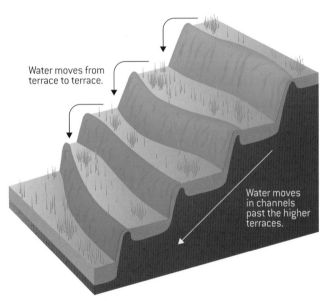

Water moves from terrace to terrace.

Water moves in channels past the higher terraces.

The subak system uses the natural run-off of water running downslope to irrigate rice fields.

The irrigation system is a complex one, requiring close coordination between all farmers in an area. Each village community has its own subaks or 'water boards' to ensure social justice and the fair distribution of water to its members, who take their water from a common source. The members of the subak have rice terraces that are irrigated from a single dam and its major canal. The subak aims to protect the dams and irrigation systems, settle disputes and arrange the communal rice festivals. There are many terraced hillsides, particularly on the south-east of the island. On one hillslope there can be many subaks.

The Balinese irrigation system is a remarkable system that is able to produce up to three crops of rice per year. The continued high rice output is believed to be due to the role played by water. The fertility of the soil is maintained by nutrients in the irrigation water, which come from higher up the volcanic slopes. These nutrients in the water replace those drawn from the soil. More recently, fertilisers have been added to ensure the soil is sufficiently fertile.

It is the management of the water down the slope and across the terrace that makes the system work. This system of water management on the rice terraces of Bali has developed over many centuries and depends on community cooperation.

GEOskills TOOLBOX

MAKING A LINE DRAWING FROM A PHOTOGRAPH

Making line drawings from photographs is an important skill for geographers. Line drawings encourage us to focus on the most valuable information in the photograph and draw attention to it by using labels or making notes. Photographs should be divided into foreground, middle ground and background when making a line drawing. For more on line drawings from photographs see pages 56 and 58.

ACTIVITIES

UNDERSTANDING

1. Describe the location of Bali. In your answer, mention latitude and longitude.
2. Describe the physical environment of Bali.
3. How have the Balinese rice farmers harvested the natural run-off of water downslope to irrigate rice?

THINKING AND APPLYING

4. Explain how social justice and equal distribution of water is managed among rice farmers in Bali.

USING YOUR SKILLS

5. Refer to the large photograph of rice terraces on sloping land in Bali.
   a. Make a line drawing of the scene in the photograph. Label the main features shown in your line drawing.
   b. What evidence is there in the photograph to suggest the climate of the area?
   c. What evidence is there that this is a carefully managed irrigation system?

What is water pollution?

Water pollution occurs when liquids or solids enter a body of water, changing the chemical, physical or biological condition of the water or making it unclean, poisonous or impure. This pollution makes the water a hazard to people and life forms that depend on it. Water pollution can occur naturally. However, we are concerned about water pollution caused by humans.

> **GEO*facts*** The ancient Romans complained about water pollution. During the reign of George III of England, a member of Parliament reportedly wrote to the Prime Minister complaining about the smell and appearance of the Thames River in London. It is reported that he wrote the letter using dirty water from the Thames instead of ink.

Heavily polluted water can lead directly to water scarcity because polluted water is of very little use unless it can be purified. Every year approximately 450 cubic kilometres of waste water are released into rivers and streams. A further 6000 cubic kilometres of clean water are needed to dilute and transport this dirty water before it can be used again. This is two-thirds of the world's available run-off.

Polluted water is a major cause of human disease, misery and death. As many as four million children die every year in developing countries as a result of severe diarrhoea caused by waterborne infection.

An outbreak of cholera in Zimbabwe in late 2008 resulted from a failure of water treatment systems, which was caused by the country's political and economic troubles. Over 1000 people died and the epidemic spread to neighbouring countries. Cholera is easily prevented by safe water treatment.

It is estimated that more than 30 per cent of the population in developing countries have no access to safe drinking water and nearly 50 per cent are without proper sanitation. In rural areas, these figures are much higher.

Water pollution caused by humans

The main types of water pollution caused by humans are:
- sewage and other oxygen-demanding wastes
- infectious agents, which are disease-causing organisms from human and animal wastes and industries such as tanning and slaughtering
- chemicals and mineral substances, including detergents, pesticides and industrial by-products
- radioactive substances from refining uranium and nuclear power stations
- sediments including soils, minerals and industrial by-products
- heat or thermal pollution, which is heated water returned to lakes and streams, for example, from power plants or steel mills.

Sewage

Human sewage causes the most widespread water pollution. Human wastes are a great risk to health for the many people who have to drink and wash in untreated water from rivers and ponds. The main source of sewage is domestic raw sewage, but urban surface run-off is also a source. Stormwater run-off in urban areas often contains large amounts of contaminants from litter, garbage and animal droppings.

An outhouse over water in a Bangladeshi slum. Floods in low-lying Bangladesh are frequent, with consequent severe water pollution problems.

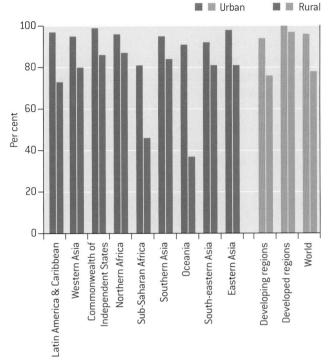

Legend: ■ ■ Urban ■ ■ Rural

Urban and rural piped water coverage, by region, 2006

Management of water quality

Most countries have environmental regulations to protect water quality. Some of these regulations are very strict, but they are not enforced all of the time. Developed countries such as Australia and the USA have had considerable success in reducing water pollution, but it remains a very severe problem in developing countries such as India and China. Making the person or company who has caused the water pollution pay to clean it up can be a very effective way to encourage people not to pollute!

 GEO*facts*

In 2007, Boeing, the aerospace company, was fined almost half a million dollars (US) for pollution run-off that went into waterways near the company's facilities in California.

GEOskills TOOLBOX

INTERPRETING PATTERNS IN GRAPHS

Bar and column graphs are useful for comparing information and interpreting patterns. The graph at the top of the page compares urban and rural piped water by region. The different colours separate the data, and the heights of the columns enables interpretation of patterns.

 GEO*facts*

In India, the major sources of water pollution are city sewage and discharge of industrial waste. Penalties for polluters are based on laws passed in 1974, decades before India's recent rapid industrial development.

ACTIVITIES →

UNDERSTANDING

1 Define water pollution.

2 How can water pollution lead to water scarcity?

3 Outline how water pollution affects health.

4 List the main forms of water pollution.

THINKING AND APPLYING

5 Why is sewage the most widespread form of water pollution?

6 Diarrhoeal diseases such as cholera, typhoid, hepatitis and schistosomiasis can be reduced by children washing their hands after going to the toilet. What prevents children in some countries from doing this?

7 Imagine a pristine lake full of fresh water has suddenly become available to a community. Outline how you feel the following groups would like to use it: tourism company, fishing cooperative, farmers, town council, conservationists. Could any of these uses lead to water pollution?

USING YOUR SKILLS

8 Refer to the graph showing urban and rural piped water coverage.

a Rank in order the regions with the highest percentage of water coverage in urban areas.

b Rank in order the regions with the highest percentage of piped water coverage in rural areas.

c What is the difference in percentage from the highest to the lowest coverage in urban areas?

d How much greater is the percentage of urban coverage in developed regions than in developing regions?

GEOTERMS

pollution: the build-up of impurities likely to be harmful to plants, animals and humans at certain concentrations

Humans are drawn to supplies of fresh water. Virtually all of the world's towns and cities are located next to a river or lake. We need water for drinking, cleaning, irrigation and transport. This most precious resource, however, is often used as a means of domestic and industrial waste disposal. When accidents occur at industrial or mining sites located near waterways, they often result in widespread water pollution that threatens the health of people and of the river they depend on.

China's rivers at risk

China is an industrial giant whose economic growth is currently outstripping that of all other countries. By 2025, China is likely to be the world's largest economic power. This rapid industrialisation brings with it many problems, and pollution of China's waterways is just one of these. It is estimated by environmentalists that 70 per cent of China's rivers and lakes are contaminated. A leading cause of water pollution comes from the location of more than half of the country's 21 000 chemical plants along the Yangtze River system. Many of these plants have not conducted environmental impact assessments and have been built in locations that directly threaten drinking water supplies, ground water, and coastal waters.

The Huaihe River is China's third largest river. It supplies water for one-sixth of the country's 1.3 billion population. The Huai River valley is one of the most densely populated areas of

China, covering Henan, Shandong, Jiangsu and Anhui provinces. The valley is a centuries-old agriculture base and now an emerging industrial belt. In addition to industrial pollution, agricultural pollution is soaring. Seventy per cent of fertilisers and pesticides used by farmers in the river valley are washed into the river.

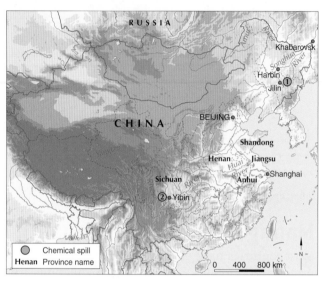

The sites of recent chemical spills into China's waterways

🐧 **GEO*facts***
- According to a World Bank report in 2007, water pollution in China is causing growing levels of cancer and diarrhoea, particularly in children under five years of age.
- 300 million Chinese lack access to clean drinking water.
- Factories and cities dump an estimated 40 to 60 billion tonnes of wastewater and sewage into China's lakes and rivers each year.

Chemical spills

On 13 November 2005, an explosion in a chemical plant in Jilin City, in China, released 100 tonnes of toxic chemicals into the Songhua River, creating a slick about 80 kilometres long. The toxic slick flowed in an already polluted river towards one of China's largest cities, Harbin, which has a population of over nine million. This city relies on the Songhua River for its water supply, and residents rushed to buy bottled water. Trucks transported 16 000 tonnes of water from nearby cities. The water supply in the Russian city of

Many industrial sites in China are located on or near waterways.

Khabarovsk, 700 kilometres downstream on the Amur River, was also affected.

This disaster came at a time when 100 of China's cities could run out of water because of waste, pollution and the degradation of the head waters of major rivers. Much of the water in China's rivers is too polluted to drink.

The chemical spill meant residents of towns near the affected Songhua River had to rely on transported water.

Three months later, a second large spill occurred on the upper reaches of the Yuexi River in southeastern Sichuan province. Toxins were released into a 100-kilometre stretch near the city of Yibin, disrupting the water supply of some 20 000 people. The frequency of such incidents provides a powerful example of the pollution challenges the Chinese Government increasingly faces, and has led authorities to reconsider the longtime trend of locating industries along rivers.

What is China doing to improve water quality?

Progress towards improving China's water quality has been slow and not always successful. After investing US$2.4 billion since 1994 in a ten-year plan to clean up the Huai River, the plan was declared a failure when 31.5 per cent of factories exceeded the maximum permitted discharge. But by 2008, 415 out of the 488 pollution control projects had been concluded. Moving forward with cleanup remains difficult because huge sums are needed to relocate or shut down polluting industries.

In 2006, China's State Environmental Protection Agency (SEPA) announced that China would invest US$125 billion to clean up its waterways. In this *Eleventh Five-Year Plan* (2006–2010), China made environmental protection its highest priority. It pledged to reduce total discharge of major pollutants by 10 per cent by 2010. China is working with the World Bank, which is lending funds for joint projects on rural and urban water conservation, pollution reduction, and sustainable urban and rural development.

ACTIVITIES

UNDERSTANDING

1. What is China's main cause of water pollution?
2. Name three of China's rivers affected by pollution.
3. What is making it difficult for China to improve its record on water pollution?

THINKING AND APPLYING

4. Why do you think so much of China's industry is located alongside the country's rivers?
5. What do you think should be of highest priority for the Chinese Government: continuing to industrialise to grow the economy and improve the living standards of its people or introducing strict environmental controls to regulate industries and force their sustainability? Do you think it is possible to do both?
6. How important do you think world opinion might be in encouraging China to work harder to deal with the problems caused by its huge population and level of industrial growth?

USING YOUR SKILLS

7. Refer to the map of China.
   a How far is it from Jilin to Harbin?
   b How far is it from Jilin to Khabarovsk?
   c How far is it from Jilin to Yibin?
   d What direction is Khabarovsk from Jilin?
   e What direction is Yibin from Jilin?
8. China is a land of many rivers. Using an atlas, tracing paper and a blank map of China, trace and mark China's river systems on the blank map.
9. Write a paragraph about the importance of China's rivers to settlement and industry.

Working geographically

KNOWLEDGE AND UNDERSTANDING

Select the alternative A, B, C or D that best answers the question.

1. The basic processes in the water cycle are
   - (A) evaporation, condensation, precipitation, infiltration and run-off.
   - (B) evaporation, precipitation, storage, infiltration and run-off.
   - (C) transpiration, condensation, precipitation, infiltration and run-off.
   - (D) transpiration, condensation, precipitation, storage and run-off.

2. When water passes through soil and rock it becomes
   - (A) brackish water.
   - (B) ground water.
   - (C) an aquifer.
   - (D) saline.

3. The supply of fresh water is a problem on parts of the Earth's surface because
   - (A) there is insufficient rain because of climate change.
   - (B) water and people are unevenly distributed.
   - (C) the Earth's population is growing too fast.
   - (D) agricultural practices use too much water.

4. A drought is
   - (A) a period of no precipitation.
   - (B) a period of unreliable precipitation.
   - (C) a period of below average precipitation.
   - (D) a period of no agricultural production.

5. Water pollution
   - (A) destroys streams.
   - (B) kills wildlife.
   - (C) reduces the amount of available fresh water.
   - (D) carries cholera.

6. Supplies of fresh water can be increased by
   - (A) using water run-off.
   - (B) using more water from underground aquifers.
   - (C) using recycled water.
   - (D) all of the above.

7. Desalination is
   - (A) making water pure by removing the salts.
   - (B) making salt water pure by removing the salts.
   - (C) making brackish water pure by removing the salts.
   - (D) making salt or brackish water pure by removing the salts.

8. A *sawah* is
   - (A) a flooded rice field.
   - (B) a water management system.
   - (C) a natural ecosystem.
   - (D) a religious ceremony to ensure enough water for use.

9. The most widespread water pollution caused by humans is the result of
   - (A) chemicals and pesticides from agriculture.
   - (B) human sewage.
   - (C) industrial waste.
   - (D) litter and garbage from cities.

10. China is attempting to improve its water quality by
    - (A) building dams.
    - (B) sustainable urban and rural development.
    - (C) reducing industrial accidents.
    - (D) preventing farmers from using pesticides.

MAPPING AND GRAPHING SKILLS

Crisis in West and Central Africa

West and Central Africa has the lowest coverage of improved drinking water and sanitation in the world, and the situation is getting worse. The rapidly expanding population in countries like Nigeria, Chad and Equitorial Guinea is outstripping any increase in coverage of access to improvements in safe drinking water. According to UNICEF, the absolute number of people without access to drinking water increased from 124 million to 157 million between 1990 and 2004. If current trends continue and the rate of progress towards the United Nations Millenium Development Goals does not improve, by 2015 about 260 million people in the region will be without access.

The region also has the highest under-five infant mortality rate of all developing regions: 191 child deaths per 1000 live births. The West and Central Africa region contains 7 of the 9 remaining countries in which Guinea worm, a disease spread through the use of contaminated water, is endemic. Ghana is particularly affected with nearly 79 per cent of the region's cases of the disease.

Improvement in access to drinking water is also hampered in the region because of civil and political unrest and the resulting movement of refugees. In addition, natural disasters such as floods further compound the problem.

11. On a blank map of Africa, mark each country listed in the table. Using the information in the table create a key to shade each country according to whether it is (a) not on track or (b) on track to meet UN Millenium Development Goals for improved access to water.

12. Create a bar graph similar to the one shown to display the information in the table for the 2004 total and the 2015 target for the countries of Mali, Sierra Leone, Togo, Gambia and Cameroon.

13. Using the information on page 380, list the problems that make achieving goals of improved access to drinking water difficult in West and Central Africa. Suggest a strategy to help overcome each of these problems.

14. According to the graph shown here, which five countries have achieved a less than 50 per cent improvement in 2004? Choose one of these countries and conduct some research into the particular problems with water faced by this country as a developing nation. Consider its proportion of urban to rural population, its natural features, sources of fresh water and causes of water pollution.

Access to improved drinking water sources in selected West and Central African countries

Percentage of population in West and Central African countries with access to improved drinking-water sources

| | U5MR* | 1990 | | | 2004 | | | MDG** Target 2015 | Progress towards the MDG target |
		Urban	Rural	Total	Urban	Rural	Total		
Benin	152	73	57	63	78	57	67	82	Insufficient
Burkina Faso	192	61	34	38	94	54	61	69	On track
Cameroon	149	77	31	50	86	44	66	75	On track
Cape Verde	36	–	–	–	86	73	80	88	–
Central African Republic	193	74	39	52	93	61	75	76	On track
Chad	200	41	13	19	41	43	42	60	On track
Congo	108	–	–	–	84	27	58	76	–
Congo, Demographic Republic of the	205	90	25	43	82	29	46	72	Not on track
Cote d'Ivoire	194	73	67	69	97	74	84	85	On track
Equatorial Guinea	204	–	–	–	45	42	43	68	–
Gabon	91	95	–	–	95	47	88	91	–
Gambia	122	95	–	–	95	77	82	90	–
Ghana	112	86	37	55	88	64	75	78	On track
Guinea	155	74	34	44	78	35	50	72	Not on track
Guinea-Bissau	203	–	–	–	79	49	59	76	–
Liberia	235	85	34	55	72	52	61	78	Not on track
Mali	219	50	29	34	78	36	50	67	On track
Mauritania	125	32	43	38	59	44	53	69	On track
Niger	259	62	35	39	80	36	46	70	Not on track
Nigeria	197	80	33	49	67	31	48	75	Not on track
Sao Tome and Principe	118	–	–	–	89	73	79	88	–
Senegal	137	89	49	65	92	60	76	83	On track
Sierra Leone	283	–	–	–	75	46	57	76	–
Togo	140	81	37	50	80	36	52	75	Not on track

* Under-five infant mortality rate   ** Millennium Development Goals

Source: Data derived from UNICEF.

eLesson

THE WATER CYCLE

This video lesson will show you the amazing continuous cycle of water in the Earth's hydrosphere. Through the processes of evaporation, condensation, run-off and rain, water is moving constantly as it is transfered from the oceans to the sky. A worksheet is attached to further your understanding.

SEARCHLIGHT ID: ELES-0062

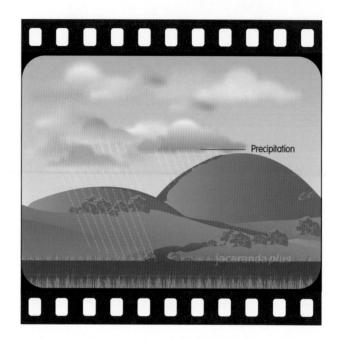

eLesson

TREATING SEWAGE

Be swept down the plug hole and learn about the processes of sewage treatment, as well as the many uses of recycled water in Australia. A worksheet is attached to further your understanding.

SEARCHLIGHT ID: ELES-0059

These ICT activities are available in this chapter's Student Resources tab inside your eBookPLUS. Visit www.jacplus.com.au to locate your digital resources.

Learning object

VIRTUAL FIELDWORK

The purpose of virtual fieldwork is to investigate the characteristics of a region, and the physical processes and human activities that form and transform the region. Because of its virtual nature, fieldwork can take place on a local, regional or global scale.

Virtual fieldwork is intended to be as real as possible, with the added advantage of interactive design. You are encouraged to participate in virtual activities to enhance your understanding and appreciation of a region and improve your geographical skills. The interactive fieldwork journal in this learning object will help you organise your fieldwork notes and prepare a final report.

The Three Gorges Dam

Through an inquiry-based approach, you will discover answers to the following questions:

1. Where is the Three Gorges Dam being built?

2. What is the purpose of the Three Gorges Dam?

3. What impact will it have on the physical environment?

4. What impact will it have on the human environment?

Download this interactive learning object and install it on your computer to investigate the issues surrounding the Three Gorges Dam by:

- exploring the plethora of data, photos, maps and drawings
- completing interactive activities
- taking virtual tours.

SEARCHLIGHT ID: LO-0338

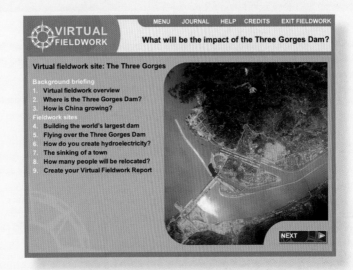

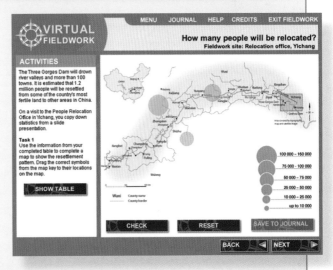

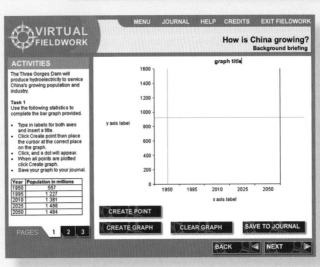

Glossary

acid rain: precipitation (e.g. rain, snow) that has a high level of acidity; that is, a pH level below 5.6 (p. 252)

active citizenship: involves individuals and groups influencing decision making at local, state, federal and global scales, and actively participating in community activities and public affairs (p. 268)

advection fog: condensation that drifts onto land as low cloud or fog (p. 130)

aerial survey: the tracking and counting of large species of animals from an aeroplane or helicopter (p. 327)

aid: charitable donations of money, food, goods and services made to countries in need (p. 222)

algal bloom: an increase in the growth of algae, due to increased nutrient levels in the water. Toxic blue-green algae make the water unsafe for human consumption. (p. 247)

alluvial plain: an area where rich sediments are deposited by flooding (p. 298)

alphanumeric grid reference: combination of letters and numbers that locate points on a map (p. 24)

alpine: the area above the tree line in mountains (p. 106)

Antarctic Treaty: an agreement signed by 42 counties in 1961 that aims to protect Antarctica and its resources (p. 188)

antiretroviral: a substance that stops or slows the activity of a retrovirus such as HIV (p. 234)

aquifer: layers of rock through which water can flow; a store for underground water (pp. 134, 371)

area reference: four numbers used to locate features on a topographic map (p. 25)

arid: having little rainfall to support vegetation (p. 116)

artesian well: a well that penetrates underground rock to release water to the surface that has been held under pressure (p. 127)

atlas: a book containing maps and information about places on the Earth (p. 8)

atmosphere: the thin, fragile layer of gases that surrounds the Earth (pp. 4, 52)

avalanche: a large mass of ice or snow separated from a mountain slope and sliding or falling suddenly downwards (p. 108)

balance of payments: measures a country's exports (goods and services leaving a country) and imports (goods and services coming into a country). Countries aim to increase wealth by increasing exports. (p. 205)

Beaufort Scale: a numerical scale from 0 to 12 used to measure wind speed (p. 61)

bias: a perspective that has a particular slant reflecting a preference or prejudice (p. 269)

biodiversity: the rich variety of all life forms on Earth, including plants and animals (pp. 77, 245, 252, 270, 350)

biosphere: living matter on Earth, including all plants and animals (p. 4)

blizzard: a snowstorm accompanied by very strong winds (p. 180)

blog: a website, usually set up and regularly updated by an individual, used to publish content, express opinions or provide running commentary on a topic. The site often invites comments from readers and provides links to other blogs. The term blog is derived from web log. (p. 209)

blue-green algae: micro-organisms that grow in water high in nutrients, such as nitrates and phosphates (p. 80)

built environment: any human addition to the land surface (p. 10)

canopy: the top layer of the forest that allows little light to pass through (p. 145)

carbon footprint: the total amount of carbon dioxide (CO2) produced to directly and indirectly support human activities. It can be measured for a country or an individual (p. 306); a measure of the impact that human activities have on the environment in terms of greenhouse gases produced; measured as units of carbon dioxide (p. 350)

carbon–oxygen cycle: process in which animals breathe in oxygen and breathe out carbon dioxide, while trees absorb carbon dioxide and produce oxygen (p. 149)

cartography: the art of drawing maps. A professional map maker is called a cartographer. (p. 20)

civil war: war between areas or parties within one country (p. 210)

climate: the long-term variation in the atmosphere, mainly relating to temperature and precipitation (p. 34); the predicted weather at a particular place, based on the average of weather events over many years (p. 288)

climate change: any change in climate over time, whether due to natural processes or human activities (pp. 44, 190, 288)

climatic zones: zones where climate is similar; the main zones are the tropics, the polar regions, and the temperate zones, which lie between them (p. 34)

commercial agriculture: type of farming that produces a surplus of products that can be sold (p. 11)

community: an identifiable group formed by people with something in common; usually based on shared space and social organisation (pp. 79, 346)

compass: an instrument for determining direction (p. 22)

conflict diamond: a diamond used to finance conflict aimed at undermining legitimate governments (p. 212)

conservation: the protection of the environment from destructive influences (p. 15)

continental drift: the theory that continents broke away and drifted from an original large land mass (p. 88)

continental plates: the large pieces of the Earth's crust that float on the magma beneath the Earth's surface. (p. 88)

continents: the seven great landmasses of the Earth (p. 36)

contour line: line drawn on a map joining places of equal height above sea level (pp. 9, 96)

conventional symbols: standard symbols that are commonly used on maps (p. 22)

core: the inner part of the Earth (p. 88)

crater: the opening on top of a volcano through which lava erupts (p. 92)

crust: the outer layer of the Earth's surface (p. 88)

culture: the body of beliefs, attitudes, skills and tools with which members of a community structure their lives and interact with their environment (pp. 82, 340)

deforestation: the process of clearing forest, usually to make way for housing or agriculture (pp. 82, 107, 156, 272, 320)

degraded: reduced in value or quality; for example, land is degraded through erosion and intensive use of the soil (pp. 104, 270)

delta: a nearly flat plain between outspreading branches of a river at its mouth (pp. 78, 132)

deltaic plain: flat area where a river(s) empties into a basin (p. 298)

deposition: the laying down of material carried by rivers, wind, ice, ocean currents or waves (p. 122)

desalination: making salt or brackish water pure by removing the dissolved salts (p. 372)

desert: an area that receives less than 250 millimetres of rainfall annually (p. 116)

desertification: the process by which useful agricultural areas on desert fringes change into desert due to poor farming practices (pp. 12, 137, 272)

developed country: a country that has high economic productivity, relatively high standards of living and a relatively democratic system of government (pp. 82, 221, 340)

developing country: a country in which most people have a low economic standard of living (pp. 82, 159, 221, 345)

diarrhoea: a condition leading to loss of fluid through bowel motions, causing dehydration. (p. 229)

dormant: sleeping, inactive, not erupting (p. 92)

drought: a period of below average precipitation (p. 12)

drylands: any area of dry climate or semi-desert (p. 270)

earthquake: series of shock waves that are generated by a disturbance of the Earth's crust (p. 91)

ecological dimension: how humans interact with environments (p. 268)

ecological footprint: measures the dependence of an individual or region on natural resources; for example, how much land and water is needed to supply energy, build roads and buildings, grow food, dispose of waste and grow forests for wood and paper (p. 258)

ecological sustainability: the ability to meet the needs of the present generation without compromising the ability of future generations to meet their needs (pp. 188, 247, 268, 319)

ecologically sustainable: describes something that meets the needs of the present population without endangering the ability of future generations to meet their needs (p. 352)

economic globalisation: the integration of national economies into the international economy (p. 204)

ecosystem: a system formed by the interactions of the living organisms (plants, animals and humans) and physical elements of an environment (pp. 10, 124, 148, 184, 252, 350)

ecotourism: nature-based tourism that involves educating tourists about the natural environment. It is ecologically sustainable tourism and injects money into local economies. (pp. 107, 299, 340)

effluent: the waste from a range of human activities that is discharged into water bodies (p. 372)

emissions: substances such as gases or particles discharged into the atmosphere (p. 300)

emissions trading scheme: buying and selling of permits to emit greenhouse gases. A permit allows emissions up to a prescribed cap or limit. (p. 306)

endangered: in danger of extinction (pp. 14, 316)

enhanced greenhouse effect: increased ability of the Earth's atmosphere to trap heat (p. 288)

environment: the surroundings of living and non-living things (p. 10)

epicentre: the point of the Earth's surface directly above the focus of an earthquake (p. 91)

erosion: wearing away of soil and rock by natural elements, such as wind and water (pp. 88, 122)

estuary: the tidal mouth of a river where the salt water of the tide meets the fresh water of the river current (p. 77)

exchange rate: specifies how much a unit of one currency is worth compared to another currency (p. 205)

extinct: animal or plant species that have died out (pp. 14, 162)

extinction: the dying out of an entire species of animal or plant (p. 316)

extreme poverty: living on less than US$1 a day (p. 220)

faulting: occurs when rocks crack and two sections move vertically, forcing up layers of rock (p. 90)

fertility rate: the average number of children a woman is likely to have in her lifetime. A rate of just over two, called the replacement level, keeps population numbers steady. (p. 236)

folding: occurs when a plate in the Earth's crust slides under another, pushing up layers of rock (p. 90)

food chain: the series of steps from producers, to consumers to decomposers — within the sequence organisms are related to one another as prey and predator with each being the food of the next member of the chain (p. 148); a group of plants and animals that feed off living things while, in turn, being eaten by others (p. 318)

food web: a complex pattern formed when a lot of food chains for an area overlap (p. 149)

fossil fuels: fuels that come from the breakdown of organic matter; for example, coal, oil and natural gas. They have formed in the ground over millions of years. (pp. 82, 246, 274, 288)

free trade: occurs where goods and services are traded between countries with no restrictions (pp. 201, 222)

fresh water: water that is not salt water (p. 366)

front: a line drawn on a weather map to show where two different air masses meet (p. 52)

gender equity: equal access of females and males to opportunities such as education and employment (p. 236)

GIS (Geographic Information Systems): a set of computer programs designed to deal with databases that are able to collect, store, retrieve, manipulate, analyse and display mapped data from the real world (pp. 5, 327)

glacier: moving rivers of ice (p. 98)

globalisation: the breakdown of traditional barriers between nations and a trend towards faster and cheaper movement around the world of people, goods, money and information (p. 200)

global scale: the whole world (p. 6)

global village: the whole world considered as being like a village, where one individual can communicate with any other and where everyone is part of a web of economic, social, cultural and political relationships (p. 200)

global warming: describes the observable trend of rising world temperatures over the past century (pp. 82, 289); the warming of the atmosphere and the Earth, which some scientists believe is caused by the burning of fossil fuels (pp. 186, 322)

greenbelt: plantations of trees for the purpose of conservation (p. 137)

greenhouse effect: the result of the sun's heat being trapped in the atmosphere rather than reflected out into space. This causes a significant increase in temperature. (p. 288)

greenhouse gas emissions: gases discharged into the atmosphere that trap heat and result in global warming and climate change; primarily carbon dioxide, methane and nitrous oxide (p. 249)

greenhouse gases: gases in the atmosphere that trap energy emitted from the Earth's surface; primarily carbon dioxide, methane and nitrous oxide (p. 288)

green movement: the name often given to people and groups who strongly support the protection of the environment (p. 332)

Greenwich Mean Time (GMT): time at the Royal Observatory in Greenwich, near London, England, which is used as the basis for standard time around the world (p. 30)

grey water: water that can be used for a second time (e.g. bath water used to water the garden) (p. 372)

grid reference: six numbers used to locate features on a topographic map (p. 24)

gross domestic product (GDP): a measure of a country's wealth; for example, a country with a GDP of $140 billion produces $140 billion worth of goods and services in a year (pp. 204, 221)

gross national product (GNP): GNP per capita gives an indication of the average standard of living in countries being compared (p. 343)

ground water: water under the surface of the ground that has seeped through soil and rock, often used for drinking and irrigation (pp. 134, 365)

habitat: the natural home of an animal or a plant; the place where it is normally found (pp. 14, 150, 316)

herbivore: a plant eater (p. 125)

hinterland: the area influenced by any settlement (p. 79)

Human Development Index (HDI): a measure of a country's level of development based on life expectancy, literacy, education and GDP per capita. The highest value is 1 and the lowest value is 0. (p. 221)

human elements of environments: any part of environments that have been built or altered by people (p. 10)

human rights: rights based on the idea that all human beings are equal, and deserve fair and equal treatment (pp. 203, 269)

humidity: the amount of water vapour in the air (p. 116)

hydrosphere: the water on the surface of the Earth in oceans, seas, lakes, rivers, rain and mist (p. 4)

iceberg: a huge piece of ice that breaks off a glacier or ice shelf and floats out to sea; most of an iceberg is below sea level (p. 183)

ice sheet: a large area of ice that completely covers more than 50 000 square kilometres of land (p. 182); area of freshwater ice that completely covers more than 50 000 square kilometres of land. There are only three ice sheets in the modern world, the Greenland ice sheet and the East and West Antarctic ice sheets. (p. 291)

ice shelf: the floating edge of an ice sheet that spills out onto the sea; it is composed of freshwater ice (p. 183)

indigenous: the descendants of the original inhabitants of an area (pp. 80, 150)

indigenous people: the descendants of the original inhabitants of an area (pp. 177, 271)

infant mortality rate (IMR): the number of deaths per 1000 babies under one year of age (p. 222)

insolation: incoming solar radiation or heat from the sun (p. 32)

International Date Line: the line of longitude at 180° (p. 30)

International Monetary Fund (IMF): international organisation that oversees the international monetary system (p. 205)

isobar: a line drawn on a map connecting all points experiencing the same barometric pressure (p. 52)

isotherm: a line joining places of equal temperature (pp. 76, 174)

ivory: a hard white substance taken from the tusks of elephants and walruses (p. 326)

katabatic winds: strong polar winds that are created as cold air descends from the polar plateau (p. 180)

land degradation: the decline in quality of the land (p. 167)

lapse rate: rate of change in temperature that occurs as the altitude increases (p. 102)

latitude: imaginary lines drawn around the Earth that run east to west (p. 26)

lava: molten rock, magma (p. 92)

leaching: occurs in areas with high rainfall, when water continually runs down through the soil, dissolving soluble minerals and carrying them into the subsoil (p. 149)

legend: used with a map to explain the meaning of signs and symbols shown on the map, also called a key (p. 22)

life expectancy: the number of years people can expect to live (p. 221)

literacy: the ability to read and write (p. 221)

lithosphere: the Earth's crust, including landforms, rocks and soil (p. 4)

local scale: the immediate neighbourhood (p. 6)

location: where something is found on the Earth's surface (p. 11)

longitude: imaginary lines drawn around the Earth from north to south (p. 26)

magma: hot molten rock under the Earth's surface (p. 90)

malnutrition: the condition suffered when a person does not get enough nutrition to sustain normal bodily functions (p. 233)

mantle: layer of the Earth between the crust and the core (p. 88)

map: a simplified plan of a place seen directly from above (p. 5)

map projection: a representation of the Earth's surface drawn on a flat grid, using latitude and longitude (p. 26)

mean temperature: average temperature (p. 175)

megacity: very large city with a population of over 10 million people (p. 278)

mitigation: implementing policies to reduce greenhouse gas emissions and enhance sinks (p. 304)

monsoon: a wind system that brings heavy rainfall over large climatic regions and reverses direction seasonally (p. 299); the seasonal change in wind direction that is experienced in much of Asia (p. 368)

monsoon Asia: part of Asia that comes under the influence of monsoons (p. 368)

natural resources: naturally occurring raw materials that are necessary or useful to people. They include soil, water, mineral deposits, fossil fuels, plants and animals. (p. 246)

NGOs: non-government organisations, such as Red Cross and Oxfam International, usually involved in humanitarian aid (p. 368)

nomad: a person who belongs to a group or tribe that moves from place to place depending on the food supply or pastures for the animals (p. 128)

nomadic: a way of life in which people move from one area to another to hunt or find food (p. 81)

non-government organisation (NGO): private organisation, usually non-profitable, with a charitable, community or environmental focus (p. 260)

non-renewable resources: resources that cannot be replenished once they have been used (e.g. oil and natural gas) (p. 246)

oasis: a fertile place in the desert (p. 123)

obesity: a body weight more than 20 per cent above what is generally considered healthy, increasing the risk of life threatening diseases such as diabetes (p. 224)

oblique: a slanting or sloping angle. When the sun's rays are at an oblique angle, a given amount of heat at high latitudes is extended over a larger area than at low latitudes. (p. 174)

ocean: a large body of salt water (p. 36)

ozone layer: a layer of gases that surround the Earth and filter out dangerous ultraviolet light from the sun (p. 186)

pack-ice: formed when sea ice breaks up during the summer (p. 183)

pandemic: a disease that spreads worldwide (p. 349)

perennial: plants with a life cycle of more than two years (p. 125)

permafrost: an area where the subsoil remains frozen throughout the year (p. 76); ground that is permanently frozen (p. 174)

perspective: a way of viewing the world (pp. 6, 201, 269)

photosynthesis: (of green plants) to capture energy in the form of sunlight and convert it to chemical energy in order to grow (p. 145); process in plants using the energy from sunlight to convert water and carbon dioxide into carbohydrates and oxygen (p. 288)

physical elements of environments: all those things that occur naturally in an area, for example, air, water, soil, flora and fauna (p. 10)

plan view: the view from directly above (p. 20)

plantation: a large area for growing crops such as coffee, palm oil and rubber for export; usually owned by a large business (p. 154)

poaching: hunting or removing animals or fish illegally (p. 326)

pollution: the build-up of impurities likely to be harmful to plants, animals and humans at certain concentrations (pp. 82, 376)

precipitation: the condensation in the atmosphere that falls as rain, hail, snow or dew (pp. 34, 61, 116, 174, 364)

predator: living thing that catches and kills another living thing for food (p. 328)

pull factors: positive characteristics of an area that attract people to move to it (p. 278)

push factors: negative characteristics of an area that cause people to leave it (p. 278)

range: to move about an area in all directions (p. 326)

renewable energy sources: energy sources that can be easily replaced in a short amount of time, such as solar and wind; non-renewable sources include fossil fuels (p. 300)

renewable resources: natural resources that, if carefully managed, can be replenished or regenerated in a relatively short amount of time. Forests, soils and fresh water are examples of renewable resources. (p. 246)

Richter scale: used to measure the energy of earthquakes (p. 91)

rift valley: a valley formed as a result of plate movements, usually long and narrow, with steep-sided mountain walls (p. 90)